LUCIAN LAMAR KNIGHT

BIOGRAPHICAL
DICTIONARY
OF
SOUTHERN AUTHORS

Originally published as

LIBRARY OF
SOUTHERN LITERATURE

VOLUME XV

BIOGRAPHICAL DICTIONARY
OF AUTHORS

COMPILED BY
LUCIAN LAMAR KNIGHT

THE MARTIN & HOYT COMPANY
ATLANTA, GEORGIA
1929

Republished by
Gale Research Company
Book Tower, Detroit, Michigan 48226
1978

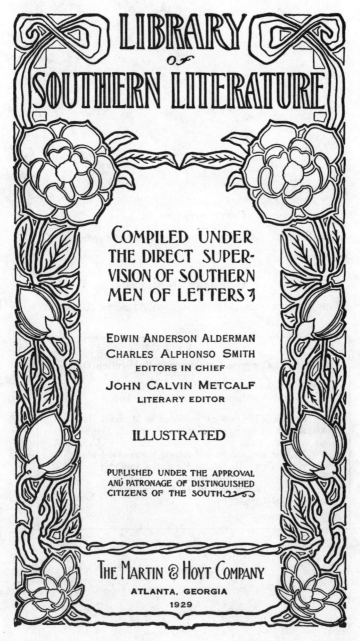

LIBRARY OF SOUTHERN LITERATURE

COMPILED UNDER THE DIRECT SUPERVISION OF SOUTHERN MEN OF LETTERS

EDWIN ANDERSON ALDERMAN
CHARLES ALPHONSO SMITH
EDITORS IN CHIEF

JOHN CALVIN METCALF
LITERARY EDITOR

ILLUSTRATED

PUBLISHED UNDER THE APPROVAL AND PATRONAGE OF DISTINGUISHED CITIZENS OF THE SOUTH

THE MARTIN & HOYT COMPANY
ATLANTA, GEORGIA
1929

Library of Congress Cataloging in Publication Data

Knight, Lucian Lamar, 1868-1933.
    Biographical dictionary of Southern authors.

    Reprint of the 1929 ed. published by Martin & Hoyt,
Atlanta, which was issued as v. 15 of Library of Southern literature, under title: Biographical dictionary of authors.
        1. American literature--Southern States--Bio-bibliog-
raphy. I. Title. II. Series: Library of Southern
literature ; v. 15.
PS261.K5   1975   810'.9'975   75-26631
ISBN 0-8103-4269-3

LIBRARY OF

SOUTHERN LITERATURE

VOLUME XV

BIOGRAPHICAL DICTIONARY
OF AUTHORS

COMPILED BY
LUCIAN LAMAR KNIGHT

EXECUTIVE BOARD

CONSULTING EDITORS

ADVISORY COUNCIL

CHARLES B. AYCOCK,
Ex-Governor, North Carolina.

WILLIAM D. BLOXHAM,
Ex-Governor, Florida.

EDWARD W. CARMACK,
Ex-U. S. Senator, Tennessee.

HENRY COHEN,
Rabbi, Texas.

CHARLES A. CULBERSON,
U.S. Senator, Texas.

DAVID R. FRANCIS,
Publicist, Missouri.

THOMAS F. GAILOR, D.D., LL.D.,
Protestant Episcopal Bishop, Tennessee.

CHARLES B. GALLOWAY, D.D., LL.D.,
Bishop M.E. Church, South, Mississippi.

JOHN TEMPLE GRAVES,
Editor and Lecturer, Georgia.

DUNCAN C. HEYWARD,
Ex-Governor, South Carolina.

RICHMOND P. HOBSON,
Congressman, Alabama.

BENJAMIN J. KEILEY, D.D.,
Resident Catholic Bishop of Georgia.

STEPHEN D. LEE,
General Commanding U.C.V., Mississippi.

W. W. MOORE, D.D., LL.D.,
President Union Theological Seminary, Virginia.

EDGAR Y. MULLINS, D.D., LL.D.,
President Southern Baptist Theological Seminary, Kentucky.

FRANCIS T. NICHOLS,
Supreme Court of Louisiana.

ISIDOR RAYNER,
U.S. Senator, Maryland.

U. M. ROSE,
Ex-President American Bar Association, Arkansas.

HOKE SMITH,
Governor of Georgia.

INTRODUCTION

THE DICTIONARY OF SOUTHERN AUTHORS is in no sense the sporadic plant of a summer's growth. It is in substance the labor of a score of years. The idea of the work was first conceived during the editor's student days at the University of Georgia, where ample opportunities for investigation were afforded by well-filled alcoves. The motive which called it forth was the desire to right what was believed to be the wrong of an unjust discrimination against this section and to show the true value and extent of the South's contributions to American letters.

In design, therefore, it was partly polemic; but the work was also intended to serve the practical end of furnishing definite and exact information concerning the South's literary statistics: to set forth succinctly the main biographical facts in regard to her writers and to present in suggestive outline the essential reference data in regard to her books. The impossibility of making an exhaustive bibliography was soon realized. To individual states, therefore, was left the task of minutely cataloguing the vast array of pamphlets and the no small number of volumes whose interest to the reader was either minor or local; and the labor of collecting only the more important materials was found to be within the scope of such an undertaking.

From year to year the work of compilation proceeded by slow degrees, but perhaps the greater part of the matter was well in hand when the privilege of incorporating it in 'The Library of Southern Literature' was offered. It is needless to add that in the effort to canvass the field with thoroughness nearly every educational institution in the South has been put under Roman tribute. Moreover, libraries, public and private, state and civic, have been ransacked; letters have been addressed to thousands of individuals through the mails; and wherever books or manuscripts bearing directly or indirectly upon Southern literature have been found, they have been freely and frequently consulted.

The result is a symposium of nearly 3,800 sketches. Yet the number might indeed have been much larger had not the eliminating test of a fixed standard of merit been rigidly applied and had not the policy been strictly enforced of excluding from the work all whose prominence before the public was not in some direct manner associated with literary activities. The meagreness of some of the sketches is due to an inability to find complete data. In hundreds of instances it was possible to secure only names and titles. If some states are more largely represented than others, it may be due to greater productivity, to prior settlement, or to more approved methods of preserving and listing their literatures. Moreover, it must be reluctantly admitted that some degree of difference has been found to exist in the zeal with which assistance has been rendered, and while coöperation has been quite general, it has not been strictly uniform

Despite the most critical and diligent research, it is possible that some writers have been omitted who should have been included and that some have been included who should have been omitted; but, under all the circumstances, the wisest judgment has been followed and the best plan of obtaining an impartial bibliography, accurate and authoritative, has been adopted. In the event anyone has been overlooked whose name deserves to appear upon this muster-roll of the South's literary hosts, it is the editor's wish that his attention be called to the matter, in order that the proper correction may be made in subsequent editions. New writers will be constantly coming to the front. The limits of the work will necessarily call for extension from time to time; for the South is growing. Not only in the realized abundance of the past, but in the promised increase of the future, this section is fabulously rich in precious ingots: an intellectual Peru whose revenues are of gold.

Lucian Lamar Knight

BIOGRAPHICAL DICTIONARY OF AUTHORS

ABBEY, RICHARD, clergyman, was born in Genesee County, N.Y., November 16, 1805, but removed to the South in early life and settled in Natchez, Miss. He was ordained to the ministry of the Methodist Episcopal Church; and, when the slavery agitation began to divide the household of faith, he took an active stand for separation. The writings of Dr. Abbey clearly evince the power which he wielded in the councils of Methodism. They include: 'Letters to Bishop Green on Apostolic Succession.' (1853), 'The Creed of All Men' (1855), 'The Ecclesiastical Constitution' (1856), 'The Church and the Ministry' (1859), 'Diuturnity, or the Comparative Age of the World' (1866), 'Ecce Ecclesia,' an answer to 'Ecce Homo' (1868), and 'The City of God and the Church Makers' (1872), besides numerous pamphlets and contributions to the religious press. For several years he was financial secretary of the M. E. Publishing House, South, with headquarters at Nashville, Tenn.

ABBOTT, BELLE KENDRICK. Author. [Ga.]. Besides numerous contributions to periodicals, she wrote an entertaining novel entitled 'Leah Mordecai' (New York, 1875). She was the first wife of Colonel B. F. Abbott, a distinguished member of the Atlanta Bar.

ABBOTT, JOHN. Entomologist. For several years he resided in Georgia and on his return to England wrote: 'The Natural History of the Rarer Lepidopterous Insects of Georgia,' edited by Sir J. E. Smith and published in London, in 1797, with one hundred and four colored plates.

ABERCROMBIE, JOHN WILLIAM. Educator. He was born in St. Clair County, Ala., May 17, 1866. On completing his collegiate studies, he chose the profession of teaching, and after filling numerous important chairs, he became, in 1902, president of the University of Alabama, his *alma mater.* Dr. Abercrombie is one of the consulting editors of 'The Library of Southern Literature.' He is also the author of numerous reports and pamphlets bearing upon educational subjects and of several published addresses. He is president of the Alabama Association of Colleges, a member of the National Council of Education and a former state senator; is a man of fine executive capacity and of ripe scholarship; and holds the degree of LL.D. from two separate institutions, besides the degree of D.C.L. He married June 8, 1891, Rosa Merrill.

ABERNETHY, ARTHUR TALMADGE, author [N.C.], was born in 1872. He wrote 'Did Washington Aspire to be King?' which was published with an address on Washington by Honorable Samuel W. Pennypacker. (New York and Washington, The Neale Publishing Company, 1906).

ABERNETHY, J. W. Editor. He published a work entitled 'The Southern Poets,' a collection of extracts from the writings of Sidney Lanier, Henry Timrod and Paul H. Hayne, with biographical and critical introductions and explanations (New York, Maynard, Merrill and Company, 1904).

1

ABRAMS, ALEXANDER ST. CLAIR. Journalist. [Ga.]. At one time he was engaged in editorial work in Atlanta, Ga., where he was associated with Henry W. Grady on the *Herald*. Afterward he located in Florida. He served in the Confederate Army and wrote a 'History of the Siege of Vicksburg' (1869).

ADAIR, JAMES. An Indian trader of distinction, who spent nearly forty years of his life among the dark-skinned natives of the Southern forest, chiefly among the Chickasaws. As the result of his observations, he published, in 1775, a work of rare interest and value, entitled 'The History of the Indian Tribes, Particularly Those Nations Adjoining the Mississippi, East and West Florida, Georgia, North and South Carolina, and Virginia.' It is one of the whimsical theories of the author that the Indian race is of Jewish origin; but, in spite of this very unscientific speculation, his book contains the most intimate account in existence of the habits and customs of the Indian tribes, to which is added an incomplete but useful vocabulary of the Indian dialects with which the author was familiar. Concerning his queer notion of the origin of the Indians, it is of interest to note that the idea was subsequently exploited by Dr. Elias Boudinot in his 'Star of the West; or an Attempt to Discover the Long-Lost Tribes of Israel,' published in 1816, but it has received little favor among scholars.

ADAMS, ANDY. Author. [Texas]. He wrote 'The Log of a Cowboy,' a narrative of real life on the hurricane deck of a Texas horse, (1903), 'The Outlet' (1905), and 'A Texas Matchmaker,' all racy stories full of humorous incidents.

ADAMS, FRANCIS COLBURN. Author. [S.C.]. He was born in 1850. Besides numerous short stories and sketches he wrote 'Uncle Tom at Home,' and 'Life and Adventures of Major Potter.'

ADAMS, HERBERT BAXTER, educator, was born at Shutesbury, Mass., April 16, 1850, and, after taking a full collegiate course at Amherst, studied at Heidelberg (Ph.D.). For several years he was professor of history at Johns Hopkins University in Baltimore, Md., and besides editing 'Studies in Historical and Political Science,' he published 'The Life and Writings of Jared Sparks.' and numerous historical monographs. He died in 1901. The University of Alabama gave him the degree of LL.D.

ADAMS, JASPER. Clergyman and educator. He was born at Medway, Mass., August 27, 1793. On completing his course at Brown University, he studied theology at Andover and became an ordained minister of the Protestant Episcopal Church. For several years he was president of the College of Charleston, S.C., and later took charge of a seminary at Pendleton, S.C. At one time his 'Moral Philosophy' (New York, 1836), was widely used in the schools. He died in Charleston, S.C., October 25, 1841.

ADAMS, JOHN HASLUP. Editor. He was born in Baltimore, Md., January 31, 1871. At the present time he is on the staff of the Baltimore *News*. Besides editorials and book reviews for his own paper, he writes occasional articles for the magazines. The sketch of Severn Teackle Wallis in 'The Library of Southern Literature,' is from the pen of Mr. Adams.

ADAMS, THOMAS ALBERT SMITH. See Biographical and Critical Sketch, Vol. I, page 1.

ADGER, JOHN B., theologian and scholar, was born in Charleston, S.C., of Scotch-Irish parentage, December 13, 1810, and died in Columbia, S.C., in 1899. For years he was a professor in the Presbyterian Theological Seminary at Columbia, and earlier in life labored among the Armenians in Asia Minor. He wrote 'My Life and Times,' a work of great value, covering almost the whole expanse of the Nineteenth Century (Richmond, Presbyterian Committee of Publication, 1899). He received the degree of D.D.

AFFLICK, MARY (Hunt). Poet. She lived first in Kentucky, and afterward in Texas and published a volume of verse entitled 'Gates Ajar and Other Poems.'

AIKEN, J. G., Mrs. Poet.]La.]. She published a volume of 'Poems' (1892).

AINSLEE, HEW. See Biographical and Critical Sketch, Vol. I, page 21.

ALBERTON, EDWIN. Author. In a volume entitled 'Florida Wilds' (New York and Washington, The Neale Publishing Company, 1907). Mr. Alberton has published a number of short stories illustrative of life in the land of blooms and of legends.

ALDERMAN, EDWIN ANDERSON, president of the University of Virginia and editor-in-chief of 'The Library of Southern Literature,' was born in Wilmington, N.C., May 15, 1861, a son of James and Susan J. Alderman. He received his collegiate education at the University of North Carolina, taking his Ph.B. degree in 1882. Whatever may have been the determining factors which led him to choose pedagogy in preference to the legal profession, it is certain that intellectually and temperamentally he was cast in the mold of the teacher. For three years he served his novitiate as superintendent of the city schools of Goldsboro, N.C. and for an equal length of time he held the office of assistant state superintendent. Then, after occupying for one year the chair of English in the State Normal College, he became professor of pedagogy in the University of North Carolina, a position which he held until his elevation to the presidency of this institution in 1896. For three years Dr. Alderman, with marked administrative skill, directed the prosperous career of his *alma mater;* and by reason of his successful work at Chapel Hill, was called in 1899 to the helm of affairs at Tulane University in New Orleans, La. Another splendid era of growth was inaugurated by his connection with this great educational plant, but in 1904 he yielded to an urgent call from the University of Virginia, and became the executive head of the historic school, which was founded by Jefferson. On broad lines he has planned for the future of this great seat of learning and in every department of the work the magnetic influence of his personality has been felt. Dr. Alderman has also been prominent on both the general and southern boards of education; and whether upon the lecture platform or in the quiet forum of letters, he is equally at home. His style both as a writer and as a speaker is distinctly individual. His published works include a 'Life of William Hooper, Signer of the Declaration of Independence,' a 'School History of North Carolina,' and a 'Life of J. L. M. Curry,' besides numerous essays and addresses on topics educational and popular, and his contributions to 'The Library of Southern Literature.' Dr. Alderman has been twice married, first, in 1886, to Emma Graves and second, in 1904, to Bessie Green Hearn. He received the degree of D.C.L. in 1882 from the University of the South and the degree of LL.D. in 1898 from Tulane, in 1902 from Johns Hopkins, in 1904 from Columbia, in 1905 from Yale, and in 1906 from the University of North Carolina.

ALEIX, L. T. EULALIE, Madame. Author. [La.]. She published in French 'Les Poésies de Lamartine' (1890).

ALEXANDER, ARCHIBALD, theologian and educator, was born in Rockbridge County, Va., April 17, 1772, and was educated at Timber Ridge Academy, afterward Washington College, at Lexington. For five years he was president of Hampden-Sidney College; and, on the organization of Princeton Seminary, he became the leading professor of this pioneer school of the prophets. From 1829 to 1850 he contributed to nearly every number of the Princeton *Review;* and, not only in the class room but in the editorial sanctum and in the pulpit, he was perhaps the most influential man of his day in molding religious thought and opinion. His writings include 'Outlines of the Evidences of Christianity,' a work which has been translated into many different tongues (1823), 'Treatise on the Canon of the Old and New Testaments' (1826), 'Lives of the Patriarchs' (1835), 'Essays on Religious Experience' (1840), 'History of African Colonization' (1846), 'History of Log College' (1846), 'History of the Israelitish Nation' (1852), 'Moral Science,' and several unpublished manuscripts, including 'The History of the Presbyterian Church in Virginia.' The College of New Jersey gave him the degree of D.D. He died at Princeton, N.J., October 22, 1851.

ALEXANDER, EDWARD PORTER. Soldier, civil engineer, railway magnate, author. He was born at Washington, Ga., May 26, 1835, and was educated at West Point. He resigned from the United States Army to enter the service of the Confederacy and became chief of artillery in Longstreet's famous corps, with the rank of brigadier. After the Civil War he became an important factor in the railway development of the South. He published in two volumes a work of much interest entitled 'The Memoirs of a Confederate,' (New York, Charles Scribner's Sons, 1907). General Alexander devotes most of his time at present to the interests of his large rice plantation on South Island, off the coast of South Carolina.

ALEXANDER, GROSS, clergyman, author, educator, was born at Scottsville, Ky., June 1, 1852. He was educated at the University of Louisville and married first, Helen M. Watts and second, Aribel Wilbur. After holding numerous important pastorates in the M. E. Church, South, he became professor of New Testament Greek and Exegesis in Vanderbilt University for seventeen years. He edited 'Homilies of Chrysostom on Galatians and Ephesians' and wrote: a 'Life of S. P. Holcomb (the Louisville Courier-Journal Company, 1888), a 'History of M.E. Church, South' (New York, Scribner's, 1894), 'The Beginnings of Methodism in the South' (Nashville, Bigham and Smith, 1897), 'The Son of Man' (*ibid.,* 1899), besides numerous contributions to church periodicals on theological subjects. He was made presiding elder of the Louisville District in 1902. Emory and Henry College gave him the degree of S.T.D.

ALEXANDER, HENRY AARON, lawyer, was born in Atlanta, Ga., October 10. 1874. He is the author of a work entitled 'Lien Laws of the Southeastern States.' (Atlanta, Ga., Southeastern Publishing Company, 1909), and represents Fulton County in the present General Assembly of Georgia, 1909-1910.

ALEXANDER, J. BELL. Author. [Ala.]. He published a volume entitled 'Malice, a Tale of Real Life in the South' (1852).

ALEXANDER, JAMES WADDELL, clergyman and educator, was born in Louisa County, Va., March 13, 1804. On completing his equipment for the ministry, he was called to pastoral work in Virginia; but later became for eleven years professor of *belles lettres* at Princeton and afterward pastor of the Fifth Avenue Presbyterian Church, of New York. Included among his published works are: 'Thoughts on Family Worship,' 'Plain Words to a Young Communicant,' 'Thoughts on Preaching,' 'The American Mechanic and Workingman,' a series of essays; and 'The Life of Archibald Alexander.' Two volumes of his 'Familiar Letters,' covering a period of forty years, were published by Dr. John Hall, who succeeded him in the New York pastorate. He died at Red Sweet Springs, Va., July 31, 1859.

ALEXANDER, JOHN BREVARD, physician, was born in Mecklenburg County, N.C., May 27, 1834, the son of R. D. and Abigail Bain Caldwell Alexander. His daughter, Annie Lowrie Alexander, M.D., was the first Southern woman to graduate in medicine. Dr. Alexander is the author of an excellent 'History of Mecklenburg County' (1902), which tells of the famous Mecklenburg Declaration of Independence, framed by the Scotch-Irish patriots of North Carolina in 1775. He resides in Charlotte, N.C.

ALEXANDER, JOHN H. Author. [Va.]. He published 'Mosby's Men,' a story of thrilling adventure delightfully told, (Washington and New York, The Neale Publishing Company, 1907).

ALEXANDER, JOHN HENRY, scientist and educator, was born in Annapolis, Md., June 26, 1812, and died in Baltimore, Md., March 2, 1867. After graduation from St. John's College, he studied law, but afterward turned his attention to science, became professor of physics in the University of Pennsylvania, and acquired an international reputation. Besides contributing to scientific journals, he edited three editions of Simm's 'Treatise on Mathematical Instruments' and published 'The History of Metallurgy of Iron,' parts I and II (1840-1842), 'Weights and Measures, Ancient and Modern,' and several collections of religious verse, among them 'Introits,' (Philadelphia, 1844), and 'Catena Dominica (1854). At his death he left in manuscript 'A Dictionary of English Surnames.' 'The Life of J. H. Alexander' was published by William Pinkney (1867), and a sketch by J. E. Hilgard was published in Vol. I of the 'Biographical Memoirs' of the National Academy of Sciences.

ALFRIEND, EDWARD MORRISON. Dramatic writer. He was born at Richmond, Va., October 25, 1843, the son of Thomas M. and Mary Ann Alfriend. His education was received at William and Mary College, at Williamsburg, Va. Most of his life has been spent at the North, and he resides at present in New York City. His writings include: 'A Woman's Ordeal,' 'A Foregone Conclusion,' 'The Louisianian,' 'Across the Potomac,' 'The Diplomats,' 'The Great Diamond Robbery,' 'His Double Life,' and several other novels.

ALFRIEND, FRANK H. Editor and author. For some time he edited the Southern Messenger, published at Richmond, Va., and wrote 'The Life of Jefferson Davis' (1868), and 'The Life of Robert E. Lee (1870), besides minor works.

ALLAIN, HELENE, Madame. Poet. [La.]. She published a volume of verse (1890).

ALLAN, ELIZABETH PRESTON. Author. The subject of this sketch was born in Lexington, Va., December 22, 1848. For several years past she has edited the 'Sunday School Literature' of the Southern Presbyterian Church and at leisure intervals has written several delightful stories for children. She has also published 'The Life and Letters of Margaret J. Preston,' her stepmother, (Boston. Houghton, Mifflin and Company, 1903). The sketch of Margaret J. Preston in 'The Library of Southern Literature' is from her pen. She married, May 14, 1874, Colonel William Allan.

ALLAN, WILLIAM, educator and historian, was born at Winchester, Va., November 12, 1837. During the Civil War he was chief of ordnance in Stonewall Jackson's Corps, with the rank of lieutenant-colonel. From 1866 to 1873 he was professor of mathematics in Washington and Lee University, and from 1873 to 1889 he was principal of McDonough School, an industrial institution near Baltimore. He wrote an important work of great interest entitled 'The Army of Northern Virginia in 1862,' with an introduction by John C. Ropes. (Boston, Houghton, Mifflin and Company, 1892), besides minor works, including 'Chancellorsville' and 'Jackson's Valley Campaign.' He died September 17, 1889. In recognition of his ripe scholarship he received the degree of LL.D.

ALLEN, D. C. Author. [Mo.]. He wrote: 'The Life and Character of Colonel Alexander W. Doniphan.' (Liberty, Mo., D. C. Allen, 1897.)

ALLEN, EDWARD ARCHIBALD. Professor of English language and literature in the University of Missouri. He was born at Suffolk, Va., October 3, 1843, and married Priscilla Armistead Sanders, of Liberty, Va. Besides numerous contributions to various magazines, he is the author of 'A School Grammar of the English Language' (Boston, D. C. Heath and Company, 1900). He also assisted in the compilation of 'The World's Best Essays' (St. Louis, Ferd. P. Kaiser Company, 1899) and 'The World's Best Orations' (ibid., 1900). In association with Dr. R. H. Jesse he also edited "Missouri Literature" (1901). For 'The Library of Southern Literature' he wrote the sketch of Thomas L. Snead. Washington and Lee gave him the degree of Litt.D. He resides in Columbia, Mo.

ALLEN, HENRY WATKINS, statesman and soldier, was born in Prince Edward County, Va., April 29, 1820. His father, a physician of some note, removed to Lexington, Mo.; but, on account of a disagreement, the youth left home before completing his studies and began to teach. In 1842, when President Sam Houston called for volunteers in the Texan War against Mexico, he enlisted upon the side of the republic. Afterward he located for the practice of law at Baton Rouge, La., acquired extensive holdings and became an important factor in politics. He rose to the rank of brigadier-general in the Confederate Army; but the explosion of a shell disabled him in both legs and resulted in placing him in the chair of governor. At the close of the struggle, he located in the City of Mexico and established a paper, *The Mexican Times*, which was printed in English. But soon after making this change of abode he died in his foreign home, April 2, 1866. An extended tour of Europe, which he made during the prime of life, bore fruit in a volume entitled: 'Travels of a Sugar Planter,' and in the year following his death Mrs. Sarah A. Dorsey published her interesting 'Recollections of Henry W. Allen,' (New York, 1867).

ALLEN, JAMES LANE. See Biographical and Critical Sketch, Vol. I, page 41.

ALLEN, JAMES LANE. One of the leading lawyers of Chicago. He was born at Lexington, Ky., March 3, 1848, and was educated at Bethany College, W. Va. He practiced law for two years at Omaha, Neb., and afterward settled in Chicago. He married, in 1870, Josephine E. Fenkell. He is the compiler of 'Allen's Hand-book of the Nebraska Code,' and is the author of several stories and sketches, including: 'The Exodus of the Children of Ham,' 'Aunt Viney's Story' and 'The Horse-Shoe Bend.'

ALLEN, JOHN MILLS. Lawyer. Often called "Private John," a soubriquet which he earned in his first race for Congress. He was born in Tishomingo County, Miss., July 8, 1846; and, after receiving an elementary education, he was admitted to the Bar. Despite his youth he served in the Confederate ranks; and it was not until the war was over that he began his legal studies. On December 24, 1872, he married Georgia Taylor, at Tupelo, Miss. Entering politics, he represented his district in Congress from 1885 to 1901. As a humorist he made a reputation which was national in extent and which rivaled even the fame of "Sunset" Cox. His speeches are models of political humor. He resides at Tupelo, Miss.

ALLEN, JOHN ROBERT. Professor of Mental and Moral Philosophy in the Southwestern University, at Georgetown, Texas, and a clergyman in the M.E. Church, South. He is a native of Iredell County, N.C. He married, October 3, 1878, Mollie Crútchfield. His books include: 'Man, Money and the Bible' (Nashville, Southern Methodist Publishing Company), and 'The Itinerant Guide' (*ibid.*). He resides in Georgetown, Texas. The Southern University gave him the degree of D.D.

ALLEN, LYMAN WHITNEY, clergyman and poet, was born in St. Louis, Mo., November 19, 1854. His father was George Otis Allen. Since 1880 he has been a minister of the Presbyterian Church; and he resides at present in Newark, N. J. As a poet he has won signal honors. He was the successful competitor for the New York *Herald's* $1,000 prize, the poem which brought him this trophy being "Abraham Lincoln—The Star of Sangamon" (New York, G. P. Putnam's Sons). He received his D.D. from Wooster.

ALLEN, PAUL, editor and author, was born in Providence, R.I., February 15, 1775. On completing his education at Brown University, he engaged in newspaper work and prepared the 'Travels of Lewis and Clarke' for the press. During the greater part of his adult life he resided in Baltimore, Md. He was a man of unusual gifts but was constantly in need of a spur. Because of this peculiar drawback he failed to redeem his engagements to write either a 'History of the Revolution' or a 'Life of Washington,' for which subscriptions were taken. Nevertheless, he published a volume of poems in 1801 and a 'Life of Alexander I' in 1818, besides a poem in twenty-five cantos, entitled "Noah," which was reduced by advice to five. At one time he suffered imprisonment for debt. He died in Baltimore, August 18, 1826.

ALLEN, WILLIAM, statesman, was born at Edenton, N.C., in 1806, and died in Ohio, July 11, 1879. The earlier part of his life was spent at Lynchburg, Va., but at the age of sixteen he made his way on foot to Ohio, where his half-sister, the mother of Allen G. Thurman, resided. Here he studied law, became an advocate of wide reputation at the Bar, served in Congress as a Democrat and at the age of thirty-one, took his seat in the United States Senate, the youngest man who was ever given the toga. He was subsequently reëlected in 1843. Later he became governor of the State. On account of his powerful voice he was called in Washington "the Ohio Gong." But he was equally vigorous in intellect, a man of strong individuality and character who left his impress upon his times.

ALLEN, WILLIAM FRANCIS. Editor. He compiled, in association with Charles Pickard and Lucy McKim, a work entitled 'The Slave Songs of the United States,' (New York, A Simpson and Company, 1867).

ALLEN, YOUNG J., for more than fifty years an honored missionary of the Methodist Episcopal Church, South, in China, was born in Burke County, Ga., in 1836. His literary work is quite voluminous, including: 'The Czar of Russia,' 'Li Hung Chang's Travels,' 'Family Prayers for Chinese Christians,' 'Illustrations of Christian Truth,' 'Life of Luther,' and 'Woman in All Lands.' He married Molly Hampton. For some time he taught English in a Chinese University; he also made numerous translations; and by reason of his blameless life and great learning he became one of the revered patriarchs of China. Emory College made him a D.D.

ALLISON, JOHN. Author. [Tenn.]. He wrote 'Dropped Stitches in Tennessee History' (1897).

ALLMOND, MARCUS BLAKEY, educator and author, was born at Stanardsville, Va., August 17, 1851. When a student at the University he won the magazine medal, a trophy which served to stimulate his latent genius of authorship, and he afterward published 'Estelle, an Idyl of Old Virginia,' 'Agricola, an Easter Idyl,' 'Fairfax, My Lord,' an historical poem, 'Outlines of Latin Syntax,' 'Lectures and Addresses' and 'Miscellaneous Poems.' In 1900 he was called to the chair of Latin and German in Hampden-Sidney College. He married, June 30, 1879, Virginia Carey Meade, a niece of Bishop Meade. The University gave him the degree of LL.D.

ALLSTON, JOSEPH BLYTH. Soldier and poet. [S.C.] He published 'Battle Songs.'

ALLSTON, WASHINGTON. See Biographical and Critical Sketch, Vol. I, page 87.

ALSOP, GEORGE. Author. The known details of his life are meager; but he was an Englishman, born in 1638, resided for several years in the Colonies and published a work of mixed prose and verse entitled: 'A Character of the Province of Maryland' (London, 1666).

ALSTON, ROBERT FRANCIS WITHERS, governor, rice planter and civil engineer, was born in All Saints' Parish S.C., April 21, 1801, and died in Georgetown. S.C., April 7, '1864. He was educated at West Point, but resigned to engage in industrial pursuits. From 1856 to 1858 he was governor of South Carolina. He wrote several volumes, among them 'Memoirs of Rice' (1843), 'Report on Public Schools' (1847), and 'Essays on Sea Coast Crops.' On account of his extensive operations he greatly stimulated the cultivation of rice in South Carolina.

ALTSHELER, JOSEPH ALEXANDER, author, was born at Three Springs, Ky., April 29, 1862. On completing his studies at Vanderbilt University, he engaged in journalistic work, first on the

Louisville *Courier-Journal* and afterward on the New York *World*. He married, May 30, 1888, Sara Boles. His stories, which are based upon dramatic incidents of American history, have proved unusually popular. They include: 'The Sun of Saratoga,' 'In Hostile Red,' 'A Soldier of Manhattan,' 'The Last Rebel,' 'A Herald of the West,' 'My Captive,' 'In Circling Camps,' 'The Wilderness Road,' 'Before the Dawn,' 'Guthrie of the Times,' 'The Candidate,' 'Forest Runners' and 'The Young Trailers.' Most of his books have been issued by D. Appleton and Company of New York, but 'The Candidate' was published by Harper and Brothers.

ANDERSON, ARCHER. [Va.]. He published several addresses which possess both historical and literary value, among them, one on "Robert E. Lee" and one on "The Battle of Chickamauga."

ANDERSON, E. M., Mrs. Poet. [N.C.]. She published a volume of verse entitled 'Memorial Poems' (Durham, N.C., The Seeman Press, 1903).

ANDERSON, FLORENCE. Author. [Ky.]. Besides a novel entitled 'Zenaida,' she published a volume of 'Poems.'

ANDERSON, GEORGE S. Baptist clergyman. [Ala.]. He published 'The Sermon Builder' (1892).

ANDERSON, L. B. Author. [Va.]. He published a volume entitled 'Biographies of Virginia Physicians of Olden Times' (1891).

ANDREW, JAMES OSGOOD. An eminent Methodist bishop. He was born in Washington, Ga., May 3, 1794, and died in Mobile, Ala., March 1, 1871. On his relations to African slavery arose the partition of the Methodist Episcopal Church. By his second wife, whom he married in 1844, he became the owner of slave property; and, being the only member of the college of bishops who possessed such an interest, he was requested to desist from the exercise of his office so long as this impediment remained. He considered this action wholly unconstitutional, and rather than submit to dictation in the management of his private affairs he was about to surrender his Episcopal seat when his colleagues from the slave-holding States dissuaded him from taking this step. Subsequently, in 1846, a convocation of delegates from the slave-holding States was held at Petersburg, Va., and the result of this independent movement was the organization of the M.E. Church, South, of which this distinguished representative became the senior bishop. He wrote on many religious topics, but only two volumes remain to tell of his arduous labors: 'Family Government' and 'Miscellanies.'

ANDREWS, CHRISTOPHER COLUMBUS. Soldier and diplomat. He was born at Hillsboro, N. C., 1829, but prior to the Civil War he removed to Minnesota; became a brigadier-general in the Union Army; was United States Minister to Sweden from 1869 to 1876 and United States Consul-general to Brazil from 1882 to 1885. His writings include: 'A History of the Campaign of Mobile' (New York, D. Van Nostrand, 1867) and 'Brazil.'

ANDREWS, D. W. Baptist clergyman. [Ala.]. He was born in 1801. Besides an interesting resumé of the North River Association (1885), he wrote a 'History of David.'

ANDREWS, ELIZA FRANCES. Educator and writer. She was born in Washington, Ga., August 1, 1840, the daughter of Judge Garnett and Annulet Ball Andrews; graduated from LaGrange Female

College and taught for several years at Wesleyan. She is an authority on botany, and her work entitled: 'Botany the Year Around'
(New York, American Book Company), is one of the popular text-
books. Besides numerous magazine articles, she has published:
'A Family Secret' (1876), 'A Mere Adventurer' (1879), 'Prince Hal'
(Philadelphia, J. B. Lippincott Company), 'The War-time Journal
of a Georgia Girl' (New York, D. Appleton and Company), and many
serials which have not appeared in book form. Miss Andrews is also
the author of some excellent verse. Her writings are characterized by
an unusual grace of diction and charm of interest. She resides in
Montgomery, Ala.

ANDREWS, GARNETT, jurist, was born near Washington, Ga.,
October 30, 1798. He became an eminent lawyer and was for
thirty years judge of the Northern Circuit of Georgia. He was
the author of an interesting work of great historical value entitled:
'Anecdotes of the Georgia Bench and Bar; or, Reminiscences of an
Old Georgia Lawyer,' only a few copies of which are extant. He was
also the author of 'A Review of Alexander H. Stephens's War Between
the States' (1872), and many newspaper and magazine articles on
political and agricultural subjects. He died in Washington, Ga.,
August 14, 1873, at his picturesque old home called "Haywood."

ANDREWS, MATTHEW PAGE, educator and editor, was born
in Shepherdstown, W.Va., July 5, 1878. From time to time he has
written for the magazines. At present he is engaged in preparing an
important work on American history, which is to be published in two
volumes. He is also editing a volume of the poems of James Ryder
Randall. He resides in Baltimore, Md.

ANDREWS, STEPHEN P. Lawyer and jurist. [La.]. He published an important legal work entitled 'A Comparison of Common
Law with French and Spanish Law' (New Orleans, 1839).

ANDRY, LAURE, Madame. Author. [La.]. She wrote in the
French language a 'Histoire de la Louisiane' (1882).

ANSPACH, FREDERICK RINEHART. Lutheran clergyman.
For more than twenty-five years the state of Maryland furnished the
field of his activities; but he was born in Pennsylvania in 1815. Besides editing the Lutheran Observer, he published 'Sons of the Sires'
(1852), 'Sepulchres of Our Departed' (1854), and 'The Two Pilgrims'
(1857), besides minor works, including a 'Discourse on the Death of
Henry Clay,' which was his first publication. He died in Baltimore,
Md., in 1867.

ANTROBUS, SUZANNE. Author. [La.]. She wrote 'The
King's Messenger, a Story of Colonial Louisiana' (1901).

APES, WILLIAM. Author. He was an Indian of the Pequoit
tribe, who was born about the year 1800, lived in the Indian Territory,
became a preacher, and published 'A Son of the Forest' (Boston,
1831), 'Experiences of Five Christian Indians of the Pequoit Tribe'
(1833), 'Indian Nullification' (1835), and a 'Eulogy of King Philip'
(1836).

ARCHDALE, JOHN. English governor of North Carolina. He
is said to have introduced rice culture into the province by distribu-
ting among some friends a bag of seed rice given to him by the
captain of a vessel from Madagascar. On returning to England, he
wrote his 'Description of the Fertile and Pleasant Province of Caro-

lina' (London, 1707). Certain scruples concerning the requisite oath restrained him from taking a seat in Parliament.

ARCHER, BRANCH T., Texan revolutionist, was born in Virginia in 1790. For several years he practiced medicine in his native state, after which he located in Texas, took an active part in the Revolution, and became first Speaker of the House and afterward Secretary of War, on the establishment of the republic. He died in Texas in 1856. He was an orator of distinction and delivered numerous public and legislative speeches, some of which were published.

ARCHER, G. W. Physician. [Md.]. At leisure intervals he exercised his imaginative gifts by writing a number of delightful stories, among them, 'Tales of Texas' and 'More Than She Could Bear,' besides medical essays.

ARMFIELD, LUCILE, Mrs. Poet. [N.C.]. She published a volume of verse entitled 'Songs from the Carolina Hills' (New York, 1902).

ARMSTRONG, GEORGE DODD, clergyman and educator, was born at Mendham, N.J., September 15, 1813. On completing his studies at Princeton, he became for several years a professor in Washington College; but in 1851 he was called to pastoral work in Norfolk, Va. He was one of the most influential Presbyterian divines of the Old Dominion. Some of his earliest contributions were made to the *Southern Literary Messenger*. Included among his writings are: 'The Doctrine of Slavery' (New York, 1857), 'Scriptural Examination of the Doctrine of Baptism,' 'The Summer of the Pestilence,' an account of the ravages of the yellow fever in Norfolk in 1857; 'The Sacraments of the New Testament' (1880), and 'The Books of Nature and Revelation' (1886). William and Mary College gave him the degree of S.T.D. He died at Norfolk, Va., May 12, 1899.

ARMSTRONG, JOSEPH L., educator, was born at Fincastle, Va., in 1857. His father was the Rev. James E. Armstrong, D.D., and his mother, Margaret Hickman. He occupies a chair in Randolph-Macon College Va., and besides magazine articles, has published a 'Grammar of English' (1889). He also wrote the sketch of John Esten Cook for 'The Library of Southern Literature.'

ARMSTRONG, SELENE AYER, editor and magazine writer, was born in Washington, Ga., September 20, 1883. Her first appearance in print was as the winner of a prize story in the Atlanta *Constitution*, written at eleven years of age. She afterward became society editor of the Atlanta *Georgian*. At present she is on the staff of the Washington (D.C.) *Times,* but contributes at frequent intervals to current magazines. Her work, though limited in volume, is characterized by an individuality of style and thought which has attracted attention in the East as well as in the South.

"ARP, BILL." See Smith, Charles H.

ARRINGTON, ALFRED W., lawyer. was born in Iredell County, N.C., in 1810, a son of Archibald Arrington, a Whig member of Congress. For some time he was an itinerant Methodist minister in Indiana; and, on account of his rare gift of eloquence, he attracted great crowds. But he left the pulpit for the Bar, locating first in one state and then in another. For six years he held a judicial position in Texas. Later he went to Chicago, where his reputation became national. Under the name of "Charles Summerfield," he frequently made literary contributions, and wrote the famous 'Apostrophe to

Water,' which was often quoted with great effect by John B. Gough. He also published 'Sketches of the Southwest' and 'The Rangers and Regulators of the Tanaha.' He died in Chicago, January 31, 1867. Two years later appeared a volume of 'Poems,' with a memoir by his wife, Leola Arrington.

ASBURY, FRANCIS, first bishop of the Methodist Episcopal Church in America, was born in Staffordsville, England, August 20, 1745, and died in Spottsylvania, Va., March 31, 1816. He was one of the earliest pioneers of Methodism, laid the foundations of this great household of faith, traveled on horseback over 270,000 miles, from first to last, and saw the denomination grow from a scattered flock of 316 members to a powerful organization of 214,000 communicants. Perhaps it is no exaggeration to say that in the literature of pioneer life there is nothing to surpass 'Asbury's Journals' in the materials of romance. They were first published in three volumes (New York, 1852). For an authentic account of this great wilderness preacher, see Strickland's 'Life of Asbury' (New York, 1858). Dr. George G. Smith has also written an excellent memoir (Nashville, 1896). Most of his ministerial labors were performed in the South.

ASHE, SAMUEL A'COURT, lawyer and editor, was born in New Hanover County, N.C., September 13, 1840. His father was William S. Ashe and his mother, Sarah Green. For several years he was editor of the Raleigh *News and Observer,* a paper to which his signal abilities gave wide influence. At the present time he is clerk to a committee of the United States Senate. Besides editing six volumes of the 'Biographical History of North Carolina,' published by C. L. Van Noppen and Company (1905-1907), to which he contributed most of the sketches, he is also the author of 'A History of North Carolina,' the first volume of which appeared in 1908. During the Civil War, Captain Ashe was an ordnance officer in the famous Battery Wagner.

ASHE, THOMAS. Author. Says Appleton's 'Cyclopedia of American Biography': "He is supposed to be the 'T. A. gent,' who visited this country on board His Majesty's ship, *Richmond,* and, on his return to England, in 1682, published 'Carolina,' a work of some pretensions descriptive of the province." The work was subsequently reprinted in 'Historical Collections of South Carolina' (1836).

ASHMORE, OTIS. Educator and astronomer. He was born in Lincoln County, Ga., March 6, 1853. He is widely known on account of the astronomical forecasts which he has made for 'Grier's Almanac;' but he has also contributed numerous articles to the magazines on scientific subjects. He resides in Savannah, Ga.

ASTROP, ROBERT. Author. He lived at Brunswick, Va., and published a volume of 'Original Poems on a Variety of Subjects, Interspersed with Tales' (Philadelphia, 1835). It contains only 132 pages, but the writer claims it to be "the largest miscellaneous collection ever published by an American author." The chief interest of the work attaches to this statement.

ATKINSON, CHARLES PRESCOTT. Methodist Episcopal clergyman and educator. He was born in Newton, Ala., August 31, 1867. Besides occasional essays, he is the author of the sketch of Clifford Lanier in 'The Library of Southern Literature,' and has an important work in preparation. Since 1904, Dr. Atkinson has held the chair of philosophy in Southern University at Greensboro, Ala. He married, October 14, 1896, Jessie Laird.

ATKINSON, GEORGE WESLEY. Congressman, governor, jurist, author. He was born in Charlestown, W.Va., June 29, 1845, and graduated from Ohio Wesleyan University in 1870. He was admitted to the Bar and became United States Marshal; served one term in Congress; occupied the office of governor from 1897 to 1901; was United States District Attorney for the Southern District of West Virginia for four years; and in 1895 became Judge of the United States Court of Claims. In politics he is a stanch Republican. He is also a Knight Templar and a Free Mason of high rank. He is, a man of strong convictions and of outspoken opinions, and despite the heavy demands of public life, has written numerous books upon historical and economic subjects, including: 'The West Virginia Pulpit,' 'The A. B. C. of the Tariff,' 'Don't: or, Negative Chips from the Blocks of Living Truths,' 'Revenue Digest, 'Prominent Men of West Virginia,' a text-book on Psychology, 'Public Addresses,' and 'After the Moonshiners.' He has also paid tribute to the poetic muse in fragmentary bits of song. The University of Nashville gave him the degree of LL.D. and the University of Virginia, the degree of D.C.L. He resides in Charlestown, W.Va.

ATKINSON, W. D. Lawyer. [Ala.]. He compiled 'The Laws of Alabama' (1890).

AUDUBON, JOHN JAMES. See Biographical and Critical Sketch, Vol. I, page 103.

AUDUBON, LUCY BAKEWELL, was the wife of the great naturalist, John James Audubon. She often shared the travels of her husband, encouraged him in his scientific labors amid sore trials and perplexities, and published 'The Life of John James Audubon: Edited by His Widow,' with an introduction by James Grant Wilson (New York, 1869). She survived her husband for more than twenty years and died at the home of her sister-in-law, in Shelbyville, Ky., June 19, 1874.

AUDUBON, MARIA R. She published a work entitled, 'Audubon and His Journals' (New York, 1897).

AUGUSTIN, GEORGE. Author. [La.]. He published 'Romances of New Orleans' (1891).

AUGUSTIN, JAMES M. Clergyman. [La.]. He wrote a 'History of the Catholic Church in Louisiana' (1893).

AUGUSTIN, JOHN. Editor and poet. He was born in New Orleans, La., February 11, 1838. At different times he held the city editorship of nearly every newspaper in New Orleans. When the Civil War began he entered the Confederate ranks; and, during the quiet intervals of camp life, wrote most of the poems which were afterward published in a volume, entitled 'War Flowers' (1865). But his prose surpasses his verse in artistic power. An article entitled "The Oaks," descriptive of the old duelling-ground of New Orleans, reveals his mastery in this respect. It is preserved in 'The Louisiana Book.' He died in New Orleans, February 5, 1888.

AUGUSTIN, MARIE. Author. [La.]. She published a novel entitled ' Le Mecandal ' (1892).

AUSTIN, MARTHA W. Author. She was born in New Orleans, La., a daughter of Major John E. and Shaulline Yerger Creath Austin, and was educated at Newcombe College, New Orleans, but subsequently took special lectures in psychology at Radcliffe College, Cambridge, Mass. As an author, she is rapidly rising into well deserved prominence. Her two books: 'Veronica' (New York, Doubleday, Page and Company) and 'Tristram and Isoult' (Boston, Richard G. Badger and Company), possess rare interest and give prophetic token of an exceptionally brilliant career. She is on the staff of the New Orleans *Picayune.*

AUSTIN, MARIA THERESA. Mother Superior, [La.]. Several volumes came from the pen of this consecrated woman, among them, a 'Life of the Venerable Clement Mary Hofbauer' (1877), a 'Life of St. Alphonsus Ligouri' (1879), a 'Life of Catharine McAuley,' foundress and first Superior of the Sisters of Mercy (1887), and 'The Annals of the Sisters of Mercy in Ireland, Great Britain and America' (1888). She was universally called "Mother Austin."

AVARY, MYRTA LOCKETT. Editor, author, poet. This well-known writer is a native of Virginia. Her father was Harwood Alexander Lockett and her mother Augusta Harper. She is the wife of Dr. James Corbin Avary, of Atlanta, Ga. For some time she resided in New York, serving on the editorial staffs of some of the leading magazines. She has specialized on sociological subjects and has written numerous stories of tenement life in the congested centers of population. She has also been interested in settlement work and in various metropolitan charities. At present she is engaged in sociological and historical work in the South. Besides frequent contributions to the periodicals of the day, she is the author of several books, among them: 'A Virginia Girl in the Civil War' (New York, D. Appleton and Company), 'Dixie After the War' (New York, Doubleday, Page and Company), and 'A Diary From Dixie' (New York, D. Appleton and Company), all of which are charming portraitures of life in the South, evincing on the part of the author a keen insight and a sympathetic touch.

AVERY, ISAAC ERWIN. See Biographical and Critical Sketch, Vol. I, page 131.

AVERY, ISAAC WHEELER, lawyer and editor, was born at St. Augustine, Fla., in 1837, and was educated at Oglethorpe University, enlisting in the Confederate Army soon after completing his studies and attaining the rank of colonel. At the close of the struggle he engaged in the practice of law; but eventually he relinquished this profession for journalism, editing first the Atlanta *Herald* and afterward the Atlanta *Capitol.* Finally he was called to the helm of the *Constitution.* He published a 'History of Georgia, 1850-1881,' an interesting resumé of an eventful period in the life of the commonwealth. He died in 1897.

AVERY, SUSAN LOOK. Reformer and writer. She was born in Conway, Mass., October 27, 1817, a daughter of Samuel and Polly Look. She married Benjamin F. Avery and became one of the pioneer advocates of equal suffrage. Besides founding the Woman's Club of Louisville, Ky., she has also written and spoken much for temperance reform; but, while her pen has been tireless and brilliant, she has left little in permanent form. At the advanced age of ninety-two years she still resides in Louisville, at the home of her daughter, Mrs. C. B. Robinson.

AVIRETT, JAMES BATTLE. Protestant Episcopal clergyman. [N.C.]. He wrote an interesting account of life in the South in ante-bellum days entitled 'The Old South, or How We Lived in Great House and Cabin Before the War' with an introduction by Dr.

Hunter McGuire (New York, F. Tennyson Neely Company, 1901). Dr. Avirett also published an important work of biography entitled 'General Turner Ashby and His Compeers.'

AYRES, BROWN, educator, was born in Memphis, Tenn., May 25, 1856. For twenty-four years, he was professor of physics in Tulane University; but is now president of the University of Tennessee. He married, July 5, 1881, Kate Allen Anderson of Lexington, Va. Dr. Ayres is one of the consulting editors of 'The Library of Southern Literature,' a ripe scholar and a fine disciplinarian. In addition to several addresses, he has published numerous scientific and educational papers. Three institutions have given him the degree of LL.D. He has also received the degrees of Ph.D. and D.C.L.

AYRES, DAISY FITZHUGH. Journalist and author. She was born in Virginia, of aristocratic colonial stock, engaged in journalistic work in Kentucky and published a novel of fascinating interest entitled 'The Conquest' (Washington and New York, The Neale Publishing Company, 1906).

BABCOCK, BERNIE. Story-writer in the interest of temperance and other reforms. She was born in Unionville, Ohio, April 28, 1866, a daughter of H. N. and Lottie B. Smade. She removed to Arkansas in early girlhood, married Wm. F. Babcock and now resides in Little Rock. She has written some excellent short stories, numerous poems, and several novels of purpose, including: 'The Daughter of a Republican,' 'The Martyr,' 'Justice to the Woman,' 'At the Mercy of the State,' 'An Uncrowned Queen,' 'By Way of the Master Passion,' 'Paul, a Victim of Justice,' and 'In Civilized Gotham.' On account of the quality and rank of the temperance literature which she has produced, Mrs. Babcock has been called the greatest temperance writer in America, and her stories are in very great demand.

BABCOCK, WILLIAM H., lawyer and author, was born in St. Louis, Mo., January 19, 1849. On completing his studies at the Columbian University Law School, he engaged in newspaper work for several years, after which he settled for the practice of law in Washington, D.C., where he still resides. At leisure intervals he has given his pen to the muse and has also written several entertaining works of fiction. His publications include: 'Lord Stirling's Stand, and Other Poems,' 'Lays from Over the Sea,' 'Cypress Beach,' 'The Brides of the Tiger,' 'An Invention of the Enemy,' 'The Clan of the Chariots,' 'The Two Last Centuries of Britain,' 'The Tower of Wye' (Philadelphia, Henry T. Coates and Company, 1901), and others. He has been twice married.

BACHMAN, CATHARINE LOUISE. Author. [S.C.]. She wrote 'The Life of John Bachman, by His Daughter.'

BACHMAN, JOHN, clergyman, author, scientist, was born in Dutchess County, N.Y., February 4, 1790, and died in Charleston, S.C., February 25, 1874. On completing his studies at Williams College he spent some time abroad, after which he entered the ministry, and for the greater part of his life was pastor of the Lutheran Chuch in Charleston. But his most important achievements were in the realm of scientific investigation. Besides assisting Audubon in his great work on ornithology, he was the chief contributor to an authoritative compendium of standard value on 'The Quadrupeds of North America,' he also wrote 'Experiments Made on the Habits of Vultures Inhabiting Carolina' (1834), 'A Monograph of the Hares of America'

(1837), 'The Design and Duties of the Christian Ministry' (1848), 'Two Letters on Hybridity' (1850), 'The Doctrine of the Unity of the Human Race Examined on the Principles of Science' (1850), a 'Defence of Luther' (1853), 'Characteristics of Genera and Species as Applied to the Doctrine of the Unity of the Human Race' (1854), 'Notice of the Types of Mankind by Nott and Glidden' (1854), an 'Examination of Professor Agassiz's Sketch of the National Provinces of the Animal World,' and numerous articles for *The Medical Journal of South Carolina.*

BACON, AUGUSTUS OCTAVIUS, United States Senator from Georgia, was born in Bryan County, Ga., October 20, 1839. On completing his studies at the University of Georgia, he shouldered his musket and went to the front. During the earlier campaigns he was adjutant of the Ninth Georgia Regiment of Infantry, but afterward became a captain. At the close of hostilities he engaged in the practice of law and became one of the foremost advocates at the Bar of Georgia. For seven consecutive terms he was elected to the State Legislature, and on five different occasions he was honored with the Speakership. In 1894 he was commissioned to serve in the United States Senate as a Democrat, was reëlected to this high office in 1900, and again in 1906 he was chosen his own successor. He is one of the ablest debaters in the Upper Chamber, an elegant and forceful public speaker, possesses an intimate knowledge of the intricate problems of legislation, and commands, whenever he speaks, the careful attention of his colleagues. On frequent occasions he has delivered literary addresses and at intervals has contributed to newspapers and reviews. He published a volume of speeches (Washington, D.C., 1901).

BACON, EUGENIA JONES, author, artist, lecturer, was born at "Green Forest," near Midway Church, in Liberty County, Ga., February 2, 1840. Her maiden name was Eugenia Jones. She married, December 8, 1858, Oliver Thomas Bacon of Savannah. After the death of her husband and only child, she spent several years abroad in the study of art, and one of her pictures was purchased by the Grand Duchess of Hesse, daughter of the late Queen Victoria. Subsequently she traveled in Europe and America. Of late years she has been engaged in literary and lecture work. She is the owner of the famous stone from Oberammergau, a curio shaped by natural processes into the image of Christ. She has written 'Lyddy, a Tale of the Old South,' a work which has elicited praise from high critics (New York, 1898); 'The Stone from Oberammergau' (New York, 1891), 'The Man of Sorrows' (London, 1896) 'The Real Stone Face' (Atlanta, 1899) and 'The Red Moon' (New York and Washington, The Neale Publishing Company, 1909), besides a story in manuscript.

BACON, JOHN HARWOOD. Author. He was born in Portland, Me., November 6, 1875, and graduated from the University of Wisconsin. He served in the Spanish-American War. Besides numerous contributions to the magazines, he has written 'The Pursuit of Phillis' (New York, Henry Holt and Company). He resides in Louisville, Ky.

BACON, JULIA, poet, was born in Macon, Ga., some time prior to the Civil War. She wrote numerous stories and poems which went the rounds of the press, and published ' Looking for the Fairies, and Other Poems.' Her descent from Nathaniel Bacon, "the Jamestown rebel," was an honor of which she often boasted. On leaving Georgia, she made her home in Beaumont. Texas. Later in life she also wrote several novels, among them: 'Broken Links' (1882) and 'The Phantom Wife; or, Guy Newton's Revenge' (1884).

BACON, MARY APPLEWHITE, educator, was born at Marietta, Ga., in 1863. On graduating from the Lucy Cobb Institute at Athens, she taught in the local schools until called to the chair of English in the Milledgeville Normal and Industrial College. She has been very successful in dialect work, portraying with equal charm and fidelity to life both the negro and the "cracker"; and her sketches which have appeared in the leading magazines and periodicals of the day have brought her wide recognition. Perhaps her best work has been in *Harper's Magazine.* Several years ago she published an arithmetic for primary grades.

BADGER, E. M., Mrs. Poet. [Texas]. She published 'Silent Influence, and Other Poems.'

BAGBY, ALFRED. Episcopal clergyman. Dr. Bagby published a work of much interest entitled 'King and Queen County, Virginia' (New York and Washington, The Neale Publishing Company, 1907), for the production of which he was equipped by an active pastorate of thirty-five years in this historic center of Virginia's political and social traditions. Dr. George W. Bagby, one of the editors of the *Southern Literary Messenger,* was his cousin.

BAGBY, DAVID YOUNG. Baptist clergyman. [Ky.]. Born in 1859. He published 'Jesus the Messiah of Prophecy' (1897) and a 'History of the New Testament.'

BAGBY, GEORGE WILLIAM. See Biographical and Critical Sketch, Vol. I, page 141.

BAILEY, JOSEPH WELDON, United States Senator from Texas, was born in Copiah County, Miss., October 3, 1863. On completing his education he settled in Gainesville, Texas, for the practice of law, won distinction in the courtroom and on the hustings by his eloquence as a speaker, represented his district in Congress for ten years, and in 1901 took his seat in the United States Senate, in which body he still serves. As a debater he has no superior on the floor of the Upper House. From time to time he has contributed to current periodicals and has delivered addresses on various themes and occasions. He is a Democrat.

BAILEY, JOSIAH WILLIAM, lawyer, was born in Warrenton, Va. The sketch of Thomas Dixon, Jr., in 'The Library of Southern Literature' is from his pen. He also wrote 'The Grounds of Democratic Hope' (1909). He resides in Raleigh, N.C.

BAILEY, THOMAS PEARCE, Jr. Educator. He was born in Georgetown, S.C., August 18, 1867, the son of an eminent physician, Dr. Thomas Pearce Bailey, and married August 1, 1895, Minneola Davis, of Marion, S.C. Dr. Bailey holds the chair of psychology in the University of Mississippi, and is also dean of the Department of Education. He has published 'Love and Law' (San Francisco, Whitaker and Ray), has contributed numerous articles to the educational and literary magazines, and bestowed much thought and study upon the negro problem. The University of South Carolina gave him the degree of Ph.D. He resides in Oxford, Miss.

BAILEY, WILLIAM HENRY, Sr., lawyer and author, was born in Pasquotank, N.C., January 22, 1831. After graduation from Caldwell College, he studied law, became Attorney-general of North Carolina, and Code Commissioner. Later he removed to Houston, Texas. Besides editing a 'Digest of North Carolina Supreme Court Decisions,' he published 'The Effect of the Civil War upon the Rights of Persons and Property Onus Probandi' (Albany, N.Y., Banks Brothers and Company), 'Conflict of Judicial Decisions,' 'The Detective Faculty' (Cincinnati, The Robert Clarke Company), and numerous legal and historical papers. Rutherford College gave him the degree of LL.D.

BAIN, CHARLES WESLEY. Educator. He was born in Portsmouth, Va., June 24, 1864, and enjoyed the best educational advantages. At the present time he is professor of ancient languages in the University of South Carolina. Bain's 'First Latin Book' (New York, University Publishing Co.) is the product of his pen, also translations from Homer (Boston, Ginn and Company) and Ovid (New York, The Macmillan Company). He resides in Columbia, S.C.

BAIRD, SAMUEL JOHN, clergyman, was born in Newark, Ohio, in 1817. After graduation from Centre College, Ky., he held pastorates both in Kentucky and in Virginia, until compelled by ill health to relinquish his labors. He made a special study of church government and published 'The Church of Christ: Its Constitution and Order,' 'A History of the Early Polity of the Presbyterian Church in the Training of Ministers,' ' Elohim Revealed in the Creation and Redemption of Man' (1859), 'A History of the New School' (1868), 'A Collection of the Acts, Deliverances and Testimonies of the Supreme Judicatory of the Presbyterian Church' (1855), and 'The Assembly's Digest' (1858).

BAKER, D. W. C. Compiler. [Texas]. He published 'The Texas Scrap-Book,' a work comprising historical, biographical, and miscellaneous literary materials.

BAKER, DANIEL, clergyman and educator, was born in Liberty County, Ga., August 17, 1891. For a number of years he was pastor of the Independent Presbyterian Church of Savannah; but in later life he became president of the Presbyterian College, at Austin, Texas, an institution which he organized and endowed. As the result of a series of meetings which he conducted in Beaufort, S.C., in 1831, three men who were destined to sway wide influence were converted, among a host of others: the Hon. Rhett W. Barnwell, Bishop Stephen Elliott, and Dr. Richard Fuller. His works include: 'Baker on Baptism,' 'Baptism in a Nutshell,' 'Affectionate Addresses to Fathers and Mothers,' and 'Revival Sermons.' He died at Austin, Texas, December 10, 1857.

BAKER, JULIA WETHERILL. Literary critic and editorial writer. She was born in Woodville, Miss., July 15, 1858, and was educated in Philadelphia, Pa. On March 3, 1886, she was united in marriage to Marion A. Baker, of New Orleans, La. She is on the editorial staff of *The Times-Democrat,* having followed in this position the gifted Lafcadio Hearn. She wields a pen of unusual brilliance and contributes to the leading magazines. In 'The Louisiana Book' (1894) an article by her entitled "Magicians and Feather Dusters" reveals the piquant charm and subtle power of this tálented writer. She is also the author of several poems of exceptional merit.

BAKER, KARLE WILSON ("Charlotte Wilson"), magazine writer, was born in Little Rock, Ark., October 13, 1878. Her literary work has appeared in several high-class periodicals. She writes with equal grace of touch in both prose and verse. Some of her contributions include: "The Love of Elia" and "A Child's Game" in *Harper's,* "Brother Singers," "The Rubber-Tired Boy," and "A Point of Honor" in the *Century;* "Bed-time," in the *Atlantic Monthly,* "An Accidental Saint," in *Collier's,* and "The End of a Philosophy," in *Putnam's.* She is at present engaged in preparing a history of Texas. She married, August 8, 1907, Thomas E. Baker. Her home is in Nacogdoches, Texas.

BAKER, WILLIAM MUMFORD, clergyman and author, was born in Washington, D.C., June 27, 1825, of Southern parents. His father was the distinguished Rev. Daniel Baker, D.D. After graduating with honors from Princeton, he entered the ministry of the Presbyterian Church. For fifteen years he was a pastor in Texas. Besides writing 'The Life of Daniel Baker, D.D.,' he also wrote: 'Inside: A Chronicle of Secession,' which was secretly published under the name of G. F. Harrington, portraying in vivid colors the existing sentiment at the South (New York, 1866). His other works, consisting largely of romantic tales, include: 'Oak Mot,' 'Mose Evans,' 'Carter Quarterman,' 'Colonel Dunwoodie,' 'The Virginians in Texas,' 'Thirlmore,' 'His Majesty Myself,' and 'Blessed Saint Certainty.' Just before his death appeared 'The Ten Theophanies,' and immediately after his death, 'The Making of a Man.' He died in Boston, Mass., August 20, 1883.

BALDWIN, JAMES MARK, educator and psychologist, was born in Columbia, S.C., January 12, 1861. His father was the Hon. Cyrus H. Baldwin, of the United States Sub-treasury. On completing his collegiate course at Princeton, he prosecuted his studies abroad. For fourteen years he was professor of psychology at Princeton, and since 1903 he has filled the same chair at Johns Hopkins. He is one of the recognized authorities of the day in the realm of psychological thought. Besides editing 'The Library of Historical Psychology' (New York, Charles Scribner's Sons), 'The Dictionary of Philosophy and Psychology' (New York, The Macmillan Company, 1901-1906), 'Johnston's Universal Encyclopœdia' (Richmond, B. F. Johnson and Company), and various periodicals, he has published a 'Hand-Book of Psychology' (New York, Henry Holt and Company, 1890), 'Elements of Psychology' (Holt, 1893), 'Mental Development in the Child and the Race' (New York, The Macmillan Company, 1896), 'Social and Ethical Interpretations in Mental Development' (Macmillan, 1898), 'The Story of the Mind' (New York, D. Appleton and Company, 1898), 'Fragments in Philosophy and Science' (New York, Charles Scribner's Sons, 1902), 'Development and Evolution' (New York, The Macmillan Company, 1902), and 'Genetic Logis,' Vol. I (Macmillan). He has also contributed to scientific journals and reviews on both sides of the water and has been the recipient of numerous honors. He married, in 1888, Helen Hayes Green of Princeton, N.J. He received the Ph.D. degree from Princeton, the Sc.D. from Oxford, England, and the LL.D. from Glasgow University and South Carolina College. Most of his books have been translated into foreign tongues.

BALDWIN, JOSEPH GLOVER. See Biographical and Critical Sketch, Vol. I, page 175.

BALL, CAROLINE AUGUSTA, poet, was born in Charleston, S.C., February 27, 1823. Her father was the Rev. Edward Rutledge, grandson of John Rutledge, the first Governor of South Carolina and Chief Justice of the Supreme Court of the United States. Her mother was Miss Shaler of Connecticut. She spent the early years of her life in the "Nutmeg" State, where she wrote the first of her charming verses; but she afterward removed to Charleston, her father having been called to one of the parish churches on the Cooper River. Here she married Mr. Isaac Ball and bore with grace and dignity a conspicuous part in the social life of the cultured metropolis. But the sorrow and suffering which weighed upon her sympathetic nature in later years was the inspiration of her best work. The most famous of her poems is the beautiful war-song called "The Jacket of Gray," which was set to music by Stratford Benjamin Woodbury. It is the opening gem of her little volume entitled 'The Jacket of Gray, and Other Poems,' which appeared in 1866.

BALLAGH, JAMES CURTIS. Educator. He was born in Brownsburg, Va., October 10, 1866, the son of the Rev. James H. and Margaret Kinnear Ballagh, and received the best educational advantages from Washington and Lee University, the University of Virginia, and Johns Hopkins University. At the last-named institution, he specialized in history, economics, and jurisprudence, winning the Stewart and the Marshall prizes. He married, July 6, 1897, Josephine Jackson. He was associate professor of biology at Tulane for some time; and in 1895 became associate professor of history at Johns Hopkins. He has traveled over the greater part of the globe, increasing by close observation his knowledge both of countries and of peoples. His writings include: 'White Servitude in the Colony of Virginia' (1895), 'The Scotch-Irish in Virginia' (1896), Introduction to Southern Economic History—I, 'The Land System' (1897), II, 'Tariff and Public Lands' (1898), 'North and South in National Expansion' (1899), 'Introduction of Slavery into North America' (1898), 'Baltimore and Municipal Reform' (1899), 'Land System of the Southwest' (1899), 'Institutional Origin of Slavery' (1899), 'Social Condition of the Ante-Bellum Negro' (1900), and 'A History of Slavery in Virginia' (1902). He has in preparation 'The Letters of Richard Henry Lee' in two volumes, and 'The Economic History of the South.' Most of his writings have been issued from the Johns Hopkins University Press, of Baltimore, Md. They are of the very greatest importance because of the light which they throw upon economic problems, and especially upon the genesis and development of slave labor in the United States. Johns Hopkins gave him the degree of Ph.D. and the University of Alabama the degree of LL.D.

BANISTER, JOHN. Botanist. [Eng. and Va.]. He published 'Curiosities in Virginia,' a work dealing largely with plant and animal life. He died in 1692.

BANKS, MARY ROSS. Author. [Ga.]. She was born in 1846. From her pen has come an interesting work entitled 'Bright Days in the Old Plantation Times.'

BANKS, NANCY H. Author. [Ky.]. She wrote 'The Little Hills' (New York, The Macmillan Company, 1905) and 'Oldfield' (Macmillan, 1906), two delightful stories.

BANKS, ROBERT W. Author. [Miss.]. Colonel Banks published a work entitled 'The Battle of Franklin' (New York and Washington, The Neale Publishing Company, 1908), in which he interestingly tells the story of the famous engagement, chiefly for the purpose of commemorating the valor of his comrade, Major E. L. Russell, who amid the terrific fire of death planted his colors on the inner breastworks of the Federals.

BARBE, WAITMAN. See Biographical and Critical Sketch, Vol. I, page 207.

BARBEE, WILLIAM J., physician and educator, was born in Winchester, Ky., in 1816, and graduated in medicine but relinquished the practice to engage in educational work. From time to time he was identified with various institutions; and he also became an able expounder of the doctrines of the Church of the Disciples. He wrote: 'Physical and Moral Aspects of Geology,' 'First Principles of Geology,' 'The Cotton Question,' 'The Scriptural Doctrine of Confirmation Without the Laying On of Hands,' 'The Life of Peter,' and other works.

BARBER, CATHARINE WEBB, editor, was born in Massachusetts but came South, settling first in Georgia and afterward in Alabama. She edited *Miss Barber's Weekly* and published 'Three Golden Links' and 'The Freemason's Fireside.' She became Mrs. Towles.

BARBOUR, JAMES, statesman, was born in Orange County, Va., June 10, 1775, and was the son of Colonel Thomas Barbour. For sixteen years he sat in the House of Delegates, and in 1812 became Governor of Virginia. Later he was sent to the Senate of the United States. In 1825 he became Secretary of War under President John Quincy Adams, and in 1828, United States Minister to England. He was in politics an ardent Whig. The anti-duelling act on the Virginia statute books is from his pen. Some of his speeches are preserved in the 'Congressional Globe.' He died in Virginia, June 8, 1842.

BARBOUR, PHILIP PENDLETON, statesman and jurist, was born in Orange County, Va., May 25, 1783. On account of some misunderstanding with his father, he was thrown upon his own resources at an early age; but made his way through the law school of William and Mary College and duly gained admission to the Bar. For many years he served in Congress; and, on account of his gifts as a parliamentarian, he was honored with the Speakership. Resigning his seat, he became an occupant of the Bench; but later he returned to Congress and in 1829 he presided over the Virginia Constitutional Convention. While making a speech in the House, in 1830, he was seized with a hemorrhage, which warned him of his frail health; and he relinquished his seat in Congress once more to spend his remaining days on the Bench, first of the United States District Court of Virginia, and afterward of the Supreme Court of the United States. Some of his speeches have been preserved in the 'Congressional Globe.' He died in Washington, D.C., February 24, 1841.

BARCIA, ANDRÉS GONZÁLES DE. Spanish historian. He published an important work reviewing the history of Florida under Spanish rule entitled 'Historia General de la Florida' (Madrid, 1723).

BARCLAY, ANTHONY. [Ga.]. He published a volume in which he gave an authentic account of the practical joke which caused the charge of plagiarism to be preferred against Richard Henry Wilde, the author of "My Life Is Like the Summer Rose," a poem which charmed Lord Byron (Savannah, Ga., 1871).

BARCLAY, JAMES TURNER, physician and author, was born in Hanover County, Va., in 1807, of Quaker stock. On receiving his medical diploma, he married Mrs. Julia A. Sowers; and for a while he owned and occupied "Monticello," the old home of Thomas Jefferson. Later he joined the followers of Alexander Campbell and spent some time in missionary work within the environs of Jerusalem. The remaining years of his life were devoted to educational work. Besides numerous papers and pamphlets, he wrote: 'The City of the

Great King,' which ranks among the standard authorities on this subject. He died in 1874.

BARCLAY, SARAH, artist and author, was born in Albemarle County, Va., and was the daughter of Dr. James Turner Barclay. It is said that by disguising herself as a Mohammedan woman she was admitted into the Tomb of David and was enabled by this ruse to get a picture of the interior to illustrate her father's book. She became the wife of Augustus Johnson, Consul-general of Syria and for some time spent her winters in Beyrout and her summers on Mt. Lebanon. Her only volume is an interesting little work entitled: 'The Howadji in Syria.' Upon her return to America she was shot by her son in a fit of insanity and the demented youth took his own life immediately afterward.

BARDE, ALEXANDRE. [La.]. He published in French a narrative of much interest entitled ' Histoire des Comités de Vigilance aux Attakapas' (St. Jean Baptiste, La., 1861).

BARKER, JACOB, financier, was born in Maine in 1779 and began his career in New York, but afterward, in 1834, settled in New Orleans, where the large fortune which he accumulated in business was despoiled by the Civil War. He published 'Incidents in the Life of Jacob Barker from 1800 to 1855' (New York, 1855). The last years of his life were spent with his son, Wharton Barker, in Philadelphia, where he died in 1871, at the age of ninety-two.

BARKSDALE, EMILY WOODSON. Author. [Va.]. She wrote 'Stella Hope: or, Under the Shadow of the Upas,' a delightful story of Southern girlhood (New York and Washington, The Neale Publishing Company, 1907).

BARKSDALE, GEORGE. Physician. [Va.]. In a work entitled 'Punch,' Dr. Barksdale portrays the present-day Virginia negro in the rural districts (New York and Washington, The Neale Publishing Company, 1907).

BARNARD, EDWARD EMERSON, astronomer, was born in Nashville, Tenn., December 16, 1857. On receiving his diploma from Vanderbilt University, he devoted his life to astronomical research. For eight years he was astronomer at the Lick Observatory in California. At present he is astronomer at the Yerkes Observatory in Wisconsin, and professor of practical astronomy in the University of Chicago. Besides sixteen comets, he discovered also the fifth satellite of Jupiter. He belongs to numerous learned societies and many honors and medals have been conferred upon him for meritorious achievements. His literary product consists mainly of contributions to scientific journals. Vanderbilt University gave him his degree of Sc.D.

BARNARD, FREDERICK AUGUSTUS PORTER. Educator and mathematician. Though born in Sheffield, Mass., in 1809, he resided for nearly thirty years in the South. He was connected with the University of Alabama for seventeen years, first in the chair of mathematics and afterward in the chair of chemistry; and with the University of Mississippi for several years, first in the chair of mathematics and afterward in the chair of astronomy, finally becoming president. In 1864 he was called to the head of Columbia College, New York, remaining for twenty-five years at the helm of this great institution. Barnard College was afterward christened in his honor.

Included among his works are the following books: 'Treatise on Arithmetic,' 'Analytical Grammar,' 'Letters on College Government,' 'History of the United States Coast Survey,' 'Recent Progress of Science,' and 'The Metric System.' He died in 1889. He received the degree of D.D. from the University of Mississippi, the degree of LL.D. from Yale, and the degree of Litt.D. from the University of New York.

BARNES, ANNIE MARIA. Story writer. She was born in Columbia, S.C., in 1857, a daughter of James Daniel and Henrietta Jackson Neville Barnes, and was educated in the public schools of Atlanta, Ga. She edited *The Little Worker,* juvenile organ of Woman's Board of Foreign Missons, M.E. Church, South. Among her numerous stories which have proven quite popular, are: "Life of David Livingston" (Nashville, Brigham and Smith), "Scenes in Pioneer Methodism" (*ibid.*), 'Gospel Among the Slaves,' 'The Ferry Maid of the Chattahoochee" (Philadelphia, Penn Publishing Company), "How Achon-hoah Found the Light" (Richmond, Presbyterian Committee of Publication), "Matouchon," "The Outstretched Hand," "Carmio," "Little Burden-Sharers," "Chonite," "Marti," "The King's Gift,' 'The Red Miriok,' 'The Little Lady of the Fort,' 'Little Betty Blew," "Mistress Moppet," "A Lass of Dorchester" (Boston, Lee and Shepard), 'Isilda,' 'Tatong,' 'The Laurel Token,' and several others. She resides in Summerville, S.C.

BARNES, JAMES, author, was born in Annapolis, Md., September 19, 1866. On completing his studies at Princeton, he accepted a position on the staff of *Scribner's Magazine,* and afterward became assistant editor of *Harper's Weekly,* a position which he resigned in 1907 to become literary editor for D. Appleton and Company. He is a writer of exceptional gifts, and the versatility of his genius is attested by the following list of his publications: 'Naval Actions of 1812' (New York, Harper and Brothers), 'For King or Country' (*ibid.*), 'A Loyal Traitor' (*ibid.*), 'Yankee Ships and Yankee Sailors' (New York, The Macmillan Company), 'Midshipman Farragut' (New York, D. Appleton and Company), 'Commodore Bainbridge' (New York, D. Appleton and Company), 'A Princetonian' (New York, G. P. Putnam's Sons), 'The Hero of Erie' (New York, D. Appleton and Company), 'Ships and Sailors' (New York, Frederick A. Stokes Company), 'David G. Farragut' (Boston, Small, Maynard and Company), 'Drake and His Yeomen' (New York, The Macmillan Company), 'The Great War Trek' (New York, D. Appleton and Company), 'With the Flag in the Channel' (*ibid.*), 'The Giant of Three Wars' (*ibid.*), 'The Unpardonable War' (New York, The Macmillan Company), 'The Son of Light-Horse Harry' (New York, Harper and Brothers), 'The Blockaders' (*ibid.*), and 'Outside the Law' (New York, D. Appleton and Company). He is a descendant of Commodore Bainbridge.

BARNETT, EVELYN SCOTT SNEAD. Literary editor of the Louisville *Courier-Journal.* She was born in Kentucky, a daughter of Charles Scott and Martha Snead, and married, June 8, 1886, Ira Sayre Barnett. Besides numerous short stories for periodicals like *The Youth's Companion* and the *Century Magazine,* she has written some very popular fiction, including: 'Mrs. Delire's Euchre Party, and Other Stories' (Boston, L. C. Page and Company), 'Paddy on the Turnpike' (1903), and 'The Dragnet,' a novel which is now in press. The sketch of George Martin in 'The Library of Southern Literature' is also from her pen.

BARNEY, JOHN. Lawyer. He repr sented Maryland in Congress from 1825 to 1829 and was the son of Commander John Barney, of the United States Navy. He died in Washington, D.C., January 26, 1856, at the age of seventy-two years, leaving unfinished a record of 'Personal Recollections of Men and Things in America and Europe.'

BARNEY, MARY. Author. She lived in Baltimore, Md., and published 'Memoirs of Commodore Barney' (Boston, 1832).

BARNWELL, LILY RIPLEY. Poet [N.C.]. She published a volume of verse entitled 'Heart Songs' (Hendersonville, N.C., 1903, paper edition).

BARNWELL, ROBERT WOODWARD, statesman, was born in Beaufort, S.C., August 10, 1801, and died in Columbia, S.C., November 25, 1882. For six years he was president of South Carolina College. He was also elected to Congress, and served in both Federal and Confederate Senates. He cast the deciding vote which made Jefferson Davis President of the Southern Confederacy, and achieved distinction at the Bar and on the hustings. He was an orator of rare gifts.

BARNWELL, ROBERT WOODWARD. Protestant Episcopal Bishop-coadjutor of Alabama. He was born in Beaufort, S.C., December 27, 1849. Bishop Barnwell published 'The Analytics of Church Government.' He died in 1900.

BARR, AMELIA E. See Biographical and Critical Sketch, Vol. I, page 231.

BARRETT, ROBERT N. Baptist clergyman. [Ky. and Texas]. He was born in 1868. His publications include: 'The Child of the Ganges' (1890), 'In the Land of the Sunrise' (1895), 'The Story of Christian Missions' (1898), and 'Our Missionary Problem.'

BARRETT, ROBERT S. Clergyman. For many years he was pastor of St. Luke's Episcopal Church of Atlanta, Ga., and published 'Thought Seeds for Holy Seasons,' 'Talks to Young Men,' and 'Character Building.' He held the degree of D.D. Dr. Barrett made frequent visits to Europe, delivered many lectures, and died some time in the 'nineties.

BARRICK, JAMES RUSSELL, poet, was born in Kentucky in 1829 and died in Georgia in 1867. For several years he was identified with leading papers. He published a number of beautiful fragments, among them, "The Poet," which appeared in the first issue of *Scott's Magazine,* and "The Sword and Pen," which appeared in the Atlanta *Constitution,* of which he was at one time the editor. He lies in an unmarked grave in Georgia's capital.

BARRINGER, RUFUS, lawyer and soldier, was born in Cabarrus County, N.C., December 2, 1821, and died in Charlotte, N.C., February 3, 1895. He studied law and won distinction at the Bar. He opposed secession but acquiesced in the result, enlisted in the Confederate Army, attained the rank of brigadier-general, and was several times wounded. At the close of hostilities he advocated acceptance of the measures of reconstruction and supported the party in power. On retiring from the practice of law, he devoted himself to literary labors and wrote interesting articles on North Carolina history and personal reminiscences.

BARRON, S. B. Author. [Texas]. During the Civil War he served in Ross's Brigade, and in later life he wrote 'The Lone Star Defenders' (New York and Washington. The Neale Publishing Company, 1906), an interesting story of his regiment.

BARROW, FRANCES ELIZABETH, author, was born in Charleston, S.C., February 22, 1822, the daughter of Charles Benton Mease. Her education was obtained in New York and it was also in that metropolis that she met and married James Barrow, Jr. She began to write for publication in 1855, adopting the pen-name of "Aunt Fanny"; and, being successful from the beginning, about twenty-five story-books for young people came from her pen. Perhaps the most popular of her writings are: 'Aunt Fanny's Story-Book,' 'Six Nightcaps,' 'Six Popguns,' 'Four Good Little Hearts,' 'Life Among Children,' and 'Take Heed.' She also wrote a novel called 'The Wife's Stratagem.' Some of her works have been translated into foreign tongues. Most of her life was spent in the Northern States.

BARRY, WILLIAM TAYLOR, lawyer, diplomat, jurist, was born in Lunenburg, Va., February 5, 1785, and died in Liverpool, England, August 3, 1835. After completing his studies at William and Mary College, he settled in Lexington, Ky., for the practice of law, and in 1810 was sent to Congress. The War of 1812 aroused his fighting blood and he went to the front. On returning home he was elected to the United States Senate but shortly resigned his commission to become Justice of the Kentucky Supreme Court. From 1829 to 1833 he was Postmaster-general, being the first incumbent of the office to enter the Cabinet. In 1835 he was appointed Minister to Spain and died on the journey to Madrid. He was an eloquent speaker and wrote and spoke with convincing power upon public questions.

BARTLETT, NAPIER. Editor and author. He was born in Georgia in 1836; but, removing to New Orleans early in life, distinguished himself in Crescent City journalism. He served with gallantry in the Confederate ranks; and, after the war, he again unsheathed the editorial pen in his adopted home. He was the author of several volumes, including: 'Clarimonde,' a novelette, 'Stories of the Crescent City,' 'A Soldier's Story of the War,' and 'The Military Record of Louisiana.' He died in 1877.

BARTLEY, JAMES AVIS, educator and poet, was born in Louisa County, Va., August 2, 1830. It is said that at the age of eleven he read the 'Æneid.' He was educated at Emory and Henry College and at the University of Virginia; and was for some time professor of English in the Baltimore Female College. His literary product is represented by two volumes of verse entitled: 'Lays of Ancient Virginia, and Other Poems' (Richmond, 1855), and 'Poems' (Charlottesville, 1882), each of which contains some graceful lines.

BARTON, SAMUEL MARX. Professor of mathematics in the University of the South. He was born in Winchester, Va., March 9, 1859, a son of Joseph M. and Mary McNeill Barton. He married, December 28, 1897, Mary Millicent Tidball. He is the author of 'An Elementary Treatise on the Theory of Equations' (Boston, D. C. Heath and Company, 1889), and 'The Elements of Plane Surveying' (*ibid.*, 1904). The University of Virginia gave him the degree of Ph.D. He resides in Sewanee, Tenn.

BARTRAM, WILLIAM. Botanist. He was born in 1739 and died in 1823. Kingsessing, Pa., was the place of his birth and death, but he spent some of his best years in the South, and his greatest work is entitled 'Travels Through North and South Carolina, Georgia, and East and West Florida,' which was published in Philadelphia in 1791. He prepared the most complete list of American birds prior to the time of Alexander Wilson. In monastic habits of life, he was very much like Henry D. Thoreau, the hermit author.

BASANIER, M. French writer. He wrote an important work entitled 'L'Histoire Notable de la Floride' (1853), in which he gives an account of the three voyages of Jean Ribalt and tells of the unsuccessful effort to found a colony of French Huguenots.

BASCOM, HENRY BIDLEMAN, bishop of the M.E. Church, South, was born in Delaware County, N.Y., of Huguenot parentage, May 27, 1796, and died in Louisville, Ky., September 8, 1850. For several years he taught in Kentucky and was for two years president of Transylvania. In 1849 he became bishop, but died within a year after his ordination. Besides editing, at one time, the *Southern Quarterly Review,* he published 'Sermons from the Pulpit,' 'Lectures on Moral and Mental Science,' and ' Methodism and Slavery.' His works were edited by the Rev. T. N. Ralston (Nashville, 1850-1856), and his memoirs were written by Dr. M. M. Henkle (Nashville, 1854). Bishop Bascom was one of the orators of Methodism. He received the degree of D.D.

BASKERVILL, WILLIAM MALONE, educator, author, literary critic, was born in Fayette County, Tenn., April 1, 1850, and died in Nashville, Tenn., September 6, 1899. He early developed a fondness for the English classics; and after completing an elective course in languages at Randolph-Macon College, he studied at Leipsic (Ph.D.). For a while he taught in Wofford College; but in 1881 he was called to the chair of English in Vanderbilt University, a position which he filled with brilliant distinction until his death. Besides contributing to current periodicals, he edited 'Andreas: a Legend of St. Andrew,' and published with J. W. Sewell an 'English Grammar for High School and College Use,' and, with J. A. Harrison, an 'Anglo-Saxon Dictionary' and an 'Anglo-Saxon Reader.' But his reputation rests mainly upon his two volume work in literary criticism entitled 'Southern Writers' (1896-1897). He was an English scholar of rare attainments, a writer of graceful diction, and a critic of keen analytical power.

BASKETT, JAMES NEWTON. See Biographical and Critical Sketch, Vol. I, page 247.

BASKETTE, GIDEON HICKS. Journalist. He was born in Rutherford County, Tenn., March 11, 1845, left college to enter the Confederate Army and served throughout the struggle. He married Annie E. McFadden and became editor of the Nashville *Banner* in 1884. He has written for periodicals numerous poems and short stories of unusual merit. The sketch of Charles Egbert Craddock in 'The Library of Southern Literature' is from his pen. He resides in Nashville, Tenn.

BASSETT, JOHN SPENCER, educator and professor of history in Trinity College, North Carolina, was born at Tarboro, N.C., September 10, 1867, and married Jessie Lewellyn, of Durham, N.C. He was called to the chair which he now occupies in 1893. His works include: 'Constitutional Beginnings of North Carolina,' 'Slavery in the State of North Carolina,' 'Slavery and Servitude in the Colony of North Carolina,' 'Anti-Slavery Leaders of North Carolina,' 'The War of the Regulation,' and 'The Federalist System' (New York, Harper and Brothers, 1905). He also edited 'The Writings of Colonel William Byrd, of Westover, Va.' (New York, Doubleday, Page and Company), and has written numerous historical sketches and papers. The writings of Dr. Bassett are marked not only by inquiring research, but also by philosophic deduction. Johns Hopkins gave him the degree of Ph.D. He resides in Durham, N.C.

BATE, WILLIAM BRIMAGE, soldier and senator, was born near Castilian Springs, Tenn., October 7, 1826. At the outbreak of the Mexican War he enlisted in one of the volunteer regiments, served with distinction, and attained the rank of lieutenant. Afterward he owned and edited a paper at Gallatin, Tenn., called *The Tenth Legion*. but in the meantime. he studied law; and, on being admitted to the Bar, rose rapidly to the front. When Tennessee seceded, he enlisted in the Confederate Army as a private, but eventually wore the stars of a major-general. He was three times desperately wounded. At the close of hostilities, he resumed the practice of law, became twice governor of Tennessee, and served in the United States Senate for eighteen years. He died in 1905.

BATES, NEWTON W. Educator. He published a 'History of the Civil Government of Alabama' (1892).

BATTEY, ROBERT, physician, was born in Augusta, Ga., November 26, 1828. After receiving his diploma from Jefferson Medical College, he settled in Rome, Ga., and became an eminent specialist. Besides editing *The Medical and Surgical Journal,* he contributed to the professional press both of this country and of England and made numerous important discoveries.

BATTLE, ARCHIBALD JOHN, Baptist clergyman and educator, was born at Powelton, Ga., September 10, 1826, a son of Dr. Cullen Battle. At one time he was president of Mercer University, at Macon. Ga., and afterward of Shorter College, at Rome, Ga. He also founded the Anniston (Ala.) College for Young Ladies. Dr. Battle published a 'Treatise, Psychological and Theological, on the Human Will.' He was one of the foremost Baptist divines of the South.

LATTLE, KEMP PLUMMER. See Biographical and Critical Sketch, Vol. I, page 269.

BATTLE, RICHARD HENRY, lawyer, was born at Lewisburg, N.C., December 3, 1835. On completing his studies, he entered the profession of law and attained high rank at the Bar. He is also at the present time president of the North Carolina Home Insurance Company of Raleigh. Though he has published no books he has delivered numerous addresses, including one at the unveiling of the bronze statue of Zebulon B. Vance, a masterpiece of biographical analysis. The sketch of Andrew Johnson in 'The Library of Southern Literature' is from his pen. He married, November 28, 1860, Annie Ruffin Ashe. The University of North Carolina gave him the degree of LL.D.

BAXTER, WILLIAM, clergyman and educator, was born in England in 1823. For many years he resided in Arkansas. He published 'Pea Ridge and Prairie Grove,' 'War Lyrics,' and 'Poems.'

BAY, W. V. N. Lawyer. He published, in 1878, 'Reminiscences of the Bench and Bar of Missouri.' (St. Louis, F. H. Thomas Co.).

BAYLOR, FRANCES COURTENAY. See Biographical and Critical Sketch, Vol. I, page 281.

BAYNE, CHARLES JOSEPH. Journalist and author. He wa: born in Milledgeville, Ga., September 28, 1870. While denied collegiate advantages, he has been a student and a traveler, has mastered several languages, and wields one of the most versatile and brilliant pens to be found in the journalistic ranks of the South. He is at present chief editorial writer on the Atlanta *Journal*. Besides two popular lectures, entitled "Drones and Dreamers" and "Things We Might Have Said," he is the author of an oriental romance: 'The Fall of Utopia,' published in 1897, and of many exquisite poems. Some of his verse appeared in book form in 1905 under the title of 'Perdita.'

BAYNE, HUGH A. Lawyer. [La.]. He published an interesting volume of fiction entitled 'Tales of Temple Bar' (1891).

BAYS, W. W. Poet. [N.C.]. The author of a collection of verse entitled 'The Superannuate and Other Poems,' (Concord, N.C., 1903, paper edition).

BEACH, CHARLES FISK, Jr. Lawyer. He was born in Kentucky, February 4, 1854, a son of the Rev. Charles Fisk Beach. He was educated at Centre College, Columbia University, and the University of Paris. He was admitted to the Bar, and practiced in New York City from 1881 to 1896. He married Annie Josephine Smyly, of New Orleans. Since 1896 he has practiced in London and in Paris. He has written extensively upon legal subjects, some of his published works being: 'The Law of Receivers' (1887), 'Wills' (1888), 'Railways' (1890), 'Private Corporations' (1891), 'Modern Equity Jurisprudence' (1892), 'Public Corporations' (1893), 'Modern Equity Practice' (1894), 'Injunctions' (1895), 'Contracts' (1897), 'Contributory Negligence' (1897). For several years he has lectured in the University of Paris.

BEALE, CHARLES WILLING. Author. Mr. Beale was born in Washington, D.C., December 9, 1845, and received his education at the University of Pennsylvania. Several works of fiction have come from his pen, among them 'The Ghost of Guir House,' 'The Secret of the Earth,' and others. He married, January 25, 1872, Maria Taylor. He resides in Arden, N.C.

BEALE, HELEN G. Author. [Va.]. She published a volume entitled 'Lansdowne.'

BEALE, MARIA TAYLOR. Author and artist. Her maiden name was Maria Taylor. She was born in Richmond, Va., January 30, 1849, and studied art in Paris. Besides numerous short stories and sketches she has published 'Jack O'Doon,' a novel of the North Carolina Coast (New York, Henry Holt and Company), and 'The White Horse in the Tree-top' (*ibid.*). She married, January 25, 1872, Charles Willing Beale. Her home is in Arden, N.C.

BEALER, ALEXANDER W. Clergyman and writer. [Ga.]. He was born near the close of the Civil War. For several years he was on the staff of the Atlanta *Journal*, but afterward, entered the Baptist ministry and is at present pastor of a church at Thomasville, Ga. Besides an occasional poem, he is the author of numerous short stories and sketches. His dialect work is perhaps his best. He is a master of negro lore and humor, and sometimes pictures

'Uncle 'Rastus'·on the lecture platform. His sister, Gertrude Bealer, who reside in New York, has also done some excellent work.

BEALL, JOHN B. [Tenn.]. He published a volume entitled 'In Barrack and Field.'

BEAN, HARRIET C. She was a writer of Augusta, Ga., born in 1823, and died in 1897, and published 'Poems—Retrospection.'

BEARD, RICHARD, clergyman and educator, was born in Sumter County, Tenn., November 27, 1799. On completing his education at Cumberland University, he became professor of languages at his *alma mater.* Later he was called to the office of president. But when the theological school was organized, he resigned the executive chair to become professor of systematic theology, an office which he held for twenty-five years. He was a leader among the Cumberland Presbyterians of the South. His published works include: 'Systematic Theology,' 'Biographical Sketches,' and 'Why I Am a Cumberland Presbyterian.' He died at Lebanon, Tenn., December 2, 1880.

BEASLEY, FREDERICK, clergyman and educator, was born near Edenton, N.C., in 1777. and was the son of a planter of some means. After receiving his diploma from Princeton, he studied theology and became an ordained minister of the Episcopal Church. For several years he was professor of moral and mental philosophy in the University of Pennsylvania. His writings include: 'American Dialogues of the Dead,' 'An Examination of the Oxford Divinity,' 'Search of Truth in the Science of the Human Mind,' 'Vindication of the Argument *a priori* in Proof of the Being and Attributes of God, from the Objection of Dr. Waterland,' 'Review of Brown's Philosophy of the Human Mind,' 'Vindication of the Fundamental Principles of Truth and Order in the Church of Christ,' and other works. He died in Elizabethtown, N. J., November 2, 1845. He received his degree of D.D. from Pennsylvania and Columbia Universities.

BEATTIE, FRANCIS ROBERT. Eminent theologian and scholar. For many years he was professor of apologetics and systematic theology in the Presbyterian Theological Seminary of Kentucky. He was born of Scotch parentage at Guelph, Ontario, in the Dominion of Canada, March 31, 1848, a son of Robert and Janet McKinley Beattie. He married, first, Jean G. Galbraith, and, second, Lily R. Satterwhite. For some time he was associate editor of the *Presbyterian Quarterly* and the *Christian Observer.* Among the numerous works on theological and doctrinal subjects that have come from his conservative pen are: 'The Utilitarian Theory of Morals' (1884), 'Methods of Theism' (1887), 'Radical Criticism' (1895), 'Presbyterian Standards' (1893), 'Calvinism and Modern Thought' (1901), and 'Christianity and Modern Evolution' (1903). Besides, he also edited the Memorial of the Westminster Assembly Celebration at Charlotte, N.C., in 1897. Dr. Beattie held the Ph.D., the D.D. and the LL.D. degrees. He died in 1906.

BEAUMONT, HENRY FRANCIS. Editor and author. He was born in Nashville, Tenn., September 8, 1878, a son of Henry Francis and Mary Fuller Plummer Beaumont. He married, April 4, 1903, Adah Pearl Terry, of Birmingham, Ala. He served in the Spanish-American War; and, while in the Philippine Islands, he founded the Manila *American,* the first newspaper published there in English. Since 1894 he has been president of the Beaumont Press Bureau. He is the author of 'Forgotten Pages in Tennessee History,' 'The

Lost Regiment' (1902), 'The Lost Letter' (1904), and 'Rulers of Alien People' (1904).

BEAUREGARD, PIERRE GUSTAVE TOUTANT. An eminent Confederate soldier. He was born in St. Bernard Parish, La., May 28, 1818, and was educated at West Point, graduating in the class of 1838. At the outbreak of the Civil War he resigned his commission in the United States Army and took charge of the fortifications at Charleston, S.C., being in command when Fort Sumter was bombarded. He rose to the full rank of general. After the surrender he became president of two insurance companies and adjutant-general of Louisiana. In 1866 he declined an appointment to the chief command of the Roumanian troops and, three years later, an honor of like character from the Khedive of Egypt was also declined. He was the author of two volumes: 'A Commentary on the Campaign and Battle of Manassas' and 'A Summary of the Art of War' (New York, Putnam's). His literary style is characterized by Professor Alcée Fortier as "mathematically precise." For further information the reader is referred to 'The Military Operations of General Beauregard' by Judge Roman. He died in New Orleans, February 20, 1893.

BECK, GEORGE, poet, was born in England in 1749; but, emigrating to America, he engaged in educational work and incidentally painted pictures. For some time he conducted a seminary for young ladies at Lexington, Ky., where he died, December 24, 1812. He wrote short poems, made numerous translations from the classics, and published "Observations of a Comet." He was a scout in Wayne's campaign against the Indians.

BECKWITH, CHARLES MINNIGRODE, Protestant Episcopal Bishop of Alabama, was born in Prince George County, Va., in 1851, a son of Dr. Thomas Stanley Beckwith and Agnes Ruffin. He was educated at the University of Georgia and at the Berkeley Divinity School, being ordained to the priesthood in 1881. Twenty years later he became the successor in office of Bishop Wilmer. Besides sermons and addresses, his works include: 'The Trinity Course of Church, in New Orleans. He was consecrated Bishop of Georgia and 'Rightly Instructed in God's Word.' He received his degree of D.D. from the University of the South.

BECKWITH, JOHN WATRUS, Protestant Episcopal Bishop of Georgia, was born at Raleigh, N.C., February 9, 1831, and on completing his education was ordained to the priesthood in the Episcopal Church, serving many important parishes, among them, Trinity Church, in New Orleans. He was consecrated Bishop of Georgia in 1868. As an orator he possessed few equals in the pulpit. His time was too much occupied in meeting the constant demands made upon him to produce books, and he published only occasional sermons and addresses. He died in 1891.

BECKWITH, PAUL. Author. [Mo.]. He published a 'History of the Beckwith Family' (1891), and 'Creoles of St. Louis' (1893),

BEDDOW, CHARLES PETER, Mrs. Author. [Ala.]. She wrote a story of Southern life entitled 'The Oracle of Moccasin Bend' (New York and Washington, the Neale Publishing Company, 1903), the scenes of which are laid around Lookout Mountain, Tenn. "Old Uncle Steve" is the oracle of the story, an ante-bellum type, full of quaint philosophy and good humor. Mrs. Beddow resides in Birmingham, Ala.

BEDFORD, GUNNING S., physician, was born in Baltimore, Md., in 1806 and died in the city of New York, September 5, 1870. For several years he taught in the medical college at Charleston, S.C., after which, in association with Dr. Valentine Nott, he founded the University Medical College of New York. He published 'Diseases of Women and Children,' and 'Principles and Practice of Obstetrics,' both of which passed into several editions and were translated into French and German.

BEDFORD, LOU SINGLETARY. Author. Mrs. Bedford was born in Kentucky and was descended from Amos Singletary, of Massachusetts, who was a figure of some prominence in the War of the Revolution. She began to write before she was fifteen; but, marrying early in life, she relinquished the pen for household duties. When her husband's health began to fail, the family residence was changed to Milton, Fla., and here it was that she took charge of the literary department of the local paper of which her husband became the editor, the Milton *Standard,* and began to renew her literary activities. Several volumes of charming verse soon came from her pen: 'A Vision, and Other Poems,' 'Gathered Leaves,' and 'Driftwood and Drifting,' the last volume also containing some prose sketches. Several years ago she made her home in Texas. Among her unpublished manuscripts is a poetical romance entitled: "Forrest Dayre."

BEDINGER, HENRY. Congressman and diplomatist. Mr. Bedinger was born near Sheperdstown, Va., in 1810. He succeeded his brother-in-law, General George Rust, as a member of Congress, and from 1853 to 1858 was Minister to Denmark. His literary gifts were of high order and he wrote a number of excellent poems.

BEE, THOMAS, patriot and jurist, was born in South Carolina in 1720. Exposing the popular cause at the outbreak of the Revolution, he jeoparded large property interests and took an active part in the exciting drama. He became lieutenant-governor of South Carolina and also represented the State in the Continental Congress. The last years of his life were spent on the bench of the United States Court for the District of South Carolina, and he compiled and published 'Reports of the District Court.'

BEER, WILLIAM, librarian, was born in Plymouth, England, in 1849, but for several years has resided in New Orleans. He is the author of an important paper entitled "The Capture of Fort Charlotte, Mobile" (Louisiana Historical Society, 1896).

BEERS, FANNIE A., Mrs. She resided in Mississippi and wrote an interesting volume entitled 'Memories: a Record of Personal Experiences and Adventures During Four years of War' (Philadelphia, J. B. Lippincott and Company). The volume contains a portrait of the author.

BELL, AGRIPPA NELSON. Physician. He was born in Northumberland County, Va., August 3, 1820. Before the war he located in Brooklyn, N.Y., where he became an eminent practitioner and wrote 'Knowledge of Living Things' (1860), and 'The Climatology and Mineral Waters of the United States' (1895), besides numerous medical papers.

BELL, HIRAM PARKS, lawyer and Congressman, was born in Jackson County, Ga., January 27, 1827. Elected to the secession convention, he opposed the ordinance but bowed to the sovereign will of the commonwealth. On the field of battle he commanded the 43rd Georgia; and, sustaining wounds which retired him from the saddle, he took his seat in the Confederate Congress. After the war he represented his district for four years in the National House of Representatives. Late in life he wrote a volume of reminiscences entitled: 'Men and Things,' which contains also a number of his speeches on public questions. He died in 1908.

BELL, J. M. Author. [Va.]. He wrote 'A Biography of Governor William Smith,' (1891).

BELL, JOHN, statesman, was born near Nashville, Tenn., February 15, 1797. On completing his education, he was duly admitted to the Bar, but his most distinguished attainments were in the sphere of politics. For several consecutive terms he served in the National House of Representatives, and in 1841 became Secretary of War under President William Henry Harrison, but resigned this office when President Tyler, who came to the Executive chair one month later, separated from the Whigs. He declined an offer of a United States senatorship; and in 1860 was nominated by the American Party for President of the United States. On the public questions of the day he spoke with great power, but few of his speeches have been preserved, except in the debates of Congress. He died at his home in Tennessee, September 10, 1869.

BELL, ORELIA KEY. She was born in Atlanta, Ga., in 1864, a daughter of Marcus A. Bell and a kinswoman of the famous author of the national anthem, Francis Scott Key. At an early age she began to write in verse, evincing a talent which attracted the attention of the best critics. It was not long before Charles A. Dana, of the New York *Sun,* paid her at the rate of a dollar a line for her poems; and she contributed to many of the periodicals. But ill health overtook this rare songster and caused her to retire all too soon from the choral ranks. Some of her best-known poems are "Po' Jo," "Gathering Roses," "Under the Laurels," and "To-day's Gethsemane." She was exceedingly clever in the writing of sonnets.

BELLAMY, ELIZABETH WHITFIELD. Author. She was born at Quincy, Fla., in 1839. Her maiden name was Croom. She wrote an interesting story, entitled 'Four Oaks,' which was published both in New York and in London and was widely read. Her other published works are: 'Kamba Thorpe,' 'The Little Joanna,' 'Old Man Gilbert,' and 'Penny Lancaster, the Story of a Georgia Farm.' She died in 1900.

BELLINGER, LUCIUS. Physician. [S.C.] He published a volume entitled 'Stray Leaves.'

BELTRAMI, J. C. Author. [La.]. He wrote in French an important work entitled 'La Découverte des Sources du Mississippi' (New Orleans, 1824).

BENEDICT, FRANK LEE. Author. He was born in Alexandria, N.Y., July 6, 1834, and was educated by private tutors at home and abroad. He is the author of several popular stories of fiction, including: 'My Daughter Elinor,' 'Miss Van Kortland,' 'John Worthington's Name,' 'Miss Dorothy's Charge,' 'Mr. Vaughn's Heir,' 'St. Simon's Niece,' 'Her Friend Lawrence,' 'Twixt Hammer and Anvil,' 'Madame,' 'The Price She Paid,' and 'A Late Remorse.' He has written also a volume of poems, 'The Shadow Worshipper,' and numerous short stories and sketches. He lives at St. Albans, W.Va.

BENET, STEPHEN VINCENT, soldier, was born at St. Augustine, Fla., January 22, 1827, and was educated at the University of Georgia and in the military school at West Point. For several years he was an instructor of cadets; but in 1869 became assistant chief of ordnance and later chief of the department, with the rank of brigadier-general. He translated 'Jomini's Political and Military History of the Campaign of Waterloo' and wrote 'Military Law and Practice of Court-Martials.'

BENJAMIN, JUDAH P. See Biographical and Critical Sketch, Vol. I, page 303.

BENNET, W. W. Clergyman. [Va.]. He published 'The Great Revival in the Southern Army' and 'Methodism in Virginia.'

BENNETT, CLAUD NATHANIEL, president of the Congressional Information Bureau, lecturer and writer, was born at Thomson, Ga., November 29, 1866. Mr. Bennett organized the splendid service over which he presides in Washington, D.C. He has delivered a number of addresses, appeared at frequent intervals upon the lecture platform and written for high-class periodicals on current topics.

BENNETT, DANIEL K. Baptist clergyman. [N.C.]. He was born in 1830 and died in 1897. He published a 'Chronology of North Carolina,' giving the dates of the most important events in the history of the State from the earliest times, with explanatory notes (New York, James M. Edney, 1858).

BENNETT, JOHN. See Biographical and Critical Sketch, Vol. I, page 323.

BENNETT, MARTHA HAINES BUTT. Author. [Va.]. She published 'Pastimes with Little Friends' and 'Leisure Moments,' besides numerous uncollected short stories and sketches for the young.

BENSON, BLACKWOOD KETCHUM. Author. He was born in Edgefield District, S.C., May 12, 1845, entered the First South Carolina Regiment of Infantry and fought until the surrender at Appomattox. He is the Southern text-book agent for some of the largest publishing houses of the East. Besides numerous compilations, he has written several stirring romances of the Civil War. Among his published works are: 'Who Goes There?' (New York, The Macmillan Company), 'The Story of a Spy in the Civil War' (*ibid.*), 'A Friend with the Countersign' (*ibid.*), 'Bayard's Courier' (*ibid.*), and 'Old Squire' (*ibid.*). He resides in Atlanta, Ga.

BENTLEY, ELLA D. [La.]. She published a volume of poems.

BENTON, THOMAS HART. See Biographical and Critical Sketch, Vol. I, page 345.

BERKELEY, SIR WILLIAM, colonial Governor of Virginia, was born near London, England, in 1610, and died in Twickenham, July 13, 1677. He was an accomplished cavalier and courtier, administered the affairs of the colony for thirty-five years, and published 'The Lost Lady,' a tragi-comedy (London, 1628), and 'Description of Virginia' (1663).

BERNARD, GEORGE S. [Va.]. He compiled and edited an interesting work entitled 'War Talks of Confederate Veterans' (Petersburg, Va., Fenn and Owen, 1892).

BERNARD, P. V. Author. [La.]. He published a volume in French entitled 'Un Ancêtre de la Sainte Alliance' (New Orleans, 1870).

BERNEY, SAFFOLD. Author. [Ala.]. He wrote 'An Industrial History of Alabama.'

BERNHEIM, G. D. Clergyman. [N.C.]. Born in 1827. He published a work entitled 'The German Settlement and Lutheran Church in North Carolina and South Carolina.'

BERRIEN, JOHN MACPHERSON, statesman and jurist, was born in New Jersey, August 23, 1781, son of Major John Berrien of the Revolution. Graduating from Princeton, he was admitted to the Georgia Bar; and, after several years of service on the Superior Court Bench, he was twice commissioned to represent his adopted commonwealth in the United States Senate. On account of his polished oratory in debate he was called "the American Cicero"; but, except in the proceedings of Congress, few of his speeches have been preserved. When Andrew Jackson became President, he received the appointment of Attorney-general; but two years later, on account of inharmonious conditions, he resigned with the other members of the Cabinet. He died in Savannah, Ga., January 1, 1856.

BERRYHILL, S. NEWTON. Journalist and poet of Mississippi. He was born in 1832 and died in 1887. He wrote some excellent verse, in which he caught the spirit of his surroundings. His best work is to be found in a volume entitled 'Backwoods Poems' (Columbus, Miss., Excelsior Printing Company, 1878).

BERTRON, OTTILIE, Mrs. Author. Her home was in Mississippi. She wrote: 'Edith,' a novel (1887) and 'Ingersoll's Attack on Christianity,' a review (1889).

BEVERLY, ROBERT. See Biographical and Critical Sketch, Vol. I, page 375.

BEYER, GEORGE EUGENE, educator, was born in Dresden, Germany, September 9, 1861. For several years he has been professor of biology in Tulane University, at New Orleans. Besides numerous monographs, he has published 'The Mounds of Louisiana' (New Orleans, Louisiana Historical Society, 1896).

BIBB, GEORGE M., statesman and jurist, was born in Virginia in 1772; and, after completing his studies at Princeton, settled in Kentucky for the practice of the law. For three separate terms he was chosen Chief Justice; twice he was commissioned United States Senator; and in 1844 he was made Secretary of the Treasury in the Cabinet of President Tyler. His only published work is his volume of 'Reports of Cases at Common Law and in Chancery in the Kentucky Court of Appeals.' He died in Georgetown, D.C., April 14, 1859.

BIEDMA, LUIS HERNANDEZ. Spanish soldier and historian. He was an officer under De Soto in the expedition for the conquest of Florida in 1538. He wrote an account of rare value entitled 'Relación

BIEN, H. M. Author. [Miss.]. He wrote: 'Ben-Beor,' an historical story divided into two parts, the first a counterpart of 'Ben-Hur' and the second a companion romance to 'The Wandering Jew.' It was published both at Vicksburg, Miss. and at Baltimore in 1892. He also wrote: 'Oriental Legends' (1883), 'Feast of Lights' (1886), 'Samson' (1885), 'Purim' (1884), 'What is Judaism?' (1888), and 'Solar Night' (1887).

de la Isla de la Florida' (1587). The work is included in the 'Colección de Varios Documentes para la Historia de la Florida' in Madrid.

BIENVILLE, JEAN BAPTISTE LE MOYNE SIEUR DE, French Governor of Louisiana, was born in Montreal, Canada, in 1680, and died in France in 1765. The part which he played in the early annals of Louisiana was both romantic and important. Among other things, he founded the city of New Orleans, which became the seat of government. His correspondence has been preserved in the 'Historical Collections of Louisiana.' He was a brother of Iberville and one of ten famous sons of Charles Le Moyne.

BIGBY, MARY CATHERINE DOUGHERTY, Mrs. Poet. [Ga.]. She was born in 1839 and was the author of numerous poems, among them "Delilah" and "The Death of Polk."

BIGGS, JOSEPH. Historian. [N.C.]. He was born in 1776, and died in 1844. He published a 'History of the Kehukee Baptist Association' (Tarboro, N.C., 1834), a continuation of Burkitt's pioneer work, important because of the light which it throws upon early State annals.

BIGHAM, MADGE ALFORD. Kindergarten teacher and writer. She was born at LaGrange, Ga., September 30, 1874, a daughter of the Rev. R. W. Bigham, D.D. In connection with her successful work in Atlanta, she has written numerous stories for children, among them: "Stories of Mother Goose Village" (1902), "Blackie, or Merry Animal Tales" (1906), "Little Folks' Land" (1907), "Flower Fairies" (1909), and "Within the Silver Moon."

BIGHAM, ROBERT WILLIAMS. Clergyman and author. For some time he was a missionary of the M.E. Church, South, to California and the Isthmus of Panama. He was born near Milledgeville, Ga., October 8, 1824. He married, first, in 1858, Charlotte Eliza Davies, and, second in 1872, Sara Jane Davies. The best of his writings are his juvenile stories, one of which, 'Vinny Leal's Trip to the Golden Shore' (Nashville, Tenn., Methodist Publishing House, 1873), is still the most popular juvenile book published by this establishment. He is also the author of 'Wine and Blood; or Uncle Viv's Story' (1875), 'California Gold Field Scenes' (1886), and 'Joe, a Boy in the War Times' (1889), all of which possess fascinating interest for the young. He died October 11, 1900, at Demorest, Ga.

BIGNEY, MARK F. Editor and poet. He was born in Nova Scotia in 1817. He settled in New Orleans, La., in 1847 and became an influential factor in journalism. He was one of the organizers of the New Orleans *City Item.* As an editor, he is said to have been cautious in forming his convictions, but courageous in maintaining them. He published, in 1867, a volume of poems entitled 'The Wreck of the Nautilus, and Other Poems,' in which there are several charming love songs. He died in New Orleans, in 1886.

BILLON, FREDERICK L. Author. [Mo.]. He published 'The Annals of St. Louis under French and Spanish Domination from 1764 to 1804' (1886).

BINGHAM, ROBERT WORTH, lawyer, was born in Orange County, N.C., November 8, 1871. At the Bar of Louisville, Ky., he has risen to prominence. In politics he has been equally successful; and, after holding the office of county attorney, has been elected mayor of Louisville. Besides numerous public addresses, he is the author of the sketch of Henry Watterson in 'The Library of Southern Literature.' He married, in 1896, Eleanor E. Miller.

BINGHAM, WILLIAM, educator, was born in North Carolina in 1835 and was educated at the University of the State, succeeding in time to the headship of the school which had been conducted successfully by both father and grandfather at Mebanesville, N.C. Among his publications are: 'A Grammar of the Latin Language,' 'A Grammar of the English Language,' and 'Cæsar's Commentaries, with Notes.'

BIRD, MARY PAGE, writer, was born in Cobham, Albemarle County, Va., in 1866. Under the pen-name of "Neil Christian" she published a story entitled 'Wedded to a Genius' (London, Bentley and Son, 1894), which brought her at once before the public. This was followed by a serial entitled 'Sir Wilfred,' which appeared in *Things and Thoughts*, a Virginia magazine. From time to time she has contributed short stories and sketches to periodicals and has also written an occasional poem. Her latest fragment of verse appeared in *Harper's*, under the title "Illusion." She married, March 1, 1892, Gilbert Bonham Bird. Her home is at Biltmore, N.C.

BIRNEY, JAMES GILLESPIE. Reformer and leader of the conservative abolitionists. He was born in Danville, Ky., February 4, 1792, and died at Perth Amboy, N. J., November 25, 1857. Freeing his own slaves, he devoted himself to the problem of gradual emancipation, and not only took the platform but seized the editorial pen. Twice was he the candidate of the Liberty party for President of the United States, polling 7,059 votes in 1840, and 62,300 votes in 1844. Disabled by a fall from his horse, the last twelve years of his life were spent in retirement as an invalid at the North. His writings include: 'Letters on Slavery and Colonization," 'American Churches the Bulwarks of American Slavery,' and 'Speeches in England.'

BIRNEY, WILLIAM, soldier, was born near Huntsville, Ala., May 29, 1819, and was the son of James G. Birney, the conservative abolitionist. His education was obtained in part abroad; and while sojourning in Paris he took an active part in the French Revolution of 1848. Enlisting upon the Union side in the Civil War he attained the rank of major-general. After the struggle, he lived for a while in Florida, but afterward moved to Washington, D.C., for the practice of law. He wrote 'The Life and Times of James G. Birney,' which was published in 1890, shortly before his death.

BISHOP, DAVID HORACE, educator, was born in Newbern, Va., August 20, 1870. Since leaving college he has been active in educational work. Besides the sketch of John H. Ingraham in 'The Library of Southern Literature,' he is the author of numerous monographs and papers preserved in the publications of the Mississippi Teachers' Association and contributes to current reviews and magazines. He is professor of English at the University of Mississippi and resides at Oxford. He is an A.M.

BISHOP, PUTNAM P. Baptist clergyman. [Fla.]. He published 'The Psychologist,' a novel (1886), 'The Heart of Man,' and 'The American Citizen.'

BLACK, SALLY. Poet. [S.C.]. She wrote 'The Chimes of St. Michael.'

BLACK, WARREN COLUMBUS. Methodist Episcopal clergyman, was born near Crystal Springs, Miss., May 24, 1848. Besides filling numerous important pastorates and achieving distinction on the lecture platform, he edited for seven years the New Orleans *Christian Advocate.* His published works include 'The Philosophy of Methodism' (1880), 'A Centennial Retrospect' (1884), 'Temperance and Teetotalism' (1886), 'Christian Manhood' (1888), 'Eternal Punishment' (1898), 'Is Man Immortal?' (1902), and 'Sermons and Addresses' (1909). Dr. Black has declined numerous calls to college chairs because of a preference for pastoral work. He married, March 24, 1865, Phoebe Marshall. The Southern University conferred upon him the degree of D.D. He resides at Meridian, Miss.

BLACK, WILLIAM H. Lawyer. He was born at Forsyth, Ga., June 10, 1868, a son of Eugene P. Black. He is the author of 'New York and New Jersey Corporations' (1902 and 1905), and 'The Real Wall Street' (1908). He resides in New York City.

BLACK, WILLIAM HENRY. Educator and divine. He was born at Centreville, Ind., March 19, 1854, a son of the Rev. Felix G. and Lydia Black. He has held numerous important pastorates, was moderator of the General Assembly of the Cumberland Presbyterian Church at Waco, Texas, in 1898, and is now president of Missouri Valley College. He has written: 'Sermons for the Sabbath School' (1886), 'God, Our Father' (1889), 'Womanhood' (1890), 'Outline Life of Paul' (1894), and 'The Life and Times of Moses' (1902). Dr. Black has been given the D.D. and the LL.D. degrees. He resides in Marshall, Mo.

BLACKBURN, GEORGE ANDREW, clergyman, was born in Green County, Tenn., October 16, 1861. His father was John N. Blackburn, and his mother Eliza Jane Ambrister. On completing his equipment for the ministry, he became pastor of the Arsenal Hill Presbyterian Church, Columbia, S.C. He has edited 'Girardeau's Discussions of Philosophical Questions' (Philadelphia, Presbyterian Board of Publication), 'Girardeau's Discussions of Theological Questions' (Richmond, Presbyterian Committee of Publication), and 'Sermons.' He married, in 1886, Annie Williams, daughter of the Rev. John L. Girardeau, D.D., of Columbia, S.C.

BLACKMAN, WILLIAM FREMONT. Educator. He was born at North Pitcher, N.Y., September 25, 1855, and was educated at Oberlin College and at Berlin. He married, in 1884, Lucy Worthington. He was for some time professor of sociology at Yale University and edited the *Yale Review* from 1893 to 1901. He then went South to assume the presidency of Rollins College. He has written 'The Making of Hawaii: a Study in Social Evolution,' in addition to numerous contributions to the periodicals. Cornell gave him the degree of Ph.D. He lives in Winter Park, Fla.

BLACKWELL, JAMES DE RUYTER. Poet. He lived in Virginia and published 'The Poetical Works of James De Ruyter Blackwell,' in three volumes (New York, 1879).

BLACKWELL, ROBERT EMORY. Educator. He was born in Warrenton, Va., November 14, 1854, a son of the Rev. John D. Blackwell, D.D., and Julia A. Blackwell. He was educated at Randolph-Macon College and at Leipsic. He married, in 1877, Theele Epia Duncan, and became president of Randolph-Macon College in 1902. He is the author, with Prof. James A. Harrison, of 'Easy Lessons in French' and, with W. W. Smith, of 'Parallel Syntax Chart' and also of an interesting article in

The Southern Methodist Review (1894) on the question: "Were the Ancients Acquainted with America?" He resides in Ashland, Va.

BLAIR, ANDREW ALEXANDER, analytical chemist, was born in Woodford County, Ky., September 20, 1848, a son of the late General Francis P. Blair. He was educated at Annapolis. Since 1881 he has been engaged in the general practice of his profession and has achieved signal distinction. Besides numerous articles in the scientific journals, particularly on the analysis of iron, he wrote the article on "Assaying" in the 'Encyclopædia Britannica.'

BLAIR, FRANCIS PRESTON, statesman and soldier, was born in Lexington, Ky., February 10, 1821, and died in St. Louis, Mo., July 8, 1875. On the issues of slavery, he joined the newly organized Republican party and served in Congress for several years prior to the war. It is claimed that he saved both Kentucky and Missouri to the Union. In the field he attained the rank of major-general. After the war he became dissatisfied with the policies of his own party and received the Democratic nomination for Vice-president. Later he served in the United States Senate. He wrote 'The Life and Public Services of General William O. Butler.'

BLAIR, FRANCIS PRESTON, statesman and editor, was born at Abingdon, Va., April 12, 1792, and died at Silver Spring, Md., October 18, 1876. For many years he edited *The Globe,* the official organ of the Democratic party, published in Washington, D.C., but most of his life was spent in Kentucky. When the slavery question emerged he became one of the organizers of the Republican party and presided over the national convention but refused to accept the nomination, declining in favor of John C. Fremont. In 1864 he made an unofficial visit to Richmond and proposed an arrangement of peace on the basis of a joint campaign against Maximilian in Mexico, and this interview is said to have led to the famous Hampton Roads Conference of February 3, 1865. After the war, he opposed reconstruction and affiliated with the Democrats. He was an influential factor in the public affairs of his time, both on the platform and in the editorial sanctum; but few of his published thoughts survive.

BLAIR, JAMES, educator, was born in Scotland in 1656, and died at Williamsburg, Va., August 1, 1743. Dr. Blair was the first president of William and Mary College, an institution for which he obtained the royal charter. He assisted in compiling 'The State of His Majesty's Colony in Virginia,' and published, in four volumes, 'Our Saviour's Divine Sermon' (1772), comprising discourses upon the Sermon on the Mount.

BLAIR, WILLIAM ALLEN. [N.C.]. He published a volume entitled 'Historic Banks and Bankers of North Carolina.'

BLAKE, LILLIE DEVEREUX. Reformer and writer. She was born August 12, 1835, in Raleigh, N.C., the daughter of George Pollock and Sarah Elizabeth Devereux, and was educated at the North. She married, first, Frank F. Q. Umsted and, second, Grenfill Blake. Her activity in the equal suffrage movement began in 1869. Besides many lectures, she has written: 'Southwold' (1859), 'Rockford' (1862), 'Fettered for Life' (1872), 'Woman's Place To-day' (1883), and 'A Daring Experiment' (1898). Her writings bear the stamp of intellectual power. For many years she has resided in New York.

BLAKE, T. C. [Tenn.]. He published 'The Old Log House, a History of the Cumberland Presbyterian Church' (1878).

BLANCHARD, AMY ELLA. Writer of popular juvenile stories. She was born in Baltimore, Md., a daughter of David Harris and Sarah Blanchard. She began to write for children in 1881, and her success was so pronounced that numerous books followed, including: 'Betty of Wye' (Philadelphia, J. B. Lippincott Company), 'Wee Babies' (New York, E. P. Dutton), 'Mistress May' (Philadelphia, George W. Jacobs and Company), 'Janet's College Career' (*ibid.*), 'Two Maryland Girls' (*ibid.*), 'Bonny Leslie of the Border' (Boston, W. A. Wilde), and 'Little Sister Annie' (Philadelphia, George W. Jacobs and Company). Her home is in Baltimore, Md.

BLAND, RICHARD, patriot, was born in Virginia, May 6, 1710. Opposed to the Stamp Act, he took an active part in the drama of resistance, becoming a delegate to the Continental Congress. He was sometimes called "the Virginia Antiquary" because of his familiar acquaintance with the antecedents of the colony from the earliest times. He wrote 'A Letter to the Clergy on the Two-Penny Act' (1760), and 'An Inquiry into the Rights of the British Colonies.' He died in Williamsburg, Va., October 26, 1776.

BLAND, RICHARD PARKS, statesman, was born near Hartford, Ky., August 19, 1835; but, after residing for some time in California and Nevada, he settled in Missouri. Becoming prominent at the Bar and in the politics of his adopted State, he was sent to Congress, where he became the author of the famous "Bland Bill," which was enacted over the veto of President Hayes in the interest of the coinage of silver. For additional information it will be necessary to consult other works. Most of his public speeches are preserved in the debates of Congress; and the story of his public career appeared soon after his death under the title of 'An American Commoner' (Columbia, Mo., 1900). He died in 1899.

BLAND, THEODRIC, physician, soldier, Member of Congress, poet, was born in Virginia in 1742. When pursuing his studies abroad, he translated the first 'Eclogue,' of Virgil, a work of some merit; but his place in the realm of letters is due to his war poem on "The Battle of Lexington." According to Dr. F. V. N. Painter (see 'Poets of Virginia'), this is the only contemporary Virginia poem in which the Revolution found echo; and in the opinion of Charles Campbell, who edited 'The Bland Papers,' it is distinguished rather for its patriotic than for its poetic merit. Still, we must remember the crudeness of the times. The author was an officer of rank in the struggle for independence; and from 1779 to 1783 he sat in the Continental Congress. He died in 1790.

BLANDIN, I. M. E., Mrs. Author. Beginning with the establishment of the Ursuline Convent in New Orleans in 1727, she interestingly narrates 'The History of Higher Education of Women in the South prior to 1860' (New York and Washington, The Neale Publishing Company, 1908).

BLECKLEY, LOGAN E., jurist and poet, was born in Rabun County, Ga., in 1827. For many years he was associate justice of the Supreme Court of the State; and, after a season of retirement, returned to the Bench, to become chief justice. His decisions, which are preserved in the 'Georgia Reports,' are characterized by simplicity of style and are illuminated by frequent flashes of wit. One of the most amusing productions of Judge Bleckley is entitled: "A Letter to Posterity." It was published in *The Green Bag,* a journal of the legal profession, and was written for the purpose of telling his remote descendants who he was; but this was only one of the many eccentricities of this unique genius. He was also the author of several rare poems, perhaps the best known being entitled "In the Matter of Rest." He was twice married, his first wife, Caroline Haralson and his second, Chloe Herring. He died in 1907.

BLEDSOE, ALBERT TAYLOR. See Biographical and Critical Sketch, Vol. I, page 395.

BLEDSOE, W. C. Baptist clergyman. [Ala.]. Born in 1847. He wrote a 'History of East Liberty Association' (1886).

BLETON, C. Author. [La.]. He published a volume in French entitled 'De la Poésie dans l'Histoire' (New Orleans, 1882).

BLOCHER, S. J. Educator. [Ark.]. He published a volume on 'The Civil Government of the United States.'

BLOSSOM, HENRY MARTYN, author, was born in St. Louis, Mo., May 10, 1866, and was educated in his native city, after which he engaged in the insurance business. But his greatest success has been in the field of authorship. He has published 'The Documents in Evidence' (St. Louis, 1901), 'Checkers, a Hard Luck Story' (Chicago, Herbert S. Stone and Company, 1903), and 'The Brother of Chuck McGann' (New York, Harper and Brothers, 1905), besides two dramatizations, 'Checkers,' and 'The Yankee Consul.' He resides in New York.

BLOUNT, ANNIE R., poet, was born near Augusta, Ga., in 1839, and was educated at the Methodist Female College, at Madison, Ga. Attention was first attracted to her gifts by her graduation essay on "The Follies of the Age." For several years after the war she edited a paper at Bainbridge, Ga., and wrote numerous poems, some of them winning prizes. Under the title of 'The Sisters,' she published a collection of her best verse. Her pen name was "Jennie Woodbine."

BLOUNT, EDWARD A. Poet. [Texas]. He published a volume of 'Poems' (1898).

BLOXHAM, WILLIAM D. Lawyer. Governor Bloxham has twice filled the executive chair of Florida, first from 1881 to 1885 and afterward from 1897 to 1901. He was born in Leon County, Fla., July 9, 1835, received his education at William and Mary College and chose the legal profession. Both at the Bar and in politics he has been a power in Florida. As an orator he is most effective and his state papers are models of vigorous and sound English. Governor Bloxham is one of the advisory council of 'The Library of Southern Literature.' He resides in Tallahassee, Fla.

BLUE, KATE LILLY. Author. [S.C.]. She wrote 'The Hand of Fate, a Romance of the Navy' (1895), 'Deathless Memory,' and numerous short stories and sketches. Her work is exceedingly clever.

BLUE, MATTHEW POWERS. [Ala.]. He published 'The Churches of Montgomery' (1878), a 'Genealogy of the Blue Family,' and a 'History of Montgomery.'

BOCOCK, JOHN HOLMES, clergyman and writer, was born in Buckingham County, Va., January 31, 1813, the son of John Thomas Bocock and Mary Flood. On completing his studies at

Amherst College he began his special equipment for the Presbyterian ministry at Union Theological Seminary in Virginia; and in course of time became an eminent minister of the gospel. He married Sarah Margaret Kemper. As a writer he was both vigorous and fearless, making frequent contributions to the leading church papers; and, after his death, a volume entitled: 'Selections from the Religious and Literary Writings of John H. Bocock, D.D.,' with a biographical sketch from the pen of C. R. Vaughan, D.D., was edited by his widow, a woman of very rare gifts. During the Civil War Dr. Bocock was a Confederate chaplain. He died July 17, 1872, at Lexington, Va.

BOCOCK, JOHN PAUL, editor and poet, was born at Harrisonburg, Va., in 1856, a son of the Rev. J. H. Bocock, D.D. On completing his education at Washington and Lee, he entered the legal profession; but by reason of his unusual literary gifts he was led into journalism and became first a member of the staff of the Philadelphia *Press* and afterward of the New York *World*. He contributed a number of splendid articles to the leading magazines of the day and was beginning to win national recognition when death arrested his young career in 1903; but a collection of his poems was issued by his wife under the title of 'Book Treasures of Mæcenas' (New York, The Knickerbocker Press), the very name indicating the classic character of the contents. He also left a manuscript entitled 'The Literary History of the Odes of Horace.'

BOCOCK, WALTER KEMPER, clergyman and editor, was a son of the Rev. J. H. Bocock, D.D., and was born at Georgetown, D.C., in 1858, receiving his education at Washington and Lee. For a number of years he engaged successfully in journalism in Philadelphia; but, yielding to an imperative conviction of duty, he relinquished this promising field of work to prepare himself for the ministry and in due time was ordained to the priesthood in the Episcopal Church and filled several important pulpits. Contemporaneously, he also engaged in editorial work; but, after his health began to fail his pen became his principal diversion. His writings include: 'Tax the Area' (New York, John W. Lovell), and 'The Social Imperative of Jesus,' in manuscript. He contributed to the leading magazines both in verse and in prose; and on the day of his death dictated an editorial. He died in 1904. Three years later a volume of his poems was issued under the title of 'The Antiphon to the Stars' (New York, The Knickerbocker Press).

BOCOCK, WILLIS HENRY, educator, was born at Halifax C. H., Va., January 4, 1865, a son of the Rev. J. H. Bocock, D.D. He was educated at Hampden-Sidney College; and after graduation was called into the service of his *alma mater*. He was made professor of Greek at the age of twenty-three. Later he also taught Latin. Incidentally he studied for a year at Berlin; and in 1894 became professor of Greek at the University of Georgia, a chair which he still retains. Professor Bocock is the author of numerous contributions to the magazines and journals on philological subjects. The sketch of William H. Hayne in 'The Library of Southern Literature' is from his pen.

BOLL, JACOB, naturalist, was born in Switzerland, May 29, 1828. He became a pupil of Louis Agassiz and spent the greater part of his life in scientific researches. For many years he resided in Texas, engaged in examining the fossiliferous and iron deposits of the State. He made numerous important discoveries and collected many rare specimens, writing much upon the line of his life's work. He died in Wilbarger County, Texas, September 29, 1880.

BOLLING, ROBERT. [Va.]. He published a 'Genealogy of the Bolling Family of Virginia' (1868).

BOLTON, SARAH TITTLE. Poet. Her maiden name was Sarah Barrett. She was born in Newport, Ky., December 18, 1815, but afterward lived in Indiana. When only sixteen she began to write verse for a newspaper, the editor of which was Nathaniel Bolton, and, falling in love with the contributor, he sued for her hand. Two of the author's best-known poems are "Left on the Battlefield," and "Paddle Your Own Canoe." In 1866 she published in New York, a volume of choice selections from her writings and afterward her complete works were published with a memoir (Indianapolis, 1866). For several years she resided at Geneva, Switzerland, during her husband's tenure of service as Consul, and wrote some very interesting letters for newspaper publication.

BOMBERGER, MAUDE A. Author. [Va.]. Miss Bomberger has garnered the results of an exhaustive inquiry into the social life of Colonial times in a work entitled 'Colonial Recipes from Old Virginia and Maryland Manors' (New York and Washington, The Neale Publishing Company, 1906), which is spiced with numerous legends and traditions.

BOND, B. W. Methodist Episcopal clergyman. He wrote 'Evidences of Christianity' (Nashville, The M. E. Publishing House, South), and a 'Life of Wesley' (*ibid.*), besides minor works.

BOND, THOMAS EMERSON, journalist and physician, was born in Baltimore, Md., in 1782, and died in New York, March 14, 1856. On account of impaired health, he retired from the successful practice of medicine and devoted himself mainly to religious journalism, becoming also a lay preacher of the M. E. Church. For twelve years he edited *The Christian Advocate and Journal,* besides contributing to other periodicals. Several strong pamphlets, bearing upon ecclesiastical topics of discussion, came from his pen, notably the controversy which resulted in the rise of the Methodist Protestants. He also wrote a 'Narrative and Defence of the Church Authorities.'

BOND, THOMAS EMERSON, Jr., journalist and physician, was born in Baltimore, Md., in 1813. For several years he was associated with his father in the editorship of *The Christian Advocate and Journal.* Just before the war, he joined the southern wing of the Church; and, after the close of hostilities, he became one of the organizers of *The Episcopal Methodist,* which was subsequently merged into *The Southern Christian Advocate.* He was a master both of humor and of sarcasm. He died in Hartford County, Md., August 18, 1872.

BONDURANT, ALEXANDER LEE, educator, was born in Buckingham County, Va., June 22, 1865. His father was Alexander J. Bondurant. He enjoyed the best educational advantages both at home and abroad and on completing his studies he devoted himself to educational work. At present he holds the chair of Latin in the University of Mississippi. Besides numerous essays on various phases of literary criticism contributed to periodicals, including *The Dial* and *The Nation,* and monographs published in the 'Collections of the Mississippi Historical Society,' he wrote the sketch of Sherwood Bonner in 'The Library of Southern Literature.' He resides at Oxford, Miss.

BONER, JOHN HENRY. See Biographical and Critical Sketch, Vol. I, page 415.

BONNELL, J. M. Educator. [Ga.]. For several years he taught at Wesleyan and afterward went to the mission field in China. He published 'The Art of Pure Composition.'

BONNER, SHERWOOD. See Biographical and Critical Sketch, Vol. I, page 439.

BONNET, MARIE MARGUERITE, author, was born in New Orleans, La., February 14, 1865, a daughter of Jean François Bonnet; but for several years past she has resided at Reading, Pa. She has been an extensive traveler and has written a number of charming stories for young people, among them: 'Sweet William' (Chicago, A. C. McClurg and Company, 1890), 'Little Marjorie's Love Story' (*ibid.*, 1891), 'Prince Tip-Top' (*ibid.*, 1892), 'My Lady' (*ibid.*, 1894), 'A Child of Tuscany' (*ibid.*, 1895), 'Pierette' (*ibid.*, 1896), 'A Little House in Pimlico' (*ibid.*, 1898), and 'Tales of an Old Château' (*ibid.*, 1900), 'Bernardo and Laurette' (*ibid.*, 1902), and 'Clotilde, a Story of Old New Orleans' (*ibid.*, 1903).

BONSAL, STEPHEN, journalist and diplomat, was born in Virginia in 1863. After completing his education abroad, he became war correspondent of the New York *Herald*, and was later for several years in the diplomatic service of the United States Government at various capitals. He has written 'Morocco as it Is,' 'The Real Condition of Cuba,' 'The Fight for Santiago,' and 'The Golden Horseshoe' (New York, The Macmillan Company, 1908), besides numerous contributions to periodicals.

BOONE, DANIEL, pioneer, was born in Pennsylvania, February 11, 1735, and died in Missouri, September 26, 1820. The fame of the great trapper is indissolubly associated with the frontier belt of Kentucky, and twenty-five years after his burial in Missouri his ashes were exhumed and re-interred near Frankfort. Though it was easier for Boone to fight Indians than to write books, still the biography which John Filson has written of Boone is virtually the backwoodsman's own account of himself. It was written almost wholly from Boone's dictation.

BOONE, HENRY BURNHAM. Author. He was born at Fall River, Mass., May 8, 1872, a son of John H. and Charlotte Boone and married, September 25, 1896, Francesca Brown, of Charlottesville, Va. He relinquished the law in 1899 to devote himself to literature. In joint authorship with Kenneth Brown, he has written: 'Eastover Court House' (New York, Harper and Brothers) and 'Redfields Succession' (*ibid.*). He is also the author of 'The Career Triumphant' (New York, D. Appleton and Company). His address is "West Cairns," Charlottesville, Va.

BOONE, WILLIAM JONES, Protestant Episcopal bishop, was born in Walterborough, S.C., July 1, 1811, and died in Shanghai, China, July 17, 1864. He was the first missionary of his church to be invested with the Episcopal honors. Twenty years of his life were spent in the Orient, and he was noted for his scholarship in the Chinese language. He not only translated the 'Prayer-book' but also assisted in producing an accurate version of the 'Scriptures.'

BOOTON, JOHN HEISKELL. From the pen of this writer appeared, at Salem, Va., in 1899, a volume entitled: 'Fugitive Lyrics,' edited, with an introduction, by William Haller Cassell; and, notwithstanding the extreme modesty of the title, it is full of poetic sparkles, evincing both a wide range and a subtle touch.

BORDEN, MATTIE FULLER, Mrs. Poet. [N.C.]. She published a collection of verse entitled 'Song Poems' (Goldsboro, N.C., 1906, paper edition).

BORDLEY, JOHN BEALE, jurist and writer, was born in Annapolis, Md., February 11, 1727, and died in Philadelphia, Pa., January 26, 1804. He was a lawyer by profession and held judicial office in Maryland, but he was also interested in husbandry, located in Philadelphia after the Revolution and published 'Forsythe on Fruit Trees, with Notes,' 'On Rotation of Crops,' 'Essays and Notes on Husbandry and Rural Affairs,' with plates (1799-1801), and 'A View of the Courses of Crops in England and Maryland' (1784).

BORUM, JOSEPH H. Clergyman. [Tenn.]. He published 'Baptist Preachers of Tennessee.' He died about 1893.

BOSHER, KATE LANGLEY, Mrs. Author. [Va.]. She has published two entertaining works of fiction, 'Bobbie, by Kate Cairns' (1900), and 'When Love is Love' (1904).

BOSSU, M., French traveler, was born about 1725. He became a captain in the royal Navy, made three journeys to America by order of his government, and was one of the first European travelers to explore Louisiana after De Soto. He published an account of his explorations in two separate works entitled 'Nouveaux Voyages aux Indies Occidentales' (Paris, 1768, two volumes), and 'Nouveaux Voyages dans l'Amérique' (Amsterdam, 1777). Both were afterward translated into English, because of the importance of his researches to historians.

BOTTS, JOHN MINOR, Congressman, was born at Dumfries, Va., September 16, 1802, and died at Culpeper, Va., January 7, 1869. He studied law, became a planter on an extensive scale, served in Congress as a Whig, supported John Quincy Adams in his plea for the right of petition in the interest of abolitionists, opposed Tyler, though a personal friend, when he changed front in 1841, and, on the dissolution of his party, joined the Americans and declined a nomination for President. He opposed secession and when hostilities began retired to his plantation, where he was put under arrest by General Winder, on the well-founded suspicion that he was writing a secret history of the conflict. The manuscript could not be found, but after the war it was brought forth, a part of it having been confided to General Mercier, the French Minister at Washington, and it formed the basis for a volume entitled: 'The Great Rebellion, Its Secret History, Rise, Progress and Disastrous Failure' (New York, 1866).

BOUCHER, JONATHAN, Episcopal clergyman, was born in England in 1738. For several years he was rector of a church at Annapolis, Md., but his violent opposition to the cause of independence made him obnoxious to his flock and he was forced to leave the colonies. He afterward published a series of lectures entitled 'A View of the Causes and Consequences of the American Revolution' (1799), which he dedicated to General Washington. He also compiled a glossary of obsolete and provincial words which the proprietors of 'Webster's Dictionary' purchased from him to be used in an English edition. He died in England in 1804.

BOULDIN, POWHATAN. Author. [Va.]. He published 'Reminiscences of John Randolph of Roanoke' (1878) and 'The Old Trunk.'

BOURGEOIS, M. Author. He was born in France, but lived for many years in Louisiana, styled himself "an old clerk of the Council of New Orleans," and published a volume entitled: 'Voyage aux Etats-Unis' (Paris, 1834).

BOURLAND, ALBERT PIKE, educator, was born near Falcon, Ark., November 14, 1861. For several years past he has filled the chair of English in Peabody College for Teachers, at Nashville, Tenn. He has published "The Teaching of English," a series of articles in the *Southwestern Journal of Education,* and 'The School and Industrial Progress.'

BOWEN, EDWIN W. Educator and author. After receiving his Ph.D. degree from Johns Hopkins University, he spent a year at the University of Leipsic. He is professor of Latin in Randolph-Macon College, Va., a student of letters, and a contributor to magazines and reviews. Dr. Bowen is also the author of a work entitled 'The Makers of American Literature' (New York and Washington, The Neale Publishing Company, 1907). It is an excellent compendium furnishing not only biographical data but critical estimates.

BOWEN, ELIZA A. Educator. [Ga.]. She was born in 1828 and died in 1898. Miss Bowen published an elementary text-book for high schools and academies entitled 'Astronomy by Observation,' besides numerous monographs on subjects educational and scientific. She also wrote an incomplete 'History of Wilkes County, Ga.'

BOWEN, JOHN WESLEY EDWARD. Clergyman and educator, of African descent. He was born in New Orleans, La., December 3, 1855, and on receiving his diploma from the University of New Orleans, he studied theology, entered the Methodist ministry, held pastorates for several years in some of the large northern cities and taught in various colleges. In 1893 he became a professor in Gammon Theological Seminary at Atlanta, Ga., and later succeeded to the office of president. His published works include: 'National Sermons,' 'University Addresses,' 'Discussions in Philosophy and Theology,' 'The United Negro,' 'The Religious History of the Negro,' 'The Educational History of the Negro,' and numerous monographs. He received his Ph.D. from Boston University and his D.D. from Gammon.

BOWEN, THOMAS JEFFERSON. Baptist missionary and explorer of the Niger region in Central Africa. He was born in Georgia in 1814. Besides a grammar for the natives among whom he labored, he published a work on 'Central Africa.' He died in 1875.

BOWERS, CHARLES WILLIAM. Journalist. He published a collection of verse entitled 'The Newspaper Waste Basket, and Other Poems' (Highland Springs, Va., 1906), concerning which the author tells us that he "personally bought the paper, cut it, set the type, printed and bound the volume."

BOWIE, WALTER WORTHINGTON. [Md.]. He published a volume entitled 'The Bowies and Their Kindred' (1899).

BOWLES, WILLIAM AUGUSTUS. An eminent chief of the Creek Indians. He was born of English parents at Frederick, Md., in 1744, but abandoned civilization to become the head of this noted tribe. He was also at one time ambassador of the United Nations of Creeks and Cherokees to the Court of London. He wrote 'The Life of George Augustus Bowles,' in which he tells the thrilling story of his own eventful career. He died in 1805.

BOYCE, JAMES PETTIGRU, clergyman and educator, was born in South Carolina, in 1827. For several years he was a professor in Furman University and was elected to fill a chair in the Southern Theological Seminary in 1858, but the outbreak of the war caused the suspension of the institution. He was sent to the South Carolina Legislature in 1862 and in 1864. For some time after the war he devoted his efforts to the resuscitation of the Southern Theological Seminary, securing pledges to the amount of $90,000. Besides publishing sermons and addresses in book form, he also contributed to the current religious periodicals. His degrees were D.D., LL.D. and S.T.D.

BOYD, C. R. Educator. [Va.]. He wrote a 'History of Washington County' and 'Geological Treatises.'

BOYD, THOMAS DUCKETT. Educator. He was born at Wytheville, Va., January 20, 1854, the son of Thomas Jefferson and Minerva French Boyd. He received the best educational advantages and became professor in the Louisiana State University from 1873 to 1888; president of the State Normal School from 1888 to 1896; and is now (1910) president of the Louisiana State University, having been elected to this positon in 1896. He married Annie F. Fuqua. He is the author of numerous reports and monographs on educational subjects, and is one of the consulting editors of 'The Library of Southern Literature.' He resides in Baton Rouge, La.

BOYD, WILLIAM KENNETH, educator, was born in Curryville, Mo., June 10, 1879. Since graduation he has been engaged in teaching. He is at present professor of history in Trinity College, Durham, N.C. Besides editing the papers of the Historical Society of Trinity College, he has contributed to various periodicals and published "The Ecclesiastical Edicts of the Theodosian Code," in the *Columbia University Studies* (1906). He was also at one time on the staff of the 'Encyclopædia Britannica.' Columbia University gave him the degree of Ph.D. The sketch of William Gaston in 'The Library of Southern Literature' is from his pen.

BOYKIN, SAMUEL, clergyman, was born in Milledgeville, Ga., November 24, 1829. He was a Baptist, edited for some time *The Christian Index* and other periodicals, and published 'Memorial of Hon. Howell Cobb' (Philadelphia, J. B. Lippincott and Company, 1870).

BOYLE, VIRGINIA FRAZER. See Biographical and Critical Sketch, Vol. II, page 463.

BOYLE, ESMERALDA. Poet and writer. [Md.]. Besides a work entitled 'Biographical Sketches of Distinguished Citizens of Maryland,' the author has also published in verse 'The Story of Felice,' 'Thistledown,' and 'Songs of Land and Sea.'

BOZMAN, JOHN LEEDS, lawyer and author, was born at Oxford, on the eastern shore of Maryland, in 1757, educated at the University of Pennsylvania, chose the legal profession, and became an eminent practitioner. Besides several law books and numerous contributions to the periodicals, he wrote a 'History of Maryland, from 1633-1660' (Baltimore, 1837). He also wrote 'An Historical and Philosophical Sketch of the Prime Causes of the Revolutionary War,' but the work was suppressed. Some occasional poems of real merit also came from the pen of this writer. He died in 1823.

BRACKENRIDGE, HENRY MARIE, jurist and author, was born in Pittsburg, Pa., May 11, 1789, a son of Hugh Henry Brackenridge. He attended school at St. Genevieve, in Louisiana, after which he studied law and located first in Baltimore and afterward in St. Louis. When only twenty-three he became district judge for the territory of Orleans, and still later district judge for the western district of Florida. He wrote a work on 'Louisiana' (Pittsburg, 1812), a 'History of the Second War with England,' 'A Voyage to South America,' in two volumes (Baltimore, 1818; London, 1820), which was praised by Humboldt, 'Recollections of Persons and Places in the West' (Philadelphia, 1834; enlarged, 1868), 'Essays on Trusts and Trustees' (Washington, 1842), a 'History of the Western Insurrection,' and a number of pamphlets, including a eulogy delivered at Pensacola, Fla., on Adams and Jefferson. He spoke both French and Spanish. He died in Pittsburg, Pa., January 18, 1871.

BRACKENRIDGE, HUGH HENRY, jurist and author, was born near Campbellton, Scotland, in 1748, and died in Carlisle, Pa., June 25, 1816. After graduating from Princeton, he taught school for several years in Maryland, and composed for his pupils a drama called "Bunker Hill" (Philadelphia, 1776). He studied theology, and, though not an ordained minister, became a chaplain in the Continental Army and published six political sermons delivered in camp. Later he studied law at Annapolis and removed to Pittsburg, where he wrote 'Incidents of the Whiskey Insurrection in Western Pennsylvania' (Philadelphia, 1795), and a political satire, 'Modern Chivalry, or the Adventures of Capt. Farrago and Teague O'Regan, His Servant,' and published several orations and miscellaneous sketches.

BRADFORD, JOSEPH, dramatic writer, was born near Nashville, Tenn., October 24, 1843, and died in Boston, Mass., April 13, 1886. His real name was William Randolph Hunter. On account of ill health, he relinquished a naval career of some promise for the stage, and chose the pseudonym by which he was afterward known. The last fifteen years of his life were spent in literary work. His best known plays are: "The Cherubs," "Our Bachelors," and "One of the Finest." In the portrayal of eccentric characters he was quite successful.

BRADFORD, MARY F. She wrote a biography of J. J. Audubon, the famous naturalist (New Orleans, 1897).

BRADLEY, A. G. [Va.]. Author of 'Sketches from Old Virginia.'

BRADLEY, HENRY STILES, clergyman and educator, was born in Jackson County, Ga., March 22, 1869. His father was Henry Stiles Bradley and his mother Susan Jackson. On completing his educational equipment, he became a professor for several years at Emory College, his *alma mater.* He was also licensed to preach by the North Georgia Conference of the M.E. Church, South; and, being impelled by his popular gifts toward the pulpit, he was assigned to Trinity Church, in Atlanta. Four years later, he was tried on a charge of heretical teaching, and after acquittal was transferred to St. Louis. In the fall of 1909 he left the fold of Methodism and accepted the call of the Piedmont Congregational Church of Worcester, Mass. He is an original thinker, outspoken and fearless. His only published work is entitled: 'Christianity as Taught by Christ,' but he has made frequent contributions to the press and delivered numerous lectures. For 'The Library of Southern Literature' he wrote the sketch of Joel Chandler Harris. The University of Georgia gave him the degree of D.D.

BRADLEY, MARY EMILY. Author. [Md. and Va.]. Born in 1835. She published 'Douglas Farm.'

BRADLEY, THOMAS BIBB. Author. [Ala.]. He was born in 1830 and died in 1855. He published in association with his cousin, Julia Pleasants, afterward Mrs. Creswell, a volume of verse entitled 'Aphelia, and Other Poems by Two Cousins of the South' (New York, 1854).

BRADSHAW, SIDNEY ERNEST, educator, was born near Covington, Tenn. His father was Sidney J. Bradshaw. He fills the chair of modern languages at Furman University, Greenville, S.C. Besides numerous monographs, he wrote the sketch of Harry Stillwell Edwards in 'The Library of Southern Literature,' and a dissertation on 'Southern Poetry Prior to 1860' (Richmond, B. F. Johnson and Company, 1900), which earned him the Ph.D. degree from the University of Virginia.

BRANCH, WILLIAM, Jr. [Va.] He wrote 'Life, and Other Poems' (1819).

BRANSON, EUGENE CUNNINGHAM, educator, was born at Morehead City, N.C., August 6, 1861. After completing his studies he devoted himself to the educational interests of the South and few men have rendered more effective service, especially in the introduction of improved methods. He is the author of several text-books, among them, 'Methods of Teaching Arithmetic' (1896), 'Methods of Teaching Reading and Spelling' (1896), and 'Branson's Common School Spellers' (1900). He has also revised Page's 'Theory and Practice of Teaching' (1899), and edited Arnold's 'Way-marks for Teachers' (1900), Shaw's 'School Hygiene' (1901), and Johnson's readers. Professor Branson is president of the State Normal School, at Athens, Ga.

BREAZEALE, J. W. M. Lawyer. [Tenn.]. He wrote 'Life, or Matters and Things in General' (1842).

BRECKINRIDGE, JOHN, clergyman and educator, was born at Cabell's Dale, near Lexington, Ky., July 4, 1797, and died at the same place August 14, 1841. For many years he labored with success in the pastorate, serving churches both in Baltimore and Philadelphia. He was also at one time chaplain of the National House of Representatives. Later he became general agent of the Presbyterian Board of Education and afterward professor of theology in the Seminary at Princeton. He possessed in an eminent degree the gift of eloquence; and was moreover a man of great learning. His controversy with Archbishop Hughes of New York bore fruit in a volume entitled: 'A Discussion of the Question: "Is the Roman Catholic Religion Inimical to Civil or Religious Liberty?" and of the Question: "Is the Presbyterian Church Inimical to Civil or Religious Liberty?"' In 1839 he published a 'Memorial of Mrs. Breckinridge.'

BRECKINRIDGE, JOHN, statesman, was born in Augusta County, Va., December 2, 1760, and died in Lexington, Ky., December

14, 1806. While a student at William and Mary College, he was elected to the Virginia House of Delegates, being at the time only nineteen. Declining an election to Congress, he located in Kentucky, becoming first attorney-general of the state and afterward United States Senator. He resigned the latter position to become Attorney-general of the United States under Jefferson. The famous Kentucky resolutions of 1798 were drafted by Mr. Breckinridge, according to numerous authorities. He also led the debate in the Senate Chamber on the annexation of Louisiana. Soon after entering the Cabinet, he died of typhoid fever. His speeches were published in book form.

BRECKINRIDGE, JOHN CABELL. See Biographical and Critical Sketch, Vol. II, page 491.

BRECKINRIDGE, ROBERT JEFFERSON. Theologian and educator. His father was John Breckinridge, United States Senator from Kentucky and member of President Jefferson's Cabinet. He was born at Cabell's Dale, Ky., March 8, 1809, and died in Danville, Ky., December 27, 1871, Equipped for the Bar, he served four consecutive terms in the Legislature and became an advocate of gradual emancipation. But he afterward relinquished the law for the ministry, and bringing his extraordinary powers of mind to bear upon the teachings of the Scriptures, he became one of the landmarks of Presbyterianism in the South. For nearly twenty years he was professor of didactic and polemic theology in the Seminary at Danville, Ky.; and the public school system of the State was in large part the offspring of his brain. Included among his published works are: 'Travels in France and Germany' (Philadelphia, 1839), 'Popery' (1841), 'Memoranda of Foreign Travel' (Baltimore, 1845), 'The Internal Evidence of Christianity' (1852), 'The Knowledge of God Objectively Considered' (New York, 1857), and 'The Knowledge of God Subjectively Considered.' Much of his time was also given to editorial work. At the outbreak of the Civil War he adhered to the cause of the Union; but one of his sons, W. C. P. Breckinridge, and his nephew, Joseph C. Breckinridge, donned the Confederate uniform.

BRECKINRIDGE, WILLIAM CAMPBELL PRESTON, lawyer and orator, was born in Baltimore, Md., August 28, 1837. Soon after completing his studies at Centre College he enlisted in the Confederate ranks and commanded a brigade of cavalry troops. For two years he engaged in editorial work, but relinquished the pen to resume the practice of law. He was afterward made professor of equity jurisprudence in Cumberland University and in 1884 was elected without opposition to Congress. On account of his oratorical gifts he wielded an immense power in debate and was always in demand on public occasions. For several terms he represented his district in the halls of national legislation. Numbers of his speeches have been preserved in pamphlet editions, in miscellaneous collections, and in the debates of Congress. Centre College made him an LL.D.

BRENNAN, JOSEPH. Editor. He was born in the north of Ireland, in 1829, but spent much of his early life in Cork. Becoming allied with the Young Ireland party, he edited for some time *The Irish Felon,* and in consequence of his bold opinions suffered imprisonment. On being released, he was made editor of *The Irishmen;* but he was soon afterward implicated in revolutionary designs and escaped to America, settling in New Orleans. He was engaged in journalism until the time of his death, which occurred in his thirtieth year. He was the author of some very rare poems, the one entitled "The Exile to His Wife" being, perhaps, the best.

BRENT, FRANK PIERCE. For many years secretary of the State Board of Education of Virginia. He was born in Mount Airy, Nelson County, Va., October 14, 1852, and enjoyed superior educational advantages, including two years at the University of Virginia, post-graduate work in Greek under Dr. Gildersleeve at Johns Hopkins University and summer school lectures at Amherst College and Harvard University. He married, December 27, 1883, Mattie Buxton Porter, of Portsmouth, Va. He has taught Latin, Greek, French, and German in some of the leading academies of Virginia and published 'Tacitus, the Latin Historian' (1876), 'The Study of the Ancient Classics' (1878), 'Bacon's Rebellion' (1892). 'The Early Settlement of the Eastern Shore of Virginia' (1890), 'The Ordinance of 1787,' a "Phi Beta Kappa" address and numerous contributions to periodicals. The sketch of Armistead C. Gordon in 'The Library of Southern Literature' is from his pen. He resides in Richmond, Va.

BRENT, HENRY JOHNSON, author, was born in Washington, D.C., in 1811, and was a grandnephew of Archbishop Carroll of Maryland. Besides editing *The Knickerbocker*, a magazine which he founded with Lewis Gaylord Clark and which flourished for over thirty years, he published a novel entitled 'Life Almost Alone' (1859), and a work entitled 'Was it a Ghost?' in which he discusses the celebrated murder of the Joyce children. He died in New York in 1880.

BREVARD, CAROLINE MAYS, educator, was born in Tallahassee, Fla., August 29, 1860. Her father was General Theodore Brevard and her mother, Mary Call. She has published a 'School History of Florida' (New York, The American Book Co., 1904), a work which ranks high, and 'Literature of the South' (New York, The Broadway Publishing Co., 1908), besides numerous articles on historical and literary subjects. She also wrote the Florida supplement for 'Frye's Grammar School Geography' (Boston: Ginn and Co., 1906), and the sketch of Caroline Lee Hentz in 'The Library of Southern Literature' is likewise from her pen. She is engaged in educational work in Tallahassee.

BREVARD, EPHRAIM, patriot and physician, was born about 1750, of Scotch-Irish parentage, but the exact locality of his birth is unknown. He was educated at Princeton; and, after equipping himself for the practice of medicine, he located at Charlotte, N.C. On the issue of taxation, his sympathies were with the colonies even to the extent of separate self-government; and his prominence in the movement resulted in his election to the post of secretary of the famous Mecklenburg Convention of May 31, 1775. He is also credited with the actual authorship of the resolutions which constituted the first formal severance of the ties of allegiance to the British crown. With six brothers, Dr. Brevard supported the cause of American independence. For some time he was a prisoner in Charleston; and so impaired was his health by this experience that soon after regaining his liberty he died, in 1783. He was buried at Hopewell; but, in the confusion of the times, his grave was unmarked and cannot to-day be identified.

BREWER, KATE. Author. [Ala.]. She wrote 'Fanciful Tales from Legends of the Adirondack Indians,' four exquisite little stories (New York and Washington, The Neale Publishing Co., 1907).

BREWER, WILLIS. Lawyer and planter. He was born in 1844, served in the Confederate Army, and represented Alabama in Congress. His work entitled 'Alabama: Her History, Resources, War Record, and Public Men' is an encyclopædia of information covering the whole period from 1540 to 1872. He has also written 'The Children of Issachar' (New York, G. P. Putnam's Sons), a work which deals with the days of reconstruction in the South.

BRICKNELL, JOHN. [N.C.]. He wrote 'The Natural History of North Carolina' (1737).

BRIDGMAN, FREDERICK ARTHUR, artist and author, was born in Tuskegee, Ala., November 10, 1847, and after studying art in New York he went to Paris, where he opened a studio. On account of his eminent attainments he was made a Knight of the Legion of Honor. He has published in English a volume entitled 'Winter in Algeria' (New York, Harper and Bros.), and in French two volumes 'Anarchy in Art,' and 'The Idol and the Ideal.' He has also composed some very difficult orchestral music. He resides in Paris.

BRIGHT, AMANDA, Mrs. Author. [Ala. and Tenn.]. She published 'The Three Bernices' (1869), and 'The Prince of Seir.'

BRINGHURST, NETTIE HOUSTON, Mrs. She was the daughter of General Sam Houston, of Texas. Occasional poems were contributed by her to the press, among the number "A Supposition," found in 'Songs of the South.'

BRISBANE, ABBOTT HALL, civil engineer and author, was born in Charleston, S.C., about 1800. He was educated at West Point, but resigned from the Army, afterward commanding a regiment of South Carolina volunteers in the war against the Seminoles, engaged in constructing railroads, taught *belles lettres,* and wrote a political novel entitled 'Ralphton, or the Young Carolinian of 1776.' He died in Summerville, S.C., September 28, 1861.

BRISCOE, MARGARET SUTTON. Author. [Md.]. She published a collection of stories entitled 'The Change of Heart' (1903). The stories, which are six in number, are entertainingly written. The author is now Mrs. Hopkins.

BROADDUS, JOHN, clergyman, was born in Caroline County, Va., November 4, 1770, and died in Salem, Va., December 1, 1846. Entering the ministry, he became an influential Baptist divine and held pastorates in Boston, Philadelphia and New York, in addition to numerous Southern cities. He wrote constantly for the press and published a 'History of the Bible,' a 'Catechism,' a 'Form of Church Discipline,' and 'Letters and Sermons,' besides two hymnbooks. Some of his manuscripts were published after his death, with a memoir by J. B. Jeter, D.D. (New York, 1852). Columbia University gave him the degree of D.D.

BROADHEAD, GARLAND CARR, geologist, was born near Charlottesville, Va., October 30, 1827. After graduation from the University of Missouri, he became assistant State geologist and was employed by the Smithsonian Institution to make collections in Missouri for the Centennial Exhibition. He published 'Missouri Geological Reports, 1855-1871' (Jefferson City, 1873), and 'Reports of the Missouri Geological Survey, 1873-1874.'

BROADUS, JOHN ALBERT. See Biographical and Critical Sketch, Vol. II, page 503.

BROCK, ROBERT ALONZO. Secretary of the Southern Historical Society, antiquarian, genealogist, historian. He was born in Richmond, Va., March 9, 1839, the son of Robert King and Elizabeth Mildred Ragland Brock. He was for eighteen years secretary of the Virginia Historical Society, and edited eleven volumes of the papers of this organization. In 1887 he was called to the position which he now holds; and more than twenty volumes of the papers of the Southern Historical Society have been edited by this painstaking scholar. He is one of the foremost literary savants in America and is a member of numerous learned bodies in the United States, Canada and Europe. He is the author of many important papers bearing upon historical and genealogical lines of research and is also registrar and historian of the Virginia Society of the Sons of the American Revolution. He resides in Richmond, Va.

BROCK, SIDNEY G. Journalist, lawyer, author. He was born in Cleveland, Ohio, April 10, 1837, a son of E. A. and M. M. Brock and was educated at Allegheny College, Meadville, Pa. He settled in Macon, Mo., for the practice of law and was mayor of the town from 1886 to 1888. He became chief of the Bureau of Statistics, United States Treasury Department, in 1889, under President Harrison, and held this position for four years. He is the author of the following works: 'The Hawaiian Islands, their History, Products, and Commerce,' 'History of the Navigation, Commerce, etc., of the Great Lakes,' 'History of the Pacific States and Alaska,' and 'The Advance of the United States for a Hundred Years, from 1790 to 1890.' He resides in Macon, Mo.

BRODHEAD, EVA WILDER. Author. [Ky.]. Besides short stories and sketches, she wrote 'One of the Visconti,' 'Diana's Livery,' and other popular novels.

BROOKE, ST. GEORGE TUCKER. He was born in Charlottesville, Va., July 22, 1844, the son of Henry Lawrence and Virginia Tucker Brooke. His maternal grandfather, Judge Henry St. George, was professor of law at the University of Virginia. He served in the Confederate Army, participating in the battles of Gettysburg, Spottsylvania, and the Wilderness, and was wounded and maimed for life at Haw's Shop, May 28, 1864. Later he was admitted to the Bar and became professor of law in the Law College of the University of West Virginia in 1878, and still holds this position. He married, August 15, 1882, Mary Harrison Brown. He is the author of 'Common Law Practice and Pleading,' in addition to numerous articles for magazines. The University of Virginia gave him the degree of LL.D. He resides in Morgantown, W.Va.

BROOKS, NATHAN COVINGTON, educator and poet, was born in Cecil County, Md., August 12, 1819. Choosing the career of an educator of youth, he organized the Baltimore Female College and became the president. During moments of relaxation he gave his pen to the muses; and his poem entitled "The South Sea Islander," won first prize in a contest which included Mrs. Sigourney, George W. Bethune and N. P. Willis among his competitors. He published: 'Scripture Anthology' (Philadelphia, 1837), 'The Literary Amaranth,' a collection of prose and verse (1840), 'The History of the Church,' a metrical composition; 'The History of the Mexican War,' a work of standard value; and several text-books and translations from the classic authors.

BROOKS, SAMUEL PALMER. Educator. He was born in Milledgeville, Ga., December 4, 1863, a son of Samuel Erskine and Aurelia E. Palmer Brooks, and was educated at Baylor and Yale Universities. He also took post-graduate work at the University of

Chicago. He married, December 24, 1893, Mattie Sime, of Cleburne, Texas. In 1902 he became president of Baylor University, his *alma mater*. Besides delivering numerous platform lectures on educational subjects, he has also contributed many articles to the magazines. Richmond College gave him the degree of LL.D. He resides in Waco, Texas.

BROOKS, ULYSSES R., lawyer and author, was born in Barnwell, S.C., October 27, 1846. His father was James Carroll Brooks, a brother of the distinguished statesman, Preston S. Brooks. His mother was Sarah Crawford Robert, the eldest daughter of Colonel Ulysses Maner Robert, a descendant of the celebrated Pierre Robert, who established the old Huguenot Church in Charleston, S.C. Despite his youth, he enlisted in the Confederate Army at the outbreak of the war and made an efficient soldier. He engaged successfully in the active practice of law until his appointment as clerk of the Supreme Court of South Carolina, a position which he still holds. During hours of relaxation he has given his cultured pen to literary diversions. Besides a work of graphic interest entitled 'Butler and his Cavalry' (1907), he has also published the first volume of a work which is destined to take high rank in the biographical literature of the State entitled 'The Bench and Bar of South Carolina' (1909). He married, December 5, 1871, Mary Jones, an adopted daughter of General James Jones. Colonel Brooks resides in Columbia, S.C.

BROUGH, CHARLES HILLMAN. He wrote: 'The History of Taxation in Mississippi,' and 'The History of Banking in Mississippi,' published by the Historical Society of the State. He received the degree of Ph.D.

BROUGHTON, LEONARD GASTON, clergyman, was born in Wake County, N.C., in 1865. He is pastor of the Tabernacle Baptist Church of Atlanta, Ga., and the organizer of the numerous departmental activities connected with this important charge. The Bible Conference, of which he is also the founder, attracts hundreds of people yearly to Atlanta. At various times Dr. Broughton has occupied the London pulpit of Dr. Campbell Morgan. He is a power in the religious world. His publications include 'The Second Coming of Christ,' 'Table Talks of Jesus,' 'The Soul-Winning Church,' 'Up from Sin,' 'The Revival of a Dead Church,' 'God's Will and My Life,' 'Salvation and the Old Theology,' 'The Plain Man and his Bible,' 'Religion and Health,' and 'Old Wine in New Bottles.' The Fleming H. Revell Company, New York and Chicago, has published most of Dr. Broughton's works.

BROWN, AARON VENABLE, statesman, was born in Brunswick County, Va., August 15, 1795, and died in Washington, D.C., March 8, 1859. After settling in Tennessee for the practice of law, he was sent to Congress; and, on the expiration of his second term, was elected governor. He was the author of the famous 'Tennessee Platform' of 1850. His last public service was performed in the office of Attorney-general under President Buchanan. Some time before his death he published a volume of his speeches. (Nashville, 1854).

BROWN, A. J. Author. He wrote a 'History of Newton County, Miss., 1834-1894' (Jackson, 1894), giving an interesting account of early settlements.

BROWN, ALBERT GALLATIN, statesman, was born in Chester District, S.C., May 31, 1813, and died near Jacksonville, Miss., June 12, 1880. Entering the legal profession, he became one of the foremost men of his adopted State. He served on the bench of the Superior Court, was several times elected to Congress, was Governor of the State from 1843 to 1848, and was twice elected to the United States Senate, resigning in 1861 when secession was thought to be the only recourse of the South under the Constitution. He published a volume of his speeches in 1859.

BROWN, ALEXANDER. Historian and planter. He was born at Glenmore, Nelson County, Va., September 5, 1843. He studied under private tutors and entered Lynchburg College, but his education was interrupted by the outbreak of the war. He served in the Confederate Army from 1861 to 1865. After the surrender he engaged in business, but subsequently relinquished commercial life for agricultural pursuits. He married, first, Caroline Augusta Caball, and, second, Sarah Randolph Caball. His literary work is mostly in the line of historical investigation; and numerous volumes have come from his pen, all of which are characterized by thoroughness of research and by vivid narrative interest. He wrote: 'New Views of Early Virginia' (1886), 'The Genesis of the United States' (1890), 'The Caballs and Their Kin' (1895), 'The First Republic in America' (1898), 'The History of Our Earliest History' (1898), 'English Politics in Early Virginia History,' and numerous magazine articles. The University of the South gave him the degree of D.C.L. and William and Mary the degree of LL.D. He died at Norwood, Va., in 1906.

BROWN, ANNA MUSE. [Ga.]. She published 'The Life and Letters of Laura A. Haygood.' Her maiden name was Anna Muse. She married Oswald Eugene Brown.

BROWN, BENJAMIN GRATZ, lawyer, was born in Lexington, Ky., May 28, 1826, and died in St. Louis, Mo., December 13, 1885. On completing his education at Yale, he was admitted to the Bar; and a speech which he delivered in the Legislature against slavery is said to have marked the beginning of free soil sentiment in Missouri. He edited for several years *The Missouri Democrat,* a paper devoted to the Republican policies. In the Union Army he commanded a brigade. After the war he was elected Governor of Missouri on the liberal Republican ticket by a majority of 40,000; and in 1872 he was the Vice-presidential candidate on the Democratic ticket with Horace Greeley. From 1863 to 1867 he served in the United States Senate; and the speeches which he delivered in this body are preserved in the 'Congressional Record.'

BROWN, DEMETRIA VAKA (Mrs. Kenneth Brown). Author. She was born Demetria Vaka, a Greek, and married, April 21, 1904, Kenneth Brown. Besides writing, in association with her husband, a story entitled 'The First Secretary,' she is also the author of a volume entitled 'Haremlik.' She resides at "West Cairns," Charlottesville, Va.

BROWN, EMMA ALICE. Poet. [Md.] She published a volume of 'Poems.'

BROWN, GEORGE WILLIAM, jurist, was born in Baltimore, Md., October 13, 1812, and died at Lake Mohonk, N.Y., September 6, 1890. He was educated at Rutgers College, studied law, became chief judge of the Appellate Court of Baltimore and professor of constitutional law in the University of Maryland. With William H. Norris, he published a 'Digest of the Maryland Reports' (Baltimore, 1847), a 'Sketch of the Life of Thomas Donaldson,' 'The Origin of Civil Growth in Maryland,' and a number of addresses on various themes.

BROWN, GLENN, architect, was born in Fauquier County, Va., September 13, 1854, a grandson of Bedford Brown, U.S. Senator from North Carolina. For years he has been one of the leading architects of Washington, D.C., and has written several works, including 'Healthy Foundations for Houses' (1885), a 'History of the U.S. Capitol' (1900), and numerous articles in technical journals.

BROWN, IDA. Educator. [Miss.]. She published 'The Story of the Ages' (1900).

BROWN, JOHN, clergyman, was born near Bremen, Germany, July 21, 1771, and died in Virginia, January 26, 1850. He belonged to the German Reformed Church, preached in the German language, and published a volume of pastoral addresses to the Germans in Virginia (1818).

BROWN, JOHN HENRY, historian, was born in Missouri in 1820. He located in Texas and wrote 'The History of Texas.'

BROWN, JOHN MASON. Historian. He wrote 'The Political Beginnings of Kentucky,' (Louisville, The Filson Club, 1889), a work which traces the historic record from the earliest days of pioneerhood to the formal admission of the State into the American union.

BROWN, JOHN THOMPSON. Educator. He holds the associate professorship of English at the University of Tennessee. Besides editing a publication for the Macmillan Company of New York, he has contributed to magazines and reviews. The sketch of George Washington Harris in 'The Library of Southern Literature' is from his pen.

BROWN, JOSEPH BROWNLEE, poet and educator, was born in Charleston, S.C., October 4, 1824, and died in Brooklyn, N.Y., October 21, 1888. He studied law but the greater part of his life was devoted to teaching, and at leisure intervals he contributed to the periodicals. He was an accomplished scholar, and besides translating 'Homer's Iliad' into hexameter verse he wrote a number of rare poems, one of which, "Thalatta! Thalatta!" is preserved in Wauchope's 'Writers of South Carolina' (Columbia, The State Company, 1909).

BROWN, JOSEPH EMERSON, governor, United States Senator, and railway president, was born in Pickens County, S.C., April 15, 1821, of sturdy Scotch-Irish stock. From circumstances of extreme poverty he rose to high eminence and great usefulness. He became Georgia's war governor, occupying the executive chair for eight years. After the war, on account of his attitude of acquiescence toward the measures of reconstruction, he suffered a reversal of popular favor; but, his judgment having been approved by time, he was first appointed and afterward twice elected by the Legislature of Georgia to the United States Senate. In early life he served on the Superior Court Bench, and later he was for many years president of the company which leased and operated the Western and Atlantic Railroad. He died in Atlanta, Ga., 1894, having amassed a fortune; but his benefactions were both wise and numerous. Long before his death, two volumes appeared which were in the main devoted to the salient events and episodes of his extraordinary career: 'History of Georgia from 1850 to 1881,' by Isaac W. Avery, and 'Life and Times of Joseph E. Brown,' by Herbert Fielder. They also contain many of his speeches.

BROWN, JOSEPH M., governor and author, was born at Canton, Ga., December 28, 1851. His father was Joseph E. Brown, Georgia's famous war governor, and his mother Elizabeth Gresham. After graduating with the first honor from Oglethorpe University, he chose the legal profession, but while pursuing his studies at Harvard his eyesight failed. For years he was general traffic manager of the Western and Atlantic Railroad and was afterward with the Seaboard. Still later he became a member of the railroad commission. From this office he was dismissed by Governor Hoke Smith, on account of an issue which rose between them over port rates. The result was that Mr. Brown entered the race for governor against Mr. Smith, and defeated him at the next election. The wielder of an accomplished pen he published in 1886 a 'History of the Atlanta Campaign,' which was followed by an historical romance entitled 'Kennesaw's Bombardment.' But his most pretentious work is 'Astyanax' (New York, The Broadway Publishing Company, 1907), an epic of early America in the preparation of which he spent thirty-five years of diligent research into Aztec and Indian antiquities and in the opinion of scholars the work is a masterpiece of archeological lore and romantic fiction. He married, February 12, 1889, Cora A. McCord. His country home is near Marietta, on a plantation which was once owned by Governor Charles J. McDonald.

BROWN, KENNETH. Author. He was born in Chicago, Ill., March 9, 1868, a son of Frank B. and Caroline Frothingham Brown. He was educated by private tutors at home and abroad, after which he spent five years at Harvard University. He was subsequently connected with some of the foremost American newspapers. He married, in 1904, Demetria Vaka, a Greek. In 1900 he made his residence at "West Cairns," near Charlottesville, Va. In collaboration with his brother-in-law, H. B. Boone, he has written two fascinating books: 'Eastover Court House' (New York, Harper and Brothers) and 'The Redfields Succession' (*ibid.*) and with Mrs. Kenneth Brown, he has written 'Sirocco' and 'The First Secretary.' He is engaged in literary work in Boston, Mass.

BROWN, MARY MITCHELL. Educator. [Texas]. She published a 'School History of Texas,' 'The Golden Wedding,' and a number of poems, including an ode to Jefferson Davis.

BROWN, SAMUEL. Physician. [Va.]. He was born in 1769 and died in 1834. He published an interesting 'Description of a Cave on Crooked Creek.'

BROWN, WALTER WIDEMAN. Educator. [S.C.]. He was born March 18, 1858. His published works include: 'Brown's Political Chart' (1882), 'How the Victory was Won' (1892), 'Money Don' Make 'Ristocrats' (1893), "Being," a poem (1893), 'Judy and other Sketches' (1895), 'The House of Haunts' (1896), and numerous political and educational articles contributed to periodicals. The writings of Professor Brown evince an intimate familiarity with negro dialect and character.

BROWN, WILLIAM GARROTT. See Biographical and Critical Sketch, Vol. II, page 531.

BROWN, WILLIAM HILL. Poet. [N.C.]. Born in 1766. He wrote a tragedy, founded upon the death of Major André and a comedy 'Ira and Isabella' (1807). He died at Murfreesboro, N.C., September 2, 1793.

BROWN, WILLIAM MONTGOMERY. Protestant Episcopal Bishop of Arkansas. He was born November 6, 1855, in Wayne County, Ohio. He married, April 19, 1885, Ella Scranton Bradford. He established numerous missions and on September 5, 1900, became Protestant Episcopal Bishop of Arkansas. He is the author of 'The Church for Americans.' Bishop Brown holds the degree of D.D. He resides in Little Rock, Ark.

BROWN, WILLIAM PERRY. Author. He was born in 1847, in the Indian Territory, where his father was an agent for the Government. Besides numerous magazine articles, he has written the following books: 'A Sea Island Romance' (New York, John B. Alder, 1888), 'Roraima' (published in London, 1898), 'Ralph Granger's Fortunes' (Akron, Ohio, Saalfield Publishing Company), 'Florida Lads' (*ibid.*, 1903), 'Sea Island Boys' and 'Vance Sevier' (*ibid.*). Most of his writings have been for boys. He resides in Glenville, W.Va.

BROWNE, ALEXANDER. Author. [Va.]. He published a work entitled 'The Genesis of the United States' (1891).

BROWNE, ANNIE GREENE. Author. [Ala.]. She published 'Fireside Battles' (1900).

BROWNE, HENRY. Clergyman. [Va.]. He published 'The Captives of Abb's Valley,' and 'The Great Supper.'

BROWNE, WILLIAM HAND, professor of English literature in Johns Hopkins University, was born December 31, 1828, a son of William and Patience Hand Browne, and is a member of the Maryland Society of the Sons of the American Revolution. Besides numerous compilations and translations, he has produced the following books: 'Maryland, the History of a Palatinate,' 'George Calvert and Cecilius Calvert, Barons Baltimore,' and 'The Life of Alexander H. Stephens,' the latter in collaboration with Richard Malcolm Johnston. For 'The Library of Southern Literature' he wrote the sketch of John B. Tabb. The most important of his translations is 'Von Falke's Greece and Rome.' Two of his principal compilations are: 'The Clarendon Dictionary of the English Language' and 'Selections from the Early Scotch Poets.' He edited *The Southern Review* from 1867 to 1868, and *The Southern Magazine* from 1870 to 1875. He also edited the 'Archives of Maryland.' At the advanced age of more than fourscore years, Dr. Browne still resides in Baltimore, Md.

BROWNING, MESHACK. Sportsman. [Md.]. He wrote an interesting volume entitled 'Forty-four Years of the Life of a Maryland Hunter' (1864).

BROWNING, RAYMOND. Poet. [N.C.] The author of a collection of verse entitled 'After-Study Meditations' (Trinity College. N.C., 1906).

BROWNLEE, ALICE VIVIAN (Mrs. James L. Cole). Author. She was born in 1874. An interesting novel has come from her pen entitled 'The Affinities' (Atlanta, Constitution Publishing Company). Her home is in Birmingham, Ala.

BROWNLOW, WILLIAM GANNAWAY. Journalist. He was sometimes called "Parson Brownlow" because for ten years he was an itinerant Methodist preacher. Born in Wythe County, Va., August 29, 1805, he enjoyed only a fair education, but was a man of tenacious and independent convictions and was early led into politics. For several years he edited *The Whig* at Knoxville, Tenn. He made himself unpopular by opposing nullification and was defeated for Congress by Andrew Jackson. Though an advocate of slavery, he opposed secession and became an avowed Unionist, with the result that his paper was confiscated and he was forced to take refuge in the North. But he returned to Tennessee during the days of reconstruction to become Governor of the State under bayonet rule and United States Senator. Later he again acquired an interest in *The Whig*. He published: 'The Iron Wheel Examined,' a reply to attacks on the Methodist Church (Nashville, 1856); 'Ought American Slavery to be Perpetuated?' a debate in which he took the affirmative side (Philadelphia, 1858), and 'Sketches of the Rise, Progress, and Decline of Secession, with a Narrative of Personal Adventures among the Rebels' (1862). He died in Knoxville, Tenn., April 29, 1877.

BRUCE, ELI METCALF, Congressman, philanthropist, orator, was born in Fleming County, Ky., February 2, 1828, and died in New York City, December 15, 1866. He acquired an immense fortune, by means of which he rendered great service to letters. As an orator he wielded an influence which made him a power in Kentucky and which sent him to Congress, and he delivered in Richmond a speech on the financial resources of the Confederacy, which is said never to have been surpassed. During the Civil War he served on the staff of General Breckinridge. He spent his means lavishly in support of the Confederate cause, to which he contributed not less than $300,000 in gold. At the close of hostilities he financed the consolidation of two Louisville papers, *The Courier* and *The Journal* and Mr. Bruce Haldeman, who is now president of the Courier Journal Publishing Company, bears the name of the distinguished philanthropist. William C. P. Breckinridge, in an editorial which appeared in the Lexington *Observer* declared that no private individual known to history surpassed Colonel Bruce in the munificence of his gifts. He is buried at Covington, Ky., where the local chapter of the U.D.C. is named in his honor.

BRUCE, JAMES DOUGLAS, educator, was born at Staunton Hill, Va., December 9, 1862, and was given the best educational advantages (M.A., University of Va.; Ph.D., Johns Hopkins). At present he occupies the chair of English language and literature in the University of Tennessee. Besides contributing to German and American philological reviews, he also writes for *The Nation*. He has edited 'The Anglo-Saxon Book of Psalms' (Baltimore, 1894), 'De Ortu Walwanii,' an Arthurian romance (Baltimore, 1899), 'Vita Meriadoci,' an Arthurian romance (Baltimore, 1900), 'La Mort d'Arthur, a middle English poem in stanzas (London, 1903), and 'La Mort d'Artes,' an old French Arthurian romance (Halle, 1909). The sketch of Richard Henry Wilde in 'The Library of Southern Literature' is from his pen.

BRUCE, JEROME. Physician. Dr. Bruce wrote an interesting work entitled 'Studies in Black and White' (New York and Washington, The Neale Publishing Company, 1906). It presents the race problem from the standpoint of ante-bellum days and incidentally unfolds a romance of engaging interest.

BRUCE, PHILIP ALEXANDER. Author. He was born at Staunton Hill, Charlotte County, Va. March 7, 1856, a son of Charles and Sarah Sedden Bruce. He was educated at the University of Virginia and at Harvard Law School, and married, October 19, 1896, Betty T. Taylor, of Norfolk, Va. He was for some years editor of the Richmond *Times* and afterward was corresponding secretary for many years of the Virginia Historical Society. His writings are in the main historical and are marked by vigor of thought and thoroughness of research. They include: 'The Plantation Negro as a Freeman' (New York, G. P. Putnam's Sons, 1889), 'Economic History of Virginia in the Seventeenth Century' (New York, Macmillan Company, 1896), 'Rise of the New South' (Barrie and Sons), 'School History of the United States' (American Book Company, 1903), 'Social Life of Virginia in the Seventeenth Century' (Richmond, Bell Book Company, 1907), an excellent 'Life of General Robert E. Lee' (Philadelphia, Jacobs and Company, 1907), and numerous contributions to English reviews and American magazines. For 'The Library of Southern Literature' he wrote the sketch of John Randolph. He is also the author of a series of articles for 'The South in the Building of the Nation.' Both William and Mary College and Washington and Lee University have conferred upon him the degree of LL.D. He resides in Norfolk, Va.

BRUCE, THOMAS. Author. [Va.]. He has published a number of very interesting stories, among them, 'Cupid and Duty,' 'That Bruisin' Lad o' Greystone Lodge' (1890), and 'Loveless Marriages.' He also wrote 'Historical Sketches of Roanoke.'

BRUCE, WILLIAM LIDDELL, Mrs. Author. From the pen of this Southern woman has come an interesting story based upon changed conditions in the Dixie cotton belt entitled 'Uncle Tom's Cabin of To-day' (New York and Washington, The Neale Publishing Company, 1906).

BRUNER, JAMES DOWDEN, educator, was born in Leitchfield, Ky., May 19, 1864. Several volumes have come from his pen, among them, 'Phonology of Pistoiese Dialect' (Baltimore: The Johns Hopkins Press, 1894), Hugo's 'Hernani' (New York, The American Book Company, 1906), Corneille's 'Le Cid' (*ibid.*, 1908), and 'Hugo's Dramatic Characters' (Boston, Ginn & Company, 1908), besides numerous minor works. At the present time he is president of Chowan Institute, at Murfreesboro, N.C. He received the degree of Ph.D. from Johns Hopkins.

BRUNNER, JOHN HAMILTON. Clergyman and educator. [Tenn.]. Born in 1825. He published 'Sunday Evening Talks' (Nashville, M. E. Publishing House, South, 1879), and 'Union of the Churches' (1884).

BRUNS, JOHN DICKSON. Physician and educator. He was born in Charleston, S.C., February 24, 1836, and died in New Orleans, La., May 20, 1883. During the Civil War he was a hospital surgeon. In 1856 he was made professor of physiology and pathology in the New Orleans School of Medicine. He wrote some graceful verse, characterized by unusual charm of description, and published 'The Life and Genius of Henry Timrod,' besides medical papers.

BRYAN, DANIEL. Poet. [Va.]. He wrote 'The Mountain Muse, or the Adventures of Daniel Boone,' 1813), and 'A Lay of Gratitude,' inspired by the visit of Lafayette (1826).

BRYAN, ELLA HOWARD, author, was born in Savannah, Ga., of distinguished colonial stock. Under the pen-name of "Clinton

Dangerfield," she contributes to current magazines, writing not only stories and sketches of sparkling interest but also excellent verse. She has published only one book, 'Behind the Veil' (Boston, Little, Brown and Company), but her work has appeared in over twenty high-class periodicals. Miss Bryan is in direct line of descent from Jonathan Bryan, who aided Oglethorpe in the settlement of the colony of Georgia.

BRYAN, EMMA LYON. Author. [Va.]. She wrote '1860-1865: a Romance of Virginia.'

BRYAN, GUY M., Congressman, author, orator, was one of the foremost public men of Texas. He served in both State and Federal Legislatures and attended the famous Charleston Convention of 1860. Colonel Bryan was a nephew of Stephen F. Austin for whom the capital of the State was named; and based largely upon the manuscripts of this early pioneer he contributed several very important chapters to Wooten's 'Comprehensive History of Texas' (Dallas, William G. Scarff, 1898).

BRYAN, MARY EDWARDS. Novelist. This popular writer of fiction was born at Fonda, Jefferson County, Ga., in 1844 and was the daughter of Major John D. and Louisa Edwards. Evincing unusual talent, she was given the best advantages; but her studies, which she began at Fletcher Institute, Thomasville, Ga., were interrupted by her marriage to Mr. Bryan, at the early age of fifteen. Later she took special college work. From 1874 to 1884 she was associate editor of *The Sunny South.* She relinquished this position to become editor first of the New York *Bazaar* and afterward of *The Half Hour,* but subsequently returned to the periodical in which her fascinating stories first appeared. She is one of the most widely read of Southern writers, and her literary work is characterized by an exquisite charm of style and incident. Among her novels are: 'Manch,' 'Wild Work,' 'Kildee,' 'Nan Haggard,' 'The Bayou Tree,' 'Uncle Ned's White Child,' 'A Stormy Wedding,' 'Ruth—An Outcast,' 'My Sin,' 'The Girl He Bought,' 'His Legal Wife,' 'A Fair Judas,' and several others. Mrs. Bryan has also written some excellent verse. She spends her winters at Cocoa, Fla.

BRYAN, WILLIAM SMITH, editor and publisher, was born in St. Charles County, Mo., January 8, 1846, became one of the foremost editors of the State, organized a publishing business, and was the first to introduce colored illustrations. His works include: 'Pioneer Families of Missouri' with Robert Rose (Philadelphia); 'Our Islands' (St. Louis, N. D. Thompson Company); 'America's War for Humanity' (*ibid.*); 'The History of the Discovery and Exploration of the Mississippi Valley' in two volumes, and 'The History of the Thirteen Colonies,' besides minor works. He resides in New York.

BRYANT, EDGAR EUGENE, lawyer, was born in Mississippi, December 9, 1861, but afterward removed to Arkansas, where he speedily rose to the front at the Bar and in public life and published 'Speeches and Addresses' (1895).

BRYANT, EDWIN, pioneer, was born in Massachusetts in 1805 and died in Louisville, Ky., in 1869. For many years he was a journalist in Kentucky, but in 1846 he headed a party of emigrants to California, and, on his return, published an account of his adventures, under the title: 'What I saw in California' (New York, 1848).

BUCHANAN, JOSEPH, inventor, was born in Washington County, Va., August 24, 1785, and died in Louisville, Ky., September 29, 1829. He removed to Tennessee, studied medicine, became a professor in the medical department of Transylvania University and patented a number of inventions, among them a steam engine, with which he ran a wagon through the streets of Louisville in 1824, and a musical instrument in which the notes were produced by glasses of different composition. He edited various papers and published 'The Philosophy of Human Nature' (Richmond, Ky., 1812).

BUCHANAN, JOSEPH RHODES, physician, was born in Frankfort, Ky., December 11, 1814, a son of Joseph Buchanan, the inventor. He studied medicine, became an eminent practitioner of the Eclectic School, taught in various institutions, and made numerous contributions to scientific thought and progress. Besides editing for several years *Buchanan's Journal of Men,* he published 'Outlines of Lectures on the Neurological System of Anthropology' (Cincinnati, 1854), 'Eclectic Practice of Medicine and Surgery,' a work which passed into several editions (Philadelphia, 1868), 'The New Education' (New York, 1882), 'Therapeutic Sarcognomy' (Boston, 1884), a 'Manual of Psychometry' (1885), and a volume on 'Cerebral Physiology.' He discovered what he called the sciences of Sarcognomy and Psychometry, and embodied them in elaborate discussions.

BUCHHOLZ, HEINRICH EWALD, editor and author, was born in Baltimore, Md., January 19, 1879. Several rich volumes have come from his pen, among them 'The Civil War' (1905), 'The Crown of the Chesapeake' (1906), 'The Governors of Maryland' (1907), and 'Maryland Country Seats' (1908). He has also edited 'Men of Mark in Maryland' and 'Edgar Allan Poe, a Centenary Tribute.' At present he is the editor of the *Merchants' and Manufacturers' Journal.* He resides in Baltimore, Md.

BUCHNER, EDWARD FRANKLIN. Educator. He was born in Paxton, Ford County, Ill., September 3, 1868, the son of Christian Jacob and Louise Caroline Lohmann Buchner; married, June 1, 1898, Hannah Louise Cable; and was for some time instructor in philosophy and pedagogy at Yale University. From 1896 to 1901 he was lecturer on psychology in the Brooklyn Institute of Arts and Sciences. In 1903 he accepted the chair of philosophy and education in the University of Alabama. He is an authority on philosophical and educational subjects. Besides numerous articles for magazines and encyclopædias, he has written 'A Study of Kant's Psychology with Reference to the Critical Philosophy' (New York, The Macmillan Company, 1897), and has also translated and edited 'The Educational Theory of Immanuel Kant' (Philadelphia, J. B. Lippincott Company, 1904). Yale gave him the degree of Ph.D.

BUCK, CHARLES W. Lawyer. He was born in Vicksburg, Miss., March 17, 1849, the son of John W. and Mary Bell Buck, married Elizabeth Crow Bullett, and was an ardent Democrat until 1896, when he adopted an independent course in politics. He is an able lawyer and a man of culture. Besides an interesting volume entitled 'Under the Sun,' he has frequently contributed to the periodicals. He resides in Louisville, Ky.

BUCK, IRVING A. Author. Captain Buck was adjutant-general on the staff of General Patrick Cleburne during the Civil War. He enjoyed the most intimate acquaintance with his superior officer and published a work of rare interest entitled 'Cleburne and His

Men' (New York and Washington, The Neale Publishing Company, 1908), in which, step by step, he traces the career of his brave commander from Shiloh and Perryville to the tragic field of Franklin.

BUCKLEY, RICHARD WALLACE. Author. [Va.]. He wrote a story of rather weird interest in which hereditary tendencies play an important part, entitled 'The Last of the Hortons' (New York and Washington, The Neale Publishing Company, 1907).

BUCKNER, R. T., Mrs. Author. [La.]. She published a volume entitled 'Toward the Gulf' (New York, 1887).

BUELL, RICHARD HOOKER, engineer, was born at Cumberland, Md., November 9, 1842, received his education at Troy Polytechnic Institute and published 'The Cadet Engineer' (Philadelphia, 1875), 'Safety-Valves' (New York, 1878), additions to Weisbach's 'Mechanics of Engineering' and treatises on heat, steam and steam-engines, besides numerous monographs.

BUIST, GEORGE, clergyman, was born in Fifeshire, Scotland, in 1770, and died in Charleston, S.C., August 31, 1808. For many years he was a pastor in Charleston; but he also conducted one of the local institutions of learning. He was a scholar of unusual attainments, having received his diploma from the University of Edinburgh; and besides contributing to the British Encyclopædia he published for school use an abridgment of 'Hume's History' and a version of the Psalms.

BULLARD, HENRY ADAMS. Jurist and educator. He was born in Groton, Mass., September 9, 1788; but, after taking his degree at Harvard University, he settled in Louisiana for the practice of law. For a time he occupied a seat in Congress; but he preferred judicial to legislative work and accepted an appointment as District Judge. Later he was promoted to the Supreme Bench of the State, remaining upon this tribunal for twelve years. He was also for some time professor of civil law in the University of Louisiana. His decisions are said to be models of judicial rhetoric. Besides compiling a 'Digest of Louisiana Laws,' he delivered eulogies upon F. X. Martin and Sargent S. Prentiss, both of which were subsequently published. He died in New Orleans, April 17, 1851.

BULLEN, MARY SWINTON LEGARÉ. [S.C.]. She published an interesting memoir of her brother, Hugh Swinton Legaré, including the diary which he kept at Brussels, and also important letters and papers (Charleston, 1848).

BULLOCH, JAMES DUNWODY, naval officer, was born in Georgia, in 1824, and died in Liverpool, England, in 1901. He served with distinction in both Atlantic and Pacific fleets, but when the Civil War began he resigned his commission to enter the Confederate service and was at once given the rank of commander. On account of his experiences in naval affairs he was sent to England as naval agent to negotiate the purchase of war vessels and supplies, and he proved to be of such value to the Government in this rôle that he was kept in England for an extended period. He purchased the *Alabama* and the *Shenandoah,* two of the most famous Confederate warships, besides also the *Florida,* and dispatched them to American waters. After the war he made England his permanent home. Captain Bulloch published in two volumes a work of much interest entitled: 'The Secret Service of the Confederate States; or, How the Confederate Cruisers were Equipped' (1883). He was an uncle of ex-President Roosevelt.

BUNNER, E. Author. [La.]. He published a 'History of Louisiana from the First Discovery and Settlement' (New York, 1855).

BURCKETT, FLORENCE. Author. [La.]. She wrote a novel entitled 'Wildmoor' (1875).

BURGESS, JOHN WILLIAM, lawyer and educator, was born in Giles County, Tenn., August 26, 1844. On completing his studies at Amherst he was admitted to the Bar, but afterward chose an educational career, for which he further prepared himself at the German universities. Since 1876 he has been professor of political science and constitutional law at Columbia University, also for many years dean of the faculty of political science. He has made frequent contributions to magazines and reviews, and among the articles which attracted widest attention were "The American University," "The Middle Period," and "Political Science and Comparative Constitutional Law." He has received the Ph.D. and the LL.D. degrees.

BURGWYN, WILLIAM HYSLOP SUMNER, lawyer and banker, was born at Jamaica Plains, Mass., July 23, 1845. His father was Henry King Burgwyn and his mother, Anna Greenough. In early childhood he was brought to the South. Enlisting in the Confederate Army when only fifteen, he was several times wounded. He graduated with the highest honors from the University of North Carolina; studied law at Harvard and practiced his profession in Baltimore, Md., until 1882, when he opened a bank at Henderson, N.C. During the Spanish-American War he commanded a regiment of North Carolina volunteers. He is the author of a 'Digest of Maryland Reports' (1878), 'Addresses on General Thomas L. Clingman and General Matt W. Ransom,' and various historical monographs. The sketch of Zebulon B. Vance in 'The Library of Southern Literature' is also from his pen. He married, November 21, 1876, Margaret Carlisle Dunlop of Richmond, Va. He is engaged in the banking business at Weldon, N.C.

BURGWYN, C. P. E. Poet. [Va.]. He wrote 'The Huguenot Lovers, and Other Poems.'

BURK, JOHN, historian and dramatist, was a native of Ireland, the date of his birth being unknown. For a time he edited *The Pole Star* in Boston, which according to Professor Brander Matthews, "remained above the horizon for barely six months and then sank forever into the darkness of night." Later he took up his residence at Petersburg, Va., for the practice of law; and, on March 4, 1803, he delivered an eloquent oration in the court-house to celebrate the election of Jefferson. His literary gifts were of high order; and besides 'The History of the Late War in Ireland' (Philadelphia, 1797), and 'The History of Virginia' (1804-1818, Vol. IV, completed by Louis Girardin and Skelton Jones), which the critics have warmly commended, he wrote several dramas, including: 'Female Patriotism; or the Death of Jean d'Arc' and 'Bunker Hill; or the Death of Warren.' He was killed on April 11, 1808, by Felix Coquebert, in a duel resulting from a political quarrel.

BURKE, JOHN W. [Ga.]. He published 'The Life of Robert Emmet.'

BURKITT, LEMUEL. Clergyman and historian. [N.C.]. He was born in 1750 and died in 1803. The earliest volume of North Carolina history came from the pen of this pioneer writer who, in association with Jesse Read, published a 'History of the Kehukee

Baptist Association' (Halifax, N.C., 1803; republished, Philadelphia, 1850).

BURNETT, FRANCES HODGSON. See Biographical and Critical Sketch, Vol. II, page 555.

BURNETT, PETER HARDEMAN, lawyer, was born in Nashville, Tenn., November 15, 1807. For many years he lived in Tennessee and Missouri; but in 1843 he went to Oregon, taking an important part in the territorial organization, and afterward located in California, when the discovery of gold began to lure the argonauts. He rose to prominence, becoming Governor of the State and Associate Justice of the Supreme Court. His writings include: 'The Path which Led a Protestant Lawyer to the Catholic Church' (New York, 1860), 'The American Theory of Government Considered with Reference to the Present Crisis' (1861), 'Recollections of an Old Pioneer' 1878), and 'Reasons Why We Should Believe in God, Love God and Obey God' (1884). From 1863 to 1880 he was president of the Pacific Bank of San Francisco.

BURNEY, STANFORD GUTHRIE. Clergyman and educator. For many years he was professor of theology in Cumberland University, Tennessee. He published 'Studies in Theology,' a 'Treatise on Elocution' and several minor works.

BURT, ARMISTEAD, lawyer and poet, was born in Abbeville District, S.C., in 1802, and became Speaker of the House of Representatives. He was quite a poet and produced three volumes of verse: 'The Coronation; or Hypocrisy Exposed,' to which was added 'Sullivan's Island, with Notes' (Charleston, 1822), 'Journeyman Weaving' (New York, 1831), and 'Poems, Chiefly Satirical' (New York, 1833). But he outgrew the poetic habit; and for the next fifty years no other work appears from his pen. He died in 1883.

BURWELL, LETITIA McCREERY. Author. [Va.]. She wrote an interesting volume entitled 'A Girl's Life in Virginia before the War,' besides short stories and sketches and quite a number of poems.

BURWELL, WILLIAM McCREERY. Editor. [Va.]. He was born in 1809 and died in 1888. At one time he conducted *DeBow's Review.* He published 'Essays on Economics,' 'White Acre Against Black Acre,' 'Exile and Empire,' and minor writings.

BUSH, GEORGE CARY. Educator. [Fla.]. He wrote 'The History of Education in Florida.'

BUTLER, MATTHEW CALBRAITH. Statesman and soldier. He was born near Greenville, S.C., March 8, 1836. Before graduation he left South Carolina College, entered the practice of law and from the start achieved signal success at the Bar. He won distinction in the Confederate Army, attaining the rank of major-general; and after the war became an active factor in the political affairs of the state. From 1877 to 1889 he represented South Carolina with distinction in the United States Senate. At the outbreak of hostilities with Spain, in 1898, he was commissioned major-general of United States volunteers; but declined to accept retirement as an army officer. He married, February 21, 1858, Maria S. Pickens. General Butler was an eloquent and effective public speaker. He wrote the sketch of General Wade Hampton for 'The Library of Southern Literature.' He died in Columbia, S.C., April 14, 1909.

BUTLER, NOBLE, educator, was born in Washington County, Pa., in 1819, but much of his life was spent in the South and he died in Louisville, Ky., having filled for years the chair of Greek and Latin in the University of Louisville. Among other text-books, he published a 'Practical and Critical English Grammar' (Louisville, 1875).

BUTLER, PIERCE, educator, was born in New Orleans, La., January 18, 1873. For some time he has been a professor in Newcomb College, in New Orleans. His published works include: 'Women of Mediæval France' (Philadelphia, Barrie and Company, 1907), a 'Life of Judah P. Benjamin' (Philadelphia, George W. Jacobs and Company, 1907), and 'Legenda Aurea,' a thesis (Baltimore, 1899). For 'The Library of Southern Literature' he wrote the sketch of Judah P. Benjamin. He received the Ph.D. degree from Johns Hopkins.

BUTLER, WILLIAM ORLANDO, lawyer and soldier, was born in Jessamine County, Ky., in 1791 and died in Carrollton, Ky., August 6, 1880. Both in the War of 1812 and in the Mexican War he achieved distinction, becoming senior major-general of volunteers and succeeding Winfield Scott in the chief command. Afterward he became the Vice-presidential condidate on the free soil ticket with Lewis Cass. In the practice of law he achieved large success. At intervals he dipped into verse, "The Boatman's Horn" being among the best known of his poems. 'The Life and Services of General William Orlando Butler,' edited by Francis P. Blair, appeared in 1848

BUTTS, SARAH HARRIET, author, was born in Columbus, Ga., September 30, 1845. She married Dr. Judson A. Butts, of Brunswick, Ga., September 30, 1867 and was regent and founder of the Brunswick chapter of the Daughters of the American Revolution. Her only literary work is entitled 'Mothers of Some Distinguished Georgians,' published by J. J. Little and Company of New York in 1902; but her memory is most beautifully embalmed in this production. She died in Brunswick, Ga., June 16, 1905.

BYARS, WILLIAM VINCENT, editor and poet, was born in Covington, Tenn., June 21, 1857. His education was chiefly directed by his father, Professor James Byars, who was quite an eminent scholar. On completing his studies he engaged in journalistic work. He acquired something of a reputation on the St. Louis papers and then became identified for several years with the New York *World*. He was also for a time on the staff of *Harper's Weekly;* but he now contributes to various publications and resides in St. Louis. His published works include: 'Tannhäuser—A Mystery' and 'The Tempting of the King.' Several fine poems have also come from his pen, some of which are preserved in 'Missouri Literature.' He married, June 15, 1880, Loula Clement, daughter of the Rev. Charles Francis Collins.

BYNUM, ENOCH EDWIN, clergyman and editor, was born in Randolph County, Ind., October 13, 1861. Dr. Bynum is an ordained minister of "the Church of God," a forceful speaker and a voluminous writer. Besides editing the *Gospel Trumpet,* he has published 'The Boys' Companion' (1890), 'Divine Healing of Soul and Body' (1892), 'The Secret of Salvation' (1896), 'The Prayer of Faith' (1899), 'The Great Physician' (1900). 'Behind the Prison Bars' (1901). 'Ordinances of the Bible' (1904), and 'Travels and Experiences in Other Lands' (1906). He resides in Moundsville, W.Va.

BYRD, ELLA BILLINGSLEY. Educator. [Ala.]. She published a novel entitled 'Marston Hall.'

BYRD, WILLIAM. See Biographical and Critical Sketch, Vol. II, page 583.

BYRNE, THOMAS SEBASTIAN. Roman Catholic Bishop of Nashville, Tenn. He was born in Hamilton, Ohio, July 29, 1842, a son of Eugene and Mary Anne Reynolds Byrne. He was ordained priest, May 22, 1869. He taught for some time in Mount St. Mary Seminary and later took charge of the cathedral at Cincinnati. In 1894 he became Bishop of Nashville. Much of his time has been given to literary work. At the World's Parliament of Religions in Chicago, he read a paper on "Man from a Catholic Point of View," which has been widely published. He has also made numerous translations and written for the religious press. He resides in Nashville, Tenn.

CABELL, EDWARD CARRINGTON, lawyer, was born in Richmond, Va., February 5, 1816, a son of William H. Cabell. On receiving his diploma from the University of Virginia, he located in Florida and served for four consecutive terms in Congress from the Peninsula State. During the war he served for a time in the Confederate ranks. It is said that a speech which he delivered in Congress resulted in the fortification of Key West. He wrote an elaborate account of Florida, which was published in *DeBow's Review.*

CABELL, JAMES ALSTON, lawyer, was born in Richmond, Va. After completing his studies, he filled for a time the chair of chemistry in Central University, Ky., studied law, became a member of the Virginia Legislature, and took high rank at the Bar. He belongs to various patriotic, historical and literary organizations, edits the *Virginia Masonic Journal,* and is the author of numerous monographs.

CABELL, I. C., Mrs. Author, of Virginia. She published a volume entitled 'Historical and Biographical Sketches.'

CABELL, JAMES BRANCH. See Biographical and Critical Sketch, Vol. II, page 609.

CABELL, JAMES LAWRENCE, physician, was born in Nelson County, Va., August 26, 1813, a son of Dr. George Cabell, Jr. While pursuing his studies abroad he was called to the chair of anatomy and surgery in the University of Virginia. During the war he was in charge of military hospitals for the Confederate Government. Besides contributing to medical journals, he published: 'The Testimony of Modern Science to the Unity of Mankind' (New York, 1858).

CABELL, JULIA MAYO, Mrs. She wrote 'An Odd Volume of Fact and Fiction' (Richmond, 1852), consisting mainly of letters of travel, interspersed with ballads, elegies and epigrams.

CABELL, MARGARET COUCH ANTHONY. Mrs. Author, of Virginia, born in 1814 and died in 1883. She published 'Recollections of Lynchburg.'

CABEZA DE VACA, ALVA NUNEZ, Spanish explorer, was born in 1507 and died in 1559. From the pen of this famous adventurer has come the earliest book on the Southern Indians, viz.; 'Voyages and Memoirs' (Madrid, 1542).

CABLE, GEORGE WASHINGTON. See Biographical and Critical Sketch, Vol. II, page 619.

CAIN, WILLIAM. Educator. [N.C.]. Born in 1847. He published several text-books on mathematics.

CALDER, ALMA. Author. [La.]. She wrote 'Miriam's Heritage,' a novel (1878).

CALDWELL, CHARLES, physician, was born in Caswell County, N.C., May 14, 1772, studied medicine in Philadelphia and served as a brigade surgeon in General Lee's command, during the whiskey insurrection of 1791-1794. He taught for some time in medical schools and also wielded an editorial pen of great power. Besides numerous essays and translations, he wrote: 'The Life and Campaigns of General Greene' (1819) and 'Memoirs of Horace Holley,' and his 'Autobiography' was published after his death from manuscript which he left. He died in Louisville, Ky., July 9, 1853.

CALDWELL, HOWARD HAYNE. Lawyer. [S.C.] He was born in 1831 and died in 1858. Mr. Caldwell published 'Oliata' (1855), 'Poems' (1858), and numerous prose articles.

CALDWELL, JAMES FITZ-JAMES. Lawyer. [S.C.]. He published: 'Gregg's Brigade of South Carolinians' (1866) and 'Letters from Europe,' and a romance of reconstruction entitled 'The Stranger' (New York and Washington, The Neale Publishing Company, 1906).

CALDWELL, J. H. Clergyman. [S.C.]. Dr. Caldwell published 'The Thurstons of the Old Palmetto State' and 'Varieties of Southern Life.'

CALDWELL, JOSEPH, clergyman and educator, was born in Lammington, N. J., April 21, 1773, and was educated at Princeton. When only twenty-three, he became professor of mathematics in the University of North Carolina; and with this institution he was identified almost uninterruptedly until the time of his death, serving it for nearly three decades in the office of president. His publications include: 'A Compendious System of Elementary Geometry' (1822) and 'Letters of Carleton.' He died at Chapel Hill, N.C., January 24, 1835. Princeton gave him the degree of D.D.

CALDWELL, JOSHUA WILLIAM. See Biographical and Critical Sketch, Vol. II, page 655.

CALDWELL, LISLE B., Methodist Episcopal clergyman and educator, was born in New York in 1834. But for many years he labored in Tennessee in both pastoral and educational lines of work and published 'The Wines of Palestine, or the Bible Defended' (1859) and 'Beyond the Grave' (1884).

CALDWELL, WILLIE WALKER, Mrs. Author. [Va.]. She published a volume entitled 'The Tie that Binds.'

CALHOUN, ALICE J. Author. She wrote a story of plantation life in the South entitled 'When the Yellow Jasmine Blooms' (New York and Washington, The Neale Publishing Company, 1907), which is well constructed. Her portrayals of negro character are excellent.

CALHOUN, JOHN CALDWELL. See Biographical and Critical Sketch, Vol. II, page 673.

CALISH, EDWARD N., clergyman, was born in Toledo, Ohio, in 1865. For several years he has resided in the South and at present occupies an important pastorate in Richmond. His publications include: 'A Book of Prayer' (1893), 'A Child's Bible' (1895), and 'The

Jew in English Literature.' He married, January 22, 1890, Gisela
Woolner. The University of Virginia gave him the Ph.D degree.

CALL, DANIEL. Lawyer. His birthplace is unknown, but he
was born about the year 1765 and died in Richmond, Va., May 20,
1840. He was a brother-in-law of Chief Justice John Marshall, and
published 'Reports of the Virginia Court of Appeals,' in six volumes,
from 1790 to 1818.

CALL, WILKINSON, United States Senator, was born in Russellville, Ky., January 9, 1834; but, locating in Florida in early life,
he was admitted to the Bar and became an important factor in the
public life of the State. Soon after the war, from which he emerged
with the rank of adjutant-general, he was elected to the United States
Senate, but was refused a seat, on account of the issues of reconstruction. However, he was again commissioned in 1879; and for eighteen
consecutive years he continued to wear the toga. He delivered
numerous public addresses, but few of his speeches have been preserved except in the debates of Congress.

CALLAHAN, JAMES MORTON. Educator, author, lecturer.
He was born in Bedford, Ind., November 4, 1864, the son of Martin I. and Sophia Oregon Tannehill Callahan, and graduated from the
University of Indiana, but took post-graduate work at the University of
Chicago and at Johns Hopkins University. Since 1902 he has been pro-
fessor of history and political science in the University of West Virignia.
His writings are characterized by great thoroughness of research and by
sound reasoning, and constitute an important contribution to the practical
thought of the day. Included among his works are: 'The Neutrality of
the American Lakes,' 'Cuba and International Relations,' 'American
Relations in the Pacific and the Far West,' 'Confederate Diplomacy,'
'American Expansion Policy,' 'The Monroe Doctrine and Inter-American
Relations,' 'The United States and Canada: a Study in International
History,' besides various historical monographs and a series of sketches
of great heroes and leaders. Dr. Callahan resides in Morgantown, W.Va.,
and most of his books have been issued by the Johns Hopkins Press, Baltimore, Md. Johns Hopkins gave him the degree of Ph.D.

CALLAWAY, MORGAN, Jr. Professor of English in the University of Texas. He was born in Cuthbert, Ga., November 2, 1862. His
father was the Rev. Morgan Callaway, D.D., for many years professor of
English at Emory College, Oxford, Ga. Morgan Callaway was educated
at Emory College and at Johns Hopkins University. His publications
include: 'The Absolute Participle in Anglo-Saxon' and 'The Appositive
Participle in Anglo-Saxon.' He has also edited 'The Select Poems of Sidney Lanier' (New York, Charles Scribner's Sons), and contributed numerous articles to the magazines, including "Jane Welsh Carlyle," "English in
Our Preparatory Schools," and "The Poetry of Sidney Lanier." Dr. Callaway is one of the assistant literary editors of 'The Library of Southern
Literature,' a man of ripe scholarship and of high rank among philologists.
Johns Hopkins gave him the degree of Ph.D. He resides in Austin, Texas.

CALLENDER, JAMES THOMAS, editor, was born in Scotland
and refugeed to this country in consequence of an article which he
published on "The Political Progress of Britain." For several years
he edited the Richmond *Recorder*. He was an uncompromising
fighter, caustic and bitter, antagonized both Washington and Adams,
and after being an ardent supporter of Jefferson, became his opponent. He wrote 'Sketches of the History of America' and 'The
Prospect before Us.' Mr. Callender was drowned in the James River
in 1813.

CALLER, MARY ALICE. Teacher of English language and literature in the Alabama Conference Female College, in Tuskegee, Ala. She comes of one of the best families of the State, her grandfather, Colonel James Caller, having been prominent in public life. She was educated at Centenary College and has held several important collegiate chairs, but since 1877 has been the teacher of English at Tuskegee. She has written an excellent 'Literary Guide for Home and School,' and a volume of verse entitled 'Poems of Nature' (1897). During the summer months she resides in Avondale, Ala.

CALVERT, GEORGE HENRY, author, was born in Prince George County, Md., January 2, 1803, and was a grandson of Lord Baltimore. After graduation from Harvard, he studied at Göttingen; and, on returning to America, he resided for some time near Baltimore, but afterward made his home at Newport, R.I., where he died May 24, 1889. For some time he edited the Baltimore *American;* but his life was devoted mainly to philosophical researches. An occasional poem gave evidence of the fact that he was also a man of artistic temperament. His published works include: 'Illustrations of Phrenology' (1832), 'A Volume from the Life of Herbert Barclay' (1833), 'Don Carlos,' a metrical translation from the German (1836), 'Count Julian,' a tragedy (1840), 'Cabiro,' which was commenced in 1840 and completed in 1864, 'Correspondence between Schiller and Goethe' a translation (1845), 'Scenes and Thoughts in Europe,' two series (1846 and 1852), 'The Battle of Lake Erie,' an oration (1853), 'Comedies and Social Science' (1856), 'Joan of Arc' (1860), 'The Gentleman, and Other Poems' (1863), 'Arnold and Andre,' an historical drama (1864), 'Ellen,' a poem (1869), 'Goethe, His Life and Works' (1872), 'Brief Essays and Brevities' (1874), 'Essays Æsthetical' (1875), and 'Wordsworth' (1875).

CAMERON, HENRY CLAY, educator, was born in Shepherdstown, Va., September 1, 1827. After graduating from Princeton, he studied theology but devoted himself to educational work for several years before applying for ordination. From 1859 to 1870 he was instructor of French at Princeton, at another time he held the office of librarian, and in 1877 he became professor of Greek. He edited for twenty years the *General Catalogue of the College of New Jersey,* wrote numerous articles for encyclopædias, notably one on "Jonathan Edwards and the Rise of Colleges in America," and published several historical pamphlets, besides a series of classical maps, in association with Professor Guyot.

CAMERON, WILLIAM EVELYN. One of the leading pub:'c men of Virginia since the war. He was born in Petersburg, Va., November 29, 1842, a son of Walker Anderson and Elizabeth Byrd Walker Cameron. His college career was interrupted by the war. He served in all the battles of Lee's army, from Seven Pines to Appomattox, and rose from private to assistant adjutant-general. He was wounded at Second Manassas. He married, October 1, 1868, Louisa Clara Egerton. He edited some of the leading newspapers of the State for ten years, and was then admitted to the Bar. He was Mayor of Petersburg from 1876 to 1882, and Governor of Virginia from 1882 to 1886. He was also a member of the Constitutional Convention of 1881. His writings include: 'The Life and Character of Robert E. Lee' (1902), 'The History of the Chicago Exposition' (1903), and 'The World's Fair' (1904). He resides in Petersburg, Va.

CAMP, GEORGE KING, journalist and poet, was born at Darien, Ga., in 1851. and. on the paternal side, was a descendant of Sir

Matthew Hale. From the University of Georgia he went to the Virginia Military Institute; and, graduating with honors, he began the practice of law. While located in Atlanta, he published a volume of poems entitled 'Whispering Winds,' and, being something of a musician, he set to music "The Memorial Window," by James Barron Hope. After an unfortunate marriage, followed by his child's death, he went to San Francisco, accepting a place on the staff of *The Examiner*, and here he published 'Shadows.'

CAMPBELL, ALEXANDER. See Biographical and Critical Sketch, Vol. II, page 711.

CAMPBELL, ALEXANDER AUGUSTUS, clergyman and physician, was born in Amherst County, Va., December 30, 1789, and died in Jackson, Tenn., May 27, 1846. At first an infidel, he was rescued from the clutches of unbelief by an attack of yellow fever; and, while actively engaged in the practice of medicine, he began the study of divinity and became an active minister. He also lectured at intervals and edited a paper. His only published work is a treatise on 'Scriptural Baptism.'

CAMPBELL, CHARLES, historian, was born in Petersburg, Va., May 1, 1807, and died in Staunton, Va., July 11, 1876. For many years he conducted a select school at Petersburg, and afterward became principal of the Anderson Seminary, located in the same town. His leisure intervals were devoted mainly to historical investigations. He contributed to numerous periodicals and published *The Bland Papers,* which ran from 1840 to 1843; 'An Introduction to the History of the Colony and Ancient Dominion of Virginia' (Richmond, 1849), 'Some Materials for a Memoir of John Daly Burk' (Albany, 1868), and 'Genealogy of the Spottswood Family.'

CAMPBELL, JESSE H. He was born in McIntosh County, Ga., February 10, 1807, became an influential divine and wrote 'Georgia Baptists: Historical and Biographical.'

CAMPBELL, JOHN ARCHIBALD. An eminent jurist. He was born at Washington, Ga., in 1811 and received his diploma from Franklin College in Athens, Ga., in 1826, when only fifteen years old. His career was one of unusual distinction. He served in the Alabama Legislature; attained the rank of colonel in the Indian wars; became Associate Justice of the Supreme Court of the United States, and Assistant Secretary of State of the Confederate States. Besides numerous political speeches, including one on "Rights of Slave States" and one on "John C. Calhoun," he published also a pamphlet entitled "Reminiscences of the Civil War." Judge Campbell received the degree of LL.D. from his *alma mater*. He died in 1889.

CAMPBELL, JOHN LYLE, chemist, was born in Rockbridge County, Va., December 17, 1818, and died at Lexington, Va., February 2, 1886. For many years he filled the chair of chemistry and geology in Washington College, afterward Washington and Lee University; and, besides contributing to scientific journals, he published 'Geology and Mineral Resources of the James River Valley' (1882) and 'Campbell's Agriculture.'

CAMPBELL, JOHN POAGE, clergyman and physician, was born in Augusta County, Va., in 1767, and died near Chillicothe, Ohio, November 4, 1814. For many years he lived in Kentucky. He was at first inclined to take an atheistic view of the universe, but was converted to Christianity by reading a volume by Dr. Jenyn's and gave up medicine to preach the gospel. He published 'The Passenger,' 'Strictures on Stone's Letters on the Atonement,' 'Vindex,' 'Letters to Rev. Mr. Craighead,' 'The Pelagian Detected,' 'An Answer to Jones,' and numerous discourses. Besides, he left in manuscript a 'History of the Western Frontier.'

CAMPBELL, JOHN WILSON. He was a bookseller of Petersburg, Va., who published a 'History of Virginia to 1781' (Philadelphia, 1813). Charles Campbell, the historian, was his son.

CAMPBELL, JOHN WILSON, jurist, was born in Augusta County, Va., February 23, 1782, and died in Delaware, Ohio., September 24, 1833. At an early age he was taken by his parents to Kentucky; but, on completing his education, he located in Ohio, became a Member of Congress and served on the Bench of the U.S. District Court. His writings were published by his wife with an introductory sketch of his life (Columbus, Ohio, 1838).

CAMPBELL, RICHARD. Jurist. He was born at Pensacola, Fla., in early colonial days and became prominent on the Bench. His work entitled 'Historical Sketches of Colonial Florida' has been an important source of information to subsequent writers. It deals chiefly with Western Florida, a section of the State with which he was most familiar, the greater part of his life having been spent in the city of his birth.

CAMPBELL, WILLIAM HENRY, educator and divine, was born in Baltimore, Md., September 14, 1808. On completing his studies at Princeton, he entered the ministry of the Dutch Reformed Church and was for many years president of Rutgers College. His published works include: 'Subjects and Modes of Baptism,' 'Influence of Christianity upon Civil and Religious Liberty,' and a 'System of Catechetical Instruction.'

CANDLER, ALLEN DANIEL. Congressman and governor. He was born in Lumpkin County, Ga., November 4, 1834, a son of Daniel G. Candler. He married, January 12, 1864, Eugenia T. Williams. He represented the Ninth District of Georgia in Congress for several years and was governor of the State for two consecutive terms. He is the author of a volume entitled 'Colonel William Candler, of Georgia: His Ancestry and Progeny' (1900), and is also the compiler and editor of 'Colonial Records of Georgia' (thirty volumes). 'Revolutionary Records of Georgia' (three volumes) and 'Confederate Records of Georgia' (six volumes). He resides in Atlanta, Ga.

CANDLER, WARREN A. Bishop of the M.E. Church, South, educator and writer. He was born in Carroll County, Ga., August 23, 1857, a son of Samuel Charles and Martha Beall Candler. He was educated at Emory College, Oxford, Ga., and married, November 21, 1877, Nettie Curtright, of LaGrange, Ga. Entering the ministry, he remained in active pastoral work until called to the presidency of Emory College, an institution founded by his distinguished kinsman, Dr. Ignatius A. Few. He also edited for some time *The Christian Advocate,* published at Nashville, Tenn. He relinquished educational work to assume the Episcopal honors; and in the high office of bishop he has frequently crossed the water to inspect the mission work of the Church in foreign fields. An eloquent advocate, whether upon the rostrum or in the pulpit, he recently electrified the city of London by an able address which he delivered before one of the great church convocations. Notwithstanding the onerous demands made upon him, Bishop Candler has found time for literary work. His writings include: a 'History of Sunday Schools' (New York, Methodist Book Concern, 1880), 'Georgia's Educational Work' (1893), 'Christus Austor' (Nashville, Southern Methodist Publishing House, 1899), 'High Living and High Lives' (1901), and 'Great Revivals and the Great Republic' (1905). Bishop Candler received from Emory College both the D.D. and the LL.D. degrees. He resides in Atlanta, Ga.

CANONGE, L. PLACIDE. See Biographical and Critical Sketch, Vol. II, page 737.

CAPERS, ELLISON, Protestant Episcopal bishop, soldier and author, was born in Charleston, S.C., October 14, 1837. After graduation from South Carolina Military Academy, he taught for some time in the same institution. During the Civil War he attained the rank of brigadier-general in the Confederate Army. At the close of hostilities he studied theology, was rector of Christ Church in Greenville, S.C., for twenty years and in 1893, became bishop. Besides minor works, he wrote the volume on South Carolina in 'The Confederate Military History' (Atlanta, Ga., The Confederate Publishing Company, 1899, twelve volumes). Bishop Capers died in 1907.

CAPERS, HENRY D., lawyer and educator, was born in South Carolina in 1830. Under the Confederate Government he was chief clerk in the Treasury Department, a position which enabled him to write with authority 'The Life of Memminger,' his best known and most important work. He also published 'Bellevue' and other novels. For many years his home has been in Georgia.

CAPERS, WILLIAM. Methodist Episcopal bishop, was born in St. Thomas Parish, S.C., January 26, 1790, and died at Anderson, S.C., January 29, 1855. The earlier days of his ministry were devoted to missionary work among the Indians and the slaves. He traveled abroad; edited at different times various publications; became prominent on the platform and in the pulpit; adhered to the Southern side when the church divided on the issues of slavery, and was made bishop in 1846. His home was one of the favorite resorts of Bishop Asbury in the pioneer days of Methodism. Besides an 'Autobiography,' which appeared after his death, with a memoir by Dr. Wightman (Nashville. Tenn., 1858), he published 'Catechisms for Negro Missions' and 'Short Sermons and Tales for Children.'

CAPPLEMAN, JOSIE FRAZEE, Mrs. Poet. She resides in Little Rock, Ark. Since the death of her husband, which occurred in 1903, she has been dependent upon the earnings of her pen; but she has compelled the favor of the public, and the respect of the critics She is the author of a volume entitled 'Heart Songs' (Richmond, B. F. Johnson), besides numerous sketches.

CARDENAS, A. DE. Spanish historian. He wrote an interesting work in which De Soto's journey to the Mississippi is described, viz.: 'Historia General de la Florida' (Madrid, 1723).

CARDOZO, ISAAC N., journalist, was born in Savannah, Ga., June 17, 1784, and was drowned in the James River, August 26, 1850. For many years he was an influential editor in Charleston, S.C., wielding a pen of rare power. He edited first *The Southern Patriot* and afterward *The Evening News*. Besides contributing to various periodicals, he published 'Notes on Political Economy' (Charleston, 1826).

CARDOZO, J. N. [S.C.]. He published 'Reminiscences of Charleston' (1866).

CAREY, WILL GAGE, magazine writer, was born in Rochelle, Ill., June 19, 1877. On completing his education at the University of Illinois, he located in the South. He is in the service of the Government, with headquarters in Atlanta, and has contributed over forty short stories to the current periodicals, some of the latest being "The Wolf," in the *Metropolitan,* "The Cardinal," in *Pearson's,* "The Renegade," in the *National,* and "Spoils of Defeat," in *Uncle Remus.*

CARLETON, HENRY, jurist and lawyer, was born in Virginia in 1785, and died in Philadelphia, Pa., March 28, 1863. For many years he resided in New Orleans, became United States District Attorney, and afterward Judge of the Supreme Court, resigning on account of ill health. He then traveled abroad, and on returning home located in Philadelphia. Besides some legal translations from the Spanish he published 'Liberty and Necessity' (Philadelphia, 1857).

CARLETON, HENRY GUY, playwright, was born at Fort Union, New Mexico, June 21, 1856. For many years Mr. Carleton resided in the South. He experienced military service in the expedition against the Kiowas and the Arapahoes in Texas, and afterward became associate editor of the New Orleans *Times.* Since 1881 he has been successfully engaged in dramatic authorship. His best known plays are: 'Memnon,' a tragedy in blank verse (1881), 'Victor Durand' (1885), 'The Pembertons' (1889), 'The Lion's Mouth' (1890), 'Ye Earlie Trouble' (1891), 'Princess Erie' (1892), 'A Gilded Fool' (1892), 'The Butterflies' (1894), 'The Impudent Young Couple' (1896), 'Ambition' (1896), 'Colinette' (1898) and 'Jack's Honeymoon' (1903). He resides in Atlantic City, N.J.

CARLISLE, JAMES HENRY. Educator. For nearly half a century he was actively identified with Wofford College, at Spartanburg, S.C. During the greater part of this time he was president of the institution and at the time of his death was president emeritus. Dr. Carlisle was born in Winnsboro, S.C., of Scotch-Irish parentage, May 4, 1825. On completing his studies at South Carolina College, he engaged in educational work. When Wofford College was organized he was called to the chair of mathematics, but he subsequently taught in nearly every department. Besides a work of much interest entitled 'The Young Astronomer,' he also wrote a 'Life of Thomas Arnold.' The Southwestern University gave him the degree of LL.D. Dr. Carlisle died in Spartanburg, S.C., October 21, 1909.

CARLISLE, JOHN GRIFFIN, lawyer and statesman, was born in Campbell (now Kenton) County, Ky., September 5, 1835. Though he received only a common school education, he rose rapidly to the front at the Bar and became an influential factor in politics. Six times he was sent to Congress and twice he was honored with the Speakership. Afterward he became United States Senator. During President Cleveland's second administration he entered the Cabinet, holding the portfolio of Secretary of the Treasury; and on his retirement from office, he located in the city of New York for the practice of law. Some of his greatest speeches were delivered on the tariff question; and these among others, have been preserved in *The Congressional Record.*

CARMACK, EDWARD WARD, journalist and Senator, was born near Castilian Springs, Tenn., November 5, 1858. He practiced for several years at Columbia, Tenn., after which he accepted a place on the staff of the Nashville *American,* and eventually became editor-in-chief. Later he accepted the editorship of the Memphis *Commercial.* He took an active part in politics, served four years in Congress, and from 1901 to 1907 was United States Senator. Few men in public life have possessed more brilliant gifts. Whether with his tongue or with his pen, he was a power in debate and was a master both of argument and of persuasion. He was a member of the advisory council of 'The Library of Southern Literature.' He married, in 1890, Elizabeth C. Dunnington. On retiring from the Senate he resumed journalistic work in Nashville, Tenn., where on November 19, 1908, he was killed by Duncan B. Cooper, in consequence of an editorial which appeared in his paper.

CARPENTER, MATTHEW T. Poet. He resided for many years at Jackson, Miss., and wrote 'Memories of the Past,' a volume of verse (New York, Baker and Scribner, 1850).

CARPENTER, STEPHEN T., author, was born in England, and before coming to the United States was distinguished in journalism, having reported the debates of Parliament. He located in Charleston, S.C., about 1803, where, in addition to editorial work, he wrote 'Memoirs of Thomas Jefferson,' an interesting work in two volumes (New York, 1809), and 'Select American Speeches, Forensic and Parliamentary, with Prefatory Remarks' (Philadelphia, 1815). Under the pen-name of Donald Campbell, he also published an account of an 'Overland Journey to India' (London, 1795; New York, 1809). He died in 1820.

CARPENTER, WILLIAM HENRY. Author. [Md.]. He was born in 1813 and died in 1899. Mr. Carpenter wrote a 'History of Georgia' and 'The Regicide's Daughter,' besides minor works.

CARR, LUCIEN, antiquarian, was born in Lincoln County, Mo., December 15, 1829, and was educated at the University of St. Louis. From 1876 to 1894 he was assistant curator of the Peabody Museum of American Archeology and Ethnology, at Cambridge, Mass. Besides sundry scientific papers, he wrote: 'Missouri, a Bone of Contention' (Boston, Houghton, Mifflin and Company) and 'The Mounds of the Mississippi Valley' (1891).

CARROLL, ANNA ELLA, writer on political topics, was born in Somerset County, Md., August 29, 1815. She wielded a pen of masculine force and vigor and, in opposition to Senator Breckenridge's speech on secession in 1861, she wrote an address, of which numberless copies were printed by the War Department. She also wrote several other pamphlets on topics of the times. On her advice, it is said that the plan of the United States Government to send a fleet down the Mississippi River was abandoned, and that instead, it was dispatched to the Tennessee River with the result that the fortunes of war were completely changed.

CARROLL, BENAJAH HARVEY, Sr. Corresponding secretary and treasurer of the Baptist Educational Commission. He was born at Carrollton, Miss., December 27, 1843, a son of Benajah Carroll. He is a graduate of Baylor University and married, first, Ellen Bell and, second, Hallie Harrison. Since 1902 he has been dean of the Theological Department of Baylor University, which institution has conferred upon him the D.D. and the LL.D. degrees. He has made frequent contributions to the religious press and has published several books and tracts (Philadelphia, American Baptist Publication Society). He resides in Waco, Texas.

CARROLL, CHARLES, of Carrollton, signer of the Declaration of Independence, was born at Annapolis, Md., September 20, 1737, and died in Baltimore, Md., November 14, 1832, at the advanced age of ninety-six, having lived to be the last survivor of the immortal band who signed the Declaration of Independence. He was one of the wealthiest land-owners of Maryland and an ardent Roman Catholic; but for the sake of his oppressed fellow-countrymen he did not hesitate to jeopardize his vast property interests. Frequent articles which he contributed to the public prints were largely instrumental in preparing the Colonies to resist the arbitrary exactions of the crown. Under the Federal Constitution he became the first United States Senator from Maryland. At his spacious and elegant home he dispensed lavish hospitality and kept an open establishment. His best biography is from the pen of John H. B. Latrobe.

CARROLL, JOHN, Roman Catholic Archbishop, was born in Upper Marlborough, Md., in 1735, and died in Georgetown, D.C., in 1817. Charles Carroll of Carrollton, the famous signer, was his cousin. He was active in the Colonial protest against British oppression; and after the Revolution, became the first Bishop of Baltimore advancing still higher when Baltimore was erected into an Archiepiscopal See. His writings, which were mainly controversial, include: 'An Address to the Roman Catholics of the United States of America,' 'A Precise View of the Principal Points of Controversy between the Protestant and Roman Churches,' 'A Review of the Important Controversy between Dr. Carroll and the Rev. Messrs. Wharton and Hawkins,' and 'A Discourse on General Washington.' St. John's College gave him the degree of LL.D.

CARTER, BERNARD M. In 1824 there appeared in London a volume entitled: 'Poems by Bernard M. Carter, of Virginia.' It contains some classic touches but the style of the author is somewhat obscure. He pays tribute to his favorite characters, going back to the time of Pocahontas.

CARTER, FELECIANA. Author. [La.]. 'Pelican Boys in Gray' (1900).

CARTER, RUSSEL KELSO, educator, was born in Baltimore, Md., November 19, 1849. For several years he taught the natural sciences in the Military Academy at Chester, Pa., and later in life became identified with the "Holiness" movement in the Methodist Church. Besides contributing to scientific journals the fruits of numerous original investigations, he wrote 'The Miracles of Healing,' 'Pastor Blumhardt' and numerous tracts. In 1886 he began the publication at Chester, Pa., of 'The Kingdom.'

CARTER, ST. LEGER LANDON. Poet. For years he was a favorite contributor to *The Southern Literary Messenger*, covering a wide range; but his touch was always light and fanciful. He published, in 1844, a volume of his verse entitled: 'Nugae by Nugator' (Baltimore). It also contained some prose selections. In contrast with the sombre product of the period, it is refreshing to the traveler to encounter this little wayside spring.

CARTER, WILLIAM PAGE. He published a volume of 138 pages entitled: 'Echoes from the Glen' (New York, 1904), which he dedicated to his friend, John Esten Cooke. Some of the best poems in the book are products of the martial sentiment, being tributes to his war comrades.

CARTWRIGHT, PETER, one of the pioneers of Methodism in the Middle West, was born in Amherst County, Va., September 1, 1785, and died near Pleasant Plains, Ill., September 25, 1872. From the clutch of dissolute habits he was marvelously rescued to become one of the foremost preachers of the age, notwithstanding an utter lack of educational equipment. He was an orator of wonderful native gifts and preached with tremendous power, especially at camp meetings and in outdoor assemblies. He opposed slavery and adhered to the Union side after secession. He published several pamphlets, of which his "Controversy with the Devil" was perhaps the most famous; and his 'Autobiography,' edited by William P. Strickland, appeared in 1856 (New York).

CARUTHERS, ELI W. Clergyman. [N.C.]. Besides a 'Life of Rev. David Caldwell, D.D.' (1842), he published a series of historical papers on "Revolutionary Incidents in the Old North State" (1854-1856). He died in 1865.

CARUTHERS, JEANNETTE. Poet. She lived at one time in Savannah, Ga. In association with others, she published a volume of verse entitled: 'Fancies, by Three Friends.' Afterward she became Mrs. Peeples of South Carolina. One of her poems, "A Web of Tatting," is preserved in 'Songs of the South.'

CARRUTHERS, WILLIAM A. See Biographical and Critical Sketch, Vol. II, page 753.

CARVER, WILLIAM O. Educator. Dr. Carver holds an important chair in the Southern Baptist Theological Seminary at Louisville, Ky., and is the author of an inspirational work entitled 'Missions in the Plan of the Ages' (New York and Chicago, The Fleming H. Revell Company, 1908).

CARWILE, JOHN BROWN. Banker. [S.C.]. Born in 1825. He published 'Reminiscences of Newberry' (1890).

CASLER, JOHN OVERTON. Jurist. He was born in Frederick County, Va., December 1, 1866. During the Civil War he served in the famous Stonewall Brigade and participated in most of the campaigns of the Army of Northern Virginia. After the close of hostilities he located in Texas and later settled in Oklahoma, where he is now an occupant of the Bench. Judge Casler wrote 'Four Years in the Stonewall Brigade' (Richmond, Va., The B. F. Johnson Company, 1893) and 'Lillian Stuart, the Heroine of the Rappahannock' (*ibid.*, 1899), a novel. He resides in Oklahoma City, Okla.

CASSELBERRY, EVANS. Lawyer. [Mo.]. He published several legal works, among them, 'Spanish Laws' and 'Missouri Land Laws.'

CASTELLANOS, HENRY C. Author. [La.] He wrote 'Episodes of Louisiana Life' (New Orleans, 1895).

CASTLEMAN, VIRGINIA CARTER. Author. She was born in Gaston, N.C., August 26, 1864, the daughter of the Rev. Robert A. and Mary Lee Castleman. She enjoyed superior educational advantages and is in charge of the musical department of Herndon Seminary, a school founded by her mother. She is a writer of excellent fiction and a contributor to various periodicals, some of her best stories being 'A Child of the Covenant,' 'Belmont,' 'Mary Shelton,' 'Roger of Fairfield,' and 'The Long Shadow.' She resides in Herndon, Va.

CATHELL, DANIEL WEBSTER, physician, was born in Worcester County, Md., November 29, 1839. For years he has been one of the leading practitioners of Baltimore, and besides numerous medi al papers, has published a work entitled 'The Physician Himself and Things that Concern His Reputation and Success.'

CAWEIN, MADISON. See Biographical and Critical Sketch, Vol. II, page 785.

CHAILLE, STANFORD EMERSON, physician and educator, was born at Natchez, Miss., July 9, 1830, and was educated at Harvard. He was for years dean of the medical department of Tulane University at New Orleans. Besides minor works, he published 'The Origin and Progress of Medical Jurisprudence.'

CHALMERS, LIONEL. Physician. He was born in Scotland in 1715 and died in Charleston, S.C., in 1777. Dr. Chalmers was an eminent practitioner. For years he recorded observations of the weather in South Carolina and published an interesting work based upon his data (London, 1776). He also wrote an 'Essay on Fevers' (Charleston, 1767), besides numerous medical papers.

CHAMBERLAYNE, CHURCHILL GIBSON, educator, was born in Richmond, Va., December 23, 1876. His father was John Hampden Chamberlayne and his mother, Mary Walker Gibson. He occupies the chair of history and English in the Country School for Boys, near Baltimore, Md. He has published several volumes containing the fruit of laborious researches into Virginia antecedents, among them, 'The Vestry Book and Register of Bristol Parish, Virginia, 1720-1789' (Richmond, 1898), two articles on 'Colonial Churches' (Richmond, The Southern Churchman Company, 1907), 'Die Heirath Richards II von England mit Anna von Luxemberg' (Halle, 1906), and is also at work on a 'History of the Virginia Parish in the Colonial Period.' He received the Ph.D. degree from Halle. The sketch of George William Bagby in 'The Library of Southern Literature' is from his pen.

CHAMBERS, BETTIE KEYES, Mrs. Writer. [Texas]. She published a 'Defence of the Women of the South.'

CHAMBERS, HENRY E., educator, was born in New Orleans, La., March 28, 1860. At the present time he is professor of English in the Boys' High School of New Orleans. He is the author of several volumes, among them a 'School History of the United States' (New York, The American Book Company, 1887), a 'Higher History of the United States' (*ibid.,* 1889), 'Search Questions in American History' (New York, University Publishing Company, 1890), 'Constitutional History of Hawaii' (Baltimore, Johns Hopkins Press, 1896), 'West Florida' (*ibid.,* 1898) and an 'Introduction to Louisiana History' (1896).

CHAMPIGNY, CHEVALIER DE, French soldier, was stationed for some time at New Orleans. In a work entitled 'La Louisiane Ensanglantée' (London, 1773), he tells of the suppression of the earliest American revolt, which occurred at New Orleans in 1767. He also wrote 'Etat Présent de la Louisiane' (Hague, 1776). Both works are rare.

CHANCELLOR, CHARLES WILLIAMS, educator and physician was born in Spottsylvania County, Va., February 19, 1833, and was educated at the University of Virginia and at Jefferson Medical College. During the Civil War he served on the staff of General Pickett. For several years he was professor of surgery and dean of Washington University, Baltimore, Md., and from 1893 to 1897 he was Consul at Havre, France.

Besides various contributions to medical journals, he has published 'Treatise on Mineral Waters' and 'The Climate of the Eastern Shore of Maryland.'

CHANCELLOR, EUSTATHIUS. Physician. Dr. Chancellor was born at Chancellorsville, Va., August 29, 1854. He began the practice of medicine in Charlottesville, Va., with his father, but in 1880 located in St. Louis, where he soon stood in the front of his profession. He wrote 'Woman in the Social Sphere' and 'The Pacific Slope,' besides numerous medical papers.

CHANDLER, AUGUSTUS B. Author. [Miss.]. Born in 1839. Besides stories and sketches, he published a number of poems.

CHANDLER, DANIEL. He was born in 1805 and died in 1866. He delivered an address before the Demosthenian and Phi Kappa societies of the University of Georgia in 1835, on "Female Educaton" which is said to have inspired the founding of the first female college ever chartered. The address was widely circulated; and, in response to the appeal which it sounded, Wesleyan Female College, at Macon, Ga., sprang into existence in 1839.

CHANDLER, JULIAN ALVIN CARROLL, editor and educator, was born in Caroline County, Va., October 29, 1872. After completing his studies at historic old William and Mary College, he attended lectures at Johns Hopkins. He taught for several years in various schools and colleges; assumed, in 1904, the editorship of Silver, Burdett and Company's standard publications; and holds at present the chair of history and political science in Richmond College. He is a writer of rare gifts and a scholar of exceptional attainments. Included among his published works are: 'Representation in Virginia' (Baltimore, The Johns Hopkins Press, 1896), 'The History of Suffrage in Virginia' (*ibid.*, 1899), 'The Geography of Virginia,' in joint authorship (New York, The Macmillan Company, 1902), 'The Makers of Virginia History' (New York and Boston, Silver, Burdett and Company, 1904), and 'The Makers of American History,' in joint authorship (*ibid.*, 1904). The sketch of Captain John Smith in 'The Library of Southern Literature' was also written by Dr. Chandler. He resides in New York. The degree of Ph.D. was conferred upon him by Johns Hopkins, and the degree of LL.D., by Richmond College. He was director of history and education at the Jamestown Exposition.

CHAPEAU, ELLEN CHAZEL. Dramatic writer. She was born in Charleston, S.C., July 6, 1844, a daughter of Pierre Auguste and Ellen Austin Chazel. She was educated at the Convent of the Sacred Heart, in New York City, and married Thomas T. Chapeau. Under the pen-name of "Esperance" she has contributed numerous short stories to the magazines. Besides a meritorious work of fiction, which appeared in 1901, entitled 'Under the Darkness of the Night' (Washington, D.C., The Neale Publishing Company), she has written several plays, including: "Madame la Marquise" and "Katherine Walton." She resides in Savannah, Ga.

CHAPELLE, PLACIDE LOUIS. Archbishop of New Orleans. He published ' The Writings and Influence of the Fathers of the Church' (Washington, 1885).

CHAPIN, SALLIE F. Novelist. [S.C.] She wrote two entertaining stories of the Civil War period in the South, entitled 'Fitzhugh St. Clair' and 'The South Carolina Rebel Boy' (1873), both of which were widely read.

CHAPMAN, A. W. Physician. [Fla.] He published an important botanical work on ' The Flora of the Southern States,' which first appeared in 1860. Another edition, revised and enlarged, was issued in 1896.

CHAPMAN, JOHN A. Educator. [S.C.]. He wrote 'Within the Vale,' a volume of verse; a 'History of South Carolina,' a 'History of Edgefield County' and 'Annals of Newberry,' besides other minor works. He also assisted in the compilation of Stephens' 'History of the United States.'

CHAPMAN, KATHARINE HOPKINS. Author. She wrote a novel entitled ' Love's Way in Dixie' (Washington and New York, The Neale Publishing Company, 1906). The portraiture which it gives of Southern life is well drawn.

CHAPMAN, NATHANIEL, physician, was born at Summer Hill, Va., May 28, 1780, and died in Philadelphia, Pa., July 1, 1853. After graduation from the University of Pennsylvania he studied abroad. He became an eminent practitioner of Philadelphia; and, for more than thirty years, taught in the medical department of the University of Pennsylvania. He was also the first president of the American Medical Association. His published works include: 'Selected Speeches' (Philadelphia, 1808), 'Elements of Therapeutics and Materia Medica' (1828), and two volumes of 'Lectures,' a compendium to which was published by Dr. N. D. Benedict.

CHAPPELL, ABSALOM HARRIS. Lawyer. He was born in Hancock County, Ga., December 18, 1801, and was educated at the famous Mount Zion Academy, taught by Dr. Beman; and afterward studied law. He became one of the foremost members of the Georgia Bar; took an influential part in State politics, and represented his district in Congress. He married, May 31, 1842, Loretta Rebecca Lamar, daughter of L. Q. C. Lamar, Sr. He was the author of 'Miscellanies of Georgia, Historical, Biographical, Descriptive,' an important work which was published in 1874. The few copies of this book which are still extant are very highly prized. He died at his home, in Columbus, Ga., December 11, 1878.

CHAPPELL, J. HARRIS. Educator. He was born at Macon, Ga., October 18, 1849, and died at Columbus, Ga., April 6, 1906. He was a son of Absalom H. and Loretta Lamar Chappell and married, in 1883, Carrie Brown. He was for several years president of the Georgia Normal and Industrial College, at Milledgeville; and the success of this splendid school is due largely to the initial impetus which it derived from the heart and brain of this devoted man. His published works are: 'Georgia History Stories' (1905), an exquisite collection, and 'Baccalaureate Addresses' (1906). He was also the author of an entertaining lecture on "Stonewall Jackson."

CHARLEVOIX, PIERRE FRANCOIS XAVIER DE. French traveler. He was born in 1682 and died in 1761. He spent some time in New Orleans and wrote the first detailed account of Louisiana entitled, 'Histoire et Déscription Générale de la Nouvelle France,' in six volumes (Paris, 1744). The work was published in English by John Gilmary Shea (New York, 1865-1872).

CHARLTON, ROBERT MILLEDGE, jurist, lawyer, poet, was born in Savannah, Ga., January 19, 1807. His father was Thomas U. P. and his mother Emily Walter Charlton. On completing his education he was admitted to the Bar and rose rapidly to the front, becoming United States District Attorney, Superior Court Judge of the Eastern Circuit, and

United States Senator, besides serving in the State Legislature and being three times elected mayor of Savannah. His literary gifts were of very high order; and, in addition to writing for the *Knickerbocker Magazine* an interesting series of sketches, descriptive of coast life, entitled: "Leaves from the Portfolio of a Georgian Lawyer," he published, in 1839, a volume of 'Poems' (Boston, 1842), which contained several beautiful fragments from the pen of his brother, Dr. T. J. Charlton; and another edition of this work was published in 1842, with some prose additions. He married, in 1829, Margaret Shick. Perhaps the best-known poem of this gifted Georgian is his thrilling historical ballad entitled: "The Death of Jasper." He died in Savannah, Ga., January 18, 1854.

CHARLTON, THOMAS USHER PULASKI, jurist and lawyer, was born near Camden, S.C., in 1781, the son of Dr. Thomas Charlton, of Frederick, Md., and Lucy Kenan. He located in Savannah, Ga.; and, before attaining his twentieth year, he represented his county in the Legislature of Georgia. He became Attorney-general and Judge of the Superior Court of the Eastern Circuit and was six times mayor of Savannah. His first wife (1803) was Emily, daughter of Thomas Walter, the author of 'Flora Caroliniana,' which was the pioneer work on Southern botany; and his second wife (1813) was Ellen Glasco. He was the author of 'The Life of Major-general James Jackson,' a work of rare interest and value (Augusta, Ga., George F. Randolph and Company, 1809). He died at Savannah, November 20, 1835.

CHARLTON, WALTER GLASCO, jurist and lawyer, was born in Savannah, Ga., June 5, 1854. His father was Robert·Milledge Charlton and his mother, Margaret Shick. Inheriting from his paternal ancestors a legal cast of mind, he was duly admitted to the Bar; and from the office of solicitor-general he rose to the Bench, becoming twice Superior Court Judge of the Eastern Circuit, an office which he still ably fills. On February 11, 1874, he married Mary Walton, daughter of Richard Malcolm Johnston. He wields an accomplished pen; and, in addition to some very graceful occasional poems, he is the author of several historical monographs and pamphlets, among them: 'The Making of Georgia' and 'Oglethorpe,' the substance of the latter being contained in an address which he delivered by invitation before the Legislature of the Commonwealth. The sketch of Richard Malcolm Johnston in 'The Library of Southern Literature' is from the pen of Judge Charlton.

CHASE, LUCIEN B., lawyer, was born in Vermont, August 14, 1817, but located in Tennessee, from which state he served in Congress from 1845 to 1849. He wrote a 'History of the Polk Administration' (New York, 1850). He died in Tennessee, December 14, 1864.

CHATTERTON, A. Poet. He published in 1787 at Baltimore a volume entitled: 'Buds of Beauty,' but no further trace or record of him can be found.

CHAUDRON, LOUIS DE VENDEL. Writer. He published 'Madame la Marquise' (1892), and other comedies.

CHAZEY, E. LIGERET DE, Madame. Author. She wrote a volume entitled 'Les Créoles' (New Orleans, 1855).

CHAUDRON, ADELAIDE DE VONDEL, Mrs. Author of a series of school readers and translator of several works from the German, including some of Mühlbach's novels.

CHEESBOROUGH, E. B. Author. [N.C.]. He published a work, in two volumes, entitled 'The Land We Love,' which is full of varied information concerning the South.

CHEEVES, E. W. FOOTE, Mrs., author, was born in Virginia. It was not until after the death of her husband that, being defrauded of the handsome property which was her rightful inheritance, she began to turn her literary gifts to account. Her only published work is entitled: 'Sketches in Prose and Verse' (Baltimore, 1849). She was related to the family of Washington.

CHEEVES, LANGDON, jurist and statesman, was born at Rocky River, S.C., September 17, 1776, and died in Columbia, S.C., June 25, 1857. For many years he represented his district in Congress and succeeded Henry Clay in the Speakership. As an orator he possessed unusual polish. Washington Irving, who was greatly impressed by his learning and eloquence said that he gave him for the first time an idea of the manner in which the Greek and Roman orators must have spoken. As an advocate at the Bar he possessed few equals; and he also at one time held judicial position. He opposed nullification, but favored secession. The last years of his life were spent in retirement on his plantation. He wrote occasional essays and reviews. Some of his speeches have been preserved in the debates of Congress.

CHESHIRE, JOSEPH BLOUNT. Protestant Episcopal Bishop of North Carolina. He was born at Tarboro, N.C., March 27, 1850, the son of the Rev. Joseph Blount and Elizabeth Toole Parker Cheshire. He was educated at Trinity College, Hartford, Conn., at the University of North Carolina, and at the University of the South. He practiced law for six years, but was ordained deacon in 1878, priest in 1880, and bishop in 1893. He is the author of numerous articles and addresses on religious subjects. Both the University of the South and the University of North Carolina have conferred upon him the degree of D.D. He resides in Raleigh, N.C.

CHESTNUT, MARY BOYKIN. [S.C.]. The author of 'A Diary from Dixie,' edited by Isabella D. Martin and Myrta Lockett Avary (New York, D. Appleton and Company, 1905). Mrs. Chestnut was the widow of James Chestnut, Jr., who was United States Senator from South Carolina from 1859 to 1861, an aide on the staff of Jefferson Davis, and afterward Confederate brigadier-general.

CHILD, JACOB. Editor. [Mo.]. He wrote 'The Pearl of Asia' (1892).

CHITTENDEN, WILLIAM LAWRENCE. See Biographical and Critical Sketch, Vol. II, page 823.

CHIVERS, THOMAS HOLLEY. See Biographical and Critical Sketch, Vol. II, page 845.

CHOPIN, KATE. See Biographical and Critical Sketch, Vol. II, page 863.

CHOUTEAU, AUGUSTE. Pioneer. With his younger brother Pierre, he founded the city of St. Louis, and his manuscripts are in the custody of the St. Louis Mercantile Library, by which institution they are kept under strict guard. He was born in New Orleans in 1739 and died in St. Louis in 1829, having reached the patriarchal age of ninety years.

CHRISTIAN, C. RUSSELL. From the pen of this author there appeared at Huntington, W.Va., in 1885, a volume of verse entitled: 'The Mountain Bard.'

CHRISTIAN, GEORGE LLEWELLYN. Lawyer. He was born in Charles City County, Va., April 13, 1841, a son of Edmund Thomas and Tabitha Rebecca Christian. He was educated at Northwood Academy, entered the Confederate Army at the outbreak of the war, and was wounded at the "bloody angle," Spottsylvania Court House. He was prepared for admission to the Bar at the Law School of the University of Virginia; married, first, Ida Morris and, second Emma Christian; and was judge of the Hustings Court of Richmond from 1878 to 1883. Later he became president of the Richmond Bar Association, president of the City Council, president of the Chamber of Commerce, president of the National Bank of Virginia, and president of the State Insurance Company of Richmond. As chairman of the committee on history of the Grand Camp of Confederate Veterans of Virginia, he has published numerous pamphlet reports upon the origin and history of the Civil War. He has also edited the *Virginia Law Journal.* For years past he has been an influential member of the Southern Historical Society. He resides in Richmond, Va.

CHRISTIAN, JOHN TYLER. Baptist clergyman. [Ky.]. His publications are mainly controversial, including: 'Immersion' (1891), 'Close Communion' (1892), 'Four Theories of Church Government' (1893), 'Heathen and Infidel Testimonies to Jesus Christ' (1894). 'Americanism or Romanism, Which?' (1895), and 'Did They Dip?' (1896).

CHRISTY, GEORGE W. Poet. [La.]. He wrote 'The Cricket and Other Poems' (1850).

CHRISTY, WILLIAM. Lawyer. [La.]. He published a 'Digest of the Decisions of the Supreme Court of Louisiana' (New Orleans, 1825).

CHURCHILL, WINSTON. Author. Though not usually included among Southern authors, he was born in St. Louis, Mo., November 10, 1871. His father was Edward Spalding Churchill and his mother, Emma Belle Blaine. He was educated at Annapolis for the career of a naval officer, but he relinquished the sea to engage in literary pursuits. His works which have placed him among the foremost writers of present-day fiction include: 'The Celebrity' (New York, The Macmillan Company), 'Richard Carvel' (*ibid.*), 'The Crisis' (*ibid.*), 'Mr. Keegan's Elopement' (*ibid.*), 'The Crossing' (*ibid.*), 'Coniston' (*ibid.*), and 'The Title Mart: A Comedy' (*ibid.*). Besides, he has also been a contributor of short stories to the magazines. For two terms he served in the Legislature of New Hampshire. He married, October 22, 1895, Mabel H. Hall. His residence is Cornish, N.H., but his postoffice, Windsor, Vt.

CLACK, MARIE LOUISE. Author. [La.]. She published a volume of war-time adventures entitled 'Our Refugee Household' (New Orleans, 1866), and a child's story entitled 'General Lee and Santa Claus.'

CLAIBORNE, F. Writer. [La.]. He published a work entitled 'The Muse, Including Occasional Poems and a Tale, the Rebel, by Himself' (1878).

CLAIBORNE, JOHN FRANCIS HAMTRAMCK. See Biographical and Critical Sketch, Vol. II, page 891.

CLAIBORNE, JOHN HERBERT. Physician. [Va.]. The author of an entertaining volume of personal recollections entitled 'Seventy-five Years in Old Virginia' (New York and Washington, The Neale Publishing Company, 1907).

CLAIBORNE, MARTHA J., Mrs., poet, was born in Virginia and published a volume entitled: 'Hawthorne Leaves,' which contains a collection of some three hundred poems, several of which are above the average in merit.

CLAIBORNE, NATHANIEL HERBERT. Lawyer and soldier. He was born in 1777 and died in 1859. He was a member of Congress from Virginia and wrote 'Notes on the War in the South,' giving biographical sketches of the principal leaders.

CLAPP, THEODORE, clergyman, was born at Easthampton, Mass., March 28, 1792, and died in Louisville, Ky., May 17, 1866. He was a graduate of Yale and preached for more than thirty-five years in New Orleans, finally turning from the Presbyterian to the Unitarian faith. He published 'Autobiographical Sketches and Recollections During Thirty-five Years' Residence in New Orleans' (Boston, 1859), besides theological works.

CLARK, CHAMP, Congressman and lawyer, was born at Lawrenceburg, Ky., March 7, 1850. His father was John Hampton Clark and his mother, Aletha Jane Beauchamp. After graduating from the Cincinnati Law School, he located in Missouri, for the practice of his profession, became prominent at the Bar and in politics, due to his unusual gifts as an advocate, and in 1893 was elected to Congress as a Democrat. He is the leader of the minority forces in the House, a parliamentarian and a debater of recognized abilities. On the lecture platform he has also attained signal success. He wrote the preface to 'Jefferson's Complete Works,' published by the Jefferson Memorial Association (1902)), a chapter in Dr. Cook's 'Old Kentucky' (1908), "Missouri from 1820 to 1869," for 'The South in the Building of the Nation,' and the sketch of Thomas H. Benton in 'The Library of Southern Literature.' He was also one of the associate editors of *Modern Eloquence*. He married, December 14, 1881, Genevieve Bennett. He resides at Bowling Green, Mo., and holds the degree of LL.D.

CLARK, CHARLES HEBER, editor, was born in Berlin, Md., July 11, 1841, and, on completing his education, engaged in journalism. At present he is editor and proprietor of the *Textile Record,* published in Philadelphia. Besides numerous articles on economic subjects, he has written several works of fiction, among them, 'Out of the Hurly Burly,' 'Elbow Room,' 'Fortunate Island,' and other stories. He resides at Conshohocken, Pa.

CLARK, DANIEL, author, was born in 1766 and died in 1813. For some time he resided in the South and wrote: 'Proofs of the Corruption of General James Wilkinson and of his Connection with Aaron Burr, with a Full Refutation of His Slanderous Allegations in Relation to the Principal Witness Against Him' (Philadelphia, 1809).

CLARK, JAMES G. Professor of mathematics at William Jewell College. He was born in the State of Virginia and was educated at the University of Virginia. He was called to his present chair in 1873. He married, first, Jennie Hume and, second, Kate Mason Morfit. Prof. Clark is the author of 'Elements of the Infinitesimal Calculus' and 'History of William Jewell College.' He resides in Liberty, Mo.

CLARK, JAMES O. A. Methodist clergyman. [Ga.]. He published 'Elijah Vindicated' (Nashville, The M.E. Publishing House, South, 1886), a work of power, 'The Camp Meeting at Troas,' and 'The Wesley Volume.' He died September 4, 1894. He held the D.D. and the LL.D. degrees.

CLARK, PEYTON NEALE. [Va.]. He published a work of much interest to genealogists entitled 'Old King William Homes and Families' (1897).

CLARK, RICHARD H., jurist, was born at Springfield, Ga., March 24, 1824. He studied law, served in the State Senate, codified the laws of Georgia in association with Thomas R. R. Cobb and David Irwin, and for years occupied a seat on the Superior Court Bench. No man of his day in Georgia was more familiar with the history of the State, or with the genealogy and relationship of individuals; and at leisure intervals he contributed to the press many delightful sketches. Some of his literary fragments have been preserved in 'Memoirs of Judge Richard H. Clark.' compiled by Mrs. Lollie Belle Wylie.

CLARK, THOMAS H. Lawyer. [Ala.]. He wrote a volume entitled 'Scenes in Alabama' (1895).

CLARK, WALTER. Chief Justice of the Supreme Court of North Carolina. He was born in Halifax County, N.C., August 19, 1846, the son of David and Anna M. Thorne Clark, and was educated at the University of North Carolina. He married, January 28, 1874, Susan W. Graham, daughter of W. A. Graham, governor, United States Senator and Secretary of the Navy. He was made a lieutenant-colonel at the age of seventeen, the youngest officer of this rank on either side in the Civil War. He was on the Superior Court Bench from 1885 to 1889; Associate Justice of the Supreme Court from 1889 to 1892, and was made Chief Justice in 1903, after a period of retirement. He is the author of an "Annotated Code of Civil Procedure' and translated from the French, Constant's 'Memoirs of Napoleon' (Springfield, Mass., G. and C. Merriam). He compiled and edited seventeen volumes of North Carolina State Records; also 'Histories of North Carolina Regiments,' in five volumes. The University of North Carolina gave him the degree of LL.D. He resides in Raleigh, N.C.

CLARK, WALTER A. Public official and writer. He was born in Brothersville, Richmond County, Ga., March 5, 1842, served in the Confederate Army, as a member of the famous Oglethorpe Infantry, and married, October 24, 1880, Sarah E. Rheney. His writings include: 'Under the Stars and Bars' (1900), an account of the adventures of the Oglethorpes from 1861 to 1865, 'A Lost Arcadia, or the Story of Old-Time Brothersville' (1909), perhaps the first distinctive effort ever made to preserve the annals of a rural community in this section; and 'Pen Pictures of the Old South.' He is also the author of some exquisite bits of verse, among the best known being: "After the Battle," "The Charge of the Boy Cadets," "Pat Cleburne's Truce at Kennesaw," "The Angel of Marye's Heights," "The Gamin's Prayer," and many others. He is treasurer and auditor of Richmond County and resides in Augusta, Ga.

CLARK, WILLIS GAYLORD. Educator. [Ala.]. He was born in 1827, and wrote a 'History of Education in Alabama' (1889), in which he traces the development of schools from the territorial days.

CLARKE, JOHN ARCHER, lawyer and poet, was a resident of Charles City County, Va. One of his poems addressed "To Mary" is preserved in 'Songs of the South.' He died in 1862 at the age of thirty.

CLARKE, J. MATT. [Tenn.]. The author of a story entitled 'Louella Blassingame' (1903).

CLARKE, JENNIE THORNLEY. Educator. [Ga.]. She compiled an exquisite collection of verse entitled 'Songs of the South' (1897).

CLARKE, KATE UPSON, Mrs. Writer. [Ala.]. Born in 1851. She wrote a novel entitled 'That Mary Anne,' besides a number of minor publications.

CLARKE, MARY BAYARD. See Biographical and Critical Sketch, Vol. II, page 915.

CLARKSON, HENRY MAZYCK, physician and poet. This cultured man of letters published a volume of verse entitled: 'Songs of Love and War' (Manassas, Va., Manassas Journal Press, 1898). It is far above the average production of the day, both in metrical skill and in imaginative power. The author touches a number of variant chords.

CLAY, ALEXANDER STEPHENS, United States Senator, was born in Cobb County, Ga., September 25, 1853. After graduating from Hiawassee College, he taught school for two years, studied law, became speaker of the House and president of the Senate of Georgia, and in 1897 took his seat in the Senate of the United States, a position to which he has twice been reëlected as a Democrat. He is an eloquent and earnest public speaker, a student of governmental problems, and occasionally a contributor to periodicals.

CLAY, CASSIUS MARCELLUS, lawyer, soldier, diplomat, was born in Madison County, Ky., October 19, 1810. On account of his strong abolition sentiments he supported Lincoln in 1861. He relinquished the mission to Russia to become major-general of volunteers, but was subsequently returned to St. Petersburg. After the war he affiliated chiefly with the Democrats. Besides a volume of his speeches, which was edited by Horace Greeley in 1848, he published, in two volumes, 'The Life Memoirs, Writings and Speeches of Cassius M. Clay' (Cincinnati, 1886). He died in 1903.

CLAY, CLEMENT CLAIBORNE. United States Senator. He was born in Huntsville, Ala., in 1816. For two years he was Judge of the Madison County Court, and from 1853 to 1861 he represented Alabama in the Senate of the United States, relinquishing his commission when his State seceded. He then took his seat in the Confederate Congress. Besides a number of speeches preserved in the *Congressional Globe,* he delivered an address in 1855 at the University of Alabama on "The Love of Truth for its Own Sake," which was printed in pamphlet form. He died in 1882.

CLAY, CLEMENT COMER, statesman. was born in Halifax County, Va., December 17, 1789, and died in Huntsville, Ala., September 9, 1866. He was at different times Congressman, Governor and United States Senator. As an orator he took high rank. He codified the laws of the State of Alabama.

CLAY, HENRY. See Biographical and Critical Sketch, Vol. III, page 937.

CLAY, MARY ROGERS. She wrote an interesting 'Genealogy of the Clays.' It was published in 1899, by the Filson Club of Louisville, in a volume which is introduced with a sketch of Henry Clay's mother, by Z. F. Smith. Several handsome portraits illuminate the work.

CLAY-CLOPTON, VIRGINIA CAROLINA, author, was born in Nash County, N.C., in 1825, and was the daughter of Dr. Peyton Randolph Tunstall and Anne Arrington. Twice married, her first husband was Clement Claiborne Clay, United States Senator from Alabama, and her second husband, Judge David Clopton. When Senator Clay was imprisoned at Fortress Monroe in 1865 with Jefferson Davis, she secured his release by dint of her own persevering efforts. She wrote a volume entitled: 'Memories of Mrs. Clay of Alabama, or, A Belle of the Fifties,' in which she interestingly portrays the social life of an eventful epoch.

CLAYTON, ALEXANDER M., jurist and lawyer, was for many years a judge of the Superior Court in Mississippi and lived to be nearly ninety years of age, dying in 1889. His address delivered at Holly Springs on the early history of Marshall County throws important light on the primitive antecedents of the commonwealth.

CLAYTON, AUGUSTIN SMITH, jurist, was born in Fredericksburg, Va., November 27, 1783, and died in Athens, Ga., June 31, 1839. He was educated at Franklin College, afterward the State University, chose the legal profession and for many years was a judge of the Superior Court. From 1831 to 1835 he served in Congress. Besides a pamphlet of 200 pages, written in the vein of satire, entitled 'The Mysterious Picture by Wrangham Fitz-ramble,' he published 'Georgia Justice,' and was also the reputed author of 'Crockett's Life of Van Buren.'

CLAYTON, JOHN, botanist, was born in Fulham. England, in 1686, but emigrated with his father to Virginia and became an enthusiastic devotee of the natural sciences, making numerous discoveries of very great value and contributing frequent papers to the scientific journals. He died December 15, 1773. Two volumes in manuscript were left behind at his death; but, when ready for the press, they were unfortunately burned. However, several of his productions, dealing with the flora of Virginia, have been preserved in the 'Philosophical Transactions.'

CLAYTON, VIRGINIA V. Author. [Ala.]. She wrote a work of much interest, portraying life in the ante-bellum days, entitled 'Black and White under the Old Regime' (Milwaukee, Wis., The Young Churchman Company, 1899). She was the widow of the late General Henry D. Clayton, one of Alabama's most distinguished sons.

CLAYTOR, GRAHAM, lawyer and author, was born in Bedford County, Va. Equipped for the Bar, he advanced rapidly to the front; and, after serving in the State Senate, he became attorney for the Commonwealth. But he was not too deeply engrossed in professional affairs to ignore the claims of literature. His powers both of imagination and of expression were unusual, and besides two interesting novels, 'Pleasant Waters' and 'Wheat and Tares,' he published a volume of verse: 'Otterdale; or Pen-Pictures of Farm Life' (Richmond, 1885).

CLELAND, JOHN. [Va.]. He was born in 1709 and died in 1789, and published 'Tombo-Chiqui' (1758). His father, Colonel Cleland, wrote for *The Spectator* under the name of "Will Honeycomb."

CLELAND, THOMAS, clergyman, was born in Fairfax County, Va., May 22, 1778; but, removing to the pioneer belt of Kentucky, he became an eminent Presbyterian minister of the Blue Grass region. Besides compiling a hymn-book, he wrote numerous tracts, among them, 'Letters on Campbellism' and 'Unitarianism Unmasked.' He died in 1858.

CLEMENS, JEREMIAH. Lawyer and author. He was born in Huntsville, Ala., in 1814, and graduated from the University of the State. In the Mexican War he achieved distinction for soldiership and valor and from 1849 to 1853 represented Alabama in the United States Senate. Opposed to secession. he nevertheless gave his allegiance to his State and became colonel of the Ninth Alabama Infantry in the Confederate Army. But, in 1864, realizing the hopelessness of the cause, he became a Unionist and advocated the reëlection of Mr. Lincoln. Besides several speeches preserved in the *Congressional Globe*, he wrote a number of novels based upon historical incidents, among them: 'Bernard Lisle,' a romance of the Texas Revolution and the Mexican War (Philadelphia, Lippincott, 1856); 'The Rivals,' a tale of the times of Aaron Burr; 'Mustang Gray,' 'Tobias Wilson' and others. He died in 1865.

CLEMENS, SAMUEL LANGHORNE. Better known to the reading public of both hemispheres under the pen-name of "Mark Twain," the foremost present-day American humorist. Mr. Clemens cannot be strictly classified among Southern authors; but he was born in Florida, Mo., November 30, 1835. He became a pilot on a Mississippi River steamboat and several of his earlier volumes contain vivid portrayals of Southern life and character. For more complete information in regard to the writings of Mark Twain consult standard works of reference.

CLEMENT, CLARA ERSKINE, author, was born in St. Louis, Mo., August 28, 1834. Her education was obtained chiefly under private tutors at home, but was supplemented by extensive travels abroad. She was twice married. Her second husband was Edwin Forbes Waters and he took her to reside in Cambridge, Mass. She possessed an unusual aptitude for the pen and began to write at an early age. Her first work was entitled: 'The Simple Story of the Orient.' Afterward she wrote: 'Legendary and Mythological Art' (Boston, 1874), 'Architects and Engravers,' 'Artists in the Nineteenth Century,' 'Eleanor Maitland,' a novel; 'Christian Symbols and Stories of the Saints,' and 'Stories of Art and Artists.' She also compiled several hand-books and made numerous translations.

CLEVELAND, HENRY. Editor. [Ga.]. He published 'Alexander H. Stephens in Public and Private, with Letters and Speeches' (Philadelphia, The National Publishing Company, 1866). He once edited *The Constitutionalist* at Augusta, Ga.

CLEVELAND, HENRY RUSSELL, author, was born in 1809, the exact place unknown, and died in St. Louis, Mo., June 12, 1843. He was educated at Harvard, became one of a brilliant coterie styled "the Five of Clubs," of which the other members were Charles Sumner, Henry W. Longfellow, Cornelius C. Felton and George S. Hilliard. He published an edition of the works of Sallust, with English notes (New York), "The Life of Henry Hudson" in Sparks's 'American Biographies,' and a number of pamphlets. George S. Hilliard published some selections from his writings, with a memoir (Boston, 1844).

CLEWELL, JOHN HENRY. President of Salem Academy and College for twenty-five years. He was born in Winston-Salem, N.C., September 19, 1855, the son of John and David Dorothea Shultz Clewell. He was educated at Moravian College and at Moravian Theological Seminary. He married Alice C. Wolle and became president of Salem Academy and College in 1884, resigning this chair in 1909. He wrote the 'History of Wachovia in North Carolina' (New York, Doubleday, Page and Company, 1902). Moravian College gave him the degree of Ph.D. He resides in Winston-Salem, N.C.

CLINGMAN, NIXON POINDEXTER. Poet. [N.C.]. He wrote both in prose and in verse, and after his death a volume of his writings appeared with the title 'A Poet and His Songs' (Baltimore, The Arundel Press, 1900). Besides a memoir, it contains several essays and some fifty poems.

CLINGMAN, THOMAS LANIER, statesman, was born in Huntsville, N.C., July 27, 1812. For several years he represented his district in Congress and was afterward sent to the United States Senate. At one time he became involved in personal difficulties with William L. Yancey and they met on the field of honor, but there was fortunately no blood shed. During the Civil War he became a brigadier-general. Besides a volume of his speeches, which he published in 1878, he also produced several minor works, including 'Follies of the Positive Philosophers.' He died in 1897.

CLINTON, GEORGE WYLIE. Bishop A. M. E. Church. He was born in Cedar Creek, S.C., March 28, 1859. He received his education at Brainerd Institute and at Livingstone College, entered the ministry of the A.M.E. Church, taught in various institutions, founded and edited *The Zion Quarterly*, became president of Atkinson College, and in 1896 succeeded to the office of bishop. Livingstone College gave him the degree of D.D. and LL.D., and Wilberface University, the degree of LL.D. His publications include: 'The Negro in the Ecumenical Conference (1901), 'The Alarm Cries' (1906), 'Tuskegee Lectures' (1907), and 'Twenty-five Years an Itinerant' (1907). He resides at Charlotte, N.C.

CLOUD, VIRGINIA WOODWOOD. See Biographical and Critical Sketch, Vol. III, page 979.

CLOVER, LEWIS P. Protestant Episcopal clergyman. [Va.]. He published an interesting work on 'Old Churches in Virginia.'

COBB, HOWELL. An American statesman. He was born in Jefferson County, Ga., in 1815, the son of John A. and Sarah Rootes Cobb, and was educated at Franklin College, afterward the State University, at Athens. He was one of the leaders of the Democratic party in Congress during the famous debates on slavery and presided with distinguished ability over the deliberations of the national House of Representatives for two years. He favored the Missouri Compromise of 1850; and, being criticized for this course, he made the race for Governor of Georgia in 1851, on a platform which advocated Constitutional Union. He held the Treasury portfolio in President Buchanan's Cabinet; but, on the election of Mr. Lincoln in 1860, he resigned this position and issued an address to the people of Georgia advocating secession as the only course left for the State to take with honor. He was made president of the Provisional Congress at Montgomery, Ala.; but he relinquished the civil for the military branch of the service and became a major-general. After the war he opposed the measures of reconstruction; and, in what is known as "the Bush Arbor Speech," he delivered one of the greatest efforts of his life, a masterpiece of denunciation and invective. It was afterward published in pamphlet form. His speeches in Congress are preserved in the *Congressional Globe*. Samuel Boykin compiled an interesting memorial volume of the distinguished Georgian (Philadelphia, J. B. Lippincott Company). He died in 1868.

COBB, HOWELL, lawyer, clergyman, editor, was born in Savannah, Ga., in 1795. While a lawyer, he was given a license to preach by the Methodist Conference. He also established and edited *The Cherokee Gazette;* and, taking an active part in politics, he became State senator. His literary product includes 'The Penal Code of Georgia' (1850), a work on legal forms, and a volume dealing with the African race in America.

COBB, JOSEPH BECKHAM, lawyer and author, was the son of Thomas W. Cobb, United States Senator from Georgia, and was born in Oglethorpe County, Ga., April 11, 1819. After graduating from the University of Georgia, he located in Noxubee County, Miss., for the practice of law. He took an active interest in politics and ran for Congress on the American ticket but was defeated. This probably influenced him to devote his leisure time to letters. His writings include: 'Creole Days; or the Siege of New Orleans,' a novel, published in Philadelphia; 'Mississippi Scenes; or Sketches of Southern Life and Adventure' and 'Leisure Hours' (New York, 1858), besides essays contributed to the *American Review.* He died at Columbus, Miss., September 15, 1858.

COBB, MARY McKINLEY, poet, was born in Milledgeville, Ga., in 1839, a daughter of William McKinley and a cousin of Carlisle McKinley. She became the wife of Judge Howell Cobb of Athens. Some exquisite hearthstone lyrics have come from her pen, among them, "Out of the Depths," "Stars My Father Loved" and "Sometimes," all of which have been preserved in Miss Rutherford's 'Southern History and Literature.'

COBB, NEEDHAM BRYAN. Baptist clergyman. [N.C.]. He published a unique volume of verse entitled 'The Poetical Geography of North Carolina' (Cambridge, Mass., The Riverside Press, 1877), besides a number of fugitive poems.

COBB, THOMAS READE ROOTES. Soldier, orator, lawyer, author. He was born at Cherry Hill, Jefferson County, Ga., in 1823, the son of John A. and Sarah Rootes Cobb, and married Marion, daughter of Chief Justice Joseph Henry Lumpkin. He took no part in politics until the election of President Lincoln, when his magnetic eloquence aroused the State to secession. On account of the dramatic appearance which he presented in this eventful crusade, he was likened to Peter the Hermit; and this appellation was all the more appropriate because of his blameless life and character. He was a member of the secession convention, a delegate to the Provisional Congress in Montgomery, and subsequently organized and commanded Cobb's famous legion. He was promoted to a brigadier-generalship, but was killed by a shell at Fredericksburg, in sight of his mother's old home, December 13, 1862. At the age of thirty-six, he wrote and published 'Cobb on Slavery,' the recognized masterpiece of legal literature upon this subject; and even at this early age he confronted no superior at the Georgia Bar. He wrote numerous articles on education, advocating both the university and the common-school system; founded the Lucy Cobb Institute at Athens in memory of his daughter; delivered numerous addresses on literary and religious subjects; and compiled a digest of Georgia laws.

COBBS, NICHOLAS HAMNER. He was born in 1796 and became, in later life, Protestant Episcopal Bishop of Alabama. He was the author of numerous tracts and essays, including: "An Answer to Some Popular Objections Against the Episcopal Church" and "The Baptismal Covenant." He died in 1861.

COCKE, PHILIP ST. GEORGE, soldier, was born in Virginia in 1808. and was educated for the Army at West Point, but resigned after two years of service to devote himself to planting in Virginia and Mississippi. He became a brigadier-general on the Confederate side during the Civil War; but in a paroxysm of insanity due to ill health he shot himself, and from the effects of the wound died, December 26, 1861. General Cocke published 'Plantation and Farm Instruction' (1852).

COCKE, SARAH COBB JOHNSON, author, was born in Selma. Ala., February 7, 1865. Her father was Dr. John M. Johnson of Paducah, Ky., and her mother, Mary Willis Cobb of Athens, Ga., both members of distinguished Southern families. The daughter married first, October 26, 1887, Dr. Hugh Hagan of Atlanta, Ga., and second, in 1903, Lucian H. Cocke of Roanoke, Va. Mrs. Cocke is a brilliant woman, writes charmingly in both negro and "cracker" dialects, and reproduces the characteristic wit and wisdom of the types which she portrays. Besides frequent contributions to high-class periodicals, she is the author of a work which is just going to press entitled 'The Test of the Rooster and the Wash Pot,' and 'Phillis Sketches.' She resides in Roanoke, Va.

COCKE, ZITELLA. Writer. [Ala.]. She published a volume of verse for juvenile readers entitled 'When Grasshoppers Hop, and Other Poems' (Boston, Dana Estes and Company, 1904), besides minor works including 'A Doric Reed.'

COCKRELL, FRANCIS MARION, soldier and statesman, was born in Johnson County, Mo., October 1, 1834, and was the son of Joseph and Nancy Cockrell. On completing his education he chose the law. At the outbreak of hostilities in 1861, he enlisted in the Confederate ranks and rose from captain to brigadier-general. From 1875 to 1905 he was United States Senator from Missouri. On retiring from the political arena, he became a member of the Interstate Commerce Commission. His speeches, which have been preserved in the *Congressional Record,* show his range of thought and his intimate familiarity with the basic principles of the Government.

COCKS, REGINALD S. [La.]. He published an interesting volume entitled 'The Flora of Louisiana' (New Orleans, 1899).

CODY, CLAUDE CARR. Educator. He was born in Georgia but afterward removed to Texas and published 'The Life and Labors of Francis Asbury Mood' (1899).

COE, CHARLES H. Writer. [Fla.]. He published a work entitled 'The Red Patriots; or, the Story of the Seminoles' (Cincinnati, The Editor Publishing Company, 1898).

COGHILL, JAMES H. Author. [Va.]. He published a volume of travels entitled: 'Abroad' (1867) and 'The Family of Coghill, from 1379 to 1879.'

COHEN, HENRY, rabbi, was born in London, England, April 7, 1863. An accomplished litterateur, he has mastered several different languages and made numerous translations. His published works include: 'Six Hundred Talmudic Sayings' (Cincinnati, 1894), 'Prayer in Bible and Talmud' (New York, 1894), and 'Hygiene and Medicine of the Talmud' (1901). To the transactions of the Jewish Historical Society he has contributed a number of important papers including "The Settlement of the Jews in Texas," "Henry Castro, Pioneer and Colonist," and others. He has also contributed numerous articles to the 'Jewish Encyclopædia' (New York, Funk and Wagnalls, 1902, *et seq.*), written for newspapers and magazines and published several important monographs. Dr. Cohen is one of the Advisory Council of 'The Library of Southern Literature,' a man of profound scholarship and of wide information. He married, March 6, 1889, Mollie Levy. He resides in Galveston, Texas.

COLCOCK, ANNIE T. Author. Two interesting novels have come from the pen of this Southern writer, 'Margaret Tudor' (1906), and 'Her American Daughter' (1908), both of which have received high praise from the critics.

COLCRAFT, HENRY ROWE. Author. [Ala.]. He wrote a novel of Indian life entitled 'Alhalla, or the Lord of Talladega; a Tale of the Creek War' (1843).

COLE, ALICE VIVIAN. [Ala.]. Her maiden name was Brownlee. She wrote a novel entitled 'The Affinities' (1890).

COLEMAN, CHARLES WASHINGTON, magazine writer and librarian, was born in Richmond, Va., November 22, 1862. His father was Dr. Charles Washington Coleman and his mother, Cynthia B. Tucker, daughter of Judge Beverley Tucker. Since 1881 he has contributed to the leading magazines, his work being mainly along historical lines; but he has also written some of the best verse of the day. He was poet at the bi-centennial celebration of William and Mary College; on the 288th anniversary of the settlement of Jamestown; and on various other historic occasions. In 1899 he became assistant librarian of Congress.

COLEMAN, CYNTHIA BEVERLEY TUCKER. Writer of numerous historical papers, also charter member and chairman for Virginia of the George Washington Memorial Association. She was born in Saline County, Mo., January 18, 1832, a daughter of Judge Beverley Tucker, of Williamsburg, Va. She married, first, in 1852, Henry Augustine Washington, of Westmoreland County, Va., and, second, in 1861, Charles Washington Coleman, M.D., of Williamsburg, Va. Besides being one of the founders and incorporators of the Association for the Preservation of Virginia Antiquities, she is also a charter member of the Society of Colonial Dames of America in the State of Virginia, the Daughters of the American Revolution and the United Daughters of the Confederacy. She resides in Williamsburg, Va.

COLEMAN, THADDEUS. Poet. [N.C.]. He published 'The Land of the Sky: an Idyl' (Asheville, N.C., 1903).

COLLENS, THOMAS WHARTON. Jurist and author. He was born in New Orleans, La., June 23, 1812. At the outset of his career, he edited a paper called *The True America;* but he afterward relinquished journalism for law, becoming, first, Judge of the City Court of New Orleans and afterward Judge of the Seventh District Court of the Parish. He was the author of two philosophical volumes which have been highly commended: 'Humanics' (1860), and 'The Eden of Labor' (1876). One of the products of his youthful genius was an historical tragedy, entitled: "The Martyr Patriots; or Louisiana in 1769," which was successfully performed at the old St. Charles Theater; but he was not beguiled by this achievement into writing another drama. The play has been preserved in 'The Louisiana Book' (1894). He died in New Orleans, November 3, 1879.

COLLIER, ROBERT LAIRD, clergyman, was born in Salisbury, Md., August 7, 1837. Originally a Methodist, he became a Unitarian, served churches in Chicago and Boston, delivered popular lectures and wrote magazine articles. He also published 'Every-day Subjects in Sunday Sermons' (Boston, 1869), 'Meditations on the Essence of Christianity' (1876) and 'English Home Life' (1885).

COLLINS, CHARLES, Methodist Episcopal clergyman and educator, was born in North Yarmouth, Me., April 17, 1813; but for twenty-four years he was president of Emory and Henry College in Virginia and at the time of his death was president of the State Female College near Memphis, Tenn. Besides magazine articles, he published 'Methodism and Calvinism Compared' (Philadelphia, 1849).

COLLINS, CLARENCE B. Writer. [Fla.]. He published a story of the Civil War entitled 'Tom and Joe' (1890).

COLLINS, JACOB C. Teacher and poet. [Miss.]. 'Poems' (Memphis, Rogers and Company, 1883).

COLLINS, LAURA G. Author. She was born in Maysville, Ky., May 6, 1826, the daughter of Reuben and Narcissa Martin Case. She was educated by private tutors and at the Young Ladies' School at Georgetown, Ky. She married, March 11, 1847, John A. Collins, of Covington, Ky. She has written many delightful poems and sketches. Her voiumes include: 'Immortelles and Asphodels' (poems); 'Bygone Tourist Days,' 'Egypt' (poems), and 'The Little Marquise.' She resides in Maysville, Ky.

COLLINS, LOUIS. Journalist and jurist. [Ky.]. He was born in 1797 and died in 1870. Judge Collins published a series of "Historical Sketches of Kentucky," which was afterward published in book form (1847). On account of the popularity of the work it was afterward revised and enlarged.

COLTHARP, JEANNETTE DOWNS, Mrs. [La.]. She wrote 'Burrell Coleman, Colored; a Tale of the Cotton Fields' (1896).

COLTON, CHARLES J. Poet. [La.]. He published a 'Volume of Various Verse' (New Orleans, 1899).

COLQUITT, ALFRED HOLT, soldier and statesman, was born in Walton County, Ga., April 20, 1824, the son of Walter T. Colquitt. On the field of battle he attained the rank of major-general and earned the soubriquet of "The Hero of Olustee." For two successive terms he was governor of Georgia, and after relinquishing this office he was twice commissioned to represent Georgia in the United States Senate. Prior to the War he also served in Congress. While not a minister of the gospel in active commission, he often occupied the pulpit of the Methodist Church. Some of his speeches have been preserved in the *Congressional Record*.

COLQUITT, MEL R., Mrs. Author. She was born in Augusta, Ga., in 1848. Her maiden name was Redmond, and she is connected by ties of kinship with the noted family of Ireland. She has contributed to the leading periodicals and her verse is specially admired. One of her poems, "The Graves Stood Tenantless," is preserved in 'Songs of the South.' For several years past she has lived in Washington, D.C.

COLQUITT, WALTER T., jurist and statesman, was born in Halifax County, Va., December 27, 1799. As an orator he possessed few equals. He achieved distinction at the Bar and on the Bench, became an eloquent minister of the gospel in the M. E. Church, and represented Georgia in Congress and in the Senate of the United States. Some of his best speeches were delivered on the hustings and in the courtroom and were never published; but happily several fragments of his senatorial eloquence have been preserved in the debates of Congress. He died in Macon, Ga., May 7, 1855.

COLWELL, STEPHEN, author, was born in Brooke County, Va., in what is now West Virginia, in 1800, studied law and practiced his profession in Pittsburg, but afterward engaged in business and at leisure intervals wrote for the press. He also published 'Politics for American Christians' (1852), 'Position of Christianity in the United States' (1855), and 'The Ways and Means of Commercial Payment' (1858), besides a pamphlet on "The South." He died in 1871.

COLYAR, ARTHUR ST. CLAIR, lawyer and author, was born in Washington County, Tenn., June 23, 1818, achieved success at the Bar, served in Congress, became an important factor in the railway and industrial development of Tennessee, and published an excellent biography of Andrew Jackson (Nashville, Marshall and Bruce, 1904).

CONANT, ALBAN JASPER, artist and author, was born in Vermont, September 24, 1821. Soon after attaining his majority, he located in St. Louis, where the remainder of his life was spent. He published a volume of exceptional interest entitled 'Footprints of Vanished Races in the Mississippi Valley' (1879). He also established an art gallery in St. Louis and painted portraits of several distinguished Americans.

'CONFEDERATE MEMORIAL ASSOCIATIONS IN THE SOUTH.' This is an important collection of historical papers published by The Confederated Southern Memorial Associations, Mrs. M. J. Behan, president (1904).

CONNELLEY, WILLIAM ELSEY, author, was born in Johnson County, Ky., March 15, 1855, but removed to Kansas, where he became an authority on the antiquities of the state and published 'James Henry Lane, the Grim Chieftain of Kansas' (Topeka, Crane and Company), 'Wyandot Folk Lore' (*ibid.*), 'Kansas Territorial Governors' (*ibid.*), 'John Brown: the Story of the Last of the Puritans' (*ibid.*), 'Life of John J. Ingalls' (Kansas City, Hudson-Kimberly Company), 'The Heckwelder Narrative' (Cleveland, The Burrows Company), and 'Donaphon's Expedition,' besides numerous contributions to periodicals.

CONNELLY, EMMA M. Author. [Ky.]. She published 'The Story of Kentucky' and 'Tiltings at Windmills.'

CONNOLLY, MICHAEL WILLIAM. Editor of the Memphis *News-Scimitar,* poet and essayist. He was born in the Dominion of Canada, March 2, 1853, and received an academic education at Montreal. He lived in Texas from 1874 to 1887, then moved to Memphis. While his editorial labors have occupied most of his time, he has contributed numerous poems,' essays, and sketches to the periodicals, and has also delivered many public addresses. His only published work is a volume of dainty verse entitled 'Poems, Wise and Otherwise.' The sketch of Judge Walter Malone in 'The Library of Southern Literature' is from his pen. He married, November 19, 1879, Lula Parham.

CONNOR, HENRY GROVES, jurist, was born in Wilmington, N.C., July 3, 1852. His father was David Connor and his mother, Mary C. Groves. He chose the legal profession, was for several years Superior Court judge, and in 1801 became associate justice of the Supreme Court of North Carolina. He is the author of a number of sketches in the 'Biographical History of North Carolina,' published by C. L. Van Noppen, besides historical monographs, essays, and addresses. For 'The Library of Southern Literature' he wrote the sketch of Kemp P. Battle.

CONNOR, ROBERT DIGGES WIMBERLEY, educator, was born at Wilson, N.C., September 26, 1878. Since graduating from the University of North Carolina he has been engaged in teaching. He is in charge of the loan fund for building schools, an office, which he holds in connection with the State Department of Public Instruction, and he is also a member of the North Carolina Historical Commission. Besides contributing to various periodicals and publications, he is the author of a work entitled 'The Story of the Old North State' (Philadelphia, J. B. Lippincott Company, 1906), and 'Cornelius Harnett: An Essay in North Carolina History' (Raleigh, Edwards and Broughton). He has contributed to 'The South in the Building of the Nation' and to 'The Biographical History of North Carolina,' and the sketch of William Gaston in 'The

Library of Southern Literature' is from his pen. He has done some excellent work for his native state. He married, December 23, 1902, Sadie Hanes.

CONVERSE, AMASSA, clergyman and journalist, was born in Virginia in 1795. Entering the ministry of the Presbyterian Church, he became a pastor of some prominence in the South, and later went to Philadelphia, where he founded *The Christian Observer*. But his sympathies were intensely Southern; and, when hostilities began, he removed his paper first to Richmond and afterward to Louisville, where it continued to be the organ of the Southern Presbyterian Church. He wrote with a virile and vigorous pen. His death occurred in Louisville, Ky., December 9, 1872.

CONVERSE, FLORENCE. Author. She was born in New Orleans, La., April 30, 1871, the daughter of George T. and Caroline Edwards Converse. She was educated at Wellesley College, from which institution she received the degree of M.A. Her mature years have been spent in the North. She is on the staff of *The Churchman*, and resides in Boston, Mass. Besides several magazine stories, she has written some interesting books which deal with life under modern conditions: 'Diana Victrix' (Boston, Houghton, Mifflin and Company), 'The Burden of Christopher, (*ibid.*), and 'Long Will.'

CONVERSE, JAMES B. Presbyterian clergyman, editor and author. He was born in Philadelphia, April 8, 1844, the son of Dr. Amasa and Flavia Booth Converse, and was educated at Princeton, N.J., after which he studied for the ministry at Union Theological Seminary, Richmond. Va. He was twice married. He assumed a pastoral charge from 1868 to 1871; and was editor of the *Christian Observer* from 1872 to 1879; an evangelist from 1879 to 1881; then again a pastor from 1881 to 1887, resuming evangelistic work in 1888. Among his published works are: 'A Summer Vacation Abroad,' 'The Bible and Land,' an argument in favor of single tax, and 'Uncle Sam's Bible, or Bible Teachings About Politics.' Besides hundreds of articles in scores of periodicals, he also wrote 'Notes on Exodus,' and circulated a petition to Christians asking them to acknowledge the authority of the Bible in civil affairs. He resides in Morristown, Tenn.

CONWAY, MONCURE DANIEL. See Biographical and Critical Sketch, Vol. III, page 1007.

COOK, EBEN. He was an early Colonial writer who published a volume of curious interest entitled 'Sot Weed Factor, or a Voyage to Maryland' (1708). "Sot Weed" was a name for tobacco.

COOK, J. F. Physician and author. [Ky.]. He published a work of much interest dealing with various phases of life in the Blue Grass State, entitled 'Old Kentucky' (New York and Washington, The Neale Publishing Company, 1908), which also contains papers by Theodore Roosevelt, Champ Clark and Reuben T. Durrett.

COOK, MARY LOUISE. Writer. [Ga.]. Her maiden name was Miss Redd. Besides a number of poems, she published 'Ante-bellum Days, or Southern Life as It Was' and 'A Woman's Perils.' She died in 1891.

COOK, RICHARD BRISCOE, clergyman, was born in Baltimore, Md. November 11, 1838, but the greater part of his life since entering the ministry has been spent in the State of Delaware. Dr. Cook has published several volumes, among them, 'The Early and Later Delaware

Baptists' (Philadelphia, The American Baptist Publication Society, 1880), 'The Story of the Baptists' (1887), 'The Story of Jesus' (1889), 'The Life and Work of Rev. C. H. Spurgeon' (1891), a 'Life of Gladstone' (1892), and 'The Life and Work of D. L. Moody' (1899), besides numerous pamphlets and papers. Dr. Cook married, in 1866, Louisa Love Kerfoot of Virginia. He resides in Wilmington, Del.

COOKE, ARTHUR BLEDSOE, educator, was born at Melton's, Louisa County, Va., June 15, 1869. His father was George Washington Cooke and his mother, Sallie Anderson. Besides contributing to current magazines, he has published 'Development of the Nature Sense in the German Lyric' (1901), 'Essays on Work and Life' (1904), and 'With the Tourist Tide' (1907). He also wrote the sketch of James A. Harrison in 'The Library of Southern Literature.' He married, in 1899, Stella Viola Crider, of Norfolk, Va. He resides in Pasadena, Cal., and holds the degree of Ph.D.

COOKE, GRACE MacGOWAN. Magazine writer. She was born in Grand Rapids, Ohio, September 11, 1863, the daughter of John Encill and Maria Johnston MacGowan. She was educated at home and married, February 17, 1887, William Cooke, of Chattanooga, Tenn. She was the first president of the Tennessee Woman's Press Club and is the author of numerous stories of unusual merit, including: 'Mistress Joy, a Tale of Natchez in 1798,' with A. B. McKinney (New York, The Century Company), 'A Story of the Sea Islands,' with Alice MacGowan (Boston, Lothrop Publishing Company), 'Hulda' (Indianapolis, The Bobbs-Merrill Company), 'A Gourd Fiddle' (Philadelphia, Henry Altemus Company), 'The Grapple' (Boston, L. C. Page and Company), and 'Their First Formal Call' (New York, Harpers), besides many contributions to magazines.

COOKE, JOHN ESTEN. See Biographical and Critical Sketch, Vol. III, page 1063.

COOKE, PHILIP PENDLETON. See Biographical and Critical Sketch, Vol. III, page 1063.

COOKE, PHILIP ST. GEORGE, soldier, was born near Leesburg, Va., June 13, 1809. After graduating from West Point he entered the United States Army, commanded a regiment in the Mexican War, and was breveted a major-general at the close of the Civil War. He published 'Scenes and Adventures in the Army, or Romance of Military Life' (Philadelphia, 1856), 'The Conquest of New Mexico and California: An Historical and Personal Narrative' (1878) and 'New Cavalry Tactics.' His daughter became the wife of the famous Confederate general, J. E. B. Stuart. He died in 1895.

COON, CHARLES LEE, educator, was born near Lincolnton, N.C., December 25, 1868. Besides numerous pamphlets on educational subjects printed by the State superintendent of North Carolina and numerous articles for school journals and daily papers, he has published 'The Beginnings of Public Education in North Carolina, 1790-1840' (Raleigh, North Carolina Historical Commission, 1908), 'Facts about Southern Educational Progress' (1905), and 'Public Taxation and Negro Schools' (1909). He married, October 21, 1903, Caroline L. Sparger. He resides at Wilson, N.C.

COOPER, CHARLES W. Poet. For many years he pursued the vocation of teaching; but reverses overtook him in later life and he died in the Soldiers' Home in Richmond. He published a volume entitled: 'The Musings of Myron' (Newmarket, Va., 1880).

COOPER, OSCAR HENRY. President of Simmons College, educator and author. He was born in Texas, November 22, 1852, a son of Dr. William Henry Cooper. He was educated at Marshall University and at Yale and took post-graduate work at Berlin. He married, November 24, 1886, Mary Bryan Stewart, of Marshall, Texas. He was president of Baylor University from 1899 to 1902 and is the author of 'Reports of State Department of Education,' 'History of Our Country,' 'Compulsory School Laws,' 'Universities and Schools,' 'Ten Years' Progress in Education in Texas,' and 'Contributions of Baptists to the Cause of Education.' Dr. Cooper holds the degree of LL.D. He resides in Abilene, Texas.

COOPER, THOMAS, educator and scientist, was born in London, England, October 22, 1759, and died in Columbia, S.C., May 11, 1840. He was educated for the Bar at Oxford, took an active part in politics, and, with James Watt, the inventor, was sent by the Democratic clubs of England on an errand to France, where his sympathies, being with the Girondists, aroused the hostility of Edmund Burke. While in France he mastered a number of chemical arts. Later, in 1795, he came to America He located in Pennsylvania, where he edited a paper in support of Democratic principles; and for boldly advocating his views he was imprisoned under the Alien and Sedition Act. He was afterward elevated to the Bench and, though impeached and removed for arbitrary conduct, he won respect for his strong legal opinions. From the professorship of chemistry in Dickinson College he was called to the corresponding chair in the College of South Carolina, where he succeeded Dr. Maxcy as president. This office he was compelled to resign on account of his peculiar religious views; and he was thereupon appointed to make a 'Digest of the Laws of South Carolina,' a work on which he was engaged at the time of his death. He also edited two volumes of the 'Emporium of Arts and Sciences,' and four volumes of Thomson's 'System of Chemistry' (1818), besides translating the works of Justinian. His other published works include: 'Letters on the Slave Trade (London, 1787), 'An Account of the Trial of Thomas Cooper of Northumberland' (Philadelphia, 1800), 'Lectures on the Elements of Political Economy' (Charleston, 1826), and numerous essays. He was a free thinker in religion. John Adams pronounced him a "talented madman" and Thomas Jefferson declared him to be "the greatest man in America in power of mind." He was closely associated with the writers and statesmen of the Eighteenth Century on both sides of the water, was dubbed "the father of political economy in America," and by his tariff and State rights teachings, prepared the way for nullification.

COPPEE, HENRY, educator, was born in Savannah, Ga., October 13, 1821. After spending two years at Yale, he entered the military academy at West Point and graduated in time to win his spurs on the fields of Mexico. For five years he taught history and ethics at West Point. Later he became professor of English at the University of Pennsylvania and afterward president of Lehigh University, which latter position he relinquished in 1875 to accept a professorship. His published works include: 'Elements of Logic,' 'Gallery of Famous Poets,' 'Elements of Rhetoric,' 'Gallery of Distinguished Poetesses,' 'Select Academic Speaker,' 'Manual of Battalion Drill,' 'Evolutions of the Line,' 'Manual of Court Martial,' 'Songs of Praise in the Christian Centuries,' 'Life and Services of General U. S. Grant,' 'Lectures on English Literature,' and 'The Conquest of Spain by the Arab-Moors,' besides various translations.

CORBIN, DIANA FONTAINE MAURY, Mrs. [Va.]. She published an interesting biography of her father, entitled 'The Life of Matthew Fontaine Maury.'

CORBIN, JOSEPH CARTER. Educator. He was born in Chillicothe, Ohio, March 26, 1833, a son of William and Susan Corbin. He was educated at the University of Ohio and married, September 11, 1866, Mary J. Ward, of Cincinnati. His life is devoted to the cause of education. He was State Superintendent of Education for Arkansas; and afterward for twenty-six years president of Branch Normal College. He has written: 'Minutes of Masonry of the Grand Lodge of Arkansas' and 'The Status of Colored Freemasons'; also numerous articles in educational journals. Dr. Corbin holds the degree of Ph.D. He resides in Pine Bluff, Ark.

CORDELL, EUGENE FAUNTLEROY, educator and physician, was born at Charlestown, W.Va., June 25, 1843. After receiving his medical degree from the University of Maryland he located in Baltimore for the practice of his profession. For twenty-one years he held the chair of materia medica in the Woman's Medical College of Baltimore and in 1903 assumed the chair of history of medicine in the University of Maryland. On account of his eminent attainments, Dr. Cordell has frequently been honored with high official positions in organizations both state and national. In addition to the professorship which he holds in the University, he is also librarian of the department of medicine. He is the founder of the American Medical College Association, of various hospitals and asylums, and of *The University Monthly,* which he edits. He has published 'The Medical Annals of Maryland' (1903) and 'The History of the University of Maryland,' in two volumes (1907), besides numerous articles, scientific, literary and historical, contributed to various periodicals, and some fifty sketches written for the 'Cyclopædia of American Medical Biography,' now in press.

CORNISH, KATE. Poet. [S.C.]. Under the pen name of "Kil Courtland" she has written a number of poems, which the Dixie Chapter of the U.D.C. at Greenville, S.C., is preparing to publish in book form.

CORNWELL, M. S., poet, was born in Hampshire County, W. Va., and reared on the farm without the advantages of a liberal education; but he possessed the gift of minstrelsy in an eminent degree and his early death alone prevented him from taking the high poetic rank to which his talents pointed. He was the editor of a country newspaper, first at Petersburg and afterward at Elkins. It was not until after his death that his poems were collected and published in book form under the title: 'Wheat and Chaff' (Romney, W.Va.), this volume being a memorial of the author by his two surviving brothers.

COSBY, FORTUNATUS. Journalist and poet of Kentucky, was born in 1802. He was the author of numerous productions of merit.

COSSETT, FRANCEWAY RANNA, clergyman and educator, was born in Claremount, N.H., April 24, 1790, and died in Lebanon, Tenn., July 3, 1863. Dr. Cossett was the first president of Cumberland University and a leader among the Cumberland Presbyterians of the South. He founded *The Banner of Peace,* which he edited for twenty years, and also wrote 'The Life and Times of Ewing' (1858).

COTTEN, SALLIE SOUTHALL, Mrs. Poet. [N.C.]. In a work entitled 'The White Doe' (Philadelphia, J. B. Lippincott Company, 1901), Mrs. Cotten tells the story of Virginia Dare, the first child of English parentage born in the New World; and incidentally the fate of Raleigh's lost colony on Roanoke Island is also sketched. The account is rendered in excellent verse.

COUNCILL, WILLIAM HOOPER. Negro educator. President for some time of the Agricultural and Mechanical College at Normal, Ala.

He was born a slave in Fayetteville, N.C., July 12, 1848, was educated at Stevenson, Ala., and married, September 5, 1885, Maria H. Weeden. He was admitted to the Supreme Court of Alabama to practice law, in 1883, but continued to teach. He organized, in 1875, the institution over which he presided until the time of his death. Besides a work entitled: 'The Lamp of Wisdom; or, Race History Illustrated,' he founded the Huntsville *Herald*, which he edited for several years. He wrote numerous articles for the magazines of the day and delivered many addresses on subjects pertaining to his race. Morris Brown College gave him the degree of Ph.D. He died in Normal, Ala., in 1909.

COURMONT, FELIX DE. Poet. [La.]. He wrote in French 'Le Taenarion,' a collection of satires (1847), 'Le Dernier de Caraibes' (1872) and other works.

COURTENAY, EDWARD HENRY, educator, was born in Maryland in 1803 and died in Charlottesville, Va., in 1853. At the time of his death he was professor of mathematics in the University of Virginia. He translated Boucharlat's 'Elementary Treatise on Mechanics,' for the use of cadets at West Point (New York, 1833), and published a textbook on 'Differential and Integral Calculus' (1855).

COURTENAY, WILLIAM A. Lawyer. [S.C.]. Captain Courtenay was several times mayor of Charleston, a veteran of the Civil War and a patron of letters. He edited the 'Charleston Year Books,' made frequent contributions to periodicals and delivered numerous addresses. The sketch of Carlisle McKinley in 'The Library of Southern Literature' is from his pen. He died in Columbia, S.C., March 17, 1908.

COWDIN, V. G., Mrs. Author. [La.]. She published a novel entitled 'Ellen, or the Fanatic's Daughter' (Mobile, 1860).

COXE, DANIEL. Physician. Dr. Coxe was an Englishman who published an archaic volume of much interest pertaining to America entitled a 'Description of the English Province of Carolana, by the Spaniards called Florida, by the French, La Louisiane, with a Map of Carolana and of the River Meschacebe' [Mississippi] (London, 1741).

COXE, HENRY CARLETON. Clergyman and educator. [Va.]. He was born in 1785 and died in 1840. He published 'Liberty and Necessity' and 'The Will,' two psychological works of much interest.

COYNER, CHARLES LUTHER. Lawyer and author. He was born in Long Grade, Augusta County, Va., February 8, 1853, the son of Addison Hyde and Elizabeth Brown Coyner; received his diploma from Wesleyan College, in Virginia, and studied law at Washington and Lee University. He married, January 4, 1884, Margaret Blair. He removed to Texas in 1877, to Missouri in 1899, and to Tennessee in 1902. In Texas he was prosecuting attorney for ten years, probate judge four years and county judge four years. He was appointed by Governor Ireland district attorney and by Governor Roberts district judge. Besides frequent contributions to magazines, he has written 'The Life of S. B. Coyner,' 'A Greenhorn in Texas,' "A Tribute" (poem), and 'Twenty Years in Texas.' He resides in Memphis, Tenn.

COYNER, ————. [Va.]. He published 'The Lost Trappers,' a sequel to the 'Clark and Lewis Expedition.'

"CRADDOCK, CHARLES EGBERT." See Murfree, Mary Noailles.

CRAFTS, WILLIAM, lawyer, editor, poet, was born in Charleston, S.C., in 1787, and educated at Harvard. On his return home he engaged in the practice of law and served for several terms in the State Legislature. He was an eloquent speaker, delivering orations on many important occasions; and in 1817 he made the Phi Beta Kappa address at his *alma mater*. For some 'time he edited the Charleston *Courier*. Possessed of an unusual poetic fancy, he frequently dropped into verse; and some time after his death a volume appeared entitled: 'Selections in Prose and Poetry, from the Miscellaneous Writings of the Late William Crafts, to which is Prefixed a Memoir of His Life' (Charleston, 1828). He died in 1826.

CRAIGHEAD, EDWIN BOONE. President of Tulane University. He was born in Ham's Prairie, Mo., March 3, 1861, and was educated at Central College. He took post-graduate work at Vanderbilt University, at Leipsic, and at Paris. He married, August 6, 1889, Kate Johnson. He was president of South Carolina Agricultural and Mechanical College, at Clemson, S.C., for four years; and afterward president of Central College, La Fayette, Mo. In 1904 he became president of Tulane University. He has contributed numerous articles to literary and educational magazines and is one of the consulting editors of 'The Library of Southern Literature.' The University of Missouri gave him the degree of LL.D. He resides in New Orleans, La.

CRANCH, CHRISTOPHER PEASE, painter and poet, was born in Alexandria, Va., March 8, 1813. Equipped for the ministry at the Harvard Divinity School, he subsequently relinquished his ambitions in this direction and began the study of art, spending seventeen years in Europe. He became an eminent painter, his specialty being landscapes; but he also wrote graceful verse and was proficient in music. He published a metrical translation of Virgil's 'Æneid' (Boston, Houghton, Mifflin and Company, 1844), a volume of poems, and 'Satan: a Libretto.' He died in Cambridge, Mass., January 20, 1892.

CRANE, ANNE MONCURE (Mrs. Seemüller), author, was born in Baltimore, Md., January 7, 1838, and died in Stuttgart, Germany, December 10, 1872. Her first novel, 'Emily Chester,' was anonymous. She afterward published 'Opportunity' and 'Reginald Archer,' besides numerous contributions to periodicals. After her marriage to August Seemüller, of New York, she went to Germany, hoping to derive some benefit from the medicinal waters, but she failed to realize this expectation and died while abroad. In 1873 a collection of her miscellaneous essays was published.

CRANE, WILLIAM CAREY, clergyman and educator, was born in Richmond, Va., March 17, 1816, and died at Independence, Texas, February 27, 1885. For more than twenty years, he was president of Baylor University, having been called to this position in 1863. Both as a scholar and as a minister of the gospel he was a man of unusual attainments and one of the foremost Baptist divines of the South. Included among his published works are 'Literary Discourses' and 'The Life of Sam Houston.'

CRAWFORD, A. MARIA, magazine writer, was born at Crawford Farm, Knox County, Tenn., March 16, 1884. Miss Crawford contributes short stories and poems of unusual merit to the leading popular magazines and is preparing to publish a volume of verse. She is engaged in journalism in Knoxville, Tenn.

CRAWFORD, J. MARSHALL. Author. [Va.]. He wrote 'Mosby and His Men' (1867).

CRAWFORD, NATHANIEL MACON, educator and clergyman, was born in Oglethorpe County, Ga., March 22, 1811, and died in Walker

County, Va., October 27, 1871. His father was the dintinguished William H. Crawford, diplomat and statesman. Entering the ministry, he became an eminent Baptist divine, noted for his scholarship and eloquence. From the chair of theology in Mercer University he was called to the executive helm, but relinquished this position to enter the faculty of the University of Mississippi. Later, he returned to Georgia and became once more the president of Mercer. Besides editing *The Christian Index,* he made frequent contributions to the religious press and published a volume entitled 'Christian Paradoxes.' (Nashville, 1858).

CRAWFORD, WILLIAM HARRIS. Diplomat and statesman. He was born in Amherst County, Va., February 24, 1772, and died in Elbert County, Ga., September 14, 1834. Before attaining his thirty-fifth year he was chosen to represent his adopted State in the United States Senate; but from this position he was called to represent the Government at the Court of France, under the empire of the first Napoleon. He was one of the handsomest men of his day; and so impressed was the French Emperor by his distinguished appearance at Court that he afterward said of Mr. Crawford that he was the only man to whom he ever felt constrained to bow. On returning home, he became Secretary of the Treasury; and such was his popularity that he was the choice of his party to succeed Mr. Monroe in the office of President. But, during the campaign, he was stricken with paralysis, due to an improper use of lobelia, and the election which was thrown into the House of Representatives resulted in the choice of Mr. Adams. The last days of the distinguished statesman were spent on the Superior Court Bench in Georgia. Few of the speeches of Mr. Crawford have been preserved except in the debates of Congress; but he stamped the impress of his genius upon the history of his times.

CREERY, WILLIAM RUFUS, educator, was born in Baltimore, Md., May 9, 1824, and died in Baltimore, Md., May 1, 1875. He graduated from Dickinson College and became professor of *belles lettres* in a college in Baltimore and later superintendent of the public schools. He prepared, in association with Professor M. A. Newell, the Maryland series of schoolbooks, including spellers and readers, besides a 'Catechism of United States History.'

CREITZBURG, A. M. Methodist Episcopal clergyman. He wrote 'Early Methodism in the Carolinas' (Nashville, The M.E. Publishing House, South).

CRESWELL, JULIA PLEASANTS, author, was born in Huntsville, Ala., August 21, 1821, and died near Shreveport, La., August 21, 1886. Her father was Colonel J. J. Pleasants, of Virginia, who, moving to Alabama, became Secretary of State. Before her marriage to Judge David Creswell, she published, in association with her cousin, Thomas Bibb Bradley, a volume of verse entitled 'Aphelia, and Other Poems, by Two Cousins of the South' (New York, 1854). Subsequent to the war, she taught school, while her husband, whose large property had been destroyed by the war, resumed the practice of his profession; and she also wrote at this time an allegorical novel entitled: 'Callamura' (Philadelphia, 1868). At her death she left a number of unpublished poems.

CRIM, MATT. Author. She spent much of her earlier life in Georgia, the first fruits of her genius appearing in the Savannah papers in the *Sunny South.* Encouraged by her success, she wrote for *The Century* a story in dialect entitled: "An Unfortunate Creetur," which brought her wide recognition; and both *Harper's* and *The Century* began to purchase her literary wares. For some time past she has resided in New York; and among the best-known products of her pen are: 'The Adventures of a Fair Rebel,' 'In Beaver Cove and Elsewhere' and 'Elizabeth, the Christian Scientist.' She is unmarried.

CRISTY, GEORGE W. Poet. [La.]. He published a volume of verse entitled 'The Cricket, and Other Poems' (1850).

CRITTENDEN, JOHN JORDAN, statesman, was born in Woodford County, Ky., September 10, 1787, and died in Frankfort, Ky., July 26, 1863. On completing his studies at William and Mary College, he chose the practice of law. At the age of twenty-eight he was elected to the United States Senate; but, after serving three years, he resigned the toga and resumed professional activities. Again, in 1835, he took his seat in the upper branch of Congress and was subsequently reëlected, but again he resigned to become Attorney-general in President Harrison's Cabinet. On the accession of President Tyler, he retired; but Henry Clay having relinquished his seat in the Senate Mr. Crittenden was appointed to succeed him and at the expiration of the term was again commissioned. But once more he resigned his seat to become governor of Kentucky; and, after completing his tenure of office, he returned to the Senate to complete his glorious career in the American House of Peers. He was an ardent Unionist. Retiring from the Senate in 1861, he was elected to the House of Representatives, where he remained until his death, which occurred two years later. The speeches of Mr. Crittenden, which have been preserved in the debates of Congress, attest his vigor of intellect and his breadth of statesmanship.

CROCKETT, DAVID. See Biographical and Critical Sketch, Vol. III, page 1083.

CROCKETT, INGRAM. Author. He was born in Henderson, Ky., February 10, 1856, a son of John W. and Louisa M. Ingram Crockett. He was educated in the public schools of his home town and married, May 17, 1887, Mary Cameron Stites. Besides numerous contributions to the magazines, he has written: 'Beneath Blue Skies and Gray' (New York, R. H. Russell), and 'A Year Book of Kentucky Woods and Fields.' His fondness for outdoor life and his intimate familiarity with nature are distinctly impressed upon his writings. He resides in Henderson, Ky.

CROSS, JANE TANDY, author, was born at Harrisburg, Ky., in 1817, a daughter of Judge Chinn. Before attaining her eighteenth year she married James P. Hardin, but he did not long survive the happy nuptials, and she afterward married Dr. Joseph Cross, a Methodist minister. She spoke fluently the Romance languages and wrote with great ease and charm. She accompanied her husband to Europe, upon his retirement from the itinerant ranks, and, on returning home, they engaged in teaching at Spartanburg, S.C. Besides several beautiful poems, one of which was inscribed to the memory of her only child by the last marriage, she wrote: 'From the Calm Centre,' 'Heart Blossoms,' 'Wayside Flowerets,' 'Duncan Adair,' 'Bible Gleanings,' 'Azile,' and 'Drift-Wood,' most of her books being for the young. She died in 1870.

CROSS, TRUEMAN, soldier, was born in Maryland, the exact time and place unknown. Attaining the rank of colonel in the United States Army, he was placed in charge of the quartermaster's department, but met his death at the hands of Mexican banditti, at Fort Brown, Texas, April 21, 1846. He published 'Military Laws of the United States.'

CROZIER, H. H. Clergyman. This author resided in Mississippi and published several books: 'The Bloody Junto, or the Escape of John

Wilkes Booth' (1869), 'The Confederate Spy' (1867), 'Fiery Trials' (1882), 'Araphel, or Falling Stars' (1884), 'The Cane of Hegobar' (1885), and 'Deep Waters' (1887).

CRUSE, MARY ANNE. Author of 'Cameron Hall,' a story of the Civil War (Philadelphia, J. B. Lippincott Company, 1867). The scenes of this stirring narrative are laid around Huntsville, Ala. She also wrote: 'Auntie's Christmas Tree' and 'Little Grandpa.'

CRUSE, PETER HOFFMAN, editor, was born in Baltimore, Md., in 1795, and educated at Princeton. Relinquishing law for journalism, he edited the Baltimore *American* for ten years and became a contributor to various magazines and periodicals. In association with John P. Kennedy he also edited *The Red Book*.

CRUZAT, J. W. [La.]. He wrote an account entitled 'The De fences of New Orleans in 1797' (Louisiana Historical Society, 1896).

CULBERSON, CHARLES A., United States Senator, was born in Dadeville, Ala., June 10, 1855. When only an infant he was taken to Texas, from which State his father, Honorable David B. Culberson, was a Representative in Congress, for twenty-two years. He graduated from the Virginia Military Institute, located in Texas for the practice of law, became prominent at the Bar and in politics, and was elected to the United States Senate in 1899, to succeed Roger Q. Mills. Six years later he was reëlected for another term. On political issues he is an ardent Democrat. Mr. Culberson is one of the ablest lawyers in the Upper House, an effective writer and an eloquent speaker on political issues and governmental problems. He is a member of the advisory council of 'The Library of Southern Literature.' He married, December 7, 1882, Sally Harrison. His place of residence is Dallas, Texas.

CULBRETH, DAVID M. R. Physician. [Va.]. Dr. Culbreth, an alumnus of the University of Virginia, has written in the reminiscent vein an exceedingly interesting volume entitled 'The University of Virginia—Memories of Her Student Life and Professors,' an elaborate work full of spicy incidents and anecdotes (New York and Washington, The Neale Publishing Company, 1908).

CUMMING, KATE. She was born in 1835 and is the author of some excellent work both in prose and in verse. Two volumes have come from her pen: 'Hospital Life in the Army of Tennessee' (1866)' and 'Gleanings From Southland' (1896).

CUMMINGS, C. C. Jurist and author. Judge Cummings was born in Virginia. During the Civil War he enlisted as a volunteer from his native State and fought throughout the struggle, losing an arm in the service of the Old Dominion. Soon after the close of hostilities he located in Texas, where he ably presided on the Bench for nearly forty years, and toward the close of his long life published in two volumes an elaborate work entitled 'Texas History' (New York and Washington, The Neale Publishing Company, 1908), in which he reviews the beginnings of the Lone Star Commonwealth.

CUMMINGS, JEREMIAH W., clergyman, was born in Washington, D.C., April 5, 1823, and died in New York January 4, 1866. He studied theology at the College of the Propaganda, in Rome, and became an effective preacher and lecturer. He published 'Italian Legends' (New York, 1859). 'Songs for Catholic Schools' (1862), 'Spiritual Progress' (1865), and 'The Silver Stole,' besides contributions to encyclopædias and periodicals.

CUMMINGS, ST. JAMES, educator, was born at Topsfield, Mass., December 22, 1858. When a lad of fourteen, he was brought to Knoxville, Tenn., by his parents, who were natives of Canada. After completing his studies at Johns Hopkins, from which institution he carried off the honors of literary prizeman, he accepted the chair of history and English literature in the South Carolina Military Academy, a position which he still retains. He is the author of 'Staves of the Triple Alliance' (1898) and 'Flamborough Head, and Other Poems,' two volumes of pronounced literary merit. The sketch of Henry J. Nott in 'The Library of Southern Literature' is also from his pen. He married, in 1896, Rosa L. Witte, of Charleston, S.C.

CUMMINS, EBENEZER HARLOW, lawyer and historian, was born in North Carolina, in 1790. On leaving college, he studied law and located in Georgia, serving for several terms in the Legislature; but afterward he entered the Marine Corps. Still later, he studied theology; and, after locating in Baltimore, he became a magistrate. He published 'A Geography of Alabama' and 'A History of the Late War,' the latter being an account of the second war with England. He died in Washington, D.C., January 17, 1835.

CUMMINS, FRANCIS, clergyman, was born near Shippensburg, Pa., in 1732, but was educated in North Carolina and spent the greater part of his life in the South. For some time he taught school, and among his pupils was Andrew Jackson. He was an ardent patriot and was present at several of the meetings of the Mecklenburg Whigs. Entering the Presbyterian ministry, after reaching middle life, he nevertheless achieved eminence and held numerous important charges. He published a volume of sermons and wrote a number of political and scientific pamphlets. He died at Greensboro, Ga., February 22, 1832, having reached the advanced age of one hundred years.

CUNNINGHAM, SUMNER ARCHIBALD. Founder of *The Confederate Veteran,* published in Nashville, Tenn. He was born in Bedford County, Tenn., July 21, 1843, the son of John Washington Campbell and Mary A. Buchanan Cunningham. He was reared on a farm and educated in the country schools of the neighborhood. He married, November 27, 1866, Laura N. Davis. He served in the Confederate Army; and after the war engaged in merchandizing at Shelbyville, Tenn. He bought and edited the Shelbyville *Commercial* and subsequently purchased the Chattanooga *Times,* which he sold in 1880 to the present owner, Adolph S. Ochs. He then launched in New York a periodical called *Our Day,* which was designed to be an exponent of Southern sentiment; but this publication was discontinued after eighteen months. In 1893 Mr. Cunningham organized and established *The Confederate Veteran,* which has ever since been the recognized literary representative of the men and memories of the Lost Cause. He resides in Nashville, Tenn.

CURRELL, WILLIAM SPENCER, educator, was born in Charleston, S.C., May 13, 1858. For several years he has filled the chair of English at Washington and Lee University, from which institution he received his Ph.D. degree. He has frequently lectured before Chautauqua assemblies and contributed to magazines and reviews. He also wrote for 'The Library of Southern Literature' the sketch of E. S. Joynes.

CURRY, JABEZ LAMAR MONROE. See Biographical and Critical Sketch, Vol. III, page 1111.

CURTIS, MARION. The author of a story which treats delicately and interestingly of the race problem in the South, entitled 'The Note of Discord' (New York, The Broadway Publishing Company, 1904).

CURTIS, MOSES ASHLEY, clergyman and scientist, was born in Massachusetts in 1808, but lived for many years in North Carolina and published 'The Edible Fungi of North Carolina' and a 'Catalogue of the Plants of North Carolina.'

CUSTIS, GEORGE WASHINGTON PARKE, author, was the adopted son of George Washington and was born at Mount Airy, Md., in 1781. Soon after completing his education, he married Mary Lee Fitzhugh and settled upon the famous estate at Arlington, his daughter in after years becoming the wife of Robert E. Lee. The splendid property having reverted to Mrs. Lee, it was confiscated after the War and converted into a burial ground for the nation's dead; but the family was subsequently reimbursed by special act of Congress. Mr. Custis was a man of distinguished attainments. He delivered numerous orations, wrote a number of plays, including 'Pocahontas, a National Drama' (Philadelphia, 1830), and published an interesting work entitled: 'Recollections of Washington,' containing a memoir by his daughter and an introductory note from the pen of B. J. Lossing. He died at Arlington, in 1857.

CUTHBERT, ALFRED, statesman, was born in Savannah, Ga., about 1784, and was educated at Princeton. For nearly ten years he served in Congress; and, in 1834, was elected to the United States Senate to succeed John Forsyth, being afterward reëlected for another full term. His speeches were characterized by unusual vigor of thought. He died at Monticello, Ga., July 9, 1856.

CUTHBERT, JAMES HAZZARD, clergyman, was born at Beaufort, S.C., December 13, 1823; and, after graduating from Princeton, he studied theology under his uncle, Rev. Richard Fuller, D.D., and became an eminent Baptist divine. For a while he served a congregation in Philadelphia; but, at the outbreak of the War, he returned to the South and held charges first in Augusta and afterward in Washington, D.C. He published 'The Life of Richard Fuller, D.D.' (New York, 1879). Forest College, N.C., gave him the degree of D.D.

CUTHBERT, JOHN A., jurist and editor, was born in Savannah, Ga., June 3, 1788, and died near Mobile Ala., September 22, 1881. Educated at Princeton, he began the study of law in New York; but, returning to Georgia, he became prominent at the Bar and was sent to Congress. Later, he edited *The Federal Union,* a paper published at Milledgeville. In 1837, he removed to Mobile and became a judge of the Circuit Court.

CUTLER, LIZZIE PETIT, author, was born in Milton, in Albemarle County, Va., in 1836, and educated at the seminary in Charlottesville, and under private tutors. Her gifts were of very high order. In 1855, she published her first novel, 'Light and Darkness,' which was reproduced in England and translated into French. She also wrote 'Household Mysteries, a Romance of Southern Life,' 'The Stars of the Crowd, or Men and Women of the Day.' Her maiden name was Lizzie Petit. In 1858, she married Mr. Cutler, a lawyer of New York.

CUTTER, GEORGE WASHINGTON. Poet. Though born in Massachusetts, in 1809, he lived many years in Kentucky and commanded a company of Kentuckians in the Mexican War. One of his best-known poems entitled: "The Song of Steam," is preserved in 'Songs of the South.' He published 'Buena Vista, and Other Poems' (Cincinnati, 1848). 'Song of Steam, and Other Poems,' and 'Poems, National and Patriotic' (Philadelphia, 1857). Under several administrations, he held an important clerkship in the United States Treasury Department. He died in Washington, D.C., in 1865.

DABNEY, CHARLES WILLIAM. President of the University of Cincinnati. He was born at Hampden-Sidney, Va., June 19, 1855, a son of the eminent Presbyterian theologian, Dr. Robert L. Dabney, who was Stonewall Jackson's chief of staff and biographer. His mother was Lavinia Morrison Dabney. He was educated at Hampden-Sidney College and at the University of Virginia, and studied also at Berlin and at Göttingen. He married, August 24, 1881, Mary Brent, of Lexington, Ky. He was the first to discover phosphate deposits in Eastern North Carolina and tin ore in Western North Carolina. This was while he was State Chemist and held the chair of chemistry in the university at Chapel Hill. He took a prominent part in establishing an industrial school at Raleigh, now the North Carolina College of Agricultural and Mechanic Arts. He was Assistant Secretary of Agriculture of the United States during the second administration of President Cleveland, and chairman of the Board of Managers of the Government exhibits at the Cotton States and International Exposition at Atlanta in 1895, and of the Tennessee Centennial Exposition in 1897. He is interested in all the problems of education and of Southern development; was president of the University of Tennessee from 1887 to 1904; and then became president of the University of Cincinnati. He has written: 'Reports of the North Carolina Agricultural Experiment Station' (1880-1887), 'Reports of the University of Tennessee Station' (1887-1899), 'Old College and New' (1894) 'A National University' (1895), 'Washington's Interest in Education' (1899), 'History of Agricultural Education' and 'Agriculture and Education.' Both Yale and Johns Hopkins have given him the degree of LL.D. He resides in Cincinnati, Ohio.

DABNEY, RICHARD, poet, was born in Louisa County, Va., of Huguenot parents, the name originally being D'Aubigny; and was the author of a work of some merit entitled: 'Poems, Original and Translated' (Philadelphia, 1815), which passed into two editions. According to Dr. Painter, his literary art is excellent but his range of thought is entirely too restricted.

DABNEY, RICHARD HEATH, educator, was born in Memphis, Tenn., March 29, 1860, the son of Virginius and Maria Heath Dabney. From the University of Virginia he went to Germany to complete his studies (Ph.D., Heidelberg). He was twice married, first to Mary A. Bentley and second to Lily H. Davis. For many years he has been professor of history at the University of Virginia and since 1905 he has been dean of the graduate department. Besides numerous historical and miscellaneous reviews and essays, his writings include: 'The Causes of the French Revolution' (New York, Henry Holt), and 'John Randolph, a Character Sketch.' He also wrote the introduction to Dr. Wayland's work entitled 'The Political Opinions of Thomas Jefferson.'

DABNEY, ROBERT LEWIS. See Biographical and Critical Sketch, Vol. III, page 1143.

DABNEY, VIRGINIUS, author, was born at Elmington, Va., in 1835. On completing his education at the State University, at Charlottesville, he began the practice of law, but he subsequently abandoned the legal profession for the more delightful paths of literature. The War upset his plans. It was his sword instead of his pen which he was called upon to unsheathe; and from 1861 to 1865 he was at the front. In the years which followed his leisure time was limited; but he wrote 'Don Miff,' which numbered four editions in six months, and 'Gold that Did Not Glitter.' Encouraged by his success, he was planning for more ambitious work when death overtook him in 1894.

DAFFAN, KATIE, educator and author, was born in Brenham, Washington County, Texas. For three years she has been president of the Texas Division of the United Daughters of the Confederacy and for two years president of the Texas Woman's Press Association, a dual honor which bears testimony to her talents. She has published several charmingly written volumes, among them, 'Woman in History' (1908), 'Texas Hero Stories' (1908), 'The Woman on the Pine Spring Road' (1909), 'My Friend, the Hypocrite' (1909), and 'Eve, a Biographical Study' (in preparation). She resides at Ennis, Texas.

DAGG, JOHN LEADLEY, theologian and educator, was born at Middleburg, Va., February 13, 1794. For eleven years he was president of Mercer University, at Macon, Ga. He lived to an advanced age and was one of the towers of strength of the Southern Baptist Church. His second wife was the widow of Rev. Noah Davis, the founder of the American Baptist Publication Society, and the mother of Dr. Noah K. Davis. His works include: 'A Manual of Theology' (1858), 'Evidences of Christianity' (1869), 'Elements of Moral Science' (1883), 'Church Order,' and an 'English Grammar,' besides minor works.

DAINGERFIELD, HENRIETTA GRAY, author, was born at Harrisonburg, Va. Her maiden name was Henrietta Gray. She married Foxhall Daingerfield, a major in the Confederate Army, and, after the War, made Kentucky her home. Though a woman of strong domestic ties, she has found time in an active life for many interests, public and philanthropic, and has written three charming little books, 'That Dear Old Sword,' a story for children (Richmond, Presbyterian Committee of Publication), 'Our Mammy, and Other Stories' (Hampton, Va., Hampton Press), and 'Frescati, a Page from Virginia History' (New York and Washington, The Neale Publishing Company).

DALCHO, FREDERICK, physician and clergyman, was born in London, England, in 1770, and died in Charleston, S.C., November 24, 1836. His father was an officer of distinction under Frederick the Great. He came to America at the invitation of an uncle, studied medicine in Baltimore, but located for the practice in Charleston, where he established the botanical gardens. At one time he also edited *The Courier.* Later he was ordained to the Episcopal priesthood and became assistant rector of St. Michael's. He published 'The Evidence of the Divinity of Our Saviour' (Charleston, 1820), an 'Historical Account of the Protestant Episcopal Church in South Carolina' (1820), and 'Ahiman Rezon,' a work for the use of freemasons.

DALSHEIMER, ALICE, poet, was born in New Orleans, La., December 1, 1845. Her maiden name was Solomon. For several years she engaged successfully in teaching and, at leisure intervals, exercised her rare literary gifts by writing short stories and sketches, in addition to several exquisite poems. Most of her work appeared over the pen name of "Sylvia Dale." Unfortunately, her writings have never appeared in book form. Two of her best-known poems are "Motherhood" and "Twilight Shadows." She died in New Orleans, January 15, 1880.

DALY, JOHN AUGUSTIN, manager and playwright, was born in Plymouth, N.C., July 20, 1838. After obtaining an elementary education in Norfolk, Va., he located in New York. where he became manager of the old Fifth Avenue Theater in West Twenty-fourth Street, then of the new Fifth Avenue Theater, at Broadway and Twenty-eighth Street. and finally of the building known as Daly's Theater, at Broadway and Thirtieth Street. He became also a dramatist of international reputation. The long list of plays which he either wrote or remodeled includes the following favorites: "Under the Gas Light," "The Railroad of Love," "Pique," "Seven-Twenty-Eight," "Horizon," "Divorce," "The Great Unknown," "Love on Crutches," and "The Last Word." He also published 'Woffington: a Tribute to the Actress and the Woman' (1888), and numerous sketches. He died in Paris in 1899.

DANA, WILLIAM COOMBS, Presbyterian clergyman, was born in Massachusetts in 1810 and died in South Carolina in 1873. Besides an account of travel entitled 'A Transatlantic Tour,' Dr. Dana published a hymnal for public worship.

DANDRIDGE, DANSKE. See Biographical and Critical Sketch, Vol. III, page 1175.

DANELLEY, ELIZABETH OTIS, Mrs., poet, was born in Georgia in 1838, but afterward removed to Texas and published 'Cactus; or, Thorns and Blossoms,' and 'Wayside Flowers.'

DANFORTH, JOSHUA NOBLE, Congregational clergyman, was born in Massachusetts in 1798 and died in Virginia in 1861. Dr. Danforth published a volume of miscellany entitled 'Gleanings and Groupings from a Pastor's Portfolio,' besides minor works.

"DANGERFIELD, CLINTON." (See Ella Howard Bryan).

DANIEL FERDINAND EUGENE. Medical journalist. He was born in Greenville County, Va., July 18, 1839, a son of R. W. T. and Hester Jordan Adams Daniel. He was educated in the public schools of Vicksburg, Miss., and at the New Orleans School of Medicine. He married, first, Minerva Patrick; second, Fannie Ragsdale Smith; and, third, Josephine Draper. He enlisted in the Confederate Army as a private, but became a surgeon. He practiced medicine and surgery in Galveston, Texas, from 1866 to 1875; at Jackson, Miss., from 1875 to 1880; and in Texas again from 1880 to 1885. He then retired from active practice to establish the *Texas Medical Journal,* which he has since continued to edit. In addition to various monographs, Dr. Daniel has written: 'Recollections of a Rebel Surgeon,' and 'The Strange Case of Dr. Bruno.' He resides in Austin, Texas.

DANIEL, JAMES WALTER, Methodist Episcopal clergyman, was born in Laurens County, S.C., August 27, 1856, of French Huguenot and Scotch-Irish stock. On the paternal side he is connected with the Virginia Harrisons and Daniels. After graduation from Newberry College, he entered the Methodist ministry. For twenty-eight years he has occupied the most prominent pulpits and on the lecture platform has likewise won distinction. He is not only an orator of rare gifts, but an author of entertaining books. During hours of relaxation he has written 'The Girl in Checks' (1886), 'Out From Under Cæsar's Frown' (1888), 'A Ramble Among Surnames' (1894). 'Cateechee of Keeowee,' an Indian legend in blank verse (1896), 'A Maid of the Foot-hills, or the Story of Reconstruction' (1905), and 'Edelano,' another Indian legend in blank verse (1909). He is an authority on names, especially such as the North American Indians have given to localities. Two brothers are likewise ministers, both men of talent. He married, first, in 1880, Emma Hunt; and, second, in 1907, Ethel S. Ragan. He resides in Columbia, S.C.

DANIEL, JOHN MONCURE, an American editor of some note, was born in Stafford County, Va., October 24, 1825. After first studying law he entered journalism, and in consequence of certain caustic editorial expressions which appeared in his paper, the Richmond *Examiner,* he became involved in several duels. In 1853 he was appointed Minister to the court of Victor Emmanuel, but on account of a breach of social etiquette at Turin, he nearly caused a rupture of diplomatic relations, especially in view of the misunderstanding between the United States and Italy, growing out of an issue in regard to naturalized citizens. At the outbreak of the Civil War he served on the staff of Gen. A. P. Hill, but his arm having been shattered, he returned to his editorial chair in Richmond. For harsh strictures upon Mr. Davis and Secretary of the Treasury Elmore, he was challenged by the latter to a duel in which he was wounded. He was a man wholly without fear but somewhat turbulent. He wrote an interesting sketch of Edgar Allan Poe for the *Southern Literary Messenger;* and his 'Writings' were edited after his death by his brother (New York, 1868). He died in Richmond, Va., March 30, 1865.

DANIEL, JOHN WARWICK. United States Senator. He was born in Lynchburg, Va., September 5, 1842, and was educated at Lynchburg College, also at Dr. Gessner Harrison's University School. He served in the Confederate Army four years, becoming chief of General Early's staff, and lost a limb on the battlefield of the Wilderness. He studied law at the University of Virginia. He was defeated for governor of Virginia, but was subsequently sent to Congress and afterward to the United States Senate, of which body he is still a member. In the upper branch of the national Legislature he is one of the most picturesque and dramatic figures. Four times he has been honored with reëlections; and though on occasions he has differed with his party on public issues, his courageous fidelity to principle and his lofty type of statesmanship have made him invincible before the people. As an orator, Senator Daniel has no superior in public life. At the dedication at the national capital of the great obelisk to Washington, Senator Daniel was Virginia's spokesman and orator and the speech which he delivered is one of the classics of American eloquence. Still another masterpiece is his eulogium upon Jefferson Davis. Senator Daniel has also been chosen to make the address on the unveiling of the statue of Robert E. Lee, in Statuary Hall, in Washington. He is the author of two important law books: 'Attachments Under the Law of Virginia' and 'Negotiable Instruments.' In recognition of his eminent attainments the degree of LL.D. has been conferred upon him by Washington and Lee University. Forced to use a crutch, he is sometimes called "the Lame Lion of Lynchburg," an affectionate epithet which embalms his fidelity to the Lost Cause. He resides in Lynchburg, Va.

DANIEL, ROBERT THOMAS. [N.C.]. Assisted by Mrs. Hardy M. Sanders, he compiled a 'Selection of Hymns and Spiritual Songs,' some eighty of which were original (Raleigh, Thomas Henderson, 1812).

DANIEL, ROYAL, journalist, was born in Newnan, Ga., September 12, 1870. Most of his life has been devoted to journalistic work and for some time past he has been on the staff of the Atlanta *Journal.* He is an authority on psychological questions; and, besides numerous contributions to the press, he is the author of a volume entitled: 'The Twilight of Consciousness,' which appeared in 1909, creating quite an impression.

DANIELS, CORA LINN. Author. This Southern lady published a work which deals with the philosophy of life after death, entitled 'As It Is to Be' (Boston, Little, Brown and Company, 1903).

DANIELS, JOSEPHUS, editor, was born in Washington, N.C., May 18, 1862. For nearly fifteen years he has been editor of the Raleigh *News and Observer,* and an influential factor in North Carolina politics.

He married, May 2, 1888, Addie W. Bagley. Besides numerous editorials and essays, he has published 'The First Fallen Hero in the Spanish-American War,' a sketch of Worth Bagley, Ensign, U.S.N. (1898).

DARBY, JOHN F. Author. He lived in Missouri and published in 1880, a volume entitled: 'Personal Recollections,' in which many racy anecdotes of the early days of the State are narrated (St. Louis, G. I. Jones and Company).

DARBY, WILLIAM, geographer, was born in Pennsylvania in 1775, but was an officer under General Jackson in Louisiana, where he resided for some time; and published a 'Geographical Description of Louisiana' (1816), an 'Emigrants' Guide to the Western Country' (1818), and a 'Geography and History of Florida' (1821).

DARDEN, FANNIE A. D., Mrs. Author. Her maiden name was Baker. She was born in Alabama, but afterward removed to Texas. Her publications include 'The Comanche Boy' and 'The Old Brigade, and Other Poems.'

DARGAN, EDWIN CHARLES. Professor in the Southern Baptist Theological Seminary, Louisville, Ky., clergyman and educator. He was born in Darlington County, S.C., November 17, 1852, a son of Dr. John O. B. and Jane Frances Lide Dargan. He was educated at Furman University and at the Southern Baptist Theological Seminary and married, June 12, 1878, Lucy A. Graves, of Orange County, Va. He has held numerous important pastorates, including the Citadel Square Baptist Church, of Charleston, S.C. In 1892 he accepted the chair which he still occupies in the Southern Baptist Theological Seminary. Both as preacher and as lecturer he has demonstrated great power. Included among his published writings are: 'Notes on Colossians' (Philadelphia, American Baptist Publication Society), 'Ecclesiology,' 'A History of Preaching,' 'The Doctrines of Our Faith,' and 'Society, Kingdom and Church' (Philadelphia, American Baptist Publication Society, 1907). He has also edited the revised edition of 'Broadus on Preparation and Delivery of Sermons.' Washington and Lee gave him the degree of D.D. and Baylor University the degree of LL.D.

DARGAN, JOHN J. Historian. [S.C.]. Colonel Dargan published an excellent 'General History of South Carolina,' besides a textbook for school purposes.

DARGAN, OLIVE TILFORD. See Biographical and Critical Sketch, Vol. III, page 1195.

D'AVEZAC, AUGUSTE GENEVIEVE VALENTIN. Lawyer. He was born on the island of St. Domingo in 1777, but during his childhood he was brought to Louisiana by his parents, who were refugees from the massacres. On completing his education in France, he settled in New Orleans and studied for the Bar under his brother-in-law, Edward Livingston. He became an advocate of great power, especially in criminal trials; and, under General Jackson, he was made Judge Advocate of the Army, at the time of the British invasion. Espousing the political fortunes of "Old Hickory," he afterward became Secretary of Legation and Chargé d'Affaires at The Hague. He wrote 'Recollections of Edward Livingston.' He died in New York, February 16, 1851.

DAVID, JEAN BAPTISTE, Roman Catholic bishop, was born near Nantes, France, in 1761, and died in Bardstown, Ky., in 1841. Bishop David established a college and published numerous theological works, including a 'Vindication of the Catholic Doctrine Concerning the Use and Veneration of Images,' an 'Address to the Brethren of Other Professions,' 'On the Rule of Faith,' 'True Piety, or the Day Well Spent,' and a Catholic hymn-book.

DAVID, URBAIN. Writer. [La.]. He published a work entitled: 'Les Anglais à la Louisiane en 1814-1815' (1845), an interesting contribution to the literature of the second war with England.

DAVIDSON, JAMES WOOD. Editor and educator. He was born in Newberry County, S.C., March 9, 1829, the son of Alexander and Sarah Davidson and was educated at South Carolina College. Before the war he taught the ancient languages. He was adjutant of the Thirteenth Regiment of South Carolina Volunteers in Stonewall Jackson's corps. After the war he entered journalism, going first to Washington and afterward to New York, where for eleven years he edited the *Evening Post*. He married Josephine Allen in 1884 and moved to Florida. He served in the State Constitutional Convention and also in the State Legislature and was in the Treasury Department at Washington for a time. Among his works are included: 'The Living Writers of the South,' 'A School History of South Carolina,' 'The Correspondent,' 'The Poetry of the Future,' and 'The Florida of To-day.' His style as a writer is characterized by choice and elegant diction and by unusual vigor and penetration of thought. At the time of his death he was compiling a 'Dictionary of Southern Authors.' He died in 1905.

DAVIDSON, ROBERT, clergyman and educator, was born in Elkton, Md., in 1750. For many years he was vice-president of Dickinson College, at Carlisle, Pa.; and, on the death of Dr. Nisbet, in 1804, became president. He was also an eminent Presbyterian divine. Besides numerous sermons, he published in verse 'An Epitome of Geography' (1784), 'The Christian's A B C' (1811), and 'The New Metrical Version of the Psalms' (1812). He died December 13, 1812.

DAVIES, SAMUEL D. Author. [Va.]. He published an interesting critique entitled 'Novels and Novel Writing.'

DAVIESS, JOSEPH HAMILTON, lawyer, was born in Bedford County, Va., March 4, 1774, and was killed in the battle of Tippecanoe, November 7, 1811. He married a sister of Chief Justice Marshall. As United States District Attorney for Kentucky, it devolved upon him to prosecute Aaron Burr. The failure of the Government to establish the guilt of the noted prisoner made him temporarily unpopular and even the subsequent exposure of the plot failed to restore him to complete favor. To vindicate himself, therefore, he published 'A View of the President's Conduct Concerning the Conspiracy of 1806.'

DAVIESS, MARIA THOMPSON, Mrs. Author. [Ky.]. She was born in 1814 and published 'Roger Sherman, a Tale of '76,' 'Woman's Love,' and a volume of 'Poems.'

DAVIESS, MARIA THOMPSON. Artist and author. Miss Daviess is a native of Harrodsburg, Ky. She has published several short stories of fascinating interest, among them, "Miss Selina Sue and the Soap-Box Babies," "Sue Saunders of Saunders Ridge" and "Some Juniors." She resides in Nashville, Tenn.

DAVIS, DUDLEY H. Poet and merchant. [W. Va.]. He published two volumes of verse entitled: 'Songs of the Age' (Baltimore, 1891), illustrated, and 'The Kingdom Gained, and Other Poems' (Richmond, 1896).

DAVIS, GARRETT M. Author. [Ky.]. He wrote, in the style of Cooper, an interesting story for boys, entitled: 'In the Footsteps of Boone' (New York and Washington, The Neale Publishing Company, 1905).

DAVIS, GEORGE. See Biographical and Critical Sketch, Vol. III, page 1225.

DAVIS, GEORGE L. L. Historian. [Md.]. He wrote a 'History of Maryland.'

DAVIS, HENRY WINTER, statesman, was born at Annapolis, Md., August 16, 1817, and died in Baltimore, Md., December 30, 1865. Choosing the profession of the law, he became one of the foremost advocates at the Maryland Bar; and from 1855 to 1865 he served in Congress, barring an interval of one term. On account of his position upon certain questions. he incurred the censure of his constituents; but he refused to surrender his convictions and retorted in language that was more positive than diplomatic. He became an avowed Unionist and was offered the nomination for Vice-president on the ticket with Mr. Lincoln, but declined. He wrote 'The War of Ormuzd and Ahriman in the Nineteenth Century' (Baltimore, 1853). His speeches were published after his death, with an introductory tribute from his colleague, John A. J. Cresswell (New York, 1867).

DAVIS, JEFFERSON. See Biographical and Critical Sketch, Vol. III, page 1243.

DAVIS, JOHN, poet, was one of the earliest of the colonial minstrels. Though a foreigner by birth, he became an adopted son of South Carolina, and on the authority of Mr. Ludwig Lewisohn. his 'Sonnet to the Whippoorwill' was probably the first production of the kind in the Palmetto State. He published in pamphlet form a number of poems and a copy of the little duodecimo is preserved in the library of the College of Charleston. In view of the remote period at which he wrote, the merit of his work is most pronounced. He always styled himself "John Davis, of Coosawhatchie."

DAVIS, JOHN A. G., lawyer, was born in Middlesex County, Va., in 1801, and died in Williamsburg, Va., November 14, 1840. For some time he was professor of law at the University of Virginia. He died from a pistol-shot wound inflicted by a student whom he was endeavoring to arrest under the rules of the institution. Included among his works are: 'Estates in Tail, Executory Devices, and Contingent Remainders Under the Virginia Statutes Modifying the Common Law' and 'Guide to Justices of the Peace.'

DAVIS, MARGARET ELLEN O'BRIEN, Mrs. Author. [Ala.]. She was born in 1870 and died in 1898. Though her pen was sheathed before she attained her intellectual prime, she produced several works of fiction which attest the high order of her gifts; among them, 'Judith, the Daughter of Judas,' a romance of the time of Nero (1891), 'John Landon, Gentleman' (1893), 'The Squire' (1894), and 'Told by the Woman' (1896), besides a number of poems. She lived in Birmingham, Ala.

DAVIS, MARTHA ANN. Poet. She published a volume of verse entitled: 'The Poems of Laura, an Original American Work' (Petersburg, Va., 1818), which contains some crude but poetic touches and is pervaded by an atmosphere of the fireside.

DAVIS, MARY EVELYN MOORE. See Biographical and Critical Sketch, Vol. III, page 1273.

DAVIS, MINNIE S. Novelist and lecturer. [Md.]. She was born in 1835. Besides minor works she wrote 'Marion Lester' (1850) and 'Clinton Forest' (1858).

DAVIS, NOAH KNOWLES. See Biographical and Critical Sketch, Vol. III, page 1309.

DAVIS, REUBEN, jurist and lawyer, was born in Tullahoma, Tenn., January 18, 1813, but removed to Mississippi, became prominent on the Bench, served in Congress from 1857 to 1861, and attained the rank of brigadier-general on the Confederate side of the struggle that ensued. He published 'Recollections of Mississippi and Mississippians' (Boston, 1889).

DAVIS, ROBERT MEANS, educator and editor, was born in Fairfield District, S.C., April 9, 1849, and died in Columbia, S.C., March 13, 1904. For twenty-three years he filled the chair of history and political economy in South Carolina College. He wielded an accomplished pen and made frequent contributions to current periodicals. Some of his work is preserved in Wauchopes' 'Writers of South Carolina' (Columbia, The State Company, 1909).

DAVIS, VARINA ANNE JEFFERSON. See Biographical and Critical Sketch, Vol. III, page 1333.

DAVIS, VARINA HOWELL. See Biographical and Critical Sketch, Vol. III, page 1349.

DAWSON, EDGAR, educator, was born in Scottsville, Va., December 22, 1872. For several years he was preceptor in history at Princeton. He now heads the department of history in the Normal College of the City of New York. Besides magazine articles and reviews, he is the author of an interesting volume of criticism entitled 'Byron and Moore.' The sketch of James Madison in 'The Library of Southern Literature' is also from his pen. He received the degree of Ph.D. from Leipsic.

DAWSON, FRANCIS WARRINGTON. See Biographical and Critical Sketch, Vol. III, page 1369.

DAWSON, FRANCIS WARRINGTON, editor, was born in London, England, May 17, 1840, and died in Charleston, S.C., the victim of an unexplained homicide, May 12, 1889. He served under Longstreet in the Gettysburg and East Tennessee Campaigns, attained high distinction in journalism and edited for some time the Charleston *News and Courier.* On account of his splendid service to public morals in the suppression of duelling, he was knighted by Leo XIII. One of his editorials entitled 'The Cash-Shannon Duel' is preserved in Wauchope's 'Writers of South Carolina' (Columbia, The State Company, 1909). In earlier life, Captain Dawson published several comedies.

DAWSON, WILLIAM C., jurist and statesman, was born in Greene County, Ga., January 4, 1798, and died at Greensboro, Ga., May 5, 1856. He was a lawyer of distinction. From 1836 to 1842 he served in Congress; and from 1849 to 1855 he was United States Senator. He was also at one time judge of the Ocmulgee Circuit. He published 'Laws of Georgia.' His speeches, which have been preserved in the 'Debates of Congress, show him to have been a man of unusual vigor of mind.

DAY, S. A., Mrs. ("Helen Hamilton Gardener"). Author. She was born in Winchester, Va., January 21, 1858, a daughter of the Rev. Alfred G. and Katherine Chenoweth. She received an excellent education, including post-graduate work in biology and medicine, in New York. She married, in 1901, Colonel S. A. Day, U.S.A., retired. She is an authority on questions of heredity. Besides numerous scientific articles, she has written many stories and sketches for the magazines. She has also written some excellent essays. Her works include: 'Men, Women, and Gods,' a volume of essays (New York, Truth Seeker Company); 'Facts and Fictions of Life'; 'Is This Your Son, My Lord?' 'Pray You, Sir, Whose Daughter?' (New York, R. F. Fenno and Company); 'Unseen Hands' (*ibid.*); 'A Thoughtless Yes' (*ibid.*); 'An Unofficial Patriot' (*ibid.*), this being a novel of the Civil War, and 'Historical Sketches of the United States Navy.' She is active in movements for the progress and development of her sex and for social and ethical reform. She resides in New York City.

DAYTON, AMOS COOPER, physician and clergyman, was born in Plainfield, N.J., September 4, 1813; but, soon after equipping himself for the practice of medicine, he settled in the South. Later, he adopted the ministerial profession, becoming first a Presbyterian and afterward a Baptist. He wrote two religious novels which were widely read at the time: 'Theodosia' and 'The Infidel's Daughter.' He died at Perry, Ga., June 11, 1865.

DEAS, ANNE IZARD. Editor. [S.C.]. Her maiden name was Anne Izard. She was the daughter of Ralph Izard, one of South Carolina's first United States Senators. She published, with a memoir, her father's 'Correspondence, 1774-1784,' a work of much interest covering the period of the American Revolution (Boston, 1844).

DEBOUCHEL, VICTOR. Author. [La.]. He wrote in French and published an interesting 'Histoire de la Louisiana' (New Orleans, 1841).

DE BOW, JAMES DUNWODY BROWNSON, editor and statistician, was born in Charleston, S.C., July 10, 1820, and died in Elizabeth, N. J., February 27, 1867. Though admitted to the Bar, his time was almost wholly devoted to literary pursuits; and after editing for several years the *Southern Quarterly Review*, he removed to New Orleans, where he established *DeBow's Commercial Review*. He also filled at one time the chair of political economy in the University of Louisiana, a position which he relinquished to become superintendent of the census. Early in his career he wrote an article on "Oregon and the Oregon Question," which attracted wide attention. He also published an 'Encyclopædia of the Trade and Commerce of the United States' in two volumes (1852), 'The Industrial Resources and Statistics of the Southwest,' in three volumes (1853), 'The Southern States in Commerce and Agriculture' (1854), and a work on mortuary statistics, besides minor publications.

DEEMS, CHARLES FORCE. Clergyman and editor. For many years he was the eloquent pastor of the Church of the Strangers in the city of New York. He was born in Baltimore, Md., in 1820; and, after graduating from Dickinson College, he became a professor in the University of North Carolina and at Randolph-Macon, and later president of Greensboro Female College. Besides writing constantly for his church periodicals, he edited five volumes of 'The Southern Methodist Pulpit' and three volumes of 'Southern Methodism,' and published two volumes of verse entitled: 'Triumphs of Peace, and Other Poems,' and 'Devotional Melodies.' His numerous other works include: 'Sermons to Young Men,' 'The Home Altar,' 'Weights and Wings,' 'Jesus: A Work on the Life of Christ,' 'Chips and Chunks for Every Fireside,' 'My Septuagint,' and 'The Life of Dr. Adam Clarke,' 'The Light of the Nations,' 'A Scotch Verdict in Evolution,' 'A Gospel of Common Sense,' 'The Gospel of Spiritual Insight,' and 'Studies in the Gospel of John.' He died in 1893. Randolph-Macon University gave him the degree of D.D., and the University of North Carolina, the degree of LL.D.

DEEMS, EDWARD MARK, clergyman and author, was born in Greensboro, N.C., April 22, 1852, the son of Dr. Charles F. Deems, the noted divine. After receiving his education at Princeton, he was ordained to the ministry of the Presbyterian Church and has since occupied Northern pulpits. He wrote: 'Memoirs of Charles Force Deems, D.D., LL.D.' (New York and Chicago, Fleming H. Revell Company), and 'Holy Days and Holidays' (New York, Funk and Wagnalls). He received his D.D. from Alfred University and his Ph.D. from the University of the City of New York.

DEERING, JOHN R. Author. He served in the Confederate Army and made an interesting contribution to the literature of the Civil War in a work entitled 'Lee and His Cause; or the Why and How of the War Between the States' (New York and Washington, The Neale Publishing Company, 1906).   :-

DE GRAFFENREIDT, CHRISTOPHER, Baron. He was born in Switzerland but came to America and published an interesting 'Narrative,' in which he gives an account of the Swiss colony at New Bern, N.C.

DEHON, THEODORE, Protestant Episcopal bishop, was born in Boston, Mass., December 8, 1776, and died in Charleston, S.C., August 6, 1817. For two years he was rector of St. Michael's Church, in Charleston, after which he was consecrated bishop of South Carolina; but he fell an early victim to yellow fever. Several of his sermons were collected after his death and published in book form (London, 1821; New York, 1857).

DEILER, JOHN HANNO. An eminent teacher of German, connected for years with the University of Louisiana and with Tulane University at New Orleans. He was born in Upper Bavaria, August 8, 1849, the son of Konrad Deiler, took a course of instruction at the Royal Normal College at Freising and also studied at the Royal Polytechnic Institute, Munich. He married, December 9, 1872, Wilhelmina Saganowski. He was principal of the German School of New Orleans, for several years, and the founder of German archives and of German vocal music societies in New Orleans. On December 15, 1898, he was made Knight of the Order of the Prussian Crown. He has written numerous German books and made frequent contributions to German periodicals.

DEJACQUE, JOSEPH. Author. [La.]. He wrote in French both prose and verse and published 'Les Lazareenes' and other works (1857).

DEJEANS, ELIZABETH (Mrs. E. J. Budgette). She is the author of a novel entitled: 'The Winning Chance' (Philadelphia, J. B. Lippincott Company, 1909), which deals with one of the most delicate of modern problems.

DE KAY, CHARLES, author, was born in Washington, D.C., July 25, 1848. For fifteen years he was literary editor and art *critic* of the New York *Times;* and, during President Cleveland's second administration, he was Consul-general at Berlin. He is a graceful writer both of prose and of verse. Several volumes have come from his pen, among them, 'The Bohemian,' 'Hesperus, and Other Poems,' 'Bird Gods, a Study of Myths and Religions in Ancient Europe,' "Essays on Ancient Ireland," in the *Century Magazine;* "Wonders of the Alphabet," in *St. Nicholas;* 'Love Poems of Louis Barnaval,' 'Life and Works of Barye, Sculptor,' 'Family Letters of Heinrich Heine,' translated from the German, two dramatic poems, "The Vision of Nimrod" and "The Vision of Esther," and several translations from the French of 'Alphonse Daudet.' He resides in New York.

DELAWARE, LORD (Thomas West). Governor of Virginia. He succeeded his father as the third Lord Delaware in 1602, and in 1609 received his appointment as governor and captain-general of Virginia. For nine years he resided in the colony and on returning to England in 1618 he died at sea. He published in 1611 'A True Relation to the Colony of Virginia,' which was reprinted in 1858.

DE LEON, EDWIN, diplomat and editor, was born in Columbia, S.C., in 1828. For several years he was engaged in editorial work chiefly in Washington, D.C., after which he became diplomatic agent in Europe and still later Consul-general in Cairo. His published works, which show him to have been a man of exceptional talents, include: 'Thirty Years of My Life on Three Continents,' 'The Khedive's Egypt,' 'Askaros Kassis, the Captain,' a novel, and 'Under the Star and Under the Crescent.' He died in 1891. Thomas Cooper De Leon, the author, is a younger brother.

DE LEON, THOMAS COOPER. Journalist, author, playwright. He was born in Columbia, S.C., May 21, 1839, a son of Dr. M. H. De Leon and was educated in the best schools, culminating with Georgetown College in the District of Columbia. He served in the Confederate Army from 1861 to 1865, and later became prominent in journalism, first in Baltimore, afterward in New York, and then in Mobile. He organized the Mobile Mardi Gras Carnival and managed it successfully for twenty-five years. From 1867 to 1873 he was sole editor of the Mobile *Register.* In 1897 he relinquished active journalism for literary work and, besides occasional appearances on the lecture platform, he has produced numerous dramas and novels of high merit. His comedy-drama, "Pluck," was produced by Lawrence Barrett in 1873; and this was followed by other plays which proved to be equally popular. Among his best-known novels are: 'Creole and Puritan,' 'The Pride of the Mercers,' 'Crag's Nest,' and 'The Puritan's Daughter.' He has also written a 'Life of Joseph Wheeler,' 'Four Years in Rebel Capitals,' 'Confederate Memories,' 'History of Creole Carnivals,' and 'Belles and Beaux of the 'Sixties.' He has also written some excellent verse, contributed many short stories to the periodicals, and made several translations. He resides in Mobile, Ala.

DELERY, FRANCOIS CHARLES, physician, was born in St. Charles Parish, La., January 28, 1815, and died in Bay St. Louis, Miss., June 12, 1880. He was educated in the medical schools of Paris, but located in New Orleans for the practice of his profession, became an eminent physician, and published a number of volumes in French, besides contributing to the newspapers.

DELPIT, ALBERT. Playwright and novelist. He was born in New Orleans, La., January 30, 1849, but, being sent by his father to France to be educated in the schools of Bordeaux and Paris, he formed attachments which made him choose the French capital as the arena of his future activities, and he returned to this country only for the purpose of adjusting his affairs. His success in Paris was pronounced.

His "Éloge de Lamartine," published in 1870, and his book of poems entitled 'L'Invasion,' published in 1872, both won prizes; and his poem "Le Repentir," written a year later, was crowned. He next essayed the dramatic rôle, and was equally successful. Several plays came from his pen, all of which were duly staged. But his greatest triumphs were reserved for the field of romance. Beginning with 'Les Compagnons du Roi,' in 1873, and ending with 'Mademoiselle de Brassier,' in 1888, he wrote about a dozen novels which brought him an international reputation. He died in New Orleans, January 4, 1893.

DEMENIL, ALEXANDER N. Physician. [Mo.]. He published a 'History of the Literature of Louisiana Territory' (St. Louis, 1904).

DE MILLE, HENRY CHURCHILL. Writer. He was born in Washington, N.C., in 1850, graduated at Columbia University in 1875, and in 1882 began to write plays for the Madison Square Theater in New York City. His dramatic works include 'Duty. or, Delmar's Daughters,' 'Sealed Instructions,' 'The Lost Paradise,' 'The Main Line,' and, in collaboration with Mr. David Belasco, 'The Wife,' 'The Charity Ball,' 'May Blossom,' 'Lord Chumley,' and 'Men and Women.' He died in Pompton, N. J., February 5, 1893. He married Matilda Beatrice Samuels, of London, England, and their elder son is William Churchill De Mille, the successful young author of 'The Warrens of Virginia,' 'Strongheart,' etc.

DENHURST, W. W. Historian. [Fla.]. He wrote a 'History of St. Augustine.'

DENNIS, JAMES TEACKLE. Writer and traveler. He published a work entitled 'On the Shores of an Inland Sea,' in which he tells of his sojourn in Alaska.

DENNY, GEORGE HUTCHESON. President of Washington and Lee University. He was born in Hanover County, Va., December 3, 1870, the son of Dr. George H. and Charlotte Denny, and was educated at Hampden-Sidney College. He married, June 1, 1899, Janie Junkin Strickler. He taught at Pantops Academy, Charlottesville, for four years, and afterward became professor of Latin and German at Hampden-Sidney College. He was made president of Washington and Lee University in 1902 and two years later became a member of the Board of Trustees of the Carnegie Foundation. Besides editing 'Cicero's Letters,' he has published 'The Subjunctive Sequence After Adjective and Substantive Predicates and Phrases.' He is one of the consulting editors of 'The Library of Southern Literature,' for which work he wrote the sketch of Robert E. Lee. The University of Virginia gave him the degree of Ph.D. and Furman University, the degree of LL.D.

DENNY, MARIE LOUISE. Author. [Texas]. She wrote an interesting story of an Alabama family in Texas, entitled 'The Doctor and the Parson' (New York and Washington, The Neale Publishing Company, 1905).

DERRY, JOSEPH TYRONE. Historian. He was born at Milledgeville, Ga., December 13, 1841, and was educated at Emory College. During the Civil War he was a member of the Oglethorpe Infantry. He taught from 1865 to 1900, and was professor of languages and history at Richmond Academy for seven years, and professor of languages and history at Wesleyan Female College for seventeen years. He married, August 5, 1862, Elizabeth D. Osborne. His writings evince the marks of thorough scholarship. They include: 'Catechetical History

of the United States'; 'Georgia's Cities, Towns, Scenery, and Resources' (1878); 'History of the United States for Schools and Academies' (1880); 'The Story of the Confederate States' (1895), the
Georgia volume in 'The Confederate Military History,' and the chapter
on "Georgia" in 'The South in the Building of the Nation.' He is also
the author of an epic poem entitled "The Strife of Brothers," which
narrates in dramatic verse the story of the Confederate struggle.
Nearly all the sketches of battles and skirmishes described in the
'Encyclopædia of Georgia' are from the pen of Professor Derry, in
addition to which he has written numerous sketches for other publications. He is also editor and compiler of 'Georgia, Historical and
Industrial' and 'Georgia's Resources and Advantages.' He resides in
Atlanta, Ga.

DE SAUSSURE, HENRY WILLIAM, jurist, was born in Poco-
taligo, S.C., August 16, 1763, and died in Charleston, S.C., March 29,
1839. As director of the United States Mint, under Washington, he
coined the first gold eagles that bore the American stamp. From 1809
to 1829 he was Chancellor of South Carolina, resigning the office on
account of impaired health. He published 'Reports of the Court of
Chancery and Court of Equity of South Carolina from the Revolution
to 1813.' While on the Bench he handed down 1,314 decisions.

DE SAUSSURE, WILMOT GIBBES, lawyer, was born in
Charleston, S.C., July 23, 1822; graduated from South Carolina College in 1840, and was admitted to the Bar. At the time of the
bombardment of Fort Sumter, he was in command of the artillery on
Morris Island. He was a man of rare culture and of peculiar eloquence.
His published addresses include: 'The Stamp Act of Great Britain and
the Resistance of the Colonies,' 'The Causes Which Led to the Surrender of Cornwallis at Yorktown,' 'The Centennial Celebration of the
Organization of the Cincinnati,' 'Memoir of General William Moultrie,' and 'The Muster Roll of the South Carolina of the Continental Line
and Militia.' Just before his death he prepared an address on the celebration by the Huguenot Society of America of the bi-centennial anniversary of the revocation of the Edict of Nantes. He died February
1, 1886.

DES LONDE, MARIE, Mrs. Author. [La.]. She wrote a
novel entitled 'The Miller of Silcot Hill' (1878).

DESSOMMES, EDWARD. Educator and author. He was born
in New Orleans, La., November 17, 1845. After completing his classical education in France, he studied medicine. But his passion for
authorship made him seize the pen. His first novel, entitled 'Femme
et Statue,' which was published in 1869, elicited from Victor Hugo,
who was then an exile at Guernsey, a compliment of unusual warmth.
This was followed by another romance entitled 'Jacques Morel.' After
the Franco-Prussian War he studied painting under two eminent
masters, and some of his work was placed on exhibition in the Paris
Salon. In 1887 he returned to New Orleans and entered the faculty
of Tulane University, occupying a chair in the department of French.

DESSOMMES, GEORGE. Author. [La.]. He published in
French a work entitled 'Tante Cydette' (New Orleans, 1888).

DEVEREUX, THOMAS POLLOCK, lawyer, was born in New
Bern, N.C., December 17, 1793, and died in Connemara, N.C., March
24, 1869. For many years he was United States District Attorney for
North Carolina and afterward Supreme Court reporter. On the death
of an uncle, he fell heir to an immense estate and the remainder of his

days were spent on his plantation. He published 'Reports of the North Carolina Supreme Court, 1826-1834,' four volumes; 'Reports in the Superior Courts, 1834-1840,' four volumes, and 'Equity Reports, 1826-1840,' four volumes.

DEVOL, GEORGE H. He wrote a story of his adventures entitled 'Forty Years a Gambler on the Mississippi' (New York, 1887).

DEW, THOMAS RODERICK, educator, was born in King and Queen County, Va., December 5, 1802, and died in Paris, France, August 6, 1846. For several years he was professor of history, metaphysics, and political economy in William and Mary College, becoming president in 1836 and holding this office until his death, which occurred while he was traveling in Europe with his bride. His published works include: 'The Policy of the Government,' 'An Essay in Favor of Slavery,' 'A Digest of the Laws, Customs, Manners, and Institutions of Ancient and Modern Nations,' a treatise on the history of the world from the earliest times to the period of the French Revolution.

DEWEY, BYRD SPILMAN. Author. She was born in Covington, Ky, February 16, 1856, a daughter of Dr. J. E. and Eliza Sarah Taylor Spilman; and grandniece of President Zachary Taylor. She was educated in the local schools of Maysville, Ky., and at Sayre Institute, Lexington, Ky. On September 25, 1877, she married Frederick Sidney Dewey. Since 1881 she has resided on the shore of Lake Worth, in Dade County, Fla. She has done some excellent literary work; and, in addition to numerous contributions to the periodicals, she has published 'Bruno' (Boston, Little, Brown and Company) and other volumes. Her Florida address is West Palm Beach.

DEVRON, GUSTAVUS. Physician and surgeon. [La.]. He wrote several important volumes, among them 'Abattoirs' (Boston, 1881), 'The Story of Medicine in Louisiana' (New Orleans, 1895), and 'Montezuma and Studies in Louisiana History.'

DEWHURST, WILLIAM W. Author. [Fla.]. He wrote a 'History of St. Augustine' (1881).

DICKERT, D. A. Soldier and author. [S.C.]. He published a 'History of Kershaw's Brigade.'

DICKISON, J. J., soldier and author, was born in Virginia, received his education in South Carolina, and located in Florida, from which state he went to the front at the outbreak of the Civil War. As an officer of cavalry he was entrusted with the defence of the eastern part of Florida and the commission was most worthily bestowed. He wrote the volume on Florida for the 'Confederate Military History' (Atlanta, Ga. The Confederate Publishing Company, 1899). By his comrades in arms he was made commander of the United Confederate Veterans of Florida with the rank of major-general.

DICKISON, MARY ELIZABETH, Mrs., author, was born in South Carolina. Mrs. Dickison has written the story of her husband's campaigns in a work entitled 'Dickison and His Men.' She also assisted in the preparation of the Florida volume of the 'Confederate Military History' (Atlanta, Ga., The Confederate Publishing Company, 1899). Her home is in Ocala, Fla.

DICKSON, ANDREW FLINN, clergyman, was born in Charleston, S.C., November 9, 1825, and died at Tuscaloosa, Ala., in 1879. Educated at Yale, he entered the Presbyterian ministry and became an influential divine, giving much of his time toward the close of his life to religious work among the negroes. He published 'Plantation Sermons,' 'The Temptation in the Desert,' and 'The Light, Is It Waning?' which gained a prize offered by Richard Fletcher.

DICKSON, HARRIS. See Biographical and Critical Sketch, Vol. III, page 1387.

DICKSON, S. O'H., Miss. Writer. [N.C.]. She published a volume of verse entitled 'Poems' (Richmond, Whittet and Shepperson, 1900), besides several novels, including 'Howard McPhlinn,' 'The Story of Marthy,' and 'Reuben Dilton.'

DICKSON, SAMUEL HENRY, physician and educator, was born in Charleston, S.C., September 20, 1798, and died in Philadelphia, Pa., March 31, 1872. He became an eminent practitioner of medicine in Charleston and afterward taught in the University of New York and in Jefferson Medical College in Philadelphia. He wrote in an elegant style not only on professional but on literary topics. Besides numerous medical works, including 'The Elements of Medicine,' 'The Practice of Medicine,' 'Essays on Pathology and Therapeutics,' he delivered an address at Yale on 'The Pursuit of Happiness,' and published a volume of verse and a pamphlet on the essential inferiority of the negro. The University of New York made him an LL.D.

DIDIER, EUGENE LEMOINE, author, was born in Baltimore, Md., in 1838. His father was Dr. Franklin James Didier and his mother Julia Lemoine. On completing his education, which was obtained partly under tutors and partly at Loyola College, he entered mercantile life; but he soon relinquished commerce for literature, a change which was more congenial to his finer temperament. Incidentally, after an apprenticeship to journalism, he became deputy-marshal of the United States Supreme Court and special secretary to Chief Justice Chase. His contributions to letters have been of great interest and value, including: 'The Life of Edgar Allan Poe,' 'The Life and Letters of Madame Bonaparte' (New York, Charles Scribner's Sons), which was translated into French and Italian; 'The Primer of Criticism,' and 'The Political Adventures of James G. Blaine,' and others. As a writer he is vigorous and lucid; as a critic, fearless and exact. To the leading periodicals of the day he has also made frequent and important contributions. His wife was Miss Louise Northrop, daughter of General L. B. Northrop. He resides in Baltimore, Md.

DIDIER, FRANKLIN JAMES, an eminent physician of Baltimore, Md., was born in 1794 and died in 1840. To the periodicals of the day, he made frequent contributions; and, years before the Civil War, he predicted the bloody clash between the rival forces within the Union. For some time he resided in France; and his wife was Julia Lemoine. He wrote: 'Didier Letters From Paris,' and 'Franklin's Letters to his Kinsfolk.'

DILLARD, JAMES HARDY. Educator, and Dean of the Academic Colleges of Tulane University. He was born in Nansemond County, Va., October 24, 1856, and was educated at Washington and Lee University. He has edited 'Selections from Wordsworth,' 'Fifty Letters of Cicero' (Boston, Ginn and Company, 1900), 'Favorite German Poems' (New York, American Book Company, 1903), and other works. Besides, he has published 'Arithmetic Exercises,' and made numerous contributions to the periodicals on educational and economic subjects. Washington and Lee University gave him the degree of Litt.D. He resides in New Orleans, La.

DILLON, MARY. Author. [Mo.]. She has published two historical novels of exceptional interest: 'The Rose of Old St. Louis' (New York, Doubleday, Page and Company, 1907), and 'The Patience of John Morland' (*ibid.*, 1909), the latter a story based upon the sensational dissolution of President Andrew Jackson's Cabinet caused by Peggy O'Neill.

DIMITRY, ALEXANDER. Diplomat and educator. He was born in New Orleans, February 7, 1805. Due to his linguistic accomplishments, he was made translator in the State Department at Washington, D.C. Three years later he became United States Minister to Costa Rica and Nicaragua; but he resigned this position in 1861 because his sympathies were with the South in the national crisis. He held official position under the Confederate Government; and in 1868 became professor of ancient languages in a college at Pass Christian, Miss. He is credited with having organized the free school system of Louisiana. In the prime of life he wrote an elaborate 'History of English Names,' which was unfortunately destroyed by fire. James R. Randall, the famous poet, considered him a master of composition. Said he: "There was something absent from the professor's nature that meaner creatures possess and utilize; and so his grand Grecian form and intellect pass away, almost without a sign, so far as this world is concerned; but I think he must, in another realm, hold high converse with Socrates and hear from the lips of Homer the undying song of Troy." He died January 30, 1883.

DIMITRY, CHARLES PATTON. Author. He was born in Washington, D.C., July 31, 1837, son of the distinguished diplomat and educator, Alexander Dimitry, his mother being Mary Powell Mills, daughter of Robert Mills, the architect of the Washington monument. He was educated at Georgetown College, and married, in 1871, Annie Elizabeth Johnston, of Alexandria, Va. He served in the Confederate Army; and after the war became identified with journalistic work in various American cities, settling eventually in New Orleans, and becoming State historian of the Louisiana Society of the Sons of the American Revolution. He has written numerous stories of exciting interest. Among his published works are: 'Guilty or Not Guilty,' 'Angela's Christmas,' 'Gold Dust and Diamonds,' 'The House in Balfour Street,' 'Two Knaves and a Queen,' 'From Exile,' 'Louisiana Families,' 'Louisiana's Story in Little Chapters,' and 'The Louisiana of the Purchase.' Competent critics have placed him among the first writers of present-day fiction. He is also the author of a number of spirited poems, his "Rhyme of Modern Venice" being one of the best.

DIMITRY, JOHN (Bull Smith). Author. He was born in Washington, D.C., December 27, 1835, a son of Dr. Alexander Dimitry, educator and diplomat. He was educated at Georgetown College; and, in 1872, married Adelaide Stewart. When his father was United States Minister to Costa Rica and Nicaragua, he was secretary of legation. On his return home he became prominent in journalism; but afterward assumed the duties of a college professor. He won, while on the New York *Mail and Express,* a prize of $500 offered for the best short story, the prize winner being a romance of singular power entitled "Le Tombeau Blanc." He was the author of epitaphs on Henry Watkins Allen, Albert Sidney Johnston, Stonewall Jackson, Edgar Allan Poe, Charlotte Temple, Charles Sumner, Jefferson Davis, and the Confederate Flag. He also wrote an historical drama in five acts entitled "The Queen's Letters." His other writings include: a 'School History and Geography of Louisiana' (New York, A.

S. Barnes and Company), 'Three Good Giants,' 'Atahualpa's Curtain,' and 'The Confederate Military History of Louisiana' (Atlanta, The Confederate Publishing Company, 1899). He died in 1901.

DINKINS, CHARLES R. Poet. [S.C.]. He wrote a volume of verse entitled 'The Lyrics of Love.'

DINKINS, JAMES. Author and banker. He was born in Madison County, Miss., April 18, 1845, a son of Alexander Hamilton and Cynthia Springs Dinkins, was educated at the North Carolina Military Institute, and entered the Confederate Army at the age of sixteen, rising to the rank of captain. He married, November 15, 1866, Sue Hart, at Canton, Miss. He was in the service of the Illinois Central Railroad for twenty-eight years, and organized the Bank of Jefferson, at Gretna, La., in 1893. He is connected with many important historical organizations; has contributed delightful war reminiscences to the periodicals; and is the author of 'From 1861 to 1865, by an Old Johnnie' (Cincinnati, Robert Clarke Company). He resides in New Orleans, La.

DINNIES, ANNA PEYRE. Poet. She was born in Georgetown, S.C., in 1816. Her maiden name was Shackleford. In 1830 she married John C. Dinnies, residing first in St. Louis and afterward in New Orleans. She wrote under the pen-name of "Moina," producing some exquisite verse which was very greatly admired. At frequent intervals she contributed to the *Catholic Standard,* a weekly edited by her husband. She published a collection of verse, arranged in twelve group , typifying bouquets of flowers and entitled 'The Floral Year' (Boston, 1847). The strings of her modest harp were attuned to the domestic endearments. Three of her poems have been preserved in 'The Louisiana Book' (1894). Perhaps the best of the number is entitled "The Wife." She died in New Orleans, August 8, 1886.

DINWIDDIE, ROBERT, colonial governor of Virginia, was born in Scotland about 1690 and died in Clifton, England, August 1, 1770 His papers have been preserved in the collections of the Virginia Historical Society at Richmond.

DINWIDDIE, WILLIAM. Author. [Va.]. Born in 1867. He published 'War Sketches.'

"DIX, DOROTHY." See Gilmer, Elizabeth Meriwether.

DIXON, AMZI CLARENCE, clergyman, was born in North Carolina, July 6, 1854, a son of the Rev. Thomas Dixon, Sr., and Amanda McAfee. On completing his education at the University of North Carolina, he entered the Baptist ministry and began at once to make his influence felt. He has held pastorates both in Baltimore and in Brooklyn, but is now located in Chicago. His published works include: 'Milk and Meat,' a volume of sermons, 'The Lights and Shadows of American Life,' 'Heaven and Earth.' 'The Christian Science Delusion' (1903), 'Present Day Life and Religion' (1905), 'Evangelism, Old and New' (1905), and 'The Young Convert's Problems' (New York, The American Tract Society, 1906). He is one of the most popular speakers of the day before Bible conferences. Thomas Dixon, Jr., the well-known author, is his brother. He is a Doctor of Divinity.

DIXON, SUSAN HOUSTON. Writer and compiler. [Texas]. She published a work of much interest entitled 'Poets and Poetry of Texas' (1885).

DIXON, SUSAN BULLETT. Writer. [Ky.]. Born in 1827. She published 'The Repeal of the Missouri Compromise and Slavery in American Politics.'

DIXON, THOMAS, Jr. See Biographical and Critical Sketch, Vol. IV, page 1405.

DOBBS, ARTHUR, colonial governor, was born in Ireland in 1684 and died at Town Creek, N.C., in 1765. For eleven years he held the office of colonial governor. He was a writer and published 'Trade and Improvement of Ireland,' 'Captain Middleton's Defence,' and 'An Account of the Countries Adjacent to Hudson's Bay.'

DODD, JAMES B., mathematician, was born in Virginia in 1807, and died in Greensburg, Ky., March 27, 1872. Besides compiling several arithmetics and algebras, he contributed to the *Southern Quarterly Review.* He was for many years a professor in Transylvania University, holding at the time of his death the office of president.

DODD, WILLIAM EDWARD. Professor of history in Randolph-Macon College, Ashland, Va. He was born in Clayton, N.C., October 21, 1869, a son of John D. and Evelyn Creech Dodd. He graduated from the Virginia Polytechnic Institute, and took a special course of study at Leipsic. He married, December 24, 1901, Mattie Johns, at Auburn, N.C. He has written: a 'Life of Nathaniel Bacon' and a 'Life of Jefferson Davis' (Philadelphia, George W. Jacobs and Company, 1907), two volumes of standard value. Besides, he has made several translations and has contributed numerous articles to the press on historical subjects. He received the Ph.D. degree from Leipsic.

DODDRIDGE, JOSEPH, clergyman, was born in Pennsylvania in 1769 and died in Virginia in 1826, having spent many years of his life in the South. He became one of the pioneer Episcopal ministers in the western part of Virginia and published 'Logan,' a dramatic composition, and 'Notes on the Settlement and Indian Wars of the Western Country in 1763-1783.'

DODGE, LOUIS. Poet. [Ark.]. He published a volume of verse entitled 'Poems.'

DODGE, RICHARD IRVING, soldier, was born in Huntsville, N.C., May 19, 1827, and was educated at West Point, becoming an officer in the United States Army with the rank of lieutenant-colonel and rendering his most important service to the Government in the campaigns against the Indians in the West. He published 'The Black Hills,' 'The Plains of the Great West,' and 'Our Wild Indians.'

DOGGETT, DANIEL SETH, bishop of the M. E. Church, South, was born in Virginia in 1810, educated at the State University, became an itinerant minister, and, after holding a professorship in Randolph-Macon College, was ordained bishop. He wrote 'The War and Its Close.' While preparing to leave for California in the discharge of his Episcopal duties, he died in Richmond, Va., October 27, 1880.

DONALDSON, JAMES LOWRY, soldier, was born in Baltimore, Md., March 17, 1814, and was educated at West Point, entering the United States Army as second-lieutenant, and attaining the rank of major-general. The suggestion of national cemeteries for the scattered remains of the soldiers and sailors who served the flag is credited to this distinguished officer. He also wrote 'Sergeant Atkins,' a tale founded upon events which occurred during the Florida war. He died in Baltimore, Md., November 4, 1885.

DONELSON, ANDREW JACKSON, diplomat and planter, was born near Nashville, Tenn., August 25, 1800, and died in Memphis, Tenn., June 26, 1871. Educated at West Point, he was aide-de-camp to his uncle, General Andrew Jackson, when the latter was territorial governor of Florida and afterward became his confidential secretary and adviser in Washington. In 1848 he was appointed Minister to Prussia. Leaving the Democratic party, he was nominated for vice-president on the American ticket with Millard Fillmore, but was defeated. His splendid estate having been destroyed by the war, he engaged in the practice of the law at Memphis, Tenn., after the close of hostilities. He published 'Reports of Explorations' (Washington, 1855).

DON LEAVY, KATHLEEN, poet, was reared and educated in Richmond, Va., and for some time edited *The Catholic Friend.* Her little volume, 'A Bunch of Flowers,' is dedicated to Pope Pius X. It exhales the devotional spirit and contains some beautiful outbursts of sentiment.

DOOLY, ISMA, journalist and magazine writer, was born in Atlanta, Ga. She has held the position of society editor on *The Constitution* for several years and has also written editorials and special articles for the paper. She contributes from time to time to leading popular magazines and reviews. The educational development of the South and the constructive work of women in organized effort for educational, industrial and social betterment furnish the lines along which her literary activities have been chiefly directed. She is a woman of brilliant gifts and of rare accomplishments.

DORMAN, C. T., Mrs. Author. [La.]. She wrote 'Under the Magnolias' (1905).

DORR, JULIA CAROLINE RIPLEY, author, was born in Charleston, S.C., February 13, 1825. On the death of her mother, she was taken by her father to the North. She married Seneca R. Dorr, of New York, but the family home was afterward transferred to Vermont. From earliest childhood she was fond of literary diversions and wrote with equal facility and grace both in prose and in verse. Her published works include: 'Farmingon,' and 'Lanmore,' novels, 'Friar Anselm and Other Poems,' "Daybreak," an Easter poem, 'Expiation,' a novel; 'Bermuda,' and 'Afternoon Songs.' She also wrote a number of essays on marriage for a New England journal.

DORR, LOUISE S. Poet. [N.C.]. She published a volume of verse entitled 'Fountain Spray and Other Poems' (Raleigh, 1885), a work of merit.

DORSEY, ANNA HANSON, author, was born in Georgetown, D.C., December 12. 1815, and became the wife of Judge Owen Dorsey, of Baltimore. In 1840 she adopted the Catholic faith. She achieved distinction as a writer, especially of stories for the young, and one of her volumes republished in Scotland is said to have been the first Catholic book issued in Scotland since the Reformation. She also wrote some very graceful poems. The following is a list of her best productions: 'The Student of Blenheim Forest,' 'Flowers of Love and Memory,' a volume of verse: 'Oriental Pearls,' 'Woodreve Manor,' 'May Brooke,' 'Cosina, the Rose of the Algonquins,' 'Nora Brady's Vow,' 'Mona, the Vestal.' 'The Flemings, or Truth Triumphant,' 'The Old Gray Rosary,' 'Guy, the Leper,' an epic poem; 'Tangled Paths,' 'The Old House at Glenarra,' 'Warp and Woof,' and 'Palms.' She wrote very little after 1887.

DORSEY, ELLA LORAINE. Author. She was born in Washington, D.C., March 2, 1853. On completing her education she engaged for several years in journalism. During the Spanish-American War she served in the hospital corps under the direct orders of the surgeon-general. Besides numerous translations from the Russian language, she has contributed to magazines and to Catholic juvenile literature and has published 'Midshipman Bob,' 'Jet, the War Mule,' 'The José-Maria,' 'Saxty's Angel,' 'The Two Tramps,' 'The Taming of Polly,' 'Pickle and Pepper,' and others. She resides in Washington, D.C., and belongs to various patriotic organizations.

DORSEY, JAMES OWEN, ethnologist, was born in Baltimore, Md., October 31, 1848, and was educated for the ministry of the Protestant Episcopal Church; but becoming interested in ethnological investigations he devoted his life to this department of research. Some of his discoveries have been of very great value to science. He has labored mainly in the service of the United States Government in the Rocky Mountain region, but has received international recognition. Included among his publications are: 'Ponka A B C Wa-ba-ru,' a primer; 'Siousan Phonology,' 'Osage War Customs,' 'Kansas Mourning and War Customs,' 'Omaha Sociology,' 'Siousan Migrations,' and 'Indian Personal Names,' most of these being pamphlets.

DORSEY, SARAH ANNE. Novelist. She was born in Natchez, Miss., in 1829, a daughter of Thomas G. Ellis, a wealthy planter, and a niece of Caroline Warfield, the novelist. She enjoyed the best educational advantages, supplemented by foreign travel, and married Samuel Dorsey, of Louisiana; after his death she returned to Natchez, and became the original owner of "Beauvoir," the famous home of Jefferson Davis, this property at her death being left to him and to his daughter, "Winnie." She was the author of numerous stories of Southern life, including: 'Agnes Graham,' 'The Vivians,' 'Castine,' 'Panola: a Tale of Louisiana,' 'Atalie,' and 'Lucia Dore,' all of which evince keen insight into character and betray an artistic touch. She also wrote 'Recollections of Henry Watkins Allen, Governor of Louisiana.' She died in 1879, while on a visit to New Orleans.

DOSKER, HENRY E. Clergyman and educator; professor of church history in the Presbyterian Seminary at Louisville, Ky. He was born in Bunschoten, in the Netherlands, February 5, 1855, a son of the Rev. Nicholas H. Dosker, and was educated at Hope College and at McCormick Theological Seminary. He married, February 21, 1882, Wilhelmina Doornink. He has held several important pastorates of the Dutch Reformed Church, and taught for several years in the Western Theological Seminary, at Holland, Mich., resigning in 1903 to accept the chair which he now occupies. His published works include: 'De Zondagschool,' 'Life of Dr. A. C. Van Raalte,' and 'Outline Studies in Ecclesiastical History.' Besides, he has written numerous articles for the religious reviews. Rutgers gave him the degree of D.D. and Central University the degree of LL.D.

DOUGHTY, WILLIAM HENRY. Physician and surgeon. [Ga.]. The author of several important medical essays and papers.

DOUGLAS, THOMAS, jurist and lawyer, was born in Connecticut in 1790, but removed to Florida in 1826, settling in St. Augustine. For nineteen years immediately following this change of residence he was United States District Attorney. Later he became Judge of the Eastern Circuit of the State, and finally was appointed to the Supreme Bench. His 'Autobiography' throws interesting light upon social and political conditions in Florida in ante-bellum days. He died at Jacksonville in 1855.

DOUGLASS, FREDERICK, an eminent orator and leader of the negro race, was born in slavery, of mixed parentage, at Tuckahoe, near Easton, Md., in 1817. He learned to read and write and under the disguise of a sailor, escaped from bondage, dropped his master's name, which was Bailey, and made his way to Massachusetts. He became an anti-slavery agitator of great power and was warmly supported by the New England abolitionists. He edited newspapers, delivered lectures, and subsequent to the war held various offices, becoming minister to Hayti. His published works include a 'Narrative' (Boston, 1844), which deals with his experience in slavery; 'My Bondage and My Freedom' (Rochester, 1855), and 'The Life and Times of Frederick Douglass' (Hartford, 1881). He died in 1895.

DOUGLAS, ROBERT MARTIN. [N.C.]. He was born in 1849, and published numerous pamphlets dealing with important phases of American history and politics.

DOUTHAT, ROBERT W. Educator and poet. [Va.]. He was one of the few survivors of Pickett's immortal charge. After the Civil War he engaged in educational work chiefly at the University of Virginia but also appeared from time to time on the lecture platform. He wrote a poem full of martial fire and enthusiasm entitled 'Gettysburg' (New York and Washington, the Neale Publishing Company, 1905).

DOVE, JOHN. Physician. [Va.]. He edited 'The Proceedings of the Grand Lodge of Masons from 1773 to 1822,' and also published a 'History of the Grand Lodge in Virginia.'

DOWD, CLEMENT, author, was a Congressman from North Carolina, serving from 1882 to 1886. He wrote a 'Life of Zebulon B. Vance' (1897).

DOWD, JEROME, editor and educator, was born in Moore County, N.C., March 18, 1864. His father was Honorable Clement Dowd. For some time he was professor of economics and sociology in Trinity College, N.C., his *alma mater*. Besides frequent contributions to periodicals he has published 'Sketches of Prominent Living North Carolinians' (1888), a 'Life of Braxton Craven' (1896), and 'Hamilton,' a tragedy (1882).

DOWD, MARY ALICE. Poet. [W.Va.]. She was born in 1855. Besides numerous uncollected poems, she published a volume entitled 'Vacation Verses.'

DOWLER, BENNETT. Author. [La.]. He wrote an interesting 'History of New Orleans' (1852).

DOWNING, FANNY MURDAUGH. Poet. She was born in Portsmouth, Va., in 1835. Her father was John W. Murdaugh, a noted lawyer of Virginia and she married Charles W. Downing, who was then Secretary of State for Florida. Some of her poems betray an exquisite touch, the best known among the number being "Pluto" and "The Legend of Catawba." She also wrote several interesting novels, among them, 'Nameless' and 'Perfect Through Suffering.' She died in 1894.

DOZIER, ORION T. Physician, inventor, poet. He was born in Marion County, Ga., August 18, 1848, the son of Dr. T. H. Dozier, and was educated in the public schools of Atlanta, Ga. He graduated in medicine from the Atlanta Medical College, and married, April 30, 1874, Elizabeth Powers. He practiced his profession in various places, but eventually settled in Birmingham, Ala. He was the originator and organizer of the Regents of the White Shield, and has held the supreme office since 1876. He also invented and patented a hame for harness, a portable elevator, and a mailing machine. He has published several volumes of poetry, including: 'Foibles of Fancy and Rhymes of the Times,' 'Poems Patriotic,' and 'Galaxy of Southern Heroes, and Other Poems.' Some of his verse is marked by unusual depth and fervor of thought. He resides in Birmingham, Ala.

DRAKE, B. M. He published 'The Negro in Literature Since the War,' a dissertation submitted for the Ph.D. degree at Vanderbilt University (Nashville, Cumberland Presbyterian Publishing House, 1898).

DRAKE, BENJAMIN, author, was born in Mason County, Ky., in 1794 and died in Cincinnati, Ohio, April 1, 1841. For several years he practiced law, but in later life he established and edited the *Western Agriculturist* and published: 'Cincinnati in 1826,' 'Life and Adventures of Black Hawk,' 'Tales and Sketches From the Queen City,' 'Life of William Henry Harrison,' and 'Life of Tecumseh,' the last being his most important production.

DRAKE, BENJAMIN M., clergyman, was born in North Carolina in 1800 and died in Mississippi in 1860. He was president of Elizabeth Female Academy, the first Methodist school in New Orleans and author of a 'Life of Rev. Elijah Steele' (Cincinnati, 1843).

DRAKE, DANIEL. Physician. [Ky.]. He wrote an interesting work entitled 'Pioneer Life in Kentucky.'

DRAKE, JEANIE. Author. [S.C.]. She wrote two very interesting stories entitled 'In Old St. Stephen's' and 'The Metropolitans.'

DRAPER, HENRY, physician and scientist, was born in Prince Edward County, Va., March 7, 1837, and died in New York, November 20, 1882. After graduating in medicine in New York, he visited the great telescope of Lord Rosse in Ireland, which gave him the inspiration for his life's work. He constructed instruments of like character and devoted himself to celestial photography, achieving important results. He also held several professorships, and published a 'Text-Book on Chemistry,' besides a number of papers bearing upon his researches. The University of New York gave him the degree of LL.D. He was a brother of Dr. John C. Draper.

DRAPER, JOHN CHRISTOPHER, physician, was born in Mecklenburg County, Va., March 31, 1835, and died in New York, December 20, 1885. For nearly twenty years he was professor of chemistry in the University of New York. He was also an eminent practitioner. Besides editorials and essays, he published a 'Text-book on Anatomy, Physiology and Hygiene' (New York, 1866), 'A Practical Laboratory Course in Medical Chemistry,' and a 'Text-Book of Medical Physics.' Trinity College gave him the degree of LL.D.

DRAPER, LYMAN COPELAND. Historian. Though of Northern birth, he resided for some time in the South, and published 'King's Mountain and Its Heroes,' an authoritative account of the famous battle of the American Revolution, together with the causes which led to the engagement (Cincinnati, Peter G. Thompson, 1881, steel engravings, maps and plans). He also wrote 'The Mecklenburg Declaration of Independence' and 'Border Forays and Adventures,' besides minor works. Dr. Draper was most exhaustive and thorough in his researches.

DRAYTON, JOHN. Jurist and lawyer. He was born in South Carolina, in 1766, and was educated in England and at Princeton. Like his father, William Henry Drayton, he chose the law for a profession; and, besides being twice elected governor of the State, he was Judge of the United States District Court, holding this latter position at the time of his death. He was the author of 'Letters Written During a Tour Through the Northern and Eastern States' and a 'View of South Carolina,' two works of much interest, and also edited his father's manuscripts under the title of 'Memoirs of the Revolution in South Carolina.' He died in 1822.

DRAYTON, WILLIAM HENRY. Colonial patriot and jurist. This early American author was born at Drayton Hall, on the Ashley River, in South Carolina, in 1742, but was educated in England. He crossed the water in the care of Chief Justice Charles Pinckney, who was taking his two sons, Charles Cotesworth and Thomas, to England to put them at school. On his return to South Carolina, eleven years later, he was admitted to the Bar and made the King's privy-councillor for the province. But he espoused the cause of the Revolution, became president of the Council of Safety and of the Provincial Congress, and Chief Justice of the State. He was also the bearer of an unsuccessful communication to the people of Georgia, proposing a merger and coalition. He died in 1779, at an early age, leaving, in addition to some important state papers, an account in manuscript of the early progress of the Revolution, which was later edited and published by his son, Governor John Drayton. While on the Supreme Bench, it devolved upon this patriot to adjudge that the King had abdicated the government in South Carolina.

DREW, COLUMBUS. Lawyer. He removed to Jacksonville, Fla., in 1845 from Washington, D.C., and held for four years the office of comptroller-general. From time to time he published a number of poems, some of which went the rounds of the press; but they have not yet been collected into book form.

DREWRY, WILLIAM SIDNEY. Educator. In a work entitled 'The Southampton Insurrection' he entertainingly discusses one of the most interesting episodes in the history of African servitude in America (New York and Washington, The Neale Publishing Company, 1905). Dr. Drewry is instructor of history in the University of Missouri.

DROMGOOLE, WILL ALLEN. See Biographical and Critical Sketch, Vol. IV, page 1431.

DU BOIS, WILLIAM E. B., educator, was born in Great Barrington, Mass., of mixed African and European descent, February 23, 1868, and after completing his studies at Fisk University, matriculated at Harvard. Still later he went to Berlin. Since 1896 he has occupied the chair of economics and history in Atlanta University, Atlanta, Ga. He has given much thought to sociological questions and has published 'The Suppression of the Slave Trade' (New York, Longmans, Green and Company, 1896), 'The Philadelphia Negro' (Boston, Ginn and Company, 1899), and 'The Souls of Black Folk' (Chicago, A. C. McClurg and Company, 1903), besides occasional contributions to current periodicals.

DU BOSE, CATHERINE ANNE. Author. She was born at Hook Norton, Oxfordshire, England, September 19, 1826, her maiden name being Richards. She came to the United States in childhood; and in 1848 married Charles W. Du Bose, a lawyer. Her works include: 'The Elliot Family,' a collection of short juvenile stories,,

'The Pastor's Household,' and numerous poems and stories contributed to the magazines. She died in Sparta, Ga., May 26, 1906.

DU BOSE, HORACE MELLARD. Clergyman and editor. He
was born in 'Choctaw County, Ala., November 7, 1858, a son of
Hezekiah and Amanda Hawkins Du Bose. Under private tutors, he studied
the classic languages and later married, first, Rosa Cheney and, second,
(Mrs.) G. V. Amis. An ordained minister of the Methodist Episcopal
Church, he has held important charges both in Texas and in California,
and was for four years editor of *The Pacific Methodist Advocate,* published
in San Francisco. Since 1898 he has been secretary of the Epworth League
and editor of *The Epworth Era,* with headquarters at Nashville, Tenn.
He is the author of 'Rupert Wise, a Poetic Romance' (Nashville,
Bigham and Smith), 'Unto the Dawn' (*ibid.*), 'Planting of the Cross'
(San Francisco, Whittaker and Ray), 'Margaret, an Idyl,' 'The Gang of
Six,' 'Life of Barbee,' 'The Symbol of Methodism,' 'The Men of Sapio
Ranch,' and numerous contributions to the religious press.

DU BOSE, JOEL CAMPBELL. Educator and author. He was
born in Gaston, Ala., December 17, 1855, of Huguenot ancestors, a
son of Benjamin Eusebius and Sarah Elizabeth Horn Du Bose. He
was educated at the University of Alabama, and married, August 8,
1883, Alice Vivian Horn. He taught for several years in some of
the leading academies of the State, and later was employed in making
special researches in the Library of Congress. Among his works are:
'Sketches of Alabama History,' articles on Robert Burns and Peter the
Great, contributed to *The Monthly* (University of Alabama), and an
article on Æschylus, contributed to *The Methodist Review.* He resides
in Birmingham, Ala.

DU BOSE, JOHN WITHERSPOON. Cotton planter and author.
He was born in Darlington County, S.C., March 5, 1836, the son of
Kimbrough Cassels and Elizabeth Witherspoon Du Bose. His education was begun in South Carolina and completed in Alabama. He
enlisted in the Confederate Army at the outbreak of the war, and
served from 1861 to 1865. Subsequently he engaged in journalistic
work. He was also for some time assistant-collaborator of the Alabama State Department of Archives and History. He is best known
by his splendid biographical work entitled 'The Life and Times of
William Lowndes Yancey,' which is an exhaustive resumé of the
stormy period which produced the great apostle and agitator of secession. His latest work is entitled 'General Joseph Wheeler and the
Army of Tennessee.' He is also the author of 'The Huguenots of the
Santee,' in addition to numerous other historical sketches and papers.
He resides in Birmingham, Ala.

DU BOSE, WILLIAM PORCHER. Dean of the Theolog-
ical Department of the University of the South. He was born in Winnsboro, S.C., in 1836, and was educated at the University of Virginia. Later
he studied theology. He served in the Confederate Army, being first adjutant and afterward chaplain. He was twice married. He entered the
Protestant Episcopal ministry in 1865, and held several important charges,
after which he became a professor in the University of the South, in which
subsequently he was made Dean of the Theological Department. Among
his works are: 'The Soteriology of the New Testament' and 'The Ecumenical Councils' (New York, Longmans, Green and Company, 1906), 'The
Ecumenical Councils' (New York, Charles Scribner's Sons), 'The Gospel
in the Gospels' (New York, Longmans, Green and Company, 1906), and
'The Gospel According to St. Paul' (*ibid.,* 1907). Columbia gave him the
degree of S.T.D.

DU CHAILLU, PAUL BELLONI. Explorer and ethnologist of very great distinction. Though his birthplace is in dispute, nevertheless, on the authority of numerous writers (See Rutherford's 'South in Literature and History,' page 576, and 'Who's Who,' 1901-1902), he was born in New Orleans, La., July 31, 1835, of French Huguenot parents. His education was obtained in Paris, and at an early age he went to Africa, where his father was operating as a trader in the French settlement at the mouth of the Gaboon River. He familiarized himself with the speech of the surrounding coast tribes and became possessed of an ambition to acquire the secrets of the great unexplored wilderness. After three years spent in America, he set out, in 1855, upon an exploring trip into the heart of equatorial Africa. On this expedition he journeyed more than eight thousand miles into the interior, with only native companions. He traversed a large area of territory previously undiscovered, and added sixty species of birds and twenty species of mammals to the known zoology of Africa. Some of his accounts, especially of the Obongo dwarfs and of the gorillas, were contradicted by scientists but were afterward confirmed by other explorers. Another expedition was made several years later and many new species were discovered. He also carried his investigations into the north of Europe. Among his published works which contain some of the most valuable contributions to the scientific literature of the times are included: 'Explorations and Adventures in Equatorial Africa,' 'A Journey to the Ashango Land,' 'Stories of the Gorilla Country,' 'Wild Life Under the Equator,' 'My Apingi Kingdom,' 'The Country of the Dwarfs,' 'The Land of the Midnight Sun,' 'The Viking Age,' 'Ivar, the Viking,' 'The People of the Great African Forest,' 'Lost in the Jungle' (New York, Harper and Brothers), 'The Land of the Long Night' (New York, Charles Scribner's Sons), 'The World of the Great Forest' (*ibid.*), 'How Animals, Birds, Reptiles, and Insects Talk, Think, Work, and Live' (*ibid.*). He died in 1903.

DUDLEY, THOMAS UNDERWOOD, Protestant Episcopal Bishop of Kentucky, was born in Richmond, Va., in 1837, and was educated at the University of the State. It was not until after enduring the hardships of army life that he began his equipment for the ministry at the Theological Seminary of Alexandria; and he was ordained in 1868, becoming bishop sixteen years later. He died in 1904. Besides many published lectures and addresses, he wrote 'A Wise Discrimination the Church's Need.' He received from St. John's College the degree of D.D., from King's his D.C.L., and from Griswold his LL.D.

DUFFEE, MARY GORDON, author, was born in Alabama in 1840. Quaint in her manner of dress and in her mode of life, she resided for many years on a lonely mountain in Blount County, making only occasional visits to the crowded centers of population. She wrote both in prose and in verse, "Cleopatra" being the best known of her poems. She published a 'History of Alabama,' and also compiled quite a number of guide-books, besides writing a series of papers on the development of Southern industries.

DUFFY, ANNIE V., Miss. Poet. [N.C.]. She published a volume of verse entitled 'Glenalban, and Other Poems' (New York, E. J. Hale & Son, 1878).

DUFFY. PATRICK LAWRENCE, clergyman and poet, is a native of South Carolina. After graduating with the first honors from St. Mary's College, Md., he studied theology, and on August 15, 1879, was ordained to the priesthood of the Roman Catholic Church in the Cathedral at Charleston, S.C., his boyhood's home. At the celebration of the centenary of St. Mary's College, in 1907, he read the "Centennial Ode," a gem which elicited the praise of Cardinal Gibbons, from whose hands he also received at this time the degree of Litt.D. Besides essays and sketches contributed to the 'Catholic Encyclopædia' and to 'The Library of Southern Literature,' he has published a volume of verse entitled 'A Wreath of Ilex' (Charleston, 1908). Redolent of the South, Father Duffy's poetry is marked by versatility of theme and treatment and points to pure and high ideals. He has lectured on "Venice," "Father Ryan, the Poet-Priest of the South," "The Ideal in Literature and Art," and "Christendom's Cathedral," the one last mentioned having been pronounced the most scholarly lecture on St. Peter's in our language. He also holds the degree of LL.D.

DUFOUR, CYPRIEN. Writer. [La.]. He published in French a volume entitled 'Esquisses Locales' (1847).

DUGAN, GEORGE E., Mrs. Poet. [Mo.]. She published a volume of verse entitled 'May Leaves' (1885). Her pen name was "May Myrtle."

DUGAS, LOUIS ALEXANDER, physician, was born in Washington, Ga., of French ancestry, January 3, 1806, and died in Augusta, Ga., October 19, 1884. After graduating from the medical department of the University of Maryland he located in Augusta, where he became an eminent practitioner. He founded the Medical College of Georgia, which afterward became a part of the university system. His numerous contributions to *The Southern Medical and Surgical Journal,* of which he was for many years the editor, attest the versatility of his talents and the wide range of his information. The University of Georgia gave him the degree of LL.D.

DUGGAN, JANIE PRITCHARD, Mrs. Author. [N.C.]. She published several stories of captivating interest, among them, 'A Mexican Ranch' (1894), 'Judith: a Story of Richmond' (1897), and 'Passion and Patience' (1899). The one first named won a prize of $500, offered by the American Baptist Publication Society of Philadelphia.

DUGGER, SHEPHERD MONROE. [N.C.]. He published 'The Balsam Groves of the Grandfather Mountains.'

DUGUE, CHARLES OSCAR, poet, was born in New Orleans, La., May 1, 1821, of French parentage, and was educated in Auvergne and Paris. While a student he wrote verse which attracted the notice of Chateaubriand. On returning to New Orleans he divided his time between law and journalism. He published 'Essais Poetiques,' 'Mila, ou la Mort de la Salle' and 'Le Cygne, ou Mingo,' 'Philosophie Morale' (1847), a volume of miscellany which contains descriptions of Southern scenery; two dramatic works based upon Louisiana legends, and an Indian romance in which Tecumseh is one of the characters (1852).

DUKE, BASIL WILSON, lawyer, was born in Scott County, Ky., May 28, 1838. At the Bar of Kentucky he early achieved very high distinction. He also served with gallantry in the Confederate Army, became brigadier-general on the death of General John H. Morgan, and afterward published a 'History of Morgan's Cavalry' (New York and Washington, The Neale Publishing Company, 1903), a work of thrilling interest. He is also the author of numerous magazine and newspaper articles. The sketch of Thomas F. Marshall in 'The Library of Southern Literature' is from the pen of General Duke. He married, July 8, 1861, Henrietta Hunt Morgan, a daughter of his illustrious commander.

DUKE, R. T. W., Jr., lawyer, was born in Charlottesville, Va., August 27, 1853. His father was Colonel R. T. W. Duke, and his mother, Elizabeth Eskridge. During the leisure intervals of an active law practice he has written an occasional poem for the magazines. The sketch of Amelie Rives in 'The Library of Southern Literature' is from his pen. For thirteen years he was judge of the Hustings Court of Charlottesville. He married, October 1, 1884, Edith R. Slaughter.

DUKE, WILLIAM, educator and clergyman, was born on Patapsco Neck, Md., September 15, 1757, and died at Elkton, Md., in 1840. For many years he engaged in teaching. He accumulated a library of some size which was presented by his daughter to St. James College. He wrote 'A Clew to Religious Truth' and contributed numerous articles to the religious press.

DULANY, DANIEL, lawyer, was born in Maryland in 1721. For many years he occupied high office in the province before the Revolution; and, while he opposed the Stamp Act, he continued to be a Loyalist. On one occasion he became involved in a controversy with Charles Carroll, of Carrollton. He published 'Considerations on the Propriety of Imposing Taxes upon the British Colonies' (London, 1766).

DUMAS, WILLIAM T. Poet and educator. He was born near Barnesville, Ga., in 1858. For fifteen years he was principal of the Sparta High School, and afterward became superintendent of the public schools of Marietta, Ga. Some of his poetry is of very high order. He has published a collection of verse entitled 'Golden Day, and Other Poems.' One of his best known productions is "The Dinner Horn."

DUMOND, ANNIE NELLES, Miss. Author. [Miss.]. She wrote 'Hard Times: the Cause and the Remedy,' 'The Life of a Book Agent,' 'Scraps on Sabbath School Influence,' and 'National Reform.'

DUNCAN, R. S. Baptist clergyman. [Mo.]. Dr. Duncan wrote a 'History of the Baptists in Missouri.'

DUNCAN, W. B. Methodist Episcopal clergyman. [S.C.]. He wrote 'Twentieth Century Sketches of South Carolina Methodism.'

DUNCAN, WILLIAM CECIL, clergyman and educator, was born in New York City, of Scotch parentage, January 4, 1824, and died in New Orleans, La., May 1, 1864. He established *The Southwestern Baptist Chronicle,* which he edited with exceptional vigor in New Orleans, and was for several years professor of Greek and Latin in the University of Louisiana. His health was always frail and the failure of his effort to save Louisiana to the Union probably hastened his death. His writings include: 'Life of John the Baptist,' 'History of the Baptists for the First Two Centuries,' and 'The Tears of Jesus.' Columbia gave him the degree of LL.D.

DUNGLESON, RICHARD JAMES, physician, was a son of Dr. Robley Dungleson, an English surgeon, and was born in Baltimore, Md., November 13, 1834. After graduating from the University of Pennsylvania he located in Philadelphia and became a practitioner of note. Besides editing his father's 'History of Medicine,' he translated Guersant's 'Surgical Diseases of Children,' and made numerous contributions to medical and scientific journals.

DUNLOP, W. S. Soldier and writer. [Ark.]. He published an interesting contribution to the literature of the Civil War entitled 'Lee's Sharpshooters' (1899).

DUNN, BALLARD S. Clergyman. He published a volume entitled: 'Brazil, the Home for Southerners' (New Orleans, 1866). He held the degree of D.D.

DUNN, JOSEPH BRAGG, clergyman, is a native of Petersburg, Va. On completing his theological studies he was admitted to orders. At the present time he is pastor of an Episcopal church in Suffolk, Va. He has published a 'History of Nansemond County,' 'The Church in the Colony,' 'George Mason,' 'George Rogers Clark,' and numerous contributions to periodicals. He also wrote the sketch of Benjamin Watkins Leigh for 'The Library of Southern Literature.' He married, November 25, 1895, Martha C. Southall.

DU PRATZ, ANTOINE SIMON LE PAGE, author, was born in France in 1689. For more than sixteen years he resided in the colony of Louisiana, traversed the region of country watered by the Arkansas River, and finally returned to France, where he died in 1775. He published a work of some interest entitled 'The History of Louisiana, or of the Western Parts of Virginia and Carolina' (Paris, 1758), which was afterward translated into English (London, 1863).

DUPUY, ANN ELIZA, author, was born in Petersburg, Va., in 1814, and died in New Orleans, La., in 1881. While employed in the capacity of a governess at Natchez, Miss., she wrote her first story, 'The Conspirators,' in which Aaron Burr is the principal character. The success of this venture encouraged her to continue, and she subsequently produced 'The Huguenot Exiles,' 'Emma Walton: or, Trials and Triumphs,' 'Céleste,' 'Florence: or, the Fatal Vow,' 'Separation,' 'Concealed Treasure,' 'Ashleigh,' and 'The Country Neighborhood.' She wrote chiefly for the New York *Ledger* and the number of her stories amounted to about forty.

DURBIN, JOHN PRICE, clergyman, was born in Bourbon County, Ky., in 1800, and died in New York, October 17, 1876. While preaching at Hamilton, Ohio, he studied at Miami University, became an eminent Methodist divine, was for several years president of Dickinson College, afterward a pastor in Philadelphia, and from 1850 to 1872, secretary of missions. He published 'Observations in Europe,' in two volumes (New York, 1844), 'Observations in Egypt, Palestine, Syria, and Asia Minor,' in two volumes (1845), and edited, with notes, Woods' 'Mosaic History of Creation' (1831). He was at one time chaplain of the Senate.

DURRETT, REUBEN THOMAS. See Biographical and Critical Sketch, Vol. IV, page 1457.

DUVAL, JOHN POPE, lawyer and soldier, was born in Richmond, Va., June 3, 1790. In the war between Texas and Mexico he enlisted upon the side of Texas and became a brigadier-general. Later he settled in Florida and achieved distinction at the Bar. Under appointment of Governor Call, he compiled a 'Digest of the Laws of Florida.' He died in 1855.

DUVAL, MARY FISHER, Mrs. Poet. [Fla.]. She belonged to the ante-bellum group of Florida writers and resided at Tallahassee.

DUVAL, MARY V. Author. [Miss.]. She was born in 1850. Her writings include: 'Students' History of Mississippi' (Louisville, Ky., 1887), 'History of Mississippi' (1887). 'Treatise on Civil Government of Mississippi' (1890), and 'Queen of the South,' a drama, with portrait of the author (1899).

DUVAL, LUCIEN, an ante-bellum Florida poet, was the author of some graceful verse, little of which, unfortunately, has been preserved.

DYER, SIDNEY, clergyman and poet, was born in Cambridge, N.Y., but spent much of his life in the South. Self-educated, he became a minister of the Gospel and was secretary of the Indian Mission at Louisville, Ky. He published: 'Voices of Nature' (Louisville, 1849), 'Psalmist for the Use of Baptist Churches' 1854), and 'Songs and Ballads' (New York, 1857). Most of his published writings were in verse.

EAGER, PATRICK HENRY, educator, was born at Warrenton, Miss., November 11, 1852. His father was the Rev. E. C. Eager. For more than thirty years he has been identified with higher educational work in Southern colleges and universities. At present he holds the chair of English in Mississippi College, at Clinton. Besides an important monograph of Lafayette Rupert Hamberlin in Vol. VII of the publications of the Mississippi Historical Society, he wrote a sketch of this same author for 'The Library of Southern Literature.' He married, September 5, 1883, Mary J. Whitfield, sister of the present Chief Justice of Mississippi.

EARLY, JOHN, bishop of the M. E. Church, South, was born in Bedford County, Va., January 1, 1786, and died in Lynchburg, Va., November 5, 1873. He was instrumental in founding Randolph-Macon College, and was both a vigorous thinker and a graceful writer, but he published little beyond an occasional message from the pulpit or platform and a pamphlet relating to the disruption of 1844.

EARLY, JUBAL ANDERSON, an eminent Confederate officer, was born in Franklin County, Va., November 3, 1816, and died in Lynchburg, Va., March 2, 1894. Soon after graduating from West Point, he resigned from the United States Army and was admitted to the Bar; but the outbreak of the War with Mexico appealed to his martial spirit and he went to the front. When Virginia seceded he followed the fortunes of his State and entered the Confederate service, attaining the rank of lieutenant-general. Subsequent to the war he practiced law in Virginia, but refused to take the oath of allegiance to the United States Government. He was an officer of dash and courage, earning his various promotions by his proven soldiership. Besides several addresses on military subjects, he published 'A Memoir of the Last Year of the War for Independence in the Confederate States of America' (1867).

EARLY, MARY WASHINGTON CABELL, Mrs., author, was born in Virginia in 1846. Besides publishing a work of much interest on 'Southern Novelists,' she also wrote 'Sambo's Banishment,' 'Virginia Before the War,' and numerous short stories and sketches.

EASBY-SMITH, JAMES STANISLAUS, educator and poet, was born in Alabama in 1870, but afterward removed to Washington, D.C. His publications include 'Songs of Sappho' (1891) and 'The New Napoleon,' a satire in verse (1896).

EASTER, MARGUERITE E. See Biographical and Critical Sketch, Vol. IV, page 1477.

EASTMAN, MARY HENDERSON. Author. She was born in Warrenton, Va., in 1818, became the wife of General Seth Eastman of the United States Army, resided for many years at Fort Snelling, and published 'Dacotah, or Legends of the Sioux' (New York, 1849), 'Romance of Indian Life' (Philadelphia, 1852), 'Aunt Phillis's Cabin,' a reply to Mrs. Stowe's famous novel, 'American Aboriginal Portfolio,' illustrated by her husband, 'Chicora' (1853), 'Tales of Fashionable Life' (1854), and numerous short stories and sketches. Her portrayals of Indian character are truthful and vivid.

EATON, JOHN H., statesman and diplomat, was born in Tennessee, in 1790; and, on being admitted to the Bar, he began the practice in Nashville. From 1829 to 1831 he was Secretary of War under President Jackson. While in office he married the famous Margaret O'Neill Timberlake, and the social insurrection which followed furnished the immediate cause for the dissolution of the Cabinet. Following this episode, he was appointed governor of Florida and afterward Minister to Spain. His place in literature is due to his 'Life of Andrew Jackson,' which he wrote in association with John Reed. It is an authoritative work, based upon long and intimate acquaintance with the subject. He died in 1856.

EATON, THOMAS TREADWELL. Clergyman and editor. Pastor of the Walnut Street Baptist Church, Louisville, Ky., for several years. He was born in Murfreesboro, Tenn., November 16, 1845, the son of Joseph H. and Esther M. Eaton, and was educated at Washington and Lee University, Lexington, Va. He was ordained to the ministry in 1870. He married, in 1872, Alice Roberts, of Nashville, Tenn. Included among the numerous volumes of this successful pastor are: 'The Angels'; 'Talks to Children'; 'Talks on Getting Married'; 'The Bible on Women's Public Speaking'; 'Wives and Husbands'; 'The Theatre'; 'Sanctification'; 'History of Walnut Street Baptist Church'; 'Cruise of the Kaiserin'; 'James Madison Pendleton.' In 1887 Dr. Eaton became the editor of *The Western Recorder.* Washington and Lee University gave him the degree of D.D. and the Southwestern Baptist University the degree of LL.D. He died in 1907.

ECHEZABAL, F. T. and J. R. [La.]. Joint authors of 'An Irish Cavalier, a Drama in Four Acts' (New Orleans, 1902).

EDMONDS, RICHARD HATHAWAY, editor, was born in Norfolk, Va., in 1857. After attending school in Baltimore he entered journalism and rose from the position of clerk to the editorial chair of the *Journal of Commerce.* In 1882 he founded the *Manufacturers' Record,* a publication devoted to the material interests of the South. For nearly thirty years he has edited this periodical, which has grown into splendid proportions and he has been the means of bringing into this section millions of dollars for investment. The files of the paper attest the manifold phases of industrialism to which his tireless and talented pen has been devoted.

EDWARDS, HARRY STILLWELL. See Biographical and Critical Sketch, Vol. IV, page 1497.

EDWARDS, JENNIE. Author. She was the wife of John N. Edwards, of Missouri. revised and re-published her husband's work, 'Shelby and His Men' (1897), and wrote 'The Life of John N. Edwards.'

EDWARDS, JOHN ELLIS, clergyman, was born in Guilford County, N.C., August 1, 1814. On completing his education at Randolph-Macon College, he entered the ministry and became one of the most prominent Methodist divines in the South, laboring for twenty-one years in Richmond. He published 'Travels in Europe' (New York, 1857), 'Life of John Wesley Childs' (Philadelphia, 1851), 'The Confederate Soldier,' and 'The Log Meeting-House' (Nashville, 1884). Randolph-Macon gave him the degree of D.D.

EDWARDS, JOHN N. Author. He lived in Missouri and published, in 1867, an interesting work entitled: 'Shelby and His Men.' It was afterward re-published in 1897 by his wife, Jennie Edwards (Kansas City, Hudson-Kimberly Company). He also wrote 'Shelby's Expedition to Mexico' (1872) and 'Noted Guerrillas' (1877).

EDWARDS, NINIAN WIRT, lawyer, was born in Frankfort, Ky., April 15, 1809, removed to Illinois, became a lawyer of distinction, and wrote at the request of the Historical Society of Illinois 'The Life and Times of Ninian Edwards' (1870).

EDWARDS, RICHARD. Writer. [Mo.]. He published 'The Great West and Her Commercial Metropolis, St. Louis' (1860), in association with Mr. Hopewell.

EDWARDS, WILLIAM EMORY, clergyman, was born in Prince Edward County, Va., June 10, 1842, and, graduating from Randolph-Macon College, he became an eminent Methodist divine. He wrote 'John Newsome, a Tale of College Life' (Nashville, 1883).

EFNOR, LOTTIE, Mrs. Writer. [Texas]. She wrote numerous short stories and sketches and published a volume of 'Poems.'

EGAN, LAVINIA. Author. [La.]. She wrote a story entitled 'A Bundle of Fagots' (1895).

EGGLESTON, GEORGE CARY. See Biographical and Critical Sketch, Vol. IV, page 1525.

EGGLESTON, JOSEPH DUPUY, Jr., educator, was born in Prince Edward County, Va., November 13, 1867. After graduating from Hampden-Sidney College he devoted himself to teaching. He resides at Worsham, Va., and holds the position of State Superintendent of Public Instruction. Besides numerous contributions to school journals and popular magazines, he is the author of the sketch of Robert Beverly in 'The Library of Southern Literature.' He married, July 18, 1896, Julia J. Johnson.

EGGLESTON, JOSEPH W. Physician. [Va.]. Dr. Eggleston has published what he calls "an old-fashioned story of an old-fashioned people" entitled 'Tuckahoe' (New York and Washington, The Neale Publishing Company, 1907), which takes the reader back to war times in the Old Dominion.

ELDER, GEORGE, A. M., educator and editor, was born at Hardin's Creek, Ky., in 1794, and died in Bardstown, Ky., in 1838. He was ordained to the Roman Catholic priesthood, organized at Bardstown, Ky., the College of St. Joseph, of which he became president, edited *The Catholic Advocate,* and published a work entitled 'The Letters of Brother Jonathan.'

ELDER, SUSAN BLANCHARD. Author. She was born at Fort Jessup, La., April 19, 1835, a daughter of General Albert G. Blanchard. She was educated in a convent of the Roman Catholic Church and married Charles D. Elder, of New Orleans. Besides many poems and dramas of exceptional merit, her literary productions include: 'The Leos of the Papacy,' 'James the Second,' 'Savonarola,' 'Ellen Fitzgerald, a Southern Tale,' and others. She has frequently contributed to Catholic periodicals.

ELKINS, WILLIAM LEWIS, astronomer, was born in New Orleans, La., April 29, 1855. After graduation from the University of

Strasburg, he was for some time associated with Sir David Gill, of the Royal Observatory, at the Cape of Good Hope, in calculating the parallaxes of the southern stars. At present he is the astronomer at the Yale Observatory, with headquarters in New Haven. From time to time he has published the results of original researches in astronomical journals.

ELLEMJAY, LOUISE ("L.M.J."). Author. [Va.]. She wrote 'The Rising Young Man,' 'Censoria Lictoria' (1859), and other interesting stories.

ELLICOTT, JOHN MORRIS, naval officer, was born at St. Inigoes, Md., September 4, 1859, and was educated at Annapolis. He participated in the famous battle of Manila Bay and in 1903 was advanced to the rank of lieutenant-commander. He wrote a novel entitled 'Justified' (1891), and a 'Life of John Ancrum Winslow' (1900), besides short stories and sketches.

ELLIOT, BENJAMIN, jurist, was born in Charleston, S.C., in 1786. Graduating from Princeton, he began the study of law; and was not long in becoming an acknowledged leader of the Bar of South Carolina. He was the author of numerous productions, historical and political, among the number, 'A Refutation of the Calumnies Circulated Against the Southern and Western States Respecting the Institution and Existence of Slavery' and 'The Military System of South Carolina.' He died in 1836.

ELLIOTT, CHARLES, clergyman, was born in Ireland in 1792. Coming to America, he studied theology, served Methodist churches in Missouri, and published 'Southwestern Methodism' (1868), in addition to minor works.

ELLIOTT, RICHARD SMITH. Writer. [Mo.]. He published a volume entitled 'Taken in Sixty Years' (1883).

ELLIOTT, SARAH BARNWELL. See Biographical and Critical Sketch, Vol. IV, page 1553.

ELLIOTT, STEPHEN, naturalist, was born in Beaufort, S.C., November 11, 1771, and died in Charleston, S.C., March 28, 1830. For twenty-eight years he was president of the State Bank of South Carolina. He was a man of means and of culture and devoted much of his time to the pursuit of scientific studies. Besides numerous contributions to the periodicals, he wrote 'The Botany of South Carolina and Georgia' and left at his death several unpublished manuscripts. His collection of books on natural history was one of the largest in the United States. For some time he was a professor in the Medical College of South Carolina, which he assisted in organizing. He was a graduate of Yale. Stephen Elliott, his son, was the first Episcopal Bishop of Georgia.

ELLIOTT, STEPHEN, Protestant Episcopal bishop, was born in Beaufort, S.C., August 31, 1806, and died in Savannah, Ga., December 21, 1866. After graduation from Harvard he practiced law first in Beaufort and afterward in Charleston. But still later he was admitted to orders, became professor of sacred literature in South Carolina College, and in 1841 was chosen the first Bishop of the Diocese of Georgia. He also served St. John's Church, Savannah, in the capacity of rector, was for a time provisional Bishop of Florida, and devoted his fortune to the cause of female education. He was a man of eloquence, of scholarship and of exceptional powers of organization. After his death a collection of his sermons was published with a memoir (1867).

ELLIOTT, WILLIAM. See Biographical and Critical Sketch, Vol. IV, page 1569.

ELLIS, JAMES TANDY. Author. [Ky.]. In a work entitled 'Sprigs o' Mint' (New York and Washington, The Neale Publishing Company, 1905), which contains both sketches and poems, the author has portrayed many delightful phases of Kentucky life and character.

ELLIS, JOHN BRECKENRIDGE. Educator and author. He was born near Hannibal, Mo., February 11, 1870, a son of Dr. John William Ellis, an eminent scholar, and was educated at Prattsburg College, Mo., in which institution he held the chair of English for eleven years. He relinquished teaching in 1902 to devote his time exclusively to literary work. Many of his stories deal with Biblical incidents. They are all charmingly written. His works include: 'In the Days of Jehu' (St. Louis, Christian Publishing Company), 'King Saul' (*ibid.*), 'Shem, a Story of the Captivity' (*ibid.*), 'The Dread and Fear of Kings' (Chicago, A. C. McClurg); 'Garcilaso' (*ibid.*), 'The Holland Wolves' (*ibid.*), 'Adnah, a Tale of the Time of Christ' (Philadelphia, George W. Jacobs and Company), 'The Red Box Clew,' 'The Ellisan Literary Year Book,' and 'The Stork's Nest,' besides stories, verses, songs, and cantatas. He resides in St. Louis, Mo.

ELLIS, LEONORA BECK. Writer. Mrs. Ellis is a native of Georgia. Her maiden name was Leonora Beck. She is a sister of Marcus W. Beck, associate justice of the Supreme Court. Before her marriage to Richard A. Ellis, on June 2, 1896, she was engaged in educational work in Atlanta, but since then she has devoted herself to literature. Besides a volume of stories entitled 'Star Heights,' she is the author of a number of magazine articles bearing upon economic and sociological conditions in the South. The Library of Congress has recently listed her series of articles on child labor, because of the interest which they possess for students of this problem. She is engaged at present in making investigations among the sponge fishers of the Florida Coast. She continues to write stories for the periodicals and also contributes an occasional poem. Among the principal magazines for which she writes are the *Review of Reviews, The Forum, Leslie's* and *The Independent.* She spends much of her time in Aripeka, Fla.

ELLISON, MATTHEW, clergyman, was born in Monroe County, Va., November 10, 1804. After organizing twenty-five Baptist churches over the South, he retired from active work, settled at Raleigh, N.C., and published: 'Dunkerism, a Plea for the Union of Baptists.'

"ELVAS, THE GENTLEMAN OF." The name of an unknown Spaniard who wrote an interesting 'Histoire de la Conquest de la Floride' (Lisbon, 1685).

ELWES, A. W. In 1825 there appeared in Richmond a volume of poems entitled: 'The Potomac Muse.' It was offered to the public by "A Lady of Virginia"; but it was copyrighted by A. W. Elwes, who may have been the author. Some of the verse betrays poetic glints. She gives her pen chiefly to Virginia's great men.

ELZAS, BARNETT ABRAHAM. Historian, rabbi, physician. Dr. Elzas was born at Eydkuhnen, Germany, December 7, 1867. His father was Dr. Abraham Elzas, clergyman and author, and his mother, Hinda Lewinthal. The son spent his earlier years in England, where, in addition to equipping himself for his theological career, he was an industrious student of the ancient and modern classics. After settling in Charleston, S.C., he studied both pharmacy and medicine, receiving his degrees in each; but his first congregational charge was in Toronto, Canada. For years past Dr. Elzas has been one of the foremost American contributors to Jewish literature. His published works include: 'Judaism, an Exposition' (1896), 'The Sabbath-School Companion' (1895-1896), 'Fifteen Historical Pamphlets relating to the Jews in South Carolina' (1902-1904), 'The Jews of South Carolina from the Earliest Times to the Present Day' (1905), 'The Old Jewish Cemeteries at Charleston, S.C.' (1903), 'Leaves from My Historical Scrap-Book,' two series (1907-1908), and 'The Jew in the South' (1909). The sketch of Penina Moise in 'The Library of Southern Literature' is also from his pen. Dr. Elzas married, June 25, 1890, Annie Samuel. South Carolina College, in 1905, gave him the degree of LL.D. He resides in Charleston, S.C.

EMMET, THOMAS ADDIS. Physician. [Va.]. The author of several important medical works including a treatise on 'The Practice and Principles of Gynecology' (Philadelphia, 1879), which has been translated into French and German. He was a grandnephew of the celebrated Irish patriot, Robert Emmet.

EMORY, JOHN, bishop of the M.E. Church, was born in Queen Anne County, Md., April 11, 1789, and died in Reistertown, Md., December 17, 1835. He was educated for the law, but turned from his legal studies to become one of the landmarks of Methodism. He founded *The Methodist Quarterly Review* and contributed most of the original articles in the first two volumes. His published works include 'The Divinity of Christ Vindicated' and 'The Defence of Our Fathers.' He was master of a style both vigorous and lucid. Thrown from his carriage, he died from the injuries which he received.

EMORY, ROBERT, clergyman and educator, was born in Philadelphia, Pa., July 29, 1814, of Southern parentage, and died in Baltimore, Md., May 18, 1848. For several years he was president of Dickinson College. Besides publishing 'The Life of Bishop Emory,' with a collection of his writings (New York, 1841), he also wrote 'The History of Methodist Discipline' and left an unfinished 'Analysis of Butler's Analogy,' which was afterward completed and published by Dr. Crooks. Columbia gave him the degree of D.D.

EMORY, WILLIAM HEMSLEY, soldier, was born in Queen Anne County, Md., September 9, 1811, and died in Washington, D.C., December 1, 1887. Educated at West Point, he entered the United States Army and rose to the rank of brigadier-general. He published 'Notes of a Military Reconnoissance in Missouri and California' (New York, 1848), and 'Report of the United States and Mexican Boundary Commission.'

ENGLAND, JOHN. Roman Catholic bishop, was born in Cork, Ireland, September 23, 1786, and died in Charleston, S.C., April 11, 1842. Before completing his theological studies, it is said that his progress was so brilliant that he was chosen to deliver public lectures on religious subjects. He took an active part in the movement for Catholic emancipation. When the See of Charleston was organized he was nominated the first bishop; and, having made up his mind to become an American citizen, he refused to take the oath of allegiance exacted of Irish bishops at the time of consecration; but, after some difficulty, he was consecrated in Cork, in 1820, and duly arrived in Charleston. He did much to suppress dueling, to foster education, and to extend Catholicism. He made four separate visits to Europe in the interest of his diocese. En route home, his ministerial labors among the steerage passengers exposed him to an infectious disorder, and he died soon after his return. He published 'An

Address Before the Hibernian Society of Savannah' (Charleston, 1824); and, after his death, his 'Works' were edited, in five volumes, by Bishop Reynolds.

ESTES, MATTHEW. This author resided at Columbus, Miss. and wrote: 'A Defence of Negro Slavery in the United States' (Montgomery, Ala., 1846).

EUSTIS, JAMES BIDDLE, statesman and diplomat, was born in New Orleans, La., August 27, 1834. Graduating from Harvard Law School, he was admitted to the New Orleans Bar and rose steadily in his profession. During the Civil War he was judge-advocate on the staffs of Generals Magruder and Johnston. He was twice sent to the United States Senate and, during President Cleveland's second term, he was commissioned to represent this country at the Court of France. For several years he was professor of law in the University of Louisiana. Several of his speeches on public questions have been preserved in the *Congressional Record.*

EVANS, CLEMENT ANSELM. Commander-in-chief of the United Confederate Veterans; lawyer, clergyman, author. He was born in Lumpkin, Ga., and was educated in the local schools. Subsequently he studied law at Augusta, Ga., and practiced his profession until the outbreak of the war, meanwhile serving as Judge of the county court and as State Senator. Entering the Confederate Army in 1861 as a major, he attained the rank of brigadier-general, and on the field of Appomattox he commanded Gordon's famous division. After the surrender he entered the ministry of the Methodist Church and preached for several years. He became a candidate for governor of Georgia in 1894, but withdrew from the race before the day of election. At the present time he is one of the prison commissioners of Georgia and on the death of General Stephen D. Lee in 1908 he was elected Commander-in-chief of the United Confederate Veterans. Besides editing 'The Confederate Military History,' in twelve volumes, a work to which he contributed several chapters, he was the orator at the unveiling of the Gordon equestrian statue, in Atlanta, and of the Davis monument, in Richmond. He resides in Atlanta.

EVANS, HUGH DAVEY, author, was born in Baltimore, Md., April 26, 1792, and died in Baltimore, Md., July 16, 1868. He studied law and became prominent at the Bar where Pinkney and Wirt were the leaders. He was an enthusiastic churchman, figured with prominence in Episcopal councils, and edited church papers. He prepared a code of laws for the Maryland Colony in Liberia and published a number of works, including: 'Essays on Pleading' (Baltimore, 1827), 'Maryland Common Law Practice' (Baltimore, 1837, revised 1867), 'Essays to Prove the Validity of Anglican Ordination' (Baltimore, 1844, revised in two volumes, 1851), 'Theophilus Americanus,' an adaptation of Canon Wadsworth's work (Philadelphia, 1851), 'Essay on the Episcopate' (1855), and 'Treatise on the Christian Doctrine of Marriage,' which appeared after his death (New York, 1870), a work of standard merit. The Rev. Hall Harrison wrote his memoir (Hartford, 1870). St. James' College gave him the degree of LL.D.

EVANS, LAWTON BRYAN. Educator. He was born in Lumpkin, Stewart County, Ga., October 27, 1862, a son of General Clement A. Evans. He married, February 15, 1887, Florence Campbell. For several years he has been superintendent of the public schools of Augusta, Ga. His published works include: a 'History of Georgia' (New York, University Publishing Company, 1898), 'Lectures on Supervision of Schools' (1904), 'Language Lessons,' 'English Grammar,' and 'Essentials of American History.'

EVANS, THOMAS J., lawyer, was born in King William County, Va., February 2, 1822, and received his education in Richmond. On being admitted to the Bar he rose to distinction and served in the State Legislature; while on the field of battle he commanded the Nineteenth Regiment of Virginia militia. Possessed of unusual skill in the art of versification, he published a volume entitled: 'Sir Francis Drake and Other Fugitive Poems' (Richmond, 1895).

EVE, MARIA LOUISA, poet, was born in Augusta, Ga., in 1848. In early childhood she evinced rare powers of mind. When only eighteen she won a prize of $100 for the best prose essay. In 1879 she won a prize of the same amount for the best poem on the yellow fever epidemic and again in 1889 she wrote her exquisite gem of verse entitled "Brier Rose," which won still another prize. At the request of the Secretary of the American Arbitration Society, she wrote a welcome to the English Peace Deputation entitled "The Lion and the Eagle," which was widely copied on both sides of the water.

EVE, PAUL FITZSIMONS, physician and surgeon, was born near Augusta, Ga., June 27, 1806, and died in Nashville, Tenn., November 3, 1877. He was an eminent practitioner and was at different times identified with the faculties of various institutions. In the line of original research he did much to advance the science of medicine, publishing over 600 articles on medical subjects. His most important works are 'Remarkable Cases in Surgery,' 'One Hundred Cases in Lithotomy,' and 'What the South and West have Done for Surgery.' For some time he edited *The Southern Medical and Surgical Journal.*

EVELINE, ROBERT, author, was an English colonist in Virginia who wrote 'Direction for Adventurers and True Description of the Healthiest, Pleasantest and Richest Plantation of New Albion, in North Virginia' (London, 1641).

EVERHART, ELFRIDA, librarian, was born of Southern parents in Jersey City, N. J., June 9, 1883. Besides several contributions to library periodicals on technical topics she has published a 'Handbook of United States Public Documents' (Minneapolis, Minn., The H. W. Wilson Co., 1909), and is engaged upon other important work. She is on the staff of the Carnegie Library of Atlanta, Ga.

EVERSHED, EMILIE, Madame. Writer. [La.]. She published in French two interesting works, entitled: 'Esquisses Poetiques' (1846), and 'Une Couronne Blanche' (1850).

EWELL, ALICE MAUDE. Author. [Va.]. Besides numerous uncollected short stories and sketches, her writings include: 'The White and the Red' (1889), 'A White Guard to Satan' (1900), 'A Long Time Ago' (New York and Washington, The Neale Publishing Company, 1906), and a volume of verse entitled 'The Heart of Old Virginia' (*ibid.*, 1908). Much of her work has appeared in *St. Nicholas.*

EWING, ELBERT WILLIAM ROBINSON. Author. [Va.]. He published 'The Dred Scott Decision Vindicated by History and Judicial Law' (1900), and 'Northern Rebellion and Southern Secession' (1904), two volumes of much interest relating to the causes of the Civil War.

EWING, FINIS, one of the founders of Cumberland Presbyterianism, was born in Bedford County, Va., June 10, 1773, and died in Lexington, Mo., July 4, 1841. As a revivalist he met with great success, but his ordination was not recognized by the Kentucky synod of the Presbyterian Church, within whose jurisdiction he labored, and, on account of some doctrinal divergence of opinion, he organized an independent movement which became the Cumberland Presbyterian Church. He published a work entitled: 'Lectures on Divinity,' which embodies the distinctive creed of the Cumberlands.

EWING, JOHN, clergyman and educator, was born in Nottingham, Md., June 22, 1732, and died in Philadelphia, Pa., September 8, 1802. For several years he was connected with the University of Pennsylvania; and his collegiate lectures on natural philosophy, including a memoir, were published in two volumes after his death. The University of Edinburgh gave him the degree of D.D.

EYSTER, NELLIE, author, was born in Frederick, Md., in 1831, a daughter of Abraham Blessing. At the age of sixteen she married David A. T. Eyster, of Harrisburg, Pa., where she resided till her removal to San Jose, Cal. She made numerous contributions to the periodicals and published in book form several delightful juveniles, including 'Sunny Hours,' 'Chincapin Charlie,' 'On the Wing,' 'Tom Harding and his Friends,' 'Lionel Wintour's Diary,' and 'Robert Brent's Three Christmas Days.' She also became active in reform work for the advancement of woman.

EZEKIEL, H. C. [Va.]. He published 'The Book Buyer' (1892).

FACKLER, S. A., editor and publisher, was born in Upson County, Ga., November 8, 1857. For forty years he has been engaged in newspaper work in rural communities and has published a play entitled 'The Ups and Downs of a Country Editor—Mostly Downs' (1909), in which he portrays with delicate humor and pathos the life with which he has long been familiar. He resides at Hazlehurst, Ga.

FAGAN, WILLIAM L., planter, was born in Wetumpka, Ala., November 20, 1838. He served in the Confederate Army, made numerous contributions to periodicals and published 'Southern War Songs' (New York, 1890), a compilation.

FAIRBANKS, GEORGE RAINSFORD. Lawyer and historian. He was born in Watertown, N.Y., in 1820. Early in life he removed to St. Augustine, Fla., and became an influential member of the Bar. For a number of years he held the office of clerk of the United States District Court; and he also served at one time in the State Senate. Enlisting in the Confederate Army at the outbreak of hostilities, he attained the rank of major. After the war he removed to Sewanee, Tenn., becoming one of the original members of the board of trustees of the University of the South. In 1880 he returned to Florida and made his home at Fernandina. He often represented the State at agricultural and forestry conventions; was president of the Florida Fruit Exchange, and edited the Florida *Weekly Mirror*. He was also made president of the Florida Historical Society, an organization which he greatly helped to promote. His published works include: 'History and Antiquities of St. Augustine,' a 'History of Florida' (1871), which is one of the best, and 'Florida: Its History and Romance' (1898). He died in 1906.

FAIRCHILD, GEORGE THOMPSON. Educator. For several years Dr. Fairchild has been vice-president and professor of English literature in Berea College, Ky., and has published a work entitled 'Rural Wealth and Welfare, Economic Principles Illustrated and Applied to Farm Life' (New York, The Macmillan Company, 1900).

FAIRMAN, HENRY CLAY, lawyer and editor, was born in Mississippi in 1849. For a while he engaged successfully in the practice of law; but he afterward went into journalism and became editor of *The Sunny South*. Besides numerous contributions to the press both in prose and in verse, he published in 1896 a volume entitled: 'The Third World, a Tale of Love and Strange Adventure' (1894).

FALCONER, THOMAS. Author. [La.]. He published 'The Expedition to Santa Fé' (New Orleans, 1842), 'The Discovery of the Mississippi,' and other works.

FALKNER, W. C. Author. [Miss.]. His writings include: 'Rapid Ramblings in Europe' (Philadelphia, J. B. Lippincott Company, 1884), 'The White Rose of Memphis,' 'The Lost Diamond' (1867), 'The Little Brick Church' (1882), and 'Henry and Ellen' (1853).

FALLIGANT, ROBERT. Jurist and poet. He was born in Savannah, Ga., in 1839, and was one of the party to seize Harper's Ferry. He was an eloquent advocate at the Bar, full of Irish fire and humor. His best poetic production is entitled "The Man of the Twelfth of May," written in commemoration of the gallantry of General John B. Gordon. He died in Savannah, January 3, 1902.

FANNIN, DAVID, freebooter, was born in Johnson County, N.C., about 1754, and died in Digby, Nova Scotia, in 1825. When the Whigs gained the ascendancy in North Carolina he went first to Florida and afterward to St. Johns, N.B., where he was sentenced to be hanged but escaped. He wrote a 'Narrative of Adventures in North Carolina,' which was edited by T. H. Wynne, and published with an introduction by John H. Wheeler, many years later (Richmond, 1861).

FARMER, C. M. Lawyer. He lived in Louisa County, Va., and published a work entitled 'The Fairy of the Stream, and Other Poems' (Richmond, 1847). It was playfully criticized by Poe; but the author of "The Raven" was not blind to the merits of the work.

FARMER, HENRY TUDOR, poet and physician, was born in England in 1782 and died in Charleston, S.C., in 1828, the greater part of his life having been spent in this Southern seaport. For some time he engaged in mercantile pursuits but he subsequently retired from business, studied medicine, and successfully practiced his profession. As a writer he possessed distinct gifts and published a volume of verse entitled: 'Imagination, the Maniac's Dream, and Other Poems,' besides a number of essays.

"FARQUHARSON, MARTHA." See Martha Finley.

FARRAR, C. S. [Miss.]. He wrote an interesting historical pamphlet entitled "The War, Its Causes and Consequences."

FARRAR, FRANK R. Jurist. [Va.]. Besides frequent articles contributed to the press, he appeared from time to time on the lecture platform. His two most popular themes were "Johnnie Reb," and "Rip Van Winkle." He died in Richmond, Va., in 1897.

FARRAR, IRENE, author, was born in Atlanta, Ga., and was the daughter of Robert M. Farrar. Her death on the threshold of young womanhood prevented the full development of her gifts, but some of her choice work was published in a volume entitled 'On the Rock' (Atlanta, Ga., James P. Harrison and Company, 1889), a miscellaneous collection of short stories and poems.

FAUQUIER, FRANCIS, colonial governor of Virginia, was born in 1720 and died in Virginia, March 3, 1768. He wrote a number of financial essays; among them, 'An Essay on Ways and Means of Raising Money for the Support of the Present War without Increasing the Public Debts" (1756).

FAVROT, HENRY L. Author. [La.]. He published an interesting account of the 'West Florida Revolution of 1810' (Louisiana Historical Society, 1895).

FAY, EDWIN W. Educator. [La.]. He wrote a 'History of Education in Louisiana' (Washington, D.C., 1898) and 'The Mostellaria of Planters.'

FELKEL, HENRY L., poet, was born in Leon County, Fla., and died in St. Augustine. He was the author of a volume entitled 'Palms and Pitcher Plants.'

FELTON, REBECCA ANN LATIMER, writer and lecturer, was born in DeKalb County, Ga., in 1835, of vigorous Southern stock. Her father was Charles Latimer and her mother Eleanor Ann Swift. On the paternal side, she is related to the Marshalls of Maryland. For more than forty years Mrs. Felton has been a contributor to newspapers and magazines, wielding a pen of rare power. Her familiarity with public issues and her brilliant and fearless style of treatment have given her articles an interest national in extent. Her scrap-books have been the fear and dread of her adversaries in debate and the most complete and perfect register of her times. Not only in the public prints but on the public platforms she has been an advocate of moral and social reforms. She has also represented her sex on the council boards of the various international expositions. She has kept apace with all the phases of current thought and has taken an active part in all the progressive movements of the day; but her first allegiance has always been to her home fireside. She resides at Cartersville, Ga. It is to be hoped that the quiet eventide of her life will be devoted to the writing of her reminiscences. She married, October 11, 1853, Dr. William H. Felton, for several years a Member of Congress, and her literary lance was first couched in the controversial tilts of Georgia politics.

FELTON, WILLIAM H., physician, clergyman, Congressman, orator, was born in Oglethorpe County, Ga., June 19, 1823, and died in Cartersville, Ga., September 24, 1909. For more than sixty years he was an ordained minister of the M. E. Church, South. But he did not become an itinerant and he took no pay for his services, deriving his income chiefly from his medical practice and from his farming interests. As an orator he was for years a power in Georgia. He represented his district in Congress for three consecutive terms, after which he served in the State Legislature and was instrumental not only in preventing a sale of the Western and Atlantic Railroad but in leasing the property at an increased rental. He married, first, Anne Carleton and, second, Rebecca Latimer. Though he published little he was matchless on the hustings and in the halls of legislation.

FENNER, CHARLES E. Lawyer. [La.]. He published an 'Oration on the Unveiling of the Statue of Robert E. Lee in New Orleans,' an important document (New Orleans, 1884).

FENOLLOSA, ERNEST FRANCISCO. Educator. He was born in Salem, Mass., February 18, 1853, and graduated with the highest honors in philosophy from Harvard in 1874. He married Mary McNeil, the well-known Southern author. For several years he was a teacher of philosophy and afterward a teacher of English in the Imperial University of Tokio, Japan. He has been the recipient of numerous decorations from the Mikado. Besides writing various monographs on oriental art for the Boston Museum, he has contributed numerous articles to the magazines on subjects relating to the Orient. He has also published two volumes of poems and 'An Outline History of Okiyo-Ye.' He resides in Spring Hill, Ala.

FENOLLOSA, MARY McNEIL. See Biographical and Critical Sketch, Vol. IV, page 1591.

FERGUSON, EMMA HENRY. Author and composer. She was born at Red Hill, Charlotte County, Va, in 1840, a daughter of John and Elvira McClelland Henry, and granddaughter of Patrick Henry, the famous orator of the American Revolution. She was educated under private tutors and afterward graduated in music at the Conservatoire in Paris. She married at Red Hill, Va., December 22, 1858, Major James B. Ferguson. Besides being the composer of the "Monogram," the "Initial" and the "Signature Waltzes," she wrote numerous stories and sketches and published a novel entitled 'Courage and Loyalty.' She died in Balham, Goochland County, Va., in 1905.

FERRELL, CHILES CLIFTON. Educator. For some time he was professor of Germanic languages in the University of Mississippi. He was born near Greenville, S.C., August 20, 1865, and was educated at Vanderbilt, pursuing post-graduate studies abroad (Ph.D., Leipzig). He married Tenney Marr Taliaferro of Birmingham, Ala. Besides numerous translations and contributions to periodicals, he has published 'Teutonic Antiquities in the Anglo-Saxon Genesis' (1893), 'Old Germanic Life; or, the Anglo-Saxon Wanderer and Seafarer' (1894), 'The Daughter of the Confederacy; her Life, Character and Writings' (1899), and 'The Medea of Euripides and the Medea of Grillparzer' (1901). The sketch of Winnie Davis in 'The Library of Southern Literature' is from the pen of Dr. Ferrell.

FESTETITS, KATE NEELY, Mrs. Author. [Va.]. Born in 1837. She published 'Ellie Randolph' and other stories for children.

FEW, WILLIAM PRESTON, educator, was born in Greenville, S.C., December 31, 1869. He is at present dean and professor of English in Trinity College, Durham, N.C. He has written for the magazines on educational and popular topics and contributed to the Child Memorial Volume of Harvard Studies and Notes in Philology and Literature. He received the degree of Ph.D. from Harvard.

FICKLEN, JOHN R., Mrs. [La.]. She published a booklet entitled 'Dream Poetry.'

FICKLEN, JOHN ROSE. Educator. He was born in Falmouth, Va., December 14, 1858. After graduation from the University of Virginia, he became assistant professor of ancient languages at the University of Louisiana, but resigned this position to continue his studies at Paris and Berlin. For a number of years he filled the chair of history and rhetoric in Tulane University, and in 1893 he became professor of history and political science in the same institution. In joint authorship with Grace Elizabeth King, he wrote a 'History of Louisiana,' which was adopted by the Louisiana State Board of Education for use in the public schools. His other writings include: 'The Indians of Louisiana' and 'The History of New Orleans.' He died in 1907.

FICKLIN, JOSEPH, mathematician, was born in Winchester, Ky., September 9, 1833. For many years he was professor of mathematics and astronomy in the University of Missouri. He published numerous textbooks, including arithmetics and algebras. The University of Wisconsin gave him the degree of LL.D.

FIELD, JOSEPH M., actor, was born in London, England, in 1810. Much of his time was spent in the South, chiefly between Mobile and St. Louis. He wrote quite a number of humorous pieces for the New Orleans *Picayune,* which was owned at the time by his brother, and he also published 'The Drama of Pokerville' (Philadelphia, 1847). He died in Mobile, Ala., January 30, 1856.

FIELD, EUGENE, poet and journalist, was born in St. Louis, Mo., September 2, 1850, and died in Chicago, Ill., November 4, 1895. Though not classed among Southern writers, due to his long residence at the North, he received his initial impetus from the South and was for years employed on Missouri newspapers. He is best known as the poet of childhood; and in this department of verse is almost peerless. His published works include: 'A Little Book of Western Verse' (1890), 'A Second Book of Verse' (1893), 'Lullaby Land' (1894), 'Love Songs of Childhood' (1894), and 'The Holy Cross and Other Tales.' In association with his brother Roswell he also wrote 'Echoes from a Sabine Farm.' He married, in 1873, Julia S. Comstock, of St. Louis.

FIELD, KATE, newspaper correspondent, was born in St. Louis, Mo., in 1838; and was the daughter of Joseph M. Field, an actor. She was educated in Massachusetts, but studied music in Italy. For some time she was European correspondent for the New York *Tribune* and other journals. She established at the national capital a weekly called *Kate Field's Washington.* She also delivered frequent lectures. Among her publications are: 'Planchette's Diary' (New York, 1868), 'Adalaide Ristori,' 'Mad on Purpose,' a comedy; 'Pen Photographs from Charles Dickens's Readings,' 'Ten Days in Spain' (Boston, Houghton, Mifflin and Company), and 'Hap-Hazard,' a volume of sketches (*ibid.*). She died in Honolulu in 1896.

FIELD, LIDA AMANDA. Educator. She was born in Dahlonega, Ga., and was the first lady librarian of the Young Men's Library, now the Carnegie Library of Atlanta. She also taught for some time at Agnes Scott College, at Decatur, Ga., and in the Atlanta public schools. She was the author of a 'Grammar School History of the United States,' which was published by the American Book Company, first in 1885 and afterward in 1897. She died in Dalton, Ga., November 29, 1908.

FIELD, MARTHA REINHARD. Journalist. She was born in Lexington, Mo., May 25, 1855. Her maiden name was Smallwood. She was united in marriage to Charles W. Field, at San Francisco; and on the death of her husband, three years later, she removed to New Orleans, securing a position on *The Times.* Later she became associated with *The Picayune.* Under the pen-name of "Catherine Cole" she gained a wide circle of readers and her "Correspondence Club" became one of the popular features of the paper. Her work is characterized by gentle humor.

FIELD, NATHANIEL, physician, was born in Jefferson County, Ky., November 7, 1805, and died in Jeffersonville, Ind., August 28, 1888. For several years he practiced medicine in Northern Alabama. Later he settled in Indiana. He espoused the doctrines of Alexander Campbell, emancipated his slaves, and, while practicing medicine, performed pastoral work without compensation. He published a humorous poem on "The Arts of Imposture and Deception" and an argument on "The State of the Dead," besides numerous lectures and contributions to medical journals.

FIELD, ROSWELL MARTIN, journalist and author, was born in St. Louis, Mo., September 1, 1851, and, on completing his education at the University of Missouri engaged in metropolitan journalism. As a writer he wields a pen of rare versatility and power. His publications include: 'In Sunflower Land' (1892), 'Echoes from a Sabine Farm' (New York, Charles Scribner's Sons, 1891), 'The Passing of Mother's Portrait' (Evanston, Ill., William S. Lord, 1901), 'The Romance of an Old Fool' (*ibid.,* 1902), 'The Bondage of Ballinger' (Chicago, Fleming H. Revell Company, 1903), and 'Little Miss Dee' (*ibid.,* 1904). Mr. Field is a brother of the late Eugene Field, the poet. He resides in Chicago, Ill.

FIELDER, HERBERT. Lawyer. [Ga.]. For many years he was prominent in state affairs and was an unsuccessful candidate for United States Senator against General John B. Gordon. He wrote 'The Life and Times of Joseph E. Brown' (Springfield, Mass., 1883).

FIERY, SAMUEL M. In the eventide of life the author found in the harp what he calls "a Lethe to the languor of old age" and published a volume entitled 'Poems' (Roanoke, Va., 1904). Most of his verse is in the vein of reminiscence, reviving tender memories of the long ago.

‹ FILHIVE, DON JUAN. Author. He resided in Arkansas on a plantation to which he gave the name of "Spain." He published in his mother-tongue a 'Description of Hot Springs' (1796).

FILLEY, C. L., Mrs. Author. [Mo.]. She wrote 'The Chapel of the Infant Jesus.'

FILSON, JOHN. Kentucky's pioneer historian. The precise date of his birth is unknown, but probably he was born about the year 1744 in East Fallowfield, Chester County, Penna. He was educated at Nottingham, Md., in the academy of Samuel Finley, who afterward became president of Princeton University. It was not until 1783 that he penetrated into the frontier belt of Kentucky, settling in Lexington; but he was not long in catching the inspiration of the soil, and, while engaged in teaching school, he gathered the data for his work. Most of his information was derived from pioneers like Daniel Boone and Levi Todd. The result was a volume entitled 'The Discovery, Settlement, and Present State of Kentucky' (Wilmington, Del., James Adams, 1784). At the same time, his map, showing the three original counties of the State, was printed in Philadelphia. Later, an appendix to the historical volume was issued in the nature of a biography of Daniel Boone; and subsequently the two parts were bound together. He left also in manuscript 'The Diary of a Journey from Philadelphia to Vincennes, Ind.,' 'An Account of a Trip by Land from Vincennes, Ind., to Louisville, Ky.,' and 'A Journal of Two Voyages by Water from Vincennes to Louisville,' also an account of an attempted voyage. The life of the pioneer was one of vicissitudes. All trace of him is lost after 1788. But the Filson Club of Louisville memorializes his genius; and from the pen of Colonel R. T. Durrett has come an interesting story of his career.

FINCK, EDWARD BERTRAM. Lawyer. He was born in Louisville, Ky., October 16, 1870, a son of C. H. and Elizabeth Jacobs Finck and was educated in private schools. His writings are cast in the philosophic mold but are characterized by the poetic touch. Besides some excellent plays, he has written two volumes: 'Pebbles' and

'Webs,' both published by John P. Morton of Louisville, Ky., in which city the author resides.

FINCK, HENRY THEOPHILUS, journalist and musical critic, was born in Bethel, Mo., September 22, 1854, and was educated in part abroad. Since 1881 he has been on the staff of the New York *Evening Post.* His writings include: 'Romantic Love and Personal Beauty' (New York, The Macmillan Company), 'Chopin, and Other Musical Essays' (New York, Charles Scribner's Sons), 'Pacific Coast Scenic Tours' (*ibid.*), 'Spain and Morocco' (*ibid.*), 'Wagner and His Works' (*ibid.*), 'Anton Seidl' (*ibid.*), 'Primitive Love and Love Stories' (*ibid.*), 'Songs and Song Writers' (*ibid.*), 'Fifty Master Songs' (Boston, Oliver Ditson Company), 'Fifty Schubert Songs' (*ibid.*), and others. He originated the theory that romantic love is a modern sentiment unknown to savages or to ancient nations.

FINLEY, EUGENIA HOWARD. Author. [Ga.]. She wrote 'Meverign, a Romance of the Philippines.'

FINLEY, JOHN, poet, was born in Rockbridge County, Va., January 11, 1797, and died in Richmond, Ind., December 23, 1866. He published a volume of verse entitled 'The Hoosier's Nest, and Other Poems.'

FINLEY, MARTHA ("Martha Farquharson"). Author. She was born at Chillicothe, Ohio, April 26, 1828, the daughter of Dr. James Brown and Maria Theresa Finley. She was educated in select schools, and was for several years herself a teacher. She is one of the most prolific story-writers of the times, devoting her pen chiefly to books for the young. She is the author of the famous 'Elsie Books,' which treat in many successive volumes of the fortunes of Elsie Dinsmore, and of the famous 'Mildred Books,' which tell in like manner of the girlhood adventures of Mildred Keith. Among her other books are included: 'Cassella,' 'An Old-Fashioned Boy,' 'Our Fred,' 'Wanted—a Pedigree,' 'Signing the Contract and What it Cost,' 'The Thorn in the Nest,' 'The Tragedy of Wild River Valley,' 'Twiddledewit,' and others. She resides in Elkton, Md.

FINN, FRANCIS JAMES, Roman Catholic clergyman and author, was born in St. Louis, Mo., October 4, 1859. At intervals of leisure he has produced numerous entertaining stories for young people, among them, 'Percy Winn' (1890), 'Tom Playfair' (1890), 'Harry Dee' (1891), 'New Faces and Old' (1894), 'The Best Foot Forward' (1898), and 'His First and Last Appearance' (1900), besides many others. He resides in Cincinnati, Ohio.

FISKE, MINNIE MADDERN, actress, was born in New Orleans, La., in 1865. Several plays have come from her pen, including "Common Clay" and "Not Guilty." She has been very successful on the stage. Her maiden name was Minnie Maddern, and she married Harrison Gray Fiske, journalist and playwright.

FITCH, WILLIAM EDWARDS. Physician. [N.C.]. He published a work of much interest entitled 'Some Neglected History of North Carolina,' in which he brings to light many hitherto obscure incidents in the early annals of the Commonwealth (New York and Washington, The Neale Publishing Company, 1906), and 'The Fitch Family in England and America.'

FITZ, JAMES. He lived in Virginia and published a volume of curious interest entitled 'A Gallery of Poetic Pictures; Comprising True

Portraits and Fancy Sketches, Interspersed with Humorous, Moral and Solemn Pieces, together with Historic, Patriotic and Sentimental Poems' (Richmond, 1857).

FITZGERALD, CHARLES. Poet. [Jackson, Miss.]. He wrote a number of exquisite odes, including one "To the Confederate Soldier." He died in 1908.

FITZGERALD, OSCAR PENN. See Biographical and Critical Sketch, Vol. IV, page 1613.

FITZHUGH, GEORGE, sociologist, was born in Prince William County, Va., July 2, 1807, and died in Huntsville, Texas, July 30, 1881. An eccentric thinker, he held that slavery was the natural and rightful condition of society which, when not founded on human servitude, tends to cannibalism. He published: 'Sociology for the South, or the Failure of Free Society' (Richmond, 1854) and 'Cannibals All; or, Slaves without Masters."

FITZHUGH, WILLIAM. Lawyer. He was born in Bedford, England, June 9, 1651, and died in Stafford County, Va., in 1701. He was the founder of the Fitzhugh family in Virginia. He left in manuscript a volume of his correspondence covering the period from 1679 to 1699. One of the same name also wrote a 'History of the Northern Neck of Virginia.'

FITZHUGH, WILLIAM HENRY, philanthropist, was born in Chatham, Va., March 8, 1792, and died in Cambridge, Md., May 21, 1830. On completing his studies at Princeton, he settled on the patrimonial domain at "Ravensworth." For several years he was vice-president of the American Colonization Society and in behalf of the cause he wrote numerous articles and delivered frequent addresses. In one of his essays he declared the labor of the slave to be a curse to the land upon which it was expended, a statement which was full of prophetic meaning.

FLAGG, EDMUND, lawyer and journalist, was born in Maine in 1815 but located in the South and was for years engaged in journalism in various Southern States, after which he was placed at the head of the Bureau of Statistics in Washington, D.C. During the last years of his life he practiced law in Virginia, where he died in 1890. He was a writer of note. Two of his novels won prizes, 'The Howard Queen' (1848) and 'Blanche of Atois' (1850). He also wrote 'Edmond Dantes,' a sequel to 'The Count of Monte Cristo' (1849), 'Venice, the City of the Sea,' his chief work in two volumes (1853), 'Mary Tudor,' a drama, and several stories in manuscript. While editing a paper at Vicksburg, Miss., he was severely wounded in a duel.

FLASH, HENRY LYNDEN. See Biographical and Critical Sketch, Vol. IV, page 1641.

FLEMING, FRANCIS P., lawyer, was born at Hibernia, Fla. After serving in the Confederate ranks, he equipped himself for the practice of law, and from the start his rise was rapid. In the office of governor, which he held for four years, he proved an efficient executive. As president of the Florida Historical Society his splendid record speaks for itself. He wrote 'Memoirs of Florida,' 'The Florida Troops in Virginia: a Memoir of Captain Seton Fleming,' and numerous historical papers. He resides in Jacksonville, Fla.

FLEMING, WALTER LYNWOOD. Professor of history in the University of West Virginia. He was born at Brundidge, Ala., April 3, 1874, a son of William Le Roy and Mary Fleming. He was educated at the Alabama Polytechnic Institute; but took a special course of instruction at Columbia (Ph.D.). He farmed one year and afterward devoted himself to teaching. He served with distinction in the Spanish-American War, and married, September 17, 1902, Mary Wright Boyd, at Auburn, Ala. Besides contributing numerous historical articles to the magazines and encyclopædias, he is the author of 'Documents Relating to Reconstruction,' 'Reconstruction of the Seceded States,' and 'The Civil War and Reconstruction in Alabama' (New York, The Macmillan Company, 1905). He has edited Lester and Wilson's 'History of the Ku Klux Klan' (Washington, D. C., the Neale Publishing Company) and 'The Documentary History of Reconstruction.' He was also one of the editors of 'The Historian's History of the World' (New York, The Outlook Company). For 'The Library of Southern Literature' he wrote the sketch of Zachary Taylor.

FLEMING, WILLIAM HENRY. Lawyer. He was born in Augusta, Ga., October 18, 1856, the son of Porter and Catherine Moragne Fleming, and received his education at the University of Georgia. He was superintendent of the Augusta public schools for four years. He studied law and rose to prominence at the Bar, representing Georgia in Congress from 1896 to 1902, and was also at one time Speaker of the Georgia House of Representatives. He married, August 22, 1900, Marie Celeste Ayer, of Rome, Ga. He is the author of a volume entitled 'The Tariff, Civil Service, Income Tax, Imperialism, The Race Problem, and Other Addresses' (Atlanta, Ga., A. B. Caldwell, 1909. His address on "Slavery and the Race Problem in the South" was published under separate covers by Dana Estes and Company, Boston, Mass. It is a masterpiece of thought and eloquence. The sketch of Col. Charles C. Jones, Jr., in 'The Library of Southern Literature' is from the pen of Mr. Fleming. He resides in Augusta, Ga.

FLINT, JOSHUA BARKER, physician and surgeon, was born in Cohasset, Mass., October 13, 1801, and died in Louisville, Ky., March 19, 1864. Dr. Flint was an eminent member of his profession and published a work on 'The Practice of Medicine' (1860), which passed into several editions.

FLINT, TIMOTHY. Clergyman. Though born at North Reading, Mass., in 1780, this Congregational minister labored for many years in the Mississippi Valley; and later in life his summer home was in Alexandria, Va. He lectured on natural history, wrote geographies, and edited periodicals. His most important work is his 'Recollections of Ten Years Passed in the Valley of the Mississippi' (1826), but he also wrote several novels, the best being 'Francis Berrian,' a tale of Mexico. He died in 1840.

FLISCH, JULIA A. Educator and author. [Ga.]. She wrote an entertaining novel entitled 'Ashes of Hopes' (New York, Funk and Wagnalls, 1886), besides minor works, including essays and sketches.

FLORY, JOHN SAMUEL, educator, was born at Broadway, Va., March 29, 1866. For several years he has been engaged in educational work and is now vice-president and professor of English in Bridgewater College, Va. Besides several monographs and pamphlets on subjects historical and critical, he has published a work entitled 'The Literary Activity of the German Baptists in the Eighteenth Century' (1908). He married, August 18, 1908, Vinnie Mikesell.

FLOYD, N. J. Author. [Va.]. He published a work entitled 'Thorns in the Flesh' (1886).

FOLSOM, JAMES M. Writer. [Ga.]. He published 'Heroes and Martyrs of Georgia' (1864).

FOLSOM, JOSEPH P. [La.]. He published a work of antiquarian interest on 'The Constitution and Laws of the Choctaws' (1869).

FOLSOM, MONTGOMERY MORGAN, journalist and poet, was born in Lowndes County, Ga., January 31, 1857, and died in Atlanta, Ga., July 2, 1898. For years he was engaged in journalistic work on Georgia papers, notably, *The Constitution* and *The Journal,* published in Atlanta, and at leisure intervals wrote for Northern newspapers and magazines. Some of his short stories were masterpieces. He was also one of the South's true poets. His only published work is a volume of verse entitled: 'Scraps of Song and Southern Scenes' (Atlanta, Ga., C. P. Byrd, 1897).

FONTAINE, FRANCIS. Author. [Ga.]. He was born in 1844 and died in 1901. Besides a number of poems, he wrote a novel entitled 'Etowah.' He was for some time a resident of Atlanta, Ga.

FONTAINE, LAMAR, civil engineer and poet, is best known to fame through the celebrated war song entitled: "All's Quiet Along the Potomac To-night," to whose disputed authorship he is one of the claimants, the others being Thaddeus Oliver and Mrs. Ethel Beers. He was born at Laberde, Texas, October 10, 1829. The story of his life reads like a tale of adventure. He was captured by the Comanche Indians and kept a prisoner for four years. He was with the Russian Army at the siege of Sebastopol and won the Iron Cross of Peter the Great for marksmanship. In the Civil War he was a scout for Stonewall Jackson and a courier for Johnston and Pemberton. He was wounded not less than sixty-seven times, and, in addition to numerous hand-to-hand encounters, he was in twenty-seven battles and fifty-seven skirmishes. When verging upon four score years he published an interesting volume entitled 'My Life and My Lectures' (New York and Washington, The Neale Publishing Company). He married, June 20, 1866, Lemuella S. Brickell. His other poems include: "Œnone," "Only a Soldier," "The Dying Prisoner at Camp Chase," and "In Memoriam."

FOOTE, HENRY STUART, lawyer and statesman, was born in Fauquier County, Va., in 1800; and, after completing his studies at Washington College, he settled first in Alabama and afterward in Mississippi, representing the latter commonwealth in the United States Senate and later becoming governor. He was an avowed Unionist; and, after relinquishing the executive reins, he went to California, but eventually he returned to Mississippi, remained a while and then settled in Nashville, Tenn. Though he fought secession, he acquiesced in the will of the people. But he never was on good terms with Mr. Davis, who was an old rival in Mississippi politics; and, following the war, he supported the administration of President Grant, who appointed him director of the Mint at New Orleans. He died in 1880. His writings include: 'Bench and Bar of the South and Southwest,' 'Texas and the Texans,' 'History of the Southern Struggle,' 'History of the Civil War; or, Scylla and Charybdis,' and 'Personal Reminiscences.' His speeches, some of which are preserved in the *Congressional Globe,* also form important contributions to the thought of the times. He died in 1880.

FOOTE, WILLIAM HENRY, clergyman, was born in Colchester, Conn., December 20, 1794, and died in Romney, W.Va., November 18, 1869. For many years he preached and taught at Romney, and during the Civil War he became a Confederate chaplain. He published 'Sketches, Historical and Biographical, of the Presbyterian Church in Virginia,'

'North Carolina Sketches,' and 'The Huguenots.' He was a graduate of Yale but studied theology at Princeton. Hampden-Sidney gave him his degree of Doctor of Divinity.

FORD, ARTHUR P. Author. [S.C.]. He wrote an interesting narrative of personal adventure entitled 'Life in the Confederate Army,' to which his wife added three entertaining stories of the same period entitled 'Some Experiences and Sketches,' by Marion Johnstone Ford, both published in one volume (New York and Washington, The Neale Publishing Company, 1906).

FORD, HENRY CLINTON, educator, was born in Charlotte County, Va., December 12, 1867. He holds the chair of English in the Virginia Military Institute at Lexington and the degree of Ph.D. from the University of Virginia. Besides the sketch of Frances Courtenay Baylor, in 'The Library of Southern Literature,' he is the author of 'Observations on Chaucer's Hours of Fame' (1899).

FORD, JAMES LAUREN, author, was born in St. Louis, Mo., July 25, 1854. On completing his education he engaged chiefly in literary pursuits. He has published 'The Literary Shop,' 'Hypnotic Tales,' 'The Third Alarm,' 'Bohemia Invaded,' 'Dr. Dodd's School,' and several other works of fiction. He resides in New York City.

FORD, SALLY ROCHESTER, author, was born at Rochester Springs, Ky., in 1828, and was educated at the Female Seminary of Georgetown. Her maiden name was Sally Rochester. With her husband, the Rev. Samuel Howard Ford, she edited *The Christian Repository* and *The Home Circle*. Her first serial story, "Grace Truman," appeared in the former periodical; and, on appearing in book form, the sales reached 30,000 copies in three years. It is semi-religious, presenting the essential tenets of the Baptist faith. She also wrote several other works: 'Mary Bunyan,' 'Romance of Free Masonry,' 'Morgan and His Men,' 'Evangel Wiseman,' and 'Earnest Quest.' On account of her zeal for evangelism, she was made president of the Woman's Missionary Union at the South.

FORD, SAMUEL HOWARD, clergyman and editor, was born in Missouri in 1823. He entered the Baptist ministry, served important congregations in various parts of the South, and edited religious papers. He published 'Historic Milestones' (1858), 'Great Pyramids of Egypt' (1880), 'Servetus, the Sixteenth-Century Martyr' (1885), and a 'Brief History of the Baptists' (1890).

FORD, THOMAS B. Author. [Ky.]. Besides some excellent lyric and dramatic verse, he published several novels. One of his poems entitled "The Siren," is preserved in 'Songs of the South.'

FOREST, WILLIAM S. Writer. [Va.]. He published 'Historical and Descriptive Sketches of Norfolk.'

FORMENTO, FELIX. Physician. [La.]. Born in 1837. He published 'Notes and Observations of Army Surgery.'

FORREST, MARY. She wrote a work entitled 'Women of the South Distinguished in Literature' (New York, Derby and Jackson, 1861). She became Mrs. Freeman.

FORRESTER, ELDRED JOHN. Baptist clergyman. [S.C.]. Born in 1853. He published 'The Baptist Position' (1893).

FORSHEY, CALEB GOLDSMITH, engineer, was born in Somerset County, Pa., July 18, 1812, and died in Carrollton, La., July 25, 1881.

He located in the South, served in the Confederate Army, and published 'The Delta of the Mississippi' (1873) and 'The Physics of the Gulf of Mexico' (1878).

FORSYTH, JOHN, diplomat and statesman, was born in Frederick County, Va., October 22, 1780, and died in Washington, D.C., October 21, 1841, while representing Georgia in the Cabinet of President Van Buren. He was an orator of unusual gifts; and settling for the practice of law at Savannah, Ga., he rose to international distinction. At three different times he was a United States Senator, twice he was sent to Congress, once he was Governor of Georgia, under two administrations he held the office of Secretary of State, and while Minister to Spain he negotiated for the purchase of Florida from Ferdinand VII. On the floor of the United States Senate, Mr. Forsyth was the intellectual peer of the ablest of his colleagues.

FORT, TOMLINSON, physician, was born in Warren County, Ga., July 11, 1787, and died in Milledgeville, Ga., May 11, 1859. For thirty years he was president of the State Bank of Georgia. He achieved eminence in his profession and published a work entitled: 'The Practice of Medicine.'

FORTIER, ALCÉE. See Biographical and Critical Sketch, Vol. IV, page 1663.

FORTIER, FLORENT. Author. [La.]. He wrote 'La Salle,' a biography of the explorer.

FORWOOD, WILLIAM STUMP, physician, was born near Darlington, Md., January 27, 1830. For several years he resided in Alabama, but afterward settled in Darlington, where he practiced medicine. He published a number of important historical pamphlets.

FOSTER, LOVELACE S., clergyman, was at one time pastor of the Senatobia Baptist Church, Senatobia, Miss. He published 'Mississippi Baptist Preachers,' quite a voluminous work (St. Louis, 1895) and 'From Error's Chain; or, the Religious Struggles of an Accomplished Young Lady' (Jackson, 1899).

FOSTER, ROBERT VERRELL. Presbyterian clergyman and educator. [Tenn.]. He was born in 1845. He holds the chair of systematic theology in the Seminary at Lebanon, Tenn. His published works include 'Introduction to the Study of Theology' (Chicago, Fleming H. Revell Company, 1889), 'Old Testament Theology' (ibid., 1890), 'Commentary on the Epistle to the Romans' (Nashville, Tenn., Cumberland Presbyterian Publishing House, 1895), 'Systematic Theology' (ibid., 1898), and 'Commentaries on the International Sunday-school Lessons (ibid, 1881), besides contributions to encyclopædias and reviews.

FOUCHÉ, L. N. Author. [La.]. He published in French 'Nouveau Recueil de Pensées' (1882).

FOWKE, GERARD. Antiquarian. [Va.]. He published 'Archæological Investigations of the James and Potomac Valleys' (1894).

FOWLES, MARY. Writer. [S.C.]. She wrote in both prose and verse and published 'The Golden Fence,' 'A Sequence of Songs,' and 'A Hero's Last Days.'

FOX, JOHN, Jr. See Biographical and Critical Sketch, Vol. IV, page 1683.

FOX, NORMAN. Baptist clergyman and educator. [Mo.]. He was born in 1836. He published 'A Layman's Ministry,' a 'Life of Honorable Nathan Bishop, Preacher and Teacher,' and a 'Life of President Rambaut.'

FOX, WALTER DENNIS. Editor and author. He was born near Murfreesboro, Tenn., July 4, 1867, the son of William F. Fox, an Irish-Canadian. He was educated at the University of Kentucky, and also took a course in a business college at Nashville, Tenn. He married, first, Josie Williams Ewing and, second, Sara Antoinette Bell. He is a writer of both prose and verse, and is also very successful in dramatic composition. His works include: 'Sam Davis, the Confederate Scout,' a tragedy written in verse (Nashville, Southern Methodist Publishing House), 'Father Carolan,' a drama, 'The Harlequin of Dreams,' a fantastic comedy, 'Almanzor,' a tragedy, 'Jean Lafitte,' an historical play, and 'Passing the Love of Women,' a romantic play. He has contributed frequently to the periodicals. His residence is in Murfreesboro, Tenn.

FRANCIS, DAVID ROWLAND, merchant and governor, was born in Richmond, Ky., October 1, 1850. His father was John B. Francis and his mother, Eliza C. Rowland. After graduating from Washington College, he engaged in business in St. Louis and became one of the foremost commercial and industrial factors of the Middle West. From 1889 to 1893 he was governor of Missouri. During the last months of President Cleveland's second administration he was Secretary of the Interior. He was also president of the Louisiana Purchase Centennial Exposition in 1904, and the phenomenal success of this great international exhibit brought him honors and decorations from foreign potentates. Besides numerous public addresses, he wrote 'A Tour of Europe in Nineteen Days.' He was also one of the advisory council of 'The Library of Southern Literature.' He married, January 20, 1876, Jane Perry. Several institutions have given him the degree of LL.D.

FRANCIS, MARY C. The author of an exceptionally life-like portrayal of Andrew Jackson entitled 'A Man of Destiny' (New York, The Federal Company, 1903).

FRANTZ, VIRGINIA J., Mrs. Poet. [Miss.]. She published a volume of verse entitled 'Ina Greenwood, and Other Poems' (1877).

FRASER, CHARLES. Artist. [S.C.]. He was born in 1782 and died in 1860. He published 'Reminiscences of Charleston.'

FREDET, PETER, author and educator, was born in Sebasat, Auvergne, France, in 1801, and died at Ellicott's Mills, Md., in 1856. Most of his adult life was spent in the neighborhood of Baltimore; and he was engaged chiefly in teaching various branches of ecclesiastical learning, besides ancient and modern histories, which were adopted as text-books in the Roman Catholic colleges of the United States and in the University of Ireland. His other works are mainly polemic, including 'Inspiration and Canon of Scripture,' 'Original Texts and Translations of the Bible,' 'Interpretation of Scripture,' 'Necessity of Baptism,' 'Effects of Baptism,' 'Lay Baptism,' and 'Doctrine of Exclusive Salvation.'

FREE, GEORGE D. Educator and editor. [Tenn.]. He was born in 1863. His published works include: a 'History of Tennessee,' 'Civil Government in the United States and Tennessee,' 'Rare Gems,' 'Marriage and Divorce,' 'Our Girls,' and 'History and Civil Government.'

FREEMAN, MARILLA WAITE, librarian, was born at Honcoye Falls, N.Y. Her father was the Rev. Samuel Alden Freeman and her mother, Sarah Allen. She holds the position of reference librarian in the Free Public Library of Louisville, Ky., and contributes to library journals and other periodicals. The sketch of Abby Meguire Roach is from her pen.

FRÉMONT, JESSIE BENTON, Mrs., author, was the second daughter of Thomas Hart Benton of Missouri and wife of John C. Frémont, the celebrated "Pathfinder," and was born in Virginia in 1824. When quite advanced in years she published a volume of unusual interest entitled 'Souvenirs of My Time' (Boston, D. Lothrop and Company, 1887). She also wrote 'The Story of the Guard,' and a sketch of her father, which appeared in her husband's 'Memoirs.'

FRÉMONT, JOHN CHARLES, explorer and soldier, was born in Savannah, Ga., January 21, 1813. His education was obtained at Charleston College; and, after passing the requisite examination, he became professor of mathematics in the Naval Academy at Annapolis. In 1842, he suggested to the Government the wisdom of making a survey of the territories and at the head of a party of twenty-eight men he was sent to explore the Rocky Mountains. This was the first of the many adventurous expeditions which earned for him the soubriquet of "the Pathfinder." Settling in California, he represented the Golden State in the Senate of the United States for the first few months of its statehood. In 1856 he was the unsuccessful candidate of the Free Soil Republicans for President of the United States. Soon after the outbreak of the Civil War, he was appointed major-general and put in command of the Western Department, with headquarters in St. Louis. Later, he was transferred to another field, due to his technical unfamiliarity with the duties of his position and to his lack of special adaptability to the work; and still later he relinquished command, after the battle of Cross Keys. General Frémont's chief service to his country was in discovering practical routes for the future march of civilization westward. From 1878 to 1882 he was governor of Arizona, and shortly before his death, he was placed on the retired list by special act of Congress. He married Jessie, the second daughter of Senator Thomas H. Benton. He died July 13, 1890. His published works include: 'Explorations' (Philadelphia, 1856) and 'Memoirs of My Life' (New York, 1886).

FRENCH, ALICE. See Biographical and Critical Sketch, Vol. IV, page 1713.

FRENCH, BENJAMIN FRANKLIN, historian, was born in Richmond, Va., June 8, 1799, and died in New York City, May 30, 1877. For many years he engaged successfully in planting in Louisiana, collected an immense library which he presented to New Orleans, and published several important volumes; among them, 'Biographia Americana,' a series of sketches (New York, 1825), 'Memoirs of Eminent Female Writers' (Philadelphia, 1827), 'Beauties of Byron, Scott, and Moore' (New York, 1828), 'Historical Collections of Louisiana' (1846-1858), 'History and Progress of the Iron Trade of the United States' (1858), and 'Historical Annals of North America' (1861).

FRENCH LITERATURE OF LOUISIANA. See Biographical and Critical Sketch, Vol. IV, page 1739.

FRENCH, SAMUEL G., soldier, was born in New Jersey, November 22, 1818. He graduated at West Point, served with distinction in the Mexican War, resigned his commission and became a planter in Mississippi, gave his sword to the Confederate cause, attained the rank of major-general, and, after the war, settled in Pensacola, Fla. He published: 'Two Wars: an Autobiography' (Nashville, The Confederate Veteran).

FRENCH, L. VIRGINIA SMITH, poet, was born in Maryland, in 1830, at the home of her grandfather, Captain Thomas Parker, an officer of the Revolution. Her maiden name was Virginia Smith. She began her literary career in Memphis, Tenn., and it was while here that her poem, "The Lost Louisiana," attracted the attention of the man who subsequently became her husband, John L. French, a wealthy planter of Louisiana. For a time she was associate editor of *The Southern Lady's Book,* published in New Orleans. Her writings include: 'Wind Whispers,' 'Legends of the South.' 'Darlingtonia.' 'My Roses,' 'One or Two,' and 'The Lady of Talo,' a drama. She died in 1881.

FRIES, ADELAIDE L. Writer. [N.C.]. She published a 'History of Salem Female Academy,' a 'History of Forsyth County, N.C.' (1898), 'The Moravians in Georgia, 1735-1740,' and an "Operetta" (1896), for which she composed both words and music.

FROST, JAMES MARION. Baptist clergyman. [Tenn.]. He was born in 1849 and published 'Pedo-baptism: Is It from Heaven or from Man?' (1890), and 'The Consistency of Restricted Communion' (1892). His daughter, Miss Margaret Frost, has also published several volumes.

FROST, WILLIAM GOODELL. Educator and divine, engaged in the work of adapting educational methods to conditions of life in the mountainous regions of the South. He was born in Le Roy, N.Y., July 2, 1854, the son of the Rev. Lewis P. and Maria Goodell Frost; was educated at Oberlin College, and also studied at Worcester and at Harvard, later taking special work at Göttingen. He was twice married and was professor of Greek at Oberlin College for thirteen years. In 1893 he became president of Berea College. He has published a 'Greek Primer' and 'Inductive Studies in Oratory,' in addition to numerous contributions to the periodicals. He holds the D.D. and the Ph.D. degrees.

FRUIT, JOHN PHELPS. Educator. He was born in Pembroke, Ky., November 22, 1855, a son of John G. Fruit. He was educated at Bethel College, in Kentucky, and also studied at Leipsic (Ph.D.). He married, December 27, 1881, Mary A. Grubbs. In 1898 he became professor of English language and literature in William Jewell College. He has frequently lectured before Chautauqua assemblies. His works include: 'The Mind and Art of Poe's Poetry' (New York, A. S. Barnes and Company), and numerous articles for the magazines. He has edited 'Lycidas' (Boston, Ginn and Company) and 'The Ancient Mariner' (Boston, B. H. Sanborn and Company). He resides at Liberty, Mo.

FRY, BENJAMIN ST. JAMES, clergyman, was born in Rutledge, Tenn., June 16, 1824. He was educated in Cincinnati, entered the Methodist itinerant ranks, edited several papers, became president of Woffington College for Young Ladies, and wrote biographies of Bishops Whatcoat, McKendree, Roberts and George, besides numerous Sabbath-school books. He held the degree of D.D.

FRY, JESSE. Poet. [N.C.]. He published a collection of verse entitled 'Selections' (Winston-Salem, 1889, paper edition).

FULKERSON, H. S. Author. [Miss.]. He wrote: 'Random Recollections of Early Days in Mississippi' (Vicksburg, 1885), and 'The Negro: Past, Present and Future' (Vicksburg, 1887).

FULLER, CAROLINE M. Author. She wrote in the vein of humor two entertaining books entitled 'The Alley-Cat's Kitten' (Boston, Little, Brown and Company, 1907), and 'The Flight of Puss Pandora' (*ibid.*, 1908), besides short stories and sketches.

FULLER, EDWIN WILEY. See Biographical and Critical Sketch, Vol. IV, page 1751.

FULLER, PHOEBE W. Educator. [S.C.]. She wrote 'Shadows Cast Before,' a work of merit, besides essays and sketches.

FULLER, RICHARD, clergyman, was born at Beaufort, S.C., April 22, 1904, and was the son of Thomas and Elizabeth Middleton Fuller. For several years he practiced law; but, relinquishing this profession for the ministry, he became one of the foremost Baptist divines of the ante-bellum days and was for more than two decades a pastor in Baltimore. His works include 'Sermons,' in four volumes, 'Correspondence with Bishop England upon the Roman Chancery,' 'Correspondence with Dr. Wayland on Slavery,' 'An Argument on Close Communion,' and others. In association with Dr. J. B. Jeter, he also compiled a hymn-book: 'The Psalmist,' which has been used by Baptists on both sides of the water. He died in Baltimore, October 20, 1876. He received the degree of D.D. from Harvard.

FULMORE, ZACHARY TAYLOR. Author. [Texas]. He was born in 1846 and published a 'Plea for Texas Literature.'

FULTON, ROBERT BURWELL. Educator. He was born in Sumter County, Ala., April 8, 1849, the son of William F. and Elizabeth K. Fulton; graduated with the highest honors from the University of Mississippi; and belongs to several of the learned societies of Europe and America. In 1892 he became chancellor of the University of Mississippi, and in 1906 superintendent of the Miller Technical School. Besides contributing articles on the "State of Mississippi" to the 'Encyclopædia Britannica' (1878 and 1902) he has delivered numerous addresses on educational subjects and written frequent reviews for educational journals. He was twice married and resides in Oxford, Miss. Three institutions have given him the degree of LL.D.

FURMAN, JAMES CLEMENT. Baptist clergyman and educator. [S.C.]. He was born in 1809. For several years he was president of Furman University, at Greenville, S.C., an institution named for his father. Besides editing *The Baptist Courier,* he published numerous sermons and addresses.

FURMAN, RICHARD, Baptist clergyman, was born in Æsopus, N.Y., in 1755, and died in Charleston, S.C., in 1825. When he preached in Virginia, Cornwallis is said to have offered a reward for his apprehension. After the Revolution he became pastor of a church in Charleston and because of his zeal for education, Furman University was named in his honor. He published numerous discourses, including one on "Washington," delivered by appointment of the Society of the Cincinnati. Brown University gave him the degree of D.D.

FURMAN, RICHARD. Baptist clergyman. [S.C.]. He was born in 1816 and died in 1886. He published 'The Pleasures of Piety, and Other Poems' (1859), besides an interesting 'Description of Table Rock, N.C.'

FUTRELLE, JACQUES, author, was born in Pike County, Ga., April 9, 1875. His father was Wiley H. H. Futrelle and his mother, Linnie Bevill. He was educated in public and private schools; and, on completing his studies, he engaged for two years in newspaper work in Atlanta. Later he engaged in theatrical management; but, again returning to the pen, he settled in New England and rose rapidly to the front by reason of his unusual talents. Besides numerous short stories, he has published 'The Chase of the Golden Plate' (New York, Dodd, Mead and Company), 'The Thinking Machine' *(ibid.)*, 'The Elusive Isabel' (Indianapolis, The Bobbs-Merrill Company), and others. He resides in Scituate, Mass.

GADSDEN, CHRISTOPHER EDWARDS, Protestant Episcopal bishop, was born in Charleston, S.C., November 25, 1785, and died in Charleston, S.C., June 24, 1852. After graduation from Yale, he studied theology and was admitted to orders. For several years he was rector of St. Philip's Church in Charleston. He was consecrated bishop in 1840. Besides editing *The Gospel Messenger,* he published several sermons, a tract on "The Prayer-book as It Is" and an essay on "The Life of Bishop Dehon" (1833).

GAILOR, THOMAS FRANK. Protestant Episcopal Bishop of Tennessee, educator and author. He was born in Jackson, Miss., September 17, 1856, and was educated at Racine College, Wis., afterward taking the theological course. He married, November 11, 1885, Ellen Douglas Cunningham. He was ordained a deacon in 1876 and a priest in 1880. He was rector of the Church of the Messiah, at Pulaski, Tenn., until chosen professor of ecclesiastical history in the University of the South in 1882. He became chaplain in 1883 and vice-chancellor in 1890. He declined the bishopric of Georgia, but in 1893 he was elected bishop-coadjutor of Tennessee by unanimous vote, and succeeded to the bishopric of Tennessee on the death of Bishop Quintard in 1898. Among his published works are: 'Apostolical Succession,' 'The Divine Event of All Time,' 'Things New and Old,' 'The Trust of the Episcopate,' 'A Manual of Devotion,' 'The Puritan Reaction,' 'The Master's Word and Church's Act,' 'Apostolic Order,' 'Christianity and Education,' and 'The Episcopal Church and Other Religious Communions.' He is a member of the advisory council of 'The Library of Southern Literature.' The D.D. and the S.T.D. degrees have each been conferred upon him by two separate institutions. He resides in Memphis.

GAINES, GEORGE STROTHER. [Miss.]. He was born in 1784 and died in 1873. He wrote 'Reminiscences of Mississippi.'

GALLAGHER, WILLIAM DAVIS. Journalist. [Ky.]. He was born in 1808. For years he edited papers in Kentucky, wrote in both prose and verse, and published "The Wreck of the Hornet," "Errato," "Miami Woods," and other poems.

GALLOWAY, CHARLES BETTS, bishop of the M. E. Church South, was born in Kosciusko, Miss., September 1, 1849; and, after graduation from the University of Mississippi, he joined the Methodist ministry and became one of the foremost divines of his generation. As an orator he possessed rare gifts and few equals. He represented his church at most of the great world-gatherings and was an influential factor in public affairs. From 1882 to 1886 he edited *The Christian Advocate.* Some of the most important pastorates in the South were filled by him prior to his elevation to the Episcopal Bench; and in his official capacity as bishop he visited the missionary stations in many parts of the world. On his thirtieth birthday he married Miss H. E. Willis. Included among his published works are: 'The Life of Bishop Linus Parker' (Nashville, Bagham and Smith), 'Hand-book of Prohibition' *(ibid.)*, 'Open Letter on Prohibition,' written in a controversy with Jefferson Davis *(ibid.)*, 'Methodism, a Child of Providence,' 'A Circuit of the Globe' *(ibid.)*,

'Modern Missions—Their Evidential Value' (*ibid.*), and 'Christianity and the American Commonwealth.' The sketch of L. Q. C. Lamar in 'The Library of Southern Literature' is also from his pen. Bishop Galloway died at his home in Jackson, Miss., May 12, 1909. The University of Mississippi gave him the degree of D.D.; Tulane and Northwestern, the degree of LL.D.

GAMBRELL, JAMES B., clergyman and educator, was born in Andersonville, N.C., August 21, 1841, served in the Confederate Army before he was of age, and completed his education at the University of Mississippi, after the close of hostilities. For fifteen years he was editor of *The Baptist Record,* published in Mississippi; in 1893 was elected president of Mercer University at Macon, Ga., and in 1896 became superintendent of Baptist Missions for Texas. Besides frequent contributions to periodicals, he published a volume entitled 'Ten Years in Texas' (1907). Furman University gave him the degree of D.D. and Wake Forest College, the degree of LL.D.

GANO, JOHN. Clergyman. [Ky.] He wrote a volume entitled, 'Biographical Sketches of the Reverend John Gano, of Frankfort, Ky.' (1806).

GANTOR, FRANZ S. Poet. [La.] He published, in twelve cantos, a poem entitled "Man" (New Orleans, 1871).

GARBER, VIRGINIA ARMISTEAD, Mrs. Author. She published a volume entitled 'Pocahontas' (New York, 1907), which revives the beautiful legend of colonial days; and besides being the author, she is also the illustrator of this artistic booklet. The work contains a reproduction of the only authentic portrait of the Indian maiden.

GARDEN, ALEXANDER, clergyman, was born in Scotland in 1785, and died in Charleston, S.C., September 27, 1856. He was a clergyman of the Church of England and published 'Six Letters to George Whitefield' and 'Two Sermons.'

GARDEN, ALEXANDER, physician and naturalist, was the son of the Rev. Alexander Garden and was born in Edinburgh, Scotland, in 1730, and died in London, England, April 15, 1791. He was eminent as a botanist and as a zoölogist. In 1775 he began a correspondence with Linnæus, to whom he furnished information on the natural history of South Carolina and who coined in his honor the term "Gardenia." He made frequent contributions to the scientific journals of the day, was famous for his investigations and discoveries, and became vice-president of the Royal Society of London.

GARDEN, ALEXANDER, soldier and author, was the son of Alexander Garden, the naturalist, and was born in Charleston, S.C., December 4, 1757. He was an aide-de-camp at one time to General Nathanael Greene and published 'Anecdotes of the Revolutionary War, with Character Sketches of Persons Most Distinguished in the Southern States for Civil and Military Services' (Charleston, 1822). The work passed into several editions, due to the important and exclusive information which it contained. He died in Charleston, S.C., February 29, 1829.

"GARDINER, HELEN HAMILTON" (Mrs. S. A. Day). Author.

GARLAND, AUGUSTUS HILL, statesman, was born in Tipton County, Tenn., June 11, 1832, was educated in Kentucky, and, after settling in Arkansas for the practice of law, was duly admitted to the Bar. He opposed secession, but adhered to the cause of the South and served in the Confederate Congress. After the war he became governor of Arkansas and served in the United States Senate from 1877 to 1885.

During President Cleveland's first administration he held the office of Attorney-general in the Cabinet; and, on relinquishing his portfolio, he resumed the practice of law in Washington, D.C., where he resided until his death, which occurred in 1899.

GARLAND, HUGH A., lawyer, was born in Nelson County, Va., June 1, 1805, and died in St. Louis, Mo., October 15, 1854. He published an excellent 'Life of John Randolph' (New York, D. Appleton and Company).

GARLAND, LANDON CABELL, educator, was born in Nelson County, Va., March 21, 1810, and was educated at Hampden-Sidney College. He achieved distinction in the educational world and at different times was connected with some of the foremost colleges and universities of the South. In 1875 he became chancellor of Vanderbilt University, at Nashville, Tenn. He was at home in any field of the natural sciences. Besides contributing to various periodicals, he published a treatise on 'Trigonometry, Plane and Spherical.'

GARLINGTON, ERNEST ALBERT. Author. [S.C.]. He wrote 'Historical Sketches of the Seventh Cavalry Regiment.'

GARNER, C. H., Miss. Author. [Miss.] She published a volume of miscellany entitled 'A Ring of Rhymes, and Short Stories' (1904).

GARNER, J. W. Author. [Miss.] He wrote 'Reconstruction in Mississippi' (New York, The Macmillan Company, 1901), an important work.

GARNETT, ALEXANDER YELVERTON PEYTON. Physician and surgeon. [Va.] He published two important medical papers on "The Potomac Marshes" and "Epidemic Jaundice," which aroused popular interest in the reclamation of swamps.

GARNETT, JAMES MERCER. Publicist and Congressman. [Va.] He was born in 1770 and died in 1843. He wrote at frequent intervals for the press on current topics of interest, was a pioneer in the cause of female education, served in Congress from Virginia for four years and published 'Constitutional Charts' (1829), 'Female Education,' and numerous essays.

GARNETT, JAMES MERCER. Philologist. He was born in Aldie, Va., April 24, 1840, the son of Theodore Stanford and Florentina Isadora Moreno Garnett and the grandson of James Mercer Garnett, Member of Congress. He graduated from the University of Virginia, and married, April 19, 1871, Kate H. Noland. He served in the Confederate Army from 1861 to 1865, attaining the rank of artillery captain. He was professor of English language and literature for fourteen years in the University of Virginia, has frequently been honored by the great educational assemblies of the country with the highest elective positions, and is an acknowledged authority on philological subjects. His literary productions include: 'Translation of Beowolf' (Boston, Ginn and Company), 'Elene, and Other Anglo-Saxon Poems' (ibid.), History of the University of Virginia,' and 'Addresses and Reviews.' Besides, he has edited 'Selections in English Prose' (ibid.), which has been reprinted several times, "Hayne's Speech," "Macbeth," and "Burke's Speech on Conciliation with America." For 'The Library of Southern Literature' he wrote the sketch of Robert Hayne. St. John's College gave him the degree of LL.D. He resides in Baltimore, Md.

GARNETT, THEODORE S. Jurist. [Va.]. During the Civil War, Judge Garnett was an aide-de-camp on the staff of General J. E. B.

Stuart, the noted Confederate cavalry officer, and his address delivered at the unveiling of the equestrian statue of his commander at Richmond, Va., on May 30, 1907, is a tribute of rare grace and fervor (New York and Washington, The Neale Publishing Company, 1907).

GARRETT, ALEXANDER CHARLES, Protestant Episcopal bishop, was born at Ballymore, Ireland, November 4, 1832, and was the son of the Rev. John G. Garrett. On completing his education at Trinity College, Dublin, he was ordained to the ministry; and, after being for three years a curate, he became a missionary in British Columbia. In 1879 he was chosen rector of St. James's Church, San Francisco, and in 1874 missionary bishop of Northern Texas. Later, when the diocese of Dallas was formed, he was given this important jurisdiction. His published works include: 'A Charge to the Clergy and Laity of North Texas,' 'Historical Continuity' (1875), 'The Eternal Sacrifice, and Other Sermons' (1881), and 'The Baldwin Lectures on the Philosophy of the Incarnation' (1891). He received the degree of D.D. from Nebraska College and the degree of LL.D. from the University of Mississippi.

GARRETT, JAMES J. Soldier and author. [Ala.]. He was born in 1837. He published 'The Forty-fourth Alabama Regiment.'

GARRETT, LEWIS. Methodist clergyman. He served a number of churches along the Kentucky and Tennessee frontier, was presiding elder in 1804 and published a work entitled 'Recollections of the West.'

GARRETT, THOMAS E. Writer. [Mo.]. He published a volume of verse entitled 'The Masque of the Muses' (1883).

GARRETT, WILLIAM. He was born in 1809. In riper years he was for some time Secretary of State of Alabama and wrote 'Reminiscences of Public Men in Alabama for Thirty Years,' an important contribution to the biographical literature of the State.

GARRETT, WILLIAM ROBERTSON, educator and author, was born at Williamsburg, Va., and was the son of Dr. Robert M. and Susan Winder Garrett. On completing his education at William and Mary College, he began the practice of law; but the war soon called him to the front, and during four years he served in the Confederate ranks. He married, November 12, 1868, Julia Flournoy Batte. After the war he engaged in educational work; and for many years he was professor of American history at Peabody Normal College, Nashville, Tenn. His writings include some very important contributions to history: 'The South Carolina Session and the Northern Boundary of Tennessee' (Nashville, M. E. Publishing House, South, 1884), "The South as a Factor in the Territorial Expansion of the United States," in the 'Confederate Military History' (Atlanta, Ga., The Confederate Publishing Company, 1899); Garrett and Goodpasture's 'History of Tennessee' (1900), and 'Geography of Tennessee' (Boston, Ginn and Company, 1902). Besides, he edited for some time *The American Historical Magazine* of Peabody Normal College. He died in 1904. The University of Nashville gave him the degree of Ph.D.

GARRISON, GEORGE PIERCE. Professor of history in the University of Texas. He was born in Carroll County, Ga., December 19, 1853, a son of P. G. and Mary Ann Curtiss Garrison, and was educated both in this country and in Scotland. He married, November 6, 1881, Annie Perkins. His writings include: 'The Civil Government of Texas' (1898), "Texas," in 'The American Commonwealth Series' (Boston, Houghton, Mifflin and Company), and "Westward Extension," in 'The American Nation,' Vol. XVII (New York, Harper and Brothers), besides various articles in the magazines and periodicals. For 'The Library of Southern Literature' he wrote the sketch of General Sam Houston. The University of Chicago gave him the degree of LL.D. He resides in Austin. Texas.

GASTON. JAMES McFADDEN. physician, was born in South Carolina in 1824. At the close of the Civil War he emigrated to Brazil, but after several years of residence he returned to the United States and located in Atlanta, Ga. He published 'Hunting a Home in Brazil.' Dr. Gaston died in Atlanta, Ga., in 1903.

GATEWOOD, JULIA GREENLEAF, Mrs. Writer. [Ala.]. Born in 1854. Her maiden name was Howard. She wrote a novel, 'Wedded Unwooed' (1892).

GATSCHET, A. S. [Ala.]. He wrote 'The Migration Legend of the Creek Indians.'

GAYARRÉ, CHARLES. See Biographical and Critical Sketch, Vol. IV, page 1773.

GAY, MARY ANN HARRIS. Author. She was born in Jones County, Ga., March 19, 1829. It is due in no small measure to the personal efforts of this patriotic woman that sufficient funds were raised for the erection of the monument at Crawfordville, Ga., to Alexander H. Stephens. She is one of the typical representatives of the ante-bellum days, devoted to the memories of her beloved Southland. Her writings, which deal most interestingly with the war period, include: 'The Pastor's Study, and Other Stories,' eleven editions of which have been issued by the Southern Methodist Publishing House, Nashville, Tenn.; 'Life in Dixie During the War' (Atlanta, C. P. Byrd, 1892, four editions); and 'The Transplanted' (Washington and New York, The Neale Publishing Company, 1907.). She resides in Decatur, Ga.

GEE, PATTIE WILLIAMS. Poet. [N.C.]. She published a volume of verse entitled 'The Palace of the Heart, and Other Poems of Love' (Boston, Richard G. Badger and Company, 1904).

GEORGE, JAMES ZACHARIAH, jurist and statesman, was born in Monroe County, Ga., in 1826, but settled in Mississippi. He served in the Mexican War and also in the Civil War, attaining the rank of brigadier-general in the Confederate Army. The measures of Reconstruction provoked his strongest opposition, and his resistance of the wrongs and outrages of this turbulent period made him widely popular. He was chief justice of the State for two years; and for eighteen years United States Senator. As an orator he possessed few equals; and as a lawyer his impress is stamped upon the Constitution of Mississippi. Besides his speeches in the *Congressional Record,* his 'Digest of Mississippi Reports' (Philadelphia, T. and J. W. Johnson) is his only published work. He died in 1897.

GERALD, FLORENCE. Writer. [Texas.] She published a number of patriotic poems under the title of 'Lays of the Republic, and Other Poems.'

GERSTAECKER, F. Author. [La.] He wrote in French an interesting work entitled 'Les Pirates du Mississippi' (Paris, 1856).

GEYER, HENRY SHEFFIE. United States Senator, was born in Fredericktown, Md.. December 9, 1790, and died in St. Louis, Mo., March 5, 1859. After settling in Missouri for the practice of his profession, he was largely instrumental in shaping the constitutional and statutory law of the commonwealth. He declined the office of Secretary of War in the Cabinet of President Fillmore, but became a condidate for the United States Senate, and, on the fortieth ballot, defeated Thomas H. Benton. He served from 1851 to 1857; and, while in Washington, was one of the counsel in the Dred Scott Case. He published 'Statutes of Missouri' (St. Louis, 1817).

GIBBES, FRANCES GUIGNARD, poet, was born in Columbia, S.C. Her only published work is a volume of verse entitled 'Poems by Frances Guignard Gibbes' (New York and Washington, The Neale Publishing Company, 1905), but it contains some very dainty fragments of song. She expects to publish soon a poetic drama. Miss Gibbes resides in Columbia, S.C., at her childhood's home, "The Green."

GIBBES, JAMES G. Author. [S.C.]. He wrote 'Who Burned Columbia?'

GIBBES, ROBERT WILSON, scientist and historian, was born in Charleston, S.C., July 8, 1809, and died in Columbia, S.C., October 15, 1866. He was twice mayor of Columbia, edited *The Daily South Carolinian* and *The Weekly Banner,* was surgeon-general of the State from 1861 to 1865, and became an eminent writer on scientific and historical topics. In the burning of Columbia, he lost his rare collection of paintings, fossils and minerals. Besides numerous articles dealing with the geological features of his native State, monographs on medical topics and papers of scientific interest, many of which were reproduced in Europe, he published in three volumes a work of very great value which he was twenty-five years in preparing, viz.: 'A Documentary History of the American Revolution Consisting of Letters and Papers Relating to the Contest for Liberty, Chiefly in South Carolina' (New York and Columbia, 1853).

GIBBONS, JAMES, Roman Catholic cardinal, was born in Baltimore, Md., July 23, 1834. At an early age he was taken by his parents to the old home in Ireland; but the family afterward returned to the United States and settled in New Orleans. The youth was sent to St. Charles College and later to St. Mary's Seminary, in Maryland. Ordained to the priesthood in 1861, he first assisted at St. Patrick's in Baltimore, then became pastor of St. Bridget's at Canton, and afterward private secretary to Archbishop Spalding and chancellor of the Arch-Diocese. In 1868 he became vicar apostolic of North Carolina, with the rank of bishop, and was later transferred to Virginia. On account of his wonderful success in fostering the interests of Catholicism, he was made archbishop in 1877; and still later in 1884 he was invested with the high office of cardinal. His work entitled: 'The Faith of Our Fathers,' has been translated into several different languages; and his other writings include: 'Our Christian Heritage' and 'The Ambassador of Christ.'

GIBBS, GEORGE. Illustrator and author. Though now a resident of Philadelphia, Pa., he was born in New Orleans, La., March 8, 1870. His father, Benjamin F. Gibbs, was a medical inspector in the United States Navy. He was educated in Geneva, Switzerland, Washington, D.C., and Annapolis. From a career in the Navy he was turned by his predilections for art; and, at some of the leading schools of the day, he studied under the best instructors. He also possessed a *penchant* for literature; and, uniting such gifts, he has become both the author and the illustrator of several interesting books which betray on every page the dramatic instinct and the artistic temperament. His writings embrace: 'Pike and Cutlass, or Hero Tales of Our Navy' (Philadelphia, J. B. Lippincott Company), 'In Search of Mademoiselle' (Philadelphia, Henry T. Coates). 'American Sea Fights,' a portfolio of drawings (New York, R. H. Russell), and 'The Love of Monsieur' (New York, Harper and Brothers).

GIBSON, J. M., lawyer, was born near Vicksburg, Miss. In 1879 he was admitted to the Bar; and after serving two terms in the Legislature, he settled in Houston, Texas. He is the author of several poems which have attracted much interest, among them, "Madaline," founded upon the love affair of Aaron Burr and Madaline Price, of Natchez, Miss.; "Zurline," "Vita et Mors," and others. In a fire which occurred in 1907 he lost several manuscripts, including a drama in blank verse, a novel, and several poems.

GIBSON, RANDALL LEE. Soldier and statesman. He was born at Spring Hill, Ky., September 10, 1832. On graduating from Yale University he took a course of law in the University of Louisiana. He enlisted in the Confederate Army and rose to very high distinction, attaining the rank of major-general. On the organization of the Board of Administrators of Tulane University, he was elected president. He represented Louisiana for several terms in the national House of Representatives, and from 1883 until the time of his death he was United States Senator. He was eloquent in debate and a volume of his select speeches appeared in 1887. He died December 15, 1892.

GIBSON, ROBERT EDWARD LEE, author, was born in Steelville, Mo., January 14, 1864. His father was Dr. Alexander Gibson. On completing his studies, he first taught school and afterward engaged in journalism in his native State; but of late years he has resided at Reno, Nev., where he is interested in mining properties. At an early age he began to write verse, contributing to the leading magazines before he was well grown. His publications include: 'Early Poems,' 'Sonnets and Lyrics' (Louisville, J. P. Martin), and 'A Miracle of St. Cuthbert.'

GIBSON, WILLIAM, surgeon and physician, was born in Baltimore, Md., in 1788, and died in Savannah, Ga., March 2, 1868. He became an eminent practitioner, taught for several years in the University of Pennsylvania, traveled extensively abroad, and published several volumes, including 'Principles and Practice of Surgery' (Philadelphia, 1824), 'Rambles in Europe,' and 'Lectures on Eminent Surgeons and Physicians of Belgium' (New York, 1841). Dr. Gibson received his medical degree at the University of Edinburgh. Some few years later he returned to Europe, participated in the battle of Waterloo on the side of the allied forces, and witnessed the downfall of Napoleon.

GIBSON, WILLIAM. Naval officer. [Md.]. He was born in 1826 and died in 1887. At intervals of leisure he exercised his poetic gifts by writing verse and published 'Poems of Many Years,' and 'The Vision of Fairy-Land, and Other Poems.'

GIELOW, MARTHA S. Author. She has published two delightful works which treat of life in the ante-bellum period, entitled 'Plantation Days' (1903) and 'The Volunteer' (1905).

GILBERT, DAVID McCONAUGHEY. Clergyman. He was born in Pennsylvania in 1836, but settled in Virginia at the beginning of his ministerial labors. He wrote: 'The Lutheran Church in Virginia' (Newmarket, 1876), and 'Muhlenberg's Ministry in Virginia' (1884), besides minor works.

GILCHRIST, ANNIE S. Writer. [Tenn.]. She wrote two interesting stories entitled 'Rosehurst' and 'Harcourt.'

GILDERSLEEVE, BASIL LANNEAU. See Biographical and Critical Sketch, Vol. IV, page 1795.

GILES, WILLIAM BRANCH, statesman, was born in Amelia County, Va., August 12, 1762, and died in Albemarle County, Va., December 4, 1830. He was educated both at Hampden-Sidney and at Princeton, became eminent at the Bar as an advocate, served in Congress for several years, succeeded William C. Nicholas in the United States Senate in 1804, and held that office until 1811. Afterward he was governor of Virginia. John Randolph compared him to Charles James Fox in power of debate. He spoke on most of the public questions of the day and published a number of letters.

GILL, GEORGE CRESWELL. Author. [Ky.]. He published a romance of Kentucky life entitled 'Beyond the Blue Grass,' which contains some very realistic portraitures (New York and Washington, The Neale Publishing Company, 1908).

GILLELAND, WILLIAM M. Writer. [Texas]. He wrote "The Burial March of General Thomas Green," "In Memory of General Ben McCulloch," and other poems.

GILLESPIE, HELENA, Mrs. Educator. [Texas]. Her maiden name was Helena West. She wrote "Tennyson's Picture" and other poems.

GILLESPIE, JOSEPH H. Clergyman and educator. [N.C.]. He published a volume of verse entitled 'Elsinore, and Other Poems' (Raleigh, Edwards and Broughton, 1888), besides numerous uncollected poems, essays, and sketches.

GILMAN, CAROLINE HOWARD. See Biographical and Critical Sketch, Vol. IV, page 1831.

GILMAN, DANIEL COIT. An eminent educator. He was born in Norwich, Conn., July 6, 1831, a son of William C. and Eliza Coit Gilman; and a descendant of Councillor John Gilman, of Exeter, N.H., an emigrant from England in 1638. He graduated from Yale University, but continued his studies at Cambridge and Berlin. Eight separate institutions conferred upon him the degree of LL.D. He married, first, Mary Ketcham and, second, Elizabeth Dwight Woolsey. He was professor of physical aand political geography at Yale from 1856 to 1872; and president of the University of California from 1872 to 1875. He was also the first president of Johns Hopkins University, holding this position from 1875 to 1902; and was the first president of the Carnegie Institution, in Washington, D.C. As an organizer he developed the very highest powers. He was a member of learned societies in both hemispheres; also a member of the United States Commission which fixed the boundary line between Venezuela and British Guiana. He was president of the Slater Fund and vice-president of the Peabody Fund. His works include: his "Bi-centennial Discourse," delivered at Norwich, Conn., in 1859, and his "Inauguration Address," delivered in Baltimore in 1876; also a 'Life of James Monroe' (Boston, Houghton, Mifflin and Company), 'University Problems,' "Introduction to De Tocqueville's Democracy in America," 'Life of James D. Dana' (New York, Harper and Brothers), 'Science and Letters in Yale,' and 'The Launching of a University' (New York, Dodd, Mead and Company). Besides, he was editor-in-chief of the 'New International Encyclopædia,' published by Dodd, Mead and Company. Dr. Gilman died in 1908.

GILMAN, SAMUEL. Clergyman and author. For nearly forty years he was pastor of the Unitarian Church, at Charleston, S.C., but was born in Gloucester, Mass., February 16, 1791, and died at Kingston, Mass., February 9, 1858. Beyond the bounds of his parish he was chiefly known through his pen. Besides numerous contributions to magazines and reviews, he made several translations, lectured at frequent intervals, and published 'Memoirs of a New England Village Choir,' 'Pleasures and Pains of a Student's Life,' and a number of poems, one of which "The History of a Ray of Light," was read before the Phi Beta Kappa Society, of Harvard, from which institution he received his degree of Doctor of Divinity.

GILMER, ELIZABETH MERIWETHER ("Dorothy Dix"). Short-story writer and journalist. She was born in Montgomery County, Tenn., November 18, 1870. She married George O. Gilmer and edited the woman's department of the New Orleans *Picayune* for five years. In 1900 she joined the staff of the New York *American* as a writer on special topics. For years the "Dorothy Dix Talks" have been famous. She is also the author of numerous stories, contributed to the magazines and periodicals. She resides in New York City.

GILMER, GEORGE ROCKINGHAM, Congressman and governor, was born in Oglethorpe County, Ga., April 11, 1790, and died at Lexington, Ga., November 15, 1859. He was several times elected to Congress and was twice governor of Georgia. In his will he substantially remembered the State University, of which for thirty years he was an honored trustee, and his memory is fragrantly embalmed in the affections of his *alma mater.* He published an interesting volume entitled 'Georgians.' It was widely read at the time because of the caustic and pungent manner in which he paid his fearless respects to sundry individuals. Only a few copies of this rare volume are now extant.

GILMOR, HARRY, soldier, was born in Baltimore, Md., January 24, 1838. On the Confederate side in the Civil War, he became conspicuous for his daring as a scout and narrowly escaped death on several occasions, besides being severely and desperately wounded. His work entitled 'Four Years in the Saddle' is full of graphic interest (New York, 1866). He died in Baltimore, Md., March 4, 1883.

GIRARD, M. D., Madame. Author. [La.]. She published in French a 'Histoire des États Unis, Suivie de l'Histoire de la Louisiane pour les Enfants' (New Orleans, 1881).

GIRARDEAU, JOHN L., Presbyterian clergyman and theological professor, was born on James Island, S.C., November 14, 1825. On completing his studies at Charleston College, he took a course in theology, entered the Presbyterian ministry and achieved eminence both in the pulpit and in the class-room. As an orator he possessed no superior. His sermon on the "Last Judgment" is said to have been the most powerful discourse on this subject since the days of Jonathan Edwards. For many years he was a professor in the Theological Seminary at Columbia, S.C. He published 'Instrumental Music in the Public Worship of the Church' (Richmond, Whittet and Shepperson, 1888), 'Calvinism and Evangelical Arminianism' (Columbia, W. J. Duffie, 1890), 'The Will in Its Theological Relations' (*ibid.,* 1891), 'Discussions of Philosophical Questions' (Richmond, Presbyterian Committee of Publication, 1900), 'Discussions of Theological Questions' (*ibid.,* 1905), and 'Sermons' (Columbia, The State Company, 1907). He married, June 24, 1849, Sarah P. Hamlin. Dr. Girardeau held both the D.D. and the LL.D. degrees. He died at Columbia, S.C., June 23, 1908.

GLASSON, WILLIAM HENRY. Professor of political economy and social science in Trinity College, N.C. He was born in Troy, N.Y., July 26, 1874, and was educated at Cornell University. He has made a specialty of the pension system of the United States. Besides editing *The South Atlantic Quarterly,* in association with Edwin

Mims, he has contributed numerous articles to the periodicals and wrote 'The History of Military Pension Legislation in the United States' (New York, The Macmillan Company, 1900). He resides in Durham, N.C., and holds the degree of Ph.D.

GLASGOW, ELLEN ANDERSEN GHOLSON. See Biographical and Critical Sketch, Vol. IV, page 1847.

GLENN, JAMES. Governor of South Carolina from 1744 to 1755. He published a 'Description of South Carolina' (London, 1761).

GLISAN, RODNEY, physician and surgeon, was born in Frederick County, Md., January 29, 1827. For several years he served in the Navy, saw much of the world on various cruises, and published a 'Journal of Army Life' (San Francisco, 1874), 'Two Years in Europe' (New York, 1887), and numerous medical works.

GODDARD, PAUL BECK, physician, was born in Baltimore, Md., January 26, 1811, and died in Philadelphia, Pa., July 3, 1866. He became an eminent practitioner in Philadelphia and wrote numerous medical works.

GODFREY, THOMAS. Dramatist and poet. [N.C.]. Mr. Godfrey wrote what is claimed to be the first American drama, entitled "The Prince of Parthia" (Philadelphia, 1765). He also wrote "The Court of Fancy" (1763), a poem modeled in part on the pseudo-Chaucer's "House of Fame." In 1767 Nathaniel Evans published a collection of his verse with a memoir. The author is buried in Wilmington, N.C.

GODMAN, JOHN D., physician, was born in Annapolis, Md., December 20, 1794, and died in Germantown, Pa., April 17, 1830. For several years he taught medicine in Cincinnati. He also practiced in Baltimore and Philadelphia. As a lecturer on anatomy he is said to have been without a rival. Besides numerous contributions to medical and scientific journals, he wrote 'American Natural History,' 'Rambles of a Naturalist,' 'Irregularities of Structure and Morbid Anatomy,' and several others. His biography was written by Dr. Sewell.

GOLDSBOROUGH, CHARLES WASHINGTON. Author. For several years he was connected in various capacities with the naval department of the United States Government. He was born in Cambridge, Md., April 18, 1779, and died in Washington, D.C., in 1843. He wrote 'The United States Naval Chronicle,' and left at his death, substantially complete, 'The History of the American Navy,' in manuscript.

GOODE, GEORGE BROWN, ichthyologist, was born of Virginia parentage in New Albany, Ind., February 13, 1851, and was descended from John Goode, of Whitby, Va. For several years he was on the scientific staff of the Smithsonian Institution in Washington, D.C., and made extensive researches and explorations. Besides a romance entitled 'Virginia Cousins' (Richmond, 1888), a work replete with incidents and pictures of Southern life, he also published numerous scientific works.

GOODE, JOHN, lawyer, was born in Bedford County, Va., May 27, 1829, and died in Norfolk, Va., July 14, 1909. For three years he served in the Confederate Congress, from 1862 to 1865, and during the legislative recesses acted as an aide on the staff of General Early. After the war he served in the Federal Congress, and still later held the office of Solicitor-general of the United States under President Cleveland. On account of the ripe old age to which he attained and the distinguished place which he filled to the very last, he was often called "the grand old man of Virginia." In the eventide of his days he wrote 'Recollections of a Lifetime,' (New York and Washington, The Neale Publishing Company, 1907), besides contributing a series of articles to the press on "Distinguished Confederate Civilians."

GOODLOE, ABBIE CARTER. See Biographical and Critical Sketch, Vol. V, page 1873.

GOODLOE, ALBERT THEODORE, clergyman and physician, was born in Tennessee but spent the greater part of his life in Arkansas. He kept a diary during the Civil War and gathered from it the material for his work entitled 'Some Rebel Relics from the Seat of War' (1893).

GOODLOE, DANIEL REAVES. Author. [N.C.]. He was born in 1814 and published two works of some interest entitled 'The Birth of the Republic' and 'Reminiscences of Washington.'

GORDON, ARMISTEAD CHURCHILL. See Biographical and Critical Sketch, Vol. V, page 1899.

GORDON, JAMES. United States Senator from Mississippi. Served with gallantry in the Confederate Army during the Civil War. At one time a reward of $10,000 was placed upon his head for alleged complicity in the assassination of President Lincoln, but he satisfied his accusers that he was innocent of any connection with the affair and on the death of Honorable A. J. McLaurin, in 1909, he was appointed by Governor Noel to be the former's successor in the United States Senate for the unexpired term. He published a volume of verse entitled: 'The Old Plantation and Other Poems,' which portrays most charmingly the variant phases of Southern life and character in antebellum days.

GORDON, JAMES LINDSAY. See Biographical and Critical Sketch, Vol. V, page 1919.

GORDON, JOHN BROWN. See Biographical and Critical Sketch, Vol. V. page 1939.

GORE, JAMES HOWARD, educator, was born at Winchester, Va., September 18, 1856, and was educated at Richmond College and at Columbian University, taking post-graduate work at the last-named institution (Ph.D.), after becoming professor of mathematics. On the United States Coast and Geodetic Survey, and also on the United States Geological Survey, he has done some very important work. His treatise on 'Geodesy' (Boston, Houghton, Mifflin and Company) is an authoritative production.

GORE, THOMAS PRYOR, Oklahoma's blind Senator, was born in Webster County, Miss., December 10, 1870. At the age of eight he lost his left eye in a scuffle with a playmate, and three years later he lost his right eye by an arrow from a cross-bow. But, in spite of this double handicap, he prosecuted his studies with the assistance of someone to read to him, and eventually he arose to an eminent position at the Bar. He settled first in Texas; and, making the race for Congress on the Populist ticket, was defeated. But he afterward became a Democrat and settled in Oklahoma, with the result that he was soon chosen to represent the State in the United States Senate. In this body, which he entered in 1907, he has been a power, amazing his colleagues by his wonderful feats of memory, whether in quoting from classic authors, or in dealing in dry statistics, by his ready repartee, and by his comprehensive grasp of governmental problems. He married Miss Nina Kay, of Palestine, Texas.

GORMAN, JOHN BERRY, physician and planter, was born in Edgefield District, S.C., February 22, 1793, and died in Talbot County,

Ga., November 12, 1864. He studied medicine at the University of Pennsylvania, became a practitioner of some note, and accumulated a fortune. He wrote 'The Philosophy of Animated Existence: or, Sketches of Living Physics' (Philadelphia, Soring and Ball, 1845). Dr. Gorman was also an artist and left a picture entitled "The Nightmare."

GORMAN, JOHN BERRY, Jr., planter and journalist, was born in Talbotton, Ga., July 22, 1839. His father was Dr. John B. Gorman, an eminent physician and writer. He published 'Around the World in '84' (Nashville, The Southern Methodist Publishing House, 1886), a narrative of travel most interestingly told.

GORMAN, OSSIAN DANIEL, journalist and educator, was born in Talbotton, Ga., October 3, 1841. His father was Dr. John Berry Gorman. He enjoyed the best educational advantages, pursuing his studies both at Columbian University and at Emory and Henry College. He is a writer of rare gifts, especially in the department of verse. His publications include 'Essays and Poems,' 'The Battle of Hampton Roads,' 'Chancellorsville,' 'Renascence,' and 'Historical Collections.' At present he is superintendent of public schools, at Talbotton. He married, first, December 6, 1864, Martha D. Holmes; and, second, October 25, 1906, Clara Jackson Redding.

GOULD, E. W. He published a volume entitled 'Fifty Years on the Mississippi' (1889).

GOULDING, FRANCIS ROBERT. Clergyman and author of distinction. His fascinating story entitled, 'The Young Marooners,' is one of the standard classics of juvenile literature, taking rank with 'Robinson Crusoe' and 'The Swiss Family Robinson.' The narrator of this delightful tale of adventure was born in Liberty County, Ga., in 1810. He came of sturdy stock, his father, the Rev. Thomas Goulding, having been the first president of the Presbyterian Theological Seminary, at Columbia, S.C. Following in the parental footsteps, he likewise achieved eminence in the pulpit. He filled numerous pastorates; and, while residing at Eatonton, Ga., he conceived the idea of the sewing-machine and constructed, in advance of Elias Howe, the first practical device for mechanical needlework ever used in this country, with pedal attachments. It is said that when the manuscript for 'The Young Marooners' was first submitted to the publishers it was rejected. But it finally emerged from the press of Martin and Company, of Philadelphia; and, taking the country by storm, it was reprinted in Scotland and England, and in various countries of Europe. According to tradition, even Martin and Company were about to decline the manuscript; but it chanced to fall into the hands of a child, and the little one was so captivated by the story that the publishers decided to take the risk. Dr. Goulding reserved the copyright, which was afterward purchased by Dodd, Mead and Company, of New York. The work has since been translated into several languages and has passed through numerous editions. Besides 'The Young Marooners,' the author also published a sequel entitled, 'The Marooners' Island,' the sales of which were enormous. His other writings include: 'Sapelo; or, Child-Life in the Tide-water,' 'Talequah; or, Life Among the Cherokees,' 'Nacoochee; or, Boy Life from Home,' and 'The Woodruff Stories.' He also made contributions to the *Army and Navy Journal*, the series being entitled: "Self-Helps." Dr. Goulding died at Roswell, Ga., August 22, 1881. He is buried in this picturesque little country town, near the childhood home of ex-President Roosevelt's mother.

GRADY, HENRY WOODFIN. See Biographical and Critical Sketch, Vol. V, page 1959.

GRAHAM, EDWARD KIDDER, educator, was born at Charlotte, N.C. His father was Archibald Graham and his mother, Eliza Owen Barry. He occupies the chair of English at the University of North Carolina. Besides magazine articles and monographs on various subjects, he is the author of the sketch of John C. McNeill in 'The Library of Southern Literature.'

GRAHAM, GEORGE W. Physician. [N.C.]. He wrote an interesting work entitled 'The Mecklenburg Declaration of Independence, May 20, 1775, and the Lives of the Signers' (New York and Washington, The Neale Publishing Company, 1905).

GRAHAM, JOSEPH A. Editor. He was born in Salisbury, Mo., September 8, 1855, and on completing his education was admitted to the Bar, but his life has been chiefly devoted to journalism. Since 1893 he has been on the staff of the St. Louis *Republic*. Besides numerous contributions to current literature, he has published a work entitled 'The Sporting Dog' (New York, The Macmillan Company, 1908), which shows him to be an authority on the subject treated.

GRAHAM, WILLIAM ALEXANDER. See Biographical and Critical Sketch, Vol. V, page 1987.

GRAINGER, JAMES MOSES, educator, was born in Knoxville, Tenn., August 12, 1879. Professor Grainger occupies a chair in the faculty of the University of North Carolina. He has published 'Studies in the Syntax of the King James Version' (Chapel Hill, N.C., The Philological Club, 1907). The sketch of Charles Alphonso Smith in 'The Biographical History of North Carolina,' and the sketch of David Crockett in 'The Library of Southern Literature,' are also from his pen.

GRANBERY, JOHN COWPER. Bishop of the Methodist Episcopal Church, South. He was born in Norfolk, Va., December 25, 1829, a son of Richard Allen and Ann Leslie Granbery. He graduated from Randolph-Macon College and held several important pastorates prior to the war. He was a chaplain in the Confederate Army from 1861 to 1865. He married, first, Jennie Massie and, second, Ella Winston. He was professor of moral philosophy and practical theology in Vanderbilt University for seven years and was elected bishop in 1882. His works include: a 'Bible Dictionary,' 'Twelve Sermons,' and 'Experience: the Crowning Evidence of the Christian Religion.' Randolph-Macon College gave him the degree of D.D. He died in Ashland, Va., in 1907.

GRASTY, JOHN S. Presbyterian clergyman. [Mo.]. He published 'Memoirs of Rev. Samuel B. McPheeters' (1871).

GRAVES, ADELIA C., Mrs. Educator. [Tenn.]. She was born in 1821 and died in 1895. Her maiden name was Adelia Spencer. She wrote 'Jephtha's Daughter,' a drama, and 'Ruined Lives'; also poems for children.

GRAVES, H. A. Methodist Episcopal clergyman. [Texas]. He published a work of biography entitled 'The Reverend Andrew Jackson Potter, the Noted Parson of the Texas Frontier.'

GRAVES, JAMES ROBINSON, Baptist clergyman and educator, was born in Vermont in 1820, but preached and taught in the South, where he was something of a leader. His published works include 'The Great Iron Wheel,' 'The Bible Doctrine of the Middle Life' (1873), 'Old Landmarkism' (1880), 'Christian Baptism' (1881), 'The Work of Christ' (1883), 'The Parables and Prophecies of Christ' (1887), 'The First Baptist Church in America' (1890), and numerous tracts and pamphlets. He died in Tennessee in 1893.

GRAVES, JOHN TEMPLE. Orator and editor. He was born at Willington Church, Abbeville County, S.C., November 9, 1856, the son of General James Porterfield and Catherine Floride Calhoun Graves, and grandson of William Calhoun, who was the eldest brother of the illustrious statesman, John C. Calhoun. He was educated at the University of Georgia and married, first, Mattie E. Simpson, of Sparta, Ga., April 17, 1878 and, second, Annie E. Cothran, of Rome, Ga., December 30, 1890. He has edited the Jacksonville (Fla.) *Union,* the Atlanta *Journal,* the Rome (Ga.) *Tribune,* the Atlanta *News,* and the Atlanta *Georgian.* At present he is editor of the New York *American.* He has been presidential elector-at-large from the states of Florida and Georgia, leading the tickets in both elections. He is an ardent Democrat, but, with allegiance to principle rather than to party, he accepted in 1908 the nomination of the Independence League for Vice-president of the United States. In 1899 he delivered his famous eulogy on Henry W. Grady, which immediately made his reputation national. He has been the orator of the New England Society, of Boston, of the New England Society of Philadelphia, of the Merchants' Club of Boston, of the New York Southern Society, of the World's Congress of Journalists, and of many other distinguished organizations. He has discussed most of the leading topics and problems of the day and has been an earnest advocate of the segregation of the races. As a lecturer before Chautauqua assemblies and lyceums, he has been in constant demand. Both as a writer and as a speaker he is a man of marvelous gifts. Besides countless editorials and sketches, he has written: 'The Florida of To-day,' a 'History of Colleton, S.C.,' 'Twelve Standard Lectures,' 'Speeches and Selections for Schools,' and 'The Negro.' He was also one of the editors of 'Eloquent Sons of the South' (Boston, The Chapple Publishing Co., 1909). He resides in New York City.

GRAVES, LOUIS, journalist, was born at Chapel Hill, N.C., August 6, 1883. He is engaged in journalistic work in New York and contributes at intervals to the magazines, his latest piece of work being "The New Cashier," in *The Atlantic Monthly.* The sketch of William Hooper in 'The Library of Southern Literature' is from his pen.

GRAVES, ROSWELL T. Baptist missionary to China. He was born in Baltimore, Md., in 1833. Dr. Graves published 'Forty Years in China, or, China in Transition' (1897).

GRAVIER, GABRIEL. Author. [La.]. He wrote in French several important works, among them, 'Les Découvertes du Cavalier de la Salle' (Paris, 1870), 'Étude sur une Carte Inconnue,' etc. (Paris, 1880), and 'Robert Cavelier de la Salle Rouen' (New York, 1886).

GRAY, A. C., journalist, contributed to 'Wooten's Comprehensive History of Texas' (Dallas, W. G. Scarffy, 1898), an important chapter on "The History of the Texas Press."

"GRAY, BARTON." (See Sass, George Henry).

GRAY, JOHN THOMPSON. Author. [Ky.]. He wrote an entertaining work replete with humor entitled 'A Kentucky Chronicle' (New York and Washington. The Neale Publishing Company, 1904).

GRAYSON, WILLIAM JOHN. See Biographical and Critical Sketch, Vol. V, page 2001.

GREEN, ALEXANDER LITTLE PAGE, clergyman, was born in Sevier County, Tenn., June 6, 1806, and died in Nashville, Tenn., July 15, 1874. He entered the itinerant ranks of Methodism and became an influential divine. At the time of the disruption in 1844 he was appointed one of the commission to adjust property rights, and he was also the principal organizer of the publishing house at Nashville. He was an acknowledged authority on Indian lore. Besides publishing 'The Church in the Wilderness,' he was preparing at the time of his death a work on 'The Fishes of North America.'

GREEN, DUFF, journalist and lawyer, was born in Kentucky, August 15, 1791, and died at Dalton, Ga., June 10, 1875. He studied law and was admitted to the Bar, but much of his time was devoted to editorial work. During the administration of John Quincy Adams he edited an opposition paper in Washington. Later, under President Jackson, he edited the administration organ; but when the breach occurred between President Jackson and Mr. Calhoun, he sided with the Vice-president. His latter years were given to developing the industrial interests of the South. He published 'Facts and Suggestions.'

GREEN, EDWIN L. Educator. He was born in Milton, Fla., December 13, 1870, the son of A. H. and L. V. Green, and was educated at Washington and Lee University and at Johns Hopkins University. In 1900 he became professor of ancient languages in the University of South Carolina, at Columbia, S.C. He is the author of an excellent 'School History of Florida.' The sketch of George McDuffie in 'The Library of Southern Literature' is also from his pen. He holds the degree of Ph.D.

GREEN, LEWIS, clergyman, was born in Kentucky in 1806, and died in Virginia in 1863. He published a contribution to Christian apologetics entitled 'Evidences of Christianity.'

GREEN, NATHAN. Educator. He was born in Winchester, Tenn., February 19, 1827, a son of Nathan and Mary Green. He graduated from Columbia University and subsequently took the law course in the same institution. He married, first, Bettie McClain and, second, Mrs. Blanche Hunter Woodward. He became professor of law in Cumberland University in 1856 and chancellor in 1873. His published works include: 'The Tall Man of Winton' and 'Sparks from a Back Log,' both of which are full of quaint humor. He resides in Lebanon, Tenn. Centre College gave him the degree of LL.D.

GREEN, THOMAS JEFFERSON, soldier, was born in Warren County, N.C., in 1801. Removing to Texas, he attained the rank of brigadier-general in the war for Texan independence; but he violated the orders of General Summerville, whose loyalty he doubted, and, with a small force, left the main body of troops and attacked the town of Mier. The result was disastrous. Officers and men were taken prisoners. In attempting to escape, they were recaptured, taken to the city of Mexico, and every tenth man was ordered to be shot by Santa Anna. Green was kept a prisoner at hard labor for several months, but was finally released. He afterward settled in California and became prominent in politics; but when the Civil War began he entered the Confederate Army and served in the Virginia campaigns. His only published work was 'The Mier Expedition.' He died at his boyhood's home in North Carolina, December 13, 1863.

GREEN, THOMAS MARSHALL. Journalist. [Ky.]. He published 'Historic Families of Kentucky' (1889), and 'The Spanish Conspiracy' (1891), besides minor works. He died in 1904 at the age of sixty-seven.

GREEN, WILLIAM. Lawyer. [Va.]. He published several law books, in addition to numerous essays upon legal topics.

GREEN, WILLIAM MARTIN. Methodist Episcopal clergyman. [Tenn.]. He wrote a 'Life of Dr. A. L. P. Green' (1877), besides also editing his papers.

GREEN, WILLIAM MERCER, Protestant Episcopal bishop, was born in Wilmington, N.C., May 2, 1798, and died in Sewanee, Tenn., February 13, 1887. He was one of the founders of the University of the South, and for several years filled the office of chancellor. He was the first bishop of the diocese of Mississippi and was called to the Episcopal office in 1850. Besides numerous sermons and addresses, he published a 'Memoir of Bishop Ravenscroft, of North Carolina,' and a 'Life of Bishop Otey, of Tennessee.'

GREENE, FRANCES NIMMO, author, was born in Tuscaloosa, Ala. From her pen have come numerous delightful stories for young people. She contributes to magazines and periodicals and has published in book form 'King Arthur and his Court' (Boston, Ginn and Company, 1901), 'With Spurs of Gold' (Boston, Little, Brown and Company, 1905), and 'Into the Night,' a novel (New York, T. Y. Crowell and Company, 1909). She has also written some excellent verse. Her home is in Montgomery, Ala.

GREENE, MARY, Mrs. [Mo.]. She published a 'Life of the Reverend Jesse Greene' (1852).

GREENHOW, ROBERT, physician and scholar, was born in Richmond, Va., in 1800 and died in San Francisco, Cal., in 1854. His mother perished in the burning of the Richmond Theater, when he was a lad of eleven years. He studied medicine, visited Europe, formed the acquaintance of Byron and other men of letters, and returned home to become an eminent writer and lecturer. He was at one time translator in the State Department at Washington; and, many years later, when he removed to the Pacific Coast, he became identified with the United States Land Commission. He published an interesting 'History of Tripoli,' 'The Discovery of the Northwest Coast of North America,' which was prepared by order of Congress and afterward enlarged into 'The History of Oregon and California,' besides several important papers.

GREENWALD, EMANUEL, clergyman, was born near Frederick, Md., January 13, 1811, and died in Lancaster, Pa., December 21, 1885. He became a leader among the Lutherans and published a number of works, among them, 'Romanism and the Reformation' (Lancaster, Pa., 1880), 'Sprinkling the True Mode of Baptism' (Philadelphia, 1876), 'Family Prayer' (1867), 'Jesus, our Table Guest' (Philadelphia, 1883), and 'Meditations for the Closet' (Lancaster, 1885).

GREENWAY, J. R. Author. [Va.]. He published a volume of miscellany entitled 'Here and There.'

GREER, HILTON ROSS, poet, was born at Hawkins, Texas, December 10, 1878. His father was Samuel J. Greer and his mother, Isabella Jane Boren. He is a clerk in the general land office of the State of Texas, but at intervals of leisure he exercises a talent for verse-making of a high order of merit. Two volumes have come from his pen, 'Sun Gleams and Gossamers' (1903), and 'The Spiders, and Other Poems' (1906). For 'The Library of Southern Literature' he wrote a sketch of J. P. Sjolander.

GREGG, ALEXANDER, Protestant Episcopal bishop, was born in Darlington District, S.C., October 8, 1819. After graduating from South Carolina College with the highest honors he practiced law for several years. But feeling called to preach he was admitted to orders, became rector of St. David's parish and in 1859 was consecrated bishop of Texas. He published a 'History of Old Cheraw,' embracing an account of the Indian tribes in the valley of the Pedee in South Carolina, of the first white settlement of the organization of St. David's parish, and of the revolutionary movements of which Cheraw was the center. He also published a 'Sketch of the Church in Texas,' besides minor works.

GREGORY, EDWARD S., journalist, clergyman, poet, was born in Lynchburg, Va., in 1843. The war interrupted his studies; and, after serving in the Confederate Army, he entered journalism, editing for some time *The Presbyterian Index-Appeal.* Later, he became an ordained clergyman of the Episcopal Church. He wrote excellent verse and published two volumes: 'Bonniebell, and Other Poems' (Lynchburg, 1880), and 'Lenore, and Other Poems' (Lynchburg, 1883), besides essays and sketches. He died in 1884.

GRESHAM, JOHN M. [Ky.]. He published a 'Biographical Cyclopædia of Kentucky.'

GRIFFIN, A. P. C. [La.]. He published an account of 'The Discovery of the Mississippi' (1887).

GRIFFIN, GILDEROY WELLS, author, was born in Louisville, Ky., March 6, 1840. For several years he practiced law, after which he entered journalism and still later held consular positions in various parts of the globe. Besides editing 'Prenticeana,' a collection of some of the literary productions of George D. Prentice, he wrote 'Studies in Literature' (1871), 'Life of George D. Prentice' (1871), 'Life of Charles S. Todd' (1873), 'Danish Days' (1874), 'A Visit to Stratford' (1875), and 'New Zealand: her Commerce and Resources' (1884).

GRIFFIN, T. M., Mrs. Poet. She was born in Alabama, but afterward removed to Texas. She contributed both prose and verse to current literature and published a volume of poems.

GRIFFITH, H. P. Educator and author. [S.C.]. He wrote a 'Life of the Reverend John G. Landrum' (Philadelphia, H. B. Garner, 1885).

GRIFFITH, MATTIE. Poet. [Ky.]. She published a volume of poems. The author was a relative of Edward Bulwer, Lord Lytton.

GRIFFITH, THOMAS W. Historian. [Md.]. He published 'The Early History of Baltimore' (1821), and 'The Annals of Baltimore' (1824).

GRIGSBY, HUGH BLAIR, historical scholar and writer, was born in Norfolk, Va., November 22, 1806, and died in Charlotte County, Va., April 28, 1881. He devoted himself to literature and agriculture and became an authority on the history of Virginia. For some time he held the office of chancellor of William and Mary College. He made frequent contributions to *The Southern Literary Messenger,* wrote numerous historical papers and published a 'Discourse on the Honorable Littleton W. Tazewell' (Norfolk, 1860). William and Mary College gave him the degree of LL.D.

GRIMES, J. H. Baptist clergyman. [Tenn.]. He wrote a 'History of Middle Tennessee Baptists' (1903).

GRIMKÉ, FREDERICK, jurist, was born in Charleston, S.C., September 1, 1791, and was a son of Judge J. F. Grimké. On completing his education he settled in Ohio, studied law, and was eventually elevated to the Bench. He published 'Ancient and Modern Literature' and 'Nature and Tendencies of Free Institutions.' He died in Chillicothe, Ohio, March 8, 1863.

GRIMKÉ, JOHN FAUCHERAUD, jurist, was born in South Carolina December 16, 1752, and died at Long Branch, N. J., August 9, 1819. For many years he occupied an honored position on the Bench of South Carolina. Toward the close of his life he became involved in litigation and an effort was made to impeach him but it was unsuccessful. He published 'Revised Edition of the Laws of South Carolina to 1789,' 'Law of Executors for South Carolina,' 'Probate Directory,' 'Public Law of South Carolina,' and 'Duty of Justices of the Peace.' Princeton gave him the degree of LL.D.

GRIMKÉ, SARAH MOORE. Reformer. Her father was Judge J. F. Grimké, of the South Carolina Bench, and she was born in Charleston, S.C., November 6, 1792, and died at Hyde Park, N.Y., December 23, 1873. Emancipating her negroes, she became an avowed foe to the system of slavery, lecturing and writing upon this subject, and also advocating women's rights. She translated Lamartine's 'Joan of Arc,' wrote 'An Epistle to the Clergy of the Southern States,' and published 'Letters on the Condition of Woman and the Equality of the Sexes.'

GRIMKÉ, THOMAS SMITH, reformer, was born in Charleston, S.C., September 26, 1786, and died near Columbus, Ohio, October 11, 1834. His father was Judge J. F. Grimké, the distinguished jurist. He became an eminent lawyer, but his best efforts were given to temperance reform, in which cause he was one of the earliest pioneers. He also endeavored to adjust the irregularities of spelling. He published 'Addresses on Science, Education, and Literature' (New Haven, 1831).

GRISWOLD, CAROLINE. [S.C.]. Poems.

GRUNDY, FELIX. Statesman. He was born in Berkeley County, Va., September 11, 1777, and died in Nashville, Tenn., December 19, 1840. For some time he was chief-justice of the Supreme Court of Appeals of Kentucky; but, finding the salary too small to enable him to make ends meet, he resigned and later removed to Tennessee. He achieved eminence in criminal law practice; became a member of Congress; was chosen a commissioner to adjust the boundary line dispute with Kentucky; was elected United States Senator; on the accession of President Van Buren, was called into the Cabinet as Attorney-general; and relinquishing this portfolio was again chosen United States Senator. Except in the 'Debates of Congress,' none of his speeches has been preserved; but he was one of the most influential of Tennessee's public men.

GUILD, JOSEPHUS C. Lawyer. [Tenn.]. He was born in 1802 and died in 1883. He published an interesting volume of recollections entitled 'Old Times in Tennessee.'

GUNBY, ANDREW AUGUSTUS. Jurist. He was born in Georgia in 1849, but settled in Louisiana for the practice of law, he became an occupant of the Bench, and published 'Colonel John Gunby of the Maryland Line' (New Orleans, 1902), and 'Louisiana Authors.'

GUNTER, BESSIE E. [Va.]. She published 'The Housekeeper's Companion.'

GUTHEIM, JAMES KOPPEL, rabbi, was born in Westphalia, November 15, 1817, and died in New Orleans, La., May 11, 1886. For years he was the minister of Temple Sinai in New Orleans, and a collection of sermons entitled 'The Temple Pulpit' is his contribution to letters.

GWIN, WILLIAM McKENDREE, United States Senator, was born in Sumter County, Tenn., October 9, 1805, and died in the city of New York, September 3, 1885. After serving for one term in Congress from Mississippi, he removed to California and was elected to the United States Senate, John C. Frémont being his colleague. At the beginning of the Civil War he was arrested on the charge of disloyalty and imprisoned until 1863, when he went to Paris and became interested in a scheme to colonize Sonoro with Southerners, but it failed to meet with success. In the campaign of 1876, he actively supported Samuel J. Tilden.

GWYN, LAURA, poet, of South Carolina, was born in 1833 and published a volume of verse entitled 'Miscellaneous Poems' (1860). She resided at one time in Greenville, where her husband was pastor of the Methodist Episcopal Church. "The Valley Flower" is perhaps the best known of her poems.

HABERSHAM, ALEXANDER WYLLY, naval officer and merchant, was born of Southern parents in the city of New York, March 24, 1826, and died in Baltimore, Md., March 26, 1883. He became a lieutenant in the navy, but resigned to engage in business in Japan. He returned at the beginning of the Civil War and was for six months a prisoner at Fort McHenry. After the close of hostilities he engaged in business in Baltimore. Besides numerous articles, he published 'My Last Cruise,' an account of the United States North Pacific exploring expedition (Philadelphia, 1857).

HAGUE, PARTHENIA ANTOINETTE, Mrs. Writer. [Fla.]. She wrote an interesting personal narrative of adventure entitled 'A Blockaded Family; or, Life in Southern Alabama during the Civil War' (1888).

HAINES, HIRAM, poet, was born in Culpeper County, Va. In the preface to his work entitled 'Mountain Buds and Blossoms, Wove in a Rustic Garland' (Petersburg, 1825), the author tells us that he was trained to the plow; but he was also editor and proprietor of *The American Constitution,* a newspaper published in Petersburg. There is a suggestion of Burns in some of the quaint mannerisms of the poet. But the chief claim of the volume does not lie in this fact. He was in love with Virginia; and the work is the first attempt to celebrate adequately the glories of the State, every river and mountain, every legend and myth receiving the homage of his harp. The opening poem of the collection is "The Virginiad."

HAINS, THORNTON JENKINS. Author. He was born in Washington, D.C., November 14, 1866, a son of General P. C. Hains, and a grandson of Admiral Thornton Hains. After an experience at sea he adopted literature as a profession. His fascinating stories which deal largely with ocean adventures, include: 'Captain Gore's Courtship' (1896), 'The Wind-Jammers' (1898), 'The Wreck of the Conemaugh' (1899), 'Mr. Trummell' (1900), 'The Cruise of the Petrel' (1901), 'The Strife of the Sea' (1903), 'The Black Barque' (1905), and 'The Voyage of the Arrow' (1906). He resides in Bensonhurst, N.Y., where he owns many small vessels.

HAKLUYT, RICHARD. Editor. [England]. He was born in 1553 and died in 1616. He published a number of important documents relating to the first attempts of the English to establish settlements in North America. Years after his death the collection was issued in four volumes (London, 1809-1812).

HALBERT, HENRY SALE. Archæologist and author. He was born in Pickens County, Ala., January 14, 1837, a son of Percival Pickens and Jane Owen Halbert, and was educated at Union University, Murfreesboro, Tenn. He served with Texas troops in campaigns against the Kiowa and Comanche Indians; also enlisted as a private in the Sixth Texas Cavalry at the outbreak of the Civil War, and fought until the close of hostilities. He taught in various schools and colleges for more than thirty years and was also colonization agent for the removal of the Choctaw Indians. He is engaged at present in historical and archæological investigations in Montgomery, Ala. Besides numerous contributions to the periodicals, he has written an excellent 'History of the Creek War of 1813-1814.'

HALE, PHILIP THOMAS. Educator and clergyman. He was born in Madison County, Ala., August 18, 1857, a son of Dr. P. P. Hale, and graduated from Howard College with high honors, afterward taking the theological course at the Southern Baptist Theological Seminary. He married, in Mayfield, Ky., December 9, 1885, Lena Lyle Bolinger. He has held numerous important pastorates, and in 1904 became president of the Southwestern Baptist University, at Jackson, Tenn., and in 1907, corresponding secretary of the Baptist Education Society of Kentucky. Besides writing 'Letters on an European Tour,' and 'Letters on a Tour Through Greece, Turkey, Egypt, and the Holy Land,' he has edited the Birmingham *Baptist*. He holds the D.D. and the LL.D. degrees.

HALE, SARAH ALICE. Missionary. [Tenn.]. She was born in 1856. She labored for several years in Mexico and published 'Mercedes, a Story of Mexico' (1894).

HALE, WILL T. See Biographical and Critical Sketch, Vol. V., page 2025.

HALL, CHARLES HENRY, clergyman, was born in Augusta, Ga., November 7, 1820. Entering the ministry of the Protestant Episcopal Church, he became an eminent divine and held numerous important pastorates, including the Church of the Epiphany, Washington, D.C., and Holy Trinity, Brooklyn, N.Y. He published 'Commentaries on the Gospels' (Philadelphia, 1867), 'Protestant Ritualism' (New York, 1871, and 'Spina Christi.' Hobart and Columbia both gave him the degree of Doctor of Divinity.

HALL, ELIZA CALVERT, author, was born in Bowling Green, Ky., February 11, 1856, a daughter of Dr. Chalmers Calvert, and was educated chiefly under private tutors. Besides numerous short stories and sketches she has published 'Aunt Jane of Kentucky' (Boston, Little, Brown and Company, 1907), an exquisite work portraying rural life in the Blue Grass region. For several years past she has also been prominent in various reform movements. She married, July 8, 1885, Major William A. Obenchain. Her home is in Bowling Green, Ky.

HALL, HARRISON, author, was born in Octarara, Md., November 5, 1785, and died in Cincinnati, Ohio, March 9, 1866. He edited 'The Portfolio' and published a work on 'Distillation,' which was reprinted in England.

HALL, JAMES. Presbyterian clergyman. He was born in 1744 and died in 1826. His work entitled 'The History of Mississippi Territory,' which was published at Salisbury, N.C., in 1801, is the first historical account of Mississippi. He also wrote an account of one of his missionary tours in North Carolina.

HALL, JOHN LESLIE. Professor of English language and literature in William and Mary College. He was born in Richmond, Va., March 2, 1856, a son of Jacob Hall, Jr., and was educated at Randolph-Macon College and at Johns Hopkins University (Ph.D.). He married, April 30, 1889, Margaret Fenwick Farland. He is an authority on Anglo-Saxon philology. Among his published works, which include some important contributions to English philology, are: a 'Translation of Beowolf' (Boston, D. C. Heath and Company), 'Old English Idylls' (Boston, Ginn and Company), 'Judith, Phœnix, and Other Anglo-Saxon Poems' (New York and Boston, Silvere, Burdett and Company). Besides, in conjunction with Professors Baskerville and Harrison, he has edited an 'Anglo-Saxon Reader' (New York, A. S. Barnes and Company). The sketch of John Tyler in 'The Library of Southern Literature' is from his pen. He resides in Williamsburg, Va.

HALL, LYMAN. Educator. For several years he was president of the Georgia School of Technology, in Atlanta, Ga.; and his death in the prime of life was due largely to his zeal for the welfare of this institution. He published a text-book on 'Algebra' (New York, 1890), and a 'Life of Henry W. Grady' (New York, 1895).

HALL, MARGARET SCOTT, writer, was born in Sumter County, Ga., October 16, 1864. Her maiden name was Margaret Melissa Scott, and her girlhood days were spent in Texas. The author's prose and verse are well known; and liberal remuneration has for some time attested the merit of her work. She has published 'Heart Leaves,' a volume of poems (Elkhart, Ind., The Mennonite Publishing Company, 1902), and 'Rhyme and Reason,' in press. She married, November 30, 1885, J. Benjamin Hall. Her home is at Kirkwood, Ga.

HALL, ROBERT PLEASANTS, lawyer and poet, was born in Chester District, S.C., December 23, 1825, and died in Macon, Ga., December 4, 1854. He was rapidly rising at the Bar, when ill health overtook him; but at leisure intervals he continued to exercise an unusual talent for verse until the end of his short life, publishing a volume of 'Poems by a South Carolinian' (Charleston, 1848), besides numerous manuscripts, among them a contemplative poem on André Chenier; "Winona," a legend of the Dakotahs, and "The Cherokee."

HALL, WILLIAM WHITTY. Physician. He was born in Paris, Ky., in 1810, and died in the city of New York, May 10, 1876. For fifteen years he practiced medicine in the South, after which he removed to New York and published *Hall's Journal of Health*. He wrote numerous medical books, including 'Health and Disease,' 'Sleep,' 'Fun Better Than Physic,' and 'Health by Good Living.'

HALLECK, REUBEN POST. Educator. He was born at Rocky Point, Long Island, N.Y., February 8, 1859, a son of the Rev. Luther Calvin and Fannie Tuthill Halleck. He enjoyed superior educational advantages, culminating with a diploma from Yale. After teaching in various academies, he became principal of the Louisville, Ky., Male High School in 1896. Besides occasional lectures on educational topics, his literary productions include: 'Psychology and Psychic Culture' (New York, D. Appleton and Company), 'The Education of the Central Nervous System' (New York, The Macmillan Company), and a 'History of English Literature' (*ibid.*).

HALLOWELL, ALICE. Writer. She was born in Maryland, but afterward lived in the District of Columbia. She published 'Forget-me-not: or, Sunshine in Affliction' (1893).

HALLUM, JOHN. Lawyer. He was born in Tennessee in 1833, but afterward settled in Arkansas. He published a 'History of Arkansas' (1887), 'The Diary of an Old Lawyer' (1895), and 'Life on the Frontier.'

HALLUM, MATTIE A. Poet. [Ark.]. Born in 1872. She published a volume of verse entitled 'Clay, and Other Poems.'

HALSEY, LEROY JONES, clergyman, was born in Goochland County, Va., in 1812. On completing his theological studies at Princeton, he entered the Presbyterian ministry, held important pastorates at Jackson, Miss., and Louisville, Ky., and was finally called to the chair of homiletics in the Theological Seminary of the Northwest, at Chicago, Ill. He published 'The Literary Attractions of the Bible' (New York, 1859), 'The Life and Pictures of the Bible' (Philadelphia, 1860), 'The Beauty of Emanuel,' 'The Life and Work of Philip Lindley,' in three volumes, 'Memoir of Lewis W. Green, D.D.' (New York, 1871), 'Living Christianity,' and 'Scotland's Place in Civilization.'

HALSTEAD, GEORGE BRUCE. Educator. He was born in South Carolina in 1853, and afterward settled in Texas. He published a series of text-books on higher mathematics.

HAM, MARION FRANKLIN. Clergyman. He was born in Harveysburg, Ohio, February 18, 1867, a son of George W. and Marcia E. Ham, and was educated in the common schools. He was for several years engaged in newspaper work, but entered the ministry in 1897. He was pastor of All Souls' Unitarian Church, of Chattanooga, Tenn., for eight years, and in 1905 became pastor of the First Unitarian Church, of Dallas, Texas. He married, January 27, 1902, Mary Louise Jenkins. He is a writer of both prose and verse. His works include: 'The Golden Shuttle,' a volume of poems, 'The Mountebank in the Pulpit,' and 'Kinchin, the Knight of Faith.'

HAMBERLIN, LA FAYETTE RUPERT. See Biographical and Critical Sketch Vol. V, page 2043.

HAMBLETON, JAMES P. Physician. He published a 'Biographical Sketch of Henry A. Wise' (1856).

HAMILL, HOWARD M. Sunday-school field worker. He was born in Lowndesboro, Ala., August 10, 1847, a son of Edward J. and Anne Hamill and graduated from East Alabama College, at Auburn. Despite his extreme youth, he served two years in the Confederate Army. He taught for some time in Missouri and Illinois; and then entered the ministry of the Methodist Church. He married, in 1885, Ada L. Tuman. He established in Illinois the first of the State Sunday-school Normal Departments. From 1896 to 1902 he was International Sunday-school field-secretary; and in 1902 became superintendent of the training work of the Methodist Episcopal Church, South. He holds the degree of D.D. In connection with his life's work, he has written: 'The Bible and Its Books,' 'Legion of Honor Normal Course of Study,' 'The Sunday-school Teacher,' and 'International Lesson History.' He resides in Nashville, Tenn.

"HAMILTON, BETSY." (See Idora Plowman Moore).

HAMILTON, JOHN WILLIAM, clergyman, was born in Weston, W.Va., March 18, 1845. He was educated in Ohio; and, entering the Methodist ministry, he founded the People's Church, in Boston. He published a 'Memorial of Jesse Lee,' 'Lives of the Methodist Bishops,' and 'The People's Church Pulpit.' Baker University gave him the degree of D.D.; Southern California and De Pauw Universities the degree of LL.D.

HAMILTON, JOSEPH GREGOIRE DE ROULLIAC, educator, was born at Hillsboro, N.C., August 6, 1878. Besides articles for reviews and magazines he has published 'Reconstruction in North Carolina' (1906), and 'Correspondence of Jonathan Worth' (1909). He is a professor in the University of North Carolina.

HAMILTON, M. J. R., Mrs. Author. [Ga.]. She wrote 'Catchet: or, The Secret Sorrow,' a novel (New York, 1873).

HAMILTON, PETER. Lawyer. He was born in 1817 and died in 1888. He compiled the Alabama Code of 1888 and framed the Alabama Debt Settlement Act. He also contributed numerous essays to law journals, some of the most important being: "The Theory of the Election of the President," "An Elective Judiciary," and "The Jury System." He was a man of distinguished attainments.

HAMILTON, PETER. JOSEPH. Lawyer and author. He was born in Mobile, Ala., March 19, 1859. His father was Peter Hamilton and his mother Anna M. Beers. After graduation from Princeton, he attended the University of Leipsic, and subsequently took law at the universities of Virginia and Alabama. He is now one of the leading members of the Mobile Bar. His works are numerous and important. They include: 'Rambles in Historic Lands' (New York, G. P. Putnam's Sons), 'Colonial Mobile' (Boston, Houghton, Mifflin and Company), 'Colonization of the South,' being Vol. III of the 'History of North America,' 'The Reconstruction Period,' being Vol. XVI of the same series, and, in collaboration with Hannis Taylor, a volume on 'International Public Law' (Chicago, Callaghan and Company). Besides, he assisted in the compilation of the Code of Alabama and other legal volumes. The sketch of Alexander B. Meek in 'The Library of Southern Literature' is from his pen. He also delivered the Bi-Centennial Oration at Mobile in 1902.

HAMILTON, WILLIAM T. Presbyterian clergyman. He was born in 1796 and died in 1884, having been for many years pastor of the Government Street Presbyterian Church, Mobile, Ala. Besides numerous published sermons and tracts, he delivered addresses at some of the leading colleges of the South, being in constant demand as an orator; and several of these addresses were printed in pamphlet form. The principal ones were on "The Importance of Knowledge," "Eloquence," "Usefulness," and "Truth."

HAMLETT, LIZZIE, Mrs. Poet. [Texas]. She published 'The Pleasures of Home, and Other Poems.'

HAMMOND, CHARLES, lawyer and editor, was born in Baltimore, Md., in 1779, and died in Cincinnati, Ohio, April 3, 1840. For several years he practiced law in Virginia but eventually moved to Ohio. He edited *The Federalist* and *The Gazette,* published a series of articles in defence of General St. Clair, and nine volumes of 'Ohio Reports' (Cincinnati, 1833-1840).

HAMMOND, HENRIETTA HARDY, Mrs. Author. [Va.]. She was born in 1854 and died in 1883. Mrs. Hammond wrote 'The Georgians' and 'A Fair Philosopher,' besides numerous short stories and sketches. The promise of an exceptionally bright career was never fulfilled, owing to her premature death.

HAMMOND, JAMES HENRY. Statesman. He was born in Newberry District, S.C., November 15, 1807, and died on Beech Island,

S.C., November 13, 1864. On completing his studies at South Carolina College, he edited at Columbia, for several years, *The Southern Times* and advocated nullification. He was an ardent supporter of Calhoun. From 1842 to 1844 he was governor of South Carolina. Several years later he took his seat in the United States Senate and served until the outbreak of hostilities. Besides numerous contributions to the press on public topics, he published 'The Pro-Slavery Argument' (Charleston, 1853), also an address on the death of John C. Calhoun, which he delivered by invitation of the city council of Charleston, and which was afterward printed in pamphlet form.

HAMMOND, JOHN. Author. He was one of Virginia's pioneer writers, born in 1635, died in 1712, and published 'Two Sisters, Leah and Rachael.'

HAMMOND, MARCUS CLAUDIUS MARCELLUS, soldier, was born in Newberry District, S.C., December 12, 1814, and died on Beech Island, S.C., January 23, 1876. He was educated at West Point but resigned from the Army on account of impaired health and became a planter. At the beginning of the Mexican War he reënlisted and was appointed paymaster. When peace was concluded he returned to agricultural pursuits. He held numerous commissions in the State militia from 1849 to 1853. Besides numerous essays on various topics, he wrote "A Critical History of the Mexican War," which appeared serially in *The Southern Quarterly Review.*

HAMMOND, WILLIAM ALEXANDER, physician and author, was born in Annapolis, Md., August 28, 1828. He resigned from the United States Army with the rank of lieutenant in the medical department to become professor of anatomy in the University of Maryland, but reënlisted at the outbreak of the Civil War, and in 1862 became surgeon-general. On the charge of irregularities in the award of liquor contracts he was court-martialed in 1864 and dismissed; but fourteen years later the case was reviewed by Act of Congress, and he was restored to the rolls on the retired list. Besides contributing to current literature, he founded and edited the *Maryland and Virginia Medical Journal* and other periodicals, and published numerous medical books, among them, 'Diseases of the Nervous System,' which has been translated into both French and Italian. He also made a number of translations and wrote several novels of fascinating interest, including 'Robert Severne' (1867), 'Lal' (1884), 'Dr. Grattan' (1884), 'Mr. Oldmixon' (1885), 'A Strong-minded Woman' (1886), and 'On the Susquehanna' (1887). He died in 1900.

HAMPTON, KATE PHELAN. (Mrs. Wade Hampton, Jr.). [S.C.]. She published 'A Flag of Truce, and Other Stories' (1898).

HAMPTON, WADE. See Biographical and Critical Sketch, Vol. V, page 2061.

HANCOCK, ELIZABETH HAZLEWOOD. Author. [Va.]. In a work entitled 'Betty Pembroke' (New York and Washington, The Neale Publishing Company, 1907), she portrays the typical Virginia girl.

HANCOCK, S. J. Author. [Ky.]. He wrote 'The Montanas,' and 'Confession, a Tale of the Stars and Clouds,' besides minor works.

HANDLIN, W. W. Author. [La.]. He published a volume of some interest entitled 'American Politics: a Moral and Political Work on the Civil War' (New Orleans, 1864).

HANDY, ALEXANDER HAMILTON, jurist, was born at Princess Anne, Md., December 25, 1809, and died at Canton, Miss., September

12, 1883. After being admitted to the Bar, he settled in Mississippi, and was for several years judge of the high court of errors. He then returned to Baltimore and for some time filled the chair of law in the University of Maryland, but eventually went back to Mississippi. He was an ardent champion of secession. His decisions, which bear the impress of his strong individuality, are embraced in volumes 26-41 of the 'Mississippi Reports.' He published in pamphlet form "Secession Considered as a Right," and "A Parallel between James the Second and Abraham Lincoln."

HANNA, ELIZABETH H., educator, was born in the state of Louisiana. Her father was James Jackson Hanna, whose family coat-of-arms, according to 'Burke's Peerage,' dates from the fifteenth century. Her mother was Ellen Cooper, daughter of Dr. Thomas Cooper, the second president of South Carolina College. She taught for thirteen years in the public schools of Atlanta, and then organized the select school of which she has ever since been the principal. She is the author of two successful plays entitled "The Court of Juno," and "High Mountain"; and also of an unpublished historical work entitled 'The Epitome of the Centuries.'

HANSON, ALEXANDER CONTEE, jurist, was born in Baltimore, Md., October 22, 1749. For some time he was private secretary and afterward aide to Washington, but ill health constrained him to resign the latter appointment. He was the first judge of the General Court of Maryland and later became chancellor of the State. Besides compiling the laws of Maryland and preparing a 'Digest of the Testamentary System,' he wrote a number of articles on political topics, and some of them have been preserved by the Historical Society of Maryland under the name of 'The Hanson Pamphlets.'

HANSON, GEORGE A. [Md.]. He published 'Old Kent, the Eastern Shore of Maryland' (1876).

HARBEN, WILL N. See Biographical and Critical Sketch, Vol. V, page 2073.

HARBY, ISAAC, editor and dramatist, was born in Charleston, S.C., of Jewish descent, in 1788 and was educated under the celebrated Dr. Best. He relinquished law for journalism and edited at different times *The Quiver* and *The Southern Patriot.* Both as a playwright and a critic he became widely known. Among his dramatic productions were "The Gordian Knot" "Alexander Severus," and "Albert." The last was founded on the history of Lorenzo de Medici. Going to New York in 1828, he contributed to *The Evening Post,* but died before the end of the year. Selections from his writings were edited in 1829 by Henry L. Pinckney and Abraham Moïse. He died in New York, November 14, 1828.

HARBY, LEE COHEN. Author. She was born in Charleston, S.C., September 7, 1849, a daughter of Marx E. and Armida Cohen. She was educated at home and married John De La Motta Harby, son of Captain L. C. Harby of the United States Navy, subsequently of the Confederate States Navy. She lived for several years in Texas, dividing her time between Galveston and Houston; afterward in New York for ten years. She now resides in Charleston, S.C., her girlhood's home. Among various other organizations, she is a member of the Incorporated Society of Authors, of London, a member of the Daughters of the American Revolution, and a director in the United Daughters of the Confederacy. She has written some excellent verse and received a prize of one hundred dollars for the words to the official flag song of Texas. Her stories, which are vividly written, include: 'Christmas Before the War,' 'In the Days When We Were Young,' 'The City of a Prince,' 'The Old Stone Fort of Nacogdoches,' 'Texan Types and Contrasts,' 'Judy Robinson, Milliner,' and 'Romance of an Old Town.' She has made frequent contributions both in prose and in verse to the periodicals, and her gifts are of the highest order.

HARDEE, WILLIAM JOSEPH. He was born in Camden County, Ga., in 1815, and was educated at West Point. After serving with distinction in Florida and Mexico, he entered the Confederate service with the rank of colonel and attained to a lieutenant-generalship. He was attached to the Army of the West until the close of the Atlanta Campaign, when he was put in command of Savannah. After the war he resided in Selma, Ala. His work on 'Rifle and Infantry Tactics,' which was published at Mobile, in 1861, is still ranked among the standard authorities. He died at Wytheville, Va., November 6, 1873, but was buried in Selma, Ala.

HARDEN, EDWARD JENKINS, lawyer and author, was born of sturdy old Revolutionary stock in Bryan County, Ga., November 19, 1813, and was the son of Thomas H. Harden, his mother being Matilda Amanda Baker, daughter of Colonel John Baker. Though a lawyer of distinguished attainments, he found time for literary diversions, and wrote 'The Life of George M. Troup' (Savannah, E. J. Purse, 1852), and 'Notes of a Short Northern Tour' (Savannah, J. H. Estill, 1869). The first work is the only authoritative biographical account in existence of one of the most commanding figures in the history of Georgia; and the second work is in Latin, the edition having been limited to one hundred copies. His wife was Sophia H. Maxwell. He died at Indian Springs, Ga., April 19, 1873.

HARDEN, WILLIAM. Librarian of the Georgia Historical Society at Savannah, in which city he was born November 11, 1844, the son of Edward J. and Sophia Harden. He left school to enter the Confederate Army and served with distinction. Later he was admitted to the Bar, and married, December 11, 1879, Mary E. Davenport. He is custodian and treasurer of the Telfair Academy of Arts and Sciences; organizer and secretary of the Georgia Society of the Sons of the American Revolution, and became librarian of the Georgia Historical Society in 1869. He is a writer on historical subjects for various magazines and periodicals.

HARDEN, WILLIAM DEARING, lawyer, was born in Athens, Ga., July 15, 1837, of the best colonial stock. His father was Thomas Hutson Harden. He was educated at Princeton University, served in the Confederate Army, practiced law in Savannah and held for fourteen years the judgeship of the city court. He published 'An Inquiry into the Truth of Dogmatic Christianity, comprising a Discussion with a Roman Catholic Bishop' (New York, G. P. Putnam's Sons, 1893).

HARDIN, CHARLOTTE PRENTISS, author, was born in New Orleans, La., December 9, 1882. Her maiden name was Charlotte Prentiss, and her grandfather was the noted orator, Sargeant S. Prentiss. She became the wife of William Johnston Hardin, July 6, 1909. Mrs. Hardin writes with an exquisite touch and much is to be expected from her pen. *The Atlantic Monthly* has published over her signature "Wind-Scents" (1907), "Chanson Louis XIII" (1908), and "Musings of a Pre-Raphaelite Painter" (1909).

HARDIN, MARTIN D., lawyer, was born on the Monongahela River, in Pennsylvania, June 21, 1780, and died at Frankfort, Ky.,

October 8, 1823. He was educated at Transylvania College, in Kentucky, became a lawyer of distinction, and succeeded William T. Barry in the United States Senate. He published 'Reports of Cases in the Kentucky Court of Appeals.'

HARDINGE, BELLE BOYD, Mrs. [Va.]. She published 'Belle Boyd in Camp and Prison.'

HARDY, ARTHUR L., lawyer and author, of Hamilton, Ga., is the author of a novel of great power entitled 'The Clutch of Circumstance' (Boston, The Mayhew Publishing Company, 1909), which deals with one of the most delicate aspects of the negro problem.

HARDY DAVID educator, was born in Vermont, in 1829. For some time he taught in the English department of Cortland Academy, at Homer, N.Y., his *alma mater*, but was afterward principal of the preparatory department of Bethel College, at Russellville, Ky. His career was brief; and, after his early death in 1857 there appeared a volume of his 'Poems' (New York, 1858), containing some delicate touches of sentiment.

HARDY, JOHN. [Ala.]. Author of 'Selma, her Institutions and her Men' (1879).

HARKEY, SIMEON WALCHER, clergyman, was born in Iredell County, N.C., December 3, 1811, settled in Illinois, and became professor of theology at the University of the State. He published 'Justification by Faith,' 'The Value of an Evangelical Ministry,' and other volumes, besides a number of addresses. At the time of his death he was engaged in compiling 'Personal Reminiscences.' Wittenberg College gave him the degree of Doctor of Divinity.

HARLAN, JOHN MARSHALL, jurist, was born in Boyle County, Ky., June 1, 1833. After receiving his collegiate education, he chose the law for a profession. At the outbreak of hostilities in 1861, he joined the Union Army and served with the rank of colonel. He was for several years attorney-general of the commonwealth, and was twice an unsuccessful candidate for governor. He served on the Louisiana Commission under appointment of President Hayes, by whom he was also elevated to the Supreme Bench of the United States, entering upon his long and useful tenure of service in 1877. His decisions, covering a period of more than thirty years, are contained in the 'Supreme Court Reports.'

"HARLAND, MARION." (See Mary Virginia Terhune).

HARMAN, HENRY E., publisher and poet, was born in Lexington, S.C., in 1866. Several volumes of verse have come from his gifted pen, among them, 'In Peaceful Valley' (1901), 'At the Gate of Dreams' (1905), and 'In Love's Domain' (Charlotte, N.C., Stone and Barringer Company, 1909). His poetry is characterized by an exquisite musical lilt, by an artistic touch, by an original power both of thought and of versification, and by an adherence to familiar themes in the development of which is betrayed the dominance of high ideals of sentiment. He married, in 1887, Ella S. Walser of Lexington, N.C. Mr. Harman resides in Atlanta, Ga.

HARNEY, JOHN HOPKINS, educator and editor, was born in Bourbon County, Ky., February 20, 1806, and died in Jefferson County, Ky., January 27, 1867. He published an 'Algebra' (Louisville, 1840), which took high rank as a text-book for advanced pupils.

HARNEY, JOHN M., poet, was born in Sussex County, Del., in 1780, but settled at Bardstown, Ky.; and, barring a residence of some few years at Savannah, Ga., most of his life was spent in the region of the Blue Grass. He wrote a volume entitled 'Crystalina, a Fairy Tale in Six Cantos' (New York, 1816), which testifies to his poetic ideals; and some time after his death various fragments from his pen went the rounds of the press, the best being one called "The Fever Dream." He died in 1823.

HARNEY, WILLIAM WALLACE. Editor and poet. [Fla.]. Besides essays and sketches he wrote numerous uncollected poems of unusual merit.

HARNEY, WILLIAM WALLACE. Journalist. He was born in Bloomington, Ind., June 20, 1831, the son of John and Martha Wallace Harney, but removed to Kentucky in early childhood. He was educated chiefly by private tutors. He taught school for several years and afterward became editor of the Louisville *Democrat.* Still later he removed to Florida. For years he has been a frequent contributor of both prose and verse to the periodicals, some of his work being of high merit. He resides in Miami, Fla.

HARPER, ROBERT GOODLOE, lawyer, was born near Fredericksburg, Va., in 1765, and died in Baltimore, Md., January 15, 1825. On completing his studies at Princeton, he settled for the practice of law in Charleston, S.C., and was soon afterward elected to Congress, in which body he served for six years and left his impress upon national legislation. He then removed to Baltimore. In the War of 1812 he was made a major-general of Maryland militia. He defended Judge Pickering and Justice Chase against charges of impeachment, and was afterward elected to the United States Senate but served only one year. He married the daughter of Charles Carroll, of Carrollton. Under the title of 'Select Works of Robert Goodloe Harper,' a collection of his papers and speeches was published in 1814.

HARPER, WILLIAM, jurist, was born on the Island of Antigua, January 17, 1790, and died in South Carolina, October 10, 1847. He became an eminent lawyer and was chancellor first of Missouri and afterward of South Carolina. Later, he became one of the judges of the Court of Appeals in the latter State. He also filled an unexpired term in the Senate of the United States. Besides an article on "Colonization," in *The Southern Review* his speech in Congress on "The Panama Mission," his eulogy on "Chancellor DeSaussure," and several addresses in favor of nullification, were published.

HARRELL, JOHN M. Lawyer. [Ark.]. As an officer of cavalry he distinguished himself in the operations of the West during the Civil War. He also achieved high rank at the Bar and wrote the volume on Arkansas in 'The Confederate Military History' (Atlanta, Ga., The Confederate Publishing Company, 1899).

HARRIS, CORRA WHITE, editorial writer and novelist of very great distinction, was born in Elbert County, Ga., March 17, 1869. She wrote at first under the pen-name of "Mrs. Lundy H. Harris." For years she has been instrumental in shaping public opinion through the columns of *The Independent,* besides contributing essays and sketches to other papers. She has also published 'The Jessica Letters' (New York, G. P. Putnam's Sons, 1908), written in collaboration with Paul Elmer More, of the New York *Evening Post,* also 'The Circuit Rider's Wife' (1910) and 'Eve's Second Husband' (1911). The last two works have given her an international reputation. She has just completed the manuscript of another story entitled: 'The Recording Angel' (1912). She resides in Nashville, Tenn.

HARRIS, CICERO WILLIS. Journalist. [N.C.]. His published works include 'A Glance at Government' (1896) and 'The Sectional Struggle: Early Tariffs and Nullification' (Philadelphia, the J. B. Lippincott Company, 1902), besides contributions to periodicals. He resides in Washington, D.C.

HARRIS, FRANCES ALLEN. Author. [Ky.]. She wrote an entertaining story of Kentucky life entitled 'Among the Meadows' (New York and Washington, The Neale Publishing Company, 1905).

HARRIS, GEORGE WASHINGTON. See Biographical and Critical Sketch, Vol. V, page 2099.

HARRIS, GILBERT D. Geologist. He published a work on 'The Geology of Louisiana' (Baton Rouge, 1899), which was afterward twice revised and enlarged.

HARRIS, HUNTER LEE. Poet. [N.C.]. He published a collection of verse entitled 'Twilight Songs and Other Youthful Poems' (1890, paper edition).

HARRIS, ISHAM GREEN, United States Senator, was born near Tullahoma, Tenn., February 10, 1818, enjoyed only meager educational advantages, but studied law and advanced rapidly to the front. Prior to the war he served two terms in Congress and was twice elected governor of Tennessee. He was an aide on the staff of General Albert Sidney Johnston, who expired in his arms on the battlefield of Shiloh. After the war he spent some time in Mexico and England, but eventually he returned to Tennessee and was four times elected to the United States Senate, serving from 1877 to 1899. He died in the latter year, while still occupying his seat.

HARRIS, JOEL CHANDLER ("Uncle Remus"). See Biographical and Critical Sketch, Vol. V, page 2111.

HARRIS, JULIAN, editor and playwright, was born in Atlanta, Ga., the eldest son of Joel Chandler Harris, the "Uncle Remus" of Southern literature. For several years he was most conspicuously identified with representative newspapers, including the Chicago *Times-Herald* and the Atlanta *Constitution*. In 1906 he organized the *Uncle Remus Magazine,* of which he became the business manager; and on the death of his father, in 1908, he succeeded to the vacant editorial chair. Some of his best literary work has appeared in this splendid periodical, and among other monographs and essays from his pen may be mentioned: "The Silence of the Whistle" (1908), "Shall the Solid South Be Shattered?" (1909), and "From the Standpoint of To-day and To-morrow" (1909). He has also written an excellent three-act farce entitled 'Peter Callender; or, the Girl from Keith's' (1909), which has been accepted by Nixon and Zimmerman of Philadelphia, but has not yet been published. Mr. Harris resides in Atlanta, Ga.

HARRIS, LOUISA, Mrs. Author. [Mo.]. She wrote 'Behind the Scenes; or, Nine Years at the Four Courts' (1893).

HARRIS, LUNDY H., Mrs. (See Carra White Harris).

HARRIS, SAMUEL SMITH, Protestant Episcopal bishop, was born in Autauga County. Ala., September 14, 1841, and died in London, England, August 24, 1888. For several years he practiced law, but convinced that it was his duty to preach he was duly ordained, held numerous important pastorates in the South, and was finally called to Chicago. On account of his eloquence he became widely popular in the pulpit. In 1878 he declined the bishopric of Quincy; but in 1879 accepted the bishopric of Michigan. Besides occasional sermons and reviews, he published the 'Bohlen Lectures' (Ann Arbor, 1882), and 'Shelton,' a novel. William and Mary College gave him the degree of D.D. and the University of Alabama, the degree of LL.D.

HARRIS, THADDEUS. Unitarian clergyman. Though he lived and died in Massachusetts, he made an important contribution to Southern literature in a work entitled 'The Biographical Memoirs of James Edward Oglethorpe, the Founder of the Colony of Georgia' (1841).

HARRIS, WILLIAM MERCER, clergyman, was born at Penfield, Ga., May 28, 1858. After completing his educational equipment he entered the Baptist ministry. At the present time he is pastor of a church in Texarkana, Texas. Besides tracts and sermons he has published several addresses and contributed to magazines and reviews. He wrote the sketch of Clarence Ousley for 'The Library of Southern Literature' and is the author of an unpublished story. He holds the degree of D.D.

HARRISON, BELLE RICHARDSON. Poet. [Ala.]. She published a volume of verse (1898).

HARRISON, BENJAMIN, signer of the Declaration of Independence, was born in Berkeley, Va., about 1740 and died in 1791. As a Member of the House of Burgesses, he opposed the Stamp Act resolutions of Patrick Henry as impolitic; but acted on the committee appointed to memorialize the King. He served with distinction in the Continental Congress for several consecutive terms, and signed the immortal documents which severed the ties of union between the Crown and the Colonies. In the Virginia convention of 1788, he opposed the ratification of the Federal Constitution, taking the position that the government was a national and not a federal power. He was several times speaker of the Virginia House of Delegates.

HARRISON, CONSTANCE CARY. See Biographical and Critical Sketch, Vol. V, page 2153.

HARRISON, EDITH OGDEN. Author. She was Edith Ogden of New Orleans, La. Since her marriage to Carter H. Harrison, Jr., she has lived in Chicago. Several charming books for children have come from her imaginative pen, among them, 'Prince Silver Wings, and Other Tales' (Chicago, A. C. McClurg and Company, 1904), 'The Star Fairies and Other Tales' (*ibid.*, 1906), 'The Moon Princess' (*ibid.*, 1907), and 'The Flaming Sword, and Other Legends of the Earth and Sky' (*ibid.*, 1909).

HARRISON, ELLENETTA. Author. [Ky.]. She wrote an interesting work of fiction entitled 'A Kentucky Romance,' and other novels.

HARRISON, GESSNER, educator and physician, was born in Harrisonburg, Va., June 26, 1807, and died near Charlottesville, Va,. April 7, 1862. He became an eminent educator and established at Belmont, Va., a classical school which attained wide celebrity throughout the South. He published 'Exposition of Some of the Laws of Latin Grammar' (New York, 1852), and 'On Greek Prepositions' (Philadelphia, 1848).

HARRISON, HALL, clergyman, was born in Anne Arundel County, Md. Entering the Episcopal ministry, he became a divine of some note. He edited 'Evans on the Christian Doctrine of Marriage' (New York, 1870), and published a 'Memoir of Hugh Davey Evans,' and a 'Life of John B. Kerfoot.'

HARRISON, JAMES A. See Biographical and Critical Sketch, Vol. V, page 2185.

HARRISON, JOHN HOFFMAN, physician, was born in Washington, D.C., August 30, 1808, and died in New Orleans, March 19, 1849. He became an eminent practitioner, achieved signal results in the treatment of yellow fever, and established the New Orleans *Medical and Surgical Journal.* Besides numerous papers, he published 'Diseases of the Mississippi Valley.'

HARRISON, WILLIAM HENRY. See Biographical and Critical Sketch, Vol. V, page 2203.

HARRISON, WILLIAM HENRY, lawyer and public official, was born in Lumpkin, Ga,, March 21, 1843. For several years he practiced law, but in 1885 he became bookkeeper for the executive department of the State of Georgia, and in 1896 tax clerk in the office of the comptroller-general. Besides sundry contributions to the historical literature of the war between the States and criticisms of publications relating to this subject, he has written verses for Southern songs and is about to publish a volume of war-time stories entitled 'The Man with the Musket.' Captain Harrison served in the Confederate Army and commanded Company E of the Thirty-first Regiment of Georgia Volunteers. From 1872 to 1883 he edited the Lumpkin *Independent.* He married, May 4, 1869, Clara R. Rockwell. He resides in Atlanta, Ga.

HARRISON, W. S. Methodist Episcopal clergyman. [Miss.]. He published 'Sermons' (1875), and 'Sam Williams, a Tale of the Old South' (1892).

HARRISON, WILLIAM POPE, clergyman and editor, was born in Georgia in 1830. Entering the ministry, he became one of the most noted scholars and divines of Southern Methodism and mastered several different languages. He published 'Theophilus Walton,' 'The High Churchman Disarmed,' 'The Living Christ,' 'The Majesty of Truth,' 'Methodist Union,' 'Lights and Shadows of Forty Years,' and, in association with Anna Maria Barnes, 'The Gospel Among the Slaves.' He also edited *The Southern Methodist Review.* Dr. Harrison held the D.D. and the LL.D. degrees.

HART, A. M. Author. [La.]. He wrote a 'History of the Mississippi Valley' (1878).

HARTSHORNE, JOSEPH, physician and surgeon, was born in Alexandria, Va., December 12, 1779, and died near Wilmington, Del., August 20, 1850. He published 'The Bones,' with an appendix and notes (1806), besides minor works.

HARVEY, CHARLES M. Political editorial writer on the St. Louis *Globe-Democrat.* He was born in Boston, Mass., October 15, 1848, a son of John and Elizabeth Harvey. In 1886 he assumed the position which he still holds. He has contributed articles on political and economic subjects to the leading magazines and newspapers and has also written the following books: 'History of the Republican Party,' 'Handbook of American Politics,' and 'History of Missouri.'

HARVEY, WILLIAM HOPE, economist, was born at Buffalo, W. Va., August 16, 1851, a son of Colonel Robert Harvey. For several years he practiced law, but afterward engaged in literary pursuits and acquired an international reputation by his ingenious treatment of the monetary question in American politics. His publications include: 'Coin's Financial School' (1894), 'A Tale of Two Nations' (1894), 'Coin's Financial School Up-to-Date' (1895), 'Patriots of America' (1895), and 'Coin on Money, Trusts and Imperialism' (1899).

HASSELL, CUSHING BIGGS. Author. [N.C.]. He was born in 1808 and died in 1880. Mr. Hassell published a 'History of the Church of God from the Creation to A.D. 1885, Including Especially the History of Kehukee Primitive Baptist Association' (Middletown, N.Y., 1886).

HATCHER, ELDRIDGE B. Baptist clergyman. [Va.]. He published a work entitled 'The Bible and the Monuments' (1897).

HATCHER, JOHN E. (G. W. Bricks). Writer. [Va.]. He published 'Kate Lyle' and 'Poems.'

HATCHER, WILLIAM E. Baptist clergyman. He wrote a 'Life of Jeremiah Bell Jeter' and 'The Pastor and the Sunday-school' (1902).

HATTON, JOHN W. Writer. [Mo.]. He published a volume of verse entitled 'The Battle of Life' (1882).

HAUGHTON, R. B. Author. [Miss.]. He wrote an important document entitled 'The Influence of the Mississippi River' (Mississippi Historical Society, 1901).

HAW, M. J., Miss. Author. [Va.]. She wrote 'The Rivals: a Tale of the Chickahominy.'

HAWKINS, BENJAMIN, statesman, was born in Warren County, N.C., August 15, 1754, and died at Hawkinsville, Ga., June 6, 1816. Fresh from his studies at Princeton, he entered the Revolution; and, on account of his proficiency in French, he was appointed by Washington interpreter between the American and French officers of his staff. He served in Congress and also became one of the first Senators from North Carolina. At the conclusion of his term of office, he was appointed agent to superintend all the Indian tribes south of the Ohio. His 'Journal of a Tour Through the Creek Country' appeared in 1797. His manuscripts are in the possession of the Georgia Historical Society at Savannah. Two of them, 'Topography' and 'Indian Character,' have been published. Hawkinsville, Ga., formerly Fort Hawkins, was named in his honor.

HAWKINS, WILLIAM GEORGE, clergyman, was born in Baltimore, Md., October 22, 1823, equipped for the Episcopal priesthood at the seminary at Alexandria, Va., and, after serving an important parish in Maryland, was called to the North. He successively occupied wide fields in Massachusetts, Pennsylvania, New York and Nebraska. He published 'The Life of J. H. W. Hawkins,' his father, who was a noted temperance reformer (Boston, 1859), and 'Young America in the Northwest' (1870), besides minor works.

HAWKS, CICERO STEPHENS, Protestant Episcopal bishop, was born at New Berne, N.C., May 26, 1812, and died in St. Louis, Mo., April 19, 1868. He gave up law for theology and studied under Bishop Freeman. New York was for some time the field of his usefulness; but in 1844 he was consecrated Bishop of Missouri. He contributed to various journals, edited two religious juvenile papers and published 'Friday Christian; or, the First-born of Pitcairn Island.' He was a brother of Dr. Francis Lister Hawks.

HAWKS, FRANCIS LISTER. See Biographical and Critical Sketch, Vol. V, page 2221.

HAWORTH, CLARENCE EVERETT, physician and educator, was born in Portland, Ohio, May 10, 1860. For several years past he has made his home in Huntington, W. Va., where he is the head of the English department of Marshall College. For ten years he owned and edited the Huntington *Herald.* Besides writing the sketch of Waitman Barbe for 'The Library of Southern Literature,' he has contributed to numerous periodicals, both sacred and secular.

HAWTHORNE, JAMES BOARDMAN, clergyman, was born in Wilcox County, Ala., May 16, 1837. Entering the ministry he became one of the most eloquent and influential Baptist divines of the country, and held leading pastorates in Nashville and Richmond. He was also for years pastor of the First Baptist Church of Atlanta, Ga., and at one time preached in New York. As an orator in his prime he possessed no superior in the pulpit. He published 'Paul and the Women' (Louisville, 1891), 'Unshaken Trust' (1898), and 'The Cloud of Witnesses' (1907), besides a number of lectures. He married, August 27, 1857, Emma Hutchisson. Dr. Hawthorne died in Richmond, Va., February 24, 1910.

HAY, CHARLES COLCOCK, poet, of South Carolina. His best known lyric is entitled "The Rose." It is preserved in Wauchope's 'Writers of South Carolina' (Columbia, The State Company, 1909), together with "A Health to Virginia," from the pen of Samuel T. Hay.

HAY, GEORGE ("Hortensius"). Lawyer. [Va.]. He wrote a 'Life of John Thompson.' He died in 1830.

HAYDEN, HORACE EDWIN, clergyman and author, was born in Catonville, Md., February 18, 1837. His father was Honorable Edwin Parsons Hayden. The son, on completing his education was admitted to orders. For more than thirty years his parish has been at Wilkes-Barre, Pa. He has published 'Virginia Genealogies' (1891), a work of the most painstaking character, a 'History of the West Virginia Soldiers' Medals' (1881), 'The Pollock Memorial' (1883), and 'The Massacre of Wyoming' (1895), besides numerous pamphlets. He has also edited, in two volumes, a work entitled 'Genealogical and Family History of the Wyoming and Lackawanna Valleys' (1906).

HAYDEN, HORACE H., scientist, was born in Windsor, Conn. October 13, 1769, and died in Baltimore, Md., January 26, 1844. He followed the dental profession, but studied geology and medicine, became vice-president of the Maryland Academy of Science and Literature, and published 'Geological Essays' (Baltimore, 1820), which Benjamin Silliman praised in the highest terms, besides numerous papers.

HAYGOOD, ATTICUS GREENE. See Biographical and Critical Sketch, Vol. V, page 2239.

HAYNE, PAUL HAMILTON. See Biographical and Critical Sketch, Vol. V, page 2265.

HAYNE, ROBERT YOUNG. See Biographical and Critical Sketch, Vol. V, page 2299.

HAYNE, WILLIAM HAMILTON. See Biographical and Critical Sketch, Vol. V, page 2317.

HAYNES, LANDON CARTER, statesman and orator, was born in Elizabethtown, Tenn., December 2, 1816, and died in Memphis, Tenn.,

February 17, 1875. On completing his education he was duly admitted to the Bar, became an important factor in State politics, and served in the Confederate States Senate throughout the entire period of the Civil War. His eloquence was of the rarest type, imaginative and brilliant. He was an uncle of Senator Robert L. Taylor.

HAYS, WILLIAM SHAKESPEARE. Ballad writer and composer. He was born in Louisville, Ky., July 19, 1837, and received an academic education. He became a reporter on the Louisville *Democrat;* afterward clerk and steamboat captain on the Ohio and Mississippi rivers; and later marine editor of both the Louisville *Courier-Journal* and the Louisville *Times.* Among his musical compositions are "Mollie Darling," "Nora O'Neill," "Shamus O'Brien," "Write Me a Letter from Home," and more than three hundred other well-known songs, for all of which he wrote both words and music. Besides, he was the author of numerous poems. He died in 1907.

HAYWOOD, JOHN. Jurist and historian. He was born in 1762 and died in 1826. He was attorney-general of North Carolina and Judge of the Superior Court in North Carolina. Afterward he removed to Tennessee and became one of the leading members of the Bar of his adopted State. He also became an industrious student of the antiquities of Tennessee, producing two works of great value: 'The Natural and Aboriginal History of Tennessee up to the First Settlement Therein by White People' and 'The Civil and Political History of Tennessee from the Earliest Settlement up to 1796.' In the second work the author tells the story of the formation of the State of Franklin and of the war that followed, narrating a chapter of Tennessee history which is very little known. His great-grandson, W. W. Haywood, republished this important work in 1901, with an introduction by Colonel A. S. Collyar (Nashville, Methodist Episcopal Publishing House).

HAZELIUS, ERNEST LEWIS. Lutheran clergyman. [S.C.]. He published a 'Life of Luther' (New York, 1813), and a 'History of the Lutheran Church in America' (Zanesville, Ohio, 1846), besides minor works.

HEADLEY, JOHN W. Author. His service in the Confederate ranks and his familiarity with state records have enabled this distinguished Southerner to produce one of the best books relating to the war. The work is entitled 'Confederate Operations in Canada and New York,' and it deals with matters which have been little discussed by historians (New York and Washington, The Neale Publishing Company, 1906).

HEADY, MORRISON. Blind and deaf poet. [Ky.]. He published 'Seen and Heard,' a volume of verse (1869).

HEARD, THOMAS JEFFERSON. Physician. He was born in Georgia in 1814 but afterward settled in Texas and published a work entitled 'The Topography and Climatology of Texas.'

HEARN, LAFCADIO. See Biographical and Critical Sketch. Vol. VI, page 2341.

HEARNE, WILLIAM T. [Mo.]. He published a 'Genealogy of the Hearne Family' (1899), in which he carries the record back to the time of the battle of Hastings.

HEATH, JAMES. Lawyer. He was born in Virginia about 1812, and published 'Edgewood,' a novel of the Revolution (1838).

HEBRON, ELLEN E. Poet. [Miss.]. She published: 'Songs from the South' (Baltimore, 1875), and 'Faith, and Other Poems' (Chicago, 1890).

HECK, WILLIAM HARRY, educator, was born at Raleigh, N.C., November 1, 1879. He is professor of education at the University of Virginia. Besides the sketch of James Madison in 'The Library of Southern Literature,' he is the author of a work entitled 'Mental Discipline and Educational Values' (New York, John Lane Company, 1909).

HELMS, W. T. Protestant Episcopal clergyman. [Tenn.]. He wrote "Moses Resisted," a poem.

HELPER, HINTON ROWAN, author, was born near Mocksville, N.C., December 27, 1829. At one time he was United States Consul at Buenos Aires. He traveled extensively over the Western Hemisphere and was the first man to suggest a railway connecting the two great continents. In 1857, he published a work which brought him into immediate prominence entitled 'The Impending Crisis of the South' (New York), in which he opposed slavery on economic grounds. More than 140,000 copies were sold between 1857 and 1861; and it was freely used by the Republicans during the campaign which resulted in the election of Mr. Lincoln. His other works include 'The Land of Gold (Baltimore, 1855), 'Nojoque: a Question for a Continent' (New York and London, 1867), 'The Negroes in Negroland, the Negroes in America, and the Negroes Generally' (New York, 1868), and 'The Three Americas Railways' (St. Louis, 1881). He resided for some time in New York and afterward settled in Washington, D.C.

HEMPHILL, CHARLES ROBERT. Theologian. Professor in the Presbyterian Theological Seminary at Louisville, Ky. He was born in Chester, S.C., April 18, 1852, the son of James and Rachael E. Hemphill, and was educated at the universities of South Carolina and Virginia. He took the theological course at Columbia, S.C., and married, September 1, 1875, Emma L. Muller. He is the author of an important essay on "The Validity and Bearing of the Testimony of Christ and His Apostles to the Mosaic Authorship of the Pentateuch." It is included in the work entitled 'Moses and His Recent Critics' (New York, Funk and Wagnalls). Two separate institutions gave him the degree of D.D., and from Hanover College he received the degree of LL.D.

HEMPHILL, JAMES CALVIN,editor, was born at Due West, S.C., of Scotch-Irish parentage, May 18, 1850. On completing his studies at Erskine College, he adopted the profession of journalism. For thirty years he lived in Charleston and at the editorial helm of the *News and Courier* wielded an influence which was felt beyond the State lines. In 1910 he assumed the editorial chair of the Richmond *Times-Dispatch*. He will this year deliver a series of lectures at Yale, and the result will doubtless be an important contribution to letters. For 'The Library of Southern Literature' he wrote the sketch of Francis W. Dawson. He married, in 1878, Rebecca M. True. In recognition of his professional attainments he has received the degree of LL.D.

HEMPHILL, JOHN, United States Senator and jurist, was born in Chester District, S.C., in 1803, and died in Richmond, Va., January 4, 1862. For some time he edited a paper in South Carolina and advocated nullification; but he afterward located in Texas, became chief justice of the Supreme Court, and in 1858 was elected to the United States Senate, serving until the outbreak of hostilities. His decisions in the 'Texas Reports'evince his robust intellect and his intimate knowledge of the law.

HEMPSTEAD, EDWARD. [La.]. He published a 'Journal of the Legislative Territory of Louisiana' (New Orleans, 1806).

*HEMPSTEAD, FAY, historian and poet, was born in Little Rock, Ark., November 24, 1847. He published his first volume of verse in 1878. Since then he has published two others, besides an authoritative 'History of the State of Arkansas,' and a smaller work on the same subject for use in the public schools. He has been the secretary of the Grand Lodge of Freemasons of the State of Arkansas for over thirty years. In 1908, he was crowned Poet-Laureate of Freemasonry, the ceremony occurring in Chicago. Only two others have received this high honor, the first of whom was Robert Burns, in 1787. Mr. Hempstead resides in Little Rock.

HEMPSTEAD, JUNIUS W. Writer. [La.]. He published a collection of short stories entitled 'After Many Days' (1898).

HENDERSON, ANNA R., poet, was born at Cheraw, S.C. From time to time she has contributed some excellent verse to the leading magazines. Her only volume of poems is entitled: 'Life and Song.' She is now engaged on a work of fiction which she expects soon to publish.

HENDERSON, ARCHIBALD, educator, was born at Salisbury, N.C., June 17, 1877. He fills the chair of mathematics at the University of North Carolina. Besides literary essays and scientific articles in current periodicals on both sides of the water, he has written 'George Bernard Shaw: His Life and Works' and 'Edinburgh,' two unpublished manuscripts. The sketch of Frances Tiernan ("Christian Reid") in 'The Library of Southern Literature,' is also from his pen. He married June 23, 1903, Minna Curtis Bynum. He holds the degree of Ph.D.

HENDERSON, G. F. R., soldier and educator, of England, wrote a masterpiece of biography, in two volumes, entitled 'Stonewall Jackson and the American Civil War' (London and New York, Longmans, Green and Company, 1898). The work deals critically and exhaustively with the campaigns of the great Confederate leader, to whose genius the author pays unstinted tribute; and coming from a non-partisan, it is almost unparalleled in the annals of literature. For years the author, who held the rank of lieutenant-colonel in the British Army, was professor of military art and history in the Staff College, England, and his work is studied in the English military schools.

HENDERSON, JOHN, United States Senator, was born in 1795, the exact place unknown, and died at Pass Christian, Miss., in 1857. He was an extreme advocate of State rights and represented Mississippi in the United States Senate as a Whig. He favored not only the annexation of Texas, but the conquest of Cuba and Mexico. He was tried for complicity in the Lopez Expedition against Cuba, but acquitted. He wrote 'A Reply to Tom Paine' (Natchez, 1820).

HENDERSON, JOHN BROOKS, Sr., United States Senator, was born in Pittsylvania County, Va., November 16, 1826. For the practice of law he located in Missouri. He was the author of the thirteenth amendment to the Constitution, abolishing slavery from the states and territories. He married, June 25, 1868, Mary N. Foote. The University of Missouri gave him the degree of LL.D.

HENDERSON, JOHN BROOKS, Jr., lawyer, was born in Louisiana, Mo., February 18, 1870. His father was John B. Henderson, United States Senator. Mr. Henderson was private secretary to John W. Foster during the latter's residence in China. He has published 'American Diplomatic Questions' (New York, The Macmillan Company, 1901).

He married, February 12, 1903, Angelica Schuyler Crosby, and resides in Washington, D.C.

HENDERSON, J. P., Miss. Writer. [Miss.]. She wrote 'Anne Balfour' (1870).

HENDERSON, MARY FOOTE, author, was born in New York in 1835, a daughter of Judge Elisha Foote, and married Senator J. B. Henderson of Missouri. She organized in St. Louis the School of Design, took an active interest in woman's suffrage, and published two volumes: 'Practical Cooking and Dinner Giving' and 'Diet for the Sick.'

HENDERSON, PHILO. Editor and poet. Besides editing a paper at Charlotte, N.C., called *The Hornet's Nest,* he wrote many poems. He died in 1852, at the age of thirty years.

HENDREE, WILLIAM WOODSON. Poet. He lived at Selma, Ala., but died in 1872 at the youthful age of twenty-one. His poem, "Mahs' Lewis's Last Ride," is preserved in 'Songs of the South.'

HENDRIX, EUGENE RUSSELL. Bishop of the Methodist Episcopal Church, South. He was born in Fayette, Mo., May 17, 1847, and married, in 1872, Annie E. Scarritt. He entered the ministry, and was president of Fayette College from 1876 to 1886, then became bishop. He founded the mission of the church in Brazil, and was chosen fraternal messenger to the British Wesleyan Conference in 1900. Bishop Hendrix is the possessor of the manuscript journal which was kept by John Wesley in America from 1836 to 1837. Among his published works are: 'Around the World,' 'Skilled Labor for the Master' (Nashville, Bigham and Smith), 'The Religion of the Incarnation' (*ibid.*), and 'The Personality of the Holy Spirit' (*ibid.*). Three separate institutions have given him the degree of LL.D. and two the degree of D.D. He resides in Kansas City, Mo.

HENING, ELIZA LEWIS, poet, was born in Virginia, in 1806, a daughter of the eminent jurist, William Waller Hening. Her poem on "Old Blanford Church," which is preserved in 'Songs of the South,' was written while visiting Petersburg with a party of friends. Conclusive evidence of her claim has been furnished by her niece, Mrs. E. V. Swann. The author afterward became Mrs. Spottswood. Later she married the Rev. J. F. Schermerhorn, of New York, and died in 1872.

HENING, WILLIAM WALLER, lawyer, was born in Virginia in 1778. He published 'The American Pleader' (1811) and 'The New Virginia Justice' (1825), two law books, besides an important legislative history entitled 'The Statutes of Virginia' (1809-1823). With William Munford he also published 'Reports of Cases in the Courts of Appeal and Chancery' (1809-1811).

HENKEL, MOSES MONTGOMERY, clergyman, was born in Pendleton County, Va., March 23, 1798, and died in Richmond, Va., in 1864. He published 'Masonic Addresses,' 'The Primary Platform of Methodism,' 'Analysis of Church Government,' 'Primitive Episcopacy,' and 'Life of Bishop Bascom.'

HENKEL, PAUL, poet and clergyman of the Lutheran faith, was born in Rowan County, N.C., December 15, 1754. He settled in New Market, Va., and piped the first poetic notes which were heard west of the Blue Ridge mountains. In 1810, he published in German a little volume entitled: 'Kurzer Zeitvertrib,' which gave intense delight to his scattered flock of Teutons. Another edition was published in 1851. He also published a work in German on 'Baptism and the Lord's Supper,' which was afterward translated into English.

HENNEMAN, JOHN BELL, educator and editor, was born at Spartanburg, S.C., January 2, 1864. After receiving his M.A. degree at the University of Virginia he obtained his Ph.D. degree at the University of Berlin. For several years he was dean of the College of Arts and Sciences in the University of the South at Sewanee, Tenn., and also editor of the Sewanee *Review.* Besides numerous essays and monographs contributed to periodicals, he edited the 'Johnson Series of English Classics' (Richmond, Va., B. F. Johnson and Company, 1900-1903); with W. P. Trent, 'The Complete Works of Thackeray,' in thirty volumes, including a bibliography (New York, Thomas Y. Crowell and Company, 1904), Shakespeare's 'Twelfth Night' (New York, Longmans, Green and Company, 1905), Thackeray's 'Henry Esmond' (New York, The Macmillan Company, 1906), Kemper Bocock's 'Antiphon to the Stars' (New York, G. P. Putnam's Sons, 1907), and, with W. P. Trent, 'Best American Tales' (New York, T. Y. Crowell and Company, 1907). From 1893 to 1900 he was professor of English in the University of Tennessee. He married, September 7, 1897, Marion, daughter of the Honorable Robert T. Hubard. For 'The Library of Southern Literature' he wrote the sketch of William P. Trent. Dr. Henneman died at Sewanee, Tenn., November 26, 1908.

HENNEPIN, LOUIS, explorer, was born in Belgium in 1640 and died in Holland in 1701. He published a 'Description de la Louisiane,' which also gives an account of the manners and customs of the savages (Paris, 1685, Italian, German, and English translation), besides numerous other works.

HENNING, JULIA R. Educator. [Va.]. She published a 'Geography of Virginia' and a volume of songs for which she also composed the music (1895).

HENRY, INA M., Mrs. Writer. [Ala.]. She published a volume of fiction entitled 'Roadside Stories' and 'None but the Brave Deserve the Fair,' a drama. Her maiden name was Porter.

HENRY, JOHN FLOURNOY, physician, was born at Henry's Mills, Ky., January 17, 1793, and died in Burlington, Iowa, November 12, 1873. He published a treatise on 'The Causes and Treatment of Cholera,' besides contributing to medical journals.

HENRY, O. (Sydney Porter), short-story writer, was born in Greensboro, N.C., in 1867. His early life was spent on a ranch in Texas. At leisure moments he acquired the rudiments of an education, became a reporter on the Houston (Tex.) *Post,* where he developed a genius for the lighter phases of fiction, followed the newspaper profession for some time in New Orleans, and finally in 1902 drifted to New York, where he found fame and fortune awaiting him in the great metropolis. Mr. Porter is one of the prime favorites of the American reading public. His stories are written in the vernacular, abound in human elements, and reveal an intimate acquaintance with various types of character. They have been collected and published in book form under the following titles: 'Cabbages and Kings' (1905), 'The Four Million' (1906), 'The Heart of the West' (1908), 'The Voice of the City' (1908), 'Options' (1909), and 'The Roads of Destiny' (1909). He died in New York in 1910.

HENRY, PATRICK. See Biographical and Critical Sketch, Vol. VI, page 2355.

HENRY, ROBERT, clergyman and educator, was born in Charleston, S.C., December 6, 1792, and died in Columbia, S.C., February 6, 1856. He was educated at the University of Edinburgh, but, returning to Charleston, he became minister to the French Huguenot congregation. For years he was also identified with South Carolina College, of which he was twice president. He wrote articles for the religious reviews, and, besides occasional sermons, published eulogies on Jonathan Maxcy and John C. Calhoun.

HENRY, WILLIAM WIRT, lawyer, was born at Red Hill, Va., February 14, 1831, and was the grandson of Patrick Henry, the famous orator. He delivered several historical addresses and wrote a 'Life of Patrick Henry.'

HENSHAW, NEVILLE GRATIOT, author, was born in St. Louis, Mo., April 23, 1880. Two charming stories have come from his pen, 'Aline of the Grand Woods' (1909) and 'The Black Violin' (1910), besides a number of contributions to current periodicals.

HENTZ, CAROLINE LEE, Mrs. See Biographical and Critical Sketch, Vol. VI, page 2375.

HENTZ, CAROLINE THÉRÈSE, writer, was born in Cincinnati, Ohio, married the Rev. J. O. Branch and lived for some time in the South, which was also the home of her parents, Dr. N. M. and Caroline Lee Hentz. She wrote a series of letters from California to the *Southern Christian Advocate* in 1875, and published a number of stories and sketches in magazines.

HENTZ, JULIA L., poet, was born at Chapel Hill, N.C., in 1829, a daughter of Dr. N. M. and Caroline Lee Hentz, was educated by her parents, and married Dr. J. W. Keyes. In 1859, she wrote a prize poem entitled "A Dream of Locust Dell." Some time after her death a volume of her verse was published by her husband. She died in 1879.

HENTZ, NICHOLAS MARCELLUS, educator and physician, was born in Versailles, France, July 25, 1797 and died in Marianna, Fla., November 4, 1856. He studied medicine and learned the art of miniature painting in Paris, emigrated to the United States, became an eminent educator, and married Caroline Lee. For many years he resided in various Southern States. He was an entomologist of repute and published 'Arachnides: or, Spiders of the United States.' He also wrote 'Tadenskund, the Last King of Lenape,' an historical novel, and 'The Valley of the Shenandoah.'

HERBERT, HILARY ABNER, Cabinet officer and Congressman. He was born in Laurensville, S.C., March 12, 1834. He was educated at the University of Alabama and at the University of Virginia. Enlisting in the Confederate service, he became colonel of the Eighth Alabama Regiment of Volunteers. On April 23, 1867, he married Ella B. Smith, of Selma, and afterward settled in Montgomery. From 1877 to 1893 he represented Alabama in Congress; and from 1893 to 1897 he held the portfolio of Secretary of the Navy in President Cleveland's Cabinet. On retiring from office, he resumed the practice of law in Washington, D.C. His speeches in Congress are preserved in the *Congressional Record*. An address which he delivered at the University of Alabama has also been printed. He is the editor of a work published in 1900 entitled 'Why the Solid South? or, Reconstruction and its Results.'

HERBERT LEILA, author, was born in Greenville, Ala., in 1868 and died in Washington, D.C., in 1897. She was the daughter of ex-Secretary of the Navy Hilary A. Herbert. On the death of her mother, she was elected to membership in the Mount Vernon Memorial Association, notwithstanding the fact that at this time she was only seventeen. During her father's tenure of service in President Cleveland's second Cabinet, she was the mistress of his household, directing its affairs and dispensing its hospitalities in a manner which was most charmingly Southern. She possessed unusual graces both of intellect and of person, was given to unostentatious acts of charity, and while cultured beyond her years, she made no display of her accomplishments for mere vanity's sake. Her only published work is entitled 'The First American: His Homes and His Households' (New York, Harper and Brothers, 1900), an exquisite production which she did not live to see in type. She died soon after her father's retirement from office, the cause of her death being indirectly due to a fall from a horse.

HEREFORD, ELIZABETH J., Mrs. Writer. She was born in Kentucky but afterward located in Texas. She published 'Rebel Rhymes.'

HEREFORD, WILLIAM R. Poet, of Missouri. One of his dialect sketches, "To Riley," is preserved in 'Missouri Literature.'

HERNDON, MARY ELIZA, author, was born in Fayette County, Ky., March 1, 1820, and was the daughter of Beverly A. Hicks, an educator. She married first Reuben Herndon. Her writings include: 'Louisa Elton,' a reply to 'Uncle Tom's Cabin' (Philadelphia, 1853), 'Bandits of Italy,' and other novels, besides a volume of 'Select Poems.' She wrote with an unusual charm of style. Her second husband was Lundsford Chiles.

HERNDON, WILLIAM LEWIS, naval officer, was born at Fredericksburg, Va., October 25, 1813, and perished at sea, September 12, 1857. He published 'Explorations of the Valley of the Amazon, Vol. I' (Washington, D.C., 1853). One of the daughters of Commander Herndon became the wife of Chester A. Arthur, afterward President of the United States.

HERRICK, SOPHIA McILVAINE BLEDSOE. Author. She was born in Gambier, Ohio, March 26, 1837, the daughter of Albert Taylor and Harriet Bledsoe, and was educated at Miss Coxe's school in Cincinnati and at Cooper Institute, in Dayton, Ohio. She married, in 1860, James B. Herrick. She taught in Baltimore from 1868 to 1872, and was also for several years associate editor and business manager of the *Southern Review,* published in Baltimore. In 1878 she was called to the editorial staff of *Scribner's Magazine* and later of *The Century Magazine.* Her books, which deal in an intimate way with scientific subjects, include: 'Chapters in Plant Life' (New York, Harper and Brothers), 'The Earth in Past Ages' (*ibid.*), 'Wonders of Plant Life' (New York, G. P. Putnam's Sons), and 'A Century of Sonnets' (New York, R. H. Russell). For 'The Library of Southern Literature' she wrote the sketch of A. T. Bledsoe. She resides in Plainfield, N.J.

HERRON, FANNY E. Author. [Fla.]. She wrote 'Glen-el-glen.'

HERTZBERG, HANS R. R. Poet. [Texas]. He published a volume of verse entitled 'Lyrics of Love'; a work of merit (New York and Washington, The Neale Publishing Company, 1906).

HEUSTIS, JABEZ WIGGINS, physician and surgeon, was born in the Dominion of Canada in 1784 and died in Talladega, Ala., in 1841. Most of his life was spent in the South. He served in the various campaigns under General Jackson and published 'Physical Observations and Medical Tracts and Researches on the Topography and Diseases of Louisiana' (New York, 1817) and other medical works.

HEWAT, ALEXANDER, historian, was born in Scotland in 1745 and died in London, England, in 1829. The records of St. Andrew's Society of Charleston, S.C., show that he was moderator of the session of the Presbyterian Church in 1762; but on the eve of the Revolution he returned to England, being a loyalist, and published 'An Historical Account of the Rise and Progress of South Carolina and Charleston' (London, 1779), besides a volume of sermons.

HEWETT, WATERMAN THOMAS, educator and author, was born at Miami, Mo., January 10, 1846. He studied Greek at Athens, attended also the German Universities, became professor of German language and literature at Cornell in 1883, a chair which he still holds. He is an authority on Goethe, taking the very highest rank in this respect among American scholars. Besides editing Goethe's 'Hermann and Dorothea' (Boston, D. C. Heath and Company), 'Uhland's Poems' (New York, the Macmillan Company), and a 'German Grammar' (*ibid.*), he has published numerous works on German literature, a 'History of Cornell' in three volumes, and numerous monographs and essays. He resides at Ithaca, N.Y. Cornell gave him the degree of Ph.D.

HEWITT, EMMA CHURCHMAN, author, was born in New Orleans in 1850. Her maiden name was Churchman. After the death of her husband, she entered professional journalism, was associate editor for several years of the *Ladies' Home Journal*, engaged in general literature, and published several volumes, among them, 'Ease in Conversation' (1887), 'Hints to Ballad Singers' (1899), 'The Little Denvers' (Philadelphia, George W. Jacobs and Company), and 'Queen of the Home,' a joint production.

HEWITT, JOHN HENRY, poet and journalist, was born in New York, July 11, 1801, and died in Baltimore, Md., October 7, 1890. He was educated at West Point, but withdrew from the institution prior to graduation on account of a dispute with the commandant. While at West Point he composed both the words and the music of his famous ballad entitled "The Minstrel's Return from the War." He settled in Baltimore, where he became identified with numerous literary ventures, and in competition with Edgar Allan Poe, won a prize for his "Song of the Winds." He also wrote plays and oratorios, editorials and essays. Some of his poems appeared in book form in 1838, but a more complete collection was published in 1877. The creations of his intellect were pure and simple and easily within the mental reach of the masses.

HEYWARD, JANIE SCREVEN. Poet. [S.C.]. She wrote a volume of verse entitled 'Wild Roses.'

HIGBEE, DOLLIE. Author. [Ky.]. She wrote an entertaining novel of life in Kentucky entitled 'God's Country.' She is now Mrs. William Geppert.

HILDRETH, EUGENIUS AUGUSTUS, physician, was born in Wheeling, W. Va., September 13, 1831, and died there, August 31, 1885. He attained professional distinction, invented surgical appliances, wrote articles upon medical subjects and published 'Biographies of Physicians of Wheeling for the Last One Hundred Years.'

HILL, AGNES LEONARD, author, was born in Louisville, Ky., January 20, 1842. Her father was Dr. Oliver Langdon Leonard and her mother, Agnes Howard. Soon after completing her studies at Henry Female College, she became the wife of Dr. L. E. Scanland; and, losing her husband several years later, she married Samuel Howe Hill. From earliest childhood she evinced a fondness for writing. Besides contributing to magazines and writing numbers of books, she has engaged extensively in religious work and has even served churches, being at one time pastor of a Congregational Church at Wollaston, England. Included among her works are: 'Myrtle Blossoms,' 'Vanquished,' 'Heights and Depths,' 'Hints on How to Talk,' 'What Makes Social Leadership,' 'Evidences of Reincarnation,' and 'Christian Science versus Common Sense.' She resides at Ravena, Ill.

HILL, BENJAMIN HARVEY. See Biographical and Critical Sketch, Vol. VI, page 2389.

HILL, BENJAMIN HARVEY, Jr., jurist, was born in Georgia and educated at the University of the State, graduating in 1869 and afterward taking a course of law. On the organization of the State Court of Appeals, he was made presiding judge. He wrote 'The Life of Senator Benjamin H. Hill,' an authoritative work which contains the most important speeches of the great orator.

HILL, BRITTON A. Lawyer. [Mo.]. He published 'Liberty and Law' (1873), 'Absolute Money' (1874), and 'Specie Resumption' (1876), besides numerous articles on political and economic subjects.

HILL, DANIEL HARVEY, soldier and educator, was born in York District, S.C., July 12, 1821, and died in Charlotte, N.C., September 25, 1899. Educated at West Point, he entered the regular army and won distinction in the Mexican War but, resigning his commission at the close of hostilities, he devoted himself to educational work. He held the chair of mathematics first at Washington College and afterward at Davidson College; but, at the beginning of the Civil War, he was superintendent of the North Carolina Military Institute at Charlotte. On the Confederate side, in the struggle which followed secession, he attained the rank of lieutenant-general. For several years after the war, he was president of the University of Arkansas, and later he became president of the Georgia Military and Agricultural College; and he also edited 'The Land We Love.' Besides frequent contributions to current literature, he published an 'Algebra,' 'A Consideration of the Sermon on the Mount,' 'The Crucifixion of Christ,' and the volume on North Carolina in 'The Confederate Military History' (Atlanta, Ga., The Confederate Publishing Company, 1899), besides several articles in 'Battles and Leaders of the Civil War.'

HILL, DANIEL HARVEY, educator, was born at Davidson College, N.C., January 15, 1859. The volumes which have come from his pen include 'North Carolina in the Civil War' (Atlanta, Ga., The Confederate Publishing Company, 1899), 'Agriculture for Beginners,' in joint authorship with Drs. Burkett and Stevens (Boston, Ginn and Company, 1903), 'The Hill Readers, a Collaboration' (Boston, Ginn and Company, 1906), and a 'Young People's History of North Carolina' (Charlotte, Stone and Barringer, 1907), besides the sketch of John Lawson in 'The Library of Southern Literature.' He is president of the North Carolina College of Agriculture and Mechanic Arts. In recognition of his literary scholarship he has been given the degree of Litt.D.

HILL, MARY CARTER. She was the first wife of Judge Benjamin H. Hill. One of her best poems, "The River," which was written on the death of Senator Benjamin H. Hill of Georgia, is preserved in 'Songs of the South.' She died in 1890.

HILL, THEOPHILUS HUNTER. See Biographical and Critical Sketch, Vol. VI, page 2417.

HILL, WALTER BARNARD. Lawyer and educator, chancellor of the University of Georgia. He was born in Talbotton, Ga., September 9, 1851, the son of Judge Barnard and Mary Clay Birch Hill, and graduated from the University of Georgia, at which institution he also studied law. From the activities of the legal profession he was called to the chancellorship of the University of Georgia in 1899. Besides being one of the compilers of the 'Code of Georgia of 1873 and 1882,' he contributed numerous articles on ethical and legal subjects to the periodicals, delivered several baccalaureate addresses which attracted wide attention, and many literary and educational addresses. He was an ardent advocate of prohibition. Three separate institutions gave him the degree of LL.D. He died in Athens, Ga., in 1905.

HILL, WALTER HENRY, clergyman and educator, was born near Lebanon, Ky., January 21, 1822. After studying medicine, he entered the order of the Jesuits, became president of St. Xavier's College, and published 'Elements of Philosophy' (Baltimore, 1873), a work which passed into numerous editions; 'Ethics,' (Baltimore, 1878), and frequent contributions to Catholic periodicals.

HILL, WILLIAM, clergyman, was born in Cumberland County, Va., March 3, 1769, and died in Winchester, Va., November 16, 1852. He published a number of sermons, and began, but failed to complete, a 'History of the Presbyterian Church in the United States.'

HILLIARD, HENRY WASHINGTON. Lawyer, clergyman, diplomat, author. He was born in Fayetteville, N.C., in 1808, an l was educated at the University of South Carolina. For three years he taught in the University of Alabama. From 1842 to 1844 he was Chargé d'Affaires in Belgium; and from 1845 to 1851 he represented Alabama in Congress. He opposed secession, but accepted the post of commissioner to Tennessee and received the appointment of brigadier-general, though he took no conspicuous part in military operations. He became a Republican on post-bellum issues; and, under the administration of President Hayes, he was United States Minister to Brazil. He was a lawyer by profession, but he joined the Methodist conference and frequently occupied the pulpit. At leisure intervals he indulged his fondness for letters and wrote: 'De Vane, a Story of Plebeians and Patricians,' in two volumes (Nashville, Methodist Episcopal Publishing House, 1884), and 'Politics and Pen-Pictures at Home and Abroad' (New York, G. P. Putnam's Sons). He was also an orator, and contested the palm with Yancey, the great advocate of secession. Some of his choice utterances are contained in 'Speeches and Addresses' (New York, Harper and Brothers, 1855). He died in Atlanta, Ga., in 1892.

HILLS, LUCIUS PERRY, writer and platform entertainer, was born in Bennington, N.Y., June 16, 1844. For more than thirty-five years he has resided in Atlanta, Ga., where most of his literary work has been done. He has published 'Echoes,' a collection of verse (1892), "When Patti Sang," an illustrated poem which passed into several editions (1894), "The Yank and the Reb," a poem issued in pamphlet form; "A Memory of Song," an illustrated poem, and a "Grant Memorial Entertainment Souvenir."

HILLYARD, M. B. Author. He published 'The New South' (Baltimore, 1887) and 'Mississippi Letters' (1876).

HILLYER, LOUISA C. [Ga.]. She wrote a memoir of her father, Dr. Shaler G. Hillyer, which was published as an appendix to the latter's 'Reminiscences of Georgia Baptists.'

HILLYER, SHALER GRANBY, clergyman and educator, was born in Wilkes County, Ga., June 20, 1809, the son of Shaler Hillyer, a native of Granby, Conn. On completing his education at the University of Georgia, he engaged in educational work, becoming a professor in Mercer University, first of rhetoric and afterward of theology; and incidentally he also preached with great power. Subsequent to the war he was for some time president of Monroe College. His first wife was Elizabeth Thompson and his second wife, Elizabeth Dagg, the daughter of Dr. John L. Dagg. Besides frequent contributions to his church papers, he wrote 'Bible Morality for the Schools' and 'Reminiscences of Georgia Baptists,' edited, with a story of the author's life by his daughter, Louisa C. Hillyer. He lived to an advanced age, dying February 19, 1900.

HILLYER, WILLIAM HURD, journalist and banker, was born in Atlanta, Ga., July 29, 1880, the son of Henry Hillyer, a prominent lawyer. For two years he was chief editorial writer on the Atlanta *Journal,* but since 1904 he has been an investment banker. His contributions have appeared from time to time in the leading periodicals of the day, including *Lippincott's, Harper's, Munsey's, The Youth's Companion, The Smart Set, Puck, St. Nicholas* and others; and among the writers of the day he deservedly takes high rank. He published in 1907 a volume of poems entitled 'Songs of the Steel Age' (Boston). At present he is engaged in writing a novel which is said to deal mainly with modern conditions. He married Mary Dunwody Jones.

HILTON, WILLIAM. Navigator. He commanded a vessel which sailed from the Barbados in 1663 and which later touched what proved to be the coast of North Carolina. He published an account of the discovery under the impression that it was the coast of Florida (London, 1664). The work is perhaps the earliest publication relating to the Carolinas.

HINDS, JOHN IREDELL DILLARD. Educator. [N.C.]. Born in 1847. He published 'The American System of Education.'

HINSDALE, LAURA F. Author. [Miss.]. She published a volume of much interest entitled 'Legends and Lyrics of the Gulf Coast' (Biloxi, Miss., The Herald Press, 1896).

HINTON, ISAAC TAYLOR, Baptist clergyman, was born in Oxford, England, July 4, 1799, and died in New Orleans, La., August 28, 1847. For several years he was pastor of the First Baptist Church of Richmond, Va. Besides assisting his brother, John Howard Hinton, in preparing 'The History and Topography of the United States' (1834), he published a 'History of Baptism' (1841), and 'Lectures on the Prophecies' (1843). He fell a victim to the yellow fever.

HITCHCOCK, HENRY. Lawyer and jurist. He was born in 1795 and died in 1839. He was a landmark of the early pioneer days in Alabama and a member of the Constitutional Convention of 1819, taking an active part in shaping the organic law of the young commonwealth. He was also for some time Chief Justice of the State. His only work is entitled 'The Alabama Justice of the Peace,' but it was the first book published in the State and it served to blaze the way for legal procedure. Consequently it is still held in high esteem. It was published by W. B. Allen, at Catawba, in 1822.

HOBBS, ROE R., author, was born in Kentucky, July 26, 1871. His father was William Vincent Hobbs, and his mother, Ollie Theresa Martin. At the age of thirteen he became a telegrapher and at the present time is chief operator for the Louisville and Nashville Railroad. He married, March 30, 1903, Emma May King. Among his exceedingly clever books are 'The Court of Pilate' (New York, R. F. Fenno and Company, 1905), 'Zoas' (Washington, The Neale Publishing Company, 1907), and 'Gates of Flame' (*ibid.*, 1906), besides frequent magazine articles. Mr. Hobbs belongs to the imaginative school of writers. He resides in Louisville, Ky.

HOBBY, ALFRED M. Poet. For some time he lived in Florida, but afterward moved to Texas. He began to attract attention many years prior to the Civil War. He published two volumes in Texas: 'Frontier from the Saddle' and 'The Sentinel's Dream of Home.'

HOBSON, ANNE. Author. [Ala.]. She wrote a story entitled 'In Old Alabama' (1903).

HOBSON, RICHMOND PEARSON. The hero of the *Merrimac*. Naval Constructor and Member of Congress. He was born in Greensboro, Ala., August 17, 1870, the son of James Marcellus and Sarah Croom Pearson Hobson, and graduated from the United States Naval Academy in 1889. He distinguished himself for skill and daring in the Spanish-American War, especially in the hazardous feat of sinking the *Merrimac* in Santiago harbor. After being rescued he was for several weeks a prisoner in Morro Castle, but was finally released. He resigned from the Navy, February 6, 1903, having achieved one of the most brilliant records in the naval history of the Government. He married, May 25, 1905, Grizelda Houston Hull. At present he is representing Alabama in Congress; and, while he has taken the leadership in the international movement for peace, he has also advocated on the floor of Congress, on the platform, and in the magazines, the policy of naval expansion. Included among his works are: 'The Sinking of the Merrimac' (New York, The Century Company, 1898) and 'Buck Jones at Annapolis' (New York, D. Appleton and Company, 1907), besides numerous contributions to the leading magazines of the day on topics connected with his profession.

HODGE, SAMUEL, clergyman and educator, was born in Sullivan County, Tenn., June 7, 1829. Entering the ministry of the Presbyterian Church he held numerous professorships and filled several important pastoral charges. He published 'The Centennial of New Bethel Presbyterian Church in Tennessee.' Iowa University gave him the degree of D.D.

HODGES, LOUISE T. Teacher and writer. She was born in Atlanta, Ga., the daughter of James Madison and Frances Collier, and was educated by private tutors. She married Benjamin F. Hodges, and was for some time connected with the public schools of Atlanta. Besides numerous poems and essays contributed to the periodicals, she has published 'Thought Blossoms From the South,' which contains many dainty bits of verse. Her daughter, Pearl, has also done some excellent work.

HODGSON, JOSEPH. Journalist. He was born in 1838, and in the Civil War was a colonel in the Confederate Army. Besides compiling 'The Alabama Manual and Statistical Register for 1869' and editing the Alabama *Journal of Education,* he wrote an interesting work entitled 'The Cradle of the Confederacy, or the Times of Troup, Quitman, and Yancey' (Mobile, 1876).

HOFFMAN, DAVID, lawyer and author, was born in Baltimore, Md., December 25, 1784, and died in New York City, November 11, 1854. He achieved distinction at the Bar of Maryland, located in Philadelphia, began a 'History of the World,' the preparation of which took him to London, returned to America to regulate his private affairs for an indefinite sojourn abroad, and died from an apoplectic attack. He completed only two volumes, bringing the narrative of civilization down to A.D. 373 (London, 1853), but another one was in type and three others were partially written. He also published 'Legal Outlines,' 'Miscellaneous Thoughts, by Anthony Grumbler,' in two volumes, 'Legal Hints,' and 'Chronicles of Cartaphilus, the Wandering Jew.' He was a man of profound scholarship and of vast information.

HOGAN, JOHN, Congressman, was born in Mollow, Ireland, January 2, 1805. For some time he was a shoemaker in Baltimore. Later he removed to the West and eventually settled in St. Louis, where he became a merchant and a banker. During four years he was mayor of St. Louis and afterward served in Congress. He published 'Thoughts About St. Louis' (St. Louis, 1857), 'The Resources of Missouri' (1858), 'Sketches of Early Western Pioneers' (1859), and 'The History of Western Methodism' (1860).

HOGAN, JOHN A. Clergyman. [La.]. He published an interesting volume entitled 'The Labors of Jesuit Fathers in the Mississippi Valley' (1904).

HOGE, JAMES, clergyman and educator, was born in Frederick County, Va., February 15, 1752, and died in Philadelphia, Pa., July 5, 1820. After serving for a short time in the Continental Army, he prepared himself for the ministry of the Presbyterian Church and became one of the landmarks of this denomination. For nearly fifteen years he was president of Hampden-Sidney College. In the opinion of John Randolph of Roanoke, he was the most eloquent man in the American pulpit. He published 'The Christian Panoply,' an answer to Paine's 'Age of Reason' (Philadelphia, 1799) and 'Sermons.'

HOGE, MOSES DRURY. See Biographical and Critical Sketch, Vol. VI, page 2435.

HOGE, PEYTON HARRISON. Clergyman. He was born at Hampden-Sidney, Va., January 6, 1858, the son of Dr. William J. Hoge, an eminent Presbyterian educator and divine. He graduated from Hampden-Sidney College and from Union Theological Seminary, in Virginia, and married, August 22, 1883, Mary Stuart Holladay. After holding numerous important pastorates, he was called, in 1899, to the Warren Street Presbyterian Church of Louisville, Ky., which charge he still retains. Two important volumes have come from his pen: 'Moses Drury Hoge—Life and Letters' (Richmond, Presbyterian Committee of Publication, 1899) and 'The Divine Tragedy—a Drama of the Christ' (New York and Chicago, Fleming H. Revell Company, 1905). Hampden-Sidney College gave him the degree of D.D.

HOGE, WILLIAM JAMES, clergyman and educator, was born at Hampden-Sidney, Va., in 1821, and died in Petersburg, Va., July 6, 1864. For several years he was professor of New Testament literature in Union Theological Seminary, in New York, and also held several metropolitan pastorates in the North; but at the beginning of the Civil

War he returned to Virginia. Besides tracts and sermons, he published 'Blind Bartimeus; or the Sightless Sinner' (New York, 1859), which was translated into most of the languages of Europe.

HOGG, THOMAS E. Writer. [Texas]. He wrote in verse 'The Fate of Marvin.'

HOLBROOK, JOHN EDWARDS, naturalist and physician, was born in Beaufort, S.C., December 30, 1794, and died in Norfolk, Mass., September 8, 1871. He took his medical degree at the University of Pennsylvania and continued his professional studies for two years in Edinburgh and London. For more than thirty years he was professor of anatomy in the Medical College of South Carolina. His first contribution to science was 'American Herpetology; or, a Description of Reptiles Inhabiting the United States,' in five volumes (Philadelphia, 1842). He next published 'The Icthyology of South Carolina' (Charleston, 1854). On account of the value of his work to science, he attracted the attention of Louis Agassiz, with whom he maintained the friendliest of relations.

HOLBROOK, SILAS PINCKNEY, author, was born in Beaufort, S.C., June 1, 1796, and died in Pineville, S.C., May 26, 1835. On completing his studies, he practiced law for some time in Massachusetts; his greatest success, however, was not achieved at the Bar but in the realm of letters. He became a contributor to the *New England Galaxy* and to the Boston *Courier,* to which, under the pen-name of "Jonathan Farbrick," he wrote "Letters from a Mariner," "Travels of a Tin Peddler," "Letters from a Boston Merchant," and "Recollections of China and Japan." They were afterward published in a volume entitled 'Sketches by a Traveler.' He also wrote the European part of 'Peter Parley's Geography,' and edited several papers. His writings are characterized by a vein of delightful humor. Dr. J. E. Holbrook, the naturalist, was his brother.

HOLCOMBE, HENRY, clergyman, was born in Prince Edward County, Va., September 22, 1762, and died in Philadelphia, Pa., May 22, 1826. After serving in the Revolution with the rank of captain, he entered the ministry and became one of the most distinguished of pioneer American Baptist divines. He filled important pastorates, edited religious journals, and established educational institutions, chiefly in the South. But in 1812 he was called to the First Baptist Church, of Philadelphia, where he labored the remainder of his days. He published 'A Funeral Discourse on the Death of Washington' and 'Lectures on Primitive Theology' (Philadelphia, 1822). He received the degree of D.D. from Brown University.

HOLCOMBE, HOSEA, clergyman, was born in Union District, S.C., July 20, 1780, and died in Jefferson County, Ala., in 1821. He published 'A Collection of Sacred Hymns' (1815), 'Anti-Mission Principles Exposed' (1836), and 'The History of Alabama Baptists' (1840).

HOLCOMBE, JAMES PHILEMON, lawyer, author, educator, was born in Lynchburg, Va., September 25, 1820, and died in Capon Springs, Va., August 26, 1873. He was well educated, completing his studies at Yale after attending the University of Virginia, was for eight years professor of law in the latter institution, became a member of the secession convention, served in the Confederate Congress, and was commissioner from the Confederate Government to Canada. For several years after the war he was principal of the Bellevue High School, in Nelson County, Va. Besides frequent contributions to periodicals, he published: 'Leading Cases on Commercial Law' (New York, 1847), 'Digests of the Decisions of the United States Supreme Court' (1848), 'Merchants' Book of Reference' (1848), and 'Literature and Letters' (1868), besides minor works.

HOLCOMBE, WILLIAM HENRY. An eminent physician and writer. He was born in Lynchburg, Va., May 29, 1825. After locating in Cincinnati, Ohio, for the practice of medicine, he was converted to homeopathy and to Swedenborgianism. Later he returned to the South, and, after sojourning in various places, he finally settled in New Orleans. On the death of two of his children in 1869 he wrote "Our Children in Heaven," a poem which a critic of some note characterized as "a work of genius, sanctified by sorrow." This marked the beginning of his literary career. His writings include: 'The Scientific Basis of Homeopathy,' 'Essays on the Spiritual Philosophy of African Slavery,' 'Poems,' 'The Sexes Here and Hereafter,' 'In Both Worlds,' 'The Other Life,' 'Southern Voices,' 'The Lost Truths of Humanity,' 'The End of the World,' 'The New Life,' 'Helps to Spiritual Growth,' and 'A Mystery of New Orleans,' the last named book being a novel which Dr. Garth Wilkinson of London pronounced a masterpiece of fiction. Still another work, 'The Truth About Homeopathy,' was published after his death, which occurred in New Orleans, November 28, 1893.

HOLDEN, EDWARD SINGLETON, astronomer, was born in St. Louis, Mo., November 5, 1846, and was educated at West Point, becoming several years later an instructor in the institution. But he resigned his commission in 1873 and became professor of mathematics in the Naval Academy at Annapolis. For three years he was president of the University of California; from 1888 to 1898 he was director of the Lick Observatory; and for several years past he has been librarian of the United States Military Academy at West Point. Besides numerous technical and scientific works, he has published 'The Life of Sir William Herschel' (New York, Charles Scribner's Sons), 'Astronomy,' with Simon Newcomb (New York, Henry Holt and Company), 'Earth and Sky' (New York, D. Appleton and Company), 'The Primer of Heraldry' (New York, The Century Company), 'Our Country's Flag' (New York, D. Appleton and Company), 'Family of the Sun' (*ibid.*), 'Essays in Astronomy' (*ibid.*), 'Stories of the Great Astronomers' (*ibid.*), 'Elementary Astronomy' (New York, Henry Holt and Company), 'Real Things in Nature' (New York, The Macmillan Company), 'The Sciences' (Boston, Ginn and Company). He received the degree of Sc.D. from the University of the Pacific and the degree of LL.D. from Columbia University.

HOLDING, ELIZABETH E., Mrs. Educator. [Mo.]. She wrote an interesting work entitled 'Joy, the Deaconess,' a novel.

HOLLAND, EDWARD CLIFFORD, poet, was born in Charleston, S.C., in 1794. He was noted as a controversialist, edited for several years the Charleston *Times,* and published a volume of patriotic verse entitled 'Odes, National Songs, and Other Poems' (Charleston, 1814). He died in Charleston, S.C., September 11, 1824.

HOLLAND, ROBERT AFTON, Protestant Episcopal clergyman, was born in Nashville, Tenn., in 1844, and was at one time a Methodist minister. Both in the pulpit and in the world of letters Dr. Holland has achieved note. His publications include: 'The Philosophy of the Real Presence,' 'The Relations of Philosophy to Agnosticism and Religion,' 'The Proof of Immortality,' 'A Midsummer Night's Dream: an Interpretation,' and 'What is the Use of Going to Church?' For some time past he has been rector of St. George's Church, St. Louis, Mo.

HOLLEY, MARY AUSTIN. Author. Her maiden name was Austin. She became the wife of Dr. Horace Holley, lived for several years in Texas, and wrote a 'History of Texas' (Baltimore, 1883), which was published long after her death. She was a kinswoman of General Austin. She died in New Orleans, August 6, 1846.

HOLLIDAY, CARL, educator and author, was born at Hanging Rock, Ohio, in 1879. His father was George H. Holliday and his mother, Lucy Sheppard. Since 1896 he has lived in the South, engaged in educational work. For a while he was instructor of English at the University of Virginia; but at the present time, he is professor of English in the Southwestern Presbyterian University, at Clarksville, Tenn. He married Winifred May Hocking. Several books have come from the facile pen of this writer, among them: a 'History of Southern Literature' (New York and Washington, The Neale Publishing Company); 'The Cotton Picker, and Other Poems,' 'Three Centuries of Southern Poetry,' 'The Literature of Colonial Virginia,' which was awarded a prize by the Virginia Colonial Dames, 'Once Upon a Time,' a volume of stories, and 'The Poetry of the South.' For 'The Library of Southern Literature' he wrote the sketch of William A. Carruthers.

HOLLISTER, W. R. In collaboration with Harry Norman, he wrote 'Five Famous Missourians' (Kansas City, Hudson-Kimberly Publishing Company).

HOLLOWAY, ELIZABETH, Mrs. Writer. [Tenn.]. Her maiden name was Elizabeth Howell. Under the title of 'Crag and Pine,' she published several entertaining stories.

HOLLOWAY, LAURA CARTER, author, was born in Nashville, Tenn., in 1848. Her maiden name was Laura Carter. On both sides of the house she came of the best stock, and her father was at one time governor of the State. At the age of fifteen she married Junius B. Holloway of Kentucky; but she was already well known to the reading public through her precocious efforts of genius. Later she became Mrs. Langford and lived in Brooklyn; but since most of her literary work had been done under the name of Laura Holloway, this continued to be the name by which she was known to the world of letters. The most successful of her books is entitled: 'The Ladies of the White House,' which is said to have been undertaken at the suggestion of Harriet Lane, and which has passed into many editions both in this country and in Europe. But she won additional praise by her work, 'The Mothers of Great Men.' She has also appeared at frequent intervals on the platform, and Henry Ward Beecher pronounced her lecture on "The Perils of the Hour; or, Woman's Place in America" to be a masterpiece.

HOLMES, GEORGE FREDERICK. See Biographical and Critical Sketch, Vol. VI, page 2465.

HOLMES, GEORGE S. [S.C.]. He published an interesting 'Sketch of the Parish Church of St. Michael's in the Province of South Carolina, 1752-1887.'

HOLMES, ISAAC EDWARD, Congressman and author, was born in Charleston, S.C., April 6, 1796, and died in Charleston, S.C., February 24, 1867. After graduation from Yale he was admitted to the Charleston Bar, became an eloquent advocate of state rights and served in Congress with distinction for twelve years. Later he removed to California, but at the outbreak of the Civil War he returned to South Carolina to share the fortunes of his people. He published a volume of delightful miscellany entitled 'The Recreations of George Taletell' (Charleston, 1822), and in conjunction with Robert J. Turnbull, a volume of political essays in support of state rights, under the pen-name of "Caroliniensis" (Charleston, 1826).

HOLMES, MARY JANE, author, was born in Brookfield, Mass.; but, upon her marriage to Daniel Holmes, a lawyer, she made her residence in Versailles, Ky., which continued for many years to be her home, and several of her stories reflect the features of her environment. Her first novel, 'Tempest and Sunshine' (New York, 1854), pictured Southern society before the war. Then followed in rapid succession numerous other stories which placed her in the front rank of writers of popular fiction. During her lifetime more than two million copies of her books were sold. With the single exception of Mrs. Stowe, who wrote 'Uncle Tom's Cabin,' no woman author in America, so it is asserted, has received such large profits from her copyrights. She ultimately removed to Brockport, N.Y., where she died in 1907. Some of her best known works are: 'The Homestead on the Hills,' 'English Orphans,' 'Lena Rivers,' 'Meadow Brook,' 'Dora Deane,' 'Marian Grey,' 'Hugh Worthington,' 'Darkness and Daylight,' 'The Cameron Pride,' 'Ethelyn's Mistake,' 'Rose Mather,' 'Mildred,' 'Daisy Thornton,' 'Forest House,' 'Château d'Or,' 'Edith Lyle,' 'Queenie Hetherington,' 'Bessie's Fortune,' 'Gretchen.' 'Millbank,' 'Dr. Hathern's Daughters,' and 'The Tracy Diamonds.'

HOLT, ANDREW JACKSON, Baptist clergyman, was born in Tennessee but afterward labored in Texas. Besides a work on 'Palestine,' he published 'Marion Heth.'

HOLT, JOHN SAUNDERS, author, was born in Mobile, Ala., December 5, 1826, and died in Natchez, Miss., February 27, 1886. After completing his education, he enlisted in a Mississippi regiment of volunteers, in command of Jefferson Davis, and served in the Mexican War. On his return home he was admitted to the Bar and was successful in building up an excellent practice; but at the outbreak of hostilities in 1861 he again went to the front, serving in the Confederate Army with the rank of lieutenant. After the war he resumed the practice of law and published, under the pen-name of "Abraham Page," several novels descriptive of Southern character: 'The Life of Abraham Page,' 'What I Know about Ben Eccles, by Abraham Page,' and 'The Quines.'

HOMES, MARY SOPHIE SHAW, author, was born in Frederick County, Md., in 1830. On the death of her father, Thomas Shaw, the family removed to New Orleans, La., where she was educated. Her first husband was Norman Rogers, who died soon after the marriage, and she later became the wife of Luther Homes. Besides contributing numerous essays and sketches to the press, under the pen-name of "Millie Mayfield," she published a volume of verse entitled 'Progression; or, the South Defended,' and the work was so favorably received that it was soon followed by a 'Wreath of Rhymes' (Philadelphia, 1870).

HOOD, JOHN BELL, an eminent Confederate officer, was born in Owenville, Ky., June 1, 1821, and died in New Orleans, La., August 30, 1879. He was educated for a military career at West Point, served with distinction in the Indian fights along the Western frontier, was severely wounded, and, at the outbreak of hostilities between the sections, he resigned. Enlisting on the Confederate side, he attained the rank of lieutenant-general and temporarily the rank of general, superseding Joseph E. Johnston at the battle of Atlanta. He was several times desperately wounded, being disabled in one arm at Gettysburg and losing a leg at Chickamauga. After the war he engaged in business in New Orleans. He wrote 'Advance and Retreat; or, Personal Experiences in the United States and Confederate Armies' (New Orleans, The Hood Orphan Memorial Fund, 1880), which was published after his death.

HOOKER, CHARLES E., Jr. Author of "The Political History of Mississippi" in Goodspeed's 'Memoirs.'

HOOKER, CHARLES E., Sr., lawyer, was born in Union District, S.C., in 1825. For several years he represented Mississippi in Congress. He attained the rank of colonel of cavalry in the Civil War, and lost an arm in defence of the South. When Jefferson Davis was arraigned for treason, he was associated with Charles O'Connor and James Lyon in defending the illustrious prisoner. From 1865 to 1868 he was attorney-general of Mississippi. He wrote: "The Confederate Military History of Mississippi," in Goodspeed's 'Memoirs,' and the volume on "Mississippi" in 'The Confederate Military History,' published in twelve volumes (Atlanta, Ga., The Confederate Publishing Company, 1899).

HOOPER, J. W. Clergyman. [Va.]. Dr. Hooper wrote 'Lead Me to the Rock,' besides minor works.

HOOPER, JOHNSON JONES. See Biographical and Critical Sketch, Vol. VI, page 2489.

HOOPER, SUE E. Writer. [Va.]. She published an entertaining volume of fiction entitled 'Ashes of Roses, and Other Stories.'

HOOPER, WILLIAM. See Biographical and Critical Sketch, Vol. VI, page 2507.

HOPE, JAMES BARRON. See Biographical and Critical Sketch, Vol. VI, page 2531.

HOPKINS, ISAAC STILES. Clergyman, educator, and lecturer. He was born in Augusta, Ga., June 20, 1841, the son of Thomas and Rebecca Hopkins; graduated from Emory College and took a course in medicine at the Medical College of Georgia. He married, first, Emily Gibson and, second, Mary Hinton. He entered the ministry of the Methodist Episcopal Church, South, and became first a professor in various departments and afterward president of Emory College, his *alma mater*. He organized the Georgia School of Technology at Atlanta, and presided for eight years over this educational institution. He has held some of the most important pastorates within the bounds of Southern Methodism. Besides frequent lectures on educational subjects, he has contributed numerous articles to the secular and religious journals. The sketch of Atticus G. Haygood, in 'The Library of Southern Literature,' is from his pen. He holds the M.D., the D.D. and the Ph.D. degrees.

HOPKINS, JOHN LIVINGSTON, jurist and lawyer, was born in Madisonville, Tenn., September 24, 1828. For several years he occupied the Bench of the Atlanta circuit and succeeded in restoring order at a time of great unrest. Until his retirement from the active practice, he was one of the leaders of the Bar of Georgia. 'The Annotated Penal Code' is the work of Judge Hopkins. On account of his legal scholarship and prestige, he was appointed chairman of the board to codify the laws of Georgia (1893-1895). Fifteen years later his annotations were accepted by the State Legislature as the basis of another revision (1909-1910). He is also the author of an important volume entitled 'The Law of Personal Injuries.' He married Mary Elizabeth Cooke. His winters are spent in Florida and his summers in Georgia.

HOPKINS, LINTON COOKE, lawyer, was born in Atlanta, Ga., April 12, 1872, a son of Judge John L. Hopkins, one of the most distinguished lawyers of Georgia. At leisure intervals he has written a number of short stories for the periodicals, among them, "Chance," in *Collier's Weekly* (1905), "How the Thing was Managed," in *Appleton's Magazine* (1906), "The Crosby Case and the Crosby Woman," in *The Reader* (1907), and "The Adventures of the Lost Bathing Suit," in *Uncle Remus*.

HORNE, IDA HARRELL, Mrs. Writer. She wrote a number of poems which went the rounds of the press, among them "Under the Snow" and "Crushed Violets."

HORRY, PETER, author, was a soldier of the Revolution who distinguished himself under General Francis Marion. Neither the time nor the place of his nativity is known, but he is supposed to have been born in South Carolina. In collaboration with the Rev. Mason L. Weems, he published a 'Life of Marion' (Philadelphia, 1824), which passed through numerous editions. The rough outline of the work was from Horry's pen and the heightened touch of romance which was given to the account by Weems is said to have made the former disclaim the credit to which he was properly entitled.

HORTON, CORINNE STOCKER, writer, was born in Orangeburg, S.C. Her maiden name was Corinne Stocker. She married, June 17, 1896, Thaddeus E. Horton. For several years she was on the editorial staff of the Atlanta *Journal*. Besides numerovs articles in high-class periodicals, most of them dealing with Southern historical characters and places, Mrs. Horton has published 'The Georgian Architecture of the Far South' (1902). She has made an exhaustive study of architectural types and has furnished to the magazines many articles illustrated from photographic views which she has taken.

HOSMER, JAMES KENDALL. For eighteen years professor of English and German literatures in Washington University, St. Louis, Mo.; clergyman and author. He was born in Northfield, Mass., January 29, 1834, the son of George W. and Hannah P. Hosmer. He was educated at Harvard and was a Unitarian pastor before the war; and after it a college professor. He served in the Union Army as a private, declining staff appointment. From 1874 to 1892 he occupied the chair of English and German literature in Washington University; and then accepted the office of librarian in the public library at Minneapolis, Minn. He was twice married. His writings include the following books: 'The Color Guard' (1864), 'The Thinking Bayonet' (1865), 'Short History of German Literature' (New York, Charles Scribner's Sons), 'Memorial of G. W. Hosmer, D.D.' (1882), 'Story of the Jews' (New York, G. P. Putnam's Sons, 1885), "Life of Samuel Adams" in the 'American Statesmen Series' (Boston, Houghton, Mifflin and Company, 1885), 'Short History of Anglo-Saxon Freedom' (New York, Charles Scribner's Sons), 'Life of Sir Henry Vane' (1888), 'Life of Thomas Hutchinson' (New York, Harper and Brothers, 1896), 'Short History of the Mississippi Valley' (*ibid.*, 1901), 'History of the Louisiana Purchase' (New York, D. Appleton and Company, 1902), and Vols. XX and XXI of the 'History of the Civil War in America' (New York, Harper and Brothers, 1907). It will be seen from this list that he has made some of the most important contributions to the literature of the day. Mention should also be made of his work in editing 'The Expedition of Lewis and Clarke.' The University of Missouri gave him the degree of Ph.D. and Washington University, the degree of LL.D.

HOSKINS, JOSEPHINE R., Mrs. Author. [La.]. She published a story entitled 'Love's Stratagem.'

HOSKINS, WILLIAM WALTON, poet, was born in Mississippi but afterward removed to Georgia, where he published a volume of verse entitled 'Atlantis and Other Poems' (Atlanta, 1894).

HOSS, ELIJAH EMBREE, bishop of the M. E. Church, South, was born in Jonesboro, Tenn., April 14, 1849. On completing his studies at Emory and Henry College, he was ordained to the ministry, filled various important pastorates on both sides of the continent, was president at different times of Martha Washington College and of Emory and Henry College, a professor in the theological department of Vanderbilt University, editor of the *Christian Advocate*, and, in 1902, became bishop. Besides contributing to the 'History of Nashville' (1888), he has published 'Discussions in Theology' (Nashville, Barbee and Smith, 1887), 'Regeneration' (*ibid.*, 1899), "The New Age," in the 'Merick Series of Lectures' (1906), and 'Southern Methodism' (1909). He also wrote the sketch of O. P. Fitzgerald for 'The Library of Southern Literature.' From Emory and Henry College he holds the D.D. and the LL.D. degrees. He is an effective speaker and an elegant writer.

HOTCHKISS, JED. Soldier and author. [Va.]. He was born in 1827 and died in 1899. During the Civil War he was topographer and staff officer in various corps in the Army of Northern Virginia. By reason of his familiarity with the ground over which rolled the tide of conflict, he rendered important assistance to William Allan in preparing 'The Battlefields of Virginia' (1867), and wrote the volume on Virginia in 'The Confederate Military History' (Atlanta, Ga., The Confederate Publishing Company, 1899), besides minor works including an interesting historical account of the city of Staunton (1878).

HOUSSAYE, S. DE LA, Madame. Author. [La.]. She wrote 'Souvenirs d'Amérique et de France' (1883) and 'La Maride Marguerite.' the story of a Virginia girl.

HOUSTON, A. C. Writer. [Va.]. He wrote 'Hugh Harrison,' a novel.

HOUSTON, DAVID, educator, was born in Monroe, N.C., February 17, 1866, and was educated at South Carolina College, completing his studies at Harvard. From 1902 to 1905 he was president of the Agricultural and Mechanical College of Texas, and from 1905 to 1908, president of the University of Texas. Since 1908 he has been chancellor of Washington University at St. Louis, Mo. Dr. Houston is one of the foremost educators of the South, a successful administrator, a fine disciplinarian and a ripe scholar. He has published 'A Critical Study of Nullification in South Carolina,' besides minor works, and is one of the consulting editors of 'The Library of Southern Literature.' He married, December 11, 1895, Helen Beall, of Austin, Texas. Tulane University and the University of Wisconsin have given him the degree of LL.D.

HOUSTON, MARGARET MOFFETT, poet, was a native of Alabama, became the second wife of General Sam Houston, wrote a number of poems, including one "To My Husband," and died in Texas in 1867.

HOUSTON, SAM. See Biographical and Critical Sketch, Vol. VI, page 2561.

HOWARD, CAROLINE E., author, was born in McIntosh County, Ga., May 5, 1835. Her maiden name was Caroline E. Shackelford. She married, July 18, 1860, Chessly B. Howard. Her published works include: 'Paths Crossed; or, Glimpses into the Early History of Methodism in Georgia' (Nashville, The M.E. Publishing House, South, 1887), 'The Do Society' (*ibid.*, 1887), and 'Annie Cooper's Friends' (*ibid.*, 1889), besides minor works.

HOWARD, FRANCES THOMAS. Author. [Ga.]. She wrote 'In and Out of the Lines,' an interesting story of Sherman's march (New York and Washington, The Neale Publishing Company, 1907).

HOWARD, H. R. Author. [Miss.]. He wrote 'The History of Virgil A. Stewart of Mississippi, and His Adventures in Capturing and Exposing the Great Western Land Pirate and His Gang' (New York, Harper and Brothers).

HOWARD, MILFORD W., lawyer, was born in Floyd County, Ga., December 18, 1862, settled in Alabama, became active in politics, was twice elected by the Populists to the national House of Representatives, and published a volume which excited much interest at the time, entitled 'If Christ Came to Congress' (1894). He resides at Fort Payne, Ala.

HOWARD, WALTER. Editor. [Ga.]. For several years he was on the staff of the Atlanta *Journal,* after which he was for some time connected with the New York *Journal,* now the New York *American,* and was sent by the latter paper to London to be the resident American editor. He wrote numerous short stories and sketches. Mr. Howard married Belle Newman, a daughter of Judge William T. Newman, United States Judge for the Northern district of Georgia. He died in 1902.

HOWE, GEORGE, Presbyterian clergyman, was born in Massachusetts in 1802 and died in Columbia, S.C., in 1883. Dr. Howe wrote a 'History of the Presbyterian Church in South Carolina.'

HOWE, ROBERT. Soldier. [N.C.]. He was born in 1732 and died in 1785. During the American Revolution he attained the rank of major-general. His memoirs were edited by A. M. Hooper and published in abridged form in the *North Carolina University Magazine,* Vols. II and IV (1853-1855).

HOWE, WILLIAM WIRT. Jurist and lawyer He was born in Canandaigua, N.Y., in 1833, the son of Henry Howe. He served in the Union Army from 1861 to 1865, and took up the practice of law in New Orleans at the close of the war, becoming Judge of the Criminal Court, Associate Justice of the Supreme Court of Louisiana, and president of the American Bar Association. In 1900 he was appointed United States Attorney for the Southern district of Louisiana. Two interesting works have come from his pen: 'The Municipal History of New Orleans' and 'Studies in the Civil Law (Boston, Little, Brown and Company). He resides in New Orleans, La.

HOWELL, ANDREW JACKSON, Jr. Writer. [N.C.]. He published a work entitled 'Cornelius Harnett, a Revolutionary Patriot' (1896).

HOWELL, CLARK. Editor. He was born in Barnwell County, S.C., September 21, 1863, a son of Captain Evan P. Howell, for many years editor-in-chief of the Atlanta *Constitution.* He graduated from the University of Georgia, and married, first, in 1887, Harriet Glascock Barrett and, second, in 1900, Annie Comer. He entered journalism, succeeding the lamented Henry W. Grady as managing editor of the Atlanta *Constitution,* in 1889, and afterward was made editor-in-chief, the position long held by his father. He has been Speaker of the House and president of the Senate of Georgia; also a member of the National Democratic Committee and a candidate for governor. Besides frequent contributions to the press, he has made numerous speeches in both sections. One of his addresses, entitled "The Man With His Hat in His Hand," was suggested by an incident in the Spanish-American War, and, not only on account of the novelty of the theme but also because of the eloquent manner in which the orator expressed the spirit of the hour, it acquired an immense popularity and was declaimed from number-less school rostrums. He assisted in the compilation of 'Modern Eloquence' (Philadelphia, Jno. D. Morris and Company, 1900) and 'Eloquent Sons of the South' (Boston, Chapple Publishing Company, 1909). Mr. Howell resides in Atlanta, Ga.

HOWELL, REDNAP. Educator and poet. He taught a school at Deep River, N.C., before the Revolution and wrote a number of patriotic airs. He also published a pamphlet entitled "A Fan for Fanning and a Touch for Tryon" (Boston, 1871).

HOWELL, ROBERT BOYTE CRAWFORD, clergyman and author, was born in Wayne County, N.C., March 10, 1801, and died in Nashville, Tenn., April 5, 1868. Dr. Howell was an eminent Baptist divine, learned and eloquent. The greater part of his ministry was spent in the pulpit of the First Baptist Church of Nashville. As a writer he was vigorous and fluent. He published 'Terms of Sacramental Communion' (Philadelphia, 1841), 'Howell on the Deaconship' (1846), 'The Way of Salvation' (1849), 'The Evils of Infant Baptism' (1851), 'The Cross' (1854), 'The Covenants' (1856), and 'The Early Baptists of Virginia' (Philadelphia, 1876), besides tracts and pamphlets. He also left a number of manuscripts. Some of his works were reproduced in England.

HOWISON, ROBERT REID. Professor of American history in the College of Fredericksburg, Va.; clergyman and author. He was born in Fredericksburg, Va., June 22, 1820, a son of Samuel and Helen Howison. He enjoyed superior educational advantages, including a course in law, and practiced this profession for a while in Richmond; later he took a course in the Union Theological Seminary at Hampden-Sidney. He was pastor of a church at Staunton, Va., for one year, after which, because of failing health, he returned to the law. He was injured in the Capitol disaster in Richmond, in 1870, and once more resumed ministerial labors. He married, November 24, 1847, Mary Elizabeth Graham. He filled numerous pastorates, and in 1894 was called to the chair of American history in the College of Fredericksburg. His literary production includes some important contributions to American history, among them: 'The History of Virginia,' in two volumes, published first in 1846, and afterward in 1848, the lives of Morgan, Marion, and Gates in 'Washington and the Generals of the American Revolution,' 'Criminal Trials,' 'God and Creation,' 'Fredericksburg, Past and Present,' and a 'Students' History of the United States.' He wrote serially a 'History of the War Between the States,' which appeared in the *Southern Literary Messenger,* a paper which was suspended in 1864; also an essay on "The New Testament Plan of Ministerial Education," which was awarded a prize of fifty dollars. Dr. Howison held both the D.D. and the LL.D. degrees. He died in 1906.

HOY, FRANK, Mrs. Author. She wrote an interesting story of war times entitled 'Adrienne' (New York and Washington, The Neale Publishing Company, 1907), the scenes of which shift from New Orleans to various parts of the South.

HUBBARD, FORDYCE MITCHELL. Author. [N.C.]. He was born in 1809 and died in 1888. He published 'Life of W. R. Davie,' 'Richard Caswell,' and 'The Harvey Family,' besides minor writings.

HUBBARD, RICHARD B., lawyer, was born in Walton County, Ga., November 1, 1836. On completing his educational equipment, he located in Texas for the practice of law and rose at once to the front. At the outbreak of hostilities in 1861, he resigned his seat in the Legislature and organized a regiment of volunteer troops. On the field of battle he served with gallantry and distinction. From 1876 to 1879 he was governor of Texas; and, during President Cleveland's first administration, he was United States Minister to Japan. On the lecture platform he also became prominent. His oratorical gifts were of very high order and frequently made him the central figure in conventional assemblies. His oration at the Philadelphia Centennial in 1876 was the masterpiece of the historic celebration. He published 'The United States in the Far East; or, Modern Japan and the Orient' (Richmond, B. F. Johnson and Company, 1900).

HUBBELL, GEORGE ALLEN. Vice-president and dean of Berea College, Berea, Ky. He was born in Springfield, Ohio, August 15, 1862, the son of Sampson R. and Emily A. Hubbell. His works include: 'A Guide in the Study of Geography,' 'The Child and the Bible, 'The Men of the Bible,' in part written by him, and 'Up From Childhood' (New York, G. P. Putnam's Sons). He holds the Ph.D. degree.

HUBNER, CHARLES WILLIAM, editor, poet, librarian, was born in Baltimore, Md., January 16, 1835. After receiving an elementary education in the common schools, he spent several years in Germany, his ancestral home. He served with gallantry in the Confederate Army and at the close of hostilities settled in Atlanta, Ga., where he has since resided. He has been connected in an editorial capacity with various magazines and periodicals, and at the present time is assistant librarian of the Carnegie Library of Atlanta. As a writer Major Hubner possesses a style which has been little affected by the modern innovations upon the old standards. It is classic both in its simplicity and in its strength; and is linked to high and beautiful ideals. There are few departments of thought to which he has not contributed; and some of the South's best poetry since the war has come from his pen. The great sovereigns of song, like Whittier and Longfellow, have been captivated by the lilt of his rhymes and by the genuineness of his poetic inspirations. He is a man of the purest life and character, a scholar of rare attainments, and a critic of fine discrimination, keen but kind in his subtle powers of analysis. The writings of Major Hubner include: 'Historical Souvenirs of Luther' (1872), 'Wild Flowers,' a volume of poems (1876) 'Cinderella,' a drama (1879), 'Modern Communism' (1880), 'Poems and Essays' (1881), 'The Wonder Stone,' a lyrical composition (1883), 'War Poets of the South' (1896), 'Representative Southern Poets' (Washington, The Neale Publishing Company, 1906), and 'Poems' (ibid., 1906). He also wrote the sketch of Frank L. Stanton for 'The Library of Southern Literature.' The versatility of his genius is attested by the merest glance at the list of his publications.

HUDNALL, RICHARD HENRY, educator, was born at Brandon, Miss., May 28, 1870. His father was Joseph Hudnall and his mother, Elizabeth Francis. Besides contributing numerous articles on literary subjects to current periodicals, he is the author of 'A Presentation of the Grammatical Inflexions in Androw of Wyntoun's "Orygynale Cronykil of Scotland"' (Leipsic, 1898). For 'The Library of Southern Literature' he wrote the sketch of F. V. N. Painter. He occupies the chair of English in the Virginia Polytechnic Institute, at Blacksburg, and holds the degree of Ph.D. from Leipzig.

HUDSON, JOSHUA HILARY, jurist, was born in Chester, S.C., January 29, 1832, and died in Greenville, S.C., July 22, 1909. Judge Hudson published an interesting volume entitled 'Reminiscences and Sketches' (1904), in which he reviews some of the dramatic episodes of his long and useful career.

HUDSON, ROBERT PAYNE. Poet. [Tenn.]. He published a volume of verse entitled 'Southern Lyrics' (Nashville, 1907).

CONGRESSIONAL LIBRARY, EXTERIOR

HUGHES, ROBERT MORTON, lawyer, was born in Abingdon, Va., September 10, 1855. His father was Robert W. Hughes, an eminent Federal jurist. As an advocate he takes high rank. In 1895 he was made president of the Virginia Bar Association, an honor which attests his legal prestige, and for ten years he was chairman of the committee on legal literature. His published works include an excellent 'Life of General Joseph E. Johnston' (New York, D. Appleton and Company, 1893), a 'Hand-Book of Admiralty Law' (St. Paul, Minn., West Publishing Company, 1901), 'Federal Procedure' (*ibid.*, 1904), and 'Maritime Liens,' Vol. XXVI, Cyc. (New York, American Law Book Company, 1907). He married, February 19, 1879, Mattie L. Smith. He resides in Norfolk, Va.

HUGHES, ROBERT WILLIAM, jurist, was born in Powhatan County, Va., June 6, 1821. On leaving college, he settled in Richmond and edited *The Examiner* until 1857. Throughout the Civil War he served in the Confederate ranks. While on the staff of *The State,* in 1868, he fought a duel with William E. Cameron, in which the latter was wounded. He afterward became United States attorney for the western district of Virginia, and still later United States judge for the eastern district of Virginia, and was also an unsuccessful Republican candidate for governor. He published 'The American Dollar,' biographies of General John B. Floyd, and General Joseph E. Johnston, and 'The Currency Question.'

HUGHES, JOHN T. Author. [Mo.]. He published in 1847 a work entitled: 'Doniphan's Expedition,' giving an account of the adventures of 1,000 Missouri volunteers, under command of A. W. Doniphan, in the Mexican War (Cincinnati, J. A. and U. P. James).

HUGHEY, G. W. Clergyman. [Mo.]. He published 'The Liquor Traffic' (1882), 'Ingersoll and Ingersollism' (1883), a 'Catechism on Beer' (1884), 'The Resurrection of the Dead' (1885), and 'The Christian Side of Faith' (1886).

HUGHSON, SHIRLEY C. Editor. [S.C.]. Besides editing 'Shelley's Letters,' he published 'Piracy on the Carolina Coast.'

HULL, AUGUSTUS LONGSTREET. Banker. He was born in Athens, Ga., September 8, 1847, and was educated at the University of Georgia, of which institution he became secretary and treasurer. He married, January 5, 1871, Callie, daughter of General Thomas R. R. Cobb. He wrote an 'Historical Sketch of the University of Georgia,' 'Campaigns of the Confederate Army,' and 'Annals of Athens, Georgia.' He died in 1909.

HULL, SUSAN R. Author. [Md.]. She wrote an interesting volume entitled 'The Boy Soldiers of the Confederacy.'

HULSE, B. M. Author. [La.]. He wrote 'The History of Claiborne Parish, Louisiana' (New Orleans, 1886).

HULSE, GEORGIANA A. (Mrs. Alexander W. McLeod), author, was born in the Naval Hospital, near Pensacola, Fla., in 1835, and was the daughter of Dr. Isaac Hulse, a surgeon in the United States Navy. Being left an orphan of tender years, she was reared by her grandparents in Baltimore. At an early age she began to contribute some unusual bits of verse to the press, and in the early 'fifties her first volume appeared: 'Sunbeams and Shadows' (New York, D. Appleton and Company). She married, in 1853, the Rev. Henry McLeod, D.D.; but, in the midst of household duties she still found time to write. Her other works are, 'Ivy Leaves from the Old Homestead,' 'Sea Drifts,' and 'Bright Memories,' which contain some very interesting sketches. Mrs. McLeod was at one time principal of the Southern Literary Institute in Baltimore. Her best known poem is entitled "Thine and Mine."

HUME, THOMAS. Educator and divine. He was born in Portsmouth, Va., the son of Rev. Thomas Hume, and was educated at Richmond College and the University of Virginia. He was a chaplain in the Confederate Army, and after the war divided his time between educational and ministerial work, holding important pastorates and professorships. He was called to the chair of English language and literature in the University of North Carolina in 1885, occupying this position until the department was divided, in 1902, when he became professor of English literature in the same institution. Besides numerous lectures on literary subjects, and frequent contributions to the magazines and periodicals, he has published the following works, whose titular mention alone indicates the scope and value of his productions: 'Helps to the Study of Hamlet,' 'Shakespeare's Moral Teaching,' and 'John Milton's Religious Opinions and Connection.' His lectures include "The Literature of the Bible." "Shakespeare," and "Tennyson." Richmond College gave him his Ph.D. and Wake Forest, his LL.D.

HUMES, THOMAS W. Writer. [Tenn.]. He published 'The Loyal Mountaineers of Tennessee.'

HUMPHREYS, DAVID. Author. [Va.]. He wrote 'Heroes and Spies of the Civil War,' a narrative interestingly told by one of the members of the original "Stonewall Brigade" (New York and Washington, The Neale Publishing Company, 1903).

HUMPHREYS, WEST HUGHES, jurist, was born in Montgomery County, Tenn., August 5, 1806, and died in Nashville, Tenn., October 5, 1883. He was educated at Transylvania University, studied law and became United States district judge by appointment of President Pierce. Afterward he held judicial office under the Confederate Government. For several years he was also Supreme Court reporter, and published eleven volumes of 'Reports of the Supreme Court of Tennessee' (Nashville, 1839-1851).

HUMPHREYS, WILTON WYLIE, educator, was born in Greenbriar County, Va., now W.Va., September 15, 1844, given the best educational advantages, both at home and abroad (Ph.D., Leipsic, LL.D., Vanderbilt), and from 1862 to 1865 fought in the artillery branch of Lee's Army in the capacity of gunner. He married, in 1877, Louise, daughter of Dr. Landon C. Garland, chancellor of Vanderbilt University. Devoting himself to educational work, he became identified with a number of leading colleges and universities, and in 1887 was called to the chair of Greek in the University of Virginia, a position which he still retains. For ten years he was chief American editor of the *Revue des Revues*, and also edited 'The Clouds of Aristophanes' (Boston, Ginn and Company), and 'The Antigone of Sophocles' (New York, Harper and Brothers), besides minor works.

HUMPHRIES, JOSEPH WILLIAM, lawyer and poet, was born in Hapeville, Ga., August 27, 1871, a son of Amos Daniel and Annis Elizabeth Humphries. The demands of the legal profession have not prevented the exercise of his unusual poetic gifts, and he has frequently made contributions in verse to the periodicals; but he has not yet published his poems in book form. Among the popular favorites of this Georgia singer are: "When She Comes," "Just for You," and "Deedee's Hands." He resides in Atlanta, Ga.

HUNDLEY, DANIEL R. Colonel of the Thirty-first Alabama Regiment, C.S.A., and author of 'Social Relations in our Southern States' (New York, H. B. Price, 1860), which received high praise from the critics. He was born in 1832.

HUNGERFORD, JAMES. Author. [Md.]. He wrote two interesting stories of ante-bellum days, 'The Old Plantation' and 'The Master of Beverley.'

HUNT, CARLETON. Author. [La.]. He published a work on 'Edward Livingston' (1901).

HUNT, CHARLES H. Author. [La.]. He wrote a 'Life of Edward Livingston,' for which an introduction was written by George Bancroft, the historian (New York, 1869).

HUNT, GAILLARD, chief of the Division of Manuscripts of the Library of Congress, was born in New Orleans, La., September 8, 1862. His father was Judge William H. Hunt, former Secretary of the Navy and United States Minister to Russia. Among the important volumes which he has published are 'The Life of James Madison' (New York, Doubleday, Page and Company, 1902), 'Disunion Sentiment in Congress in 1794' (Washington, D.C., Lowdermilk and Company, 1905), 'The Life of John C. Calhoun' (Philadelphia, George W. Jacobs and Company, 1908), the 'History of the Seal of the United States' (1909), 'The American Passport' (1898), and 'The Department of State' (1898), besides numerous contributions to magazines on topics historical and governmental. He also edited 'Fragments of Revolutionary History' (1891), the 'Writings of James Madison,' in eight volumes (New York, G. P. Putnam's Sons, 1900-1909), and 'The First Forty Years of Washington Society' (New York, Charles Scribner's Sons, 1906). The sketch of Molly Elliot Seawell in 'The Library of Southern Literature' is also from his pen. He married, October 24, 1901, Mary Goodfellow.

HUNT, JAMES H. Writer. [Mo.]. With G. W. Westbrook he published 'The Mormon War in Missouri' (1844).

HUNT, LOUISE LIVINGSTON. [La.]. She wrote a 'Memoir of Mrs. Edward Livingston' (New York, 1886).

HUNT, RANDALL, lawyer, educator, orator, was born in South Carolina in 1807, but when a young man settled in New Orleans, La. His peculiar gifts impelled him toward the forum of eloquence. In politics he was an ardent Whig, and when the issue of secession arose he became an avowed Unionist. But he opposed the expediency rather than the right of the state to secede. In 1866 he was chosen United States Senator, but was not seated on account of the political complications of the reconstruction period. For more than forty years he was professor of constitutional law in the University of Louisiana, now Tulane University, and for seventeen years he was president of the institution. Both in vigor of intellect and in power of oratory he is said to have been the peer of Judah P. Benjamin. He died in New Orleans, La., March 22, 1892, in his eighty-fifth year. One of his speeches has been preserved in 'The Louisiana Book' (1894).

HUNT, THOMAS POAGE, clergyman, was born in Charlotte County, Va., in 1794, and died in Wyoming Valley, Pa., December 3, 1876. He was educated at Hampden-Sidney College, and, after achieving some note in the Presbyterian pulpit, he went upon the temperance platform. He published a 'History of Jesse Johnson and His Times,' 'It Will Not Injure Me,' 'Death by Measure,' 'Wedding-days of Former Times,' and 'Liquor-selling, a History of Fraud.'

HUNT, WILLIAM HENRY, jurist and diplomat, was born in South Carolina in 1824, and died in St. Petersburg, Russia, February 27, 1884. He settled in New Orleans for the practice of law, supported the cause of the Union, and became a judge of the Court of Claims, Secretary of the Navy in the Cabinet of President Hayes, and Minister to Russia under President Arthur. He published a memorial of his brother entitled 'Randall Hunt: Selected Letters and Speeches' (New Orleans, 1896).

HUNTER, ALEXANDER. Author. Major Hunter served with gallantry in the Confederate Army and published 'Johnny Reb and Billy Yank' (New York and Washington, The Neale Publishing Company, 1906), an interesting narrative written in a vein of rare good humor, and 'The Huntsman in the South' (*ibid.*, 1907).

HUNTER, JOHN DUNN, adventurer and author, published a work entitled 'Manners and Customs of Several Indian Tribes Located West of the Mississippi' (1823). The records are silent concerning when and where he was born, but he spent his youthful days among the Osage and Kansas Indians. He abandoned his forest life in 1817, made his way down the Mississippi River, and acquired the English language at schools in New Orleans. Later he traveled extensively over Europe and America, but finally settled among the Indians on the Texas frontier, where he was murdered by the red men on account of the failure of an abortive enterprise, in which they were leagued with him against Mexico. The value of his work is problematical. General Cass considered it a tissue of falsehood. But this opinion is by no means universal among the critics.

HUNTER, MARTHA T. [Va.]. The daughter of the distinguished statesman, Robert M. T. Hunter, she wrote an interesting memoir of her father, to which was added an address on his life by Colonel L. Q. Washington (New York and Washington, The Neale Publishing Company, 1907).

HUNTER, ROBERT MERCER TALIAFERRO, statesman, was born in Essex County, Va., April 21, 1809, and died in the same place, July 18, 1887. He was educated at the University of Virginia, chose the profession of law, and in 1836 was elected to Congress. Twice successively reëlected, he was made Speaker of the National House during his third term of service; but, defeated at the polls in the ensuing campaign, he was again returned in 1844, and two years later he was sent to the United States Senate, in which body he remained until 1861. He advocated secession, was a member of the Provisional Confederate Congress, served for a time in the office of Secretary of State, and was finally elected to the Confederate Senate, where he remained until the Confederacy was overthrown. He was one of the peace commissioners to confer with Mr. Lincoln at Hampton Roads. In 1874 he was an unsuccessful candidate for the United States Senate, but later was elected treasurer of the State of Virginia. He was one of the most conspicuous figures in the political arena during the turbulent ante-bellum days.

HUNTINGTON, FRANCES IRWIN, Miss. Author. [Miss.]. She wrote 'The Wife of the Sun: a Legend of Natchez,' which appeared in 1892.

HURLBUT, WILLIAM HENRY, journalist, was born in Charleston, S.C., July 3, 1827, educated at Harvard, and gave up an expected career in the ministry to enter journalism. For some time he was on the staff of the New York *Times* and afterward became identified with the New York *World*. From 1876 to 1883 he was editor-in-chief of the latter newspaper. On relinquishing active journalism he went to Europe, where he has since resided. Besides contributing to periodicals on both sides of the water, he published 'Gan-Eden' (Boston, 1854), and 'General Mc-Clellan and the Conduct of the War' (New York, 1864).

HUTCHINS, JAMES H., writer, was born in North Carolina, but afterward settled in Texas. He published a number of poems, some of which were published under the title of 'Funeral Odes.'

HUTCHINS, THOMAS. Geographer. He lived and died at the North, but much of his life was spent in the South. He fought in the Southern campaign of the Revolution under General Nathanael Greene and published among other volumes a 'Topographical Description of Virginia, Pennsylvania, Maryland, and North Carolina (London, 1778), and a 'History, Narrative, and Topographical Description of Louisiana and West Florida' (Philadelphia, 1784).

HUTCHINSON, I. R. Clergyman. He published an interesting volume entitled 'Recollections of Forty-five Years in the Presbyterian Ministry in Mississippi, Louisiana, and Texas' (1874).

HUTSON, CHARLES WOODWARD. Professor of history in the Agricultural and Mechanical College, at College Station, Texas. He was born in McPhersonville, S.C., September 23, 1840, the son of William Ferguson and Sophronia Palmer Hutson. He graduated from the University of South Carolina, and married, July 5, 1871, Miss M. J. Lockett. He was called to his present chair in 1893. His most important contributions to literature are: 'Out of a Besieged City' (New York, John B. Alden), 'The Beginnings of Civilization' (ibid.), 'The Story of Beryl' (ibid.), 'French Ltierature' (ibid.), and 'The Story of Language' (Chicago, A. C. McClurg and Company).

IBERVILLE, PIERRE LE MOYNE, SIEUR D', founder of the colony of Louisiana, was born in Montreal, Canada, July 16, 1661, and died in Havana, Cuba, July 9, 1706. At the age of fourteen he entered the French Navy and rose to high rank. He built old Fort Biloxi, the first post on the Mississippi, but afterward transferred the seat of the colony to Mobile, on account of an epidemic. His own health was undermined by malignant fever and his life prematurely shortened. 'The Narrative of a Voyage' (1698) is preserved in the French historical collection.

IMLAY, GILBERT. Kentucky's first novelist. Though born in New Jersey about the year 1755, he settled in Louisville soon after the close of the Revolution; and it was during the years that immediately followed this removal that he wrote his interesting story entitled: 'The Emigrants.' It is the tale of an English merchant, who, losing his fortune by an unexpected turn, emigrated to America with his children. It was first published in three small volumes, attractively bound in marbled calf. He was also the author of an important work entitled 'A Topographical Description of the Western Territory of North America,' consisting of a series of eleven letters written from Kentucky to a friend in England. Both works were issued from the London press. The author's sojourn in Kentucky lasted about eight years. After this time, he went to England, forming an unhappy alliance with Mary Wollstonecraft. He subsequently separated from her and she favored the suit of William Godwin, an only daughter of this marriage becoming the wife of the poet, Shelley, who in his turn played the deserter. The date of Imlay's death is unknown. It is said that in 1793 he laid before the French Directory plans for the capture of New Orleans.

INGERSOLL, HENRY HULBERT, lawyer, was born in Oberlin, Ohio, January 20, 1844, but settled in the South, and was for several years dean of the law school of the University of Tennessee. Besides editing 'Barton's Suit in Equity' (1886), he published 'Ingersoll on Corporations' (1902), and several minor works. He resides in Knoxville, Tenn.

INGLE, EDWARD, editor and author, was born in Baltimore, Md., May 17, 1861. After graduation from Johns Hopkins, he devoted himself to literary pursuits. His writings include 'The Parish Institutions of Maryland' (1883), 'Captain Richard Ingle, the Maryland Pirate and Rebel' (1884), 'Local Institutions of Virginia' (1885), 'The Negro in the District of Columbia' (1893), 'Southern Side-lights,' 'In the Maze,' and 'The Realism of Southern Dreams of Material Progress,' besides numerous contributions to magazines and reviews. He is on the staff of the *Manufacturers' Record.*

INGLEHART, FANNY C. G. Author. [Miss.]. She wrote 'Face to Face with Mexicans.'

INGRAHAM, JOSEPH HOLT. See Biographical and Critical Sketch, Vol. VI, page 2591.

INGRAHAM, PRENTISS, soldier and author, was born in Natchez, Miss., in 1843, and was the son of Joseph Holt Ingraham, the distinguished novelist. Before his education at Jefferson College was finished, the bugle-call to battle was sounded and he entered the Confederate Army, attaining the rank of captain. The result of the war disheartened him; and, being inured to the hardships of the field, he went to Mexico and enlisted under Juarez against Maximilian. But he became involved in a duel with a brother officer, was wounded, and resigned. He next went to Prussia; and, after the defeat of the Austrians at Sadowa, he joined the Cretans in the revolt against Turkey. Then began his journeyings around the globe. It was in London that his genius for authorship was quickened by the success of some satirical sketches which he sent to *Pall Mall;* and, returning home to engage in literary pursuits, he was again seized with the fighting fever by the outbreak of the Spanish-American War, and it is said that he raised the first Cuban flag which ever floated from an armed vessel at sea. But his thrilling adventures are too numerous to be cited in this connection. He wrote with marvelous rapidity, completing one of his novels in four days; and among his books are included: 'A Desert Prince,' 'Rais el Rais,' 'Zuleika: a Tale of Crete,' 'Montezuma,' 'Merle, the Mutineer,' 'The Duelist,' 'Honors Are Easy,' 'The Blue Blockader,' 'The Wandering Jew of the Sea,' 'A Cuban Coquette,' 'Led by Destiny,' 'A Prince of the Plains,' 'A Knight in Buckskin,' 'The Sergeant's Daughter,' 'Pearl of the Prairie,' and many others. Under the pressure of work, which brought him an income of $7,000 a year, his health failed, and he died in Beauvoir, Miss., in 1904.

IRBY, RICHARD. Writer. [Va.]. He wrote a 'Sketch of the Nottoway Grays' and a 'History of Randolph-Macon College' (1898).

IREDELL, JAMES, jurist, was born in Lewes, England, October 5, 1750, and died in Edenton, N.C., October 20, 1799. He was only seventeen when he came to this country; and, beginning the study of law soon after his arrival, he achieved distinction at the Bar. At the outbreak of the Revolution he not only resigned the lucrative office of collector of customs, but relinquished the prospect of inheriting a fortune from an English uncle. In 1787 he was appointed a commissioner to compile and revise the laws of the State, and the result of his labor was given the name of 'Iredell's Revisal.' Under appointment of Washington, he became associate justice of the Supreme Court in 1790. He left at his death the manuscript of a treatise on 'Pleading.' Some of his papers and speeches have been preserved in 'The Life and Correspondence of James Iredell,' edited by Griffith J. McRee.

IREDELL, JAMES, United States Senator, was born in Edenton, N.C., November 2, 1788, and died in the same place April 13, 1853. He was educated at Princeton, chose the profession of law, became Superior Court judge, governor of the State, and United States Senator. For many years he also reported the decisions of the Supreme Court of the State, his reports of law cases filling thirteen volumes and of equity cases eight volumes. Besides, he was one of the three commissioners to codify the laws of North Carolina in 1837. He published also a 'Treatise on the Law of Executors and Administrators' and a 'Digest of all the Reported Cases in North Carolina.'

IRION, ALFRED BRIGGS. [La.]. He published a work entitled 'Boaz: His Tribulations' (1874), in which he dealt with the woes of the Southern planter just after the Civil War.

IRVING, JOHN BEAUFAIN, artist, was born in Charleston, S.C., November 26, 1825, and died in New York City, April 20, 1877. As an artist he took high rank. He also published a volume of 'Essays.'

IRVING, THEODORE. Protestant Episcopal clergyman and educator. Dr. Irving was not a product of the South, but in his excellent work of two volumes entitled 'The Conquest of Florida by Hernando de Soto' (Philadelphia, 1845), he made an important contribution to the literature of the Peninsula State. He was a nephew of Washington Irving and a scholar of rare attainments.

IVORY, BERTHA MAY. Author. [Mo.]. She published a volume of verse entitled 'A Collection of Roses' and a 'Life of Archbishop Kenrick.'

IZARD, RALPH, statesman, was born in Charleston, S.C., in 1742, and died at South Bay, near Charleston, S.C., November 30, 1804. He came of the oldest colonial stock in the Palmetto State. his grandfather having been one of the founders of South Carolina. After graduation from Cambridge, England, he married Alice Delaney of New York, and resided abroad for several years. During the early part of the Revolution he quit England for France, served the patriotic cause in Europe until 1780, when he returned home to occupy a seat in the Continental Congress. He is said to have been instrumental in the appointment of General Nathanael Greene to the command of the Southern Department, and to have pledged his vast estate to secure ships of war. When the Federal Constitution was adopted in 1789, he took his seat in the United States Senate. His daughter, Anne Izard Deas, published his 'Correspondence, 1774-1784,' with a memoir of her father (1844), a work of much interest because of the period which it covers.

JACKSON, ANDREW. See Biographical and Critical Sketch, Vol. VI, page 2613.

JACKSON, HENRY ROOTES. See Biographical and Critical Sketch, Vol. VI, page 2635.

JACKSON, JAMES, jurist, was born in Jefferson County, Ga., October 18, 1819, and died in Atlanta, Ga., January 13, 1887. For several years before the war he was an occupant of the Superior Court Bench. From 1859 to 1861 he was a Member of Congress from Georgia, and in 1875 he was appointed associate-justice of the Supreme Court of Georgia, afterward becoming chief-justice. He possessed oratorical gifts of high order. His decisions are preserved in the 'Georgia Reports.' Fragments of his oratory may be found in the *Congressional Record* and in Vol. II of Knight's 'Famous Georgians.' He was a grandson of Governor James Jackson.

JACKSON, JAMES, soldier and statesman, was born in Devonshire, England, September 21, 1757, and died in Washington, D.C., March 16, 1806. Coming to this country when a lad, he settled in Savannah, Ga., became an officer of distinction in the Revolution, served the State in the chair of governor, and was twice commissioned to represent Georgia in the Senate of the United States. While serving in the Upper House of Congress, the measure known as the Yazoo Fraud Bill was enacted into law. It conveyed for a mere pittance millions of acres of wild lands belonging to the State of Georgia. Resigning his seat in the Senate, he returned home, entered the State Legislature, caused the iniquitous act to be rescinded, and, in the open square before the State House, called down fire from heaven by means of a sun-glass to consume the records of the transaction. As an outcome of this dramatic affair, he was drawn into several duels, and his death, which occurred in Washington, D.C., while he was still in office, was due indirectly to wounds received upon the field of honor. His biography was published in 1809 by T. U. P. Charlton.

JACKSON, MARY ANNA (Mrs. "Stonewall" Jackson), author, was born in Mecklenburg County, N.C., and was the daughter of the Rev Robert Hall, D.D., and Mary Graham Morrison. On completing her education, she became the second wife of Thomas Jonathan Jackson afterward the illustrious Confederate leader who was killed at Chancellorsville. The date of her marriage was July 16, 1857. Her life has been one of beautiful devotion to the memory of her noble husband and to the Lost Cause. She is the author of an exquisite work entitled 'Memoirs of Stonewall Jackson' (Louisville, The Courier-Journal Press), which gives us glimpses into the ideal home life of the Christian soldier and hero.

JACOBS, THORNWELL, clergyman and journalist, was born in Clinton, S.C., February 15, 1877, and educated at Clinton College and at Princeton. Much of his time is given to literary work. For several years he was editor of the *Taylor-Trotwood Magazine,* published at Nashville, Tenn., but is now editor of the *Presbyterian of the South,* published in Atlanta, Ga. Three delightful volumes have come from his pen, viz.: 'Sinful Sadday,' a collection of sketches, 'The Shadow of Attacoa,' and 'The Law of the White Circle.' On June 30, 1903, he married Maud K. Lesh, of Newton Centre, Mass.

JACQUES, DANIEL HARRISON, physician, was born about 1825, the place unknown, and died near Fernandina, Fla., August 28, 1877. Besides practicing his profession, he edited the *Rural Carolinian,* and published 'Hints Toward Physical Perfection; or, the Philosophy of Human Beauty' (New York, 1859), 'The Garden' (New York, 1861), and 'The Farm,' with an Essay by John J. Thomas (New York, 1866), besides numerous minor writings.

JAMES, BENJAMIN, lawyer, was born in Stafford County, Va., April 22, 1768, and died in Laurens District, S.C., November 15, 1825. He achieved some prominence at the Bar and published a 'Digest of the Statute and Common Law of Carolina' (Columbia, 1814).

JAMES, HENRY AMMON, lawyer, was born in Baltimore, Md., April 24, 1854. On completing his studies at Yale, he settled for the practice of law in the city of New York and published 'Communism in America' (New York, 1879).

JAMES, SAMUEL HUMPHREYS. Author. He was born at Cottage Oaks, La., December 12, 1857, the son of Dr. Dan James, and enjoyed the best educational advantages both at home and abroad. His literary career began when he attended the University of Virginia and was chief editor of the *University Magazine* and medalist.

He contributed numerous articles to the periodicals, one of which, a travesty on the picking of cotton, was copied on both sides of the water, causing a break in the cotton markets of Europe. Mr. Jones is said to be the owner of the largest pecan grove in the world, at Mound, La. He is the author of two interesting volumes: 'A Woman of New Orleans' and 'A Prince of Good Fellows.'

JAMISON, CECILIA VIETS. Author. She was born in Canada, in 1848, the daughter of Viets and Elizabeth Bruce Dakin, and was educated in private schools in Canada, New York, Boston, and Paris. In 1878 she married Samuel Jamison, a lawyer of New Orleans, and removed to the Crescent City. Her literary career, which brought her marked distinction, began in 1872, and her charming stories were given to the public through *Appleton's Journal, Harper's Magazine*, and *St. Nicholas*. The following are the titles of some of her books: 'Woven of Many Threads' (1872), 'A Crown from the Spear' (1874), 'Ropes of Sand' (1876), 'My Bonnie Lass' (1877), 'Story of an Enthusiast' (1888), 'Lady Jane' (New York, Charles Scribner's Sons, 1889), 'Toinette's Philip' (*ibid.*, 1894), 'Seraph' (*ibid.*, 1896), 'Thistledown' (*ibid.*, 1903), and 'The Penhallow Family' (*ibid.*, 1905). She spends the summer on the coast of Massachusetts and the winter in New Orleans.

JAMISON, DAVID F. Planter and soldier. [S.C.]. He was born in 1810 and died in 1860. He wrote 'The Life and Times of Bertrand du Guesclin: a History of the Fourteenth Century' (1864), which was published after his death.

JANNEY, SAMUEL M. See Biographical and Critical Sketch, Vol. VI, page 2655.

JANVIER, MARGARET THOMPSON. Author. Under the pen-name of "Margaret Vandegrift," she has written numerous juvenile stories and verses. She was born in Louisiana in 1844, but now resides at Morristown, N.J. Her writings, which are widely popular with young readers, include: 'Under the Dog Star' (Philadelphia, Henry T. Coates and Company), 'Clover Beach' (*ibid.*), 'Little Helpers' (*ibid.*), 'The Dead Doll, and Other Verses' (*ibid.*), 'The Queen's Body-Guard' (*ibid.*), 'Doris and Theodora' (*ibid.*), 'Rose Raymond's Wards' (*ibid.*), 'Ways and Means' (*ibid.*), 'Holidays at Home' (*ibid.*), 'The Absent-minded Fairy' (*ibid.*), and 'Little Belle, and Other Stories.'

JARRATT, DEVEREAUX. Protestant Episcopal clergyman, [Va.]. He was born in 1733 and died in 1801. In some of his doctrinal views he was inclined to be heretical. He published three volumes of 'Sermons' (1793-1794), and a series of letters entitled 'Thoughts on Some Important Subjects in Divinity (1791), which was afterward republished as an 'Autobiography' (1806).

JAY, HAMILTON. Poet. He settled in Florida during the days of reconstruction, was for some time secretary to Senator Conover, and was afterward postmaster at Live Oak, where he resided until his death. At leisure intervals he exercised his rare gifts for verse making, and produced a number of poems.

JAYNE, ANSELM HELM. Lawyer. [Miss.]. He was born in 1856. Besides minor writings, he published a 'History of Mississippi.'

JEFFERSON, THOMAS. See Biographical and Critical Sketch, Vol. VI, page 2677.

JEFFREY, ROSA VERTNER JOHNSON, author, was born in Natchez, Miss., in 1828. Her maiden name was Rosa Griffith. She began to contribute verse to the press when quite young, employing the pen-name of "Rosa"; but the merit of her work was of such high order that the guise was soon penetrated and the identity of the author discovered. She was twice married; first, to Claude M. Johnson of Louisiana, and, second, to Alexander Jeffrey of New York. She was living in the North during the Civil War and enjoyed exceptional advantages for publishing her novels, 'Woodburn' and 'Marsh.' She is said to have been the first woman whose literary work attracted wide recognition throughout the United States. Her poetic volumes are entitled: 'Poems by Rosa,' 'Darsy Dare and Baby Power,' and 'The Crimson Hand, and Other Poems.' Several dramas have also come from her pen. She was only fifteen when she wrote her well-known poem, "The Legend of the Opal."

JEFFRIES, FAYETTE. [Va.]. He wrote an interesting autobiography of invalidism entitled 'Crippled Fayette.'

JEFFRIES, MILLARD DUDLEY. Clergyman. [Va.]. He published 'Sanctification as Taught in the Scriptures.'

JEMISON, LOUISA, Mrs. ("Ellery Sinclair"). She was born in Alabama, but afterward removed to Texas. She published a story entitled: 'Christie's Choice' (1886).

JENKINS, BURRIS ATKINS. Clergyman and educator. He was born in Kansas City, Mo., October 2, 1869, the son of Andrew T. Jenkins, and was educated at Bethany College and at Harvard University. He married, May 23, 1894, Mattie Hocker. He entered the ministry of the Church of Christ, and in 1901 became president of the University of Kentucky at Lexington. He is the author of a volume entitled 'Heroes of Faith' (New York, Funk and Wagnalls).

JENNINGS, N A. [Texas]. Author of 'A Texas Ranger' (1899).

JENNINGS, JOHN JOSEPH, editor, was born in St. Louis, Mo., March 1, 1853. His father was Michael Jennings and his mother, Mary O'Meara. For several years he was dramatic editor of the St. Louis *Globe-Democrat*. At the present time he is on the staff of the New York *Evening World*. Besides exposing the fallacy of the Shakespeare-Bacon cipher of Ignatius Donnelly, he has written humorous poems and sketches, remodeled plays, and published 'Theatrical and Circus Life' (1882), and 'Widow Magoogin' (New York, G. W. Dillingham, 1900).

JERVEY, CAROLINE HOWARD GILMAN. Author. Her father was Samuel Gilman, D.D., an eminent Unitarian divine of Charleston, S.C., and her mother, Caroline Howard Gilman, the famous writer. She was born in Charleston. S.C., June 1, 1823, and died there January 29, 1877. She married, first, Nelson Glover, and afterward Lewis Jervey. Besides numerous poems and stories for the magazines, she published 'Vernon Grove' and 'Helen Courtenay's Promise,' two delightfully written volumes of fiction.

JERVEY, THEODORE DEHON. Lawyer. The subject of this sketch was born in Charleston, S.C., August 19, 1859. He has attained high rank at the South Carolina Bar. His writings include: 'The Elder Brother,' a novel which deals with reconstruction days in South Carolina (Washington, D.C., The Neale Publishing Company, 1905), and 'Robert Y. Hayne and His Times' (New York. The Macmillan Company, 1909), both of which are volumes of unusual interest.

JESSE, RICHARD HENRY, educator, was born at Epping Forest, Lancaster County, Va., March 1, 1853. His father was William T. Jesse and his mother, Mary Claybrook. After graduation from the University of Virginia, he chose the profession of teaching. From 1884 to 1891 he was professor of Latin in Tulane University, at New Orleans, after which he became president of the University of Missouri, a position which he ably filled for eighteen years. On account of impaired health, he resigned his executive duties in 1908, and retired upon a pension from the Carnegie Foundation, which he received in recognition of his eminent services to education. Besides numerous published articles and addresses, he compiled 'Missouri Literature,' in association with E. A. Allen (Columbia, Mo., E. W. Stephens, 1901). Dr. Jesse is also one of the consulting editors of 'The Library of Southern Literature.' Tulane University, the University of Wisconsin, and South Carolina College have given him the degree of LL.D.

JETER, JEREMIAH BEIL, clergyman and author, was born in Bedford County, Va., in 1802, and attained to very high eminence in the Baptist Church, preaching for a time in Richmond and afterward laboring in St. Louis. He also edited *The Religious Herald*. His works are numerous, including a 'Life of A. W. Clopton' (1837), a 'Memoir of Mrs. Henrietta Shuck,' the first American woman to become a missionary to China (1845), a 'Memoir of Andrew Broaddus' (1850), 'The Mirror,' 'Campbellism Examined' (1854), 'Campbellism Re-examined,' 'The Christian Mirror' (1858), 'The Seal of Heaven' (1871), a 'Life of Rev. Daniel De Witt' (1876), and, toward the end of his pilgrimage, 'The Recollections of a Long Life' (1878). He also assisted Dr. Richard Fuller to compile 'The Psalmist.' The 'Life of the Rev. Dr. J. B. Jeter' appeared in 1882 from the pen of the Rev. William E. Hatcher. He died in Richmond, Va., February 25, 1880.

JETT, JAMES. Writer. [Va.]. He has published 'A Virginia Tragedy,' and other stories.

JEWELL, HORACE. Methodist clergyman. [Ark.]. He wrote a 'History of Methodism in Arkansas' (1893).

JOHN, I. G. Methodist clergyman. [Texas]. He published a work on 'Methodist Missions.'

JOHNS, ANNIE. Author. [S.C.]. She wrote 'Cooleemee: a Tale of Southern Life.'

JOHNS, JOHN, Protestant Episcopal bishop, was born in New Castle, Del., July 10, 1796, and died in Fairfax County, Va., April 6, 1876. For more than thirty years he was bishop of Virginia, and from 1849 to 1854 was president of William and Mary College. He published a 'Memorial of Bishop Meade' (Baltimore, 1857). William and Mary College gave him the degree of LL.D.; Princeton, Columbia, and New York, the degree of S.T.D.

JOHNSON, ANDREW. See Biographical and Critical Sketch, Vol. VI, page 2719.

JOHNSON, BRADLEY TYLER, lawyer, soldier, author, was born in Frederick, Md., September 29, 1829. His father was Charles Worthington Johnson and his mother, Eleanor Murdock Tyler. After graduation from Princeton, he studied law at Harvard, and was duly admitted to the Bar. During the Civil War he attained the rank of brigadier-general in the Confederate Army. As a lawyer he met few equals in the courtroom. In politics a Democrat, he was in his prime a power on the hustings. Besides editing 'Chase's Decisions,' he wrote 'The Foundations of Maryland,' a 'Memoir of Joseph E. Johnston,' a "Life of Washington," in the 'Great Commanders Series' (New York, D. Appleton and Company, 1886), and the volume on Maryland in 'The Confederate Military History' (Atlanta, Ga., The Confederate Publishing Company, 1899).

JOHNSON, HERSCHEL VESPASIAN, jurist and statesman, was born in Burke County, Ga., September 18, 1812, and died in Jefferson County, Ga., August 16, 1880. He was educated at the University of Georgia, chose the profession of law, in which he attained eminence, and in 1848 succeeded Walter T. Colquitt in the United States Senate, the latter having resigned his seat. On completing his tenure of service, he became judge of the Ocmulgee circuit, and held this office until his election to the governorship. He twice filled the gubernatorial chair of Georgia, and in 1860 was an unsuccessful candidate for Vice-president of the United States on the ticket with Stephen A. Douglas. He opposed secession, but acquiesced in the majority decision, and represented Georgia with distinction in the Confederate Senate until the overthrow of the Confederate Government. In 1868 he was again elected to the United States Senate, but, under the Reconstruction Acts of Congress, was not allowed to take his seat. He afterward returned for eight years to the Superior Court Bench. As an orator, Georgia has produced few equals to Herschel V. Johnson. He was also a writer of exquisite grace and polish.

JOHNSON, JOHN. Clergyman. He was born in Charleston, S.C., December 25, 1829, the son of Dr. Joseph J. and Catharine Bonneau Johnson, and was educated at the University of Virginia. He married, in 1865, Floride Cantey, of Camden, S.C., and followed for some time the profession of civil engineering, was in charge of Fort Sumter for fifteen months, and was twice wounded during the bombardment. After the war he was ordained to the ministry of the Protestant Episcopal Church, becoming rector of St. Philip's Church, in Charleston, in 1871. His writings include: 'The Defence of Charleston Harbor, 1863-1865,' and two important contributions which appeared in the *Church Review*: "A Socialist's Plea for the Observance of Sunday" and "The Outlook of Toleration." The University of the South gave him his D.D. and Charleston College, his LL.D. He died in 1907.

JOHNSON, JOSEPH, physician, was born in Charleston, S.C., June 15, 1776, received his medical degree at the University of Pennsylvania, became an eminent practitioner of Charleston, was for several years president of the local branch of the United States Bank, and died in Charleston, October 6, 1862. He published 'Traditions and Reminiscences of the Revolution' (Charleston, 1851).

JOHNSON, LUTHER APELLES. Educator. [Miss.]. Born in 1858. He wrote 'The Foundation Principles of Literature.'

JOHNSON, REVERDY, statesman and diplomat, was born in Annapolis, Md., May 21, 1796, educated at St. John's College and achieved eminence at the Bar and in politics. Under President Taylor he became Attorney-general, and in 1845 was sent to the United States Senate as a Whig, but, refusing to be governed by party dictates, he resigned the latter office in 1846, and for twenty years continued uninterruptedly and successfully the practice of his profession. He then returned to the United States Senate, where he advocated the readmission of the seceding states without delay; and in 1868 he resigned to become United States Minister to England. He died in Annapolis, February 10, 1876. In conjunction with Thomas Harris, he reported the decisions of the Maryland Court of Appeals, in seven volumes.

JOHNSON, RICHARD MENTOR, statesman, was born in Bryant's Station, Ky., October 17, 1781, and died in Frankfort, Ky., November 19, 1850. Entering the legal profession, he achieved eminence at the Bar and for twelve years served in Congress. He organized and commanded a regiment in the War of 1812 and was desperately wounded in the battle of the Thames. Later he was chosen to fill the unexpired term of John J. Crittenden in the United States Senate, and was subsequently elected for another six years. On relinquishing his commission, he was repeatedly returned to Congress. In 1835, he was chosen Vice-president of the United States on the ticket with Martin Van Buren. His speeches, which have been preserved in the 'Debates of Congress' are characterized by vigorous treatment and, by wide information.

JOHNSON, RICHARD W., soldier, was born near Smithland, Ky., February 7, 1827, educated at West Point, achieved distinction in the Union Army during the Civil War, retired from the military service of the Government with the rank of brigadier-general in 1867, and published 'The Life of General George H. Thomas' (Philadelphia, 1881), and 'A Soldier's Reminiscences of Peace and War' (1886).

JOHNSON, THOMAS, statesman, was born at St. Leonard's, Md., November 4, 1732, and died at Rose Hill, Md., October 25, 1819. As deputy from Maryland in the Continental Congress at Philadelphia, he nominated Washington for the post of commander-in-chief. He was the first governor of Maryland under the rule of the commonwealth, and was twice reëlected. For many years he adorned the Supreme Bench of the State, and, on the resignation of John Rutledge, declined the office of Chief Justice of the Supreme Court of the United States. He was a man of wide influence, an effective speaker, and a writer of rare gifts.

JOHNSON, THOMAS. Poet. He was the earliest minstrel whose notes were heard in the land of the Blue Grass. The exact date of his birth is unknown, but he first saw the light in Virginia about the year 1760. At an early period he settled in Danville, Ky., and some time later he published a small duodecimo volume of poems entitled 'The Kentucky Miscellany' (Lexington, Ky., 1796). It passed into four editions; but the only extant copy of this primitive work is in the library of Colonel Reuben T. Durrett of Louisville. The poet was unfortunately a man of erratic genius and dissolute habits. He disappeared from Danville about the year 1825, and all efforts to trace him were unsuccessful.

JOHNSON, THOMAS CARY, clergyman, author, educator, was born at Fishbok Hill, W.Va., July 19, 1859. After graduating from Hampden-Sidney College, he took post-graduate work at the University of Virginia and also at Yale, and prosecuted his theological studies at Union, in Virginia. For several years he engaged in active pastoral work, but in 1892 became professor of ecclesiastical history at Union, a chair which he still retains. Several volumes of standard merit have come from his pen, including a 'History of the Southern Presbyterian Church' (New York, Charles Scribner's Sons, 1894), 'John Calvin and the Genevan Reformation,' a sketch (Richmond, Presbyterian Committee of Publication, 1900), 'Life and Letters of Robert Lewis Dabney' (*ibid.*, 1903), 'Life and Letters of Benjamin M. Palmer' (*ibid.*, 1906), 'Virginia Presbyterianism and Religious Liberty' (1907), and 'Introduction to Christian Missions' (1909). For 'The Library of Southern Literature' he wrote the sketch of Benjamin M. Palmer. He married, December 26, 1894, Ella F. Bocock. Hampden-Sidney gave him the D.D. and the LL.D. degrees.

JOHNSON, WILLIAM, jurist, was born in Charleston, S.C., December 27, 1771, and received his education at Princeton. Achieving eminence at the Bar, he was first appointed judge of the Court of Common Pleas and afterward elevated to the Supreme Court of the United States. On the latter Bench he maintained an independent course. He quarreled with Jefferson over the Embargo Act, and took so emphatic a stand against nullification, which was the popular doctrine in South Carolina, that he found it necessary to leave his home State; and he settled in the North. But he survived this change of residence for only a brief time, dying in Brooklyn, N.Y., August 11, 1834. He was the author of a work which contains some very pronounced views on 'The Life and Correspondence of Major-general Nathanael Greene,' which was published in 1822. Princeton gave him the degree of LL.D.

JOHNSON, WILLIAM BULLIEN. Clergyman. He was born on St. John's Island, S.C., June 13, 1782, and died in Greenville, S.C., January 10, 1862. He was a Baptist, served churches in Columbia, S.C., and Savannah, Ga., became principal of a seminary in Greenville, and published 'Infant Baptism Argued from Analogy,' 'Memoir of Nathan P. Knapp' and other works, besides editing 'Knapp's Select Sermons.' Brown University gave him the degree of D.D.

JOHNSON, WILLIAM HENRY. Author. [S.C.]. Born in 1845. He wrote 'The King's Henchman.'

JOHNSTON, ANNIE FELLOWS. Author. She was born in Evansville, Ind., in 1863, the daughter of the Rev. Albion and Mary Erskine Fellows. She was educated in the public schools of Indiana and at the State University of Iowa. She married, in 1888, William L. Johnston (deceased). She has been one of the most frequent and popular contributors to the periodicals of the day, and her stories are well represented in the following list: 'Big Brother,' 'The Little Colonel,' 'Joel, a Boy of Galilee,' 'In League With Israel,' 'Ole Mammy's Torment,' 'The Gate of the Giant Scissors,' 'Two Little Knights of Kentucky,' 'The Little Colonel's House Party,' 'The Little Colonel's Holidays,' 'The Little Colonel's Hero,' 'Cicely,' 'Asa Holmes; or, At the Cross Roads,' 'Flip's Islands of Providence,' 'The Little Colonel at Boarding School,' 'The Little Colonel in Arizona,' 'The Quilt that Jack Built,' 'The Little Colonel's Christmas Vacation,' 'In the Desert of Waiting,' and 'Three Weavers.' Most of Mrs. Johnston's writings have been for young readers. She is a Southerner by adoption only, but she has caught into her books the atmosphere of her Kentucky surroundings, and in her portraitures of child-life has emphasized the Southern characteristics. With her sister, Mrs. Albion Fellows Bacon, she is also the joint author of a volume of poems. Her home is at Pewee Valley, Ky. L. C. Page and Company, Boston, have published most of her books.

JOHNSTON, EDWARD WILLIAM. Author. [S.C.]. He published a 'Life of Hugh Swinton Legaré,' an interesting biographical work.

JOHNSTON, ELIZABETH BRYANT. Author. [Ky.]. She wrote 'The Days that Are No More.'

JOHNSTON, FREDERICK. [Va.]. He was born in 1811 and died in 1894. He published 'Old Virginia Clerks' (1888).

JOHNSTON, GEORGE. Writer. [Md.]. He published 'Wild Southern Scenes' (1859) and a 'History of Cecil County, Md.' (1881).

JOHNSTON, GEORGE DOHERTY. Lawyer. soldier, educator. lecturer. He was born in Hillsboro, N.C., May 30, 1832, the son of George M. and Mary Johnston. He entered the Confederate Army as second-lieutenant of the Fourth Alabama Regiment and became brigadier-general. He was wounded at Murfreesboro and Atlanta. After the war he divided his time between educational work and the practice of law and was State Senator and United States Civil Service Commissioner. He was three times married. His literary production embraces three lectures which were widely delivered with effective results: "Memories of the Old South," "The Confederate War," and "Jefferson Davis." He resides in Tuscaloosa, Ala.

JOHNSTON, JOSEPH EGGLESTON, an eminent Confederate officer, was born near Farmville, Va., February 7, 1807, educated at West Point in the class with Robert E. Lee, served in the Seminole and Mexican Wars, resigned his commission as quartermaster-general in the United States Army and offered his services to the Confederate Government, rising by virtue of his proven soldiership to the full rank of general. On the eve of the battle of Atlanta, he was superseded by General Hood, but it proved to be a tactical mistake, and he was restored to command. He died in Washington, D.C., March 21, 1891. In the opinion of many critics, he possessed no superior in the art of military maneuverings. During his career he was wounded ten times. One of the best works bearing upon the bloody grapple of the 'sixties has come from the pen of this gallant fighter, entitled 'A Narrative of Military Operations Directed During the Late War between the States' (New York, D. Appleton and Company, 1874).

JOHNSTON, JOSIAH STODDARD. See Biographical and Critical Sketch, Vol. VI, page 2741.

JOHNSTON, MARGARET A. Author. [La.]. She published a story entitled 'In Arcadia' (New Orleans, 1893).

JOHNSTON, MARY. See Biographical and Critical Sketch, Vol. VI, page 2757.

JOHNSTON, RICHARD MALCOLM. See Biographical and Critical Sketch, Vol. VI, page 2781.

JOHNSTON, WILLIAM PRESTON. See Biographical and Critical Sketch, Vol. VII, page 2813.

JOHNSTONE, JOB, jurist, was born in Fairfield County, S.C., June 7, 1793, and died in Newberry, S.C., April 15, 1862. He abandoned medicine for law and became an eminent jurist, filling the office of chancellor of the State for twenty-one years. His decisions are preserved in Hill's 'Chancery Reports,' Strobhart's 'Equity,' Cheeve's 'Equity,' and McCord's 'Chancery Reports.'

JONAS, S. A., editor and poet, was an officer in the Confederate Army and a member of the first Constitutional Convention which was held in Mississippi after the Civil War. Major Jonas is the recognized author of the famous poem entitled "Lines on the Back of a Confederate Note," a gem which has often been reproduced without due credit. He resides in Aberdeen, Miss., where he edits *The Examiner,* a newspaper which has been a power in Mississippi journalism since reconstruction.

JONES, ALEXANDER, physician and author, was born in North Carolina about 1802 and died in the city of New York August 20, 1853. Settling in Mississippi for the practice of medicine, he became interested in the culture of cotton and made several improvements in the cotton-gin. He afterward became a resident of New York. His published works include: 'Cuba in 1851,' an 'Historical Sketch of the Electric Telegraph,' and 'The Cymri of Seventy-six; or, the Welshmen of the Revolution.'

JONES, ALICE ILGENFRITZ. Author. [La.]. She wrote an interesting work of fiction entitled 'The Chevalier de St. Denis' (Chicago, 1900).

JONES, ANSON, president of the republic of Texas, was born in Great Barrington, Mass., January 20, 1798, and died in Houston, Texas, January 8, 1858. On the eve of the war for Texan independence, he located on the Texan frontier, took an active part in the struggle, held commissions in military and civil affairs, was Minister from Texas to the United States Government, Vice-president and afterward President of the republic. He opposed annexation, lost his popularity, became unbalanced in mind, and finally died by his own hand. His 'Journal' was published privately in 1859.

JONES, BUEHRING H. Writer. [W.Va.]. He was born in 1823, and published 'The Sunny Land; or, Prison Prose and Poetry.'

JONES, CADWALLADER. [S.C.]. He published a 'Genealogical History of the Iones Family' (1900).

JONES, CHARLES COLCOCK, Jr. See Biographical and Critical Sketch, Vol. VII, page 2835.

JONES, CHARLES COLCOCK, Sr., clergyman, was born in Liberty County, Ga., December 20, 1804, and was for many years pastor of the First Presbyterian Church, of Savannah, but returned to the old homestead in 1832 to labor among the slaves. In later life he alternated between missionary work on the plantations and educational work in the theological seminary at Columbia, S.C. He published 'Religious Instruction for Negroes in the Southern States,' 'Suggestions on the Instruction of Negroes in the South,' and a 'History of the Church of God,' edited by his son, Charles C. Jones, Jr.

JONES, CHARLES EDGEWORTH, lawyer and author, was born in New York City, July 27, 1867, of Southern parentage, the son of Colonel Charles C. Jones, Jr., the distinguished Georgia historian. His education was received at the University of Georgia; and, on completing his studies, he began the practice of law in Augusta. His writings include: 'Colonel Charles C. Jones, Jr., LL.D., Sketch' (1889), 'Education in Georgia' (1889), 'Political and Judicial Divisions of the Commonwealth of Georgia' (1892), 'In Memoriam, Charles C. Jones, Jr.' (1893), 'History of Georgia,' which appeared serially in the Atlanta *Constitution* (1899), and 'Georgia in the Civil War' (1909).

JONES, HUGH, clergyman, was born in England, in 1669, and died in Cecil County, Md., September 8, 1760. For sixty years he was an ordained minister of the Church of England, serving parishes in Maryland and in Virginia, and was also at one time professor of mathematics in William and Mary College. He published 'The Present State of Virginia' (London, 1724), a volume of rare and curious interest.

JONES, IREDELL. He published 'The South Carolina College Cadets.'

JONES, JOHN BEAUCHAMP, author, was born in Baltimore, Md., in 1810. For many years he was engaged in journalism, and in 1857 established in Philadelphia *The Southern Monitor,* devoted to the interests of the South. His writings are full of life and color and cover a wide range of subjects. They include 'Books of Visions' (1847), "Rural Sports," a poem (1848), 'The Western Merchant' (1848), 'Wild Western Scenes' (1849), 'The Rival Belles' (1852), 'Adventures of Colonel Vandercomb' (1852), 'The Monarchist' (1853), 'Life and Adventures of a Country Merchant' (1854), 'Freaks of Fortune' (1854), and a 'Rebel Clerk's War Diary of the Confederate States Capitol' (1866). He died in 1866.

JONES, JOHN G., Methodist Episcopal clergyman, wrote a work entitled 'The History of Methodism in Mississippi.' He planned to write two volumes but finished only one, covering the period from 1799 to 1817. It is an important contribution not only to religious history but also to the history of pioneer life in Mississippi. Another product of his pen is 'The Bishop's Council.'

JONES, JOHN P. Author. [Mo.]. He published a number of historical accounts, including 'The Spanish Expedition to Missouri in 1799,' 'Early Travel in Missouri,' and 'The Missouri River and the Indians.'

JONES, JOHN WILLIAM. Clergyman and author. For many years chaplain-general of the United Confederate Veterans. He was born at Louisa Court House, Va., September 25, 1836, the son of Francis William and Ann Pendleton Jones, and was educated at the University of Virginia and at the Southern Baptist Theological Seminary. He married, December 20, 1860, Judith Page Helm. He was under appointment as missionary to China when the war opened, but enlisted for the struggle and became, first, private, and afterward chaplain. He assisted in conducting revivals, in which more than fifteen thousand of Lee's soldiers professed conversion; and of this number he personally baptized four hundred and sixteen converts. He was also chaplain of Washington College during the incumbency of General Lee as president. Besides serving the Southern Baptist Church in field work, he often lectured on Lee and Jackson, and seldom failed to mingle with his war comrades in annual reunions. His works, which deal with the war period, include 'Personal Reminiscences, Anecdotes and Letters of Robert E. Lee' (Washington, D.C., The Neale Publishing Company), in the preparation of which he was given access to all the personal manuscripts and documents in the possession of the family; 'The Army of Northern Virginia Memorial Volume,' 'Christ in the Camp,' and 'School History of the United States.' He also edited fourteen volumes of Southern historical papers. The sketch of Jefferson Davis in 'The Library of Southern Literature' is from his pen. Dr. Jones died at the home of his son, the Rev. Carter Helm Jones, in Columbus, Ga., in 1909; but his remains were taken to Virginia for burial.

JONES, JOSEPH, physician and educator, was born in Liberty County, Ga., September 6, 1833, and was the son of the Rev. Charles C. Jones, D.D. He became an eminent practitioner of medicine and also held chairs at different times in various institutions, including the University of Georgia, the Medical College of Nashville, and Tulane University. Besides many important contributions to the scientific and educational journals, he wrote 'Explorations of the Aboriginal Remains of Tennessee,' 'Medical and Surgical Memoirs,' 'Investigations, Chemical and Physiological, Relative to Certain American Vertebrata,' and other works. He died in New Orleans, February 17, 1896.

JONES, JOSEPH SEAWELL, author, was born about 1811, probably in North Carolina. He graduated from the Harvard Law School, practiced his profession with success, and published a 'Defence of North Carolina in the Revolution' (1834), and 'Memorials of North Carolina' (1838).

JONES, MARY. Writer. [Ky.]. She wrote an interesting 'History of Campbell County, Ky.' (1876).

JONES, PLUMMER F., Presbyterian clergyman, was born in New Store, Buckingham County, Va., August 29, 1875. Besides numerous contributions to high-class periodicals he has published an entertaining volume entitled 'Shamrock Land' (New York, Moffat, Yard and Company, 1908), and is at present engaged upon other manuscripts. He resides at Arvonia, Va.

JONES, RICHARD. Educator. He was born in Berlin, Wis., July 18, 1855, the son of John A. and Ann Davies Jones. He studied at Oxford, Munich, and Heidelberg, and married, December 28, 1881, Carrie Holmes Grinnell, daughter of Congressman J. B. Grinnell. He became professor of literature in Vanderbilt University in 1899. His works evince ripe scholarship and laborious research. They include: 'The Growth of the Idylls of the King' (Philadelphia, J. B. Lippincott Company), 'The Arthurian Legends' (in the Warner Library), and 'College Entrance English.' Also, he has edited 'The Tragedy of Macbeth' (New York, D. Appleton and Company), 'The Merchant of Venice' (*ibid.*), and 'The History of English Literature' (*ibid.*), besides contributing to American and European magazines. Dr. Jones received his Ph.D. degree from Heidelberg. He resides in Nashville, Tenn.

JONES, RICHARD WATSON, educator, was born in Virginia in 1837 and was educated at Randolph-Macon. For five years he was president of Martha Washington College, and for two years president of Emory and Henry College. Afterward he became professor of chemistry in the University of Mississippi. He has edited various publications and written numerous monographs. Mississippi College gave him the degree of LL.D.

JONES, SAMUEL PORTER, evangelist and lecturer, was born in Oak Bowery, Ala., October 16, 1847, and died while en route from Oklahoma City, Okla., to his home in Cartersville, Ga., October 15, 1906. He practiced law for two years with indifferent success due to intemperate habits; but after the death of his father he experienced conversion and became the greatest revivalist of his day and generation on either side of the water. In the quality of humor he was perhaps never excelled, and for years he was one of the prime favorites of the lecture lyceum. He published 'Sermons and Sayings of Sam Jones' (1885), 'Quit Your Meanness' (1886), 'Sam Jones's Own Book' (1886), and 'Thunderbolts' (1896). Since his death have appeared: 'The Life and Sayings of Sam P. Jones' edited by his wife (Atlanta, Ga., The Franklin-Turner Company, 1907), 'Famous Stories of Sam P. Jones,' by the Rev. George R. Stuart (New York and Chicago, Fleming H. Revell and Company, 1908), and 'Popular Lectures of Sam P. Jones,' edited by his wife (*ibid.*, 1909).

JONES, THOMAS GOODE. Lawyer and jurist. He was born in Macon, Ga., November 26, 1844. In the Civil War he was an officer on the staff of General John B. Gordon, attaining the rank of major; and to him was assigned the duty of carrying a flag of truce to General Sheridan at Appomattox. On December 20, 1866, he was united in marriage to Gena C. Bird. He began the practice of law in Montgomery, Ala., and rose rapidly to the front. He commanded the Second Regiment of Alabama State troops for ten years and took an active part in suppressing the famous riots in Birmingham in 1883 and 1888. From 1890 to 1894 he was governor of Alabama and assumed personal command of the troops during the great strike of 1894. For nearly eight years he has been United States District Judge for the Middle and Northern Districts of Alabama. He framed the laws regulating the employment of military force in the suppression of riots and for other purposes; compiled eighteen volumes of 'Alabama Supreme Court Reports'; and prepared the 'Code of Ethics of the Alabama State Bar Association.' His address on "The Last Days of the Army of Northern Virginia," delivered for his war comrades in Richmond, is an interesting contribution to the literature of the great conflict. On the field of battle he was several times wounded.

JONES, WILEY. Clergyman. [Va.]. He published 'The Gospel of the Kingdom.'

JONES, WILLIAM HITE. [Va.]. He published a work on economics entitled 'Federal Taxes and State Expenses.'

JONES, WILLIAM LOUIS, educator, physician, editor, was born in Liberty County, Ga., in 1827, of the same noted stock which has produced the Le Contes. After graduating from the University of Georgia, he studied at Harvard under Agassiz, his companion at Cambridge being his cousin, Joseph Le Conte; and he also accompanied his distinguished preceptor on a tour of investigation to the Florida reefs. For a time he practiced medicine; but, at later periods, he filled chairs in science at the University of Georgia, first in one branch and then in another; and he also edited *The Southern Cultivator*. Both to the scientific journals and to the secular newspapers he has been a contributor of thoughtful articles for more than fifty years.

JORDAN, CORNELIA JANE MATTHEWS, Mrs., poet, was born in Lynchburg, Va., January 11, 1830. She possessed unusual gifts and among the plaintive war minstrels of Virginia she is entitled to high rank. Two rich volumes have come from the pen of this author: 'Flowers of Hope and Memory' (Richmond, 1861), and 'Echoes from the Cannon' (Buffalo, N.Y., 1899). Her poem on "Corinth" appeared in 1865. On account of the sentiment which it breathed, the entire edition was seized by General Terry, who was provost-marshal at the time, condemned and burned. But the song survived the flames. Her poem on "Richmond" is perhaps the finest tribute in verse ever paid to the capital of the Confederacy; and her poems, "The Battle of Manassas" and "The Death of Jackson," are also widely admired.

JORDAN, FRANK MARION. Baptist clergyman. [N.C.]. He published 'The Life and Labors of Elder F. M. Jordan' (1899).

JORDAN, RICHARD, Quaker preacher, was born in Norfolk County, Va., December 19, 1756, and died in Newton, N.J., October 14, 1826. For nearly fifty years he was a minister of the Society of Friends, traversing the whole eastern part of the United States and visiting Europe. He wrote an autobiographic account of his labors, entitled 'The Journal of Richard Jordan,' which was published many years after his death (Philadelphia, 1870).

JORDAN, THOMAS, soldier, was born in Luray, Va., September 30, 1819. He was educated at West Point, served in the Indian and Mexican campaigns, resigned his captain's commission to enter the Confederate ranks and became a brigadier-general. After the war he went to Cuba, where he succeeded to the chief command of the Revolutionists, but he afterward returned home and edited for some time the Memphis *Appeal*. Besides contributing to periodicals, he published, in association with J. B. Pryor, 'The Campaigns of Lieutenant-general Forrest' (New York, 1868).

JOSCELYN, JEP., Major. The author, who is supposed to have served under General Sherman, wrote 'Tar-Heel Rhymes in Vernacular Verse' (1866).

JOSSELYN, ROBERT, poet, was born in Massachusetts, in 1810, but was admitted to the Bar in Virginia and afterward settled in Mississippi. He served under Jefferson Davis in the Mexican War. Later he removed to Texas. He published three volumes of verse. One of his best known poems is entitled "The Last Tear I Shed," a satire on the times. He died in 1884.

JOUVENAT, M. M., Mrs. Poet. [Texas]. One of her fragments, "The Message of the Flowers," is preserved in 'Songs of the South.' She lived in Sherman, Texas.

JOYCE, W. H. H. Cergyman. [Va.]. He published a work in three volumes entitled 'Things and Thoughts' (Winchester, Va., 1903).

JOYNER, JAMES YADKIN, educator, was born in Davidson County, N.C., August 7, 1862. His father was John Joyner and his mother, Sallie A. Wooten. For several years he was professor of English in the State Normal and Industrial College of North Carolina. At present he is superintendent of public instruction. Besides official reports, from 1902 to 1909, he is the author of numerous pamphlets and monographs on educational subjects. The sketch of Calvin H. Wiley in 'The Library of Southern Literature' is also from his pen.

JOYNES, EDWARD SOUTHEY. See Biographical and Critical Sketch, Vol. VII, page 2859.

JULAP, GILES. Poet. He lived at Chotank, Va., and wrote a poem in two books, published in 1802, entitled "The Glosser." It is not a composition of the first rank; and, in the postscript to his preface, the author adds for the information of posterity: "The tax on whiskey is put down. Huzza for the Ancient Dominion! Vive old liberty pole!"

JULIAN, ISAAC HOOVER. Journalist. He was born rear Centreville, Ind., June 19, 1823, the son of Isaac and Rebecca Hoover Julian. He was self-educated, twice married, and lived for some time in Indiana. He was admitted to the Bar; but, becoming interested in the anti-slavery and temperance reforms, he took up the editorial pen. In 1873 he moved to San Marcos, Texas, editing *The Free Press* for seventeen years, and *The People's Era* for ten years. Besides contributions in both prose and verse to the periodicals, he has published: 'Sketches of the Early History of the White-water Valley' (1857), 'Late Gathered Leaves in Verse and Prose,' and 'Outline History of the Julian and Hoover Families.'

KARNS, THOMAS C. Educator. [Tenn.]. He published 'The Government of the People of Tennessee' (1896).

KAVANAUGH, BENJAMIN TAYLOR, clergyman and physician, was born in Jefferson County, Ky., April 28, 1805, and died in Boonesborough, Ky., July 3, 1898. He was both a physician and a minister. During the Civil War he was a surgeon in the Confederate Army; and after the close of hostilities he became a professor in Soule University in the department of mental and moral science. He published 'Electricity the Motor Power of the Solar System' (New York, 1886), 'The Great Central Valley of North America,' and 'Notes of a Western Rambler.' Bishop H. H. Kavanaugh was his brother.

KEARNEY, BELLE. Author, and lecturer for the Women's Christian Temperance Union. She was born on a plantation near Vernon, Miss., enjoyed excellent educational advantages, and spent several years in teaching. She is an ardent advocate of temperance reform, and has traveled over Europe and America on extended lecture tours, making eloquent pleas for temperance before great assemblies. She has also pleaded her cause in the periodicals. She is the author of an interesting volume entitled 'The Slaveholder's Daughter.' She resides at Flora, Miss.

KEENER, JOHN CHRISTIAN. Bishop of the Methodist Episcopal Church, South, for more than thirty years. He was born in Baltimore, Md., February 7, 1819, engaged in business for several years in Baltimore, and then entered the itinerant ranks of Southern Methodism. He preached first in Alabama, and afterward became pastor in New Orleans, resigning his charge to become presiding elder. During the war, he was superintendent of all the chaplains west of the Mississippi. From 1865 to 1870 he edited the New Orleans *Christian Advocate*, and was then elevated to the Episcopal Bench. Besides numerous articles for the secular and religious press, he wrote: 'The Post Oak Circuit, or Studies in Bible Truths,' and 'The Garden of Eden and the Flood.' He died in New Orleans in 1906. Bishop Keener received both the D.D. and the LL.D. degrees.

KEIFFER, ALDINE S., poet, was born in Missouri but the greater part of his life was spent in the Old Dominion, and he became one of the favorite songsters of the Valley. Before he was eighteen he edited *The Musical Advocate*. At the beginning of the war he enlisted in the Army of Northern Virginia and was at the first battle of Manassas. Many of his stirring stanzas are echoes of his life in the bivouac and on the field. He published a volume entitled: 'Hours of Fancy; or, Vision and Vigil' (Dayton, Va., 1881). Some of his minor lyrics have been set to music.

KEILEY, ANTHONY M. Author. [Va.]. He wrote 'In Vinculis; or, the Prisoner of War' (1866).

KEITH, ISAAC STOCKTON, clergyman, was born in Newton, Pa., January 20, 1755, and died in Charleston, S.C., December 13, 1813. On completing his studies at Princeton he entered the Presbyterian ministry and was for more than twenty-five years pastor of the First Presbyterian Church of Charleston, S.C. The Rev. Andrew Flinn edited a volume of his 'Sermons and Addresses' (Charleston, 1810).

KELL, JOHN McINTOSH. Under Captain Semmes, he was first lieutenant of the famous Confederate warship, the *Alabama*, which was sunk in the English Channel, after one of the most brilliant careers in the annals of the sea. He was born in McIntosh County, Ga., in 1828. For many years after the war he was adjutant-general of the State of Georgia; and except for his extreme modesty he might have claimed any office in the gift of his fellow citizens. It was not without much persuasion that he was induced to commit his reminiscences to the pen. But he finally wrote for the *Century Magazine* an article entitled "Battles and Leaders of the Civil War," and this was followed by his 'Recollections of a Naval Life' (Washington, The Neale Publishing Company). He died at "Sunny Side," near Griffin, in 1900.

KELLER, HELEN ADAMS. See Biographical and Critical Sketch, Vol. VII, page 2875.

KELLEY, DAVID CAMPBELL. Clergyman. He was born in Leesville, Tenn., December 25, 1833, a son of John and Margaret Kelley. He was twice married. Besides holding numerous important pastorates, he was an unsuccessful candidate for Governor of Tennessee on the Prohibition ticket in 1890, and was the projector of the scheme from which Vanderbilt University and the Nashville College for Young Ladies were evolved. Among his works are:

'Short Method with Modern Doubt' (Nashville, Southern Methodist Publishing House), 'Bishop or Conference' (*ibid.*), and 'Life of Mrs. M. L. Kelley' (*ibid.*). He died in 1909.

KELLOGG, SANFORD C. Author. [Va.]. Colonel Kellogg was an aide on the staff of General George H. Thomas of the United States Army during the Civil War. He wrote an interesting work entitled 'The Shenandoah Valley and Virginia, 1861-1865' (New York and Washington, The Neale Publishing Company, 1908), in which he treats of the Virginia campaigns from the Federal point of view.

KELLY, JAMES MADISON, lawyer, was born in Washington County, Ga., in 1795, and died in Perry, Ga., January 17, 1849. He chose the legal profession, was several times elected to the Legislature, and, on the organization of the Supreme Court of the State, became the first reporter and published five volumes of 'Georgia Reports' (1846-1848).

KEMBLE, FRANCES ANNE, an English actress of note, who became the wife of Pierce Butler, a Georgia planter, who divorced her in 1849. Besides numerous other volumes she published 'The Journal of a Residence on a Georgia Plantation' in 1838-1839 (New York, Harper and Brothers, 1857), in which she harshly criticised the institution of slavery, but her feelings were doubtless embittered and her views somewhat distorted by her domestic relations. She died in London in 1893, at the advanced age of eighty-four.

KEMPER, CHARLES PENDLETON, educator and lecturer, was born in Louisa County, Va. His father was Charles S. Kemper and his mother, Mary Pendleton. For several years he was engaged in educational work. But of late years has been in business in Vicksburg, Miss. and has also appeared at frequent intervals on the lecture platform, much to the delight of his many admirers. He is the author of a number of dialect poems, including "Dem Back Times," "A New Year Idyl," "In Sassafras Diggin' Root Time," and others of like charm and power, recalling the old days of the South. He has also written numerous prose articles. The sketch of Harris Dickson in 'The Library of Southern Literature' is from his pen.

KEMPER, JAMES LAWSON, soldier and governor, was born in Madison County, Va., June 11, 1823, graduated from Washington College, became a captain in the Mexican War, and a brigadier-general in the Civil War. At Gettysburg he was wounded and taken prisoner. In 1874 he was elected governor of Virginia, and retiring from office engaged in planting. He published a volume of 'Messages to the Legislature' (Richmond, 1876).

KENDALL, AMOS, editor and Cabinet officer, was born in Dunstable, Mass., August 16, 1789, and died in Washington, D.C., November 11, 1869. For several years he edited Democratic newspapers in Kentucky, wielded great power for Andrew Jackson, and became Postmaster-general in the latter's Cabinet. Harriet Martineau considered him the genius of the administration. He purchased an interest in the telegraph patents of Samuel F. B. Morse, and eventually acquired immense wealth. He published 'The Life of Andrew Jackson, Private, Military, and Civil' (New York, 1843), a series of articles in the Washington *Star*, opposing secession, and a number of pamphlets. After his death his 'Autobiography' was edited by William Stickney (Boston, 1872).

KENDALL, GEORGE WILKINS, journalist, was born in Amherst, N.H., August 22, 1809, and died near Bowie, Texas, October 22, 1867. After learning the printers' trade, he came South, settled in New

Orleans, and established *The Picayune* in association with F. A. Lumsden In 1841 he joined the Santa Fé Expedition, only to fall into the hands of the Mexicans, but was afterward released, and when formal hostilities began he rendered important service to General Taylor and furnished his paper war news by means of pony expresses. Later he settled in Texas and acquired a fortune. He wrote a 'Narrative of the Santa Fé Expedition,' in two volumes (New York, 1844; London, 1845), and 'The War between the United States and Mexico,' with twelve colored plates by Carl Nebel (New York, 1851).

KENDALL, ISOLINE RODD, writer, was born in New Orleans, La., October 11, 1873. Her maiden name was Isoline Rodd. She married, July 1, 1903, John Smith Kendall. Some excellent newspaper and magazine articles have come from her pen. The sketch of George W. Cable in 'The Library of Southern Literature' was written by Mrs. Kendall.

KENDALL, JOHN SMITH, journalist, was born in Ocean Springs, Miss., April 9, 1874, a son of John I. and Mary E. Smith Kendall. For some time he has been literary editor of the New Orleans *Picayune,* for which paper he was also war correspondent during the Spanish-American hostilities. Besides numerous articles on foreign travel which have appeared in his paper, Mr. Kendall has published 'The Picayune Guide to New Orleans' (1900, revised, 1909). 'The Picayune Frog Circus' (New Orleans, F. F. Hansell and Brother, 1903), 'A Midsummer Trip to Nicaragua' (New Orleans, The Picayune, 1905), 'Seven Mexican Cities' (*ibid.*, 1906), and the article on "New Orleans" in 'Appleton's Encyclopædia.' He is also a contributor to magazines. The sketch of Eliza J. Nicholson in 'The Library of Southern Literature' is from Mr. Kendall's pen. He married, July 1, 1903, Isoline Rodd.

KENLY, JOHN REESE, lawyer and soldier, was born in Baltimore, Md., in 1822, served in both Mexican and Civil Wars under the United States flag, achieved distinction at the Bar, and published 'Memoirs of a Maryland Volunteer in the Mexican War' (1873).

KENNEDY, JOHN PENDLETON. See Biographical and Critical Sketch, Vol. VII, page 2897.

KENNEDY, SARA BEAUMONT. Author. She was born in Somerville, Tenn., the daughter of Dr. Robert H. and Nora Devereux Cannon. She graduated from St. Mary's Protestant Episcopal School, Raleigh, N.C., and married, January 10, 1888, Walker Kennedy. Besides journalistic work on the Memphis papers, she has contributed stories to some of the leading magazines. She has also written some excellent verse, her war poems of the Revolution being specially admired. 'Jocelyn Cheshire' (New York, Doubleday, Page and Company) and 'The Wooing of Judith (*ibid.*) are two of Mrs. Kennedy's best stories. They are breezily written and entertaining, and evince an observant eye for modern types and conditions.

KENNEDY, WALKER, journalist, was born in Louisville, Ky., June 8, 1857, the son of James and Kate E. Kennedy. He was educated in the public schools of his home town, and married, January 10, 1888, Sara Beaumont Cannon. At various times he was connected in an editorial capacity with some of the leading Southern newspapers, including the Louisville *Courier-Journal,* the Memphis *Appeal,* and the Nashville *American,* and in 1896 he became editor of the Memphis *Commercial Appeal,* on which he labored for thirteen years. He was a contributor of racy sketches and stories to such periodicals as *Life, Puck,* the *Saturday Evening Post,* the *Century Magazine,* and the *North American Review.* His books include: 'In the Dwellings of Science' (New York, Dodd, Mead and Company), 'Javanben Seir' (New York, Frederick A. Stokes), and 'The Secret of the Wet Woods.' He died in Memphis, Tenn., November 12, 1909.

KENNEDY, WILLIAM, author, was born near Paisley, Scotland, December 26, 1799, and died near London, England, in 1849. For many years he was the British Consul at Galveston, Texas, and he published two works of very great interest entitled 'The Rise, Progress, and Prospects of the Republic of Texas,' in two volumes (London, 1841), and 'Texas, its Geography, Natural History, and Topography' (New York, 1844). He also published several volumes of verse, including 'Fitful Fancies' (1827).

KENNEY, M. M., antiquarian and author. Contributed to 'Wooten's Comprehensive History of Texas' (Dallas, Wm. G. Scarff, 1898) an important chapter on "The Indian Tribes of Texas," which contains some very rare ethnological data, besides narrating in a manner both graphic and simple, many thrilling episodes of pioneer days along the frontier.

KENRICK, FRANCIS PATRICK, Roman Catholic archbishop, was born in Dublin, Ireland, December 3, 1797, and died in Baltimore, Md., July 6, 1863. On the death of Archbishop Eccleson he was chosen to succeed him in the spiritual oversight of the See of Baltimore, and also appointed by the Pope apostolic delegate to preside at a council of all the archbishops and bishops in the United States. As a theologian and scholar it is doubtful if the Mother Church has produced his superior. His writings include 'Letters of Omicron to Omega' (1826), 'Theologia Dogmatica' (Philadelphia, 1840, in four volumes; Baltimore, 1857, three volumes), 'Theologia Moralis' (Philadelphia, 1841-1843, three volumes), 'The Primacy of the Apostolic See Vindicated' (Baltimore, 1855), 'The Catholic Doctrine of Justification' (Philadelphia, 1841), a 'Treatise on Baptism' (1843), a 'Vindication of the Catholic Church,' and 'Four Sermons Preached in the Cathedral at Bardstown' (1829), besides several minor works. He also translated, with copious notes, the New Testament Scriptures, and portions of the Old, being dissatisfied with the textual departures of the English Catholic Bibles from the Rheims and the Douay standards.

KENRICK, PETER RICHARD, Roman Catholic archbishop, was born in Dublin, Ireland, August 17, 1806, and was a brother of Archbishop F. P. Kenrick, whose strong intellectual traits he shared in an eminent degree. He taught in various Catholic institutions, founded a magazine called *The Catholic Cabinet,* and became archbishop of St. Louis. During the Civil War he ministered to the sick and wounded on both sides. He organized schools and reformatories, delivered frequent lectures, and published 'The Holy House of Loretto; or, an Examination of the Historical Evidence of its Miraculous Translation,' and 'Anglican Ordinations.' He died in 1896.

KENT, CHARLES WILLIAM, educator and editor, was born at Louisa, C.H., Va., September 27, 1860. His father was Robert Meredith Kent and his mother, Sarah Garland Hunter. After graduation from the University of Virginia, he became head master of the University School at Charleston, S.C., an institution of which he was joint founder. Later he pursued post-graduate studies at the German universities; Göttingen, Berlin, and Leipzig. For several years he was professor of English and modern languages at the University of Tennessee, and in 1893 became professor of English literature, rhetoric, and *belles lettres* in Linden Kent Memorial School of English Literature at the University of Virginia, a chair which he still occupies. Dr. Kent is a lecturer of great charm and power on topics connected with American and English literature, and notably upon the poets of the South. He is the author of several volumes, including 'Teutonic Antiquities in Andreas and Elene' (Leipzig, 1887), 'Shakespeare Note-Book' (Boston, Ginn and Company), 1897), and 'Graphic Representations of English and American Literature' (New York, Henry Holt and Company, 1898). He has also edited a number of standard works, among them, 'Cynewulf's Elene' (Boston, Ginn and Company, 1888), 'Idyls of the Lawn' (Charlottesville, 1899), 'Selected Poems from Burns' (New York, Silver, Burdett and Company, 1901), Tennyson's 'The Princess' (Richmond B. F. Johnson Company, 1901), 'Poe Memorial Volume' (Charlottesville, 1901), Poe's 'Poems,' Vol. VII of the Virginia edition of his works (New York, T. Y. Crowell and Company, 1902), 'Poe's Poems in Pocket Classics' (New York, The Macmillan Company, 1904), and 'The Book of the Poe Centenary' (Charlottesville, 1909). Dr. Kent is also the literary editor of 'The Library of Southern Literature,' a work whose monumental character testifies alike to his tireless research and to his broad scholarship. The vast amount of labor which Dr. Kent has expended upon this great enterprise, the keen analytical power which he has brought to bear upon his task, and the soundness of his judgment in the matter of literary values entitle him to the lasting gratitude of an appreciative Southland. He has received from the University of Virginia the degree of M.A.; from Leipzig, the degree of Ph.D., and from the University of Alabama, the degree of LL.D.

KEPLINGER, E. M., Mrs. Author. [La.]. She published a novel which was quite popular, entitled 'Berenice' (New Orleans, 1878).

KERCHEVAL, SAMUEL. Historian. [Va.]. He published a 'History of the Valley of Virginia' (1833, revised, 1850).

KERLIN, ROBERT THOMAS. Clergyman and educator. He was born in Newcastle, Mo., March 22, 1866; graduated from Central College, Fayette, Mo., and studied also at Johns Hopkins Uninversity, at Chicago and at Harvard. Then followed an extended sojourn abroad. On returning home, he divided his time between ministerial and educational work, having been received into the Conference of the Methodist Episcopal Church, South. At present he is professor of English in the State Normal School, at Warrensburg, Mo. His writings include: 'Mainly for Myself,' 'The Lyrical Diversions of a Village Parson (Kansas City, Hudson Kimberly Publishing Company), 'The Camp Life of the Third Regiment' (*ibid.*), and 'The Church of the Fathers' (Nashville, Southern Methodist Publishing House), besides numerous contributions to the press. He was a chaplain in the Spanish-American War.

KERN, ALFRED ALLAN, educator, was born in Salem, Va., November 29, 1879. His father was John A. Kern and his mother, Margaret Eskridge. He occupies the chair of English in Millsaps College, Jackson, Miss., and holds the degree of Ph.D. He is the author of a work entitled 'The Ancestry of Chaucer' (1906). The sketch of Irwin Russell in 'The Library of Southern Literature' is also from his pen.

KERN, JOHN ADAM, Methodist Episcopal clergyman and educator, was born in Frederick County, Va., April 23, 1846. For several years past he has filled the chair of practical theology in Vanderbilt University at Nashville, Tenn. He wrote 'The Ministry to the Congregation: a work on Homiletics' (Nashville, Barbee and Smith, 1897). Washington and Lee University gave him the degree of D.D.

KERNAN, WILL HUBBARD, poet, was born in Bellefontaine, Ohio, November 5, 1845, and died in Memphis, Tenn., January 28, 1905. He was educated for the Bar, but relinquished law to enter journalism.

For years he was connected with Southern newspapers and considered Memphis his home. He was undoubtedly a genius. His poem entitled "Southland" alone entitles him to high rank. He published only one volume of verse 'The Flaming Meteor' (Chicago, Charles H. Kerr and Company, 1892), but there are still many of his song-fragments extant, from which another exquisite collection can be made. His favorite pen-name was "Kenneth Lamar."

KERNEY, MARTIN JOSEPH, educator and author, was born in Lewiston, Md., in 1819, and died in Baltimore, Md., March 16, 1861. For several years he successfully conducted an academy in Baltimore and at leisure hours compiled text-books adapted to Catholic methods of instruction. On the list of his publications are included 'Compendium of History,' 'Class Book of History,' an adaptation of 'Murray's Grammar,' a 'Catechism of Scripture History,' 'The Columbian Arithmetic' and several others.

KERR, HUGH, poet, was born in Ireland but lived for many years in Texas, where he died in 1843. He wrote a 'Poetical Description of Texas' (1838).

KERR, JAMES EDWIN. Poet. [S.C.]. He published a volume of verse entitled 'Songs as They Came' (1898).

KERR, JOHN LEEDS, lawyer, was born near Annapolis, Md., January 15, 1780, and died near Easton, Md., February 21, 1844. He engaged successfully in the practice of law, served for several terms in Congress, and, on the death of John S. Spence was chosen by the Legislature to fill his unexpired term in the United States Senate. He edited 'The History of Maryland,' by his uncle, John L. Bozeman.

KERR, ROBERT POLLOCK, clergyman, was born in 1850 and was for many years pastor of a church in Savannah. He published 'Presbyterianism for the People' (1883), 'History of Presbyterianism' (1886), 'Hymns of the Ages' (1891), and 'The Voice of God in History.'

KERR, WASHINGTON CARUTHERS, geologist, was born in Alamance County, N.C., May 24, 1827, and died in Asheville, N.C., August 9, 1885. For several years he was state geologist of North Carolina. He contributed to the proceedings of scientific societies numerous important papers and published two volumes of 'Geological Reports' (Raleigh, 1875-1881).

KESTER, VAUGHAN, author, was born at New Brunswick, N.J., September 12, 1869. His education was obtained in the common schools of Mount Vernon, Ohio, and under private tutors at Cleveland, Ohio. He married, August 31, 1898, Jessie B. Jennings, and was for some time on the staff of the *Cosmopolitan Magazine*. He was also connected with the International Literary and News Syndicates, at Irvington-on-the-Hudson. His contributions to the periodicals have been numerous, consisting mainly of short stories and poems. He has also written two plays which have been well received. His two novels: "The Manager of the B. and R." (*Harper's Magazine*) and "The Fortunes of the Landrays" (*McClure's Magazine*), are deservedly popular. He resides at Wood Lawn Mansion, Accotink, Va.

KETCHUM, ANNIE CHAMBERS, educator, lecturer, author, was born in Scott County, Ky., in 1824. Her maiden name was Annie Chambers. She was married, first, to Mr. Bradford, and afterward to Mr. Ketchum, the latter being killed in the Civil War. For several years she was principal of the Memphis High School. It was not until the outbreak of hostilities between the North and the South that she began to write for the press; but she received immediate recognition. Perhaps her best known poem is "Benny's Christmas," which has been the juvenile favorite of two generations. It was inspired by the childish prattle of her own promising boy, who attained the years of manhood only to die of cholera. Besides two volumes of verse entitled 'Christmas Poems' and 'Lotus Flowers,' she was also the author of two interesting novels: 'Nellie Bracken' and 'Rilla Motto.'

KEY, FRANCIS SCOTT. Author of our national anthem, "The Star-Spangled Banner," and a lawyer of distinction. He was born in Frederick County, Md., in 1780, and was educated at St. John's College, at Annapolis. Most of his life was spent at the national seat of government, and he held for many years the office of district-attorney for the District of Columbia. It was toward the close of the second war with England that the stirring lines of his famous melody were written. The immediate occasion was furnished by the attack on Fort McHenry, in Baltimore Harbor, in 1814. To secure the release of a friend, who was a prisoner on a British war vessel, he boarded the hostile ship. The effort was successful, but he was not allowed to return to shore until after the attack on the fort. It was while engaged in watching the flag during the long night hours of this detention from dusk to dawn that he caught the inspiration of the song which has immortalized him, and the words were written upon an old envelope. Under the title of 'Poems,' a collection of his verse has been published, and the volume is introduced with a sketch from the pen of Chief Justice Roger B. Taney, an intimate friend of the author. On the precise spot that was occupied by the flag at Fort McHenry a memorial tablet has been placed by order of Congress. He died in 1843.

KEYES, EDWARD LAWRENCE, surgeon, was born in Charleston, S.C., August 28, 1843. After studying in France, he located in New York, where he became an eminent specialist and wrote a number of medical essays and monographs. The University of New York gave him the degree of LL.D.

KEYES, WADE. Lawyer. [Ala.]. He was born in 1821 and died in 1879. He published two law-books, one on 'Realty' (1853), and one on 'Chattels' (1853).

KILBY, L. CLAY. Author. [Va.]. He published a story entitled 'Vernon Lonsdale' (1876).

KILLEBREW, JOSEPH BUCKNER. Statistical expert and railway official. He was born in Montgomery County, Tenn., May 29, 1840, a son of Bryan Whitfield and Elizabeth Smith Ligon Killebrew. He graduated from the University of North Carolina, and afterward pursued legal and scientific studies. He married, December 3, 1857, Mary Catharine Wimberly. He was Commissioner of Agriculture for Tennessee for ten years, afterward special expert for the Tenth Federal Census on Tobacco in the United States, and was also one of the editors of the 'Standard Dictionary.' Besides numerous articles contributed to the magazines and encyclopædias, he published: 'The Resources of Tennessee,' 'The Geology of Tennessee,' 'The Life of James C. Warner,' and numerous writings upon the subject of tobacco. He died in Nashville, Tenn., in 1906.

KIMBALL, RICHARD BURLEY, lawyer, author, railway magnate, was born in Plainville, N.H., October 11, 1816, and died in New York City, December 28, 1892. He founded the town of Kimball, Texas and built part of the first railway system constructed in the State. He was a

writer of very great distinction and published 'St. Ledger; or the Threads
of Life,' a metaphysical novel (1850), which was translated into foreign
languages; 'Cuba and the Cubans' (1851), 'Undercurrents of Wall Street'
(1861), 'Was He Successful?' (1863), 'In the Tropics' (1863), 'The Prince
of Kashna' (1865), 'Lectures before the New York Law Institute' (1870),
and 'Stories of Exceptional Life.' Just before his death he read the
proofs of his last work, entitled, 'Half a Century of Recollections' (1893).

KING, BEN. Poet. [Ky.]. As a writer of whimsical verse he
enjoyed wide popularity, his best known production being the serio-comic
favorite, "If I Should Die To-night." At the time of his death, in 1894,
a collection of his poems was published under the title of 'Ben King's
Verse,' and four years later another edition was issued, with a memoir
by Opie Reed.

KING, GRACE ELIZABETH. See Biographical and Critical
Sketch, Vol. VII, page 2927.

KING, SUSAN PETIGRU. Author. [S.C.]. She was born in
1826 and died in 1875. She wrote 'Busy Moments of an Idle Woman,'
'Sylvia's World,' 'Lily,' 'Gerald Gray's Wife,' and other excellent stories.
Mrs. King was a native of Charleston.

KING, WILBURN HILL. Lawyer and planter. He was born
in Cullodenville, Crawford County, Ga., June 10, 1839, the son of
Alexander and Mary Douglas King, and was educated at Americus,
Ga. He studied both medicine and law, but chose the latter as a
profession, and settled in Texas. He married, in 1867, Lucy Furman.
He served four years in the Confederate Army, enlisting as a private
but rising to the rank of a brigadier-general, and was for ten years
adjutant-general of the State. He wrote 'A History of the Texas Rangers'
(see 'Yoakum's History of Texas,' revised edition), besides numerous
contributions to the periodicals.

KING, WILLIAM, physician, of Georgia, wrote an interesting
volume of essays entitled 'A Sure Possession; or, Some Thoughts of a
Layman' (Atlanta, A. B. Caldwell, 1909). It crystallizes the experience
of nearly eighty years. Julia, the eldest daughter of Dr. King, married
Henry W. Grady, the distinguished journalist and orator; and Mrs.
William King, his wife, a gifted woman, has for years been a contributor
to the press.

KING, WILLIAM RUFUS. Vice-president of the United States.
He was born in North Carolina, in 1786, and for several years represented the State in Congress. But in 1818 he settled in Alabama,
becoming a delegate to the first Constitutional Convention and afterward receiving a commission in the United States Senate, which was
frequently renewed. Under President Tyler he was Minister to
France. In 1852 he was elected Vice-president of the United States
on the ticket with Franklin Pierce; but, before the inauguration, his
health became suddenly impaired and he made a trip to Havana. By
special act of Congress he was allowed to take the oath of office in
the Cuban capital; but he did not live to enter upon his high duties,
dying soon after his return home, in 1853. While not an orator, Mr.
King was a statesman whose impress has been left upon his times,
and some of his speeches in the *Congressional Globe* are characterized
by unusual force of logic and breadth of vision.

KING, WILLIS PERCIVAL, physician and surgeon, was born in
Macon County, Mo., December 21, 1839. Growing up in a settlement without school advantages, he ran away at the age of fourteen; and by work-

ing in the summer he was enabled to attend school. After receiving his diploma from the St. Louis Medical College, he pursued post-graduate studies in the East, and afterward settled in Kansas City, where he became one of the foremost practitioners of the State. His literary gifts are of very high order; and, in addition to numerous poems, he published: 'Stories of a Country Doctor,' 'Perjury for Pay,' and 'Quacks and Quackery in Missouri,' besides medical works.

KINGSBURY, THEODORE BRYANT. Editor. [N.C.]. He was born in 1828. Besides numerous essays on literary and historical subjects, he published a 'History of Granville County, N.C.,' and a work on 'Baptism.'

KINKEAD, ELEANOR TALBOT. Author. She was born in Kentucky, the daughter of William B. and Elizabeth de la Fontaine Shelby Kinkead; also a great-granddaughter of Isaac Shelby, an officer in the Revolution. She was educated at the State College of Kentucky and by her father, a scholar of classical attainments. She is the author of several charming volumes, among them: ''Gainst Wind and Tide' (Chicago, Rand, McNally and Company), 'Young Greer of Kentucky' (*ibid.*), 'Florida Alexander' (Chicago, A. C. McClurg), 'The Invisible Bond' (New York, Moffat, Yard and Company), and 'The Courage of Blackburn Blair' (*ibid.*). She resides at Lexington, Ky.

KINKEAD, ELIZABETH SHELBY. Lecturer and author. She was born in Kentucky, the daughter of Judge William B. and Elizabeth de la Fontaine Shelby Kinkead, and was educated at the State College of Kentucky, and by her father. In 1893 she was called to the department of English in the State College of Kentucky, her *alma mater.* In 1900 she was one of the lecturers at Chautauqua, N.Y. Her best known work is 'A History of Kentucky,' which appeared in 1896 (New York, The American Book Company). She resides in Lexington, Ky.

KINLOCH, FRANCIS, patriot, was born in Charleston, S.C., March 7, 1755, received his education in England, and returned home to serve with distinction in the American Revolution. He was severely wounded at the siege of Savannah in 1779. He was several times sent to the Legislature, was an occupant of the Bench, and was also a member of the convention that framed the constitution of South Carolina. For several years he resided with his family abroad, but eventually returned to Charleston. He published 'Letters from Geneva,' in two volumes (Boston), and 'Eulogy on Washington' (Georgetown, 1800). He died in Charleston, S.C., February 8, 1826.

KIRKLAND, JAMES HAMPTON. Educator. He was born in Spartanburg, S.C., September 9, 1859, a son of the Rev. W. C. and Virginia Kirkland. He graduated from Wofford College, and also took a course of study at Leipsic. He married, in 1895, Mary Henderson, of Knoxville, Tenn. He was professor of Latin in Vanderbilt University for several years, and in 1893 became chancellor. He is one of the consulting editors of 'The Library of Southern Literature.' Besides editing 'Satires and Epistles of Horace' (Boston, B. H. Sanborn and Company), he has published numerous monographs and reviews. Dr. Kirkland has received the Ph.D. degree from Leipsic, the LL.D. from the University of North Carolina and the D.C.L. degree from the University of the South. He resides in Nashville, Tenn.

KIRKLAND, T. H. [S.C.]. In association with R. M. Kennedy he published 'Historic Camden.'

KIRKWOOD, DANIEL, educator and mathematician, was born in Bradenbaugh, Md., September 27, 1814, and held the chair of mathematics at different times in various institutions. Besides contributing to scientific journals, he published 'Meteoric Astronomy' (1867), 'Comets and Meteors' (1873), and 'The Asteroids and Minor Planets between Mars and Jupiter' (1887). He died in 1895.

KIRTLEY, JAMES ADDISON, Baptist clergyman [Ky.], was born in 1822. He published a 'History of Bullittsburg Church' (1872), 'The Design of Baptism' (1873), and 'Cody's Theology Examined' (1893).

KITTRELL, NORMAN G. Jurist. Judge Kittrell resides in Houston, Texas, where he ably presides on the Superior Court Bench. His story of reconstruction days in the South entitled 'Ned, Nigger an' Gent'man,' is considered one of the best (New York and Washington, The Neale Publishing Company, 1907). The work has been dramatized and staged with successful results.

KNIGHT, JAMES, physician, was born at Taneytown, Md., February 14, 1810, and died in New York City, October 24, 1887. Dr. Knight became an eminent practitioner. After locating in New York he converted his private home into a hospital until permanent quarters were built. He published 'The Improvement of Health in Children and Adults by Natural Means' (1875), 'Orthopædia; or, a Practical Treatise on the Aberrations of the Human Form' (1874), and minor works.

KNIGHT, LUCIAN LAMAR, editor and author, was born in Atlanta, Ga., February 9, 1868. His father was George Walton Knight, an officer in both Mexican and Civil Wars, and his mother, Clara Corinne Daniel. On his father's side he numbers among his kindred George Walton, one of the signers of the Declaration of Independence from Georgia; on his mother's he is closely related to both the Lamars and the Cobbs. After graduating with distinction from the University of Georgia, at which institution he won the debator's medal and received a speaker's place in his junior year on three separate awards, viz.; scholarship, composition, and oratory, he read law under Judge Richard F. Lyon, at Macon, Ga. But his penchant was for literature, and relinquishing Blackstone, he accepted a position on the editorial staff of the Atlanta *Constitution*, of which his kinsman, the lamented Henry W. Grady, was long editor. Ten years of his life were devoted to journalism and then, feeling impelled toward the ministry, he entered the theological seminary at Princeton. While here he also took post-graduate work in the university and received his degree of Master of Arts. Before completing his studies he was called to the Central Presbyterian Church of Washington, D.C., but ill health necessitated an abandonment of his ministerial career. After several months spent in foreign travel, he returned home but little improved, and on the advice of his physician he went to Southern California, where he remained for two years, spending most of his time on Catalina Island, twenty-seven miles off the coast. It was here that Mr. Knight wrote his two elaborate biographical volumes entitled 'Reminiscences of Famous Georgians' (Atlanta, Ga., The Franklin-Turner Company, 1907-1908), a work which passed into two editions. At the invitation of his *alma mater* he crossed the continent to deliver the alumni address at the University of Georgia, and took for his subject, "Lee's Old War Horse; an Appeal Before the Bar of Public Opinion on Behalf of Lieutenant-general James Longstreet." On recovering his health he accepted the associate-editorship of the Atlanta *Georgian,* a chair which he still occupies. Besides contributing to 'The Library of Southern Literature' the sketches of two Georgians, Benjamin H. Hill and Thomas E. Watson, Mr. Knight compiled the 'Dictionary of Southern Authors,' Vol. XV. He also assisted in the compilation of

'Memoirs of Georgia' (1895), 'Modern Eloquence' (1900), and other works. Mr. Knight has delivered literary and historical addresses in various parts of the South.   *Charles Alphonso Smith.*

KNOX, T. W. Author. [La.]. He published a volume entitled 'Camp Fire and Cotton Field, and Residence on a Louisiana Plantation' (1865).

KOENIGSBERG, M. Author. [Ala.]. He published 'Southern Martyrs: Alabama's White Regiments During the Spanish-American War' (1898).

KOLLOCK, HENRY, clergyman, was born in New Providence, N. J., December 14, 1778, was educated for the ministry, taught and preached for several years at Princeton, and became, in 1806, pastor of the Independent Presbyterian Church, of Savannah, Ga. He was an orator of unusual attainments. His sermons, in four volumes, were published, with a memoir, by his brother (Savannah, 1822). He expected to write a biography of John Calvin, and spent several months abroad to collect material, but he was prevented from accomplishing this task by ill health. He died in Savannah, Ga., December 29, 1819. Harvard gave him the degree of D.D.

KOUNS, NATHAN CHAPMAN, author, was born in Fulton, Mo., December 17, 1833. On completing his education, he was admitted to the Bar. At the outbreak of the war, he enlisted in the Confederate Army, participated in numerous engagements, and was several times wounded. For many years after the war, he was state librarian of Missouri. He published two historical novels of rare interest and power: 'Dorcas, the Daughter of Faustina' (New York, Fords, Howard and Hulbert), and 'Arius, the Libyan.'

KRAUTH, CHARLES PORTERFIELD, Lutheran clergyman, was born in Martinsburg, Va., March 17, 1823, and died in Philadelphia, January 2, 1883. He served congregations in Maryland and Virginia and afterward located in Philadelphia, where he taught in the Lutheran Theological Seminary and in the University of Pennsylvania. His most important work is 'The Conservative Reformation' (Philadelphia, 1872), but he also wrote 'Christian Liberty' (1860), 'Infant Baptism' (1874), and numerous other volumes, besides editing and translating several works on theology and producing at intervals a number of religious poems. He also published 'Winter and Spring in the Danish West Indies.' (1854).

KREBS, JOHN MICHAEL, clergyman, was born in Hagerstown, Md., May 6, 1804, and died in the city of New York, September 30, 1867. He received his collegiate education at Dickinson College and his theological equipment at Princeton. For nearly forty years he was pastor of the Rutgers Street Presbyterian Church, of New York. He published 'The Private, Domestic, and Social Life of Jesus Christ, a Model for Youth' (Philadelphia, 1849), and 'The Presbyterian Psalmist.'

KROEGER, ADOLPH ERNST. Editor. [Mo.]. He was born in 1837 and died in 1882. He wrote 'The Minnesingers of Germany' (1873), 'Our Forms of Government and the Problems of the Future' (1862), and made several translations.

KYLE, RUBY BERYL. Author. [Ala.]. She wrote a novel entitled 'Paul St. Paul, a Son of the People' (1895).

LA BORDE, MAXIMILIAN, educator and physician, was born in Edgefield, S.C., June 5, 1804, and died in Columbia, S.C., November 6, 1873. For several years he practiced medicine, but afterward became professor of logic and literature in South Carolina College; and, when this institution was merged into the University of South Carolina, he was called to the head of the school of English. He published 'An Introduction to Physiology' (New York, 1855), a 'History of South Carolina College' (Charleston, 1859), one of the best works of the kind extant, 'The Story of Lethea and Verona' (1860), and 'The Suburban House and an Old Lady' (1861), besides contributions to various magazines.

LA BREE, BEN. Soldier, author, editor. [Ky.]. He published 'The Pictorial Battles of the Civil War,' a 'History of the Confederate States Navy,' 'Camp Fires of the Confederacy,' and 'The Confederate Soldier in the Civil War' (Louisville, Ky., The Courier-Journal Company, 1895).

LACEY, GEORGE S. Lawyer. [La.]. He was the author of a work on 'The Holy Eucharist' (Philadelphia, 1869).

LACLOTTE, H. Author. [La.]. He published a 'View of the Battle of New Orleans, with Key,' an exceedingly rare book (1815).

LA COSTE. MARIE RAVENEL DE, poet and educator, whose famous war lyric entitled "Somebody's Darling," is perhaps the best known poem of the Civil War period in America, on the Southern side at least, spent her early days in Savannah, where she was engaged in teaching when hostilities began in 1861. Her father was Henri de la Coste and her mother Angèle Pérony d'Istria, both natives of France. Though the gifted author has written nothing in years for publication, and has shunned rather than courted the applause which her masterpiece has called forth, she still lives in the enjoyment of good health and is temporarily residing in Washington, D.C. Due to an extreme reticence it has been difficult to obtain from Miss La Coste even the barest information in regard to herself. Consequently, neither the date nor place of her birth can be given. But the greater part of her life has been devoted to the teaching of French. The inspiration of her tender and pathetic song was furnished by the scenes which she doubtless witnessed with her own eyes in the Confederate hospitals, while a resident of Savannah, where she also wrote in similar vein another exquisite song entitled "Beautiful Hands." Miss Rutherford is inclined to think that "The Boy Soldier," which was published during the same period by an unknown "Lady of Savannah" emanated from the pen of this same talented woman. It is certainly to be regretted that one so richly endowed with spiritual and mental graces should not only have ceased so early to write for publication, but should also have cloistered herself so completely from a world whose admiration for her genius is an undivided unit.

LACY, J. HORACE. Writer. [Va.]. He published a number of interesting historical sketches.

LADD, CATHERINE. Educator. Her maiden name was Stratton. She was born in Richmond, Va., October 28, 1809, and at the age of nineteen married G. W. Ladd, a portrait and miniature painter. For several years she conducted successfully a select school at Winnsborough, S.C. She also contributed stories and sketches to the popular magazines, besides an occasional poem of rare grace, and also advocated in the press the encouragement of white labor and of manufacturing industries in the South. She wrote under various pen-names. During the war, she gave her whole thought to the care of the sick and wounded soldiers. Her school property was destroyed by General Sherman, but she resumed teaching for a while after the war closed and then retired to a farm near Buckhead, S.C.

LADD, JOSEPH BROWN, physician and poet, was born at Newport, R.I., in 1764, but settled in Charleston, S.C., at the close of the Revolution and was killed in a duel which resulted from a newspaper controversy in 1786. He published in the year of his death a volume entitled 'The Poems of Arouet' (Charleston, 1786), and several years later his 'Literary Remains' were collected by his sister and introduced with a biographical sketch from the pen of W. B. Chittenden (New York, 1832). Many of his poems were inspired by his sweetheart, Amanda. His rhymes are skilfully turned; and his first work is said to have been done at the age of ten.

LAFFERTY, JOHN JAMES. Clergyman. He was born in Virginia in 1837, and enjoyed fine educational advantages, including a course at the University of Virginia. He entered the ministry, and for thirty years was editor of the Richmond *Christian Advocate.* He served four years in the Confederate ranks, holding the commission of major of cavalry and operating chiefly on the upper waters of the Potomac, outside the Confederate lines. He invented a process of milling. Besides delivering many popular lectures, he has published: 'A Geography of Virginia' and 'Sketches of Virginia Methodist Ministers.' Washington and Lee University gave him the degree of LL.D. He resides in Richmond, Va.

LA HARPE, BERNARD DE. Author. [La.]. He published in the French language an interesting 'Journal Historique de l'Establissement des Français à la Louisiane, 1698-1720' (New Orleans, 1831).

LAIDLEY, THEODORE THADDEUS SOBIESKI, soldier, was born in Guyandotte, Va., April 14, 1822, and died in Palatka, Fla., April 4, 1886. He was educated at West Point, served forty years in the Army and retired with the rank of colonel. Besides compiling 'The Ordnance Manual of 1861,' which was a standard for years, he also published 'Instructions in Rifle Practice' (Philadelphia, 1879).

LAMAR, JAMES S., clergyman and author, was born in Gwinnett County, Ga., in 1829, and became an influential minister of the Christian Church. His work entitled 'The Organon of Scripture; or, the Inductive Method of Biblical Interpretation' (1860), takes high rank among theological books. Dr. Lamar also published several other volumes. He was the father of Joseph R. Lamar, former associate-justice of the Supreme Court of Georgia.

LAMAR, JOHN BASIL. Planter and writer. He was born in Milledgeville, Ga., November 5, 1812. He was a member of the State secession convention, and was a man of large means and of liberal culture. Under the title of "Homespun Yarns" he wrote numerous stories for the magazines, from one of which, "The Blacksmith of the Mountain Pass," it is said that Charles Dickens derived the central idea of "Colonel Quagg's Conversion," which appeared in *Household Words* soon after the great novelist returned from his American tour. Colonel Lamar never married. He was killed in the battle of Crampton's Gap, in Maryland, September 14, 1862, while serving on the staff of his brother-in-law, General Howell Cobb.

LAMAR, JOSEPH RUCKER, jurist and lawyer, was born in Ruckersville, Ga., in 1857. His father was the Rev. James S. Lamar and his mother, Mary Rucker. He received his education at the University of Georgia, at Bethany College, and at Washington and Lee. He studied law, won early distinction at the Bar, was appointed one of the commissioners to codify the laws of Georgia in 1895, and later occupied a seat on the Supreme Court Bench. He is a man of ripe scholarship, and, besides numerous addresses, has published several monographs.

"LAMAR, KENNETH." See Will Hubbard Kernan.

LAMAR, LUCIUS QUINTUS CINCINNATUS. See Biographical and Critical Sketch, Vol. VII, page 2963.

LAMAR, LUCIUS QUINTUS CINCINNATUS, Sr. Jurist. He was the father of L. Q. C. Lamar of Mississippi and a brother of Mirabeau B. Lamar, president of the republic of Texas. He was born near Eatonton, Ga., July 15, 1797, and died in Milledgeville, Ga., July 4 1834. For several years he adorned the Superior Court Bench, and, in addition to revising Clayton's 'Georgia Justice,' he compiled 'The Laws of Georgia from 1810 to 1819.' He was a man of unusual culture, courtly in his manners and exceptional in his attainments; but unhappily he possessed an organism of extreme sensitiveness, and to this unfortunate handicap his untimely deat't is attributed.

LAMAR, MIRABEAU BONAPARTE. See Biographical and Critical Sketch, Vol. VII, page 2987.

LAMBERT, MARY E., Mrs., author, was born in Cahaba, Ala., November 6, 1835. Her maiden name was Mary E. Perine. She was educated at the North, and on her return home she married John M. Tucker, of Milledgeville, Ga. The death of her husband turned her thoughts in the direction of literature, and she began to write for Northern periodicals. In 1871 she married Col. James H. Lambert, of the Philadelphia *Press*. Besides extensive editorial work, she published a volume of verse entitled 'Poems' (1867); 'Loew's Bridge, a Broadway Idyl' (1868) and a 'Life of Mark M. Pomeroy' (1868).

LANCE, WILLIAM, author, was born in Charleston, S.C., in 1791 and died in Texas in 1840. He attained high rank both as a lawyer and as a scholar. Besides a number of political essays, he wrote in Latin a 'Life of Washington' (Charleston, 1834).

LANDRUM, J. O. B. [S.C.]. He wrote a 'Colonial and Revolutionary History of Upper South Carolina' (1897).

LANE, ELEANOR McCARTNEY. See Biographical and Critical Sketch, Vol. VII, page 3003.

LANE, JAMES H. Educator and soldier. [N.C.]. He wrote 'Lane's North Carolina Brigade,' and other historical papers.

LANE, J. J. Educator. [Texas]. He contributed to 'Wooten's Comprehensive History of Texas' (Dallas, W. G. Scarff, 1898) an important chapter on "The History of the Educational System of Texas."

LANGLOIS, FATHER A. Clergyman. He published a 'Botany of Louisiana' (1892).

LANGSTON, JOHN MERCER, educator, was born a slave, of African parents, in Louisa County, Va., December 14, 1829, but was emancipated at the age of six, studied law, achieved distinction at the Bar, was for several years dean of the law department of Howard University and later, under President Grant, was United States Minister and Consul-general to Hayti. Besides numerous contributions to the press, he published a volume of addresses entitled 'Freedom and Citizenship' (Washington, 1883).

LANIER. CLIFFORD. See Biographical and Critical Sketch, Vol. VII, page 3021.

LANIER, HENRY WYSHAM. Author. [Ga.]. He published 'The Romance of Piscator' (New York, Henry Holt and Company, 1904).

LANIER, JOHN JABEZ, Protestant Episcopal clergyman, is a native of South Carolina, a deep student of theological problems and a forceful writer. His published works include: 'The Harmony of Some Relations in Nature and in Grace' ·(1908), 'The Kinship of God and Man,' a work of three volumes comprising 'Good and Evil' (1902), 'The Master-Key,' and 'The American Church.' As a thinker he is courageous and independent. He resides in Washington, Ga.

LANIER, SIDNEY. See Biographical and Critical Sketch, Vol. VII, page 3041.

LANTZ, EMILY EMERSON, journalist, was born in Lancaster, Pa., of aristocratic colonial stock. Miss Lantz is on the staff of the Baltimore *Sun*, and, in addition to her newspaper work, she contributes both prose and verse to current magazines. The sketch of Lucy M. Thurston in 'The Library of Southern Literature' is from her pen.

LA SALLE, ROBERT CAVELIER, Sieur DE, explorer, was born in Rouen, France, November 22, 1643, and died in Texas, March 20, 1687. He discovered the Ohio River and was the first to explore the Mississippi for any very great distance. His memoirs (1678) are published in the French historical collection.

LATANÉ, JOHN HOLLADAY. Educator. He was born in Staunton, Va., April 1, 1869, the son of Bishop James Allen Latané, of the Reformed Episcopal Church. He was educated at Baltimore City College and at Johns Hopkins University (Ph.D.). He has been identified with the chair of history in several leading institutions, and has frequently lectured before student bodies on historical subjects. Among his published works are included: 'Early Relations Between Maryland and Virginia' (Baltimore, Johns Hopkins Press, 1895), 'Diplomatic Relations of the United States and Spanish America' (*ibid.,* 1900), and 'America as a World Power' (New York, Harper and Brothers, 1907). He also wrote the sketch of Moncure D. Conway for 'The Library of Southern Literature.' Dr. Latané is an authority on international law and diplomatic relations. He resides in Lexington, Va.

LATHERS, RICHARD, merchant, was born in Georgetown, S.C., about 1820. For some time he engaged successfully in mercantile pursuits in his home town, but eventually removed to New York, established himself in business, and became president of the Great Western Marine Insurance Company, accumulating a fortune of large proportions. He published 'Notes of a Life of Sixty Years.'

LATIL, ALEXANDER. Poet. [La.]. During the greater part of his life he suffered from invalidism. On this account his poetry is tinctured with sadness, but his work is nevertheless soulful. He published 'Éssais Poétiques' (1841).

LATOUR, A. LACARRIÉRE, French soldier and historian, published an 'Historical Manual of the War in West Florida and Louisiana.' The book was written in French and translated for the author into English.

LATROBE, BENJAMIN HENRY, architect, was born in Yorkshire, England, May 1, 1764, a descendant of Henry Boneval de la Trobe, who emigrated from France to Holland on the revocation of the Edict of Nantes. He was educated at the University of Leipzig, served in the

Prussian Army, and was twice wounded. On coming to the United States, Mr. Latrobe settled in Virginia. He engineered the James River and Appomattox Canal and built the penitentiary in Richmond. Later, when the capitol building in Washington was destroyed by the British, he was one of the architects who remodeled the new structure. He died in New Orleans, La., September 3, 1820, leaving an important manuscript, which was edited by his son, J. H. B. Latrobe, entitled 'The Journal of Latrobe' (New York, D. Appleton and Company, 1905).

LATROBE, JOHN HAZLEHURST BONEVAL, lawyer, inventor, colonizer, author, was born in Philadelphia, Pa., of French extraction, May 4, 1803, and was educated for the Army at West Point, but he resigned prior to graduation and settled in Baltimore, Md., for the practice of law. For more than sixty years he was an eloquent advocate at the Bar, but along with his professional triumphs he is remembered for his pioneer labors in the scheme of negro colonization in Liberia, on the west coast of Africa, and for his invention of the stove which bears his name. He also published numerous works, among them, a 'Biography of Charles Carroll of Carrollton' (Philadelphia, 1824), a 'History of Mason and Dixon's Line' (Philadelphia, 1854), 'Personal Recollections of the Baltimore and Ohio Railroad' (Baltimore, 1858), 'Hints for Six Months in Europe' (Philadelphia, 1859), 'Odds and Ends' (Baltimore, 1876), a 'History of Maryland in Liberia' (Baltimore, 1885), 'Reminiscences of West Point in 1818 and 1822' (Baltimore, 1887), besides law-books, books for children, and several novelettes. He was also one of the founders of the Maryland Institute. He died in Baltimore, Md., in 1891.

LAUDONNIÉRE, RENÉ DE, French Colonist, accompanied Ribault, who was sent by Coligny to found a colony of Huguenots in Florida, but the enterprise met with disaster at the hands of the Spaniards. Ribault was killed and Laudonnière narrowly escaped. He wrote a 'Histoire Notable de la Florida' (Paris, 1586).

LAURENS, JOHN, soldier, was born in Charleston, S.C., in 1753, and was the son of the Honorable Henry Laurens. During the Revolution he was an aide on the staff of Washington, and by reason of his familiarity with foreign languages he was of great service in conducting correspondence with European officers. But he also participated in the active fighting and was several times wounded. In 1781 he was sent on a special errand to France to negotiate a loan, which he consummated successfully. He acquitted himself with heroic distinction at the battle of Yorktown; but, several months after the surrender of Cornwallis, while on the staff of General Greene, he was killed in an insignificant skirmish. Due to his chivalrous characteristics, he was styled "the Bayard of the Revolution." The military papers of the gallant officer, together with a memoir by William Gilmore Simms, were published in 1867 (New York, The Bradford Club).

LAURENS, HENRY. See Biographical and Critical Sketch, Vol. VII, page 3079.

LAWSON, JOHN. See Biographical and Critical Sketch, Vol. VII, page 3097.

LAWSON, THOMAS, soldier, was born in Virginia in 1781 and died at Norfolk, Va., May 15, 1861. He was chief medical officer of the United States forces in the Mexican War and was breveted a brigadier-general. He published an important report on 'Sickness and Mortality in the United States Army, 1819-1839' (1840), and a 'Meteorological Register.'

LAY, HENRY CHAMPLIN, Protestant Episcopal bishop, was born in Richmond, Va., December 6, 1823, and died in Easton, Md., September 17, 1885. For eleven years he was rector of the Church of the Nativity at Huntsville, Ala. In 1859 he became missionary bishop of Arkansas, and in 1868, bishop of the diocese of Easton. He wrote 'Letters to a Man Bewildered,' 'Tracts for Missionary Use,' 'Studies in the Church' (New York, 1872), and 'The Church and the Nation' (New York, 1885). Hobart College gave him the degree of D.D. and Cambridge, England, the degree of LL.D.

LAY, JAMES H. Lawyer. [Mo.]. He wrote a 'History of Benton County' (1876).

LAYTON, THOMAS. Author. [La.]. He wrote a volume entitled 'The Apparitions of Our Lady of Lourdes' (New Orleans, 1879).

LEACH, LUCY MAYNARD, Mrs. Poet. [N.C.]. She published a volume of verse entitled 'Scattered Leaves' (New York, E. J. Hale and Son, 1877), a work of merit.

LEACHMAN, WELTHEA BRYANT, Mrs. Poet. [Texas]. She was born in 1847. Mrs. Leachman published a volume of verse entitled 'Bitter Sweet, and Other Poems.'

LEAWELL, ZACHARY TAYLOR, clergyman, was born in 1847. Besides numerous pamphlets, he wrote 'Baptist Annals; or, Twenty-two Years with Mississippi Baptists, 1877-1899' (Philadelphia, American Baptist Publication Society, 1899).

LE CLERCQ, CHRÉTIEN. French missionary. He wrote an important work, covering the period of his long sojourn in America entitled the 'Premier Établissement de la Foi dans la Nouvelle France,' in two volumes (1691), which has been translated into English by John G. Shea.

LE CONTE, JOHN, one of the most distinguished of American scientists, was a son of Louis Le Conte, the noted botanist, and a brother of Joseph Le Conte, the famous geologist; and was born in Liberty County, Ga., in 1818. He was educated at the University of Georgia, and at the College of Physicians and Surgeons, of New York. For a while he practiced medicine in Savannah, Ga., and then began his long career of educational work. He taught at the University of Georgia, at South Carolina College, and at the University of California, being the organizer and for some time the executive head of the last-named institution. Though he specialized in the department of physics, it was said of him by Joseph Le Conte that his intimate acquaintance with nature embraced the whole realm of phenomena. In addition to numberless papers bearing upon important investigations and discoveries, he published two important volumes: 'The Philosophy of Medicine' and 'The Study of the Physical Sciences,' and contributed to scientific journals of Europe and America. He also belonged to the learned bodies of both hemispheres. He died at Berkeley, Cal., in 1891. His wife was Miss Josephine Graham, of New York. John and Joseph Le Conte have been called "the Gemini of the scientific heavens."

LE CONTE, JOSEPH. See Biographical and Critical Sketch, Vol. VII, page 3117.

LE CONTE, LOUIS, an eminent naturalist, was born near Shrewsbury, N.J., in 1782, and was the father of John and Joseph Le Conte. He settled in Liberty County, Ga., where he developed a botanical garden which attracted visitors from all parts of the globe. He wrote little; and for the reason that he was more concerned about his experiments than in taking care of his fame, others have appropriated the fruits of his labors; but he was one of the most original thinkers in the realm of scientific investigation on either side of the Atlantic. The manuscripts which he left at his death were destroyed in the burning of Columbia, S.C., and the world is distinctly poorer because of this loss to the literature of scientific research. Not only in the world of plant life, but among the rocks, with the animals, and in the department of mathematics, this wonderful man was equally at home. The celebrated Le Conte pear has been named in his honor. He died in 1838.

LEDERER, JOHN. Explorer. He penetrated the Alleghenies in 1669-1670 and published in Latin an account of his discoveries, which was translated by Sir William Talbot and entitled 'The Discoveries of John Lederer in Three Several Marches from Virginia to the West of Carolina and Other Parts of the Continent, with a Map' (London, 1672).

LEE, ADDIE McGRATH. Author. [La.]. She published a collection of charming stories descriptive of Southern life entitled 'Playin' 'Possum, and Other Pine-woods Stories' (Baton Rouge, La., 1895).

LEE, ALBERT, editor of *Collier's Weekly,* was born in New Orleans, La., May 11, 1868. For some time after graduating from Yale he was on the staff of the New York *Sun,* and later he was with the Harpers. He is the author of a number of stories, all of which are exceedingly clever, among them, 'Tommy Toddles' (New York, Harper and Brothers, 1896), 'Four for a Fortune' (*ibid.,* 1898), and several others.

LEE, ARTHUR, diplomat and physician, was born in Westmoreland County, Va., in 1740, the youngest son of Thomas Lee, a brother to "Light-horse Harry" and to Richard Henry Lee. He was one of the American representatives in Europe during the War of the Revolution. Dr. Lee first came into prominence as a controversialist in the public prints. He wrote the "Monitor Letters," addressed "An Appeal to the British Nation," and answered the famous "Letters of Junius."

LEE, CHARLES CARTER, poet, was the author of a work entitled 'Virginia Georgics,' written for the Hole and Corner Club of Powhatan (Richmond, 1858). It contains touches of scholarship and humor, and is pervaded by the refreshing breath of the fields.

LEE, FITZHUGH, an eminent soldier and civilian, was born in Clermont, Va., November 19, 1835, and was the son of Commodore Sydney Smith Lee. He was educated at West Point, and, entering the United States Army, was wounded in a fight with the Indians. At the outbreak of hostilities in 1861, he resigned his commission, enlisted in the Confederate Army, became major-general of cavalry, and achieved signal distinction in the field. Subsequent to the war, he was elected governor of Virginia, and later appointed Consul-general at Havana. During the Spanish-American War he served with the rank of major-general of volunteers, and afterward became military governor of the province of Havana. He was eventually retired with the rank of brigadier-general in the United States Army. Besides several contributions to the magazines and periodicals, he published a biography of his uncle, Robert E. Lee (New York, D. Appleton and Company, 1899), and 'Cuba's Struggle Against Spain.' He died in Richmond, Va., in 1905.

LEE, GEORGE TAYLOR. Author. [Va.]. He wrote a story of Blue Ridge mountaineer life in the Old Dominion entitled 'A Virginia Feud' (New York and Washington, The Neale Publishing Company, 1907).

LEE, GUY CARLETON, for some time editor-in-chief of the International Literary Syndicate and literary editor of the Baltimore *Sun.* On completing his studies at Dickinson College, in 1895, he took a course of law at the University of North Carolina and was duly admitted to the Bar. For several years he was an instructor in history at Johns Hopkins and afterward a lecturer on comparative politics at Columbian. Included among his writings are: 'Hincmar: an Introduction to the Study of the Church in the Ninth Century' (1898), 'Public Speaking' (New York, G. P. Putnam's Sons, 1899), 'Historical Jurisprudence' (New York, The Macmillan Company, 1900), 'Source Book of English History' (New York, Henry Holt and Company, 1900), 'The True History of the War between the States' (Philadelphia, J. B. Lippincott Company, 1903), and 'Robert E. Lee' (Philadelphia, George W. Jacobs Company, 1905). Besides, in the capacity of editor-in-chief, he compiled: 'The World's Orators,' in ten volumes (New York, G. P. Putnam's Sons, 1900), 'The History of Woman,' in ten volumes (Philadelphia, George Barrie and Son, 1902-1903), 'The History of North America,' in twenty volumes (*ibid.,* 1903-1905), and 'Southern Prose Writers, 1606-1744' (Baltimore, 1905). He has also been a frequent contributor to the current periodicals. Johns Hopkins gave him the degree of Ph.D.

LEE, HENRY. An eminent soldier and patriot, the "Light-horse" Harry of the American Revolution and father of General Robert E. Lee. He was the son of Henry Lee and Lucy Grimes, the famous lowland beauty who captured the heart of Washington. He was born in Westmoreland County, Va., in 1756, and was educated at Princeton University. At the outbreak of hostilities with England he enlisted in the Continental Army with the rank of captain, and was subsequently advanced to the rank of general. After the war he served in the Legislature of Virginia. He was wounded in a riot, in Baltimore, while taking the part of a friend, Alexander C. Hanson, an editor, and went to Cuba to regain his health. On the return voyage he stopped at the home of General Nathanael Greene's daughter, Mrs. Shaw, on Cumberland Island, where he died, in 1818, and was buried. It was through his marriage with his cousin, Matilda Lee, that he acquired Stratford House, the home in which his distinguished son was born; but the latter was the fruit of his marriage to Anne Hill Carter. He was the author of a work of much interest entitled. 'Memoirs of the War in the Southern Department of the United States,' edited by his sons, Henry and Robert E. Lee. On the death of Washington, he pronounced the famous eulogy in which he designated his illustrious chieftain as "first in war, first in peace, and first in the hearts of his countrymen."

LEE, HENRY, Jr., author, was born in Westmoreland County. Va., in 1787, a son of "Light-horse" Harry Lee of the Revolution, and an elder brother of General Robert E. Lee. Several books came from his pen. 'The Campaign of 1761 in the Carolinas' was written to repel an attack upon his father's soldiership in Judge William Johnson's 'Life and Correspondence of Major-general Nathanael Greene.' His other works were: 'Observations on the Writings of Thomas Jefferson' (New York, 1832, and Philadelphia, 1839), 'The Life of Arthur Lee,' containing his political and literary papers, in two volumes (Boston, 1829), and 'The Life of Napoleon' (New York, 1835). He contemplated an elaborate biography of the Emperor of the French, but death intervened and he completed only one volume, bringing the work down to the close of the first Italian campaign. He died in Paris in 1837.

LEE, IVY LEDBETTER, writer of magazine articles and publicity agent, was born in Cedartown, Ga., July 16, 1877, a son of Rev.

James Wideman Lee, D.D., and was educated at Emory College and at Princeton, taking post-graduate studies at Columbia and Harvard. He married Cornelia Bartlett, daughter of Horace R. Bigelow, of St. Paul. For some time he worked on the New York papers and in 1903 took charge of the publicity campaign of the Citizens' Union. Subsequently he became press representative of the Pennsylvania Railroad, of the anthracite coal operators and of other corporate interests, and in 1909 he accepted an agency for American interests in London. He is the author of numerous monographs and sketches contributed to the leading magazines and periodicals.

LEE, JAMES WIDEMAN, clergyman, author, editor, was born in Rockbridge, Ga., November 28, 1849. His father was Zachary J. Lee, and his mother Emily Harris Wideman. On graduating from Emory College, he was ordained to the ministry of the M.E. Church, South; and, in the fruitful years which followed, some of the most important pastorates in the gift of his denomination were filled by him, including St. John's Church in St. Louis, and Trinity Church in Atlanta. After occupying the pulpit of this last-named church for the second full term of years, he became in 1909 pastor of Park Street Methodist Church of Atlanta. He married, in 1875, Emma Eufaula Ledbetter. Besides editing, in four volumes, 'The Self-Interpreting Bible,' for which he obtained the illustrations on a special trip to Palestine, he also edited for some time *The Illustrated Southern Methodist Magazine*, published at St. Louis. As a writer of books he is noted. The list includes: 'The Making of a Man,' which has been translated into oriental tongues, 'Earthly Footsteps of the Man of Galilee,' with Bishop John H. Vincent; 'Henry W. Grady, Orator and Man' (New York and Chicago, Fleming H. Revell Company), 'History of Methodism,' 'Romance of Palestine,' and 'History of Jerusalem.' He also wrote the sketch of Henry W. Grady in 'The Library of Southern Literature.' On account of his eminent attainments, Dr. Lee has been frequently mentioned for a seat on the Episcopal Bench.

LEE, JESSE, clergyman, was born in Prince George County, Va., March 12, 1758, and died in Baltimore, Md., September 12, 1816. Entering the ministry of the Methodist Church, he devoted the greater part of his life to the work of organizing mission stations and of preaching the gospel along the frontier. Later he became an assistant to Bishop Asbury. For several years he was chaplain of the National House of Representatives, and in 1814 was given the same office in the United States Senate. His labors, especially in New England, earned for him the title of "the Apostle of Methodism." He published the first history which appeared in this country of the Methodist movement, an authority for years upon the subject. It was entitled 'A History of Methodism.' From the pen of his nephew, Leroy M. Lee, appeared his 'Life and Times' (Richmond, 1848).

LEE, LEROY MADISON, clergyman, was born in Petersburg, Va., April 30, 1808, and died in Ashland, Va., April 20, 1882. He became an eminent Methodist divine, edited for many years, in Richmond, *The Christian Advocate*, and published 'The Life and Times of Jesse Lee,' 'Advice to a Young Convert,' and 'The Great Supper not Calvinistic.'

LEE, MARY ELIZABETH, author, was born in Charleston, S.C., of an old aristocratic family, and instructed by private tutors until reaching the age of ten, when she was sent to the best private schools. She wrote numerous sketches of rare interest and published, in 1883, her interesting 'Historical Tales for Youth.' Following her early death, which occurred in 1849, at the age of thirty-six, a volume of her poems was edited by S. Gilman, D.D. Her writings evince the touch of genius, but are tinged with pathos.

LEE, RICHARD HENRY, an American patriot and statesman, was born at Stratford, Va., a son of Thomas Lee, president of the Virginia Council. He was one of the leaders in the revolt against British oppression, and wrote the famous resolution which he introduced in the Continental Congress, on June 7, 1776, declaring that "these United Colonies are, and of right ought to be, free and independent States; and that all political connection between them and the State of Great Britain is, and ought to be, totally dissolved." As an orator he possessed commanding gifts. 'The Memoirs of Richard Henry Lee,' in two volumes (Philadelphia, 1825), edited by his grandson, form an important contribution to the literature of the early life of the nation. It contains some of his most important letters and speeches.

LEE, RICHARD HENRY, Jr., author, was born in Westmoreland County, Va., in 1802, and was the grandson of the distinguished patriot of the same name. Besides writing 'Memoirs of the Life of Richard Henry Lee,' in two volumes (Philadelphia, 1825), he wrote also 'The Life of Arthur Lee,' in two volumes (Boston, 1829), and 'The Life of Harriet Preble' (New York, 1856). His works form interesting contributions to the literature of one of the most noted of American families. He died in 1865.

LEE, ROBERT EDWARD. See Biographical and Critical Sketch, Vol. VII, page 3145.

LEE, ROBERT EDWARD, Jr. Planter. He was born in Arlington, Va., October 27, 1843, the son of General Robert E. Lee, commander of the Army of Northern Virginia, and Mary Custis Lee. He was educated at Charlottesville, and married, March 28, 1894, Juliet Carter. He served in the Confederate Army from 1862 to 1865. After the war he chose the life of a planter; and at leisure intervals wrote 'Recollections and Letters of General Robert E. Lee' (New York, Doubleday, Page and Company, 1904), which is one of the most intimate and important works bearing upon the career of the illustrious soldier. He resides in West Point, Va.

LEE, SAMUEL PHILLIPS, Naval officer, was the grandson of Richard Henry Lee, of the Revolution, and was born in Fairfax County, Va., February 13, 1812, educated at Annapolis, entered the United States Navy, and attained the rank of rear-admiral. During the Civil War he rendered gallant service to the Union, especially in charge of the Mississippi squadron at the time of Hood's advance upon Nashville, Tenn. Before his retirement, in 1873, he was in active command of the North Atlantic Fleet. He published "The Cruise of the Dolphin" in the 'Reports of the United States Naval Department' (Washington, 1854).

LEE, STEPHEN DILL, soldier and educator, was born in Charleston, S.C., September 22, 1833. After graduating at West Point, he served with distinction in the United States Army until the outbreak of the Civil War, when he resigned his commission to enter the Confederate service, in which he attained the rank of lieutenant-general, and won a record for soldiership which few surpassed. For many years he was president of the Agricultural and Mechanical College of Mississippi. President McKinley appointed him commissioner of the National Park at Vicksburg; and, on the death of General John B. Gordon, he was elected commander-in-chief of the United Confederate Veterans. Besides a chapter on "The South Since the War," in the 'Confederate Military History' (Atlanta, Ga., The Confederate Publishing Company, 1899), he wrote numerous papers on educational and historical subjects. Tulane University gave him the degree of LL.D. General Lee died at his home in Columbus, Miss., in 1908.

LEE, SUSAN PENDLETON, Mrs. [Va.]. She wrote a 'Life of General William N. Pendleton' and a 'History of the United States' (1896, revised 1900).

LEES, J. T. Little is known of this author except that in 1831 he published at Wheeling, in what was then the State of Virginia, a work entitled: 'The Musings of Carol, containing an Essay on Liberty; the Desperado, a Tale of the Ocean; and Other Original Poems.'

LEFEVRE, ARTHUR, educator and editor, was born in Baltimore, Md., June 4, 1863, and educated at Baltimore City College and the University of Virginia. Besides numerous contributions to educational journals, he has published a text-book on Algebra. He resides in Dallas, Tex., where he owns and edits the *Texas School Journal*.

LEFEVRE, GEORGE, zoölogist and educator, was born in Baltimore, Md., September 16, 1869. He was educated in the public schools of Baltimore and at Johns Hopkins (Ph.D.), and since 1899 he has been professor of zoölogy and curator of the Zoölogical Museum of the University of Missouri.

LEGARÉ, HUGH SWINTON. See Biographical and Critical Sketch, Vol. VII, page 3169.

LEGARÉ, JAMES MATTHEW. See Biographical and Critical Sketch, Vol. VII, page 3191.

LEHMAN, E. A., Miss. Poet. [N.C.]. She published a volume of 'Poems' (New York, The Grafton Press, 1904).

LEIGH, BENJAMIN WATKINS. See Biographical and Critical Sketch, Vol. VII, page 3205.

LEIGH, FRANCES BUTLER, author, was born in Philadelphia. Her father was Pierce Butler, a Georgian planter, and her mother the noted English actress, Frances Anne Kemble. When her parents separated in 1849, she remained with her father; but in 1871 married an English clergyman, the Rev. John Wentworth Leigh, and afterward made her residence in England, where she published 'Ten Years on a Georgia Plantation Since the War' (1883), an authoritative work on social and economic conditions among the coast negroes.

LEIGH, WILLIAM, Jr., educator, was born in Halifax County, Va., July 12, 1883, and was educated at the University of Virginia. While an undergraduate he was editor-in-chief of the *University Magazine* and evinced literary gifts of high order. Since graduation he has engaged in teaching. The sketch of William Byrd in 'The Library of Southern Literature' is from his pen.

LEIGHTON, WILLIAM, poet, was born in Cambridge, Mass., June 22, 1833. After graduation from Harvard he settled in Wheeling, W.Va., and engaged in the manufacture of glass. At leisure intervals he published 'Godwin,' a tragedy (1876), "Change, the Whisper of the Sphinx," a philosophical poem (1878), 'Shakespeare,' a sketch (1879), 'Shakespeare's Dream, and Other Poems' (1881), "The Subjection of Hamlet," an essay (1882), and "The Price of the Present Paid by the Past," a poem (1883).

LEMLY, HENRY ROWAN, soldier and writer, was born in North Carolina, January 12, 1851. He was educated at West Point, attained the rank of captain and was retired at his own request after thirty years of service. Besides numerous magazine articles, he translated 'Upton's Infantry Regulations' into Spanish, and numerous Spanish works into English.

LEONARD, MARY FINLEY. Author. , She was born in Philadelphia, Pa., January 11, 1862, the daughter of Lafayette and Elizabeth Finley Leonard. In early childhood she removed with her parents to Louisville, Ky., where she received her education in private schools. Besides contributing many short stories to the magazines, she has published the following works of fiction, all of which are pervaded by an atmosphere of Southern life: 'The Story of the Big Front Door,' 'Half a Dozen Thinking-Caps,' 'The Candle and the Cat,' 'The Spectacle Man,' 'Mr. Pat's Little Girl,' 'How the Two Ends Met,' 'The Pleasant Street Partnership,' 'It All Came True,' and 'On Hyacinth Hill.' Most of her writings have been for children and youth and have been published by Thomas Y. Crowell and Company, New York.

LEPOUZE, CONSTANT. Poet. He published in French 'Poésies Diverses' (1838), and translated some of the 'Odes of Horace.'

LESCARBOT, MARC. French lawyer and traveler. He wrote an erratic work of much interest entitled 'Histoire de la Nouvelle France' (1609).

LESLIE, FRANK, Mrs. Editor and publisher. She was born in New Orleans, La., in 1851. Her maiden name was Miriam Florence Foline, and her parentage was French Huguenot. She enjoyed superior educational advantages, and while still young married Frank Leslie, the famous New York publisher. On the death of her husband she succeeded to his business, which was somewhat involved, by reason of careless management; and such was her intelligent grasp of the commercial helm that she soon put the establishment upon a paying basis. Later, she leased the business to a syndicate and made an extended European tour. By special legislative act she took the name of Mrs. Frank Leslie, but, on retiring to private life, she became the Baroness de Bazus, having derived this title from her forebears. She was for many years both publisher and editor of *Frank Leslie's Magazine.* She resides in New York City.

LESTER, J. C. Author. [Tenn.]. Major Lester served in the Confederate Army, was one of the six original members of the parent chapter of the famous Ku Klux Klan, which arose in Tennessee during reconstruction, and wrote in collaboration with D. L. Wilson, 'The Ku Klux Klan: its Origin, Growth, and Disbandment,' with introduction and notes by Walter L. Fleming, Ph.D. (New York and Washington, The Neale Publishing Company, 1907).

LEQUEUX, H. D. Author. [S.C.]. He published a miscellaneous collection of both prose and verse entitled 'Palmetto Leaves' (1892, paper edition).

LE SUEUR, M. French explorer. He wrote an interesting 'Journal of a Voyage up the Mississippi' (1699).

LEVEQUE, JOSEPH MARK. Journalist. He was born in Louisiana, August 26, 1868, and was educated at Collegiate Institute, Baton Rouge, also at Vanderbilt University. He taught for some time in Texas and then entered journalism, becoming identified with the New York papers; but he afterward returned to Texas and later settled in New Orleans. He is editor and owner of *The Harlequin,* and is the author of two comic operas, which have proven quite popular: "The Swimming Girl" and "King Capital."

LE VERT, OCTAVIA WALTON. See Biographical and Critical Sketch, Vol. VII, page 3221.

LEVY, SAMUEL YATES. [Ga.]. He was born in 1827 and published 'The Italian Bride,' a drama.

LEWIS, ESTELLE ANNA BLANCHE ROBINSON, author, was born near Baltimore, Md., of Anglo-Spanish parentage, in 1824, and died in London, England, November 24, 1880. She began to write when a school-girl and at the age of twenty published 'Records of the Heart,' which contains some of her best minor verses (New York, 1844). While in Italy she wrote 'Helemah: or, the Fall of Montezuma' (New York, 1864), a tragedy which was widely admired; but her best dramatic effort was 'Sappho of Lesbos' (London, 1868), which reached seven editions. She also wrote 'The Child of the Sea, and Other Poems' (New York, 1848), 'The Myths of the Minstrel' (1852), 'Poems' (London, 1866), and 'The King's Stratagem,' a tragedy (1869). Edgar Allan Poe was her first patron, and Lamartine called her "the female Petrarch." She married Sidney D. Lewis of Brooklyn, N.Y.

LEWIS, JOHN. Poet. He lived in Virginia and published a work entitled: 'Flowers and Weeds of the Old Dominion' (Frankfort, Ky., 1857). It contains some contributions from his own pen, but is devoted mainly to the poetic effusions of three Virginia writers: Mrs. Jean Wood, Mrs. Littleford, and John Moncure Lewis. One of the same name but probably not the same person wrote 'Young Kate; or, the Rescue,' a tale of the Great Kenawha.

LEWIS, JUDD MORTIMER, poet, was born in Fulton, N.Y., September 13, 1867, but the inspirations of song which have brought him fame have come from the South. He is on the staff of the *Post,* in Houston, Texas, and contributes both prose and verse to the columns of that journal. He has published two volumes of verse: 'Sing the South' (1905), and 'Lilts o' Love' (1906). He married, September 24, 1894, Mary Bartley.

LEWIS, MARY, poet, was born in Augusta County, Va., in 1828, and died in Decatur, Ga., April 14, 1893. Her father was the Rev. Francis McFarland, D.D., and her mother, Mary Ann Bent. In 1849 she became the wife of Dr. William Wellington Lewis of Roanoke, Va. Mrs. Lewis was a woman of rare gifts and published a volume of verse entitled 'Heart Echoes' (Baltimore, 1868). Her daughter, Mrs. F. H. Gaines, is also gifted as a writer, and has done some excellent dialect work in both prose and verse.

LEWIS, MERIWETHER, explorer, was born near Charlottesville, Va., August 18, 1774, and died near Nashville, Tenn., October 8, 1809. Of an adventurous nature he was recommended by Jefferson to Congress for the command of an expedition across the continent and in association with Captain William Clark he undertook the perilous enterprise, traversing unexplored regions, from the confluence of the Missouri and Mississippi rivers to the mouth of the Columbia. By way of reward he was given large grants of land and made governor of the territory of Missouri. From materials which were furnished chiefly by him, Nicholas Biddle and Paul Allen wrote a memoir of the expedition in two volumes, to which Thomas Jefferson wrote the introductory memoir (Philadelphia, 1814). The work was subsequently enlarged, with additions by Alexander McVickar (New York, 1843). During one of his moods of depression the explorer took his own life, while en route to Washington.

LEWIS, WILLIAM TERRELL. Compiler. [Miss.]. He was born in 1811 and died in 1893. The author resided at Perryville, Miss. He published: 'The Genealogy of the Lewis Family in America' (Louisville, 1893).

LEWISOHN, LUDWIG, author and lecturer, was born in Berlin, Germany, May 30, 1882. At one time he was engaged in journalism in Charleston, S.C. He wrote 'The History of Literature in South Carolina,' a work which was serialized in the Charleston *News and Courier,* June-August, 1903, and 'The Broken Seal,' a novel (New York, B. W. Dodge and Company), besides numerous poems, stories and essays in current periodicals. The sketches of Washington Allston and of J. M. Legaré, in 'The Library of Southern Literature,' were written by Mr. Lewisohn. He resides in the city of New York.

LEY, JOHN C., clergyman and author, was born in 1822. Entering the ministry of the M.E. Church, South, he located in Florida and assisted in the establishment of Methodism in the Peninsula State. In his 'Reminiscences of Fifty Years' he interestingly records his personal observations and experiences. He died in Jacksonville, Fla., August 19, 1907, at the age of eighty-five.

LEYBURN, JOHN, clergyman, was born in Lexington, Va., April 25, 1814. On completing his educational equipment, he entered the Presbyterian ministry and for twenty years was pastor of a church in Baltimore, Md. He also edited at one time *The Presbyterian,* a religious paper published in Philadelphia. His writings include: 'The Soldier of the Cross' (New York and Edinburgh, 1853), 'Hints to Young Men from the Parable of the Prodigal Son,' and 'Lectures on 'he Journeyings of the Children of Israel,' illustrated from his travels. Hampden-Sidney gave him the degree of D.D.

LIEBER, FRANCIS, educator, was born in Berlin, Germany, March 4, 1800, and died in New York City, October 2, 1872. He served in the Prussian Army and took part in the Greek Revolution, enjoyed the advantages of the best German universities, and became one of the foremost of the world's scholars. For more than twenty years he was professor of political economy in the University of South Carolina, after which he was called to the same chair in Columbia College, New York. While in the South he produced his most important works: 'A Manual of Political Ethics,' in two volumes (Boston, 1838), 'Legal and Political Hermaneutics' (1839), 'Great Events Described by Great Historians' (1847), 'The West, and Other Poems' (1848), and 'Civil Liberty and Self-Government,' in two volumes (Philadelphia, 1852). He also wrote 'Reminiscences of Niebuhr,' 'Laws of Property,' 'The Origin and Development of the First Constituents of Civilization,' made numerous translations and edited nine volumes of the 'Encyclopædia Americana.' Lieber's 'Miscellaneous Writings' were published in two volumes (Philadelphia, 1880), and his correspondence was edited by Thomas S. Perry (Boston, 1882). He was a member of numerous learned societies on both sides of the water.

LIÉS, EUGENE. Poet. [La.]. He published 'The Preludes,' a collection of poems (1846).

LINCECUM, GIDEON, naturalist, was born in Hancock County, Ga., April 22, 1793, and died in Brenham, Tex., November 28, 1874. He became an eminent physician, though largely self-educated; was also at one time county judge in Lowndas County, Miss., but his most successful work was in the realm of the natural sciences. He corresponded with men of international note like Darwin and Humboldt; was an intimate friend of Agassiz; made frequent contributions to scientific journals; collected many rare specimens which he gave to museums and institutes, and belonged to numerous learned societies. He left several manuscripts, including a work on 'The Traditions of the Choctaw Indians,' among whom he lived at one time; a 'Medical History of the Southern States, and an autobiography, the last being still in the possession of his daughter. He specialized for fourteen years in the study of ants.

LINCOLN, ABRAHAM. President of the United States from 1861 to 1865. Though he cannot be strictly classified among the makers of Southern literature, he was nevertheless born in Hardin County, Ky., February 12, 1809, of Southern parentage. For more complete information in regard to Mr. Lincoln, his political addresses, his state papers, etc., consult the standard biographies and encyclopædias.

LINCOLN, REXFORD J. Author. [La.]. He wrote 'A Tale of Pagan Rome' (New Orleans, 1900).

LIND, G. DALLAS. Physician. [Mo.]. He published 'The Races of Man,' 'The Religions of the World,' 'Great Educators,' 'Primæval Man,' and 'The Human Body.'

LINDESAY, M. BATTERHAM. Poet. [N.C.] The author of a volume of verse entitled 'The First Shearing' (Richmond, Va., Whittet and Shepperson, 1904).

LINDSAY, JOHN SUMMERFIELD, Protestant Episcopal clergyman, was born of Scotch lineage in Williamsburg, Va., March 19, 1842. For several years he was rector of a church at Warrenton, Va., after which he was called to Georgetown, D.C. In 1887 he declined the bishopric of Easton, Md., and for twenty years past he has been rector of St. Paul's Church in Boston. He has published 'St. John's Church,' 'Hamilton Parish,' and 'The True American Citizen,' besides numerous sermons and review articles. The University of the South gave him the degree of LL.D.

LINDSAY, MARGARET ISABELLA. Author. [Va.]. She published 'The Lindsays of America' (1889).

LINDSEY, BENJAMIN BARR, jurist and reformer, was born in Jackson, Madison County, Tenn., November 25, 1869. His father was Landy T. Lindsey, and his mother, Letitia Ann Barr. On completing his education he engaged successfully in the practice of law and in 1900 became County Court judge and judge of the Juvenile Court of Denver, Colo. In connection with the reform movement to rescue youthful offenders, he has earned an international reputation. Moreover, on account of the persistent and effective warfare which he has waged against crime in general at this gateway to the Rocky Mountain region, his life has been repeatedly threatened. Both openly and furtively the most painstaking efforts have been made to blacken his reputation and to weaken his power. Even traps have been set to ensnare him unawares. But no amount of intimidation has caused him for one moment to relinquish his stubborn fight. Besides various pamphlets and papers relating to the subject of crime, not only in its legal but also in its psychological and sociological aspects, he has published 'The Problem of the Children' (1904) and 'The Beast and the Jungle' (1909), both of which deal powerfully with the evils which menace American childhood.

LINDSEY, MARIA, music teacher and writer, was born on a farm near Frankfort, Ky., February 18, 1863. At leisure moments she has exercised her literary gifts by writing some very delightful stories, one of which, "The Lions at Pleasureville," a story of woman's club life, which appeared in *Leslie's Monthly* for April, 1905, was widely copied. Miss Lindsey resides in Frankfort, Ky.

LINDSLEY, JOHN BERRIEN, college chancellor, clergyman, and editor, was born in Princeton, N.J., October 24, 1822, and died in Nashville, Tenn., December 7, 1897. After graduating from the University of Nashville, he studied theology and was ordained to the Presbyterian ministry, but most of his life was devoted to educational work. For twenty years he was chancellor of the University of Nashville, and he also occupied the chair of chemistry in the same institution. Later he was professor of materia medica in the Tennessee College of Pharmacy. Besides editing the Nashville *Journal of Medicine and Surgery,* he published 'Our Ruin; Its Causes, and Its Cure' (1868), and 'The Military Annals of Tennessee,' giving a review of military operations during the Civil War, with regimental histories and memorial rolls compiled from original and official sources (Nashville, J. M. Lindsley and Company, 1886; electroplated and printed by the M.E. Publishing House, South), a work of great value. He married, February 9, 1857, Sally McGavock. He held the degree of D.D.

LINDSLEY, PHILIP, clergyman, educator and writer, was born near Morristown, N.J., December 21, 1786, and died in Nashville, Tenn., May 25, 1855. He was the son of Isaac and Phoebe Lindsley. For several years he was president of the University of Nashville. 'The Works of Philip Lindsley,' in three volumes (Philadelphia, J. B. Lippincott and Company), constitute his literary memorials. They are divided: Vol. I, 'Educational Discourses'; Vol. II, 'Religious Discourses'; Vol. III, 'Miscellaneous Discourses and Essays.' He is the subject of an extended notice in Sprague's 'Annals of the American Pulpit,' from which it appears that he wielded an immense influence upon the cause of education not only in Tennessee but throughout the whole Southwest.

LINDSLEY, PHILIP, lawyer and author, was born in Nashville, Tenn., August 2, 1842. His father was N. L. Lindsley and his mother, Julia Stevens. He married, April 28, 1869, Louisa G. Dickinson, the only sister of the present Secretary of War, J. M. Dickinson. He possesses a rich fund of anecdote and a keen sense of humor, and besides occasional poems and sketches, has published 'The Humor of the Court-room' (1899), a work of rare charm, which the author has cast in the mold of the drama and which has evoked the most enthusiastic praise of critics, North and South; 'The History of Greater Dallas' (1909), and 'The Circuit Judge' (1909).

LINK, SAMUEL ALBERT. Educator. He was born near Lebanon, Tenn., July 10, 1848, the son of William B. and Amanda Randolph Link, and was educated at Ewing College, in Illinois, also at the University of Nashville. He read law, but never practiced. He married, in 1875, Sallie A. Deboe. He engaged in the profession of teaching and pursued this line of work for several years with distinguished success, but latterly has given much of his time to literary work. Among his writings may be mentioned: a 'Sketch of Paul Havne' (Nashville, Southern Methodist Publishing House), 'Pioneers of Southern Literature,' in two volumes (*ibid.*), and numerous monographs of Southern poets and eminent Americans. The sketch of Will T. Hale in 'The Library of Southern Literature' is also from his pen. He is a frequent contributor to the *Methodist Quarterly* and to the *Christian Advocate.* He resides in Thomasville, Tenn.

LINN, E. A. [Mo.]. In association with N. Sargent, he wrote a 'Life of Lewis Fields Lind' (1857).

LINN, JOHN F., author, was born in Ireland in 1798 and died in Texas in 1885. He published a volume of personal reminiscences entitled: 'Fifty Years in Texas.'

LINN, LEWIS FIELDS, United States Senator, was born near Louisville, Ky., November 5, 1795, and died at Sainte Genevieve, Mo., October 3, 1843. He studied medicine and settled for practice in Missouri, achieving very great distinction, but he also took an interest in public affairs and, on the death of Alexander Buchner, was appointed to fill the unexpired term in the United States Senate and was subsequently twice re-commissioned by the State Legislature to a seat in this high forum. Some of his speeches have been preserved in the 'Debates of Congress.'

LIPSCOMB, ABNER SMITH, jurist, was born near Abbeville, S.C., February 10, 1789, and died near Austin, Texas, December 3, 1857. He studied law under John C. Calhoun and achieved success at the Bar, becoming chief justice of the Supreme Court of Alabama. Afterward he settled in Texas, where he became Secretary of State under President Lamar, and later associate justice of the Supreme Court. His decisions are published in Minor's, Stewart's and Stewart and Porter's 'Alabama Reports,' and in the first seventeen volumes of the 'Texas Reports.'

LIPSCOMB, ANDREW ADGATE. Shakespearean scholar and educator. He was born in Georgetown, D.C., September 6, 1816. He enjoyed the best educational advantages, and entered the ministry of the Methodist Episcopal Church; but, after filling numerous important pastorates, he left the itinerant ranks on account of impaired health. At one time he was president of Tuskeegee Female College and afterward chancellor of the University of Georgia. He was a man of great eloquence and of profound learning, an authority on Shakespeare, and a writer of excellent verse, one of his best poems being "Chastened Grief," which was written on the death of his son, Professor F. A. Lipscomb. In personal appearance Dr. Lipscomb was a man of unusual attractiveness, his massive brow, his long curly hair and his dignified demeanor making him an object of universal interest. Dr. Lipscomb received both the D.D. and the LL.D. degrees. He died at Athens, Ga., in 1890.

LIPSCOMB, DABNEY, educator, was born in Columbus, Miss., March 6, 1859, a son of Dr. W. L. Lipscomb, an eminent and influential physician. After completing his studies at the University of Mississippi, he taught for three years in the public schools and for thirteen years in the State Agricultural and Military College. Still later he became professor of English in the University of Mississippi. At present he ably fills the chair of civics and economics in the Mississippi Industrial Institute. He has traveled abroad, received frequent honors at the hands of his colleagues in state and national assemblies, and written numerous historical and educational papers. Especially notable have been the articles contributed by him to the publications of the Mississippi Historical Society. The sketch of T. A. S. Adams in 'The Library of Southern Literature' is from Professor Lipscomb's pen. He has also published several addresses. He resides in Columbus, Miss.

LITSEY, EDWIN CARLILE, one of the rising novelists of the State of Kentucky, was born at Beechland, Ky., June 3, 1874. Besides 'The Princess of Gramfalon,' in which he first caught the ear of the public, he has written 'The Love Story of Abner Stone' (New York, A. S. Barnes and Company, 1906), and 'The Race of the Swift' (Boston, Little, Brown and Company, 1908). He has also published a volume of essays. Since seventeen he has been in the banking business. His residence is in Lebanon, Ky.

LITTELL, WILLIAM, lawyer, was born in New Jersey in 1780 and died in Frankfort, Ky., in 1825. He attained eminence at the Bar of Kentucky, and published an entertaining volume entitled 'Festoons of

Fancy' (1820), which contains poems and essays, both humorous and sentimental. He also published 'The Statute Law of Kentucky,' in five volumes (1808-1819), a 'Digest,' in two volumes (1822), 'Reports of Cases at Common Law and in Chancery, Decided by the Court of Appeals of Kentucky,' in four volumes (1822-1824), and 'Selected Cases' (1825).

"LITTLE, FRANCES." See Mrs. Frances Caldwell McCauley.

LITTLE, JOHN BUCKNER. Author. [Ala.]. He wrote a 'History of Butler County' (1885), and a 'History of Marengo County' (1887).

LITTLE, LUCIUS P. Author. [Ky.]. He wrote an interesting work entitled 'Times and Contemporaries of Ben Hardin' (1887)

LITTLEPAGE, LEWIS, diplomat, was born in Hanover County, Va., December 19, 1762, and died in Fredericksburg, Va., July 19, 1802. For many years he lived abroad and under Stanislaus, King of Poland, was Ambassador to Russia. Some of his writings have been published.

LITTLETON, JESSE TALBOT, educator, was born in Portsmouth, Va., October 27, 1856. On completing his academic studies he devoted himself to teaching. He holds at present the chair of modern languages in Southern University at Greensboro, Ala. Besides numerous contributions to current periodicals, including the *Quarterly Review* published at Nashville, Tenn., he wrote in excellent verse "The Story of Captain Smith and Pocahontas" (1907). He married, December 26, 1882, Lulie Rosser.

LIVERMORE, SAMUEL, lawyer, was born in 1786, the place of his birth unknown, and died in New Orleans, La., in 1833. He graduated from Harvard, studied law, and achieved high professional eminence at the Bar of New Orleans, publishing 'A Treatise on the Law of Principal and Agent and of Sales by Auction,' two volumes (Baltimore, 1818), and 'Dissertations on the Questions Which Arise from the Contrariety of the Positive Laws of Different States and Nations' (New Orleans, 1828).

LIVINGSTON, EDWARD, lawyer, was a son of Robert R. Livingston, the distinguished diplomat and statesman. For many years of his life he practiced law in New Orleans, where he published a 'System of Penal Law for the State of Louisiana' (New Orleans, 1825), besides numerous other legal works. His career was full of dramatic interest. Mr. Livingston's second wife was Louise D'Avezac, a New Orleans lady of rare gifts.

LLOYD, ANNIE CREIGHT, Mrs. Author. [Ala.]. She wrote several novels, among them, 'Garnet,' 'Hagar,' and 'Pearl.'

LLOYD, FRANCIS BARTOW. Lawyer and journalist. [Ala.]. Under the pen-name of "Rufus Saunders, the Sage of Rocky Creek," he published some very characteristic sketches of country life, which were edited and published in book form by his widow (1898).

LLOYD, WILLA D. Poet. [Texas]. She was born in 1866, and wrote 'Christmas Chimes, and Other Poems.'

LOCHRANE, OSBORNE AUGUSTUS, jurist, was born in Middleton, Ireland, August 22, 1829, and died in Atlanta, Ga., June 17, 1887. He was a youth of seventeen when he crossed the Atlantic, and, studying law under difficulties, he arose steadily to the front, becoming one of the ablest practitioners at the Bar. For several years he occupied the Superior Court Bench, and in 1871 was appointed chief justice of the Supreme

Court of Georgia. He possessed in an eminent degree the gift of Irish eloquence, and some of his flashes of oratory have been perserved in Knight's 'Famous Georgians.

LODGE, LEE DAVIS. Educator. He was born in Montgomery County, Md., November 24, 1865, a son of the Rev. James L. and Alice Virginia Warfield Lodge. He enjoyed superior educational advantages and was twice married. He engaged in educational work, and in 1899 became president of Limestone College, at Gaffney, S.C. Besides numerous essays and reviews, he has written an interesting 'Study in Corneille' (Baltimore, John Murphy Company) and other works. Columbian University gave him the degree of Ph.D.

LOEWENSTEIN, LOUIS J. Writer. [La.]. He published a 'History of the St. Louis Cathedral' (New Orleans, 1882).

LOFTON, GEORGE A. Baptist clergyman. [Tenn.]. He published an entertaining series of 'Character Sketches,' besides tracts and sermons.

LOGAN, CORNELIUS AMBROSIUS, dramatist, was born in Baltimore, Md., May 4, 1806, and died on the Ohio River, near Wheeling, W.Va., February 23, 1853. While an actor by profession, he wrote a number of successful plays, among them "Yankee Land" (1834), "The Wag of Maine" (1835), "The Wool Dealer," "Removing the Deposits," "Astarte," "A Hundred Years Hence," and "Chloroform." He also wrote stories and sketches, besides a number of poems.

LOGAN, GEORGE, physician, was born in Charleston, S.C., January 4, 1778, and died in New Orleans, La., February 13, 1861. He received his medical degree from the University of Pennsylvania and for more than fifty years practiced his profession in Charleston. He published a popular work on 'The Diseases of Children.'

LOGAN, JOHN HENRY, physician and educator, was born in Abbeville District, S.C., November 5, 1822, and died in Atlanta, Ga., March 28, 1885. For several years he taught and practiced at Abbeville, but when the war began he enlisted in a Confederate regiment and served as a surgeon. After the war he settled for a time in Alabama, but eventually removed to Atlanta, Ga., where he became a professor in the Atlanta Medical College. He wrote a 'History of the Upper Country of South Carolina,' only the first volume of which was completed (Charleston, 1859), and 'The Students' Manual of Chemico-Physics' (Atlanta, 1879).

LOGAN, JOHN RANDOLPH, Baptist clergyman of North Carolina, was born in 1811 and died in 1884. He published an interesting historical account entitled 'The Broad River and King's Mountain Association from 1800 to 1882' (1887).

LOGAN, MARGARET ANN, poet, was born in Charleston, S.C., just before the war but she became a resident of Vicksburg, Miss. In addition to writing for the papers, she published a volume of verse entitled: 'Sweet Alyssum.'

LOGAN, THOMAS MULDROP, physician, was born in Charleston, S.C., January 31, 1808, received his medical diploma from the Charleston Medical College, and settled in California for the practice of his profession. Later he gave his attention largely to meteorological lines of investigation and published 'The Topography of California,' 'The Climate of California,' and 'Meteorological Observations at Sacramento,' besides contributing to the 'Transactions of the American Medical Association.'

LOMAX, ELIZABETH WINTER PAYNE, writer, was born in Fauquier County, Va., January 17, 1854. Besides numerous short stories and sketches for magazines and articles for newspapers, Mrs. Lomax has published 'A Consul to China.' The sketch of Julia Magruder in 'The Library of Southern Literature' is also from her pen. She married, February 20, 1873, Lindsay L. Lomax, a major-general in the Army of Northern Virginia. Her home is at Gettysburg, Pa.

LOMAX, JOHN AVERY, educator and writer, was born in Goodman, Miss., September 23, 1872. For several years he has occupied the chair of English in the Agricultural and Military College of Texas. Besides numerous magazine articles, he has written some excellent verse and has just completed a work which is now in press entitled 'The Songs of the Cowboys.' He wrote for 'The Library of Southern Literature' the sketch of William A. Chittenden.

LOMAX, JOHN TAYLOE, jurist, was born at Port Tobacco, Va., in 1781, and died in Fredericksburg, Va., October 10, 1862. For some time he was a professor in the law school of the University of Virginia, and afterward for many years an occupant of the Supreme Bench of the State. He published a 'Digest of the Laws Respecting Real Property Generally Adopted and in Use in the United States,' in three volumes (Philadelphia, 1839), and a 'Treatise on the Law of Executors and Administrators Generally in Use in the United States,' in two volumes (Richmond, 1856).

LOMAX, JUDITH, poet, was born in Virginia, and, in 1813, published a volume entitled: 'The Notes of an American Lyre' (Richmond). It is crude and simple, but the author disclaims any ambitious pretentions.

LONG, ARMISTEAD LINDSAY, soldier, was born in Campbell County, Va., September 23, 1827, graduated from West Point, and entered the United States Army; but, at the outbreak of hostilities in 1861, he resigned his commission, enlisted in the Confederate Army, was for some time on the staff of General Lee, and in 1863 became brigadier-general, participating in most of the Virginia campaigns. He published an authoritative volume dealing chiefly with the military record of the South's great commander, entitled 'Memoirs of Robert E. Lee' (New York, 1886).

LONG, CHARLES CHAILLÉ, soldier and lawyer, was born in Princess Anne, Md., July 2, 1842. After serving with the rank of captain in the Union Army during the Civil War, he was appointed lieutenant-colonel in the Egyptian Army in 1869, and later became chief of staff to the commander-in-chief, General Gordon. For several years he endured the brunt of the African campaigns and encountered some of the most thrilling adventures. On returning to America he studied law and went back to Egypt to practice in the international courts; but in 1882 he settled in Paris. He published several volumes of unique interest, among them, 'Central Africa: Naked Truths of Naked People' (New York, Harper and Brothers, 1876), and 'The Three Prophets: Chinese Gordon, the Mahdi, and Aribi Pasha' (New York, D. Appleton and Company.).

LONG, CHARLES MASSIE. Educator. Both a student and a teacher of history, Dr. Long has made an interesting contribution to the literature of the Old Dominion, in a work entitled 'Virginia County Names' (New York and Washington, The Neale Publishing Company, 1908).

LONG, CRAWFORD W., physician and surgeon, the discoverer of anæsthesia, was born in Danielsville, Ga., November 1, 1815, and died at Athens, Ga., June 10, 1878. After graduation from Franklin College, now the University of Georgia, he continued his studies in the medical department of the University of Pennsylvania and then located in Jefferson, Ga., for the practice of his profession. It was in this little town of North Georgia that in making certain laboratory experiments he discovered the peculiar effects of sulphuric ether and performed, without pain, the first surgical operation known to the scientific world, while the patient was in a state of unconsciousness produced by inhaling the gas. Investigation has fully established the claims of the Georgia physician. He anticipated Wells by two years and eight months, and Morton by not less than four years. The letters and papers of Dr. Long bearing upon his discovery are among the most important contributions to the literature of medicine.

LONG, ELLEN CALL, Mrs. Author. She was born in Tallahassee, Fla., September 9, 1825, and was the daughter of Governor Richard Keith Call. One of the most gifted women of the State, she produced several books: 'Florida Breezes,' 'Jackson and Packingham,' 'Silk Culture in Florida,' and a number of historical papers and pamphlets. She died at Tallahassee, December 18, 1905. Among her unpublished manuscripts was a complete 'History of Florida.'

LONGSTREET, AUGUSTUS BALDWIN. See Biographical and Critical Sketch, Vol. VII, page 3241.

LONGSTREET, HELEN DORTCH. Author and journalist. She is a daughter of the late Colonel James S. Dortch, a prominent member of the Georgia Bar, and was born in Franklin County, Ga., on a plantation which was ceded to one of her ancestors for service in the American Revolution. She was for several years prominent in Georgia journalism, and also assistant State Librarian under Captain John Milledge. She married, September 8, 1897, Lieutenant-general James Longstreet, and wrote 'Lee and Longstreet at High Tide' (1904), a volume in which she reviews the charge against her illustrious husband of disobedience to Lee's orders at Gettysburg; also an historical novel entitled 'The Shadows of Our Skies' (1909), and a sketch entitled "My Old Black Mammy." She has held the office of postmistress at Gainesville, Ga., for several years.

LONGSTREET, JAMES, commander of the First Corps of the Army of Northern Virginia, was born in Edgefield, S.C., January 8, 1821, a son of James Longstreet, planter, and a nephew of Judge Augustus B. Longstreet, the author of 'Georgia Scenes.' His paternal grandfather, William Longstreet, anticipated Fulton in applying steam to navigation but failed to procure a patent. The proof of this priority of invention is recorded in the Georgia archives. After graduating from West Point in the class of 1842, James Longstreet won his first military spurs in the Mexican War, being wounded in the assault upon Chapultepec. He entered the Confederate service with the rank of brigadier-general, and rose to the rank of lieutenant-general, participating in some of the most decisive engagements of the war and sustaining severe wounds in the battle of the Wilderness from the accidental fire of his own men. On the cessation of hostilities he became a Republican in politics, believing that the welfare of the South could be best subserved by giving support to the dominant party in politics. His life was saddened by the constant fire of criticism to which he was exposed at the hands of his own people for taking this course, and by the charge which was preferred against him some time after General Lee's death of having disobeyed orders at the battle of Gettysburg. But he lived to witness a change in the tide of popular opposition. He was at one time Surveyor of the port at New Orleans; afterward Minister to Turkey; and later United States Marshal for the Northern District of Georgia. He was twice married; first, March 8, 1848, to Marie Louise Garland, and, second, September 8, 1897, to Helen Dortch. The eventide of his life was spent in writing his splendid work: 'From Manassas to Appomattox' (Philadelphia, J. B. Lippincott Company). He died in Gainesville, Ga., January 2, 1904, while holding the office of postmaster. General Longstreet bore the soubriquet of "Lee's Old War Horse."

LOONEY, LOUISA PRESTON. Author. She was born in Memphis, Tenn., a daughter of Robert F. and Louisa M. Looney. Her education was obtained in the schools of Memphis and was supplemented by extensive travel. Besides numerous magazine articles, she has written 'Tennessee Sketches' (Chicago, A. C. McClurg), a series of delightful pen pictures of life in Tennessee. She was for three years president of the Woman's Club of Memphis.

LORD, ALICE, Mrs. Writer. [Md.]. She published a work entitled 'The Days of Lamb and Coleridge' (1894).

LORD, WILLIAM WILBERFORCE, Protestant Episcopal clergyman, was born in the State of New York in 1819, but was for many years rector of a church at Vicksburg, Miss., and served in the Confederate Army as chaplain. He published a volume of verse entitled 'Poems' (1845), which was praised by Wordsworth and criticized by Poe. He also wrote 'Christ in Hades' (1851), and 'André, a Tragedy' (1856).

LORIMER, GEORGE CLAUD, clergyman, was born in Edinburgh, Scotland, in 1838, and died in the city of New York in 1904, but most of his earlier life was spent in the South. He was educated at Georgetown College, in Kentucky, and occupied several important pastorates in the Blue Grass State, before being called to the North. He filled the leading Baptist pulpits of Chicago, Boston, and New York. Besides editing 'The People's Bible History Prepared in the Light of Recent Investigations,' he published 'Under the Evergreens,' 'The Great Conflict,' 'Studies in Social Life,' 'The Argument for Christianity,' and 'Messages of To-day for the Men of To-morrow.' Georgetown College gave him the degree of LL.D.

LORIMER, GEORGE HORACE, editor and author, was born in Louisville, Ky., October 6, 1868. His father was the Rev. George C. Lorimer, D.D., the distinguished Baptist divine, and his mother, Belle Burford. He enjoyed the finest educational advantages, completing his studies at Yale. In 1893 he married Alma Viola, daughter of Judge Alfred Ennis, of Chicago. For several years he has been the successful and popular editor-in-chief of the *Saturday Evening Post*. His published works include: 'Letters from a Self-made Merchant to His Son' (Boston, Small, Maynard and Company), 'Old Gorgon Graham' (New York, Doubleday, Page and Company), 'Jack Spurlock—Prodigal' (*ibid.*), and 'The False Gods' (New York, D. Appleton and Company). His residence is at Wyncote, Pa.

LOUGHBOROUGH, MARY WEBSTER, Mrs. Writer. [Ark.]. She was born in 1836 and died in 1887. She wrote an interesting personal narrative of war time adventure entitled 'My Cave Life in Vicksburg' (1864), and numerous stories, among them, one entitled "For Better, for Worse."

LOVEJOY, WILLIAM P. Methodist Episcopal clergyman. [Ga.]. He wrote 'The Mission of the Church' (1900).

LOVEMAN, ROBERT. He was born in Cleveland, Ohio, April 11, 1864, the son of David R. and Esther Black Loveman. His academic education was obtained at Dalton, Ga., and his collegiate education at the University of Alabama. Extensive travel abroad has given him a wide acquaintance with men. His poems, which are mostly cast in diminutive molds, are gems of verse, familiar to the readers of the best magazines. His tuneful wares have been gathered into book form from time to time under the following titles: 'Poems' (three separate volumes, 1889, 1889, 1897), 'A Book of Verses' (Philadelphia, J. B. Lippincott Company), 'The Gates of Silence, With Interludes of Song' (New York, G. P. Putnam's Sons), 'Songs From a Georgia Garden,' and 'Echoes From the Gates of Silence' (Philadelphia, J. B. Lippincott Company). He resides in Dalton, Ga.

LOVETT, HOWARD MERIWEATHER, Mrs. Author. [Ga.]. She wrote a number of delightful stories for children, some of which are soon to be published in a volume, entitled 'Grandmother Stories from the Land of Used-to-Be.' She resides at Girard, Ga.

LOWE, JOHN, poet, was born near New Galloway, Scotland, in 1750, and died in Culpeper County, Va., in 1798. For many years he was a tutor in the family of George Washington and subsequently opened a boarding-school at Fredericksburg, Va. He possessed no little talent for verse making. His poetical compositions were published in Cromek's 'Remains of Nithesdale and Galloway,' with a memoir by the Rev. Mr. Gillespie. Some few fragments may also be found in James Grant Wilson's 'Poets and Poetry of Scotland' (New York, 1876).

LOWNDES, RAWLINS, statesman, was born in the British West Indies in 1722 and died in Charleston, S.C., in 1800. While an associate judge, under appointment from the Crown, he delivered the majority opinion of the Bench in oposition to the chief justice, favoring the legality of public proceedings without the employment of stamped paper. During the Revolution he was president of the province and on the fall of Charleston into the hands of the British, was taken prisoner. He opposed the adoption of the Federal Constitution because it centralized too much power in the Federal Government; and, in one of his impassioned outbursts he declared: "I wish for no other epitaph than this: 'Here lies one who opposed the Federal Constitution, holding it to be fatal to the liberties of his country.'" He published nothing except an occasional speech or letter addressed to the public.

LOWNDES, WILLIAM JONES, statesman, was born in Charleston, S.C., February 7, 1782, and died at sea, November 22, 1822. On completing his education, he spent some time in European travel, partly for mental culture and partly to improve his health, which was none too robust. He was a man of extraordinary endowment, and nothing save his early death prevented him from plucking the very highest laurels of statesmanship. From 1811 to 1822 he served in Congress with the most brilliant distinction. Withdrawing from public life, he embarked for England, hoping that a change of scene might restore him to his wonted vigor, but he died on the voyage across the Atlantic. Henry Clay declared him to be the wisest man in his circle of acquaintances. Except in the 'Debates of Congress' few of the speeches of Mr. Lowndes have been preserved.

LOWRY, ROBERT, governor, was born in South Carolina in 1830. He located in Mississippi for the practice of law, attained the rank of brigadier-general in the Confederate Army, was twice wounded, and filled the office of governor of the State for two terms. With William H. McCardle, he wrote a 'History of Mississippi, from the Discovery of the Great River to the Death of Jefferson Davis' (Jackson, R. H. Henry and Company, 1891). For school purposes an abridgment of this work was also published.

LUCAS, DANIEL BEDINGER. See Biographical and Critical Sketch, Vol. VII, page 3267.

LUCAS, VIRGINIA. Poet. [W.Va.]. She was a sister of Daniel Bedinger Lewis. She wrote some very charming verse and published 'The Maid of Northumberland,' a drama of the Civil War, and 'Ballads and Madrigals,' both of which are included in her brother's work, 'A Wreath of Eglantine.'

LUCEY, THOMAS ELMORE. Poet. Also an interpreter of character, styled by his admirers "the poet-entertainer of the Ozarks." He was born near Monroe, N.C., January 15, 1874, and was educated in country newspaper offices. Afterward he took a special course of study at the Perry School of Oratory and Dramatic Art, in St. Louis, Mo. He is widely known by reason of his work on Chautauqua platforms and in lyceum lecture courses. He has written some very popular verse. His writings include: 'Etchings by an Optimist,' 'Through Prairie Meadows,' a volume of poems, and 'At the Altar of Atonement,' a drama. He resides in Hartford, Ark.

LUDLOW, NOAH MILLER, actor and author, was born in New York, July 4, 1795, and died in St. Louis, Mo., January 9, 1886. For years he resided in the South, was one of the successful old-time comedians of ante-bellum days, and published 'Dramatic Life,' with anecdotes and sketches of the actors who have appeared on the stage in the Mississippi Valley (St. Louis, G. I. Jones, 1880).

LUMPKIN, JOSEPH HENRY, jurist, was born in Oglethorpe County, Ga., December 23, 1799, and died in Athens, Ga., June 4, 1867. On completing his studies at Princeton, he read law, became an eminent advocate and won numerous legal victories. But impaired health made it necessary for him to relinquish the active practice for some time and he made an extended tour of Europe. On returning home, he was chosen one of the first triumvirate of judges to occupy the Bench of the newly-organized Supreme Court; and from 1845 to 1867 he wore the ermine of this august tribunal, for the greater part of this time holding the rank of chief justice. He was an orator of the very rarest gifts, and, under the old system of procedure, he rendered his decisions in open court with the most dramatic effect. The first thirty-six volumes of the 'Georgia Reports' contain the judicial productions of Judge Lumpkin.

LUMPKIN, WILSON, statesman, was born in Pittsylvania County, Va., January 14, 1783, and died in Athens, Ga., December 28, 1870. He studied law, became an eminent practitioner, served in Congress from 1815 to 1817 and from 1829 to 1831, was governor of Georgia and filled in the United States Senate the unexpired term of John P. King. He left an autobiography, in two large volumes of manuscript, containing many important sidelights upon American politics.

LUPTON, NATHANIEL THOMAS, educator and chemist, was born in Frederick County, Va., December 13, 1830. For three years he was president of the University of Alabama, afterward professor of chemistry in Vanderbilt University and dean of the School of Pharmacy: and still later State chemist of Alabama and professor of chemistry in the Agricultural College of Alabama. Besides minor contributions to technical literature, he published 'The Elementary Principles of Scientific Agriculture' (New York, 1880). The University of North Carolina gave him the degree of LL.D.

LUSSAN, A. Author. [La.]. He wrote an excellent tragedy in French entitled 'Les Martyrs de la Louisiane' (1839).

LUTHER, JOHN HILL, Baptist clergyman, was born in Rhode Island but labored for many years in Texas. Besides a volume of 'Sermons,' he published 'My Verses.'

LYDE, AUGUSTUS FOSTER. Poet. [N.C.]. The author of a volume of verse entitled 'Buds of Spring.' He died in 1834, at the age of twenty-one. Some of his work is quoted in 'Wood-notes,' Vol. I, page 202.

LYLE, EUGENE P., Jr., author, was born in Dallas, Texas, December 31, 1873. His father was Eugene P. Lyle, Sr., and his mother, Mary E. Angers. On completing his studies, he engaged in newspaper work but was drawn by popular appreciation into making frequent contributions to the magazines. He married Ethel Magill, of Kansas City, Mo. Two volumes have come from his pen, viz.: 'The Lone Star' (New York, Doubleday, Page and Company) and 'The Missourian' (*ibid.*). His residence is at Evergreen Farm, City Point, Prince Edward County, Va.

LYNCH, JAMES DANIEL, lawyer, author, poet, was born in Mecklenburg County, Va., January 6, 1836, received his education at the University of North Carolina, raised a company of cavalry under General Polk, and sustained severe wounds in a fight at Lafayette, Ga. He practiced law for some time at West Point, Miss., but abandoned the legal profession for literary pursuits. He published 'The Bench and Bar of Mississippi,' 'The Bench and Bar of Texas,' and 'The Industrial History of Texas,' besides numerous minor works. He also wrote poems of unusual merit, the best known being "The Clock of Destiny," "The Star of Texas," "The Siege of the Alamo" and "Columbia Saluting the Nations," the last-named production being an ode which was adopted as the national salutation of the Columbian Exposition. Few men have possessed more varied gifts.

LYNCH, PATRICK NIESEN, Roman Catholic bishop, was born in Clones, Ireland, March 10, 1817, and died in Charleston, S.C., February 26, 1882. On account of the reverses of war, it was incumbent upon him during the last years of his life to raise the sum of one hundred and fifty thousand dollars for the purpose of restoring the church property of his diocese, but he succeeded in accomplishing the task, stupendous though it was at that time of destitution. He wrote numerous articles for the reviews and edited Deharbe's 'Series of Catechisms.' His papers on "The Vatican Council" and "The Blood of St. James" were afterward published in book form.

LYNCH, WILLIAM FRANCIS, naval officer, was born in Norfolk, Va., in 1801, and died in Baltimore, Md., October 17, 1865. He was educated at Annapolis, entered the United States Navy, planned an expedition to explore the source of the Jordan, and the bed of the Dead Sea, and conducted the enterprise to success. At the beginning of the Civil War he resigned his commission and entered the Confederate service, receiving the commission of flag officer in command of the defences of North Carolina. He published a 'Narrative of the United States Expedition to the River Jordan and the Dead Sea' (Philadelphia, 1849), and 'Naval Life; or, Observations Afloat and Ashore' (New York, 1851).

LYNDE, FRANCIS. Author. He was born in Lewiston, N.Y., November 12, 1856, and enjoyed fair educational advantages, supplemented by home studies. For many years he was engaged in the

Railway Mail Service, but in 1893 took up literary work. His intimate knowledge of men is delightfully portrayed in his character sketches. His contributions to the magazines have been deservedly popular; and among his stories are: 'A Case in Equity' (Philadelphia, J. B. Lippincott Company), 'A Question of Courage' (*ibid.*), 'A Romance in Transit' (New York, Charles Scribner's Sons), 'The Helpers,' 'A Private Chivalry' (New York, D. Appleton and Company), 'The Master of Appleby' (Indianapolis, Bobbs-Merrill Company), 'The Grafters' (New York, Harper and Brothers), 'A Fool for Love' (*ibid.*), 'The Quickening' (*ibid.*), 'The Empire Builders' (*ibid.*), 'The King of Arcadia' (*ibid.*), and others. He resides at Lookout Mountain, near Chattanooga, Tenn.

LYNE, MONCURE. Author. [Texas]. She wrote an entertaining romance of the Texas Revolution entitled 'The Grito; or, From the Alamo to San Jacinto,' in which the pendulum swings between love and war (New York and Washington, The Neale Publishing Company, 1905).

LYNES, JESSE COLTON, educator, editor, chemist, was born on the Cooper river near Charleston, S.C., October 6, 1844. His father was Samuel Lynes and his mother, Sarah Jeanne Du Bois. He enjoyed the best educational advantages, supplemented by foreign travel. From 1889 to 1892 he was president of the Georgia Military and Agricultural College at Milledgeville, Ga., and from 1900 to 1906 professor of chemistry and geology at the South Carolina Military Academy, at Charleston, S.C. He belongs to numerous scientific bodies. His publications include a 'Laboratory Manual of the Physical Sciences' (1903) and a 'Laboratory Manual of Chemical Experiments' (1905), besides contributions to periodicals. Colonel Lynes resides on his plantation "Ormewood" near Atlanta, Ga., and delivers occasional lectures before agricultural colleges and farmers' institutes. He served with gallantry in the Confederate Army during the Civil War. The University of Paris gave him the degree of Ph.D.

LYON, ANNE BOZEMAN. Writer. She was born in Mobile, Ala., February 25, 1860, a daughter of Thomas T. A. and Mary Coffee Lyon. She was educated partly in Mobile and partly in New Orleans. Her earliest writings took the form of verse, contributed to the Louisville *Courier-Journal* and other newspapers; but of late her work has been chiefly in prose. She has made special investigations into the colonial records of Alabama and Louisiana, and her researches have borne fruit in numerous historical papers. She has also contributed many stories and sketches to the periodicals, her dialect work being particularly admired. 'Early Missions of the South' and an interesting novel entitled 'No Saint' are also from her pen. She resides in Mobile, Ala.

McADOO, MARY FAITH FLOYD. Author. She was born at St. Mary's, Ga. Her maiden name was Mary Floyd. She married William Gibbs McAdoo, professor of English in the University of Tennessee, now deceased. Besides contributing the chapters on "Journalism" and "Literature" in Goodspeed's 'History of Tennessee,' she has written several novels, among them 'The Nereid' and 'Eagle Bend.' She resides in Knoxville, Tenn.

McADOO, WILLIAM GIBBS, jurist, was born near Knoxville, Tenn., April 4, 1820, received his education at the University of East Tennessee, served in the Mexican War, was for some time solicitor-general of the Knoxville Circuit, attained the rank of a captain in the Confederate Army; and, settling in Georgia after the close of hostilities, became an occupant of the Bench. He published several addresses and, in association with Professor H. C. White, wrote 'Elementary Geology of Tennessee.'

McAFEE, ROBERT BRECKINRIDGE, lawyer, was born in Mercer County, Ky., in 1784, and died there March 12, 1849. He served in the War of 1812, studied law, became lieutenant-governor of the State, declined an election to Congress, and resided for four years at Bogota, Colombia from 1833 to 1837, in the office of the United States Chargé d'Affaires. He wrote a 'History of the War of 1812' (Lexington, Ky., 1816), and was also the author of an unpublished journal containing much information in regard to early Kentucky annals.

McALLISTER, JAMES GRAY, clergyman and educator, was born in Covington, Va., November 27, 1872. Besides numerous monographs, he has published several sermons, among them, "Recognition in Heaven" (1902), and "The Book Preëminent." For 'The Library of Southern Literature' he wrote the sketch of Robert Lewis Dabney. He married, May 18, 1904, Miss Meta E. Russell. Dr. McAllister was president of Hampden-Sidney College from 1905 to 1908. Washington and Jefferson College and Central University have both conferred upon him the degree of D.D. He resides at Hot Springs, Va.

McALLISTER, JOHN MERIWETHER, genealogist and author, of Georgia, published, in collaboration with Lura Boulton Tandy, a work of very great value entitled 'Genealogies of the Lewis and Kindred Families' (Columbia, Mo., E. W. Stephens Company, 1906). Mr. McAllister devoted the mellow years of his life to this important work, but died before it came from the press.

McALLISTER, MATTHEW HALL, jurist, was born in Savannah, Ga., November 26, 1800, and died in San Francisco, Cal., December 19, 1865. He was educated at Princeton, studied law, became prominent at the Georgia Bar and was narrowly defeated for governor. In 1850 he settled in San Francisco and five years later was elevated to the Bench of the first United States Circuit Court of California. He was the author of a volume of legal opinions which was published by his son, and also of a 'Eulogy on Andrew Jackson.'

McANALLY, DAVID RICE, clergyman, was born in Granger County, Tenn., February 17, 1810, studied for the ministry, and became an eminent pioneer landmark of Methodism. For several years he was president of the East Tennessee Female Institute. In 1851 he became editor of *The Christian Advocate*, and superintendent of the Methodist Book Concern, with headquarters in St. Louis, Mo. He was also long associated with Horace Mann in efforts to improve the common school system. Besides numerous tracts and sermons, he published: 'Life of Martha Laurens Ramsey' (St. Louis, 1852), 'Life and Times of the Reverend William Patton' (1856), 'Life and Times of the Reverend Dr. Samuel Patton' (1857), 'Life and Labors of Bishop Marvine' (1878), and 'History of Methodism in Missouri' (1881).

McANALLY, DAVID RICE, Jr., author, of Missouri, published in 1886 a volume entitled 'Irish Wonders' (Boston, Houghton, Mifflin and Company).

McBRIDE, JAMES, physician, was born in Williamsburg County, S.C., in 1784, and died in Charleston, S.C., in 1817. He was educated at Yale and for several years successfully practiced medicine in Charleston; but he was also an ardent student of botany and contributed numerous papers to the scientific periodicals.

McBRYDE, JOHN McLAUREN, Jr., educator, was born near Charlottesville, Va., March 18, 1870. His father is Dr. J. M. McBryde, president emeritus of the Virginia Polytechnic Institute, at Blacksburg. Besides 'A Study of Cowley's Dardeis,' he has contributed numerous articles to educational and philological journals, and a sketch in negro dialect to the *Atlantic Monthly.* For 'The Library of Southern Literature' he wrote the sketch of Mary Greenway McClelland. He is a professor in Sweet Briar College, Sweet Briar, Va., and holds the degree of Ph.D.

McCABE, JAMES DABNEY, Jr., author, was born in Richmond, Va., in 1842, of an old line of Scotch-Irish progenitors, reaching back to the time of the Crusades. Before completing his education, which was obtained in private schools and at the Virginia Military Institute, he enjoyed a reputation for successful authorship, publishing, in 1860, a work entitled: 'Fanaticism and Its Results, by a Southerner.' Then followed his "The Aide-de-Camp," a story of the war, which appeared serially in *The Magnolia Weekly,* a periodical of Richmond; and several plays; but his attention was turned to more serious work by the loss of "Lee's Right Arm," and his 'Life of Lieutenant-general T. J. Jackson, by an Ex-Cadet,' appeared next. He also wrote 'A Memoir of General Albert Sidney Johnston,' 'The Life and Campaigns of General Robert E. Lee,' 'The Gray Jackets,' a compilation of war-time humor, 'Paris by Gaslight and Sunlight,' 'Young Folks Abroad,' 'Pathways of the Holy Land,' 'Centennial History of the United States,' 'The Life of Garfield,' and a number of poems, besides translating two stories from the French. He died in 1883

McCABE, JAMES DABNEY, Sr., clergyman and editor, was born in Richmond, Va., April 15, 1808, and died in Baltimore, Md., August 1, 1875. He was first a Methodist, but afterward entered the Protestant Episcopal priesthood and became an eminent divine, serving important parishes and twice declining the bishopric. He edited *The Olive Branch* and *The Odd Fellow's Magazine,* and published a 'Masonic Text-book.'

McCABE, JOHN COLLINS, clergyman and poet, was born in Richmond, Va., November 12, 1810, and died in Chambersburg, Pa., February 26, 1875. At an early age he left school to enter commercial life, but an unusual aptitude for composition induced him to devote his odd moments to authorship and he contributed a poem to the first number of the *Southern Literary Messenger.* Edgar Allan Poe, its editor, became deeply interested in him, and this circumstance led to future contributions. He also wrote for other periodicals. Some of his essays and sketches attracted wide attention. He later entered the Protestant Episcopal ministry and served numerous important parishes. For three years during the Civil War he was chaplain of Libby Prison in Richmond. The materials of several years of diligent research into the historical antecedents of Virginia were given by him to Bishop Meade for his well-known work. Some of his earlier poems were published under the modest title of 'Scraps' (Richmond, 1835). William and Mary College gave him the degree of D.D.

McCABE, W. GORDON. See Biographical and Critical Sketch, Vol. VIII, page 3459.

McCAINE, ALEXANDER, clergyman, was born in Ireland about 1775 and died in Montgomery, Ala., June 1, 1856. He was one of the most eloquent of Methodist divines. After the adverse decision of the general conference of 1824, with reference to lay representation in the councils of the church, he published a treatise in support of his views entitled 'History and Mystery of Methodist Episcopacy' (Baltimore, 1829), which called forth Bishop Emory's 'Defence of Our Fathers.'

McCALL, HUGH, historian and soldier, was born in South Carolina, in 1767. On account of his fondness for military life, he became an ensign in the United States Army and remained in the service until he attained the rank of major. During his last years he was military storekeeper, first at Savannah and afterward at Charleston. He published in two volumes a 'History of Georgia' (Savannah, Seymour and Williams, 1811, Vol. I; William T. Williams, 1816, Vol. II). A. B. Caldwell of Atlanta has lately reissued the work (1909). Major McCall died at Savannah, Ga., July 9, 1824.

"McCALL, SIDNEY." See Mary McNeill Fenollosa.

McCALLA, WILLIAM LATTA, clergyman, was born near Lexington, Ky., November 25, 1788, and died in Louisiana, October 12, 1859. Entering the ministry of the Presbyterian Church, he filled important charges, first in Augusta, Ga., and afterward in Philadelphia, Pa. On account of ill health he then went to Texas. Still later he was called to Missouri, and finally he settled in Alabama. He engaged for a time in missionary work among the boatmen at St. Louis. As a controversialist, he possessed superior gifts, and held numerous debates with representative men of varying views. Besides sermons and essays, he published 'The Doctorate of Divinity,' 'Adventures in Texas, Chiefly in 1840,' and a collection of psalms and hymns in French.

McCALEB, THEODORE HOWARD. Jurist and educator. He was born in Pendleton District, S. C., February 10, 1810. By appointment of President Polk he was United States District Judge of Louisiana for several years. He was also professor of international law in the Louisiana State University for seventeen years, and became president of the institution. His oration on Henry Clay, delivered in 1852, was a model of eloquent diction (see 'The Louisiana Book,' 1894). He wrote numerous monographs on legal and educational subjects. His death occurred at Hermitage Plantation, Miss., April 29, 1864.

McCALEB, THOMAS. Author and compiler. He wrote 'Anthony Melgrave' (New York, 1892) and compiled 'The Louisiana Book' (New Orleans, R. F. Straughan, 1894).

McCANTS, ELLIOTT CRAYTON. Author. [S.C.]. Besides a romance of the Civil War entitled 'One of the Gray Jackets,' he has published a story of the post-bellum period entitled 'In the Red Hills' (New York, Doubleday, Page and Company, 1904), in which he furnishes an excellent portrayal of South Carolina types; also a volume of short stories. He resides in Anderson, S.C.

McCARDELL, ROY LARCOM, journalist and author, was born at Hagerstown, Md., June 30, 1870. For some time he was a reporter on the Birmingham *Age-Herald*. Afterward he settled in New York, became identified with several of the metropolitan papers, made a reputation for humorous and satirical writings, and contributed both prose and verse to periodicals. He is also the author of several volumes, including 'The Wage Slaves of New York' (New York, G. W. Dillingham and Company, 1898), 'Old Love and Lavender' (New York, Godfrey A. S. Wieners, 1900), 'Rise and Shine Stories' (1903), 'Conversations of a Chorus Girl' (New York, Street and Smith, 1903), 'Mr. and Mrs. Nagg' (1906), 'The Jarr Family' (1907), and others. He has also composed several musical comedies. He resides in New York City.

McCARTHY, CARLTON. Publisher. He was born in Richmond, Va., in 1847. His education was interrupted by the outbreak of the war, and, enlisting in the famous Richmond Howitzers, he served the Confederate cause until the surrender at Appomattox. Subsequent to the war, he farmed for several years, and later became a publisher in Richmond. He was mayor for some time, holding the office from 1904 to 1908. Though a man of business, he has found time to garner in literary fields. His writings include: 'Walks About Richmond' (out of print), 'Soldier Life in the Army of Northern Virginia' (Richmond, B. F. Johnson), and 'Our Distinguished Fellow-Citizen' (out of print). He resides in Richmond, Va.

McCARTHY, HARRY. An actor, who composed the famous war ballad entitled "The Bonnie Blue Flag." It was sung by his sister in one of the variety theaters of New Orleans. What became of the author of this familiar song no one seems to know.

McCAULEY, CHARLES ADAM HOKE, soldier, was born in Middletown, Md., July 13, 1847, was educated at West Point, and entered the United States Army; but, becoming interested in natural science, he accompanied the Red River exploring expedition in the capacity of ornithologist. Captain McCauley invented, in 1871, the military method of signaling by means of mirrors. At the present time he is assistant quartermaster-general, with headquarters in Washington, D.C. He has published 'Ornithology of the Red River Region of Texas,' 'The San Juan Reconnoissance in Colorado and New Mexico,' and various official reports.

McCAULEY, FRANCES CALDWELL, Mrs. ("Frances Little"). Author. [Ky.]. This talented woman has recently caught the attention of the public with her charming story entitled 'The Lady of the Decoration' (New York, The Century Company, 1908).

McCLELLAND, H. B. Author. [Va.]. He published 'The Life of General J. E. B. Stuart' (1885).

McCLELLAND, MARY GREENWAY. See Biographical and Critical Sketch, Vol. VIII, page 3477.

McCLUNG, JOHN ALEXANDER, clergyman and lawyer, was born in Washington, Ky., September 25, 1804, and perished in the Niagara River, August 7, 1859. He was a nephew of Chief Justice John Marshall. For a while he relinquished the Presbyterian ministry to practice law, but he was licensed for the second time in 1851 and served churches at various points. He was a man of exceptional gifts. Besides frequent contributions to the press, he wrote 'Sketches of Western Adventure' (Philadelphia, 1832). Some time after his tragic death, his biography appeared from the pen of Henry Waller (Covington, Ky., 1873).

McCLURG, JAMES, physician and man of letters, was born at Hampton, Va., and graduated from William and Mary College in the class with Thomas Jefferson. He studied medicine in Edinburgh and Paris, and became an eminent practitioner. His literary gifts were of high order, but he wrote only for the entertainment of his friends. One of his compositions, an "Essay on Human Bile," which was written abroad, is said to have been translated into several European languages. In joint authorship with Judge St. George Tucker he wrote "The Belles of Williamsburg," a poem.

McCONNELL, ANDREW. Editor. He was born in Blount County, Ala., in 1873, received a collegiate education, and married, in 1898, Marion Daniel. He inaugurated the Alkahest Lyceum system, a coöperative plan for furnishing Southern towns with lecture entertainments; and was also the founder of the McConnell Library Association, which supplies free lecture courses to public libraries. In addition to lectures on "The Philosophy of Life," "Openings for Great Men," and "The Larger Education," he is the author of a volume of poems entitled 'Echoes From the Heart.' He resides in Englewood, near Chicago, Ill.

McCONNELL, JOHN PRESTON, educator, was born at Mack, Scott County, Va., February 22, 1866. On completing his studies, he became a professor in Milligan College, Tenn., and, in 1904, accepted the chair of history and economics in Emory and Henry College, Va. Besides numerous historical and educational pamphlets, he has published "Negroes and their Treatment in Virginia from 1865 to 1867" (1909), "Virginia in the New Nation, 1865-1909," for 'The South in the Building of the Nation,' and the sketch of William Henry Harrison in 'The Library of Southern Literature.' The University of Virginia gave him the degree of Ph.D.

McCONNELL, JOSEPH MOORE, educator, was born at McConnellsville, S.C., November 29, 1875. His father was Captain John D. McConnell. Besides the sketch of James K. Polk in 'The Library of Southern Literature,' he has published a work of much value on 'Southern Oratory' (New York, The Macmillan Company, 1909). He married, August 3, 1905, Eliza Howard Riggs. He occupies the chair of history and economics in Davidson College and holds the degree of Ph. D.

McCONNELL, MARION DANIEL. Writer. She was born at Newnan, Ga., a daughter of the Rev. F. M. Daniel, and was educated at the Atlanta Female Institute. She married, in 1898, Andrew M. McConnell. She was for some time editor of *The Alkahest*. Besides frequent contributions to the periodicals, in both prose and verse, she has published 'The Life Beautiful' and 'Sheaves of Song,' the latter a volume of poems. She resides in Englewood, near Chicago, Ill.

McCORD, DAVID JAMES, lawyer, was born at Fort Motte, S.C., in 1797, and died in Columbia, S. C., May 12, 1855. He compiled and edited the 'Statutes at Large of South Carolina,' a work which had been begun by Dr. Thomas Cooper; and, besides numerous contributions to the magazines and reviews, he published 'Reports of Cases Determined in the Constitutional Convention of South Carolina,' four volumes, and 'Chancery Cases in the Court of Appeals of South Carolina,' two volumes. Between 1828 and 1830 he traveled in Europe and witnessed the revolution in Paris.

McCORD, LOUISA S. See Biographical and Critical Sketch, Vol. VIII, page 3505.

McCORVEY, THOMAS CHALMERS, educator, was born in Monroe County, Ala., August 18, 1852. His father was Murdock McCorvey and his mother, Lydia Ronaldson. Since graduation he has been a member of the faculty of the University of Alabama, his *alma mater*. In 1888 he became professor of history and economics, a chair which he still retains. Besides contributing articles on historical and literary subjects to various magazines and reviews, he has published 'The Government of the People of the State of Alabama' (Philadelphia, Eldredge and Brother, 1895), "Henry Tutwiler and the Influence of the University of Virginia on Education in Alabama," in the *Methodist Review*, September-October, 1899; "The Mission of Francis Scott Key to Alabama in 1833," in the publications of the Alabama Historical Society, Vol. IV; "The Masses and Classes in Southern Politics," in 'The South in the Building of the Nation,' and the sketch of Samuel Minturn Peck, in 'The Library of Southern Literature.' He married, July 22 1880, Netta Tutwiler. The University of Alabama gave him the degree of LL.D.

McCRADY, EDWARD. See Biographical and Critical Sketch. Vol. VIII, page 3531.

McCULLOH, JAMES HAINES, antiquarian, was born in Maryland about 1793. He received his medical degree from the University of Pennsylvania, but, after serving as garrison surgeon in the War of 1812, he devoted himself mainly to archæological studies. In 1836 he succeeded his father as collector of the port of Baltimore, and was also at one time president of the National Bank of Baltimore. He published 'Researches on America, being an Attempt to Settle Some Points Relative to the Aborigines of America' (Baltimore, 1816), 'Researches, Philosophical and Antiquarian, Concerning the Aboriginal History of America,' 'Analytical Investigations Concerning the Credibility of the Scriptures,' 'An Important Exposition of the Evidences and Doctrines of the Christian Religion, Addressed to the Better Classes of Society,' and other works. He was a thinker of original force and a writer of exceptional vigor of style.

McDAVID, MITTIE OWEN. Author. [Va.]. She wrote an entertaining little book entitled 'Princess Pocahontas' (New York and Washington, The Neale Publishing Company, 1907).

McDONALD, F. M., Miss. Author. [Va.]. She wrote a story entitled 'Who Was the Patriot?'

McDONNOLD, B. W. He was the author of an interesting 'History of the Cumberland Presbyterian Church (Nashville, Board of Publication of the Cumberland Presbyterian Church, 1888). He was given both the D.D. and the LL.D. degrees.

McDOWELL, KATE GOLDSBORO. Poet. [Ky.]. She published a volume of verse entitled 'Unfolding Leaves of Tender Thought' (1898).

McDOWELL, SILAS, author, was born in York District, S.C., May 10, 1793, and died in Macon County, N.C., July 14, 1879. Left an orphan at an early age, his life was one of hardships, but he acquired a trade and incidentally a knowledge of books. But he was chiefly characterized by his ardent love of nature and by his descriptive touch in portraying the features of his environment. One of his sketches, "Above the Clouds," was extensively copied in the newspapers and was followed by others, giving pen pictures of the North Carolina mountains. He also wrote articles for publication on various topics of industrial and scientific interest.

McDUFFIE, GEORGE. See Biographical and Critical Sketch, Vol. VIII, page 3547.

McEACHIN, R. B., writer, was born in Alabama, but afterward moved to Texas. Besides occasional short stories and sketches, he wrote 'Youthful Days, and Other Poems.'

McELLIGOTT, JAMES NAPOLEON, educator, was born in Richmond, Va., October 3, 1812, and died in the city of New York, October 22, 1866. Much of his time was spent in teaching and in compiling textbooks. In 1849 he opened a private school in New York and conducted it successfully until his death. He also edited for some time *The Teachers' Advocate.* Besides Greek and Hebrew grammars, he published a 'Manual, Analytical and Synthetical, of Orthography and Definition' (New York, 1845), 'The Young Analyzer,' 'The Humorous Speaker,' and 'The American Debater.' He also wrote hymns, and left an unfinished Latin grammar in manuscript. Harrodsburg College gave him the degree of LL.D.

McELROY, LUCY CLEAVER. Author. [Ky.]. Her father was Dr. W. W. Cleaver, a physician of Lebanon, Ky. She began her literary career by contributing racy sketches to the Louisville *Courier-Journal.* Her most ambitious work is entitled 'Juletty: a Story of Old Kentucky' (New York, Thomas Y. Crowell and Company, 1901).

McFERRIN, ANDERSON PURDY, clergyman, was born in Rutherford County, Tenn., February 25, 1818, was a brother of Dr. J. B. McFerrin, and published 'Sermons for the Times' and 'Heavenly Shadows and Hymns.'

McFERRIN, JOHN BERRY, clergyman, was born in Rutherford County, Tenn., June 15, 1807, and died in Nashville, Tenn., May 10, 1887. For many years he was secretary of the Board of Missions of the M. E. Church, South. At one time he also edited *The Christian Advocate;* and he was twice appointed agent for its books. He was a man of wide influence in the councils of his denomination and was a delegate to the ecumenical conference in London in 1881. Besides frequent contributions to religious and secular periodicals, he wrote 'The History of Methodism in Tennessee,' an authoritative work of great value, in three volumes (Nashville, M.E. Publishing House, South). Some time after his death, a memorial volume of Dr. McFerrin appeared from the pen of Bishop O. P. Fitzgerald. Randolph-Macon gave him the degree of D.D.

McGARY, ELIZABETH VISERE. Author. [Texas]. She wrote 'An American Girl in Mexico' (1904).

McGARVEY, JOHN WILLIAM. Educator and divine. For nearly forty years he was president of the College of the Bible, at Lexington, Ky., and for an equal length of time was connected with various religious newspapers. He was born in Hopkinsville, Ky., March 1, 1829, and married, March 23, 1853, Ottie Hix, of Fayette, Mo. His writings, which are almost wholly religious include: 'Commentaries on Acts,' 'Commentaries on Matthew and Mark,' 'Lands of the Bible,' 'Text and Canon of the New Testament,' 'Credibility, and Inspiration of the New Testament,' 'Sermons,' 'Jesus and Jonah' and the 'Authorship of Deuteronomy.' They were published by the Standard Publishing Company, Cincinnati, Ohio. He holds both the D.D. and the LL.D degrees.

McGEHEE, MONTFORD. Author. [N.C.]. He was born in 1822 and published a 'Life of Governor William A. Graham' (1877).

McGHEE, ZACH, journalist, was born in Cokesbury, S.C., in 1881. For some time past he has been engaged in newspaper work in Washington, D.C., as correspondent for Southern newspapers, including the Columbia *State* and the Charlotte *Observer.* He is the author of a volume entitled 'The Dark Corner' (1908), besides minor writings. He married, in 1907, Helen Irwin, since deceased.

McGILL, ANNA BLANCHE, journalist, was born in Louisville, Ky., in 1874. Her father was Benjamin Harden McGill and her mother, Bridget Corcoran. For several years she has been a contributor to high-class periodicals. She also wrote the sketch of Abby Carter Goodloe in 'The Library of Southern Literature.' Miss McGill is assistant book reviewer on the staff of the Louisville *Courier-Journal.*

McGILL, JOHN, Roman Catholic bishop, was born of Irish parentage, in Philadelphia, Pa., November 4, 1809, and died in Richmond, Va., January 14, 1872. His early life was spent in Kentucky. On completing his studies at the College of St. Joseph, he practiced law for several years, after which he entered the ministry, and in 1850 was consecrated bishop of the See of Richmond. He wrote two able works entitled 'The True Church' and 'Faith the Victory.' He also translated Audin's 'Life of Calvin' (Louisville, 1847).

McGIRT, JAMES EPHRAIM, negro poet, of North Carolina, wrote 'Avenging the Maine, and Other Poems' (Raleigh, 1900), 'Some Simple Songs' (Philadelphia), 'A Mystery, and Other Poems' (*ibid.*), and 'For Your Sweet Sake.' (*ibid.*).

McGLOIN, FRANK. Jurist and editor. He was born in Ireland, February 22, 1846, but was brought by his parents to New Orleans in early childhood. His education was obtained in the public schools of New Orleans and at St. Mary's College in Missouri. He served in the Confederate Army toward the close of the Civil War, and after the cessation of hostilities began the study of law in New Orleans. In 1880 he was elected Judge of the Court of Appeals of New Orleans, and was subsequently reëlected. For seven years he edited *The Holy Family,* a Catholic periodical of New Orleans. His writings in both prose and verse are characterized by the emotional touch which is peculiar to the Irish temperament. They include "The Conquest of Europe," a poem (1874), and 'The Story of Norodom, King of Cambodia: a Romance of the East' (1882).

McGRADY, THOMAS. Clergyman, author, lecturer. He was born in Lexington, Ky., June 6, 1863, enjoyed fine educational advantages, and, after preparing for the ministry, was ordained Roman Catholic priest, at Galveston, Texas, in 1887. He held numerous important pastorates. His social and economic views expressed on the lecture platform and in the pulpit exposed him to severe criticism and his case was presented to the highest ecclesiastical authorities. The result was that he was requested to retract some of his more radical statements. But he refused to comply with this order, and rather than sacrifice his convictions he preferred to sever his church relations. Consequently he withdrew from the ministry in 1902 to devote his time to law and lecture work. His writings embrace: 'The Mistakes of Ingersoll,' 'The Two Kingdoms,' 'Beyond the Black Ocean,' 'City of Angels,' 'A Voice From England,' and 'The Clerical Capitalist.' He resides in Newport, Ky.

McGUFFY, WILLIAM HOLMES, educator, was born in Washington County, Pa., September 23, 1800, and died at Charlottesville, Va., May 4, 1873. For nearly thirty years he occupied the chair of moral philosophy and political economy in the University of Virginia. He published a series of text-books including geographies and spellers, which became standards.

McGUIRE, HUNTER HOLMES, physician and surgeon, was born in Winchester, Va., October 11, 1835. During the Civil War he was medical director of the Army of the Shenandoah, and when hostilities closed he became professor of surgery in the Virginia Medical College at Richmond. Besides numerous medical papers and contributions to scientific journals on medical topics, he wrote an account of the death of Stonewall Jackson, reciting in detail the tragic circumstances, of which he was an eye-witness.

McGUIRE, JUDITH WALKER BROCKENBROUGH, Mrs., author, was born in Richmond, Va., in 1813, and was the wife of an Episcopal clergyman. Besides an interesting biography of General Lee, she wrote 'The Diary of a Southern Refugee,' which gives an exact portraiture of war times in the South.

McILWAYNE, RICHARD, Presbyterian clergyman and educator, was born in Petersburg, Va., May 20, 1834. For more than twenty years he was president of Hampden-Sidney College at Farmville, Va. During the Civil War he was a Confederate chaplain. Dr. McIlwayne was a landmark of Presbyterianism and his work entitled 'Memories of Three Score Years and Ten' (New York and Washington, The Neale Publishing Company, 1908), is an interesting commentary upon his times, full of delightful episodes and incidents.

McINTOSH, ATWELL CAMPBELL, lawyer and educator, was born in Fayetteville, N.C., November 3, 1859. On completing his education he was admitted to the Bar; and while still engaged in the general practice of his profession, is also professor of law in Trinity College, Durham, N.C. He is the author of an important legal text-book entitled 'Selected Cases on the Law of Contracts' (Raleigh, N.C., Edwards and Broughton, 1908). He married, January 13, 1887, Carrie Seagle of Newton, N.C.

McINTOSH, MARIA JANE, author, was born in Sunbury, Ga., in 1803, and died in Morristown, N.J., February 25, 1878. Her father was the gallant Captain James McKay McIntosh, of the United States Navy. She enjoyed the best educational advantages of the day and in 1835 removed to New York; but, having lost her fortune, she began to devote her unusual talents to authorship. Under the pen-name of "Aunt Kitty," she published a juvenile entitled 'Blind Alice,' and it proved to be so popular that it was immediately followed by others of like character, and the series was afterward issued in one volume of 'Aunt Kitty's Tales.' At the suggestion of Macready, the famous English tragedian, her subsequent volumes were reprinted in England. They include: 'Conquest and Self Conquest' (1844), 'Praise and Principle' (1845), 'Two Lives, to Seem and to Be' (1846), 'Charms and Counter Charms' (1848), 'Woman in America: Her Work and Reward' (1850), 'The Lofty and the Lowly' (1852), 'Evenings at Donaldson Manor' (1852), 'Emily Herbert' (1855), 'Violet; or, the Cross and Crown' (1856), 'Meta Gray' (1858), and 'Two Pictures' (1863). The stories of Miss McIntosh attracted wide attention on both sides of the water.

McKAY, ANNIE E., Mrs. Author. [Va.]. She published an interesting novel entitled 'A Latter Day Saint.'

McKENNEY, THOMAS LORRAINE, author, was born in Hopewell, Md., March 21, 1785, and died in the city of New York, February 19, 1859. For some time he was engaged in commercial life, but in 1816 he was appointed superintendent of the United States trade with the Indian tribes and was later put in charge of the bureau of Indian affairs. At one time he was a special commissioner with Lewis Cass to negotiate a treaty with the Chippewa Indians at Fond du Lac. He published 'Sketches of a Tour to the Lakes' (Baltimore, 1827) and in association with James Hall a 'History of the Indian Tribes,' in three volumes, illustrated with 120 colored portraits, a work which commanded an enormous price in the market and which was sold chiefly to libraries. He also wrote 'Essays on the Spirit of Jacksonianism,' dealing with the fight against the bank of the United States (Philadelphia, 1835) and 'Memoirs, Official and Personal, with Sketches of Travel among the Northern and Southern Indians' (New York, 1846).

McKIM, RANDOLPH HARRISON, clergyman and author, was born in Baltimore, Md., April 15, 1842, and after receiving his diploma from the University of Virginia, was in due season admitted to orders. He served in the Confederate Army, making an efficient soldier. Dr. McKim has held numerous important charges ranging from New York to New Orleans, and in 1889 became rector of Epiphany Church in Washington, D.C. Later he was also made dean of the Theological Seminary of Virginia. His published works include: 'A Vindication of Protestant Principles' (New York, Thomas Whittaker, 1879), 'The Nature of the Christian Ministry (*ibid.*, 1880), 'Future Punishment' (*ibid.*, 1883), 'Bread in the Desert, and Other Sermons' (*ibid.*, 1887), 'Christ and Modern Unbelief' (*ibid.*, 1893), 'Leo XIII at the Bar of History' (Washington, 1897), and 'Present Day Problems of Christian Thought' (New York, Thomas Whittaker, 1900). Washington and Lee University gave him the degree of D.D.

McKINLEY, CARLYLE. See Biographical and Critical Sketch, Vol. VIII, page 3567.

McKINNEY, ANNIE VALENTINE BOOTH. Author. She was born in Warren County, Miss., a daughter of Colonel S. S. and Anne Valentine Booth, and was educated at Hillman College, Clinton, Miss. She married, February 14, 1878, Samuel McKinney, of Vicksburg, Miss. She has been president of the Tennessee Woman's Press and Author's Club and also president of the Knoxville Chapter of the Daughters of the American Revolution. Besides numerous stories contributed to the leading magazines, she is the author, in collaboration with Grace MacGowan Cooke, of 'Mistress Joy, a Tale of Natchez in 1798' (Cincinnati, Robert Clarke Company). The sketch of Will N. Harben in 'The Library of Southern Literature' is from her pen. She resides in Knoxville, Tenn.

McKINNEY, KATE SLAUGHTER. Story-writer and poet. She was born in London, Ky., February 6, 1857, a daughter of James Love Slaughter, and was educated at Daughters' College, Harrodsburg, Ky. She married, May 7, 1878, James I. McKinney, superintendent of the Louisville and Nashville Railroad. Under the pen-name of "Katydid," she wrote numerous poems of merit which were published in book form in 1887. She is also the author of several published songs and a number of excellent short stories contributed to the periodicals. She resides in Montgomery, Ala.

McKINSEY, FOLGER, poet and editor, was born in Elleton, Md., August 29, 1866. Under the pen-name of "the Bentztown Bard" he has written some of the most exquisite newspaper verse of the day. He is on the staff of the Baltimore *Sun,* and daily, amid the grind of the journalistic mill, produces a song, which seldom fails to catch the ear of the public. He has published 'A Rose of the Old Regime, and Other Poems of Home Love and Childhood' (Baltimore, The Doxey Book Shop Company, 1908). He married, January 4, 1886, Frances H. Dungan.

McLAUGHLIN, J. FAIRFAX, author, wrote 'The American Cyclops, the Hero of New Orleans and the Spoiler of Silver Spoons,' dubbed LL.D. by Pasquino (Baltimore, 1868). The work is an amusing commentary upon General Butler.

McLAWS, (EMILY) LAFAYETTE. Author. She was born in Augusta, Ga., April 28, 1874, a daughter of Major Huguenin and Sarah Twiggs McLaws, and a niece of General LaFayette McLaws, an officer of distinction in the Army of Northern Virginia. She was educated under private tutors and at select schools in Boston and speaks four modern languages, besides English. She has contributed numerous stories to the magazines and has published: 'When the Land Was Young,' 'Jezebel,' 'Maid of Athens,' and 'The Welding,' all of which are charmingly written. She resides in New York City.

McLEARY, J. H., author, of Texas, wrote a "History of Green's Brigade," which has been preserved in 'Wooten's Comprehensive History of Texas' (Dallas, W. G. Scarff, 1898).

McLEOD, GEORGIANA A. HULSE, Mrs., educator, of Florida, published 'Sunbeams and Shadows' and 'Ivy Leaves from the Old Homestead.'

McLOUGHLIN, J. J. Author. [La.]. He wrote an interesting volume of fiction recently published, entitled 'A Creole Courtship, and Other Stories.'

McMAHON, JOHN VAN LEAR, lawyer, was born in Maryland in 1800, received his educational equipment at Princeton, studied law and achieved eminence at the Maryland Bar. On account of his oratorical gifts, he wielded an influence of wide extent on the political hustings, but he never sought or accepted public office, being more than content with his professional emoluments. He published 'An Historical View of Maryland,' a work of very great value dealing with the early colonial days. He died in Cumberland, Md., June 15, 1871. St. John's College gave him the degree of LL.D.

McMILLAN, HAMILTON. Writer. [N.C.]. He published 'Sir Walter Raleigh's Lost Colony' (1888).

McNEILL, DUNCAN. [N.C.]. He published 'Brief Selections of Poems and Speeches' (1853).

McNEILL, JOHN CHARLES. See Biographical and Critical Sketch, Vol. VIII, page 3583.

McNUTT, HUGH M. Writer. [Ala.]. Besides a number of sketches, he wrote 'The Old Treasurer,' a drama in three acts (1893).

McPHEETERS, WILLIAM MARCELLUS, physician, was born in Raleigh, N.C., December 3, 1815, studied medicine, located in St. Louis for the practice of his profession, and achieved distinction. During the Civil War he was chief surgeon on the staff of General Churchill for three years, and also medical director on the staff of General Price. At the close of hostilities he resumed the practice in St. Louis. Besides editing the St. Louis *Medical and Surgical Journal* for nearly twenty years, he published a 'History of the Cholera Epidemic in St. Louis in 1849,' besides numerous papers.

McPHERSON, JOHN HANSON THOMAS. Educator. He was born in Baltimore, Md., October 3, 1865, son of John H. T. and Sallie Cooke McPherson, and descendant of Robert and Janet McPherson, who came from the Scotch Highlands in 1738. He was educated at Johns Hopkins University and married, at Geneva, Switzerland, June 23, 1892, Georgia Adama Rathbone, who died November 13, 1893. He was instructor in history for one year in the University of Michigan, and became professor of history and political science in the University of Georgia in 1891. He is also lecturer on Roman law in the University of Georgia Law School, and is a member of the board of judges of the National Hall of Fame. His writings include: 'The History of Liberia' (Baltimore, Johns Hopkins Press, 1891), 'The Civil Government of Georgia' (Philadelphia, Eldredge and Brother, 1898), and 'The History and Government of Georgia' (1908). The sketch of General Henry R. Jackson in 'The Library of Southern Literature' is from his pen. Johns Hopkins conferred upon him the degree of LL.D. He resides at Athens, Ga.

McQUEARY, HOWARD. Clergyman. [Va.]. He published 'Topics of the Times' (1886) and 'Evolution and Christianity' (1889).

McQUEEN, ANNE. Author. [Fla.]. She has published a number of excellent short stories in dialect, both negro and cracker.

McREE, GRIFFITH JOHN, lawyer, was born in Wilmington, N.C., September 20, 1820, received his education at Princeton, and became an eminent member of the Bar. He married Penelope, daughter of Governor, James Iredell, and published, in two volumes, the biography of his father-in-law (Philadelphia, 1857). He died in Wilmington, N.C., April 29, 1872.

McSHERRY, JAMES, author, was born in Frederick County, Md., July 29, 1819, received his academic education at St. Mary's College, located at Gettysburg, Pa., for the practice of law, but eventually returned to Maryland. He was a devout Roman Catholic and contributed for years to the *United States Catholic Magazine*. He also published 'The History of Maryland, 1634-1848,' 'Père Jean; or, the Jesuit Missionary,' and 'Willitoft; or, the Days of James the First.' The last named work was subsequently translated into German. He died in Frederick County, Md., July 13, 1869.

McSHERRY, RICHARD, physician, was born in Martinsburg, W.Va., November 21, 1817, and died in Baltimore, Md., October 7, 1885. Entering the medical corps of the Army, he served under General Zachary Taylor in the Seminole War, but resigned to become assistant surgeon in the Navy, and on the United States frigate *Constitution* made a tour of the globe. Under General Scott, in the Mexican War, he was surgeon to a battalion of marines. For several years he was a professor in the medical department of the University of Maryland and later became the first president of the Baltimore Academy of Medicine. He wrote 'El Puchero; or, a Mixed Dish from Mexico' (Philadelphia, 1850), 'Essays' (Baltimore, 1869), and 'Health and How to Promote It' (New York, 1883).

McTYEIRE, HOLLAND NIMMONS, bishop of the M.E. Church, South, was born in Barnwell District, S.C., in 1824, and was educated at Randolph-Macon College, entering the itinerant ranks of Methodism and advancing rapidly to the front until, in 1866, at the General Conference of the M.E. Church, South, in New Orleans, he was made bishop. For more than twenty-five years he wore the episcopal honors. His writings include: 'The Duties of Christian Masters,' a work written in ante-bellum days for the benefit of slave-holders; a 'Catechism of Church Government,' a 'History of Methodist Discipline,' a 'History of Methodism,' 'Rules of Order,' and 'Passing Through the Gates,' a volume of sermons. He was also for some time editor of *The Christian Advocate* and was trustee of the gift of $1,000,000, which was made by Commodore Vanderbilt to the cause of education in the South, and which bore fruit in the great university which honors the name of the generous founder.

McVEA, EMILY W., educator, was born in Clinton, La., February 16, 1867. She began her life's work as teacher in St. Mary's School for Girls, in Raleigh, N.C., later for two years she was instructor of English in the University of Tennessee, and at the present time is assistant professor of English and dean of women in the University of Cincinnati. She is the author of articles on Madison, Marshall, Poe, and Lanier in the 'Encyclopædia Americana,' besides numerous monographs and papers on educational and general topics. For 'The Library of Southern Literature' she wrote the sketch of Susan Dabney Smedes.

MAC GOWAN, ALICE. Author. She was born in Perrysburg, Ohio, December 10, 1858, a daughter of Colonel John E. and Malvina Johnson MacGowan, and was educated in the public schools of Chattanooga, Tenn., also under the direction of her father at home. Full of the spirit of adventure, she rode alone through the Black Mountain region, a distance of one thousand miles, from Western North Carolina to Chattanooga, Tenn., in 1900, making the journey in eight weeks. Included among her stories, which are all pervaded by an atmosphere of outdoor life, are: 'The Last Word' (Boston, L. C. Page and Company), 'Return' (*ibid.*), 'Hulda' (Indianapolis, Bobbs-Merrill Company), and 'The Wiving of Lance Cleaverage.' Nearly all of her books have been written in collaboration with her sister, Grace MacGowan Cooke. She resides in Nashville, Tenn.

MACHEN, MINNIE GRESHAM, Mrs., author, was born in Georgia, a daughter of Honorable John J. Gresham, a lawyer of distinction. Since her marriage she has resided in Baltimore, Md. Mrs. Machen has published an interesting work entitled 'The Bible in Browning' (1903).

MACK, FLORA LATHAM, Mrs. Poet. She wrote an historical poem called "Old Jamestown," which revives in ballad measure the days of the first permanent English settlement in North America.

MACKAY, FRANKLIN H. Poet. [S.C.]. He published 'Laus Infantium, and Other Poems.'

MACKEY, ALBERT GALLATIN, physician and author, was born in Charleston, S.C., March 12, 1807, and died at Fortress Monroe, Va., June 20, 1881. For several years he taught and practiced medicine in Charleston, but in 1844 he relinquished medicine for literature. The subject of Freemasonry was the inspiration of most of his labors in this line, and he not only edited papers but published books in the interest of the craft. Almost unaided he acquired the ancient and modern languages in order to open the mysterious treasure house of knowledge; and he frequently appeared upon the lecture platform. His publications include: 'A Lexicon of Freemasonry' (New York, 1845), 'The Mystic Tie' (Charleston, 1849), 'Book of the Chapter' (New York, 1858), 'A History of Freemasonry in South Carolina,' 'A Manual of the Lodge,' 'Cryptic Masonry,' 'Masonic Ritualist,' 'Symbolism of Freemasonry,' 'A Text-book of Masonic Jurisprudence,' 'Masonic Parliamentary Law,' and 'The Encyclopædia of Freemasonry,' the latter being his most important and comprehensive work. On both sides of the water, he is an authority of the very highest rank.

MACKEY, JOHN, physician and editor, was born in Charleston, S.C., in 1765, and for several years engaged successfully in the practice of medicine. Afterward he embarked in editorial work and the latter part of his life was spent in teaching. He published 'The American Teacher's Assistant and Self Instructor's Guide' (Charleston, 1820), the most comprehensive work on arithmetic which had appeared up to this time. He died in Charleston, S.C., December 14, 1831.

MACKEY, ROBERT. Clergyman. [Tenn.]. He published a volume of verse entitled 'Kyle Stuart, and Other Poems' (1834).

MACLEAN, CLARA DARGAN, novelist and poet, was born on a plantation near Winnsboro, S.C., October 11, 1841. Her father was Dr. Kemp Strother Dargan. She was educated in the home schools and at Salem, N.C. For several years she engaged in educational work, and at leisure intervals exercised an unusual literary gift by contributing to the periodicals sometimes a poem, sometimes a story, but always something bright. She has published several novels: 'Riverlands' (1864), 'Light o' Love' (1890), 'Helen Howard,' and others. She usually spends the winter in Florida. In 1871 she married Judge Joseph A. Maclean. Her son, Stuart Maclean, a journalist of Minneapolis, has written a number of poems and essays of merit.

MACON, JOHN ALFRED. Journalist. [Ala.]. Born in 1851. He published 'Uncle Gabe Tucker,' 'Christmas at the Quarters,' and other poems in dialect.

MACON, NATHANIEL, statesman, was born in Warren County, N.C., December 17, 1757. Before completing his education at Princeton, he shouldered his musket and participated in the struggle for independence. He was elected to the State senate while he was in the field and it was not until he was urged by General Greene to accept this post of honor that he yielded. When the United States Constitution was first submitted to the vote of North Carolina he opposed it because it conferred too much power upon the general Government. From 1791 to 1815 he served in Congress, wielding for six years the gavel of speaker; and from 1815 to 1828 he was United States Senator. He refused to accept any office which was not the immediate gift of the people and he opposed every legislative impulse toward centralization of power. He adhered to the very highest standard of rectitude and in the opinion of John Randolph was the purest and wisest man of his time. He spoke with telling effect but seldom at great length. Benton said of his last moments that they lacked nothing except the hemlock to make them suggest the deathbed of Socrates. He died at the old homestead in Warren County, N.C., June 29, 1837. 'The Life of Nathaniel Macon' (Baltimore, 1840), was written by Edward R. Cotten, but the work is very inferior.

MADDEN, EVA A. Author. Though now a resident of Italy, she was born and reared in the State of Kentucky, which is still the home of her sister, Mrs. George Madden Martin. Several charming historical books for children have come from her pen, among them, 'Two Royal Foes.'

MADISON, DOROTHY, the most famous "Mistress of the White House," was born in North Carolina, May 20, 1768, and was the daughter of John Payne, a Virginia Quaker, who subsequently removed to Philadelphia. Her first husband was John Todd; but, being left a widow, she gave her hand to James Madison. When the latter became Secretary of State she accompanied him to Washington and frequently presided at the White House for President Jefferson; then followed eight years of social sway in her own right. On account of her many fascinating charms, she has ever since been the model of the executive queens. She left interesting materials which afterward took the form of 'Memoirs and Letters of Dolly Madison' (Boston, Houghton, Mifflin and Company), edited by her grandniece. She died July 12, 1849.

MADISON, JAMES, first Protestant Episcopal bishop of Virginia, was born near Port Republic, Va., August 27, 1749, and died in Williamsburg, Va., March 5, 1812. For several years he held a professorship in William and Mary College; and, leave of absence having been given him for the purpose, he went to England, where he was ordained to the priesthood in the chapel of Fulham Palace by the bishop of London. On his return home to resume his professorship, he was made president of the institution, an office which he continued to hold until his death. He presided over the first convention of the Episcopal Church in Virginia and was also the first bishop of the diocese. Besides several sermons, he published a 'Eulogy on Washington' and papers in *Barton's Journal.* William and Mary College, gave him the degree of LL.D.

MADISON, JAMES. See Biographical and Critical Sketch, Vol. VIII, page 3283.

MAFFITT, EMMA MARTIN, author, was the wife of Captain John Newland Maffitt, Jr., and published an interesting biography of her husband entitled 'The Life and Services of John Newland Maffitt' (New York and Washington, The Neale Publishing Company, 1905). The latter was for some time an officer in the United States Army, and afterward in command of blockade runners transporting supplies to the Confederate Armies.

MAFFITT, JOHN NEWLAND, clergyman and author, was born in Dublin, Ireland, December 28, 1795, but, emigrating to America, he became a minister of the Methodist Episcopal Church and preached to large congregations. For a while he edited the *Western Methodist,* at Nashville, Tenn., and was also professor of elocution at LaGrange Female College (Ga.). He wielded a pen of unusual versatility and published: 'Literary and Religious Sketches' (New York, 1832), 'Pulpit Sketches' (Boston, 1828), "Ireland," a poem (Louisville, 1839), and 'Poems' (Louisville, 1839). He died in Mobile, Ala., May 28, 1850.

MAGILL, MARY TUDOR. See Biographical and Critical Sketch, Vol. VIII, page 3305.

MAGNESS, EDGAR. Banker. [Ala.]. He published 'Tramp Tales of Europe' (1895).

MAGRUDER, ALLAN B. Author. [Va.]. He published a "Life of John Marshall," in the 'American Statesman Series' (Boston, Houghton, Mifflin and Company, 1895).

MAGRUDER, ALLAN BOWIE, United States Senator, was born in Kentucky, about 1775, and died in Opelousas, La., April 16, 1822. He studied law in Lexington, Ky., but removed to Louisiana to practice. From the start he met with success, and the climax to his career was reached in his appointment to the United States Senate in 1812. He published 'Reflections on the Cession of Louisiana,' and 'The Character of Mr. Jefferson,' besides leaving in manuscript an unfinished history of the North American Indians.

MAGRUDER, HARRIET FUQUA. Educator. Her maiden name was Harriet Fuqua. She was born in Baton Rouge, La., of Scotch-Irish and French Huguenot stock and married Heman Bangs Magruder. She wrote a 'Child's History of Louisiana' (Boston, D. C. Heath and Company, 1909), which has been adopted by the State Board of Education. Mrs. Magruder is teacher in history in the Baton Rouge High School.

MAGRUDER, JULIA. See Biographical and Critical Sketch, Vol. VIII, page 3321.

MAHAN, MILO, clergyman, was born in Suffolk, Va., May 24, 1819, and died in Baltimore, Md., September 3, 1870. For several years he was professor of church history in a theological seminary in New York, and afterward became rector of St. Paul's Church in Baltimore. He published 'The Exercise of Faith' (Philadelphia, 1851), 'The History of the Church During the First Three Centuries,' (New York, 1860), and several other volumes. His works were published collectively after his death, with a 'Memoir' by Rev. John J. Hopkins, Jr., (New York, 1872-1875). William and Mary College made him a D.D.

MAJORS, ALEXANDER, author, lived in Missouri and published in 1893 an interesting work entitled: 'Seventy Years on the Frontier' (Chicago, Rand, McNally and Company).

MALLARD, ROBERT QUARTERMAN, Presbyterian clergyman, was born in Liberty County, Ga., in 1830. For years he was pastor of the Napoleon Avenue Presbyterian Church of New Orleans, and besides editing the *Southwestern Presbyterian,* he published 'Plantation Life before Emancipation' (1892).

MALLARY, CHARLES DUTTON, clergyman, was born in Poultney, Vt., January 23, 1801, and died near Albany, Ga., July 31, 1864. He achieved distinction in the Baptist ministry, and, during the greater part of his life, labored in Georgia, where he filled numerous important pastorates. He published 'The Life of Edmund Botsford' (Charleston, 1832), 'Memoir of Jesse Mercer' (Philadelphia, 1844), and 'Soul Prosperity' (Charleston, 1860).

MALLARY, MARY JEANIE DAGG, Mrs. Author. [Ga.]. She published several works of fiction, among them, 'Horace Wilde,' 'Elsie Lee,' 'Rosalie Wynnton,' 'Jack,' 'Picciola; or, the Power of Conscience,' 'Aunt Clara's School,' and 'Won by a Boy.'

MALLORY, STEPHEN RUSSELL, statesman, was born in Trinidad, in the West Indies, in 1813, and died in Pensacola, Fla., November 9, 1873. He achieved distinction at the Bar, became a member of the Bench, served in the operations against the Seminole Indians, and from 1851 to 1861 held the commission of United States Senator, resigning his seat at the outbreak of hostilities. In the Cabinet of President Davis, he held the Secretaryship of the Navy from the organization till the overthrow of the Confederate Government. When he entered upon the discharge of his duties there was not a ship to defend the cause or to bear the flag of the young nation. The work of building a navy devolved upon him; but he undertook the task in hand with an intelligent grasp of the situation and the history of this important branch of the service bears testimony to his genius for administration. On May 20, 1865, he was arrested at LaGrange, Ga., in company with Benjamin H. Hill, and imprisoned for several months in Fort LaFayette, in New York Harbor, until released on parole. In the 'Debates of Congress' several of his speeches have been preserved.

MALONE, WALTER. See Biographical and Critical Sketch, Vol. VIII, page 3343.

MANGUM, ADOLPHUS WILLIAMSON. Methodist Episcopal clergyman and educator, [N. C.]. He was born in 1834 and died in 1890. He published 'Morven and Linda,' a collection of verse (1864), and 'Myrtle Leaves,' a volume of miscellany (1858).

MANGUM, WILLIE PERSON, United States Senator, was born in Orange County, N.C., in 1792 and died at Red Mountain, N.C., September 14, 1861. He received his education at the University of North Carolina, studied law, became a judge of the superior court, served in Congress for several terms, and twice represented North Carolina in the United States Senate. He wielded a powerful influence not only in state but in national affairs and in the campaign of 1837 received the electoral vote of South Carolina for president. His death was the result of nervous depression caused by the loss of his only son in the first battle of Manassas.

MANLY, BASIL, Sr., clergyman and educator, was born in Chatham County, N.C., January 28, 1798 and died in Greenville, S.C., December 21, 1868. He became an eminent Baptist educator and divine. For eighteen years he was president of the University of Alabama. He led in the movement which resulted in the organization of the Southern Baptist convention in 1845 and also in the effort to establish the Southern Baptist

Theological Seminary, which was opened at Greenville, S.C. in 1850. He published occasional sermons and addresses, made frequent contributions to periodicals, and, with his son Basil, compiled 'The Baptist Psalmody' (Charleston, 1850). From the pen of Dr. J. P. Boyce appeared his 'Memoir' in 1869. He received the degree of D.D.

MANLY, BASIL, Jr., clergyman and educator, was born in Edgefield County, S.C., December 19, 1825, graduated from the University of Alabama and pursued his theological studies at Princeton. For some time he was pastor of the First Baptist Church, of Richmond, Va. Afterward he became president of the Richmond Female Institute; and on the organization of the Southern Baptist Theological Seminary, at Greenville, S.C., he became one of the professors. Still later, he was for eight years president of Georgetown College, in Kentucky; and also at different times he edited religious periodicals. Besides sermons and addresses, he published 'The Bible Doctrine of Inspiration,' 'A Call to the Ministry,' 'A Sunday School Catechism' and 'The Baptist Psalmody' in association with his father. He died in 1892. The University of Alabama gave him the degree of D.D., and the Agricultural College at Auburn, the degree of LL.D.

MANLY, JOHN MATTHEWS, educator and editor, was born in Sumter County, Ala., September 2, 1865. After graduation from Furman University, he studied at Harvard. For seven years he was professor of English in Brown University and since 1898 he has filled the same chair in the University of Chicago. He has edited 'Macbeth' (New York, Longmans Greene & Company, 1896), 'Specimens of the Pre-Shakesperean Drama (Boston, Ginn & Company, 1897), and 'English Poetry' (*ibid.*, 1907).

MANLY, LOUISE, author, was born in Richmond, Va., July 10, 1857. Her father was Rev. Basil Manly, Jr., D.D., and her mother, Charlotte Whitfield. On completing her education in this country, she spent two years abroad; and, for several years after her return, she taught school in various parts of the South. In 1895 she published her 'Southern Literature' (Richmond: B. F. Johnson Company), a work which has been of very great value both in arousing public interest and in supplying important information. She also wrote a 'History of Alabama for Children' and a 'History of Judson Institute,' and assisted in editing 'English Poets.' The sketch of Augusta Evans Wilson in 'The Library of Southern Literature' is also from her pen. She resides at Fairhope, Ala.

MANN, AMBROSE DUDLEY, diplomat, was born at Hanover Court House, Va., April 26, 1801, and educated at West Point but resigned before graduation. For many years he was in the diplomatic service of the government, holding first the office of consul at Bremen and later becoming minister to Switzerland. On his return home he was made assistant Secretary of State, under President Pierce. During the Civil War he was one of the special commissioners sent by the Confederate Government to Europe. The last years of his life were devoted to the writing of his 'Memoirs' (1888).

MANNING, ESTELLE H., author, of Kentucky, has achieved some note in Washington journalism, and written a story entitled 'Hafiz.'

MANNING, THOMAS COURTLAND, diplomat and jurist, was born in Edenton, N.C., in 1831 and died in New York City, October 11, 1887. He received his education at the University of North Carolina, chose the profession of law, and attained high honors on the Bench. He served with distinction in the Confederate Army, was three times a member of the Supreme Court of Louisiana, was commissioned to the United States Senate in 1880 but was not allowed to take his seat, and in 1886 received from President Cleveland the appointment of Minister to Mexico. His decisions are preserved in the 'Louisiana Reports.'

MANSFIELD, BLANCHE McMANUS, writer and illustrator, was born in Louisiana and was educated partly in New Orleans and partly in Paris. Her stories for young people are exceedingly clever. They include: 'The True Mother Goose,' 'Childhood Songs of Long Ago,' 'Colonial Monographs,' 'Told in the Twilight' and 'Bachelor Ballads.' As an illustrator of books and periodicals she also takes high rank. Twelve illustrations in color were made by her for Kipling's 'Ballads and Ditties.' She married in 1898, M. F. Mansfield. Her home is in New York City.

MANSHIP, ANDREW, clergyman, was born in Caroline County, Md., June 23, 1824. Entering the ministry of the Methodist Church, he became an influential divine, and labored for the greater part of his time in Philadelphia, chiefly in the work of missions. He published 'Thirteen Years in the Itineracy' (Philadelphia, 1856), 'Cherished Memories,' 'Reminiscences from the Saddle-Bags of a Methodist Preacher,' 'History of Gospel Tents and Experience' and 'Forty Years in the Wilderness,' besides compiling 'The Patriot's Hymn Book' and 'National Jewels.'

MANSHIP, LUTHER, former lieutenant-governor of Mississippi, lecturer and writer, was born in Jackson, Miss., April 16, 1856. On the lecture platform he is one of the popular favorites, ranking with George R. Wendling and Bob Taylor. As an interpreter of the antebellum negro he is without a superior. Among his principal themes are 'Song and Story,' 'The Dialects of the Nations,' 'Lights and Shadows of Slavery Days' and 'From the Big House to the Cabin.' He married, in 1881, Belmont Phelps. He resides in Jackson, Miss.

MARCHMONT, JOHN. Author. He wrote 'Thirty-four Years: a Story of Southern Life' (1877).

MAREAN, BEATRICE, author, was born in Iowa, but since her marriage to Dr. W. H. Marean, of Memphis, Tenn., she has made her home in the South. At first she wrote merely for diversion but her stories and sketches proved so popular that she was encouraged to undertake more serious work. Her first book 'The Tragedies of Oakhurst' (1891) was translated into French and German; others rapidly followed, including 'Won at Last,' 'Judge Mortimer's Crime,' 'When a Woman Loves,' 'Her Shadowed Life,' 'The Firemen's Heart,' 'Cherry,' 'The Sign of the Cross,' 'Camella,' and several others. The writings of Mrs. Marean abound in dramatic situations and are characterized by a style which is most intensely realistic.

MARIGNY, BERNARD DE. Author. [La.]. He published in French 'Reflexions sur la Politique des États-Unis' (1854), 'Statistique de l'Espagne' and other works.

MARKELL, CATHERINE SUE, writer, was born in Frederick County, Md., February 28, 1828 and wrote 'Barbara Frietchie's Town' (Baltimore, 1893). She was the mother of Charles F. Markell, the author.

MARKELL, CHARLES FREDERICK. Author. He was born in Frederick, Md., October 16, 1855, the son of Frederick and Catherine Sue Markell, and received an excellent education, including a course of law in Columbia University. He was admitted to the Bar and served in the Maryland Legislature. Afterward he was Secretary of Legation to Brazil and later Chargé d'Affaires. He induced the Government of Brazil to remove an excessive tax on wheat flour from the United States. He married, January 28, 1902, Sue Markell Rogan. His writings are in both prose and verse, and include: 'Chamodine, and Other Poems,' 'The Chaskell Papers,' and 'Ypiranga: a Love Tale of the Brazils.' He resides in Birmingham, Ala.

MARKS, ELIAS, physician and educator, was born in Charleston, S.C., December 2, 1790 and died in Washington, D.C., in 1886. He received his medical diploma from the College of Physicians and Surgeons in New York and, after practicing his profession for some time in the metropolis, he returned to South Carolina, became president of Columbia Female College and later founded Barhamsville Collegiate Institute, near Columbia. Besides writing many fugitive poems, he translated 'The Aphorisms of Hippocrates' and 'Elfrede of Guldal, a Scandinavian Legend,' and left a treatise on philosophy and an unfinished novel.

MARQUIS, DON ROBERT PERRY, editor, was born in Walnut, Ill., July 29, 1878. For several years he has been engaged in journalistic work in the South, writing over the signature of Don Marquis. At the present time he is associate editor of the *Uncle Remus Magazine*, published in Atlanta, Ga. Whether in the realm of verse or of prose, his touch is artistic, his imagination tropical, and his work popular. Besides editorials, he has written numerous short stories and sketches which vie with his fragments of song in subtleness of appeal. He married, June 8, 1909, Reina Melcher.

MARR, FRANCES HARRISON, poet, was born in Warrenton, Va., of French and Scotch parentage, in 1835. For several years after the war she taught school and incidentally began to write more for amusement than with any serious desire to enter the ranks of authorship, but she won a prize offered by a Georgia paper and this encouragement stimulated her genius to such an extent that two volumes of verse were in time published, 'Heart Life in Song' and 'Virginia, and Other Poems.'

MARR, JANE BARRON HOPE. Writer. [Va.]. She published 'Stories and Papers,' a volume of fiction dealing with the days of Governor Spottswood.

MARSHALL, ALEXANDER KEITH, lawyer, was born in Fauquier County, Va., in 1770 and died in Mason County, Ky., February 7, 1825. He chose the profession of law, located in Kentucky, became one of the ablest pioneer lawyers of his day, was for years clerk and afterward reporter of the court of appeals and edited, in three volumes, 'Decisions of the Court of Appeals of Kentucky, 1817-1821.'

MARSHALL, ANNIE WARREN, Mrs., poet, was born in Louisville, Ky., some time before the war, but afterward located in New Mexico. Her poem, "A Magnolia Blossom," preserved in 'Songs of the South,' reveals an artistic touch. It is to be regretted that she did not write more.

MARSHALL, CHARLES, lawyer, was born in Warrenton, Va., October 3, 1830, received his education at the University of Virginia, and taught mathematics for several years at the University of Indiana. Later he practiced law in Baltimore. During the Civil War he was an aide on the staff of his kinsman, Robert E. Lee, and was charged with the duty of preparing the official reports of the Army of Northern Virginia. After the surrender at Appomattox, he resumed the practice of law in Baltimore. He occasionally appeared on the lecture platform, and also contributed articles to the magazines. He died in 1902.

MARSHALL, HUMPHREY, statesman, was born in Westmoreland County, Va., in 1756, and died near Frankfort, Ky., July 1, 1841. After serving in the Revolution with the rank of captain, he located in Kentucky, married his cousin, by whom he was taught to read, became an active factor in the early political affairs of the Blue Grass State, and from 1795 to 1801 held the commission of United States Senator. In a series of published letters he forced the resignation of Judge Sebastian from the Bench of the Court of Appeals by establishing the fact that for years he had been the paid pensioner of Spain, and he also took a conspicuous part in thwarting the plans of Aaron Burr. In 1809, he fought a duel with Henry Clay, in which the latter was wounded. He was the author of a 'History of Kentucky,' in two volumes (Frankfort, 1824), but the work deals largely with the events of his own period.

MARSHALL, JOHN. See Biographical and Critical Sketch, Vol. VIII, page 3369.

MARSHALL, JOHN JAY, jurist, was born in Woodford County, Ky., August 4, 1785, and died in Louisville, Ky., in 1846. He received his education at Princeton, chose the profession of law, was for several years reporter of the Court of Appeals, and from 1836 till his death was judge of the Circuit Court of Louisville. In the financial crisis of 1837 he lost his property by reason of the generous support which he gave to embarrassed friends. He published 'Reports of Cases at Law and Equity in the Court of Appeals of Kentucky' in seven volumes (Frankfort, 1831-1834).

MARSHALL, NELLY NICHOL, author, was born in Louisville, Ky., May 8, 1845, and began to write for periodicals during the Civil War. She afterward married Colonel John J. McAfee. Some of her stories were exceedingly popular, and she also wrote occasional poems of unusual merit. Among her novels may be included 'Eleanor Morton, or, Life in Dixie' (New York, 1865), 'Sodom Apples,' 'Fireside Gleanings' (Chicago, 1866), 'As by Fire' (New York, 1869), 'Wearing the Cross' (Cincinnati, 1868), 'Passion; or, Bartered and Sold' (Louisville, 1876), and 'A Criminal Through Love.'

MARSHALL, THOMAS ALEXANDER, jurist, was born in Augusta County, Ky., March 29, 1812, settled in Mississippi, achieved eminence at the Bar, became judge of the Vicksburg Circuit Court, and edited Swede's and Marshall's 'Reports of the Supreme Court of Mississippi' (Vicksburg, 1857).

MARSHALL. THOMAS FRANCIS. See Biographical an ' Critical Sketch, Vol. VIII, page 3395.

MARTIN, DÉSIRÉE, Mlle. Author. [La.]. She published in French 'Les Veilles d'une Sœur' (New Orleans, 1877).

MARTIN, ELLEN. Author. She resided at Vicksburg, Miss., and published 'The Feet of Clay,' a novel (New York, 1881).

MARTIN, FERNANDO WOOD. Educator. He was born in Volga, W.Va., May 5, 1863, a son of Washington and Matilda Cool Martin. and was educated in this country and at Leipsic. He married, in 1889, Emma Herron. He occupies the chair of chemistry in Randolph-Macon College, and is the author of 'Qualitative Analysis with the Blow Pipe,' also of a 'Text-Book on Inorganic Chemistry.' He resides at College Park, Va. Syracuse University gave him the degree of Ph.D.

MARTIN, FRANCOIS-XAVIER. Jurist and historian. He was born in Marseilles, France, March 17, 1762, and at the age of eighteen he emigrated to Martinique; but. after a sojourn of several years on the island, he came to Newbern, N.C. He became in time an eminent member of the Bar, translated and compiled many important law-books, and wrote an excellent 'History of North Carolina.' In 1809 President Madison appointed him Judge of the Territory of Mississippi, but he was subsequently transferred to the Bench of the City Court of the Territory of Orleans. Later he became attorney-general of Louisiana and Chief Justice of the Supreme Court of that State, retiring to private life in 1845. He also wrote an interesting 'History of New Orleans.' It is devoid of ornamentation but replete with interest. He died in 1846.

MARTIN, GEORGE MADDEN. See Biographical and Critical Sketch, Vol. VIII, page 3413.

MARTIN, JOSEPH HAMILTON, clergyman and poet, was born in Dandridge, Jefferson County, Tenn., August 11, 1825, the son of Hugh and Sarah Russell Martin. For many years he was pastor of the First Presbyterian Church of Atlanta. He was the author of some very beautiful hymns and poems, his best production in verse being "The Dove," written in the style of Poe's "Raven," but intended to answer the doubts of this morbid masterpiece. He also wrote an historical poem called "Smith and Pocahontas" (Richmond, 1862), and an interesting account of the Mecklenburg Declaration of Independence (New York, 1876), is also from his pen. He died at Georgetown, Ky., January 7, 1887.

MARTIN, L. A. Lawyer. [Mo.]. He published 'Hallowe'en, and Other Poems.'

MARTIN, LUTHER, lawyer, was born in New Brunswick, N.J., February 9, 1748, and died in New York City July 10, 1826. For the practice of law he located in Maryland and became one of the foremost advocates of his time. He defended Samuel Chase against the charge of impeachment before the United States Senate and Aaron Burr against the charge of treason at Richmond. He published a 'Defence of Captain Cresap,' whose daughter he married, a series of pamphlets on 'Modern Gratitude' and a number of 'Speeches.' He spent his last days in New York City, the guest of Aaron Burr.

MARTIN, MARGARET MAXWELL, author, was born in Dumfries, Scotland, July 12, 1807, but was brought to the United States in early childhood by her parents, who settled in Columbia, S.C., and in 1836 she married Rev. William Martin. For seventeen years she taught in a girls' seminary at Columbia, and, at leisure intervals, wrote for publication. Her writings include: 'Day-Spring; or, Light to Them That Sit in Darkness' (Nashville, 1854), 'Sabbath-school Offering,' a collection of poems and tales, 'Christianity in Earnest,' 'Heroines of Early Methodism,' written in association with her husband (Nashville, 1858), 'Religious Poems,' 'Flowers and Fruits; or, Poems for Young People,' and 'Scenes and Scenery of South Carolina.'

MARTIN, SALLIE M. DAVIS. Writer. [S.C.]. She published 'Lalla de Vere' and 'The Women of France.'

MARTIN, THOMAS RICAUD. Author. He published a work of much interest to historical students entitled 'The Great Parliamentary Battle and Farewell Addresses of the Southern Senators on the Eve of the Civil War' (New York and Washington, The Neale Publishing Company, 1904).

MARTIN, WALTER DRANE, writer, was born at Waverly, near Columbus, Miss., March 15, 1870, and is a grandson of Mortimer A. Martin, for seventeen years circuit court judge in Tennessee and of Gustavius A. Henry, an ex-Confederate States Senator and orator of distinction. Mr. Martin has published a volume of verse entitled 'Lenora and other

Poems' (Nashville, Smith and Lamar, illustrated, 1909). He is engaged in business in Clarksville, Tenn.

MARTIN, WILLIAM MAXWELL, educator and poet, was born in Columbia, S.C., June 4, 1837. After graduating from Wofford College, he taught school in Columbia until the outbreak of the war. He was a man of rare talent, a writer of excellent verse and a speaker of unusual graces. Under the title of 'Lyrics and Sketches' (1861), a volume of his miscellaneous writings appeared soon after his death, which occurred in Columbia, S.C., February 21, 1861, the result of exposure on the field of battle. During the whole of an inclement night he stood by his gun and contracted a chill which developed into typhoid fever.

MARVIN, ENOCH MATHER, Methodist Episcopal bishop, was born in Warren County, Mo., June 12, 1823, and died in St. Louis, Mo., December 3, 1877. Only a few months before his death he was sent to the Orient to ordain native preachers. Bishop Marvin wrote 'To the East by the West' (1877), an interesting account of his travels, and several treatises including 'The Work of Christ.' He received the D.D. and the LL.D. degrees.

MARX, DAVID, rabbi, was born in New Orleans, La., April 29, 1872. Besides being an associate editor of the *Jewish American,* he has published an interesting series of articles on 'The Women of Israel,' several sermons and numerous contributions to periodicals. He married, October 15, 1901, Eleanor Rosenfeld. Dr. Marx is a man of unusual acquirements and of broad sympathies. He resides in Atlanta, Ga.

MASDEVALL, JOSEPH. Physician. [La.]. He published in French the first bound volume to be printed in the territory of Louisiana, entitled 'Médicaments et Précis de la Méthode de M. Masdevall, docteur de Médecine du Roi d'Espagne Charles IV' (New Orleans, 1796).

MASON, EMILY VIRGINIA. Author. She was born in Lexington, Ky., October 15, 1815, a daughter of John T. and Eliza Mason. Her brother, S. T. Mason, was the first Governor of the State of Michigan. She was educated at Troy, N.Y., and served during the war in the Confederate hospitals, nursing the wounded soldiers. After the war she resided in Paris for fifteen years, being assistant principal of an American school for girls. Her writings include: 'The Life of General Robert E. Lee' (1871) and 'Memories of a Hospital Matron.' Besides, she edited 'Southern Poems of the War' and 'The Journal of a Young Lady of Virginia in 1798.' She is living, at the advanced age of ninety-four, in Georgetown, D.C.

MASON, GEORGE, statesman, was born in Stafford County, Va., in 1725, and died near his birthplace October 7, 1792. He espoused the patriotic cause, drafted the declaration of rights and the constitution of Virginia in 1775, opposed the importation of additional slaves, served in Congress, became a member of the convention that framed the Constitution, and, with Patrick Henry, fought the ratification of the document. In the opinion of James Madison he was the ablest debater of the day. When the Upper House was created he was elected the first United States Senator from Virginia, but declined the honor. Some of his writings are preserved in a volume of 'Speeches and State Papers.'

MASON, ISABEL S. Poet. Mrs. Mason comes of aristocratic stock, being a descendant of the Fitz-Randolphs. Her father was Charles F. Baker of Louisville, Ky., and her mother Annie E. Clark, a writer of excellent verse. She married Dr. Charles T. Mason. The maternal gift has been inherited in an eminent degree by the daughter. Besides fre-

quent contributions to high-class periodicals, she has published an artistic
little volume entitled 'Songs by the Way' (1909). She resides at Clear
Spring, Md.

MASON, JAMES MURRAY, statesman, was born in Fairfax
County, Va., November 3, 1798, and died near Alexandria, Va., April 28,
1871. After graduating from the University of Pennsylvania, he read
law, became successful in the practice, served one term in Congress and
declined a reëlection. Later he accepted an appointment to the United
States Senate, and was subsequently twice returned. He advocated
states rights with great warmth. During the war period he was one of
the commissioners sent by the Confederate Government to Europe. 'The
Public Life and Diplomatic Correspondence of James M. Mason' has
been published by his daughter, Virginia Mason.

MASON, VIRGINIA. Author. [Va.]. She was a daughter of
James M. Mason, United States Senator and Confederate States Com-
missioner. She published an interesting biography of her father entitled
'The Public Life and Diplomatic Correspondence of James M. Mason'
(New York and Washington, The Neale Publishing Company, 1903).

MASSIE, ROBERT KINLOCH, clergyman and educator, was
born at Charlottesville, Va., February 4, 1864. His father was Nathaniel
Harden Massie and his mother, Eliza Nelson. He occupies the chair of
church history in the Theological Seminary of the Episcopal Church, near
Alexandria, Va. Besides the sketch of Mason L. Weems in 'The Library
of Southern Literature' he has published occasional sermons and addresses. He holds the degree of D.D.

MASSEY, JOHN E. Baptist clergyman and lieutenant-governor.
For years he was an impressive figure in the public life of Virginia and
his 'Autobiography' is a work of much interest (New York and Washington, The Neale Publishing Company, 1909).

MASSEY, ROBERT JEHU, physician and writer, was born in
Morgan County, Ga., October 16, 1828, and received his diploma in medicine from the Medical College of Georgia. During the Civil War he
was instrumental in saving the state library from destruction at the hands
of General Sherman. Dr. Massey has published nothing in book form,
but for fifty years he has contributed to popular magazines and newspapers; and worthy of special note have been his reminiscences of ante-
bellum days. Besides more than one hundred sketches written for 'Men
of Mark in Georgia,' he has contributed to other works. At frequent intervals he also writes for the *Uncle Remus Magazine*. He married, June
16, 1850, Sarah Elizabeth Copeland. He resides in Atlanta, Ga.

MATHES, J. HARVEY. Author. He wrote a 'Life of General
N. B. Forrest' (New York, D. Appleton and Company, 1902).

MATTHEWS, (JAMES) BRANDER, educator and author, was
born in New Orleans, La., February 21, 1852. After graduating from
Columbia College he studied law, but literature proved to be more attractive to his talents. In 1892 he became professor of dramatic literature at Columbia, a chair which he still holds. He has attained high
rank in the realm of letters by reason of his critical and imaginative
work. Among his numerous writings are included 'French Dramatists of
the Nineteenth Century,' 'The Last Meeting,' a story, 'A Secret of the
Sea and Other Stories,' 'A Family Tree, and Other Stories,' 'American-
isms and Briticisms,' 'Vignettes of Manhattan,' 'Tales of Phantasy and
Fact,' 'Peter Stuyvesant,' a comedy (with Bronson Howard), 'The Historical Novel,' 'The Action and the Word,' 'The Development of the

Drama,' and 'Recreations of an Anthologist.' He holds the degree of LL.D. from Columbia, the degree of Litt.D. from Yale and the degree of D.C.L. from the University of the South.

MATTHEWS, JOHN, clergyman and educator, was born in Guilford County, N.C., January 19, 1792, and died in New Albany, Ind., May 19, 1848. He held numerous important pulpits in the South and in 1836 became president of the Presbyterian Theological Seminary, at Hanover, Ind. Besides numerous sermons, he published 'Divine Purpose Displayed in the Works of Providence and Grace' and 'The Influence of the Bible.' Washington College conferred upon him the degree of D.D.

MATTHEWS, MARK ALLISON, clergyman, was born at Calhoun, Ga., September 24, 1867. He received the best educational advantages, entered the Presbyterian ministry and after filling important pulpits in the South, he was called to the First Presbyterian Church of Seattle, Wash., where he preaches to the largest and wealthiest congregation on the Pacific Coast. As an orator he possesses in the rarest degree both personal magnetism and dramatic power, and his sermonic literature besides exhibiting the oratorical graces which are natural to one of such gifts, evinces also an independence of thought which proves him to be a man who does not lack in any sense of the word the courage of his convictions. He married, August 24, 1904, Grace Owen Jones.

MAURY, ANN, author, a cousin of Matthew F. Maury, was born in Liverpool, England, in 1803, and died in New York City, in 1876. She published 'The Memoirs of a Huguenot Family' (New York, 1856), a work which sets forth the autobiography of her ancestor, the Rev. James Fontaine, and a journal of travels in America. The appendix to the work contains a translation of the Edict of Nantes and other historical documents of interest.

MAURY, DABNEY HERNDON, soldier, was born in Fredericksburg, Va., May 21, 1822, received his education at the University of Virginia and at the United States Military Academy, served in the Mexican War, was severely wounded at Cerro Gordo, and in recognition of his gallantry was presented with a sword by the citizens of Fredericksburg and the Legislature of Virginia. Later he taught at West Point. When Virginia seceded in 1861, he espoused the fortunes of the Confederacy and attained the rank of major-general. He organized the Southern Historical Society in 1868 and, during President Cleveland's first administration, was United States Minister to Colombia. He published a military text-book entitled 'Skirmish Drill for Mounted Troops.' He died in 1900.

MAURY, MATTHEW FONTAINE. See Biographical and Critical Sketch, Vol. VIII, page 3435.

MAURY, SARAH MYTTON, author, was born in Liverpool, England, November 1, 1803, and died in Virginia in 1849. Her maiden name was Hughes, and she married William, the eldest son of James Maury. On the trip to America, an epidemic of smallpox broke out among the steerage passengers, a circumstance which caused her to inaugurate a crusade on both sides of the water for better sanitary regulations on

MAXCY, JONATHAN, educator, was born in Attleborough, Mass., September 2, 1768, and died in Columbia, S.C., June 4, 1820. He was the first president of South Carolina College, occupying the executive chair for sixteen years. 'The Literary Remains of the Rev. Jonathan Maxcy, D.D., with a Memoir of his Life by Romeo Elton, D.D.' (New York, 1844).

emigrant vessels. She published 'Etchings from the Caracci' (Liverpool, 1842), 'The Englishwoman in America,' 'The Statesmen of America in 1846,' and 'The Progress of the Catholic Church in America.'

MAXEY, EDWIN. Educator and lawyer. He was born in Royal, Pa., October 26, 1869, a son of Thomas and Ann Price Maxey, and received an excellent education, including a course at the Chicago Law School. In 1903 he became professor of constitutional and international law at the West Virginia University. He has published numerous monographs on political and legal subjects, in addition to the following works: 'Some Questions of Larger Politics' (New York, The Abbey Press, 1901), 'Triumphs of American Diplomacy' (New York, Brentano's, 1905), 'International Law' (St. Louis, F. H. Thomas Law Book Company, 1906), and 'Suffrage Extension in Rhode Island.' He holds the dregrees of D.C.L. and of LL.D.

MAXEY, SAMUEL BELL, United States Senator, soldier and lawyer, was born in Tompkinsville, Ky., March 30, 1825, of Huguenot ancestry, and was educated at West Point. During the Mexican War he was breveted first lieutenant for gallantry; but soon after the close of hostilities he resigned from the United States Army and settled in Paris, Texas for the practice of law. At the outbreak of hostilities in 1861, he organized the Ninth Texas Infantry, went to the front, and attained the rank of major-general. From 1875 to 1881 he served in the United States Senate. General Maxey contributed to 'Wooten's Comprehensive History of Texas' (Dallas, Wm. G. Scarff, 1898), two very important chapters on "The Annexation of Texas to the United States" and "The Mexican War, 1845-1848." He was engaged in writing another chapter on "The Natural Growth and Material Development of the State" when death arrested his pen.

MAXWELL, AUGUSTUS EMMET, jurist, was born in Elberton, Ga., September 21, 1820, received his education at the University of Virginia, studied law, settled in Florida for the practice of his profession, and served in Congress from 1853 to 1857. During the greater part of the Civil War period he was a Confederate Senator. He was afterward elevated to the Supreme Bench of the State. Still later he became judge of the first circuit of Florida, and he closed his splendid career in the ermine of the chief justiceship. Some of his speeches have been preserved in the records of the Federal and Confederate Houses of Congress; while some of his decisions are contained in the 'Florida Reports.'

MAXWELL, GEORGE TROUP, physician, was born in Bryan County, Ga., August 6, 1827, studied medicine, became an eminent practitioner, first in Florida and afterward in Georgia, commanded a brigade of Confederate troops during the Civil War, settled in Delaware at the close of hostilities, invented the laryngoscope, and published 'An Exposition of the Liability of the Negro Race to Yellow Fever,' besides numerous contributions to periodicals.

MAXWELL, H. V. Author. [Tenn.]. He wrote 'Chilhowee: a Legend of the Great Smoky Mountains' (1897).

MAXWELL, HU. This author was a product of West Virginia; but into his volume entitled 'Idyls of the Golden Shore' (New York, 1889), he has woven the scenery of the far-distant slope of the Pacific. Even to the most casual reader it is evident that the poet belongs to an exceptional group; and the work is considerably above the average in merit.

MAXWELL, THOMAS, merchant, was born in England, but afterward lived in Alabama and published 'The King Bee's Dream,' a poem.

MAXWELL, WILLIAM, educator and poet, was born in Norfolk, Va., in 1784 and died near Williamsburg, Va., in 1857. For several years he practiced law with success, after graduating from Yale; but he relinquished his profession to become president of Hampden-Sidney College. He published a volume of 'Poems' (Philadelphia, 1812), which passed into two editions; and also became interested in the antiquities of the state, establishing, in 1848, the Virginia Historical Register and editing the first six volumes. The best of his poems is "A Naval Song," inspired by the War of 1812. Hampden-Sidney College gave him the degree of LL.D.

MAYER, ALFRED MARSHALL, physicist, was born in Baltimore, Md., November 13, 1836, received his education at St. Mary's College, and became an eminent authority in various branches of science, especially in physics. At different times he was identified with some of the leading colleges and universities, but the most fruitful years of his life were given to the Stevens Institute of Technology, at Hoboken, N.J. In the realm of original research he made many useful and important discoveries, contributed at frequent intervals to the *American Journal of Science,* wrote numerous articles for encyclopædias, and published 'Lecture Notes on Physics,' 'The Earth a Great Magnet,' 'Light,' in association with Charles Barnard, 'Sound,' and 'Sport with Gun and Rod in American Woods and Rivers.' He died in 1897. Pennsylvania College gave him the degree of Ph.D.

MAYER, BRANTZ, author, was born in Baltimore, Md., September 27, 1809. On completing his studies at St. Mary's College, he made an extended tour of the Old World, began the practice of law on his return home, became Secretary of Legation in Mexico, in 1843, and afterward organized the Historical Society of Maryland. During the Civil War he espoused the Union cause and held the office of paymaster, which he retained for several years after the close of hostilities. He published 'Mexico as It Was and as It Is' (Philadelphia, 1844), 'Mexico: Aztec, Spanish, and Republican,' in two volumes (Hartford, 1861), 'Captain Canot; or, Twenty Years of an African Slaver,' founded on fact (New York, 1854). "Observations on American History and Archæology," in 'Smithsonian Contributions to Knowledge' (Washington, 1856), 'Mexican Antiquities' (Philadelphia, 1858), 'Memoir of Jared Sparks,' and 'Baltimore.' He also contributed to the Historical Society "The Journal of Charles Carroll during his Mission to Canada," and other interesting papers, He died in Baltimore, Md., March 21, 1879.

MAYES, EDWARD. Lawyer and educator. He was born in Hines County, Miss., December 15, 1846, a son of Daniel Mayes, graduated from the University of Mississippi, and afterward took the law course in the same institution. He married, May 11, 1869, Frances Eliza Lamar, daughter of L. Q. C. Lamar. He served in the Confederate Army, and later was for many years professor of law in the University of Mississippi, and chancellor from 1889 to 1892, subsequently professor of law in Millsaps College. Besides a 'History of Education in Mississippi,' he has written an exhaustive biography of L. Q. C. Lamar, portraying his times and including his speeches (Nashville, Methodist Episcopal Publishing House, South, 1895). Mississippi College gave him the degree of LL.D. He resides in Jackson, Miss.

MAYNARD SALLIE B. HILLYER, Mrs., author, was born in Georgia in 1841 and died in Texas in 1882. She wrote 'The Two Heroines; or, the Valley Farm,' besides several poems.

MAYO, JOSEPH. Author. [Va.]. He published a novel of Southern life entitled 'Woodburne,' the scenes of which are laid on both sides of the Potomac.

MAYO, ROBERT, author, was born in Powhatan County, Va., April 25, 1784, and died in Washington, D.C., October 31, 1864. After graduating from the University of Pennsylvania, he practiced medicine in Richmond, Va., for several years, and then entered the Civil Service at Washington. Free access to the Government files furnished him ample material for authorship, and he published a number of books, including a 'View of Ancient Geography and History' (Philadelphia, 1813), a 'New System of Mythology,' in four volumes (1815-1819), 'Pension Laws of the United States, 1776-1833' (Washington, 1833), a 'Synopsis of the Revenue System of the United States,' in two volumes (1847), and 'The Treasury Department: Its Origin, Organization, and Operation' (1847).

MEAD, EDWARD CAMPBELL. Author. He was born in Newton, Mass., January 12, 1837, a son of the Rev. Zachariah Mead, and was educated at Ridgeway Academy in Virginia. He married and engaged in business, but afterward took up farming on account of impaired health and made an extended voyage in early life to Australia and the East Indies. He is a frequent contributor to the periodicals, writing in both prose and verse. Especially important are his researches into Virginia antecedents. Included among his works are: 'Genealogical History of the Lee Family of Virginia and Maryland' (New York University Publishing Company, 1866), 'Biographical Sketch of Anna M. Chalmers,' and 'Historic Homes of the Southwest Mountains of Virginia,' in two volumes. He resides in Keswick, Va.

MEAD, F. Writer. [La.]. He published a volume of verse entitled 'Leaves of Thought' (1868).

MEADE, WILLIAM, Protestant Episcopal bishop, was born near Millwood, Va., November 11, 1789, and died in Richmond, Va., March 14, 1862. After receiving his diploma from Princeton, he studied theology and in due time was ordained to the priesthood. The gifts which he brought to the ministerial office were of the very highest order; his rise was therefore rapid; and, on his return from Europe, in 1841, after an extended visit, he was made bishop of the diocese. Conscientious scruples against slavery induced him to emancipate his negroes, but the experiment proved so disastrous to the blacks that he ceased to recommend this course to others. Included among his published works are 'Old Churches, Ministers and Families of Virginia,' in two volumes (Philadelphia, 1857), a work of rare value to the student of Virginia antiquities 'Lectures on the Pastoral Office,' 'Reasons for Loving the Episcopal Church,' 'The Bible and the Classics,' 'Pastoral Letters on the Duty of Affording Religious Instruction to Those in Bondage,' 'Companion to the Font and the Pulpit,' 'Family Prayer,' and others. From the pen of the Rev. John Johns, D.D., appeared an interesting 'Memorial of Bishop Meade.' William and Mary College conferred upon him the degree of D.D.

MEANS, ALEXANDER. Clergyman, educator, poet, physician. He was born in Statesville, N.C., February 6, 1801. Possessing one of the keenest intellects of his time, he foresaw the triumphs of electricity and predicted the motor car and the telegraph years in advance of the announcement of either invention. His eloquence was of the rarest type, and he not only filled many important pulpits but also took part in public affairs. He was a delegate to the Secession Convention in Georgia, and spoke against the policy of separating from the Union. He was the fourth president of Emory College and the first State Chemist of Georgia, receiving this latter appointment from the governor. He held important chairs from time to time in both literary and medical institutions, wrote learnedly upon many subjects, and published, in addition to numerous sermons and tracts, 'A Cluster of Poems for the Home and Heart.' He died in 1883. Besides the M.D. degree, he also held the D.D. and the LL.D.

MEANS, CELINA E., Mrs. Author. [S.C.]. Besides an interesting novel entitled 'Thirty-four Years,' she wrote 'Palmetto Stories,' an entertaining collection (New York, The Macmillan Company, 1908). Mrs. Means died in Columbia, S.C., in 1909.

MEEK, ALEXANDER BEAUFORT. See Biographical and Critical Sketch, Vol. VIII, page 3599.

MEEKINS, LYNN ROBY, journalist and author, was born in Salem, Md., November 14, 1862. For seventeen years he was literary editor of the Baltimore *American;* for two years managing editor of the *Saturday Evening Post,* and for four years editor-in-chief of the Baltimore *Herald.* Besides numerous stories and sketches contributed to magazines, he has published 'The Robb's Island Wreck' (New York, Stone and Kimball, 1894), 'Some of Our People' (1898), and 'Adam Rush' (Philadelphia, J. B. Lippincott Company, 1902). He married, November 5, 1891, Kate Owings.

MEIGS, RETURN JONATHAN, lawyer, was born in Clark County, Ky., April 14, 1801, achieved eminence at the Bar, became United States Attorney for the middle district of Tennessee and afterward clerk of the Supreme Court. He published 'Reports of Cases in the Supreme Court of Tennessee,' 'Digest of the Decisions of the Former Superior Courts of Law and Equity and of the Supreme Court of Errors and Appeals in the State of Tennessee,' and 'The Code of Tennessee,' compiled in association with William F. Cooper.

MELL, PATRICK HUES, clergyman and educator, was born in Walthourville, Ga., July 19, 1814, and was the son of Major Benjamin Mell and Cynthia Sumner. Most of his life was devoted to educational work; and for many years he was chancellor of the University of Georgia. As a parliamentarian he was without a peer in the South; and, covering a period of more than three decades, he moderated the assemblies of his Baptist brethren. He was twice married; first, to Lurene Howard Cooper, in 1840, and, second, to Eliza E. Cooper, in 1861. His published works include: 'Baptism,' 'Corrective Church Discipline,' 'Parliamentary Practice,' 'Slavery,' 'Calvinism,' 'Predestination,' 'God's Providential Government,' 'Philosophy of Prayer,' 'Church Polity,' 'College Government,' 'Dormitory System,' 'Keeping the Sabbath,' and 'Coming to Christ.' He died at Athens, Ga., January 26, 1888. Dr. Mell received the degree of D.D. from the University of Georgia and the degree of LL.D. from Howard.

MELL, PATRICK HUES, educator, was born in Penfield, Ga., May 24, 1850. His father was Patrick Hues Mell, the distinguished parliamentarian and chancellor of the University of Georgia, and his mother was Lurene Howard Cooper. He was educated at the University of Georgia, at Athens. For fourteen years he was professor of geology and botany at the Alabama Polytechnic Institute, and later for seven years was president of the South Carolina Agricultural and Mechanical College, at Clemson, S.C. On June 15, 1875, he married Annie R. White. Besides numerous papers and pamphlets bearing upon scientific subjects, he is the author of an interesting 'Life of Patrick Hues Mell' (Louisville Baptist Book Concern, 1895), and a volume entitled 'Biological Laboratory Methods' (New York, **The**

Macmillan Company, 1896). He has also revised 'Mell's Parliamentary Practice' (Louisville, Baptist Book Concern), and 'White's Gardening for the South' (Richmond, B. F. Johnson Company). The University of South Carolina gave him the degree of LL.D.

MELLEN, GEORGE FREDERICK, educator and writer, was born at Pierce's Springs, Miss., June 27, 1859. On completing his course at the University of Alabama, he studied at Leipsic (Ph.D.). In 1891 he became professor of Greek and French in the University of Tennessee, a chair which he filled for several years. Besides numerous contributions to magazines and newspapers, he contributed important chapters to Rule's 'History of Knoxville' and to 'The South in the Building of the Nation.' The sketch of J. G. Baldwin in 'The Library of Southern Literature' is also from his pen.

MELTON, WIGHTMAN FLETCHER, educator, was born at Ripley, Tenn., September 26, 1867. His father was the Rev. Isaac Q. Melton, and his mother, Frances Louisa Ellis. He occupies the chair of English at Emory College, Oxford, Ga. Besides numerous stories and sketches for periodicals, both religious and secular, he has published 'The Preacher's Son' (Nashville, M.E. Publishing House, South) and 'The Rhetoric of John Donne's Verse' (Baltimore, 1906). He has also edited Ruskin's 'Crown of Wild Olive' and 'Queen of the Air' (New York, The Macmillan Company, 1909). The sketch of Edward Coote Pinkney in 'The Library of Southern Literature' is from his pen. He received the degree of Ph.D. from Johns Hopkins University.

MEMMINGER, CHARLES GUSTAVUS, financier and statesman, was born in Wurtemburg, Germany, January 9, 1803, and died in Charleston, S.C., March 7, 1888. He was brought to America when an infant, received his education at South Carolina College, chose the profession of law, was for nearly twenty years chairman of the finance committee of the South Carolina House of Representatives, and from 1861 to 1864 held the Treasury portfolio in the Confederate Cabinet. He opposed nullification and wrote a work, satirizing the advocates of the doctrine entitled 'The Book of Nullification' (Charleston, 1832).

MEMMINGER, ROBERT WITHERS. Protestant Episcopal clergyman. [S.C.]. He published 'What is Religion?' 'Present Issues' (1873), and 'Reflections of a Recluse' (1878).

MENKEN, ADAH ISAACS, actress and poet, was born near New Orleans, La., June 15, 1835, and died in Paris, France, August 10, 1868. Her father was a Spanish Jew and her mother a native of Bordeaux. She married Alexander Menken, a musician, from whom she was subsequently divorced; and later in life she married, first, John C. Heenan, and Robert H. Newell, from both of whom she was likewise separated. On the stage she attained some note; and after retiring she published over the signature of "Indigena" a volume of verse entitled 'Memories.' When she died, at the age of thirty-three, she was Mrs. James Barclay.

MERCER, CHARLES FENTON, lawyer and soldier, was born in Fredericksburg, Va., June 6, 1778, and died near Alexandria, Va., May 4, 1858. During the War of 1812 he commanded the defences at Norfolk, with the rank of brigadier-general. He also served in Congress for twenty-four years and was the first president of the Chesapeake and Ohio Canal. Opposed to slavery, General Mercer conferred with eminent men of several countries in the interest of abolition. He published 'The Weakness and Inefficiency of the United States Government' (1863).

MERCER, JESSE, one of the pioneer Baptist divines and philanthropists of Georgia, was born in Halifax County, N.C., December 16, 1769, and died in Washington, Ga., September 6, 1841. For fifty years he preached the gospel with wonderful power. Possessed of large means, he gave liberally to Mercer University, an institution which was named in his honor, and he also purchased and edited *The Christian Index,* which he afterward presented to the Georgia Baptists. For eighteen years in succession he was president of the State convention. Perhaps no man of his day was more influential in molding religious opinion, whether in the pulpit or in the editorial sanctum. He received the degree of D.D.

MERCER, MARGARET, educator, was born in Annapolis, Md., in 1792, and died in Virginia in 1846. On account of deep-seated convictions, she voluntarily reduced herself from affluence to poverty by releasing her slaves. For twenty years she taught school in Virginia and prepared two volumes for her pupils: 'Studies for Bible Classes' and 'Ethics: a Series of Lectures to Young Ladies.' Caspar Morris published her 'Memoir' (Philadelphia, 1848).

MERCIER, ALFRED. See Biographical and Critical Sketch, Vol. VIII, page 3629.

MERIWETHER, ELIZABETH AVERY. Author. She was born in Bolivar, Tenn., in 1832, married Minor Meriwether, and is the mother of the well-known author, Lee Meriwether. Some very excellent stories have come from her pen, among them: 'The Master of Red Leaf,' 'Black and White,' 'The Ku Klux Klan,' and 'My First and Last Love.' She resides in St. Louis, Mo.

MERIWETHER, LEE. Lawyer and author. He was born in Columbus, Miss., December 25, 1862, a son of Minor and Elizabeth Avery Meriwether, and was educated in Memphis, Tenn., but settled in St. Louis for the practice of law. Some time during the 'eighties, he took an extended trip abroad, "roughing it" from Gibraltar to the Bosphorus. He was afterward appointed by the United States Secretary of the Interior to prepare a report on the condition of European laborers. At another time he was special agent for the Department of the Interior and collected data in regard to labor in the United States and in the Philippines. Subsequently he was made Commissioner of Labor in Missouri. Several books have come from his busy pen, among them: 'A Tramp Trip, or How to See Europe on Fifty Cents a Day' (New York, Harper and Brothers, 1887), 'The Tramp at Home' (*ibid.,* 1890), 'Afloat and Ashore on the Mediterranean,' (New York, Charles Scribner's Sons, 1892), 'Miss Chunk' (1899), and 'A Lord's Courtship' (Boston, Laird and Lee, 1900). He resides in St. Louis, Mo.

MERIWETHER, LIDE SMITH, Mrs., poet, was born in Virginia in 1829, but most of her life was spent in Memphis, Tenn. In association with her sister, Virginia French, she published a volume of verse entitled 'One or Two.'

MERRICK, CAROLINE E. Author. [La.]. She wrote an interesting volume entitled 'Old Times in Dixie Land' (New York, 1901).

MERRICK, E. T., Jr. Lawyer. [La.]. He published several works, including 'The Louisiana Civil Code, Annotated' (1902), 'Roger B. Taney' (1903), and 'The Louisiana Purchase' (1904).

MERRIMON, MAUD L. Writer. [N.C.]. She wrote a memoir of her father, Judge A. S. Merrimon (1895).

MÉRY, GASTON ÉTIENNE, explorer, was born in Baton Rouge, La., in 1793, and died in France in 1844. He fought under General Jackson at New Orleans and published 'La Légende du Corsair La Fitte' (Tours 1841), 'Observations sur le Commerce, des États-Unis' (Paris, 1842), and 'La Politique Américaine et les Indiens' (1843).

MESSENGER, LILLIAN ROZELL, author, was born in Kentucky, a daughter of Dr. F. O. Rozell, and was educated at Forest Hill Institute, near Memphis, Tenn. She married, in 1868, North A. Messenger, an editor of Tuscumbia, Ala., and, after the death of her husband, she settled in Washington, D.C., where she engaged in journalistic and literary work. She published several delightful volumes, including 'Threads of Fate,' 'Fragments from an Old Inn,' 'The Vision of Gold,' 'The Southern Cross,' and 'In the Heart of America.'

METCALF, JOHN CALVIN, educator, was born in Christian County, Ky., August 7, 1865. His father was John C. Metcalf and his mother, Victoria Willis. He holds the chair of English in Richmond College, and at leisure intervals devotes his pen to literary activities. Besides contributing to encyclopædias, he has published 'Literature and the Moral Law, and Other Essays,' "The English in the South," a chapter written for 'The South in the Building of the Nation,' and several lectures and addresses. He also wrote the sketch of George C. Eggleston in 'The Library of Southern Literature.' He married Ruth C. Sharp.

METCALF, SAMUEL L., physician, was born near Winchester, Va., September 21, 1798, and died at Cape May, N.J., July 17, 1856. He was educated in Kentucky and practiced first in Mississippi and afterward in Tennessee, but removed eventually to New York. He gave much attention to scientific research, made two extended visits to England, and published 'Narratives of Indian Warfare in the West' (Lexington, 1821), 'New Theory of Terrestrial Magnetism' (New York, 1833), and 'Caloric; Its Agencies in the Phenomena of Nature,' in two volumes (London, 1843; New York, 1853). He was almost equally well known on both sides of the Atlantic.

MEZES, SIDNEY EDWARD, educator, was born in the State of California, September 23, 1863, and was educated at the University of California and at Harvard. He became associate professor of philosophy in the University of Texas in 1897, professor of this department and dean of the College of Arts in 1900, and, on the resignation of Dr. Houston in 1908, president, an honor which he received unexpectedly while traveling abroad. He has published an important text-book on 'Ethics, Descriptive and Explanatory' (1901), besides his co-authorship interest in another work entitled 'The Conception of God' (1897). Harvard gave him the degree of Ph.D.

MICHARD, J. Educator and poet. In 1860 there appeared in Richmond a volume entitled 'Religio Poetæ: a Trilogy, by J. Michard, Professor of Modern Languages.' It is too mystical and deep to win popular favor, but it contains some fine passages, showing that the author possessed in an unusual degree the poetic gift.

MICHEL, WILLIAM MIDDLETON, physician and scientist, was born in Charleston, S.C., January 22, 1822. He attained high professional rank, edited the *Confederate States Medical and Surgical Journal,* taught in South Carolina Medical College, and published the result of his researches 'On the Development of the Opossum,' which brought him into controversy with Agassiz.

MIDDLETON, ARTHUR, signer of the Declaration of Independence, was born at Middleton Place, S.C., on the Ashley River, June 26,

1742, and died at Goose Creek, S.C., January 1, 1787. He was educated at Cambridge, England, and spent two years in traveling abroad. He espoused the patriotic cause, succeeded his father, Henry Middleton, in the Continental Congress, signed the immortal scroll of freedom, declined the governorship of South Carolina, on the fall of Charleston was made a political prisoner and after being exchanged, resumed his seat at Philadelphia. Subsequent to the war he served in the State Senate. Over the signature of "Andrew Marvel" he wrote several effective political essays; and having acquired the stenographic art, he also reported the debates in which he participated. He is said to have owned fifty thousand acres and eight hundred slaves.

MIDDLETON, HENRY, author, was born in Paris, France, but of South Carolina parentage, March 16, 1797, and died in Washington, D.C., March 15, 1876. His father was Henry Middleton, an American diplomat, and his grandfather, Arthur Middleton, the signer. He was educated at West Point; but relinquishing army life after a time, he chose the legal profession, and became a writer of distinction upon economic topics. He was an enthusiastic advocate of free trade; and this important issue inspired numerous articles from his pen. In an essay on "Prospects of Disunion" he strongly opposed nullification. He also wrote: 'The Government and the Currency' (New York, 1850), 'Economical Causes of Slavery in the United States and Obstacles to Abolition' (London, 1857), 'The Government of India,' and 'Universal Suffrage.'

MIDDLETON, JOHN IZARD, author, was born at Middleton Place, S.C., in 1785, and died in Paris, France, in 1849. He was educated at Cambridge, England, married the daughter of M. Falconet, a banker of Naples, resided first in Italy and then in France, and published 'Grecian Remains in Italy,' the first contribution made by an American to the literature of classic antiquities (London, 1812).

MILBURN, W. H., Mrs. Poet. [Va.]. She wrote 'Poems of Faith and Affection.'

MILBURN, WILLIAM HENRY. The blind chaplain of Congress. Though born in Philadelphia, he resided for several years in the South, where he occupied Methodist pulpits, Mobile and Montgomery supplying his principal fields. He published 'Rifle, Axe and Saddle-Bags, the Symbols of Western Character and Civilization' (New York, 1856), 'Ten Years of a Preacher's Life; Chapters from an Autobiography' (New York, 1859), and 'The Pioneers, Preachers and People of the Mississippi Valley' (New York, 1860).

MILES, GEORGE HENRY. See Biographical and Critical Sketch, Vol. VIII, page 3641.

MILES, JAMES WARLEY, clergyman, was born in Charleston, S.C., November 24, 1818. He was an accomplished divine and scholar of the Episcopal Church, who wrote 'Philosophic Theology; or, Ultimate Grounds of all Religious Belief Based on Reason' (Charleston, 1849). He also published occasional poems. Besides the classic and sacred tongues, he also mastered Turkish and Persian. He died in Charleston, S.C., in 1875.

MILFORT, LE CLERC, French traveler and writer, was born in 1750 and died in 1817 in France. For some time he sojourned in the Territory of Alabama, and wrote 'Mémoire, ou Coup d'Œil Rapide sur mes Différents Voyages et mon Séjour dans la Nation Creëk' (1802).

MILLAR, ALEXANDER COPELAND. Educator. He was born in McKeesport, Pa., May 17, 1861, the son of W. J. and Ellen

Millar. He removed to Missouri in childhood, and graduated from Central College. He married, June 27, 1887, Elizabeth Harwood. His life has been largely devoted to educational work; and for fifteen years he was president of Central Collegiate Institute. At present his labors are given chiefly to the great educational commission of the Methodist Church, South. As an advocate of good roads, he led the movement that resulted in an amendment to the Constitution of Arkansas, authorizing counties to levy a road tax. He edits the *Arkansas Methodist*, and he is also a minister of the gospel. Besides a work entitled 'Twentieth Century Educational Problems' (Philadelphia, Hinds and Noble) he is the author of a poem called "Together, Yes, Together," written in answer to the English Laureate's poem of the same title. He resides in Little Rock, Ark.

MILLARD, JUNIUS WILLIAM. Clergyman. He was born in Sampson County, N.C., January 23, 1870, was educated at Wake Forest College and at Southern Baptist Theological Seminary and married, November 4, 1870, Mary Frances Weakley. He was for nine years pastor of Eutaw Place Baptist Church, Baltimore, Md., and became pastor of the Ponce De Leon Avenue Baptist Church in 1905. He is the author of a volume entitled 'Life's To-morrows,' published in 1908. He has received the degree of D.D.

MILLER, ALEXANDER McVEIGH, Mrs. Author. Her maiden name was Mittie F. C. Points. She was born in West Virginia in 1858. Her writings are characterized by vivid imagination and by rapid movement of plot. She became one of the most popular contributors of the day to New York periodicals, most of her stories appearing in serial form. She wrote 'Laurel Vane,' 'Lancaster's Choice,' 'Lady Gray's Pride,' 'The Senator's Bride,' 'The Senator's Favorite,' 'Nina's Peril,' 'A Little Southern Beauty,' 'A Golden Barrier,' 'Little Sweetheart,' 'Rosamond,' 'Sworn to Silence,' and several others, besides also a number of uncollected poems.

MILLER, ANDREW JAMES. Journalist and author. He was born in La Grange, September 4, 1855, the son of Thomas C. and Elizabeth Miller, was educated at the University of Georgia, and married in 1881, Ella Stephens. He edited for three years *The Tribune* at Evansville, Ind., headed the scientific exploration party to Central America in 1889, and several years later joined the newspaper syndicate expedition to South America. His style as a writer is graphic and fluent. Besides numerous short stories and sketches contributed to the magazines, he has published: 'Old School Days,' 'The Making of a Pirate,' and 'The Toastmaster.' He resides in Llano, Texas.

MILLER, ELVIRA, SYDNOR, Miss, poet, was born in Virginia during the Civil War, but subsequently became a resident of Louisville, Ky., and a favorite writer on the Louisville *Times*. She published a volume of verse entitled 'Songs of the Heart.'

MILLER, GUSTAVUS HINDMAN. Merchant and author. He was born on a ranch in Texas, September 4, 1857, the son of Franklin L. and Emily McGee Miller, and was educated in the common schools. He married, in 1878, Tennessee Jameson. His busy mercantile life has not kept him from devoting his evenings to literary pursuits; and from his pen have come some very bright stories, among them: 'Lucy Dalton,' 'Is Marriage a Failure?' and 'What's in a Dream?' He resides in Chattanooga, Tenn.

MILLER, HOMER VIRGIL MILTON, physician and senator, was born in South Carolina in 1814, and died in Atlanta, Ga., in 1897. He began his career at Cassville, Ga., and taking an active interest in politics, he won by his dynamic oratory on the stump the soubriquet of "the Demosthenes of the Mountains." During the Civil War he served the Confederacy as a surgeon. He taught in medical colleges, attended the Constitutional Convention of 1868, was elected to the United States Senate in 1870, and delivered numerous public addresses. He also contributed to medical magazines. Dr. Miller was one of the best informed men of his day in the South.

MILLER, L. D. Educator and author. For years he was connected with the public schools of Alabama and published a 'History of Alabama,' which is both authoritative and exhaustive, beginning with the expedition of De Soto (Birmingham, Ala., Roberts and Son, 1902).

MILLER, MARY AYER. Author. [N.C.]. Her maiden name was Mary Ayer. Besides several books for Sunday-schools, she wrote occasional poems, and published a collection of verse entitled 'Wood-notes.'

MILLER, M. C., Mrs. Author. [La.]. She wrote 'Severed at Gettysburg' and 'Love and Rebellion.'

MILLER, SAMUEL FREEMAN. Jurist. [Ky.]. He was born in 1816 and died in 1890. Judge Miller wrote 'The Supreme Court of the United States,' a series of interesting biographies.

MILLER, STEPHEN FRANKS, lawyer and author, was born in North Carolina, in 1810, and died in Oglethorpe, Ga., in 1867. For some time he successfully practiced law, but a bronchial affection compelled him to engage in other pursuits; and in various places he edited newspapers and periodicals. He also published several volumes, among them, 'The Bench and Bar of Georgia' (Philadelphia, J. B. Lippincott and Company), in two volumes, 'Wilkins Wilder; or, the Successful Man,' and 'Memoir of General Blackshear.'

MILLER, WALTER, educator, was born in Ashland County, Ohio, May 5, 1864. After completing his studies at the University of Michigan, he studied abroad. Since 1902 he has been professor of Greek at Tulane University, New Orleans. Besides numerous contributions to magazines and reviews, he has published a 'Latin Prose Composition for College Use' (Boston, B. H. Sanborn and Company, 1890), a 'History of the Akropolis at Athens' (1893), 'The Old and the New' (Palo Alto, Cal., The Stanford University Press, 1898), and 'Stella's Sea Beasts' (Washington, D.C., The Government Press, 1899). He wrote for 'The Library of Southern Literature' the sketch of William B. Smith.

MILLIGAN, ROBERT, clergyman and educator, was born in County Tyrone, Ireland, July 25, 1814, and died in Lexington, Ky., March 20, 1875. Most of his life was devoted to educational work. He entered the ministry of the Disciples of Christ, became associate editor of the *Millennial Harbinger,* of which Alexander Campbell was the founder and editor-in-chief, taught in Kentucky University, and published several theological works; among them, 'Prayer' (1863), 'Reason and Revelation' (1867), 'The Scheme of Redemption' (1868), 'The Great Commission' (1871), an 'Analysis of the New Testament' (1874), and a 'Commentary on the Epistle to the Hebrews' (1875).

MILLS, ROBERT, architect, was born in Charleston, S.C., August 12, 1781, and died in Washington, D.C., March 3, 1855. He studied architecture under Benjamin H. Latrobe, became an eminent architect, designed the fireproof wings of Independence Hall, the single arch bridge across the Schuylkill, and the Washington monument, the latter being the tallest memorial structure in the world. For many years he was United States architect and supervised the construction of many of the public buildings in Washington. He published 'Statistics of South Carolina,' with an atlas of the State, 'The American Pharos; or, Light-house Guide,' and 'Guide to the National Executive Offices.'

MILLS, ROGER QUARLES, statesman, was born in Todd County, Ky., March 30, 1832. On completing his education he located in Texas for the practice of law and became distinguished as an advocate. He enlisted in the Confederate Army at the outbreak of the Civil War, commanded a brigade and received a number of wounds. For nearly twenty years he served in the National House. In 1892 he was appointed to fill the unexpired term of John H. Reagan in the United States Senate, and was subsequently elected for another full term. He married, January 7, 1858, Caroline R. Jones. In the legislative councils at Washington, Senator Mills was an acknowledged leader. His speeches are masterpieces of thought and logic.

MILNER, JOHN TURNER. Civil engineer. He was born in 1826 and died in 1898. He was at one time in the State Senate of Alabama, and was the author of a book entitled 'Alabama as It Was, as It Is, and as It Will Be,' besides numerous monographs on industrial and economic subjects.

MILTON, GEORGE FORT, editor and publisher, was born in Macon, Ga., July 16, 1869. For several years he has been principal owner of two of the South's leading newspapers, the Knoxville *Sentinel* and the Chattanooga *News,* and has also been an active factor in politics. Twice he was a delegate to national Democratic conventions. Besides contributing to current periodicals like the *North American Review* and the *American Journal of Politics,* he has published two important pamphlets, viz.: 'The Constitution of Tennessee Considered with Reference to the Constitutions of Other States' (1897), and 'Compulsory Education in the Southern States' (1908). He married, first, February 3, 1893, Caroline McCall; and, second, September 19, 1904, Abby Crawford.

MIMS, EDWIN, educator, was born in Richmond, Ark., May 27, 1872, being the son of Andrew J. and Cornelia Mims, and was educated at Vanderbilt. From 1894 to 1909 he occupied the chair of English at Trinity College, Durham, N.C., resigning to head the same department at the State University, Chapel Hill, N.C. In 1902 he became editor of the *South Atlantic Quarterly,* and besides editing Carlyle's "Essay on Burns" for the 'Gateway Series of English Classics' (New York, The American Book Company) and 'Selections from Henry Van Dyke' (New York, Charles Scribner's Sons), he is the author of an excellent 'Life of Sidney Lanier' (Boston, Houghton, Mifflin and Company), the sketch of Thomas Nelson Page in Baskerville's 'Southern Writers,' Vol. II, and the sketch of Paul H. Hayne in 'The Library of Southern Literature.' From time to time he has also written for the various periodicals. He received his Ph.D. from Cornell.

MINES, FLAVEL SCOTT, clergyman was born in Leesburg, Va., December 31, 1811, and died in San Francisco, Cal., in 1852. He was at one time pastor of a Presbyterian church in the city of New York, but experienced a change of religious faith, resigned, took orders in the Episcopal ministry and organized the first church of his denomination on the Pacific Coast. He wrote 'A Presbyterian Clergyman Looking for the Church' (New York, 1850).

MINIFIE, WILLIAM, author, was born in Devonshire, England, August 14, 1805, and died in Baltimore, Md., October 24, 1880. He was an architect by profession and a bookseller by trade. Afterward he became a professor in the Maryland School of Art. He published a 'Text-book of Mechanical Drawing' (Baltimore, 1849), a 'Text-book of Geometrical Drawing' (1853), "Essay on the Theory and Application of Color" (1854), and 'Lectures on Drawing and Design' (1854).

MINNEGERODE, CHARLES G., Protestant Episcopal clergyman, was born in Germany in 1814 and died in Virginia in 1894. He published 'Sermons.'

MINOR, BENJAMIN BLAKE, lawyer and educator, was born in Essex County, Va., in 1818, and died in Richmond, Va., in 1904. For years Dr. Minor owned and edited *The Southern Literary Messenger,* to which some of the foremost ante-bellum writers were contributors; and his work entitled 'The Southern Literary Messenger, 1834-1864' (New York and Washington, The Neale Publishing Company, 1900), is full of fascinating interest to lovers of literature. He also edited 'Wythe's Chancery Reports,' with a memoir, lectured on astronomical and Biblical subjects, and contributed to periodicals. He married, May 26, 1842, Virginia Maury, daughter of Bishop Otey of Tennessee. The University of Missouri gave him the degree of LL.D.

MINOR, JOHN BARBEE, lawyer and educator, was born in Louisa County, Va., June 2, 1813, became a law professor of very wide reputation in the University of Virginia, with which institution he was connected for many years, and published 'The Virginia Reports of 1799-1900,' 'Synopsis of the Law of Crimes and Punishments,' and 'The Institutes of Common and Statute Law.'

MINOR, LUCIAN, educator and lawyer, was born in Louisa County, Va., in 1802, and died in Williamsburg, Va., in 1858. For twenty-four years he was commonwealth attorney, and from 1856 till his death he was professor of law in William and Mary College. Besides contributing to periodicals, he wrote part of John A. G. Davis's 'Guide to Justices,' added notes to Call's 'Virginia Reports,' condensed the four volumes of Hening and Mumford's 'Reports' into one, adding subsequent decisions and enactments, 'Reasons for Abolishing the Liquor Traffic,' pamphlet, and "Notes of Travel in New England," which were published after his death in the *Atlantic Monthly,* under the supervision of James Russell Lowell.

MINOR, RALEIGH COLSTON, educator and lawyer, was born near Charlottesville, Va., January 24, 1869. His father was John B. Minor, for many years connected with the law department of the University of Virginia. On completing his education, he studied law, was called to teach in the law department of his *alma mater* in the capacity of assistant, and since 1899 has been professor of law. His publications include 'Law of Tax Titles in Virginia' and 'Conflict of Laws' (Boston, Little, Brown and Company).

MINOR, VIRGINIA L. Author. [Va.]. She published 'Historical and Biographical Sketches.'

MITCHELL, EDWARD COPPEE, lawyer, was born in Savannah, Ga., July 24, 1836, and died in Philadelphia, Pa., January 25, 1887. He achieved distinction at the Northern Bar, and was for many years connected with the legal department of the University of Pennsylvania. Besides editing 'Tudor's Leading Cases,' he published 'Separate Use in Pennsylvania,' 'Contracts for the Sale of Land in Pennsylvania' and 'The Equitable Relation of the Buyer and Seller of Land under Contract and before Conveyance.' Hobart College gave him the degree of LL.D.

MITCHELL, ELISHA, clergyman and educator, was born in Washington, Conn., August 19, 1793, and died on Black Mountain, N.C.,

June 27, 1857. For more tha.i twenty-five years he was connected with the scientific department of the University of North Carolina. He lost his life in a snow-storm while endeavoring to ascertain the height of Black Dome; but his body was recovered from the pool into which it fell, and entombed on the highest peak of the mountain, which is to-day called bv the name of the ill-fated explorer. He published 'Elements of Geology, with an Outline of the Geology of North Carolina,' and numerous reports. The University of Alabama gave him the degree of D.D.

MITCHELL, FRANCES LETCHER. Author. [Ga.]. She published 'Georgia Land and People,' an interesting story of the State (Atlanta, The Franklin Printing Company, 1893). Miss Mitchell resides in Athens, Ga.

MITCHELL, JAMES C., lawyer, was born in Mecklenburg County, N.C., about 1790, and died near Jackson, Miss., August 7, 1843. He practiced law for several years in Tennessee and served for two years in Congress, after which he became judge of the Circuit Court. In 1837 he located in Mississippi. He published 'Mitchell's Justice.'

MITCHELL, JOHN KEARSLEY, physician and author, was born of Scotch parentage at Shepherdstown, Va., May 12, 1798, and died in Philadelphia, Pa., April 4, 1858. After receiving his medical diploma he became a ship-surgeon, and made three voyages to the Orient. He then located in Philadelphia, becoming an eminent practitioner and professor. He also edited periodicals and delivered popular scientific lectures. His literary gifts were of very high order. He wrote both prose and verse and published "St. Helena, a Poem by a Yankee" (1821), 'Indecision: a Tale of the Far West, and Other Poems' (Philadelphia, 1831), 'On the Wisdom, Goodness and Power of God, Illustrated in the Properties of Water' (1834), 'On the Cryptogamous Origin of Malarious and Epidemic Fevers,' and 'Five Essays on Various Chemical and Medical Subjects' (1858). His son, Dr. Silas Weir Mitchell, is one of the most noted of living surgeons and authors.

MITCHELL, ORMSBY MACKNIGHT, astronomer, was born in Morganfield, Ky., July 28, 1809, and died in Beaufort, S.C., October 30, 1862. He was educated at West Point in the class with Robert E. Lee and Joseph E. Johnston, but resigned from the Army and became an eminent writer and teacher in the astronomical branches, inventing the chronograph. During the Civil War he attained the rank of brigadier-general on the Union side. He was a member of scientific societies of both Europe and America, and published 'The Planetary and Siderial Worlds' (New York, 1848), 'The Orbs of Heaven' (1851), 'A Concise Elementary Treatise of the Sun, Planets, Satellites, and Comets' (1860), and 'The Astronomy of the Bible' (1863). His son, Frederick A. Mitchell, wrote his memoir (Boston, 1887). Washington University made him an LL.D. and Harvard an A.M.

MITCHELL, WILL WARD. Poet. [Mo.]. He published 'Joel, and Other Poems' (1903) and 'A Wreath of Autumn' (1905).

MOHR, CARL THEODOR. Scientist. He was born in Germany, in 1824, but came to this country on completing his education. He was one of the argonauts who crossed the great plains in 1849; later he accompanied Kappler on an exploring expedition to Dutch Guiana; and for the Tenth United States Census he explored the forests of the Gulf States. He was for several years botanist of the Geological Survey of Alabama and agent of the Forestry Division of the United States Department of Agriculture. Besides many important papers bearing upon the botanical products of this section, he wrote: 'The Timber Pines of the Southern United States' and

'Plant Life of Alabama,' both of which were published by the United States Department of Agriculture, at Washington, D.C. His intimate knowledge of the Southern forests has yielded some very important results. He died in 1901.

MOISE, PENINA. See Biographical and Critical Sketch, Vol. VIII, page 3663.

MONETTE, JOHN WESLEY, physician, was born in Ohio, April 3, 1803, died in Madison Parish, La., March 1, 1851. After graduating from the Kentucky Medical College, he located in Mississippi, became a practitioner of note and a member of the Legislature, and wrote a 'History of the Discovery and Settlement of the Mississippi Valley,' in two volumes (New York, Harper and Brothers, 1848). At his death he left the manuscript of an important work on 'Rivers of the Southwest.'

MONEY, HERNANDO DE SOTO, United States Senator, was born in Holmes County, Miss., August 26, 1839. Soon after completing his studies at the University of Mississippi, hostilities began, and he entered the Confederate ranks. When peace was restored, he began the practice of law, represented his district in Congress for fourteen years, and, on the death of James Z. George, was appointed to fill the unexpired term in the United States Senate. Later he was twice commissioned by the Legislature to occupy the same high seat, and in 1909 became minority leader. On most of the public questions of the day he has spoken with great power and earnestness.

MONROE, JAMES. See Biographical and Critical Sketch, Vol. VIII, page 3675.

MONTAGUE, ANDREW JACKSON, governor, lawyer and educator, was born in Campbell County, Va., October 3, 1862. His father was Robert Latane Montague, and his mother, Cordelia Gay Eubank. He chose the legal profession, filled the office of attorney-general four years, and in 1902 became governor of Virginia. Since retiring from the executive chair, in 1906, he has been dean of the law school of Richmond College. Besides occasional articles and addresses, he is the author of the sketch of John Marshall, in 'The Library of Southern Literature.' He married, December 11, 1889, Elizabeth Hoskins. Brown University gave him the degree of LL.D.

MONTAGUE, ANDREW PHILIP, educator, was born in Essex County, Va., September 27, 1854. His father was Howard W. Montague and his mother, Mildred C. Broaddus. After graduation from the University of Virginia, he devoted himself to educational work. Since 1902 he has been president of Howard College at East Lake, Ala. He has edited 'Selected Letters of Cicero' (Philadelphia, Eldredge and Brother, 1890), and 'Selected Letters of Pliny' (*ibid.*, 1893). The University of Virginia gave him the degree of Ph.D., and Columbian University, the degree of LL.D.

MONTAGUE, MARGARET PRESCOTT, author, was born at White Sulphur Springs, W.Va., November 26, 1878. Her father was Russell W. Montague. She was educated at home and in private schools. Her published works include 'The Poet, Miss Kate and I' (New York, The Baker and Taylor Company, 1905), and 'The Sowing of Alderson Cree' (*ibid.*, 1907).

MONTGOMERY, SIR ROBERT, colonist, was born in Ayr, Scotland, about 1680 and died in Ireland in 1731. He designed to plant a colony in what is now the State of Georgia, giving it the name of the "Margravate of Azalia." The climate he declared to be the most salubrious under the sun. Sir Robert's dream failed to materialize, but the splendid project is embalmed in his 'Discourse Concerning the Designed Establishment of a New Colony to the South of South Carolina, in the Most Delightful Country of the Universe' (London, 1717).

MOODY, EDWIN F. Author. [Miss.]. He wrote 'Bob Rutherford and His Wife' (1888) and 'Helen Vernon' (1890).

MOODY, HENRY A. Physician. [Ala.]. He wrote a novel entitled 'A City without a Name' (1897).

MOOMAW, BENJAMIN C. Horticulturist and poet. At the opening of the Jamestown Exposition, on May 13, 1907, the tercentenary poem was read by this talented Virginian, to whom was entrusted the honor of signalizing the event in song. Both in scope of thought and in power of expression the ode which he composed was worthy of the historic occasion. Entitled "Freedom's Empire," it pictured the outgrowth of the first English colony, which, in 1607, was planted at the mouth of the James, and portrayed the influence of this pioneer settlement upon civilization. Mr. Moomaw is also the author of a collection of poems in pamphlet form, which appeared in 1900, entitled: 'Songs in the Night,' but he has recently withdrawn the work from publication and is preparing to bring out another volume which will contain his best productions up to date. He was born in Botetourt County, Va., December 23, 1852. His home is at Ben, in Alleghany County, of the same state, and his chief occupation and enjoyment is in the cultivation of plants and flowers. He married Margaret Ellen Bowman.

MOORE, EDWARD A. Author. [Va.]. He published an exceedingly graphic narrative of personal adventures entitled 'The Story of a Cannoneer under Stonewall Jackson,' to which Captain Robert E. Lee, Jr., and the Honorable Henry St. George Tucker furnished introductions (New York and Washington, The Neale Publishing Company, 1900).

MOORE, FRANK. He compiled and edited 'Songs and Ballads of the Southern People, 1861-1865' (New York, D. Appleton and Company, 1886).

MOORE, FREDERICK WIGHTMAN. Educator. He was born in Lyme, Conn., October 18, 1863, graduated from Yale University and became professor of history and economics in Vanderbilt University and dean of the academic faculty of that institution. Besides translating 'Outlines of Sociology,' by Dr. Ludwig Gumplowitz, he has also written two papers of rare historical interest and value entitled "Representation in the National Congress from the Seceding States" and "The Course of Louisiana Politics from 1862 to 1866." The sketch of Andrew Jackson in 'The Library of Southern Literature' is from his pen. Yale gave him the degree of Ph.D. He resides in Nashville, Tenn.

MOORE, HIGHT C., Baptist clergyman and educator, was born in Globe, Caldwell County, N.C., January 28, 1871. The published works of Dr. Moore include: 'Seaside Sermons' (Morehead City, N.C., 1891), 'Select Poetry of North Carolina' (Raleigh, N.C., Edwards and Broughton, 1894), 'Books of the Bible' (Nashville, Tenn., Baptist Sunday-school Board, 1902), and a 'Bibliography of the Poetic Literature of North Carolina (Chapel Hill, N.C., 1907). The sketch of Theophilus H. Hill in 'The Library of Southern Literature' is also from his pen. He resides in Raleigh, N.C., where he edits the *Biblical Recorder*, the official organ of North Carolina Baptists. He married, May 2, 1893, Laura Peterson.

MOORE, IDORA PLOWMAN ("Betsy Hamilton"), author, was born near Talladega, Ala., in 1843, and was the daughter of General

William B. McClellan, a Scotchman of the line of William Wallace. At an early age she became the wife of Albert W. Plowman, a lawyer of her native town; and, being left a widow soon thereafter, she began to write stories and sketches in "cracker" dialect for the local papers, her first effort being entitled: "Betsy's Trip to Town." She won instant success; and, under the name of "Betsy Hamilton," she became one of the favorite contributors to the current periodicals. Later she married Captain M. V. Moore and moved to Auburn, Ala. She was equally unique in impersonating the characters which she described with her pen; and for years she delighted the public with her dramatic readings.

MOORE, JOHN C. Soldier and author. [Mo.]. He commanded a regiment during the Civil War and wrote the volume on "Missouri" in 'The Confederate Military History' (Atlanta, Ga., The Confederate Publishing Company, 1899), besides numerous ably written historical papers.

MOORE, JOHN TROTWOOD. See Biographical and Critical Sketch, Vol. VIII, page 3693.

MOORE, JOHN WHEELER. Author. [N.C.]. Born in 1833. He wrote a 'History of North Carolina.'

MOORE, JOSIAH STAUNTON. Merchant and capitalist. He was born in Richmond, Va., June 18, 1843, the son of James Robert and Maria Louisa Higgins Moore. His education was interrupted by the outbreak of the war; and, entering the Confederate Army, he served in Pickett's immortal division. He was captured at Five Forks, the last pitched battle of the war, and was held a prisoner at Point Lookout until June 16, 1865, more than two months after General Lee surrendered. He married Jennie E. Owens, and became one of the leading merchants of Richmond, engaging in the wholesale grocery business. He held numerous positions of trust and honor, but found time for literary diversions. His writings include: 'A Trans-Atlantic Itinerary,' 'Reminiscences, Letters, and Miscellanies,' and 'History of Henrico Parish and Old St. John's Church,' besides frequent contributions to the press. He resides in Richmond, Va.

MOORE, M. A., Sr. He was an eminent physician who wrote 'The Life of General Edward Lacy, with a List of Battles and Skirmishes in South Carolina during the Revolution.' The book was published in Spartanburg, S.C., in 1859.

MOORE, MARTIN V. Educator. He wrote 'The Rhyme of the Southern Rivers,' with notes, historical, traditional, geographical and etymological (Nashville, The M.E. Publishing House, South, 1897), 'The Recollections of a Gray Jacket,' and numerous contributions to newspapers and magazines. For some time Captain Moore was a professor in the college at Auburn, Ala.

MOORE, MATHEW HENRY. Methodist Episcopal clergyman. [N.C.]. He was born in 1857. He wrote 'Pioneers of Methodism in North Carolina and Virginia' (Nashville, Tenn., The M.E. Publishing House, South, 1884).

MOORE, MAURICE. See Biographical and Critical Sketch, Vol. VIII, page 3707.

MOORE, MINNIE WILSON, Mrs. Author. For many years she has resided at Kissimmee, Fla., and her study of Indian life and character has borne fruit in an entertaining work entitled 'The Seminoles of Florida,' which gives an account of the Indians now living in the Everglades.

MOORE, THOMAS VERNON, clergyman, was born in Newville, Pa., February 1, 1818, and died in Nashville, Tenn., August 5, 1871. For several years he was pastor of a church in Richmond, Va., and afterward accepted a call to Nashville. With Dr. Moses D. Hodge, he edited the *Central Presbyterian.* Besides contributing to current periodicals, he published 'Commentaries on Haggai, Zachariah, and Malachi' (Philadelphia, 1856), 'Last Words of Jesus' (1859), 'God's University; or, the Family a School, a Government and a Church' (Richmond, 1864), and 'The Culdee Church.' He was a graduate of Princeton.

MOORE, W. H. Poet. [N.C.]. The author of 'Virginia Dare: a Story of Colonial Days,' written in verse (Raleigh, 1904), a work of merit.

MOORE, WALTER WILLIAM. Clergyman and educator. He was born in Charlotte, N.C., June 14, 1857, a son of Isaac Hudson and Martha Parks Moore. He graduated from Davidson College, N.C., and from Union Theological Seminary, Va., and married, May 18, 1886, Loula S. Fries. He became professor of Hebrew in Union Theological Seminary in 1883 and president of the institution in 1904. Besides numerous contributions to religious reviews and periodicals, he has written a volume of wide popularity entitled 'A Year in Europe' (Richmond, Presbyterian Committee of Publication, 1904). The sketch of Moses D. Hoge in 'The Library of Southern Literature' is also from his pen. Central University gave him the degree of D.D. and Davidson College the degree of LL.D. He resides in Richmond, Va.

MOORE, WILLIAM THOMAS, clergyman and educator, was born in Henry County, Ky., August 27, 1832. After graduation from Bethany College he entered the ministry of the Disciples of Christ. For ten years he was pastor of a church in London, Eng., and edited the *Christian Commonwealth.* He was also at one time a professor in Kentucky University and later dean of the Columbia Bible College. Besides editing 'Lectures on the Pentateuch,' by Alexander Campbell, he published 'Views of Life,' 'Conversations of the Unity Club' (London, 1888), 'The Fundamental Error of Christendom,' 'The Life of Timothy Coop' (London, 1889), 'Man Preparing for Other Worlds' (St. Louis, Christian Publishing Company), 'Preacher Problems' (New York, Fleming H. Revell Company), and 'At Seventy-five, and Other Poems' (St. Louis, Christian Publishing Company). Butler University gave him the degree of LL.D.

MOORMAN, R. B. Writer. [Va.]. He published 'Sketches of Travel in Europe.'

MORAN, JANE W. BLACKBURN, Mrs. Author. [Va.]. She was born in 1842 and wrote 'Miss Washington of Virginia.'

MORAN, WILLIAM HENRY WADSWORTH. Editor. [Va.]. He published 'From Schoolroom to Bar' (1892), and 'Face to Face,' a volume of poems (1893).

MORDECAI, ALFRED, soldier, was born in Warrentown, N.C., January 3, 1804, and died in Philadelphia, October 23, 1887. He was educated at West Point, graduating first in his class, attained the rank of major in the Mexican War, resigned in 1861, and later accepted an engineering offer from Mexico. For twenty years he was treasurer of the Pennsylvania Canal Company, with headquarters in Philadelphia. He published: 'Digest of Military Laws,' 'Ordnance Manual for the Use of Officers in the United States Army,' 'Reports of Experiments on Gunpowder,' and 'Artillery for the United States Land Service, as Devised and Arranged by the Ordnance Board,' illustrated with plates.

•

MORDECAI, SAMUEL FOX, lawyer and educator, was born in Richmond, Va., December 12, 1852. At the present time he is professor of law in Trinity College, Durham, N.C. His writings embrace several legal works of standard value, viz.: 'Mechanics' Liens' (1897), 'Lex Scripta' (1905), 'Mordecai's Law Lectures' (1907), and 'Notes to the Negotiable Instruments Law of North Carolina' (1897). He married, November 10, 1875, Betty Grimes.

MORE, PAUL ELMER, author, was born in St. Louis, Mo., December 12, 1864, and was educated at Washington and Harvard Universities. For two years he taught Sanscrit at Bryn Mawr. His published works include: 'The Great Refusal' (New York, Harper and Brothers), 'A Century of Indian Epigrams' (*ibid.*), 'The Judgment of Socrates' (*ibid.*), a translation of 'Prometheus Bound' (*ibid.*), and a 'Life of Benjamin Franklin,' besides numerous articles on classic and oriental literatures. He resides at East Orange, N.J.

MOREHEAD, CHARLES SLAUGHTER, Congressman and governor, was born in Nelson County, Ky., July 7, 1802, and died near Greenville, Miss., December 23, 1868. For several years he was attorney-general of Kentucky, served in Congress from 1847 to 1851, and occupied the office of governor from 1855 to 1859. His endeavors to bring about the secession of Kentucky occasioned his arrest in 1861, but after imprisonment for some time in Fort Lafayette his friends secured his release and he went to England. On returning to the United States he settled upon a plantation near Greenville, Miss., where he spent his few remaining days. In association with Judge Mason Brown, he published a 'Digest of the State Laws of Kentucky to 1834.'

MOREHEAD, JAMES TURNER, United States Senator and governor, was born in Bullitt County, Ky., May 24, 1797, and died in Covington, Ky., December 28, 1854. On completing his studies at college, he chose the legal profession, achieved eminence at the Bar, became governor of Kentucky, and from 1841 to 1847 served in the United States Senate. He published 'An Address Commemorative of the First Settlers of Kentucky at Boonesborough' (Frankfort, 1840), and 'Practice and Procedure of Law in Kentucky' (1846).

MOREHEAD, JOSEPH M. [N.C.]. He published in verse an 'Address to Battle-Ground Oak' (Greensboro, N.C., 1904, paper edition).

MORFIT, CAMPBELL, chemist, was born in Herculaneum, Mo., November 19, 1820. After graduating from Columbian College, he took up the study of chemistry, made himself proficient in this branch, became professor of chemistry in the University of Maryland, and in 1861 removed to London. Besides numerous scientific papers, he published 'Chemistry as Applied to the Manufacture of Soaps and Candles' (Philadelphia, 1847), 'Progress of Chemical Arts,' with Dr. James C. Booth (Washington, 1851), 'The Arts of Tanning and Currying' (Philadelphia, 1852), 'Oleic Soaps' (London, 1871), and 'Chemical and Pharmaceutical Manipulations.'

MORGAN, JAMES BRAINERD, poet, was born in Berkeley County, Va. Two volumes of verse have come from his pen: 'Song Sermons, and Other Poems' (Richmond, 1892) and 'Strollings in Song-land' (Richmond, 1893).

MORGAN, JOHN TYLER. Statesman. He was born in Athens, Tenn., in 1824, but in early life he crossed into Alabama and became an important factor in the political affairs of his adopted State. As a lawyer he early took front rank. He was a delegate to the Secession Convention, and in the field service of the Confederacy became a brigadier-general. After the war he practiced law for several years, at Selma, Ala.; and, from 1877 to 1907, he represented Alabama in the Senate of the United States. He was one of the ablest debaters in that body, familiar with every phase of national legislation and ready to discuss with illuminating argument any public issue. His senatorial speeches have been preserved in the *Congressional Record*. Though he favored the Nicaraguan route which was rejected by the Administration, he is recognized as the originator of the Isthmian Canal project, this having been his favorite theme for years. He died in Washington, D.C., in 1907.

MORGAN, THOMAS G. Lawyer. [La.]. He compiled a 'Civil Code of the State of Louisiana' (New Orleans, 1857).

MORGAN, TOM P. Humorist. He was born in East Lyme, Conn., December 1, 1864, a son of Joseph P. and Mary A. Morgan. He enjoyed very fair educational advantages and moved to Kansas in early life; afterward to Arkansas. He has contributed to most of the leading periodicals of the day, including *Puck, The Smart Set,* and *Town Topics*. His sketches and portraitures are characterized by pungent humor. He resides in Rogers, Ark.

MORGAN, WILLIAM, mason, was born in Culpeper County, Va., about 1775, and served under General Jackson at New Orleans. The report was circulated in 1826 that he was on the eve of exposing the secrets of masonry and not long thereafter he strangely and suddenly disappeared. Efforts to find him were fruitless. Thereupon a war against masonry was inaugurated, political organizations were effected, and what purported to be Morgan's book was published under the title of 'Illustrations of Freemasonry by One of the Fraternity Who Has Devoted Thirty Years to the Subject,' with an account of the kidnapping of the author. Later it was published under the title of 'Freemasonry Exposed and Explained.' But the excitement over the affair eventually subsided. As an episode it was full of sensational and dramatic interest and various works have appeared upon the subject; among them, 'The Broken Seal; or, the Morgan Abduction and Murder,' by S. D. Greene (New York, 1870), a 'History of the Morgan Affair,' by Robert Morris (New York, 1852), and 'American Political Anti-Masonry' (New York, 1879).

MORINIÉRE, EMMANUEL DE LA. An eloquent Jesuit priest. He was born at Basse-Terre, Guadeloupe, April 17, 1856, but was educated in New Orleans. On account of his rare gifts as an orator his rise to distinction was rapid, and soon after his ordination he took front rank in the Roman Catholic pulpit. His lecture on "Chivalry" is preserved in 'The Louisiana Book' (1894). He now resides in Mobile, Ala.

MORRIS, GEORGE VAN DERVEER, clergyman and author, was born in Bridgeton, N.J., December 5, 1867, a son of Dr. George K. Morris, a distinguished minister. On completing his studies, he was licensed to preach by the M.E. Church, North, but for several years Kentucky has been the field of his labors. Instead of devoting his pen to grave theological problems, he has written several entertaining works of fiction: 'A Man for a' That' (Chicago, The Western Methodist Publishing House, 1904), 'A Fairy Tale of Love' (Washington, The Neale Publishing Company, 1906), and 'Polly' (*ibid.*, 1907). He has received the D.D. and the LL.D. degrees.

MORRIS, JOHN, educator, was born in Goochland County, Va., June 23, 1863. His father was Major Charles Morris, for many years his predecessor in the chair of English at the University of Georgia. Besides articles in philological journals, he has published 'The Organic History of English Words' (1909). The sketch of "Bill Arp" in 'The Library of Southern Literature' is also from his pen. He married, June 23, 1904. Gretchen McC. Gallagher.

MORRIS, JOHN GOTTLIEB. Clergyman. Dr. Morris founded Trinity English Lutheran Church, in Baltimore, Md., and served it as pastor for more than thirty years. He was an extensive traveler and an eminent theologian and scholar. His published works are numerous. They include: 'A Popular Exposition of the Gospels,' in two volumes (1840), 'The Blind Girl of Wittenberg' (1856), a 'Life of John Arndt' (1853), a 'Life of Catharine de Bora' (1856), 'Fifty Years in the Lutheran Ministry' (1878), and several others, besides also a number of translations. He died in 1895, at the age of ninety-two.

MORRIS, ROBERT, author, was born in Massachusetts, August 31, 1818. and died in LaGrange, Ky., July 31, 1888. For the greater part of his life he resided in the South. He was an active freemason and wrote and lectured on the subject of freemasonry. At one time he was also president of Oldham College, at LaGrange, Ky., where he resided for many years. He published 'Lights and Shadows of Freemasonry' (Louisville, 1852), 'History of the Morgan Affair' (New York, 1852), 'Code of Masonic Law' (Louisville, 1855), 'History of Freemasonry in Kentucky' (Frankfort, 1859), 'Freemasonry in the Holy Land' (New York, 1882), and 'The Poetry of Freemasonry.'

MORRIS, ROBERT HUGH, clergyman, poet, lecturer, was born in Bluffton, Ga., August 9, 1876, a son of Rev. W. J. Morris, and received his education partly at Emory College, Oxford, Ga., and partly at Princeton, where he attended both the University and the Seminary, obtaining his M.A. degree in 1905. Dr. Morris is at present pastor of the First Presbyterian Church of Evanston, Ill., to which charge he was recently called from the pastorate of Oak Lane Presbyterian Church, Philadelphia, Pa. As an orator he has perhaps no superior of his age in the pulpit. On the lecture platform he has also acquired distinction; and from time to time he contributes an occasional poem to current periodicals. He has written most charmingly of his travels abroad. Northwestern University conferred upon him, in 1909, the degree of D.D.

MORRIS, THOMAS ASBURY, Methodist Episcopal bishop, was born near Shepherdstown, Va., April 28, 1794, and died in Springfield, Ohio, September 2, 1874. For some years he was a skeptic, but in 1813 he experienced conversion, joined the Ohio Conference of the Methodist Church, became one of the most effective pioneer preachers of the Middle West, and in 1836 was ordained to the office of bishop. At one time he edited *The Western Christian Advocate,* in Cincinnati. His published works include a volume of sermons, 'Church Polity,' 'Essays, Biographical Sketches, and Notes of Travel,' and 'Sketches of Western Methodism.' McKenzie College gave him his D.D. degree.

MORRISON, HENRY CLAY, bishop of the M.E. Church, South, was born in Montgomery County, Tenn., May 30, 1842. On completing his studies, he taught school for several years, entered the ministry of the M.E. Church, South, occupied the most important pulpits within the bounds of the Louisville Conference, after which he was transferred to the Atlanta Conference, became secretary of the Board of Missions, lifted an indebtedness of $140,000, and, in 1898, was called to the office of bishop. He is one of the most eloquent divines of his denomination. Besides occasional sermons and addresses, he has published a volume entitled 'Arrows From Two Quivers,' and contributed to religious and secular periodicals. He holds the degree of D.D.

MORROW, THOMAS VAUGHN, physician, was born in Kentucky, in 1804, and died in Cincinnati, Ohio, July 16, 1850. Under the patronage of Bishop Philander Chase, he founded at Worthington, Ohio, a reformed school of medicine, which was afterward transferred to Cincinnati and reorganized under the name of the American Eclectic Medical Institute, in which he taught for the remainder of his life. He published 'The Practice of Medicine' (1852).

MORSE, ALEXANDER PORTER, Lawyer. [La.]. He was born in 1842, and wrote 'Citizenship by Birth and Naturalization.'

MORTON, JENNIE C., Mrs. Secretary and treasurer of the Kentucky State Historical Society, editor and poet. Mrs. Morton is the recognized founder of the organization with which she has for years been identified, and her contributions to the historical literature of Kentucky have been both numerous and important. Besides editing the *Register*, she is constantly engaged in writing historical essays and sketches. She is also a poet of rare mental and spiritual endowment; and from her ode to the memory of Governor Goebel were taken the lines which have been inscribed upon his monument. She has recently published in verse a work which the critics have praised in very high terms, entitled 'Her Dearest Friend' (1909), an epic of love and religion. She resides in Lexington, Ky.

MOSBY, ELLA F. Author. [Va.]. She was born in 1846 and wrote 'The Ideal Life' (1877), numerous short stories and sketches, and occasional poems.

MOSBY, JOHN SINGLETON, lawyer, was born in Powhatan County, Va., December 6, 1833. He was educated at the University of Virginia, and chose the profession of law. During the Civil War, he was colonel of the famous band of partisan rangers, an independent cavalry command, which bore his name and which inflicted great damage upon the foe by intercepting communications and destroying supply trains in the rear of the Federal Army. He practiced law in Virginia for several years after the war, became a Republican, and supported Grant for President of the United States. He was Consul at Hongkong from 1878 to 1885; and on returning to this country settled in San Francisco. He is the author of an exceedingly interesting volume entitled 'War Reminiscences' (New York, Dodd, Mead and Company, 1887), which gives an account of his exploits.

MOSBY, MARY WEBSTER, author, was born in Henrico County, Va., in 1791, and died in Richmond, Va., November 19, 1844. Her maiden name was Webster. She was adopted by her grandfather, Robert Pleasants, a Quaker planter, who freed more than a hundred of his slaves. She married John Garland Mosby. Under the pen-name of "M. M. Webster," she made frequent contributions to current literature, and published a volume entitled 'Pocahontas' (Philadelphia, 1840) which treats of the legend of the Indian heroine, from whom, through her maternal grandfather, Thomas Mann Randolph, she traced descent.

MOSS, LEMUEL, educator and divine, was born near Burlington, Ky., December 27, 1829. Entering the Baptist ministry, he became an eminent minister of this denomination, held numerous theological professorships, was for a time president of the University of Chicago and afterward, from 1875 to 1884, president of the University of Indiana. He edited several church papers and published 'Annals of the United States Christian Commission' (Philadelphia, 1866). Rochester University conferred upon him the degrees of D.D. and LL.D.

MOULTRIE, WILLIAM, patriot and soldier of the Revolution, was born in England in 1731, and died in Charleston, S.C., September 27, 1805. Though several of his family remained loyal to the Crown, he espoused the colonial cause, became one of the most conspicuous figures in the military operations, was taken prisoner at the fall of Charleston, and, on being released, was made major-general by act of Congress. He was twice governor of South Carolina; and, after retiring to private life, he devoted the remainder of his days to the preparation of his 'Memoirs of the American Revolution,' a work of two volumes, dealing with the campaigns in North and South Carolina and Georgia (New York, 1802).

MOUNT, MARY W., Mrs. Writer. [La.]. She published 'Notables of New Orleans in Art, Music, Poetry, Sculpture and the Drama' (1896).

MUDD, NETTIE. Author. [Va.]. She published a biography of her distinguished father entitled: 'The Life of Dr. Samuel A. Mudd' (New York and Washington, The Neale Publishing Company, 1900). From start to finish this work is replete with interest. It tells the story of one who was unjustly implicated in the assassination of Abraham Lincoln and throws fresh light upon one of the most thrilling of historic chapters. The author has performed her labor of love exceedingly well.

MUENCH, FRANCIS, educator, was born in Germany in 1836. For several years he taught in South Carolina. Besides translating Bryant's works into German, he published 'Palmetto Lyrics' (1896), and 'Luther Lyrics' (1898).

MUIR, JAMES, Presbyterian clergyman, was born in Scotland, in 1757, and died in Virginia, in 1820. He published an 'Examination of Paine's Age of Reason.'

MULLANEY, PATRICK FRANCIS (Brother Azarias), educator, was born in Ireland, June 29, 1847, but brought to the United States when a child, and at the age of fifteen he joined the Brothers of the Christian Schools. For many years he was president of Rock Hill College, at Ellicott City, Md. Besides lectures on Dante and Aristotle, which he read before the Concord School of Philosophy, he published a volume of essays entitled 'Phases of Thought and Criticism' (Boston, Houghton, Mifflin and Company). He died, August 20, 1893.

MULLER, ALBERT A., clergyman and poet, was born in Charleston, S.C., about the year 1800, entered the ministry on completing his education and moved to the West. He was a minor poet; and, before leaving his native town, he published a volume of verse. One of the fragments of his genius was the introductory piece in the American edition of Moore's 'Sacred Melodies.'

MULLINS, EDGAR YOUNG, clergyman and educator, was born in Franklin County, Miss., January 5, 1860. On completing his educational equipment he was ordained to the ministry and was for several years pastor of the Lee Street Baptist Church of Baltimore. He also edited *The Evangel.* In 1899 he became president of the Southern Baptist Theological Seminary at Louisville, Ky. Dr. Mullins is one of the most distinguished theologians and divines of his denomination, the author of an important work, 'Is Christianity True?' (1905), and one of the advisory council of 'The Library of Southern Literature.' His wife is also the author of a work entitled 'Face to Face; or, the Story of a Child.' He has received both the D.D. and the LL.D. degrees.

MUNFORD, B. B. Author. [Va.]. He wrote 'Virginia's Attitude Toward Slavery and Secession' (New York, Longmans, Green and Company, 1909), an important contribution to the apologetic literature of the war between the states.

MUNFORD, ROBERT. Soldier and dramatist. He was an officer in the Revolution and, in addition to several poems, wrote two plays: 'The Candidates' and 'The Patriots,' which deal in a vein of satire with the foibles of his time and are full of the grandiloquent forms of speech which are characteristic of the Eighteenth Century molds. His works were not published until after his death. They appeared in 1798 under the title, 'A Collection of Poems and Plays, by the late Colonel Robert Munford.'

MUNFORD, WILLIAM, lawyer and poet, was born in Mecklenburg County, Va., in 1775, and was the son of Robert Munford, the dramatist. After receiving his education at William and Mary College, he was admitted to the Bar and soon became prominent in the politics of the State. It is said that his classical tastes were developed under the eminent George Wythe, who was his instructor in law. Besides a work entitled: 'Poems and Compositions in Prose' (Richmond, 1798), in which there are some delicate touches of thought, he also made an excellent translation in verse of Homer's 'Iliad,' which was published in two volumes by a Boston firm. He died in 1825.

MUNROE, KIRK. Author of books chiefly for boys. He was born near Prairie du Chien, Wis., September 15, 1856, and was edu cated at Harvard University. Much of the material which he wove into his earlier stories was gathered while a civil engineer in the employ of the Northern Pacific and the Southern Pacific railways. He was the first editor of Harper's 'Round Table.' On May 21, 1880, he married Mary, daughter of Amelia Barr, the novelist; and soon afterward established his residence in southern Florida. Most of his later stories reflect the local color of his subtropical surroundings. Besides editing 'Eminent Men of Our Time,' he is the author of a multitude of books, some of the best known being found in the following list: 'The Golden Days of '49,' 'The White Conquerors,' 'At War With Pontiac,' 'Through Swamp and Glade,' 'The Coral Ship,' 'In Pirate Waters,' 'Forward, March,' 'Under the Great Bear,' 'Children of the Coast.' 'A Sun of Satsuma,' 'The Blue Dragon,' 'The Outcast Warrior' (New York, D. Appleton and Company), and many others. He resides in Cocoanut Grove, Dade County, Fla.

MUNSON, JOHN W. One of Mosby's men. He published 'Reminiscences of a Mosby Guerilla' (New York, Moffit, Yard and Company, 1906).

MURAT, CHARLES LOUIS NAPOLEON ACHILLÉ, son of the King of Naples, Joachim Murat, was born in Paris, France, January 21, 1801, and died near Tallahassee, Fla., April 15, 1847. For some time after the overthrow of the Napoleonic power, he resided in Austria, but on reaching his majority, he came to the United States, toured the principal cities, and finally purchased near Tallahassee, an extensive plantation, on which he spent the remainder of his life. When Lafayette visited this country he met him in Baltimore and accompanied him to Virginia; and while on this trip he made the acquaintance of the beautiful Virginia woman who afterward became his wife, Catharina Dudley, a grandniece of Washington. For several years he practiced law in Tallahassee; but most of his time was given to his splendid estate, which he beautified and improved. He served in a campaign against the Seminoles, took an unobtrusive but deep interest in public affairs and published 'Lettres d'un Citoyen des Étas-Unis à ses Amis, d'Europe' (Paris, 1830) and 'Ésquisses Morales et Politiques sur les États-Unis d'Amérique' (Paris, 1838), the latter of which was in two volumes. Both works were widely read. Murat was a man of engaging manners and of rare accomplishments. He died childless, leaving a fortune to his widow; but his vast estate was destroyed during the Civil War. However, she received an annuity of 20,000 francs from Napoleon III, and when she visited France was greeted with great cordiality at the Imperial Court.

MURFEE, HOPSON OWEN, educator, was born in Marion, Ala., December 11, 1875. After completing his studies at the University of Virginia, he adopted the profession of teaching. Besides occasional articles for the press, he is the author of the sketch of William G. Brown in 'The Library of Southern Literature.' He married, June 26, 1901, Mary McQueer Smith. He resides in Marion, Ala., where he is superintendent of schools.

MURFREE, FANNIE D., author, a sister of Mary Noailles Murfree, otherwise known as "Charles Egbert Craddock." [Tenn.]. She published 'Felicia,' an interesting novel.

MURFREE, MARY NOAILLES. See Biographical and Critical Sketch, Vol. VIII, page 3721.

MURPHEY, ARCHIBALD DE BOW. See Biographical and Critical Sketch, Vol. IX, page 3747.

MURPHEY, EDGAR GARDNER, clergyman, author, educator, was born near Fort Smith, Ark., August 31, 1869 and was educated at the University of the South, where, after completing his collegiate studies, he took a course in theology. Later he attended lectures at Columbia University. He was ordained to the ministry of the Protestant Episcopal Church, at San Antonio, Texas, in 1890 and served parishes in San Antonio and Laredo, Texas, Chillicothe, Ohio, Kingston, N.Y., and Montgomery, Ala. On account of ill health, he withdrew from active pastoral work in 1902, but continued to give much thought to economic and reform movements. The wide scope of his usefulness is attested by the most casual survey of his phenomenal activities. He organized the Southern society for the consideration of the race problem and became the executive secretary of this body which met in National Conference in Montgomery in 1900. As the first chairman of the Alabama Child Labor Committee he initiated the movement which resulted in the National Child Labor Committee, of which he became the first secretary; but when this organization endorsed the "Beveridge Bill" he withdrew. Later he became identified with the Southern Education Board to which he gave his most enthusiastic and loyal support. By special act of the Carnegie Foundation he was granted a pension in 1908 in recognition of his distinguished service to education. His writings include: 'Words for the Church' (1896), 'The Larger Life' (1896), 'The Christian's Life' (1899), 'The Present South; a Discussion of Certain Industrial, Educational and Political Issues' (1904), 'The Basis of Ascendancy; a Discussion of Certain Principles of Public Policy Involved in the Development of the Southern States' (1909) and 'Issues, Southern and National' (1910), besides numerous contributions to periodicals.

MURPHY, JEANNETTE ROBINSON, dramatic soprano and lecturer, was born in Jefferson, Ky., but resides in New York, spending her winters usually in Florida. On the lecture platform she has been quite successful. She is the author of some excellent dialect work both in prose and in verse and has recently published a volume entitled 'Southern Thoughts for Northern Thinkers, and African Music in America.'

MURPHY, JOHN ALBERT, author, was a native of North Carolina, but moved to the West prior to the war, locating first in Missouri and afterward in Texas. He published 'The First Fallen Soldier of 1861,' the same being an account of Henry Wyatt of North Carolina, and 'Cosmostoria,' a work of verse most favorably mentioned in 'Poets and Poetry of Texas.'

MURPHY, ROSALIE MILLER, author, was born in South Carolina but afterward lived in Alabama, and finally removed to New York. She wrote 'Destiny; or, Life As It Is,' 'Mistrust,' and a volume of verse entitled 'Waifs.'

MURRAH, WILLIAM BELTON. Educator and divine, president of Millsaps College, Miss. He was born in Pickensville, Ala., in 1852, a son of the Rev. William Murrah, D.D., and received excellent educational advantages. He married, in 1861, Beulah Fitzhugh, and joined the Mississippi Conference of the Methodist Episcopal Church, South, in 1876. He held numerous important pastorates prior to assuming educational work and attended the Ecumenical Conference in London in 1901. Besides contributing to the religious press, he has delivered many popular lectures and addresses. He resides in Jackson, Miss. Centenary College gave him the degree of D.D. and Wofford College the degree of LL.D.

MURRAY, CHARLES THEODORE. Journalist. He was born in Goshen, Ind., March 30, 1843, the son of Charles L. and Ann E. Murray. He was educated at the Indiana University and at the Columbian Law School, and married, May 25, 1871, Ada M. Nealy. He served in the Union Army and was wounded at Stone River in 1862. During the famous Tilden campaign of 1876, he was shot through the lungs. For twenty years he was Washington correspondent, and for ten years was syndicate and special writer in New York. He was in Paris at the time of the celebrated Dreyfus riots. His life being so full of dramatic episodes, his writings have been naturally spiced and tinctured by his adventures. Included among his best known novels are: 'Sub Rosa' (1880), 'Summer Girls' (1885), 'A Modern Gipsy' (1897), and 'Mademoiselle Fouchette' (Philadelphia, J. B. Lippincott Company, 1902). He has also contributed numerous short stories and sketches to the periodicals. He resides in Wardensville, W. Va.

MURRAY, JAMES ORMSBEE, clergyman and educator, was born in Camden, S.C. On completing his education he entered the ministry of the Congregational Church and held many important pastorates at the North; but in 1875 he was made professor of English literature at Princeton, a place which he held for several years, becoming later also dean. He wrote 'Francis Wayland' (Boston, Houghton, Mifflin and Company), and papers and sketches.

MUSICK, JOHN ROY, author, was born in St. Louis County, Mo., February 28, 1849. He studied law but abandoned the legal profession to engage in literary pursuits. He wrote a number of delightful stories of fiction, some of them based upon historical episodes. The list includes: 'The Banker of Bedford,' 'Brother Against Brother,' 'Calamity Row,' 'A Century Too Soon,' 'A Story of Bacon's Rebellion,' 'The Witch of Salem,' 'Hawaii,' 'Cuba Libre,' and 'Lights and Shadows of Our War with Spain' (New York, 1898). Besides, he published the 'Columbian Historical Novels,' covering the whole period of American history in twelve dramatic tales.

MYERS, E. H., Methodist Episcopal clergyman, wrote an interesting historical work entitled 'The Disruption of the Methodist Episcopal Church' (Nashville, M.E. Publishing House. South).

MYERS, KATIE BRUCE. Author. [Ga.]. She published 'Hope Deferred,' a novel (1904).

MYERS, MINNIE WALTER. Author. She published 'Romance and Realism of the Southern Gulf Coast' (Cincinnati, The Robert Clarke Company, 1898).

NADAL, BERNARD HARRISON, clergyman and educator, was born in Talbot County, Md., March 27, 1812, and died in Madison, N.J., June 20, 1870. For many years he labored in the South. He occupied several important Methodist pulpits and taught for some time in Drew Theological Seminary, becoming president on the death of Dr. McClintock. Dickinson College gave him the degree of D.D. He published 'Essays on Church History,' and in 1873 a volume of his sermons entitled 'New Life Dawning' was edited by Professor Henry A. Butts, with a memoir (New York).

NADAL, EHRMAN SYME, author, was born in Lewisburg, W.Va., February 13, 1843. At different periods he was Secretary of Legation at London, and was also for several years on the editorial staff of the New York *Evening Post*. He wrote 'Impressions of London Social Life,' 'Essays at Home and Elsewhere,' and 'Zweibach; or, Notes of a Professional Exile.'

NAGLE, J. E. Physician. [La.]. He published a number of poems, one of which was entitled 'A Home that I Love.'

NAVARRO, MARY ANDERSON DE. Retired actress. Though born in Sacramento, Cal., July 28, 1859, she spent her girlhood days in Louisville, Ky., and received her education at the Ursuline Convent. She became the foremost actress on the American stage, famed for her beauty not only of person but of character. She married, in 1889, Antonio de Navarro, relinquished her dramatic career, and made her home in England. Her only volume is entitled 'A Few Memories.'

NEALE, WALTER, publisher, author, editor, was born in Eastville, Va., January 21, 1873, and is president of the Neale Publishing Company of Washington and New York. In collaboration with Elizabeth H. Hancock, he wrote 'The Betrayal,' an historico-political novel (1910), besides editing two important works: 'A Southern Anthology' (1910), and 'Masterpieces of Southern Poetry' (1910). He married, June 9, 1897, Margaret Ella Stuart of Charleston, S.C.

NEESE, GEORGE M. Author. [Va.]. Mr. Neese was a gunner under General J. E. B. Stuart in the Army of Northern Virginia. He wrote an interesting work entitled 'Three Years in the Confederate Horse Artillery' (New York and Washington, The Neale Publishing Company, 1909). The introduction was written by Senator John W. Daniel.

NELSON, KATHLEEN GRAY. Author. She was born in Atlanta, Ga., the daughter of John A. and Katherine Gray Smith and married, December 3, 1891, Levi D. Nelson. For three years she was on the staff of the New York *World*. Besides many short stories and sketches for current magazines, she published in 1898 a volume of intense interest, entitled 'Tuen, Slave and Empress,' an account of the extraordinary rise to power of the late Empress Dowager of China. On a recent trip abroad she gathered the material for an Egyptian romance on which she is now engaged. She resides in New York City.

NEVILLE, L., author, of Virginia, wrote 'Edith Allen,' a story of life in Virginia.

NEWBERRY, SAMUEL HENDERSON. Poet, of Bland, Va. The volume of 426 pages which has come from the pen of Mr. Newberry is entitled: 'Eagle Oak, and Other Poems.' It reflects the picturesque scenery of the southwestern part of the State.

NEWMAN, ALBERT HENRY. Clergyman and educator. Since 1881 Dr. Newman has filled the chair of church history in McMaster University, Toronto, Canada. He was born in Edgefield County, S.C., August 25, 1852, and was educated at Mercer University at Macon, Ga. He married, in 1873, Mary Augusta Ware, of Seale, Ala. His published works include: 'The Baptist Churches of the United States' (New York, Charles Scribner's Sons, 1894), a 'History of Anti-Pedo Baptism to A.D. 1609' (Philadelphia, The American Baptist Publication Society, 1897), a 'Manual of Church History,' in two volumes' (*ibid.*, 1900-1901), and 'A Century of Baptist Achievement' (*ibid.*, 1901), besides numerous translations and contributions to encyclopædias and reviews.

NEWMAN, CAROL MONTGOMERY, educator, was born in Wytheville, Va., October 29, 1879. He occupies a chair in the Virginia Polytechnic Institute and holds the Ph.D. degree. He has published 'Virginia Literature' (1903), and edited 'DeQuincey's Essays' (1905). The sketch of Henry Norwood in 'The Library of Southern Literature' is also from his pen. He married, in 1902, Carrie A. Fain.

NEWMAN, EUGENE WILLIAM, newspaper writer, was born in Barren County, Ky., May 3, 1845. Under the pen-name of "Savoyard," he has written some of the best political essays and monographs upon public men and events which have appeared in newspaper columns since the war. The writer's style is vigorous and trenchant. He is a wellspring of delightful reminiscences of the American capital, a critic both kind and severe, and a student of broad range and thorough research. He has published only one volume, 'Savoyard's Essays' (New York and Washington, The Neale Publishing Company, 1904). For some time he was connected with the Louisville *Courier-Journal,* but of late years he has been on the staff of the Washington *Post.* He married, first, in 1865, Emily Clark; and, second, in 1885, Florence Newman.

NEWTON, VIRGINIUS. [Va.]. He published several historical sketches including 'The Confederate Navy' and 'The Ram Merrimac.'

NICHOLAS, SAMUEL SMITH, jurist, was born in Lexington, Ky., in 1796, and died in Louisville, Ky., November 27, 1869. For several years he was a merchant in New Orleans, but he afterward studied law, settled in Kentucky, became a judge of the Court of Appeals, assisted in compiling the revised code of Kentucky, and wrote a volume of 'Essays on Constitutional Law' (Louisville, 1857).

NICHOLS, EDWARD WEST. Educator. [Va.]. He published several text-books on mathematics.

NICHOLS, JOSEPHINE HAMILTON. Author. [La.]. She wrote 'Bayou Triste: a Story of Louisiana' (New York, 1902).

NICHOLSON, ALFRED OSBORN POPE, United States Senator and jurist, was born in Williamson County, Tenn., August 31, 1808, and died in Columbia, Tenn., March 23, 1876. For several years he edited newspapers with great vigor, in addition to meeting the demands of an active law practice. He also became an important factor in political affairs, declined a Cabinet portfolio under President Pierce, and held a commission in the United States Senate from 1857 to 1861. Twice during the Civil War he was arrested at Columbia and imprisoned. At the close of hostilities he was made chief justice of the State. He was the author of a document addressed to aspirants for the Presidency in 1848, which became famous under the name of "The Nicholson Letter."

NICHOLSON, ELIZA JANE. See Biographical and Critical Sketch, Vol. IX, page 3767.

NICHOLSON, J. W. Educator. [La.]. He published text-books on mathematics.

NICHOLSON, WILLIAM RUFUS. Clergyman. [Miss.]. He was born in 1822 and published a work on eschatology entitled 'The Blessedness of Heaven.'

NICOLASSEN, GEORGE FREDERICK, educator, was born in Baltimore, Md., December 15, 1857. He is vice-chancellor and professor of Greek in the Southwestern Presbyterian University at Clarksville, Tenn., and the author of 'Notes on Latin and Greek' (Baltimore, 1890) and 'Greek Notes—Revised' (Baltimore, 1896). The sketch of Will T. Hale in 'The Library of Southern Literature' is also from his pen. He holds the degree of Ph.D. from Johns Hopkins.

NILES, HEZEKIAH. Editor. For twenty-five years he edited in Baltimore, Md., a periodical called *Niles Register*, which was found to be so important as a source of information concerning American history that thirty-two volumes were reprinted. Besides 'Quill Driving,' a series of humorous essays, he published 'Principles and Acts of the Revolution' (1822).

NISBET, EUGENIUS ARISTIDES, jurist and orator, was born near Union Point, in Greene County, Ga., December 7, 1803, and died in Macon, Ga., March 18, 1871. He received his collegiate education at the University of Georgia, after which he studied law in the office of Judge Clayton, at Athens, Ga., and under Judge Gould, at Litchfield, Conn. From 1839 to 1843 he served in Congress. Judge Nisbet was a Whig until the final dissolution of this famous old party, when he became a Democrat. On the organization of the Supreme Court of Georgia, in 1845, he became one of the noted triumvirate which included Joseph Henry Lumpkin and Hiram Warner, but he left the Bench in 1853 and resumed the active practice of his profession. He was a member of the secession convention of 1861 and drafted the ordinance which separated Georgia from the Union. The judicial decisions of Judge Nisbet are embraced in the first fourteen volumes of 'Georgia Reports' (1845-1853). They are characterized not only by profound legal scholarship but also by wide familiarity with general literature. He was a man of rare intellectual and moral culture, an able jurist, and an orator of few equals at the Bar of his native commonwealth.

NIXON, RICHARD. Lawyer. He was born in Edinburgh, Scotland, March 21, 1860. For several years he was the Washington correspondent of the New Orleans *Times-Democrat*. He afterward settled in Portland, Ore., for the practice of law. He is the author of some fine sonnets, three of which are preserved in 'The Louisiana Book,' (1894).

NOBLE, MARY ELLA. Writer. [Ga.]. Poems. She became Mrs. Allen.

NOLL, ARTHUR HOWARD. Clergyman and author. He was born in Caldwell, N.J., February 4, 1855, a son of Arthur B., and Mary Hamilton Noll, was well educated in schools taught by his father, and practiced law in New Jersey until 1882. He engaged in railroading in Mexico and became cashier of the Mexican Central Railway, in the City of Mexico. Afterward he entered the ministry of the Protestant Episcopal Church and was ordained in 1888. He has held numerous important parishes; but since 1902 has been registrar and lecturer on medical jurisprudence in the University of the South. He married, October 26, 1887, Florence, daughter of Dr. Thomas Dunn English, of Newark, N.J. His writings include: 'A Short History of Mexico' (Chicago, A. C. McClurg, 1890), 'From Empire to Republic' (*ibid.*, 1903) ; 'History of the Church in the Diocese of Tennessee' (1900); 'Confirmation', three lectures (1903); 'The Peruvians' (1905); and, in association with Dr. B. J. Ramage, 'A History of the Northern States Subsequent to the War' (1905). He has also edited 'The Little Giant, and Other Wonder Tales,' by Thomas Dunn English, and 'Dr. Quintard, Chaplain C.S.A. and Second Bishop of Tennessee,' besides numerous magazine articles. He resides in Sewanee, Tenn.

NOLTE, VINCENT. Author. For many years he was a resident of New Orleans, La., and published an interesting account of travel entitled 'Fifty Years in Both Hemispheres.'

NORMAN, BENJAMIN MOORE, author, was born in Hudson, N.Y., December 22, 1809, and died near Summit, Miss., February 1, 1900. For a number of years he resided in New Orleans, La. He wrote 'Rambles in Yucatan' (New York, 1843), 'New Orleans and Its Environs' (New Orleans, 1845), and 'Rambles by Land and Water' (New York, 1845).

NORMAN, HARRY. In collaboration with W. R. Hollister he wrote 'Five Famous Missourians' (Kansas City, Hudson-Kimberly Publishing Company).

NORRIS, THADDEUS, author, was born in Warrenton, Va., August 15, 1811, and died in Philadelphia, Pa., April 10, 1877. He was an ardent lover of angling and wrote 'The American Anglers' Book' (Philadelphia, 1864) and 'American Fish Culture' (1868). He became a manufacturer in Philadelphia.

NORTHEN, WILLIAM J., governor, educator, planter, editor, was born in Jones County, Ga., July 9, 1835, a son of Peter and Louisa Northen, graduated from Mercer University at Macon, Ga., and was for many years principal of the famous academy at Mount Zion. He married, December 19, 1860, Mattie M. Neel. He served as a private in the Confederate ranks for four years, and after the war resumed teaching, but soon gave it up because of impaired health and began to farm. He became president of the State Agricultural Society and governor of Georgia, holding the latter position from 1890 to 1894. Afterward he was made manager of the Georgia Immigration and Investment Bureau. He wrote the chapter on "Georgia's Industrial Resources" in 'Memoirs of Georgia' (1895), and also edited 'Men of Mark in Georgia,' (Atlanta, A. B. Caldwell), a work of several volumes. Mercer University gave him the degree of LL.D. He resides in Atlanta, Ga.

NORTON, GEORGE HATLEY, clergyman, was born in Ontario County, N.Y., of Virginia parentage, in 1824, and was a brother of the

Rev. John Nicholas Norton, D.D. He was for twelve years rector of St. James's Church at Warrenton, Va., and in 1859 was called to St. Paul's Church, Alexandria, Va., where he remained for more than thirty years. He contributed to various periodicals and published an 'Inquiry into the Nature and Extent of the Holy Catholic Church' (Philadelphia, 1853). William and Mary College gave him the degree of D.D.

NORTON, JOHN NICHOLAS, clergyman and author, was born in Waterloo, N.Y., of Virginia parentage, in 1820, and died in Louisville, Ky., January 18, 1881 For twenty-four years he was rector of the Church of the Ascension, at Frankfort, Ky., after which he accepted a call to Louisville, where he spent his last days. He published 'The Boy Who Was Trained to be a Clergyman' (Philadelphia, 1854), 'Full Proof of the Ministry' (New York, 1855), 'Lives of the Bishops of the Protestant Episcopal Church' (1857-1859), a 'Life of George Washington' (1860), a 'Life of Benjamin Franklin' (1861), a 'Life of Archbishop Cranmer' (1863), a 'Life of Archbishop Laud' (1864), 'Short Sermons' (1868), 'Sketches Literary and Theological' (1872), and two volumes of sermons entitled 'The King's Ferry-boat' (1876), and 'The Old Paths' (1880). Several institutions gave him the degree of D.D. He wielded a pen of unusual grace.

NORWOOD, HENRY. See Biographical and Critical Sketch, Vol. IX, page 3781.

NORWOOD, THOMAS MANSON. Jurist and author. He was born in Talbot County, Ga., April 26, 1830, graduated from Emory College, Oxford, Ga., and married, June 2, 1853, Anna M. Hendree. Later he was admitted to the Bar. During the Civil War he was a private in the Confederate Army. From 1871 to 1877 he represented Georgia in the United States Senate, and in 1880, was the unsuccessful candidate of the minority faction of the Democratic party for governor of Georgia against Alfred H. Colquitt. He became judge of the City Court of Savannah in 1896. As a writer the style of Judge Norwood is caustic and brilliant. His works include: 'Plutocracy, or American White Slavery', a politico-social novel (1888), 'Mother Goose Carved by a Commentator' (1900), and 'Patriotism—Democracy or Empire?' a satirical production (1900). He resides in Savannah, Ga.

NOTT, ARTHUR HOWARD, educator, was born in Tennessee, but now resides in New Jersey. He wrote a 'Short History of Mexico.'

NOTT, HENRY JUNIUS. See Biographical and Critical Sketch, Vol. IX, page 3797.

NOTT, JOSIAH CLARK, physician and ethnologist, was born in Columbia, S.C., March 24, 1804, and died in Mobile, Ala., March 31, 1873 After receiving his medical diploma from the University of Pennsylvania, he remained in the institution for two years as demonstrator of anatomy under Dr. Philip S. Physic, and then studied abroad. Later he established at Mobile, Ala., a medical college which the State endowed and made a part of the university system. He became an eminent authority in the realm of antiquarian research. Besides numerous articles to scientific journals, he published 'Two Lectures on the Connection between the Biblical and the Physical History of Man' (New York, 1849), 'The Physical History of the Jewish Race' (Charleston, 1850), 'Types of Mankind,' in association with G. R. Gliddon (Philadelphia, 1854), and 'Indigenous Races of the Earth.'

NOURSE, JAMES DUNCAN, author, was born in Bardstown, Ky., September 26, 1817, and died in St. Louis, Mo., June 1, 1854. For journalism he relinquished both law and medicine, edited various newspapers, including the St. Louis *Intelligencer,* contributed to magazines, and wrote two novels, 'The Forest Knight' and 'Leavenworth: a Story of the Mississippi,' besides a series of lectures which he published under the title of 'God in History; or, the Past and Its Legacies' (Louisville, 1852).

NOURSE, JOSEPH EVERETT, educator, was born in Washington, D.C., April 17, 1819. For thirty years he was a professor in the Naval Academy at Annapolis. He was also licensed to preach by the Presbyterian Church, and frequently occupied pulpits in the district, and sometimes in Virginia. He published 'The Maritime Canal of Suez' (Washington, 1869; extended, 1884), 'Memoir of the Founding and Progress of the United States Naval Observatory' (1873), Medals Awarded to American Arctic Explorers by Foreign Societies' (1876), 'Narrative of the Second Arctic Exploration by Charles F. Hall' (1879), 'American Explorations in the Ice Zones, Prepared from Official Sources' (Boston, 1884), and other works.

NOYES, JAMES OSCAR, author, was born in Cayuga County, N.Y., June 14, 1829, and died in New Orleans, La., September 11, 1872. After completing his education he spent some time abroad, chiefly as correspondent for American newspapers. On his return home he became proprietor of the *Knickerbocker Magazine,* which he edited for several years. The latter part of his life was spent in New Orleans. He published 'Roumania' (1857) and 'The Gypsies' (1858).

OATES, WILLIAM CALVIN. Soldier and lawyer. He was born in Pike County, Ala., December 1, 1835, a son of William O. and Sarah Oates, and received fair educational advantages. He enlisted in the Confederate Army, fighting in twenty-seven battles, and losing his right arm. He married, in 1882, Sallie Toney, of Eufaula, Ala., was a member of the Constitutional Conventions of 1875 and 1901, a Representative in Congress from the Third Alabama District for many years and governor of the State; but was defeated for the United State Senate because he opposed the free coinage of silver. At the outbreak of the Spanish-American War, in 1898, he was appointed brigadier-general of United States volunteers. He is the author of a volume entitled: 'The War Between the Union and the Confederacy, and Its Lost Opportunities' (New York and Washington, The Neale Publishing Company, 1900). He resides in Montgomery, Ala.

O'BRIEN, JOHN, Roman Catholic clergyman and educator, was born in Ireland in 1841 and died in Emmetsburg, Md., in 1879. Besides minor works, he wrote a 'History of the Mass,' which has passed through fourteen editions.

OCKENDEN, INA MARIE PORTER. Author. She was born in Alabama, a daughter of Judge B. F. Porter, was educated at South Alabama Female College and married, first, in 1868, G. L. Henry and, second, in 1888, Albion Ockenden. She taught for several years, but after 1878 devoted herself entirely to literary work. She is the author of numerous poems of merit which have appeared from time to time in the magazines and periodicals, and also of many excellent short stories. Her best known poem is entitled "Southria." It appeared in 1875. She was for some time the correspondent of several English and Scotch papers. Mrs. Ockenden has received a number of prizes for literary work. She resides in Montgomery, Ala.

O'CONNELL, JEREMIAH JOSEPH, clergyman, was born in the County of Cork, Ireland, November 21, 1821, came to America in early life, locating at Charleston, became an eminent Catholic priest, established missions, organized colleges, delivered lectures, and published 'Catholicity in the Carolinas and Georgia' (New York, 1878).

O'CONNOR, FLORENCE J. Author. [La.]. She wrote 'The Heroine of the Confederacy: Louisiana' (London, date not given).

ODUM, MARY HUNT McCALEB ("L'Eclair"), author, was born in Kentucky, but afterward removed first to Mississippi and then to Texas. She wrote occasional verses and published 'Hood's Last Charge, and Other Poems.'

O'FERRALL, CHARLES TRIPLETT, Congressman and governor, was born in Frederick County, Va., October 21, 1840, and died in Richmond, Va., September 22, 1905. He attained the rank of colonel in the Confederate Army and received a number of wounds, one through the lungs. After the war he studied law and became a judge of the County Court for six years, a member of Congress for twelve years, and governor of Virginia. He was twice married; first, in 1862, to Annie McLain, and second, in 1881, to Jennie Knight Danforth. He published an interesting commentary upon his times entitled 'Forty Years of Active Service—Autobiographical' (New York and Washington, The Neale Publishing Company, 1904), besides numerous political essays and speeches. He was a Democrat of life-long allegiance, but refused to support Bryan on a free silver platform.

OGDEN, OTTO N. Author. [La.]. He published 'Halimah, a Legend of the Tangipahoa' (1891), and 'Dominic Yon,' a volume of poems.

OGDEN, ROBERT NASH. Jurist and poet. He was born in Baton Rouge, La., May 5, 1839, served with distinction in the Confederate Army, and became prominent in Louisiana politics. In 1886 he was appointed Judge of the Court of Appeals of New Orleans. Besides a novel, entitled 'Who Did It?' published in 1880, he is the author of some excellent verse, including a poem entitled "Recollections of the Past."

OGLESBY, THADDEUS KOSCIUSKO, author, was born near Booneville, Mo., of Georgia parentage, in 1847. He was one of the youngest soldiers in the Confederate service, and when paroled at Greensboro, N.C., was under eighteen. For several years he was private secretary to Alexander H. Stephens. He relinquished law for literature and wrote 'Some Truths of History: a Vindication of the South' (1903, revised and enlarged, 1909), which has received enthusiastic praise from the highest critics. Besides contributing to current periodicals, he also furnished several articles to the 'New International Encyclopædia' (New York, Dodd, Mead and Company).

OGLETHORPE, JAMES EDWARD, founder of the colony of Georgia, philanthropist and soldier, was born in London, England, December 21, 1698, and died at Cranham Hall, Essex, England, January 30, 1785. He was of noble blood, his father being Sir Theophilus Oglethorpe. The martial instinct impelled him toward the army, and on the Continent he served under Prince Eugene and the Duke of Marlborough. For thirty-two years he was a Member of Parliament. One of his first legislative efforts was to devise plans for the relief of indigent but honest debtors in the prisons of England, and the colony of Georgia in the new world was largely the offspring of this benevolent enterprise. Besides pledging his own immense fortune to the project, he also interested other men of wealth and character; accompanied the expedition to America, conducted the military operations against the Spaniards, and shared for years the vicissitudes of the colonists. In 1775 he declined the command of the English forces in America, due partly to his extreme age and partly to his reluctance to take up arms against the colony he had planted. He was a man of culture, an intimate associate of Samuel Johnson and Alexander Pope, and a writer of force. In the collections of the Georgia Historical Society are preserved his "New and Accurate Account of the Colonies of South Carolina and Georgia," his letters to the trustees of the colony, and his memoirs of the St. Augustine campaign. The most complete life of General Oglethorpe was written by Robert Wright (London, 1867).

O'HARA, THEODORE. See Biographical and Critical Sketch, Vol. IX, page 3827.

OHL, MAUDE ("Annulet Andrews"). Author. Over the penname of "Annulet Andrews" this gifted woman has contributed both prose and verse to the leading magazines. She is also the author of an exceptionally interesting work of fiction entitled 'The Wife of Narcissus.' Born at Washington, Ga., she comes of one of Georgia's best families. For a number of years she edited the society page of the Atlanta *Constitution;* and in the early nineties she married Josiah Kingsley Ohl, who was then city editor of the paper, but who is now manager of the New York *Herald's* Oriental Bureau.

"OLD FIELD TEACHER." [N.C.]. The author's identity is unknown. But he published a volume of verse entitled 'Attempts at Rhyming,' a work of much interest (Raleigh, Thomas J. Lemay, 1839).

OLIPHANT, BLOSSOM D. Author. [Tenn.]. She wrote 'Mrs. Lemon's Neighbors.'

OLIVE, JOHNSON. Baptist clergyman. [N.C.]. He was born in 1816 and died in 1885. He published an 'Autobiography.'

OLIVER, JAMES McCARTY. Author. He wrote 'The Battle of Franklin,' 'The Little Girl at the Fort,' and other works. In the preface to a volume (Philadelphia, J. B. Lippincott Company), dated September 23, 1869, his address is given as "Lake, Mississippi."

OLIVER, THADDEUS, lawyer and poet, was born in Jeffersonville, Twiggs County, Ga., December 25, 1826, and died in a hospital in Charleston, S.C., August 21, 1864, the result of a wound received in battle. During the administration of Herschel V. Johnson he held the office of solicitor-general of the Chattahoochee Circuit. He was an eloquent advocate before the jury, a man of culture and a poet of singular power. There is abundant evidence for his claim to the authorship of the famous war lyric, "All's Quiet Along the Potomac To-night," despite the fact that two other claimants contest the honor, Lamar Fontaine and Ethel Lynn Beers. Several other fugitive poems from the pen of Mr. Oliver betray the same delicate and rhythmic touch. They include "Rain in the Heart" and "My Soul Is Dark as Starless Night." He married, in 1849, Sarah Penelope, daughter of Hugh Lawson.

OLMSTED, ALEXANDER FISHER, educator and chemist, was born at Chapel Hill, N.C., December 20, 1822, and died in New Haven,

Conn., May 5, 1853. He was educated at Yale, filled for a while the chair of chemistry in the University of North Carolina, and published 'Elements of Chemistry' (New Haven, 1851).

OLMSTED, FRANCIS ALLYN, physician, was born in Chapel Hill, N.C., July 14, 1819, and died in New Haven, Conn., July 19, 1844. He was educated at Yale, took a sea voyage to the Sandwich Islands for his health, became a practitioner of medicine, and published 'Incidents of a Whaling Voyage' (New York, 1841).

O'MALLEY, CHARLES J., lawyer, editor, poet, was born near Waverly, Ala., February 9, 1857. On his father's side he comes of the famous O'Malley family of Ireland; on his mother's side he is English and Spanish. For twenty years he has been engaged in editorial lines of work. He is a writer of exquisite grace and polish, and from time to time has produced verse which has been widely copied. His books include: 'Out of the White Mist,' a volume of poems (1875), 'Out of Arcady,' a volume of poems, 'The Building of the Moon, and Other Poems' (Evansville, Ind., Keller Publishing Company, 1894), 'Songs of Southern Kentucky' (Cincinnati, Pratt Publishing Company, 1903), 'The White Shepherd,' a sketch (Chicago, J. S. Hyland and Company, 1904), 'Thistledrift,' poems and epigrams (Chicago, The New World Company, 1908), 'Songs of Dawn' (Chicago, J. S. Hyland and Company, 1909), and three serial stories, "Kentucky People," "Drouth," and "Deluded." Mr. O'Malley's work, which is typically Southern, has appeared in most of the high-class magazines. He married, October 16, 1882, Sallie M. Hill. He is at present editor of the *New World,* a paper published in Chicago, Ill. The degree of Litt.D. has been conferred upon him in recognition of his literary attainments.

O'MALLEY, SALLIE M. Educator and novelist. Her maiden name was Sallie M. Hill. She was born in Centerville. Ind., of Southern parentage. Her father was a cousin of General A. P. Hill, the famous Confederate leader, and her mother a Miss Wilson of Lexington, Va. She enjoyed the best educational advantages and for several years engaged in teaching, but the popular encouragement which her first excursions into authorship evoked finally persuaded her to adopt literature as her profession, and she has since written many delightful volumes of fiction. They include: 'The Story of Seven Swans' (Mount Vernon, Ind., The Advocate Company, 1893), 'An Heir of Dreams' (New York, Benziger Brothers, 1898), 'On the Frontier' (*ibid.*, 1902), 'The White Flame' (Chicago, The Nazareth Company, 1905), 'Tales of the Old Bonne Femme' (Boston, Bouquet Publishing Company, 1906), and 'Beyond the Purple Hills' (Chicago, The Extension, 1907), besides other stories in manuscript. Her work is characterized by creative force and by artistic charm. She married, October 16, 1882, Charles J. O'Malley. Her home is in Chicago. Ill.

O'NEALL, JOHN BELTON, jurist, was born on Bush River, S.C., April 10, 1793, and died near Newberry, S.C., September 27, 1863. He was educated at South Carolina College, chose the legal profession, became judge of the Court of Appeals and major-general of the State militia, advocated temperance reform with great eloquence and power, and published 'The Bench and Bar of South Carolina,' in two volumes (Charleston, 1859), a 'Digest of the Negro Law' (1848), and 'Annals of Newberry' (1858).

ONDERDONK, HENRY A. Author. [Md.]. He published a 'History of Maryland' (1878).

OPIE, JOHN N. Lawyer. [Va.]. He was born in 1845 and published an interesting personal narrative entitled 'A Rebel Cavalryman with Lee, Stuart and Jackson' (1899).

ORGAIN, KATE ALMA, Mrs. Author. [Texas]. Mrs. Orgain has published a work of much interest designed with special reference to school use, entitled 'Southern Authors in Poetry and Prose' (New York and Washington, The Neale Publishing Comany, 1907), a collection of biographical and critical essays, supplemented by numerous selections.

ORME, RICHARD McALLISTER, Jr., editor, was born in Georgia, about 1830. For several years he edited at Milledgeville, Ga., the *Southern Recorder*, a paper once edited by his distinguished father. Later he removed to Savannah. Besides numerous political essays and editorials, he wrote 'Dr. Devine and the Devil' (Savannah, 1894).

ORR, JAMES LAWRENCE, statesman, was born near Anderson, S.C., May 12, 1822, and died in St. Petersburg, Russia, May 5, 1873. He was educated at the University of Virginia, studied law, established and edited the *Gazette*, at Anderson, S.C., opposed nullification, became prominent in politics and at the Bar, and served in Congress for five consecutive terms. He recognized the right but opposed the policy of secession. Nevertheless, he espoused the Confederate side in the struggle which ensued, commanded a regiment in the field for several months, and sat in the Confederate Senate from 1862 to 1865. At the close of hostilities he became governor of South Carolina, under President Johnson's plan of reconstruction, supported the Republican policies, became Circuit Court judge, and received in 1872, from President Grant, the appointment of United States Minister to Russia. Some of his speeches have been preserved in the 'Debates of Congress,' and in the 'Proceedings of the Confederate Senate.'

ORRICK, JESSE LEWIS, merchant, was born in Cumberland, Md., October 21, 1874. For some time he was engaged in journalistic work, but is now credit manager of one of the wholesale establishments of Cumberland. He has contributed some very delightful articles to magazines and newspapers and has written the sketch of John Pendleton Kennedy for 'The Library of Southern Literature.' He married, October 24, 1900, Nannie Oliver Bentley. He resides in Cumberland, Md.

OSBORNE, Mrs. Author. [N.C.]. She wrote a novel entitled 'Under Golden Skies' (1878).

OTEY, JAMES HERVEY, Protestant Episcopal bishop, was born in Liberty, Va., January 27, 1800, and died in Memphis, Tenn., April 23, 1863. He was educated at the University of North Carolina, after which he studied theology, received his ordination to the priesthood, and became eventually bishop of Tennessee. He published a volume entitled 'Unity of the Church, and Other Discourses' (Vicksburg, 1852).

OTTS, JOHN MARTIN PHILIP, clergyman, was born in Union, S.C., in 1838; and, after graduating from Davidson College, he prepared himself for the ministry of the Presbyterian Church at Columbia Theological Seminary. Before his ordination he married Miss Leila McCrary, of Greensboro, Ala. For several years the South furnished his field of work, but he afterward took charge of important pastorates in the North. He visited Palestine and Egypt, and on his return lectured on 'Explorations in Bible Lands.' Among his published works are included: 'Nicodemus with Jesus,' 'Light and Life for a Dead World,' 'The Southern Pen and Pulpit,' 'Interdenominational Literature,' 'The Gospel of

Honesty,' 'Laconisms,' 'The Fifth Gospel,' 'Unsettled Questions,' 'At Mother's Knee,' and 'Christ and the Cherubim.' He died in 1901. Dr. Otts held the D.D. and the LL.D. degrees.

OUSLEY, CLARENCE. See Biographical and Critical Sketch, Vol. IX, page 3837.

OVERALL, JOHN WILFORD. Editor and poet. He was born in the famous Shenandoah Valley of Virginia, September 25, 1822, but early in life settled in New Orleans and became prominent in journalism. Later he undertook editorial work for papers in other cities, going finally to New York to edit *The Mercury.* He wrote 'A Catechism of the Constitution,' in which he maintained that delegated power was a trust. He possessed the poetic instinct well developed, and left some charming leaflets of song. One of the best is entitled "To a Miniature."

OVERTON, JOHN, jurist, was born in Louisa·County, Va., April 9, 1766, and died near Nashville, Tenn., April 13, 1833. He studied law and began to practice in Nashville, Tenn., in association with Andrew Jackson, whom he afterward succeeded on the Circuit Bench, became an authority of the law pertaining to land titles, and was for several years an occupant of the Supreme Bench of the State. He wrote 'Overton's Reports,' an important series of volumes covering the period from 1791 to 1817 and dealing with rights and titles to land in the State of Tennessee.

OWEN, GARONWY, clergyman and poet, was born in North Wales, January 13, 1722, and died in St. Andrew's Parish, Va., between 1770 and 1780. He was a scholar of ripe attainments, a minister of the Church of England, and a poet of delicate sensibilities. He came to America in 1757, taught for three years in William and Mary College, and then resumed pastoral labors. 'The Poetical Works of Rev. Garonwy Owen, with His Life and Correspondence,' was edited by Rev. Robert Jones (London, 1876). Some of his countrymen in 1831 erected a tablet to his memory in the cathedral church at Bangor.

OWEN, MARIE BANKHEAD, short story writer and playwright, was born in Mississippi in 1869. For several years past she has contributed to leading Southern periodicals like the *Taylor-Trotwood* and the *Uncle Remus* magazines, and has also written in collaboration with Margaret Mayo a play entitled 'The Transgression.' Her style is piquant and bright. On April 12, 1893 she became the wife of Thomas M. Owen, the distinguished archæologist of Montgomery, Ala.

OWEN, MARY ALICIA. Author. She was born in St. Joseph, Mo., January 29, 1858, a daughter of the Hon. James A. Owen, and was educated in private schools and at Vassar. She is credited with having made some important discoveries in "voodoo" magic, while engaged in making folk-lore researches. She also enjoys the somewhat unusual distinction of having been admitted to tribal membership with the Indians; and from the intimate knowledge which she gained in their secret councils she has written interestingly concerning their habits and customs. Later in life she turned her attention to the gypsies. Her writings, which possess very great interest both to the general reader and to the scientific student, include: 'Ole Rabbit's Plantation Stories,' 'Voodoo Tales,' 'The Daughter of Alouette,' 'An Ozark Gypsy,' 'Folk-Lore of the Musquakie Indians,' and 'Oracles and Witches.' She resides in St. Joseph, Mo.

OWEN, THOMAS McADORY, lawyer, historian and director of the Alabama State Department of Archives and History, was born

in Jonesboro, Ala., December 15, 1866. On completing his studies at
the University of Alabama he was admitted to the Bar in Birmingham,
and practiced his profession successfully for fourteen years, when he
retired to engage in literary pursuits. From early youth he was possessed
of a passion for historical research, and after graduation he began to
give definite shape and direction to his interest in antiquities, especially
in the Southern field, and in ten years was the owner of one of the
largest and richest collections of Southern Americana known, including
manuscripts, newspaper files and pamphlets. Through his active and
constructive leadership the Alabama State Department of Archives and
History was established by legislative act, February 27, 1901, the first
organization of the kind in existence; and he was called to the head of
this important bureau. In 1902 Mississippi copied the plan without altera-
tion, and in substantial form it is now employed in West Virginia, North
Carolina, South Carolina and Arkansas, while in other states efforts
have been made for similar legislation. It has likewise received the
endorsement of the most eminent authorities. Dr. Owen has been secretary of the Sons of the Revolution in Alabama and of the Alabama
Historical Society, since the date of organization; he was also one of
the founders of the Southern History Association in Washington,
D.C., and was for two years commander-in-chief of the United Sons
of Confederate Veterans. He was married, April 12, 1893, to Marie,
daughter of John H. Bankhead, now senior United States Senator from
Alabama. His literary work is extensive. Besides editing the publications of his department, the 'Transactions of the Alabama Historical
Society' (Vols. I-IV, 1898-1903), and the 'Report of the Alabama History
Commission' (1901), he has published a 'City Code of Bessemer' (1888),
a 'Bibliography of Alabama' (1897), a 'Bibliography of Mississippi' (1900),
'Annals of Alabama, 1819-1900,' an addendum to Pickett's 'History of Alabama' (1900), separate genealogies of the Lester, Strother, Eaton, Stansel,
Lacey, Kelly, Fisher and Ross families, a 'History of the Great Seal of
Alabama,' sketch of Ephraim Kirby, the first Superior Court judge in what
is now Alabama, and numerous short papers. He was also one of the
founders of the *Gulf States Historical Magazine*, which he edited, 1902-
1903. The University of Alabama in 1904 gave him the degree of LL.D.

OWEN, WILLIAM MILLER. Author. He was born in Cincinnati, Ohio, January 10, 1862, but he lived in the South long enough
prior to the war to become an ardent champion of the cause of Dixie;
and when hostilities began, he went to Virginia with the Washington
Artillery, serving with gallantry until the surrender of Lee. His work
entitled 'In Camp and Battle with the Washington Artillery' is thor-
oughly pervaded by the martial spirit. He contributed to some of the
leading magazines of the day, including *Scribner's Magazine* and the
Century Magazine; and also assisted Mrs. Jefferson Davis in preparing
the military chapters of her 'Memoirs.' He died in New Orleans,
January 10, 1893, on the anniversary of his birth.

PAGE, CURTIS HIDDEN, educator and editor, was born in
Greenwood, Mo., April 4, 1870. After graduation from Harvard he
studied at the University of Paris, and later became adjunct professor
of Romance languages in Columbia University, New York. He has translated 'Cyrano de Bergerac's Voyage to the Moon' (New York, Doubleday,
Page and Company, 1899), 'Songs and Sonnets of Ronsard' (Boston,
Houghton, Mifflin and Company, 1903), and 'The Best Plays of Molière,'
in two volumes (New York, G. P. Putnam's Sons, 1907). He has edited
'The British Poets of the Nineteenth Century' (Boston, B. H. Sanborn
and Company, 1904), 'Rabelais' (New York, G. P. Putnam's Sons, 1905),
'The Chief American Poets' (Boston, Houghton, Mifflin and Company,
1905), and 'The Golden Treasury of American Songs and Lyrics' (New

York, The Macmillan Company, 1907). Besides occasional poems, he also contributes stories and essays to high-class periodicals.

PAGE, JAMES M. Author. Mr. Page, a Pennsylvanian oy oirth, was second lieutenant in Company A, Michigan Cavalry; but he deserves a place in Southern literature because of a work which he published entitled 'The True Story of Andersonville; a Defence of Major Henry Wirz' (New York and Washington, The Neale Publishing Company, 1907). He spent seven months in Andersonville, and with the ample opportunities for observation furnished by this protracted sojourn behind the walls, he says that Secretary Stanton is the man to blame for the 13,000 graves at this famous prison.

PAGE, JOHN, governor, was born in Rosewell, Va., April 17, 1744, and died in Richmond, Va., October 11, 1808. He was educated at William and Mary College, studied law, served three terms in Congress, following the adoption of the Federal Constitution, and in the office of governor of Virginia succeeded James Monroe. Though partial to theological studies, he declined to take orders. He published 'Addresses to the People' (1796-1900), and left at his death the materials for a memoir of his times, besides letters from Revolutionary leaders; but most of this matter was unfortunately lost.

PAGE, RICHARD CHANNING MOORE, physician, was born at Turkey Hill, Va., January 2, 1841, left the University of Virginia before completing his studies to enter the Confederate Army and was wounded at the battle of Gettysburg; studied medicine after the war and in 1885 became a professor in the New York Polyclinic Institute. Besides contributing to various medical journals, he published a 'Genealogy of the Page Family in Virginia,' (New York, 1882), a 'Sketch of Page's Battery,' and a 'Chart of Physical Diagnosis.'

PAGE, ROSEWELL, lawyer, was born in Hanover County, Va., November 21 1858. His father was Major John Page and his mother, Elizabeth Burwell Nelson. At leisure intervals, he has exercised his talent for authorship by writing articles on current topics, occasional poems, and short stories and sketches. Some of his most delightful bits of fiction are "Zeke Waxcomb's Will," "Hackit's Bail Bond," "The Parson's Grip," "Fiddler Rake's Fiddle" and "How Rich Joined the Army," all of which have appeared in popular magazines. The sketch of Ellen Glasgow in 'The Library of Southern Literature' is also from his pen. He married, February 16, 1898, Ruth Nelson.

PAGE, THOMAS JEFFERSON, naval officer, was born in Shelly, Va., January 4, 1808. Entering the United States Navy, he attained the rank of commodore. In 1853 he was put in charge of an expedition to explore the tributaries of the Rio de la Plata, a commission which he successfully accomplished after an absence of three years and four months. When Virginia seceded in 1861, he resigned his commission and entered the service of the Confederate Government, declining from the Italian Ministry of Marine the post of admiral. At the close of hostilities he located in the Argentine Republic. He published 'La Plata: the Argentine Confederation and Paraguay,' a work in which he gave a descriptive account of his explorations covering several thousand miles. (New York. 1859.)

PAGE, THOMAS NELSON. See Biographical and Critical Sketch, Vol. IX, page 3849.

PAGE, WALTER HINES, editor, was born in Cary, N.C., August 15, 1855, the son of A. F. Page, and was educated at Bingham School and at Randolph-Macon College, completing his studies at Johns Hopkins. From 1890 to 1895 he was editor of the *Forum;* afterward, for several years, he was literary adviser to Houghton, Mifflin and Company and also editor of the *Atlantic;* but since the establishment of the *World's Work* he has been the editor of this publication. He is also a member of the publishing firm of Doubleday, Page and Company, New York. His work entitled: 'The Rebuilding of Old Commonwealths' is an important contribution to serious letters. He married Alice, daughter of Dr. William Wilson, of Michigan. His home is at Englewood, N. J.

PAGE, WILLIAM. Naval officer. [Va.]. He published an 'Exploration of the Valley of the Amazon.'

PAGE, WILLIAM A. Writer. [Va.]. He published an antebellum portraiture entitled 'Uncle Robin in His Cabin in Virginia' (1853).

PAINE, ROBERT, bishop of the M.E. Church, South, was born in Pearson County, N.C., November 12, 1799 and died in Aberdeen, Miss., October 20, 1882. For sixteen years he was president of LaGrange College, Ala. He attended the general conference of 1844 and participated in the debate which preceded the division of the church. On the organization of the seceding branch, he was elected bishop. He published, in two volumes, 'The Life of Bishop McKendree,' a work which deals interestingly with an important period in the history of Methodism.

PAINTER, F. V. N. See Biographical and Critical Sketch, Vol. IX, page 3889.

PALLEN, CONDÉ BENOIST, journalist and author, was born in St. Louis, Mo., December 5, 1858, and was engaged for several years in active journalism. Besides editing various Catholic publications he has contributed to current literature and published in book form the following works: 'The Philosophy of Literature' (St. Louis, 1897), 'Epochs of Literature' (*ibid.,* 1898), 'What is Liberalism' (*ibid.,* 1899), "The New Rubaiyat," a poem, (*ibid.,* 1899), 'The feast of Thalarchus,' a dramatic composition, (Boston, Small, Maynard and Company, 1901), 'The Death of Sir Lancelot, and Other Poems' (*ibid.,* 1902), and 'The Meaning of the Idyls of the King' (New York, The American Book Company, 1904). He resides in New York. Georgetown University gave him the degree of LL.D.

PALMER, BENJAMIN MORGAN. See Biographical and Critical Sketch, Vol. IX, page 3907.

PALMER, BENJAMIN MORGAN, clergyman, was born in Philadelphia, Pa., September 25, 1781, and died in Charleston, S.C., October 9, 1847. He became an eminent Presbyterian divine, was for several years pastor of a church in Beaufort, and, from 1817 to 1835, pastor of a church in Charleston. Dr. B. M. Palmer, of New Orleans, was his nephew. In addition to numerous sermons, he published 'The Family Companion' (Charleston, 1835). South Carolina College gave him his degree of D.D.

PALMER, HENRIETTA LEE, author, was born in Baltimore, Md., February 6, 1834. Her maiden name was Henrietta Lee. She was educated at Patapsco Institute, Md., and in 1855 became the wife of Dr. John Williamson Palmer. The gift of expression inclined her toward literature; and, besides contributing to numerous periodicals, she translated 'The Lady Tartuffe' for Rachel, the actress, and wrote 'The Stratford Gallery, or the Shakespeare Sisterhood' (New York, 1858) and 'Home Life in the Bible' (Boston, 1882).

PALMER, JOHN WILLIAMSON, physician and poet, best known through his famous war lyric entitled: 'Stonewall Jackson's Way,' was born in Baltimore, Md., in 1825, the son of Dr. James C. Palmer. He studied medicine at the University of Maryland; and, crossing the continent in the days of the gold fever, he became the first city physician of San Francisco. He married, in 1855, Henrietta Lee, a well known writer. During the Burmese War he was surgeon on one of the ships of the East India Company; and it was at this time that his literary career began with contributions to the leading American magazines. Soon after the outbreak of hostilities between the North and the South, he became staff correspondent of The New York *Tribune.* His pen-name was "John Coventry." As a writer he was graphic and fluent but his fame rests chiefly upon his verse. Besides several volumes of his poems, he published: 'Beauties and Curiosities of Engraving,' 'A Portfolio of Autograph Etchings,' and a novel, 'After His Kind.' He died in 1906.

PALMER, MARY STANLEY BUNCE, author, was born in Beaufort, S.C., a daughter of the Rev. Benjamin M. Palmer, D.D., an eminent Presbyterian divine; and she was tutored, in Charleston, by the Misses Ramsay, daughters of the distinguished historian, David Ramsay. In 1835, she married Charles E. Dana, of New York; but the early death of her husband brought her back to Charleston and she afterward married Rev. Robert D. Shindler, D.D., an Episcopalian clergyman, by whom her leanings toward Unitarianism are said to have been overcome. She was the author of some exquisite poems and several novels, the former of which were called forth by her domestic bereavements. Her works include: 'The Southern Harp,' 'The Northern Harp,' 'The Parted Family, and Other Poems,' 'Charles Morton, or, The Young Patriot,' 'Letters to Relatives and Friends,' written to explain her doubts in regard to the Trinity; 'Forecastle Tom' and others. Her best known poem is entitled "Pass Under the Rod."

PARIS, JOHN. Methodist Protestant clergyman. [N.C.]. He published a 'History of the Methodist Protestant Church' (Baltimore, Sherwood and Company, 1849), besides minor works.

PARISH, SAMUEL CLAIBORNE. Author. [Ark.]. He wrote an interesting volume of personal memories entitled 'Reminiscences and Sketches.'

PARK, ROBERT EMORY, former State Treasurer of Georgia, planter and educator, was born in LaGrange, Ga., January 13, 1843 and died in Atlanta, Ga., May 7, 1909. He wrote an important historical sketch of 'The Twelfth Alabama Regiment' (Richmond, William Ellis Jones, 1906). It was compiled largely from the author's "War and Prison Diary" which appeared as a serial in the Southern Historical Society Papers (1876-1877). An earlier portion of the diary was lost on the field of battle but was recovered in 1888 and appeared in Vol. XXVI of the same publication. Captain Park was three times married. His last wife, who survived him, was Mrs. Emily Hendree Stuart, a lady of rare personal and intellectual charm.

PARKER, EDWARD FROST. Physician and surgeon. [S.C.]. He published a 'History of Surgery in South Carolina.'

PARKER, NATHAN H. Writer. [Mo.]. He published a 'Missouri Hand Book' (1865), a 'Geological Map of Missouri' (1865), and 'Missouri as It Is' (1867).

PARKER, WILLIAM HARWAR. Naval officer. For twenty years he served with distinction in the United States Navy and participated in the War with Mexico. At the outbreak of hostilities in 1861 he resigned his commission and gave his services to the South. For several years he was president of the Maryland Agricultural College and, during President Cleveland's second administration he was United States Minister to Korea. Besides 'Talks on Astronomy,' Lieutenant Parker wrote 'Recollections of a Naval Officer' (1883), and a "History of the Confederate States Navy," for 'The Confederate Military History' (Atlanta, Ga., The Confederate Publishing Company, 1899). The last mentioned work was completed just before his death.

PARKER, W. W. Physician. [Va.]. He published 'The Rise and Decline of Homeopathy' and 'Forty Years a Doctor.'

PARKINSON, WILLIAM, clergyman and historian, was born in Frederick County, Md., November 8, 1774, and died in New York City, March 10, 1848. For thirty-five years he was pastor of the First Baptist Church, of New York, resigning in 1841 on account of charges which impaired his usefulness in the pulpit but of which he was found to be innocent upon legal investigation. He published 'Ecclesiastical History' (New York, 1813), 'Public Ministry of the World' (1818), and 'Sermons on Deuteronomy XXXII,' in two volumes, (1831).

PARRISH, JOHN, clergyman, was born in Baltimore, Md., November 7, 1729, and died in Baltimore, Md., October 21, 1807. He belonged to the Society of Friends and succeeded Anthony Benezet in pleading the cause of the African race. He published 'Remarks on the Slavery of the Black People' (Philadelphia, 1806).

PARSONS, H. C. Poet and man of affairs. For several years he was the owner of the famous Natural Bridge and much of his life was spent in developing the material resources of his state; but he also moved in the higher realm of thought. He published a volume entitled: 'The Reaper, and Other Poems' (New York, 1884), the title member of which group is dedicated to Cyrus H. McCormick, the celebrated inventor.

PASCHALL, EDWIN, educator and editor, was born in Mecklenburg County, Va., in 1799 and died in Nolenville, Tenn., June 5, 1869. He taught in various Tennessee schools, was editor of several papers, and published 'Old Times; or, Tennessee History' (1869).

PASCHALL, GEORGE WASHINGTON, jurist, was born in Greene County, Ga., November 23, 1812, and died in Washington, D.C., February 16, 1878. He married Sarah, the only daughter of the Cherokee chief, John Ridge, and moved to Arkansas, where he became justice of the Supreme Court. Afterward he moved to Texas and still later to Washington, D.C., where he was instrumental in founding the law department of Georgetown University and became the first professor of jurisprudence. Judge Paschall published an 'Annotated Digest of the Laws of Texas' (1866, revised 1872), an 'Annotated Constitution of the United States' (1868, revised 1876), 'The Decisions of the Supreme Court of Texas, in five volumes, (1869-1871), besides numerous addresses. He also wrote for *Harper's Magazine* a "Sketch of the Last Days of Sam Houston" (1866).

PATE, HENRY CLAY. [Va.]. He published 'Sketches of Virginia.'

PATE, J. THOMAS. Methodist Episcopal clergyman. [S.C.]. He published 'Father Ryan and his Poems,' 'Life in the Shadow of Sin and Want,' 'Early Christianity,' 'The History of Sunday Schools,' 'Sermons,' and 'Lectures.'

PATTEN, FRANK. Clergyman. He wrote "Reminiscences of the Chickasaw Indians," which appeared in the *Electra* (1884-1885).

PATTERSON, JAMES KENNEDY. Educator. He was born in Glasgow, Scotland, March 26, 1833, a son of Andrew and Janet Kennedy Patterson. His elementary education was obtained in Scotland and his collegiate education at Hanover College, in Indiana. He married, December 27, 1857, Lucelia, daughter of Captain Charles F. Wing, of Greenville, Ky. He held numerous important professorships in leading colleges, and in 1869 became president of the State College of Kentucky. He has represented this country in many scientific gatherings abroad, and in the early eighties he successfully led a fight in Kentucky to sustain the constitutionality of an act levying a tax for the support of the State University. He is a Fellow both of the Royal Historical Society of Great Britain and of the Scotch Society of Antiquities. Besides numerous lectures and papers, he is the author of an important report of the International Congress of Geographical Sciences at Paris, in 1875, and of other contributions of value to the scientific thought and information of the day. Hanover and Lafayette colleges gave him the degree of LL.D. He resides in Lexington, Ky.

PATTERSON, JOHN. See Biographical and Critical Sketch, Vol. IX, page 3935.

PATTIE, JAMES OHIO, explorer, was born in Bracken County, Ky., accompanied his father on an expedition into New Mexico, escaped the tragic death which befell his parent at the hands of the Indians, and, returning home, brought his journal of the adventurous enterprise which was edited by Timothy Flint and published under the title of 'The Personal Narrative of James O. Pattie' (Cincinnati, 1833).

PATTON, JOHN M. Clergyman. [Va.]. He published 'The Death of Death.'

PATTON, JOHN SHELTON, librarian, was born in Augusta County, Va., January 10, 1857. His father was Alfred Taylor Patton and his mother, Virginia Harris. He has published 'The University of Virginia; Glimpses of its Past and Present,' in joint authorship with Sallie J. Doswell (1900), and 'Jefferson, Cabell and the University of Virginia' (Washington, The Neale Publishing Company, 1906). He married, June 10, 1881, Beatrice Faber. He is librarian of the University of Virginia.

PAXTON, ALEXANDER S. Author. [Va.]. He wrote an interesting volume of reminiscences in which many delightful incidents of life in the Shenandoah Valley of Virginia fifty years ago are recalled. The work is entitled 'Memory Days' (New York and Washington, The Neale Publishing Company, 1907).

PAXTON, JOHN GALLATIN. He published an interesting collection of letters written from field and camp by his father, Brigadier-general Elisha Franklin Paxton, who was killed while leading his brigade at the battle of Chancellorsville. The collection is prefaced by a memoir (New York and Washington, The Neale Publishing Company, 1907).

PAXTON, WILLIAM M. [Mo.]. He published a volume of genealogical data on 'The Marshall Family' (1875).

PAYNE, ODESSA STRICKLAND, author, was born in Marietta, Ga., September 7, 1857. Her maiden name was Odessa Strickland. Under the pen-name of "Faith Mills," her first literary work was published in

The Sunny South. She has written 'Psyche' (1885), 'Esther Ferrall's Experiment' (1909), and 'The Mission Girl' (1908), three interesting stories, the latter in association with her son, Lamar S. Srickland, with whom also she conducts the story department of *The Golden Age.* Besides, she is the author of several minor works. Mrs. Payne resides at Smyrna, Ga. She married, December 24, 1879, Benjamin F. Payne, a lawyer.

PAYNE, RAPHAEL SEMMES, banker, was born in Warrenton, Va., June 3, 1860. His father was Major Rice W. Payne and his mother, America Semmes. Besides a series of sketches of the post-bellum period in Virginia for the Baltimore *Sun,* he is the author of the sketch of Raphael Semmes in 'The Library of Southern Literature.' He married, June 6, 1905, Mary Dunlop Thomas. He is engaged in business in Baltimore, and resides at "Mecca," Pikesville, Md.

PEACOCK, J. S. Physician and author. [La.]. He wrote 'The Creole Orphans,' a novel (New Orleans, 1855).

PEACOCK, THOMAS BROWER. Author. He was born in Cambridge, Ohio, April 16, 1866, a son of Thomas William and Naomi Carson Peacock, and was educated at Zanesville, Ohio. He is the inventor and patentee of numerous devices, including a fire-escape and a railroad switch, is successful as a lecturer, and his writings in both prose and verse betray the touch of true genius. He wrote the "Columbian Ode" for the opening of the World's Fair at Chicago. His poems have been published in book form from time to time and embrace the following volumes: 'Poems,' a collection which appeared in 1872 when he was only sixteen years old; 'The Vendetta, and Other Poems,' The Rhyme of the Border War,' and 'Poems of the Plains and Songs of the Solitudes.' Besides, he has written several plays. He resides in Kansas City, Mo.

PEARSON, ABEL. Clergyman. [Tenn.]. He published a work on 'The Principles of the Divine Government' (1833).

PEARSON, JAMES LARKIN. Poet. [N.C.]. He published 'Early Poems' (Moravian Falls, N. C., 1903, paper edition), 'A Pilgrimage to Mount Vernon' (*ibid.,* 1903, paper edition), and 'Pearson's Poems' (*ibid.,* 1906, paper edition).

PECK, JOHN MASON. Baptist clergyman. Though of Northern birth, he labored for several years in Kentucky, where he established a school of theology at Covington. He published a 'Life of Daniel Boone,' an 'Emigrant's Guide to the West' (Boston, 1836) and 'Father Clark, or, the Pioneer Preacher' (New York, 1855), besides editing 'Annals of the West.' At the time of his death he left important manuscripts, which were edited by the Rev. Rufus Babcock under the title of 'Forty Years of Pioneer Life: a Memoir of John Mason Peck, Edited from his Journal and Correspondence' (Philadelphia, 1864).

PECK, SAMUEL MINTURN. See Biographical and Critical Sketch, Vol. IX, page 3951.

PECK, SARAH ELIZABETH. Author. [Ala.]. Besides a number of short stories and sketches, she published a 'Dictionary of Similes and Figures.'

PECK, WILLIAM HENRY, educator and author, was born in Augusta, Ga., December 30, 1830 and died in Jacksonville, Fla., February 4, 1892. After graduation from Harvard, he located in New Orleans for several years and became professor of *belles-lettres* in the University of Louisiana. Later he went to New York but finally returned to Georgia, where he devoted the remainder of his days to literary pursuits, barring short intervals when he was president of the Masonic Female College, and professor in the Le Vert Female College, both Georgia institutions. For the greater part of the time he resided in Atlanta. Professor Peck was one of the most popular serial story writers of his day and was paid by the New York *Ledger* as high as five thousand dollars for single productions. Most of his work was projected along historical lines. He wrote 'The McDonalds,' 'The Stone-cutter of Lisbon,' 'The Queen's Secret,' 'The Miller of Marseilles,' 'The Flower Girl of London,' 'The King's Messenger,' 'The Conspirators of New Orleans,' and numerous other novels.

PEEK, COMER L. Author. [Ga.]. He wrote an entertaining story of the Civil War entitled 'Lorna Carswell' (New York and Washington, The Neale Publishing Company, 1906). The author was born on a plantation in Georgia.

PEELE, WILLIAM J. [N.C.]. He edited 'Lives of Distinguished North Carolinians' (1899).

PEERS, BENJAMIN ORRS, clergyman and educator, was born in Loudon County, Va., in 1800 and died in Louisville, Ky., August 20, 1842. He was first a Presbyterian and afterward an Episcopalian in religious views. He became an educator of note, originated the system of common school education in Kentucky, and published 'American Education,' with an introduction by Francis Lister Hawks (New York, 1838).

PELL, EDWARD LEIGH. Clergyman and editor. He was born in Raleigh, N.C., September 7, 1861, a son of the Rev. William E. Pell, and was educated at the University of North Carolina; but before graduation he accepted an offer of editorial work. He married, December 21, 1881, Lucy Hardison. He entered the ministry of the Methodist Episcopal Church, South, but withdrew from the active ranks after ten years of pastoral work. Later he became a lecturer on biblical subjects and editor of *The Bible Reader*, and finally president of the Robert Harding Company (Inc.) and the B. F. Johnson Publishing Company, of Richmond, Va. His writings include: 'The Art of Enjoying the Bible', 'Life of Dwight L. Moody,' (Richmond, B. F. Johnson), 'The Bright Side of Humanity,' 'Life of McKinley,' 'Commentary on the Sunday-school Lessons' (1899-1905), 'Superintendent's Book of Prayer,' 'Letters to a Sunday-school Teacher,' 'The Life Worth While,' and 'Little Guide-Posts in the Way of Life.' Emory College gave him the degree of LL.D. He resides in Richmond, Va.

PELTON, MABELL SHIPPIE CLARKE. Author. She was born in Boston, Mass., November 14, 1864, a daughter of Augustus May and Frances Dexter Clarke. She was educated in Boston, but received the degree of A.M., from the University of North Carolina. She married, October 17, 1884, F. A. Pelton, since deceased. She is the author of an interesting story of her adopted State entitled 'A Tar-Heel Baron,' (Philadelphia, J. B. Lippincott Company). She resides in Arden, N.C.

PENDLETON, EDMUND, patriot and statesman was born in Caroline County, Va., September 9, 1721, and died in Richmond, Va., October 23, 1803. With few educational advantages, he rose to high distinction at the Bar and in politics. Elected to the House of Burgesses, he took the view that the Stamp Act did not bind the inhabitants of Virginia. Afterward he sat in the Continental Congress. As president of the convention, he was virtually at the head of governmental affairs till the adoption of the State Constitution. He also drafted the resolutions by which the delegates from Virginia were instructed to propose a declaration of independence in Congress. As the representative of the cavalier or planter class, he was the opponent of Patrick Henry on numerous public issues. Under the State Government, he was twice Speaker of the House of Representatives; when the Court of Chancery was organized, he was chosen to preside; and later, on the establishment of the Court of Appeals, he became president of this tribunal also. Jefferson said of Pendleton that he was the ablest man he ever met in debate.

PENDLETON, EDMUND MONROE, chemist and physician, was born in Eatonton, Ga., March 19, 1815, and died in Atlanta, Ga., January 26, 1884. After practicing medicine for several years he turned his attention to agriculture, originated the formulas for making fertilizers which bear his name, and was the first to employ animal matter and cotton-seed in the manufacture of fertilizers. For some time he held the chair of agriculture at the University of Georgia. He wrote in both prose and verse, contributing to various periodicals, and published 'Scientific Agriculture' (New York, 1874).

PENDLETON, JAMES MADISON, clergyman, was born in Spottsylvania County, Va., November 29, 1811, entered the ministry of the Baptist Church, occupied a pastorate for twenty years at Bowling Green, Ky., and taught theology for a time in Union University at Murfreesboro, Tenn.; but he was an avowed opponent of slavery and in 1862 settled in Pennsylvania. He published: 'Three Reasons Why I Am a Baptist,' (Cincinnati, 1853), a work which passed into numerous editions; 'Sermons' (Nashville, 1859), 'Church Manual' (Philadelphia, 1868), 'Christian Doctrines,' 'Distinctive Principles of Baptists,' 'Brief Notes on the New Testament,' with Rev. George W. Clark, D.D., 'The Atonement of Christ,' and 'Old Landmarks Reset.' Denison University gave him the degree of D.D.

PENDLETON, LOUIS [BEAUREGARD], author, was born in Ware County, Ga., of Revolutionary stock, April 21, 1861, his father being Philip C. Pendleton, an editor of distinction, who established at Macon, in 1840, the *Southern Lady's Book.* After completing his education at the North, he contributed to *The Sunny South* under the pseudonym of "Richard Penfield" an imaginative serial entitled "Louelle," which was written when he was only nineteen. It opened wide the gates of authorship and he has since written a number of successful volumes of fiction, among them 'Bewitched,' a novel of South Georgia life; 'In the Wire Grass' (New York, D. Appleton and Company, 1889), 'King Tom and the Runaways,' a story of adventure in the Georgia swamp (*ibid.,* 1890), 'The Sons of Ham,' a study of the race problem in narrative form (Boston, Roberts Brothers, 1895), 'The Wedding Garment' (*ibid.,* 1894), 'In the Okefinokee' (*ibid.*), 'Curita,' a Cuban romance (Boston, Lamson, Wolffe and Company), 'Corona of the Nanlahalas,' a tale of the North Carolina mountains (London, Sampson, Low and Company), 'Lost King Ammon,' 'In Assyrian Tents,' 'A Forest Drama,' (Philadelphia, Henry T. Coates and Company), and 'In the Camp of the Creeks,' a story of the Indian uprising in Georgia in 1836. The latest production of his pen is 'The Life of Alexander H. Stephens' (Philadelphia, George W. Jacobs and Company), an excellent portrayal of the great commoner and sage of Liberty Hall. For several years he has resided at Bryn Athyn, Pa.

PENDLETON, WILLIAM NELSON, soldier and clergyman, was born in Richmond, Va., December 26, 1809, and died in Lexington, Va., January 15, 1883. He was educated at West Point and became assistant professor of mathematics in the military academy but resigned to accept the chair of mathematics in Bristol College, Tenn. Later he was ordained to the Episcopal priesthood, and in 1853 became rector of the church in Lexington. At the outbreak of the Civil War he joined the Confederate Army as captain of artillery, became commander of the artillery of the Army of Northern Virginia, with the rank of brigadier-general, and participated in nearly every engagement from Manassas to Appomattox. At the close of hostilities he returned to the church at Lexington. General Lee was one of his parishioners. Dr. Pendleton published 'Science a Witness for the Bible' (London, 1860). Alexandria Theological Seminary gave him his degree of D.D.

PENICK, CHARLES CLIFTON, Protestant Episcopal missionary bishop, was born in Charlotte County, Va., December 9, 1843. On completing his collegiate studies, he enlisted in the Confederate Army and served in Pickett's immortal division. After the war he began his equipment for the ministry at the Alexandria Seminary; and was ordained to the priesthood in 1870. Seven years later he was consecrated bishop to Cape Palmas, West Africa. He married Mary Hoge. Included among his published works are: 'More Than a Prophet,' 'Advice to the Church in Africa,' 'Hopes, Perils and Struggles of the Negro in America,' 'What Can the Church Do for the Negro in the United States,' 'Everlasting Life,' 'The Dead Memories: Lessons and Duties of the Confederacy,' 'The Science of Missions,' 'The Social Side of Christ's Life' and 'The Conquest of the World by Christianity.'

PENNY, KATE SPEAKE, author, was born in Alabama and resided for many years at Huntsville, where her childhood and youth were largely spent, but her present home is in Birmingham. Her father was Judge Henry Clay Speake, for twenty-seven years an occupant of the Bench of the Eighth Judicial Circuit, and her mother, Carolyn Mayhew, a native of Oxford, Ohio, and the author of a volume of poems entitled 'Home Echoes.' Mrs. Penny's chief claim to literary distinction rests upon a work of fiction entitled 'A Woman's Problem.' It was widely popular, not only in the United States but also in Canada, and was largely instrumental in furthering the cause of temperance reform.

PENNY, VIRGINIA, author, was born in Louisville, Ky., January 18, 1826, received her education at the girls' seminary in Steubenville, Ohio, taught for several years along the sectional border, and became an eloquent champion of her sex, advocating the enlargement of woman's sphere of industrial activities. She published 'The Employment of Women' (Boston, 1863), 'Five Hundred Occupations Adapted to Women' (Philadelphia, 1868) and 'Think and Act.'

PENNYPACKER, ANNA J. HARDWICKE, Mrs., educator, was born in Virginia in 1861, but afterward removed to Texas, where she engaged in educational work and wrote a 'History of Texas' (1888, revised and enlarged, 1895).

PERCY, GEORGE, colonial governor of Virginia, was born in Northumberland County, England, in 1586, and died in England in 1632. He succeeded Captain John Smith as governor of the Colony of Virginia and published a work on the 'Plantations of the Southerne Colonie in Virginia by the English' (London, 1606), a work of much interest which gives in detail the incidents of the first voyage and the early movements of the Jamestown colonists.

PERCY, WILLIAM, clergyman, was born in Bedworth, England, September 15, 1744, and died in London, England, July 13, 1819. He was sent by Lady Huntington to take charge of Bethesda Orphanage, near Savannah, the famous institution established by Whitefield. He espoused the patriotic cause, officiated at St. Michael's Church, in Charleston, S.C. from 1777 to 1780, went back to England for a stay of twenty years, returned to Charleston in 1804 for a sojourn of twelve years, and finally went back for the last time to England. He published an apologetic work on the Episcopal Church and several religious and devotional books. South Carolina College gave him the degree of D.D.

PERRIN, W. H. Journalist. He compiled a work of very great value entitled 'The Pioneer Press of Kentucky,' which narrates the story of newspaper enterprise in the Blue Grass State from 1787 to 1830. It was published by the Filson Club of Louisville and illustrated with facsimile reproductions of some of the old prints.

PERRY, BENJAMIN FRANKLIN, lawyer, was born in Pendleton District, S.C., November 20, 1805, and died in Greenville, S.C., December 3, 1886. He chose the legal profession, but for several years edited newspapers and opposed nullification and secession. He espoused the Confederate cause when the sentiment of his State was registered, and held judicial office under the Confederate Government. Later he was made provisional governor and was also elected to the United States Senate but was not seated. He published 'Reminiscences of Public Men' (Philadelphia, 1883; revised in 1889 by his son), and left in manuscript several sketches of eminent Americans which were subsequently edited by his wife, entitled 'Sketches of Eminent American Statesmen, with Speeches and Letters of Governor Perry, Prefaced by an Outline of the Author's Life' (Philadelphia, 1887).

PETER, ROBERT. Physician. [Ky.]. He wrote a 'History of Transylvania University,' assisted by his daughter (1896).

PETERKIN, GEORGE WILLIAM. First Protestant Episcopal bishop of West Virginia. He was born in Washington County, Md., March 21, 1841, a son of the Rev. Joshua Peterkin, D.D. He was twice married, was consecrated bishop of West Virginia in 1878 and edited 'Records of the Protestant Episcopal Church of Virginia and West Virginia,' 1903. Kenyon College gave him the degree of D.D. and Washington and Lee University the degree of LL.D. He resides in Parkersburg, W. Va.

PETERSON, MATTIE J. Author. [N.C.]. She published in one volume 'Little Pansy: a Novel, and Miscellaneous Poetry' (Wilmington, N.C., 1890).

PETIGRU, JAMES LEWIS, statesman, was born in Abbeville District, S.C., March 10, 1789, and died in Charleston, S.C., March 3, 1863. He was of Scotch-Irish lineage on the one side and of Huguenot on the other. He achieved eminence at the Bar, succeeding Robert Y. Hayne in the office of Attorney-general. Among the men of wealth and position in the State, he was almost alone in opposing nullification, and it made him unpopular, but he remained unrivaled at the Bar. He also opposed secession, but was too advanced in years to participate actively in the discussion. The great work of his life was the codification of the laws of South Carolina (Charleston, 1862). But he also published 'A Semi-Centennial Oration, delivered at the College of South Carolina' (Columbia, 1855) and 'An Address before the South Carolina Historical Society' (Charleston, 1858). William J. Grayson published his biography in 1866.

PETRIE, GEORGE, educator, was born in Montgomery, Ala., April 10, 1866. His father was George L. Petrie and his mother, Mary Cooper. He holds the chair of Latin and history in the Alabama Polytechnic Institute, a position to which he was called in 1891. He has executed some very important work in the line of archæological research, including "Montgomery," in 'Historic Towns of the Southern States.' "W. F. Samford" and "The Final Estimate of Yancey," in the 'Transactions of the Historical Society of Alabama': 'The Doctrine of Secession Historically Traced' and "Alabama, 1819-1865," in 'The South in the Building of the Nation,' and the sketch of William L. Yancey in 'The Library of Southern Literature,' besides numerous historical papers. He has also edited two volumes of 'Studies in Southern History' by advanced students of the Alabama Polytechnic Institute. Johns Hopkins gave him the degree of Ph.D.

PETTIGREW, JAMES JOHNSTON. See Biographical and Critical Sketch, Vol. IX, page 3981.

PETTUS, EDMUND WINSTON, United States Senator, was born in Limestone County, Ala., July 6, 1821. After graduating from Clinton College, Tenn., he studied law, became a lieutenant in the Mexican War and a brigadier-general in the war between the States. He took no part in politics until his election to the United States Senate, in 1900, and, on the floor of the Upper Chamber was distinguished for his sound judgment and his wide legal information. On one occasion he paid his respects to the oratorical propensities of Senator Beveridge in a speech which made him famous. He was twice reëlected, but died in 1907 before entering upon his third term.

PETTUS, MAIA. Author. She was born in Elkmont, Ala., in 1873, a daughter of Dr. J. A. Pettus, and graduated from Cox College, Atlanta, Ga. Besides being a contributor to various magazines, she is the author of a charming novel entitled 'The Princess of Glendale.' The story is descriptive of home life on an ante-bellum Southern plantation; but it also conducts the reader into the turbulent war period and sketches General Forrest, the great cavalry leader, and Sam Davis, the typical Southern hero. Another novel is entitled 'Meta's Heritage.' The Neale Publishing Company, Washington, D.C., are her publishers.

PEYTON, JESSE ENLOWS, merchant, was born in Maysville, Ky., November 1, 1815, and died in Haddonfield, N.J., April 28, 1897. He settled in Philadelphia, achieved success in the business world, raised forty thousand dollars to save the home of Henry Clay, and was one of the earliest promoters of the Centennial Exposition of 1876. He published 'Reminiscences of Philadelphia during the Past Fifty Years' (Philadelphia, 1888).

PEYTON, JOHN LEWIS, author, was born in Staunton, Va., September 15, 1824, received his law diploma from the University of Virginia, and settled in Chicago. During the Civil War he became an agent for the Confederate Government in Europe, and later ran the blockade at Charleston, S.C. His publications include: 'Pacific Railway Communication and the Trade of China,' 'The American Crisis' (London, 1866), 'Over the Alleghanies and Across the Prairies,' 'The Adventures of my Grandfather,' 'Memoir of William M. Peyton,' 'Memorials of Nature and Art' and 'History of Augusta County, Va.' (Staunton, 1882).

PHELAN, JAMES, Congressman, was born in Aberdeen, Miss., December 7, 1856. After leaving the Kentucky Military Institute, he studied at Leipsic (Ph.D.). He settled in Memphis for the practice of law, owned and edited *The Avalanche,* and represented his district in Congress. He wrote 'Philip Massinger and his Plays' (Leipsic, 1878), and 'Tennessee; the Making of a State' (Boston, 1888).

PHELPS, ALBERT CARRUTHERS, journalist, was born in New Orleans, La., December 29, 1875. His father was Albert Gallatin Phelps and his mother, Annie Carruthers. While a freshman in Tulane University he began to write for the *Evening Post* of New York. At present he is an editorial writer on the New Orleans *Item.* Besides numerous articles for leading magazines and newspapers, he is the author of 'Louisiana, a Record of Expansion' (Boston, Houghton, Mifflin and Company, 1905). The sketch of Grace King in 'The Library of Southern Literature' is also from his pen.

PHELPS, ALMIRA HART LINCOLN, Mrs., educator, author, scientist, was born in Berlin, Conn., July 13, 1793, and died in Baltimore, Md., July 15, 1884. Her father was Samuel Hart. On completing her education she began to teach school, but in 1817 she married Simeon Lincoln and it was not until his death in 1823 that she resumed her profession. Eight years later she married Judge John Phelps; and in 1841, in association with her husband, she took charge of Patapsco Institute near Baltimore; and after her husband's death, which occurred in 1849, she conducted the school alone for several years, when she finally retired. Mrs. Phelps took deep interest in scientific studies, became a member of the American Association for the Advancement of Science and produced a number of text-books, which are marked by an exceptionally luminous style of treatment. They include: 'Familiar Lectures in Botany' (1829), a 'Dictionary of Chemistry' (1830), a 'Botany for Beginners' (1831), a 'Geology for Beginners' (1832), 'The Female Student or Fireside Friend' (1833), a 'Chemistry for Beginners' (1834), 'Lectures on Natural Philosophy' (1835), 'Lectures on Chemistry' (1837), and 'Hours with My Pupils' (1869). She also edited at one time a periodical entitled *Our Country,* and wrote several interesting stories, among them, 'Caroline Westerly' (1833), 'Ida Norman' (1850), and 'Christian Households' (1860). Mrs. Phelps was a lineal descendant of Thomas Hooker, one of the founders of Hartford, Conn.

PHIFER, C. L. Writer. [Mo.]. He published 'Annals of the Earth,' 'Weather Wisdom,' 'Love and Law,' a collection of sonnets, and numerous poems.

PHILIPS, SAMUEL, clergyman, was born near Hagerstown, Md., June 14, 1823, became an eminent Presbyterian divine and educator, holding professorships at Dickinson and Muhlenberg, and published 'Gethsemane and the Cross' (Boonesborough, Md., 1851), 'The Christian Home' (Springfield, Mass., 1861), and 'The Voice of Blood' (Philadelphia, 1863).

PHILLIPS, JOHN H. Author. [Ky.]. He was born in 1853 and published 'Old Tales and Modern Ideals.'

PHILLIPS, S. K. [Tenn.]. He published 'Immortelles.'

PHILLIPS, ULRICH B., educator, was born in LaGrange, Ga., November 4, 1877. After completing his studies at the University of Georgia, he took post-graduate work at Columbia University for his Ph.D. degree. At the present time he is professor of history at Tulane University, New Orleans, La. Besides numerous articles on Southern economic, social and political history for current reviews he has published 'Georgia and State Rights' (1902), 'History of Transportation in the Eastern Cotton Belt' (1908), and 'Plantation and Frontier Documents' in two volumes (Cleveland, Ohio, A. H. Clark Company, 1909. Dr. Phillips is a member of the Historical Manuscript Commission of the American Historical Society and adjunct member for Georgia of the Public Archives Commission.

PIATT, SARAH MORGAN BRYAN. See Biographical and Critical Sketch, Vol. IX, page 4003.

PICKARD, WILLIAM LOWNDES. Baptist clergyman. [Ga.]. He was born in 1861. He wrote a novel entitled 'Under the War Flags' (1895).

PICKENS, FRANCIS WILKINSON, statesman, was born in St. Paul's Parish, S.C., April 7, 1805, and died in Edgefield, S. C., January 25, 1869. He chose the profession of law, became prominent in the politics of the State, advocating the doctrine of nullification, served in Congress from 1834 to 1843, represented the United States Government at the Court of St. Petersburg, and on his return home became governor of South Carolina. He was an orator of unusual gifts, and delivered frequent addresses on literary topics, besides political speeches on the hustings and in the forum.

PICKETT, ALBERT J. See Biographical and Critical Sketch, Vol. IX, page 4017.

PICKETT. LA SALLE CORBELL, author, was born in Chuckatuck, Va., May 16, 1848, a daughter of John D. and Elizabeth Corbell. Soon after completing her education at Lynchburg College, she became the wife of Major-general George Edward Pickett. It was on September 15, 1863, that the marriage was celebrated, barely two months after the immortal charge which he led at Gettysburg. She began to contribute to the press in early girlhood. Besides numerous short poems and sketches, she is the author of the following books: 'Pickett and His Men,' (Washington, The Neale Publishing Company, 1899), 'Kunnoo Spirits,' 'Yule Log,' 'Ebil Eye,' 'Jinny,' 'Digging Through to Manila,' and monographs of some of the great figures of the Civil War. In dialect work she is at her best. On the lecture platform she has also gained some note, her favorite theme being the folk-lore of the South. For some time past she has made her home in Washington, D.C.

PICKETT, L. L. Methodist Episcopal clergyman. [Texas]. He published 'A Shot at the Foe,' 'Leaves from the Tree of Life,' and 'The Sabbath Day.'

PICKETT, THOMAS EDWARD. physician and surgeon, was born near Maysville, Ky., January 11, 1841. On completing his medical equipment he engaged at once in the practice and rose to the very front of his profession. At intervals of leisure, he has brought the resources of an unusual mind to bear upon some of the most interesting problems of scholarship. His most important work is entitled 'The Quest of a Lost Race,' which was recently published by the Filson Club, of Louisville. It is based upon the theory of Paul Du Chaillu to the effect that the English are descended from the Scandinavians rather than from the Teutons. His earlier writings include: 'The Testimony of the Mounds,' which was published originally in the 'History of Kentucky,' by Collins; 'The Hypothetical Migration of Morbus Americanus' (London, Cassell, 1889), and 'A Soldier of the Civil War.' The last named volume presents an interesting portraiture of the hero of Gettysburg, George E. Pickett. He married, June 18, 1878, Abby, daughter of Hamilton Gray. Dr. Pickett holds the degree of LL.D.

PIERCE, GEORGE FOSTER. Bishop of the Methodist Episcopal Church, South, clergyman and educator. Because of his superb eloquence he was styled "the Demosthenes of Southern Methodism." His father was the famous Dr. Lovick Pierce, who was scarcely less distinguished as an orator. He was born in Green County, Ga., February 3, 1811, and died in Sparta, Ga., September 3. 1884. He was the first president of Wesleyan Female College. which claims the distinction of being the first chartered institution in the world for the higher education of woman; and he was also the third president of Emory College. For more than thirty years he adorned the Episcopal Bench. Some of his best efforts have been published in a volume entitled 'Sermons and Addresses' (Nashville, Publishing House of the Methodist Episcopal Church, South); and Dr. George G. Smith, in a work entitled, 'The Life and Times of Bishop Pierce,' has preserved a number of additional extracts. Robert Toombs regarded Bishop Pierce as the most symmetrical man he ever knew: "the handsomest in person, the most gifted in intellect, and the purest in life." He held the degrees of D.D. and of LL.D.

PIERCE, HENRY NILES, clergyman, was born in Pawtucket, R.I., in 1820; and, after finishing his preparations for the ministry of the Episcopal Church, he settled in Texas. Later he became rector of Trinity Church, in New Orleans, and of St. John's, in Mobile. He sometimes dipped into verse; and his published works include a volume entitled: 'The Agnostic, and Other Poems.' He also published a volume of 'Addresses' and a volume of 'Sermons.' His wife was Nannie Hayward Sheppard, of Matagorda, Texas. He died in 1899. William and Mary College gave him the degree of LL.D. and the University of Alabama the degree of D.D.

PIERCE, WILLIAM, statesman, was born in Georgia about 1740 and died about 1806. During the Revolution he was an aide on the staff of General Nathanael Greene, and in recognition of his gallantry was presented with a sword by the Continental Congress, in which body he afterward served. He was also a member of the convention that framed the Constitution but, being opposed to the plan of federation, he withdrew without signing the instrument. He published in one of the newspapers of Savannah his impressions of the membership of the convention, and they are preserved in the Force collection of the library of Congress.

PIKE, ALBERT. See Biographical and Critical Sketch, Vol. IX, page 4037.

PILLING, JAMES CONSTANTINE, ethnologist, was born in Washington, D.C., November 16, 1846. While connected with the geological survey in the Rocky Mountains, he began to tabulate the vocabularies of the various Indian dialects. Later he became chief clerk in the Ethnological Bureau. He published a 'Bibliography of the Languages of the North American Indians' (Washington, 1885), 'Bibliography of the Eskimoan Languages' (1887), 'Bibliography of the Siouan Languages' (1887), besides various memoirs on ethnological subjects.

PILSBURY, CHARLES A. Writer. [La.]. He was born in 1839. He published 'Pepita and I,' a volume of poems.

PINCKNEY, CHARLES, statesman, was born in Charleston, S.C., in 1758, studied law, was made a prisoner at the fall of Charleston, in 1780, took part in the proceedings of the convention that framed the Federal Constitution, and became governor of South Carolina, United States Senator, United States Minister to Spain and Member of Congress. He was the founder of the old Republican or Democratic party in South Carolina, advocated free schools, and over the signature of "Republican," wrote many strong political articles which were instrumental in Jefferson's election. He was a cousin of Charles Cotesworth Pinckney, with whom he disagreed in politics. Princeton made him an LL.D.

PINCKNEY, CHARLES COTESWORTH, statesman and diplomat, was born in Charleston, S.C., February 25, 1746, obtained his education in England, studied law, served with distinction in the Revolution. and was made a prisoner at the fall of Charleston in 1780. He represented South Carolina in the convention that framed the Federal Constitution, wrote the clause which forbids any religious test as a qualification for office and when the instrument was adopted, became in politics an ardent Federalist. He declined two Cabinet offers but accepted the mission to France and while at Court made the famous reply to Talleyrand: "Millions for defence, but not one cent for tribute." On his return home he received from Washington a major-general's commission. He was the third president-general of the Society of the Cincinnati. The Federalists twice nominated him for President of the United States. He died in Charleston, S.C., August 16, 1825.

PINCKNEY, ELIZA LUCAS. [S.C.]. She was born in 1721 and died in 1792. She kept an interesting journal of events, extending from 1739 to 1761, which was published together with some of her letters (1850).

PINCKNEY, GUSTAVUS MEMMINGER, author, was born in Charleston, S.C., July 29, 1872, of distinguished Southern stock. On completing his education he chose a literary career, for which he was qualified by unusual talents, and he has already attained high rank among writers. He has published a 'Life of John C. Calhoun' (Charleston, Walker, Evans and Cogswell, 1903), 'The Coming Crisis and Three Ideas' (*ibid.,* 1905), and 'Fruits and Specimens from my Acre' (*ibid.,* 1907), besides an edition of McKinley's 'Appeal to Pharaoh.' He married, September 17, 1907, Mary W. Middleton. He resides in Charleston, S.C.

PINCKNEY, HENRY LAURENS, lawyer and editor, was born in Charleston, S.C., September 24, 1794, received his education at South Carolina College, and chose the profession of law but never practiced. He was three times mayor of Charleston, served one term in Congress, under the administration of President Pierce, was collector of the Port of Charleston, and for eighteen years was tax-collector of the parishes of St. Philip and St. Michael. He founded and edited for fifteen years the Charleston *Mercury,* an organ of State rights, and, besides numerous public addresses, he wrote memoirs of Jonathan Maxcv, Robert Y. Hayne, and Andrew Jackson. He died in Charleston, S.C., February 3, 1863.

PINCKNEY, MARIA. Author. She was the daughter of Charles Cotesworth Pinckney and a niece of Arthur Middleton, a signer of the Declaration of Independence. She was a woman of unusual force of mind and a student of public questions. Besides numerous letters, she wrote a work in defence of nullification.

PINCKNEY, THOMAS, diplomat, was born in Charleston, S.C., October 23, 1750, accompanied his brother, Charles Cotesworth, to England to receive his education, served in the Revolution, became governor of South Carolina, United States Minister to England, and Member of Congress, and was also sent upon an important mission to Spain. He received the nomination of the Federalists for Vice-president of the United States in 1796; and President Madison during the War of 1812 advanced him to the rank of major-general. He succeeded his brother as president-general of the Cincinnati. His death occurred in Charleston, S.C., November 2, 1828.

PINER, H. L., author, was born in Kentucky in 1858, but afterward removed to Texas. He wrote 'Ruth, a Romance of the Civil War,' 'The Great Sherman Tornado' (1896), and a number of poems.

PINKNEY, EDWARD COOTE. See Biographical and Critical Sketch, Vol. IX, page 4063.

PINKNEY, FREDERICK, poet and editor, was born at sea, October 14, 1804, and died in Baltimore, Md., June 13, 1873. He was a son of William Pinkney and a brother of Edward Coote Pinkney. At different times he edited *The Marylander* and the Baltimore *Patriot;* and, during the Civil War, published numerous songs and poems, which were quite popular.

PINKNEY, NINIAN, Jr., surgeon, was born in Annapolis, Md., June 7, 1811 and died near Easton, Md., December 15, 1877. He entered the United States Navy, was fleet surgeon of the Mississippi Squadron during the Civil War and became medical director with the rank of commodore in 1871. St. John's College gave him the degree of LL.D. He delivered on patriotic themes numerous addresses which were afterward published.

PINKNEY, NINIAN, Sr., soldier and author, was born in Baltimore, Md., in 1776, entered the United States Army and attained the rank of colonel. As a result of a tour of France, he published an entertaining volume entitled 'Travels in the South of France and in the Interior of the Provinces of Provence and Languedoc by a Route never before Performed' (London, 1809). Leigh Hunt said of this work that "it set all the idle world to going to France to live on the charming banks of the Loire." William Pinkney was his brother. He died in Baltimore, Md., December 16, 1825.

PINKNEY, WILLIAM, statesman, was born in Annapolis, Md., March 17, 1764, and died in Washington, D. C., February 25, 1822. Though his father was a loyalist, he gave his youthful enthusiasm to the patriotic cause, studied law, achieved distinction at the Bar, became Attorney-general of the United States, advocated the War of 1812, represented the United States Government at the Court of Russia, and served both in the National House and Senate. With James Monroe, he was also at one time special commissioner to England, remaining in London for several years as resident minister, after Mr. Monroe's return to America. He was one of the foremost public men and one of the ablest lawyers of his day. Edward Coote Pinkney, one of his sons, attained high distinction in literature, but died on the threshold of manhood.

PINKNEY, WILLIAM, Protestant Episcopal bishop, was born at Annapolis, Md., April 17, 1810, and died in Cockeysville, Md., July 4, 1883. He received his education at St. John's College, entered the Episcopal priesthood, became rector of the Church of the Ascension in Washington, D.C. and, on the death of Bishop Whittingham, succeeded to the vacant chair of the diocese of Maryland. He received the degree of D.D. from St. John's and the degree of LL.D. from Columbian University and from William and Mary College. He published a 'Life' of his uncle, William Pinkney (New York, 1853) and a 'Memoir of John H. Alexander, LL.D.' (Baltimore, 1867).

PINSON, W. W., Methodist Episcopal clergyman, was born in Georgia. Dr. Pinson wrote an interesting story illustrative of life in the South at the close of the Civil War (Akron, Ohio, The Saalfield Publishing Company, 1903).

PISE, CHARLES CHRISTOPHER, clergyman and poet, was born at Annapolis, Md., in 1802, and became a Catholic priest of distinguished attainments. As a poet he also achieved distinction and was a frequent contributor to the *Knickerbocker Magazine.* He published 'Pleasures of Religion and Other Poems' and 'Acts of the Apostles done into Blank Verse.' He died in 1880.

PITKIN, HELEN. Journalist. She was born in New Orleans, La., August 8, 1877, a daughter of John Robert Graham Pitkin, United States Minister to the Argentine Republic under President Harrison. She was educated by private instruction and at Newcomb College. For some time she was on the staff of the *Times-Democrat*. Her writings include: 'Over the Hills,' a poem of some length, and 'An Angel by Brevet,' (Philadelphia, J. B. Lippincott Company). She resides in New Orleans, La.

PITT, S. E. W., Mrs., poet, was born in Wallonia, Ky., in 1865. Her father was John S. Wall, a Confederate soldier and her mother, Letitia Baker. Her only published work is a volume of verse entitled 'Poems Dear to the Heart' (1909). She married, August 1, 1890, G. L. Pitt, a lawyer. She resides in Clarksville, Tenn.

PITTMAN, H. D., Mrs. Author. [Ky.]. Besides an interesting genealogical work entitled 'Americans of Gentle Birth,' she has published two entertaining works of fiction: 'The Belle of the Blue Grass Country,' which deals with the love affair of a Harvard man, and 'The Heart of Kentucky' (New York and Washington, The Neale Publishing Company, 1908).

PITTS, J. R. S. Physician [Miss.]. He published the 'Life and Bloody Career of the Executed Criminal, James Copeland, the Great Land Pirate' (1874).

PITZER, ALEXANDER WHITE, clergyman, educator and author, was born in Salem, Va., September 14, 1834. His father was Bernard Pitzer and his mother, Frances White. After completing his theological studies he was ordained to the ministry and served his initial pastorate in Leavenworth, Kan. During the Civil War he was a missionary within the Confederate lines. At the close of hostilities he organized in Washington, D.C., the Central Presbyterian Church which was for years the only church which belonged to the Southern wing of this denomination at the national capital. On this account it was called "the rebel church" but hostility was eventually outgrown and the organization prospered. For nearly forty years Dr. Pitzer ministered to this congregation; and he is still the beloved pastor emeritus. He has always been an ardent advocate of organic union and also an enthusiastic revisionist, both of the English version of the Scriptures and of the ecclesiastical standards. For more than thirty-five years he was president of the Washington City Bible Society, and he was also professor of Biblical theology in Howard University for fourteen years. He has published 'Ecce Deus Homo' (Philadelphia, J. B. Lippincott Company, 1868), 'Christ, The Teacher of Men (*ibid.*, 1877), 'The New Life' (Philadelphia. The Presbyterian Board of Publication, 1884), 'Confidence in Christ' (*ibid.*, 1890), 'The Manifold Ministry of the Holy Spirit' (*ibid.*, 1894), 'Predestination' (*ibid.*, 1899). and 'The Blessed Hope,' in which he sets forth the pre-millennial view of the second coming of Christ. Besides he has also contributed constantly to periodicals. He married, August 20, 1860, Laura McClanahan. He received the degree of D.D. from Arkansas College and the degree of LL.D. from Howard.

PLATT, WILLIAM HENRY. Episcopal clergyman. Though born in the State of New York, April 16, 1821, the greater part of his ministry was spent in the South, chiefly in Virginia, Kentucky and Alabama. He published 'Art Culture' (1873), 'The Influence of Religion in the Development of Jurisprudence' (1877), 'After Death, What?' (1878}, 'Unity of Law or Legal Morality' (1879), and 'God in and Man Out,' a reply to Ingersoll' (1883), besides minor works. William and Mary College gave him the degree of LL.D.

PLEASANTS, MARY W. Educator. [Va.]. She published 'The Triumph of an Idea, or Two Hearts Revealed,' and numerous stories translated from the German.

PLEASANTS, WILLIAM HENRY, educator, was born in Henrico County, Va., January 29, 1829, at "Piquenocque," the Indian name of his father's country seat. Besides numerous critical essays he has made several translations from Latin and German authors, including a brochure entitled 'The Destruction of Columbia, S.C.' (1902). The account of the burning of the famous South Carolina Capitol was written by an old German who witnessed the spectacle and who told the story in his own tongue. It loses nothing in the way of dramatic interest from the professor's translation. The sketch of Mary Johnston in 'The Library of Southern Literature' is also from his pen. He married, October 15, 1852, Araminta Smoot. He holds the chair of ancient languages in Hollins Institute, Hollins, Va.

PLUMER, WILLIAM SWAN, clergyman and educator, was born at Griersburg, now Darlington, Pa., in 1802, but was brought to the South when only nine years old; and his career as a teacher began in Virginia at the early age of sixteen. Later, he prepared more fully for his life's work at Princeton; and, after filling several pastorates, he became a professor in Western Theological Seminary, at Alleghany, Pa., and afterward in Columbia Theological Seminary, at Columbia, S.C. More than twenty-five volumes came from the pen of this rugged philosopher of Presbyterianism, the list including: 'The Promises of God,' 'Thoughts Worth Remembering,' 'The Bible Tone,' 'Rome Against the Bible,' 'The Church and Her Enemies,' 'Vital Goodness,' 'Rock of Our Salvation,' 'Grace of Christ,' 'Love of God,' 'Jehovah-Jireh,' 'Earnest Hours,' 'Commentary on the Epistle to the Romans,' 'Commentary on the Epistle to the Hebrews,' and 'Studies in the Book of Psalms.' He died at Columbia, S.C., in 1880. Princeton, Lafayette and Washington Colleges gave him the degree of D.D. and the University of Mississippi the degree of LL.D.

POE, CLARENCE HAMILTON, editor and publisher, was born in Chatham County, N.C., January 10, 1881. Besides contributing to high class periodicals, he has written 'Cotton; its Cultivation, Marketing and Manufacture' (New York, Doubleday, Page and Company, 1906) and 'A Southerner in Europe' (1908), which has passed already into two editions. He is also editor and chief owner of *The Progressive Farmer,*' published at Raleigh, N.C.

POE, EDGAR ALLAN. See Biographical and Critical Sketch, Vol. IX, page 4079.

POINSETT, JOEL ROBERTS. Statesman and diplomat. He was born in Charleston, S.C., March 2, 1779 and died in Statesburg, S.C., December 12, 1851. Besides serving for two consecutive terms in Congress, he held the portfolio of War under President Van Buren, and represented the Government on several diplomatic errands of special importance including one to Mexico, which resulted in his formal appointment as United States Minister. He published 'Notes on Mexico, with an Historical Sketch of the Revolution' (Philadelphia, 1824), and left numerous unpublished manuscripts. From time to time he wrote political and scientific essays. Columbia gave him the degree of LL.D. Dr. Poinsett was something of a botanist, and a Mexican flower which he introduced into this country was named in his honor 'Poinsettia Pulcherina.'

POINTS, MARIE LOUISE. Author. [La.]. Besides a 'Picayune Guide' (1903), she has published an entertaining series entitled 'Stories of New Orleans.'

POLK, JAMES KNOX. See Biographical and Critical Sketch, Vol. IX, page 4127.

POLK, WILLIAM MECKLENBURG, physician, was born in Ashwood, Maury County, Tenn., August 15, 1844, received his medical diploma from the New York College of Physicians and Surgeons, and became a professor first in Bellevue College and afterward in the University of New York. Besides a life of his father, Leonidas Polk, bishop and general (1889), he has published several important papers bearing upon the treatment of female diseases.

POLLARD, EDWARD ALBERT. See Biographical and Critical Sketch, Vol. IX, page 4147.

POLLARD, HENRY RIVES, editor, was born in Nelson County, Va., August 29, 1833, and died in Richmond, Va., November 24, 1868. From time to time he was identified with various papers but eventually established with his brother, E. A. Pollard, in Richmond, *The Southern Opinion.* He was fatally shot from an upper window on the opposite side of the street by James Grant, who considered himself aggrieved by an article which appeared in the paper. Mr. Pollard wrote numerous historical and political essays and sketches.

POLLARD, MARIE ANTOINETTE NATHALIE GRANIER. Lecturer and poet. Her first husband was James R. Dowell, but she separated from him during the Civil War and afterward married E. A. Pollard, the author. On the death of the latter, she took the public platform, canvassed the State of California for the Democratic ticket in 1876, and later lectured on popular themes. She was an ardent advocate of temperance and wrote a number of poems.

POLLEY, J. B. Author. He served with gallantry during the Civil War under General Hood and contributed to the literature of the conflict, two volumes of much interest entitled 'A Soldier's Letters to Charming Nellie' (New York and Washington, The Neale Publishing Company, 1906) and 'Hood's Texas Brigade' (*ibid.*, 1908).

POOL, BETTY FRESHWATER. Author. [N.C.]. She published a miscellaneous collection of prose and verse entitled 'The Eyrie and Other Southern Stories' (New York, The Broadway Publishing Company, 1905), a work of merit.

POOLE, MARY BELLE. Author. [La.]. She wrote a novel entitled 'Down Fate's Walk' (1896).

POPE, JOHN, United States Senator and governor, was born in Prince William County, Va., in 1770 and died in Springfield, Ky., July 12, 1845. He settled in Lexington, Ky., for the practice of law, achieved eminence at the Bar, represented the State in the United States Senate from 1807 to 1813, and, during a part of this time, was president *pro tem.* From 1829 to 1835 he was territorial governor of Arkansas; and returning to Kentucky he served in Congress for three consecutive terms. He was an eloquent public speaker.

POPE, JOHN, soldier, was educated at West Point, served in the Mexican War with distinction, received a captain's commission for his gallantry at the battle of Buena Vista, and attained the rank of major-general in the Union Army during the Civil War. Prior to the outbreak of hostilities in 1861 he conducted an expedition to explore the Red River of the North. He published 'The Campaign in Virginia, of July and August, 1862' (Washington, 1865), and "Explorations from the Red River to the Rio Grande" in 'Pacific Railroad Reports.' He died in 1892.

POPE, JOHN HUNTER, physician, was born in Washington, Ga., February 12, 1845. After graduating from the University of Virginia he practiced medicine in Marshall, Texas. Besides a 'History of the Epidemic of Yellow Fever,' he wrote a number of reports and monographs on medical topics.

POPE, MARY E. FOOTE, educator, was born in Alabama, but afterward lived in Tennessee and published occasional poems of unusual merit.

POPE, WILLIAM P. Author. [Ark.]. He wrote an interesting series of personal reminiscences entitled 'Early Days in Arkansas.' He died in 1895.

PORCHER, FRANCIS PEYRE, physician and botanist, was born in St. John's, Berkeley, S.C., December 14, 1825, received his diploma from the Medical College of South Carolina, and became an eminent practitioner of Charleston. During the Civil War he was in charge of the Confederate hospitals at Norfolk, Va.; and for several years after the war he edited the Charleston *Medical Journal and Review*. He was also an enthusiastic botanist and gave much thought to this important branch of science. Among his published works are included: 'A Medico-Botanical Catalogue of the Plants and Ferns of St. John's, Berkeley, S.C.' (Charleston, 1847), 'A Sketch of the Medical Botany of South Carolina' (Philadelphia, 1849), 'The Medicinal, Poisonous, and Dietetic Properties of the Cryptogamic Plants of the United States' (New York, 1854), 'Illustrations of Disease with the Microscope' (Charleston, 1861), and 'Resources of the Southern Fields and Forests, Medical, Economical, and Agricultural,' published by order of the surgeon-general of the Confederate States (Richmond, 1863; revised, Charleston, 1869).

PORTER, ANTHONY TURNER, Protestant Episcopal clergyman, was born in 1828 and was for many years a resident of Charleston, S.C. He published an interesting autobiographical work entitled 'Led on Step by Step.'

PORTER, BENJAMIN FICKLING, lawyer, was born in Charleston, S.C., in 1808. He practiced medicine for a while, but relinquished it for law. He became the Supreme Court reporter of Alabama, and was afterward elected to the Bench, but declined the honor. He was frequently an orator on public occasions, contributed to periodicals, translated the 'Elements of the Institutes of Hienneccius' and published 'Reports of the Supreme Court of Alabama,' nine volumes (Tuscaloosa, 1835-1840), 'Office of Executors and Administrators,' and a collection of poems.

PORTER, DUVAL, author, was born in Appomattox County, Va., in 1844, and was the son of Madison C. Porter. He was given the best educational advantages, including a course at Columbia. From his earliest boyhood he was fond of literary diversions and began to write at fourteen for the local papers. Besides being a man of letters, he is also an accomplished linguist, and is familiar with German, French, Spanish and Italian, among modern languages, in addition to Greek and Latin. He is the author of some charming productions both in prose and in verse. His works include: 'Alphonso, and Other Poems,' 'Mere Places and Things,' 'Wasted Talents,' 'The Lost Cause, and Other Poems,' 'Adventures of an Office-seeker,' 'The Same Old Fool,' and 'Lyrics of the Lost Cause.' He resides at Cascade, Va.

PORTER, JAMES DAVIS. Jurist, planter, governor, and railway president. He was born in Paris, Tenn., December 7, 1828, and was educated at the University of Nashville. He married Susanna, daughter of General John H. Dunlop, served in the Confederate Army and was adjutant-general on the staff of Major-general Cheatham. For several years he was Judge of the Twelfth Judicial Circuit, and from 1874 to 1878 was governor of Tennessee. He was also a delegate to the constitutional convention of 1870, and was for some time president of the Nashville and Chattanooga Railway. He was Assistant Secretary of State under President Cleveland's first administration and United States Envoy to Chile under the second. He is the author of 'The Confederate Military History of Tennessee,' (Atlanta, Confederate Publishing Company). The University of Nashville gave him the degree of LL.D. He resides in Paris, Tenn.

PORTER, SYDNEY (See Henry, O., page 194).

PORY, JOHN, colonist, was born in England in 1570 and died in Virginia about 1635. He was speaker of the first legislative assembly to be held in the New World, assisted Hakluyt in his geographical work, and wrote an account of his excursions among the Indians, which was published in John Smith's 'General Historie.'

POST, MELVILLE D. See Biographical and Critical Sketch, Vol. IX, page 4167.

POST, T. M. Educator. [Mo.]. He was born in 1810 and died in 1866. He published a 'Life of the Rev. Dr. T. A. Post,' and 'Skeptical Era in Modern History.' Dr. Post occupied a chair for several years in Washington University, St. Louis, Mo.

POTTER, HENRY, jurist, was born in Granville County, N.C., in 1765, and died in Fayetteville, N.Y., December 20, 1857. He studied law, and for more than half a century was an occupant of the Bench of the United States District Court of North Carolina. He was also for fifty-seven years a trustee of the University of North Carolina. He published 'Duties of a Justice of the Peace' (Raleigh, 1816), and in association with John L. Taylor and Bartlett Yancey compiled a revision of the 'Law of the State of North Carolina,' in two volumes (Raleigh, 1821).

POTTER, MARY EUGENIA GUILLOT, Mrs. Editor. [Texas]. Mrs. Potter was born in 1864. Besides editing *Dixieland,* she has published a number of excellent poems, among them one entitled "Gibraltar."

POTTER, NATHANIEL, physician, was born in Caroline County, Md., in 1770, and died in Baltimore, Md., January 2, 1843. He received his diploma from the University of Pennsylvania, became an eminent practitioner, assisted in the organization of the Medical College of Maryland, and edited for a time the *Maryland Medical and Surgical Journal.* He published 'Medical Properties and Deleterious Qualities of Arsenic' (Baltimore, 1805), 'A Memoir on Contagion with Respect to Yellow Fever', and edited, with notes explanatory and critical, John Armstrong's 'Practical Illustrations of the Typhus Fever' (Baltimore, 1821), and in association with Samuel Calhoun, two editions of George Gregory's 'Elements of Theory and Practice of Medicine,' two volumes (Philadelphia, 1826-1829).

POTTER, REUBEN M., Texan pioneer, was born in New Jersey in 1802 but lived in Texas during the early days and wrote "The Hymn of the Alamo," "The Old Texan Hunter," and other poems commemorative of pioneer life in the Lone Star commonwealth.

POWELL, E. L. Clergyman. For several years he has been pastor of one of the leading churches of the Disciples of Christ in Louisville, Ky., a contributor to current religious periodicals, and a leader in ecclesiastical councils. Dr. Powell has published several theological works, the best known of which, perhaps, is a series of lectures on Savon-arola, the reformer and martyr of Florence.

POWELL, L. P. Author. He wrote 'Historic Towns of the Southern States' (1890).

POWELL, MARY ELLA, Miss, musician, was born in Atlanta, Ga., May 2, 1863. Three very delightful volumes have come from her pen: 'Clio' (1879), 'Winona' (1890), and 'Women Who Laugh.' For several years past she has resided in New York, where she is engaged in educational work.

POWELL, WILLIAM BYRD, physician, was born in Bourbon County, Ky., January 8, 1799, and died in Henderson, Ky., July 3, 1867. For some time he was a professor in the Medical College of Louisiana. Later he organized the Memphis Medical Institute, becoming professor of cerebral physiology; and he afterward held the same chair in the Eclectic Medical Institute of Cincinnati. His collection of skulls numbered more than five hundred. He began to prosecute his investigations into the physi-ology of the brain among the Indians. He published 'Natural History of the Human Temperament' (Cincinnati, 1856), and, with Dr. Robert S. Newton, 'The Eclectic Practice of Medicine,' and 'Eclectic Treatise of the Diseases of Children.'

POWER, FREDERICK DUNGLISON, clergyman, author, editor, was born near Yorktown, Va., January 23, 1851. His father was Dr. Robert H. Power and his mother, Abigail M. Jencks. He entered the min-istry of the Disciples of Christ on completing his preparatory studies; and for thirty-four years has been pastor of the church which President Gar-field attended, in Washington, D.C., known since the President's death by the name of Garfield Memorial. He was also chaplain of the Forty-seventh Congress. Dr. Power is one of the strongest personal forces in the ranks of his denomination. He has published 'Bible Doctrine for Young Disci-ples' (1899), 'Sketches of Our Pioneers' (1898), 'Life of W. K. Pendleton, LL.D., President of Bethany College' (1902), 'Story of My Pastorate' (1899), and 'Thoughts of Thirty Years' (1905). He also wrote the sketch of Alexander Campbell for 'The Library of Southern Literature.' On the lecture platform and in the editorial sanctum Dr. Power has further extended the sphere of his useful activities. Bethany College, his *alma mater,* gave him the degree of LL.D. He married, March 17, 1874, Emily B. Alsop.

POWERS, WILLIAM DUDLEY, clergyman and author, was born in Richmond, Va., March 2, 1849, his parents being William Hazard and Mary Johnston Powers. On completing his educational equipment, he was ordained to the priesthood in the Protestant Episcopal Church, and has since been rector of many important congregations. He married, December 2, 1880, Mary Bullock Howard. For some time past his field of labor has been in the Northwest, at Flint, Mich. He writes with ease, both in prose and in verse, and several volumes have come from his pen: 'Nature's Vespers,' 'Why Not and Why' (New York, D. Appleton and Company), 'The Light Shineth,' and 'Uncle Isaac; or, Old Days in the South' (Richmond, B. F. Johnson Company). Two editions of the last-named work have been issued. He received the degree of D.D. from the University of the South.

POYAS, CATHARINE GENDRON, poet, was born in Charles-ton, S.C., April 27, 1813, and was educated in the local schools and under tutors. Her writings were chiefly in verse, including 'Huguenot Daugh-ters, and Other Poems' (Charleston, 1849), 'Year of Grace' (*ibid.,* 1869), and 'In Memory of the Rev. C. P. Gadsden, and Other Poems' (*ibid.*, 1871). She died in Charleston, February 7, 1882.

POYAS, ELIZABETH ANNE. Author. Under the title of "The Ancient Lady," she published several small books and pamphlets relating to the homes and genealogies of South Carolina. Her daughter, Catharine G. Poyas, was a writer of distinction.

POYDRAS, JULIEN, philanthropist, was born in Nantes, France, April 3, 1746, and died in Point Coupée, La., June 25, 1824. He was the first delegate to Congress from the territory of Orleans, and donated $300,000 to public institutions. He published 'La Prise du Morne du Baton Rouge' (New Orleans, La., 1779), the earliest pamphlet printed in New Orleans.

PRENTICE, GEORGE D. See Biographical and Critical Sketch, Vol. IX, page 4189.

PRENTISS, SARGENT SMITH. See Biographical and Critical Sketch, Vol. X, page 4209.

PRESTON, JOHN SMITH, planter and orator, was born near Abingdon, Va., April 20, 1809, and died in Columbia, S.C., May 1, 1881. Possessed of large means, he collected paintings and sculptures and encouraged artists. On the return of the Palmetto Regiment from the Mexican War, he delivered a speech of welcome which made him famous. Later his reputation was still further enhanced by numerous addresses on commemorative occasions. But his greatest effort was on the floor of the Secession Convention in support of the policy of withdrawal from the Union. At the outbreak of hostilities he enlisted in the Confederate Army and attained the rank of brigadier-general. For several years after the war he resided abroad. General Preston was more than six feet in height, a man of broad culture and of fine intellect. He married Caroline, daughter of General Wade Hampton. His orations, a number of which have been published in book form, bear testimony to his gifts.

PRESTON, MARGARET JUNKIN. See Biographical and Critical Sketch, Vol. X, page 4235.

PRESTON, THOMAS LEWIS, planter, was born in Botetourt County, Va., November 28, 1812. After completing his studies at the State University, he read law but never practiced, and for several years engaged successfully in the manufacture of salt. During the Civil War he served on the staff of General Joseph E. Johnston. He published 'The Life of Elizabeth Russell, the Wife of William Campbell, of King's Mountain' (University of Virginia, 1880).

PRESTON, WILLIAM CAMPBELL. See Biographical and Critical Sketch, Vol. X, page 4255.

PRICE, ANNA. Author. [Va.]. She wrote a number of stories for religious periodicals.

PRICE, SAMUEL W. Soldier and artist. General Price wrote a volume of rare interest and value entitled: 'Old Masters of the Blue Grass' (Louisville, Ky., The Filson Club, 1902), which gives interesting biographical sketches of the famous artists of the State, including Jouett, Bush, Frazer, Grimes, and Hart, together with artistic reproductions from the work of each. He also wrote a sketch of Colonel Joseph Crockett, which was published in a volume which contains also a sketch of James Francis Leonard (*ibid.*, 1909).

PRICE, THOMAS RANDOLPH. Educator. [Va.]. He was born in 1839 and died in 1903. He published 'The Teaching of the Mother Tongue.'

PRINCE, OLIVER HILLHOUSE, lawyer, was born in Connecticut, about 1787, and died at sea, October 9, 1837. He settled in Georgia for the practice of law, and was one of the five commissioners to lay out the city of Macon. He achieved distinction at the Bar and also wrote numerous sketches, one of which, "The Militia Drill," has been preserved by Judge A. B. Longstreet in 'Georgia Scenes.' He also published a 'Digest of the Laws of Georgia to December, 1820.' On returning home from New York by steamer, he perished off the coast of Cape Hatteras.

PRINCE, OLIVER HILLHOUSE, Jr. [Ga.]. He was born in 1823 and died in 1875. He published a humorous series of writings entitled 'Billy Woodpile's Letters.'

PRYOR, ROGER ATKINSON, jurist, was born in Dinwiddie County, Va., July 19, 1828, his father being the Rev. Theodoric B. Pryor, and his mother, Lucy Atkinson. He was educated at Hampden-Sidney College; and soon after graduation he married Sara A. Rice. Though admitted to the Bar in 1849, he gave much of his time to editorial work, first in Petersburg and then in Richmond. In 1855 he was United States Special Envoy to Greece; and from 1859 to 1861 he served in Congress, declining the seat on being reëlected. He was subsequently chosen to the Congress of the Confederate States. Later he resigned to take the field, becoming a brigadier-general; but, dissatisfied, he relinquished his commission and reënlisted as a private. He was made a prisoner at Petersburg. Removing to New York after the war, he became one of the leaders of the Bar of the metropolis. From 1894 to 1899 he was judge of the Court of Common Pleas. Besides his numerous speeches, he has published many important papers and sketches. Hampden-Sidney College gave him the degree of LL.D.

PRYOR, SARA AGNES. See Biographical and Critical Sketch, Vol. X, page 4273.

PUGH, EDWARD WILLIAMS. Physician. [N.C.]. Born in 1850. He published a number of poems.

PUGH, ELIZA LOFTON, author, was born in Bayou Lafourche, La., in 1841. Her father was Colonel George Phillips and her mother a daughter of Judge John Rhea. On completing her education in New Orleans, she married William W. Pugh, a planter. Under the pen-name of "Arria" she wrote two novels: 'Not a Hero' (New York, 1867) and 'In a Crucible' (Philadelphia, 1871).

PUGH, JAMES LAWRENCE, United States Senator, was born in Burke County, Ga., December 12, 1820, but at an early age removed to Alabama, studied law, served in both Federal and Confederate Congresses, and for several terms represented Alabama in the United States Senate. He was an able debater and an eloquent public speaker. He died in Washington, D.C., in 1907.

PURDY, AMELIA V. McCARTY. Poet. [Texas]. She was born in 1845 and died in 1881. She published "First Fruits," "Vocation," and other poems.

PUREFOY, GEORGE W. Baptist clergyman. He published an important historical account entitled 'The Sandy Creek Baptist Association, 1758-1858' (New York, Sheldon and Company, 1859).

PURINTON, DANIEL BOARDMAN. He was born in Virginia, February 15, 1850, a son of the Rev. Jesse M. Purinton, D.D., and was educated at West Virginia University. He married Florence A. Lyon. From 1878 to 1890 he held successively the chairs of logic, mathematics, and metaphysics in the University of West Virginia; was president of Denison University for eleven years; and in 1901 became president of the University of West Virginia, an office which he still holds. His most important work is entitled, 'Christian Theism.' The University of Nashville gave him the degree of Ph.D. and Denison College the degree of LL.D. He resides in Morgantown, W.Va.

PURVIS, EVELYN MARTIN, educator, was born at Free Run, Miss., December 23, 1873. Besides a number of fragments which have appeared in periodicals, she is the author of a volume of 'Poems' (1903). She is engaged in teaching at Eden, Miss.

PURYEAR, CHARLES. Educator. [Va.]. He has published several text-books on mathematics.

PUTNAM, ALGERNON WALDO, author, was born in Marietta, Ohio, March 11, 1799, and died in Nashville, Tenn., January 20, 1869. After being admitted to the Bar he practiced first in Mississippi, but subsequently removed to Tennessee, locating in Nashville, became president of the Tennessee Historical Society, and published 'History of Middle Tennessee' (Nashville, 1859), 'Life and Times of General James Robertson' (1859), and "Life of General John Sevier," in Wheeler's 'History of North Carolina.'

PUTNAM, SALLIE A., Mrs., poet, was born in Madison Court House, Va., in 1845. Her maiden name was Sallie Brock. She was educated by private tutors and began at an early age to evince unusual literary gifts. In 1883 she married Rev. Richard Putnam of New York. Under the pen-name of "Virginia Madison," she wrote for the press and published: 'Richmond During the War,' 'Kenneth, My King,' and 'Southern Amaranth.'

PYRNELLE, LOUISA CLARKE, author, was born on her father's plantation, "Ittabena," near Uniontown, Ala., in 1852, of distinguished colonial stock, a daughter of Dr. Richard Clarke, who came from Petersburg, Va., and of Elizabeth Bates, who formerly lived in Mobile. When the war commenced, Louisa was only a slip of a girl. Her education was, therefore, rudely interrupted; and the failure of the Southern cause entailed reverses which denied her further opportunities. At sixteen she became a governess; and began in this way her career of teaching. She supplied by studious habit the lack of collegiate advantages, and developing a talent not only for creative authorship but also for dramatic recitation, she went North to avail herself of the best instruction. Here she attracted the attention of Mrs. Siddons, the famous actress, who made her a tempting offer; but eventually she returned to the South, where she married, in 1880, R. H. Pyrnelle, since deceased. Her married life was an ideally happy one and inspired her most successful efforts. Whether in writing stories for children or in describing plantation scenes of the old South, her pen has caught the fancy of the public and she stands to-day in the front rank of Southern prose writers. Her published works include: 'Diddy, Dumps and Tot' (New York, Harper and Brothers, 1882), 'The Courtship and Marriage of Aunt Flora' (Birmingham, 1895), and 'Miss Lil Tweety' (New York, Harper and Brothers, 1907), besides numerous uncollected short stories and sketches.

QUARLES, JAMES ADDISON. Educator and divine. He was born in Cooper County, Mo., April 30, 1837, a son of Colonel James and Sarah Ann Quarles, and was educated at the University of Virginia and at Princeton Theological Seminary. He married Caroline Wallace Field. He became professor of philosophy in Washington and Lee University, in 1886. Besides numerous reviews and articles on secular and religious subjects, he published in 1884 a 'Life of F. T. Kemper.' Westminster College gave him the degree of D.D. and Central University the degree of LL.D. He died in Lexington, Va., in 1907.

QUAYLE, WILLIAM ALFRED, clergyman and author, was born in Parkville, Mo., June 25, 1860. On completing his education he entered the ministry of the M.E. Church. His published works include: 'The Poet's Poet, and Other Essays' (1898), 'A Study in Current Social Theories' (1899), 'A Hero, and Some Other Folk' (1900), 'The Blessed Life' (1901), 'In God's Out-of-Doors' (1902), 'Eternity in the Heart' (1904), and 'The Prairies and the Sea' (1905). He holds the D.D. and the Litt.D. degrees and is at present pastor of St. James M.E. Church, Chicago, Ill.

QUINN, MINNIE. Author of a volume entitled 'Violets and Apple Blossoms.' For several years she taught in the public schools of Atlanta, Ga., but now resides in Texas.

QUINTARD, CHARLES TODD, Protestant Episcopal bishop, was born in Stamford, Conn., December 22, 1824, of Huguenot ancestry, received his degree in medicine from the University of the City of New York, and practiced his profession for some time in Georgia. But in 1855 he took orders, became an eminent Episcopal divine, served the First Tennessee Regiment in the capacity of chaplain, to which were also frequently added the duties of physician and surgeon; and in 1865 he was consecrated bishop of Tennessee. He reëstablished the University of the South, at Sewanee, and became the first vice-chancellor. He received the degree of D.D. from Columbia, and the degree of LL.D. from Cambridge, England. Some of his sermons have been published in book form; and they evince both scholarship and thought.

QUISENBERRY, ANDERSON Q. Journalist. For many years he resided in Kentucky, but at present his home is in Washington, D.C. What is said to be the most fascinating volume in many respects issued by the Filson Club, of Louisville, is from the pen of this writer. It is entitled: 'Lopez's Expeditions to Cuba, 1850-1851.' He intended originally to write a novel based upon the incidents which he narrates.

QUITMAN, JOHN ANTHONY, soldier and statesman, was born in Rhinebeck, N.Y., September 1, 1799, and died in Natchez, Miss., July 17, 1858. He was educated for the Lutheran ministry; but, preferring the law, he settled for the practice of his profession at Natchez, Miss., became eminent at the Bar and in politics, rose to the rank of major-general in the Mexican War, became governor of the State, served repeatedly in Congress, and received votes for the vice-presidency in two national Democratic Conventions. He was an ardent advocate of states' rights and also favored the annexation of Cuba. 'The Life and Correspondence of John A. Quitman, Major-general, U.S.A., and Governor of the State of Mississippi' was published by J. F. H. Claiborne (New York, 1860).

RADER, PERRY S. Author. [Mo.]. He wrote a 'School History of Missouri' (1891).

RAGSDALE, LULAH. Author. [Miss.]. She published 'A Shadow's Shadow' (1893), 'Sweet Mistress Prue,' a drama and numerous uncollected poems.

RAINES, C. W. Lawyer. [Texas]. He published a 'Bibliography of Texas' (1896).

RAINS, GEORGE WASHINGTON, soldier and educator, was born in Craven County, N.C., in 1817, received his education at West Point, and served with distinction in the Mexican War and in the troubles with the Seminole Indians. Later he resigned to enter business. At the outbreak of the Civil War he established at Augusta, Ga., the famous Confederate powder works, of which he remained in charge until the close of hostilities. He attained the rank of brigadier-general. Subsequent to the war, he engaged in educational work. He published a treatise on 'Steam Portable Engines' (Newburg, N.Y., 1860), a 'History of the Confederate Powder Works' (Augusta, 1882), 'Analytical and Applied Chemistry' (Augusta, 1872), and 'Chemical Analysis' (New York, 1879).

RALSTON, THOMAS NEELY, clergyman, was born in Bourbon County, Ky., March 3, 1806, received his education at Georgetown College, and became an eminent Methodist divine and educator. Wesleyan University made him a D.D. He published 'Elements of Divinity' (Louisville, 1847), 'Evidences, Morals, and Institutions of Christianity' (Nashville, 1870), 'Ecce Unitas' (Cincinnati, 1870), and 'Bible Truths' (1879).

RAMAGE, BURR JAMES, lawyer, was born in Newberry, S.C., July 1, 1858. For several years he was a member of the faculty of the University of the South, at Sewanee, Tenn. At the present time he is special attorney before the Bureau of Corporations in the Department of Commerce and Labor in Washington, D.C. From 1900 to 1904 he was associate editor of the Sewanee *Review*. Besides numerous documents for the Government, he has written magazine and newspaper articles on historical, economic and legal subjects. The sketch of Hugh Swinton Legaré in 'The Library of Southern Literature' is from his pen. He married, February 24, 1897, Harriet Page Bird.

RAMSAY, DAVID. See Biographical and Critical Sketch, Vol. X, page 4295.

RAMSAY, FRANKLIN PIERCE, clergyman, was born in Pike County, Ala., March 30, 1856. Dr. Ramsay has not only attained distinction in the pulpit, but has also published several theological works, among them, an 'Exposition of the Book of Church Order' (Richmond, Va., The Presbyterian Committee of Publication, 1898), 'The Question' (New York and Washington, The Neale Publishing Company, 1909), and 'A Study of Genesis' (in press). He resides in Chicago, Ill.

RAMSAY, JAMES GATTYS McGREGOR. Physician and historian. Most of his life was spent in Tennessee, where he died, in 1884, at the advanced age of eighty-eight. He published 'Annals of Tennessee' (Philadelphia, J. B. Lippincott Company).

RAMSAY, ROBERT LEE, educator, was born in Sumter, S.C., December 14, 1880. After graduating, he became an instructor in English at the University of Missouri. He has published 'Magnyfycence: a Moral Play by John Skelton,' edited with introduction, notes, and glossary for the Early English Text Society (London, 1906), 'The West Saxon Psalms,' edited from the manuscript, in collaboration with Professor J. W. Bright, of Johns Hopkins, for the Belles-lettres Series (Boston and London, 1907), and 'Principles of Modern Punctuation,' issued by the department of journalism, University of Missouri, in 1908. He received the Ph.D. degree from Johns Hopkins.

RANCK, GEORGE W. Author. He was born in Louisville, Ky., was educated at the University of Kentucky. His wife was Helen Carty. He devoted much time to historical research, especially in Kentucky archives, and published the following books: 'History of Lexington, Ky.' (Cincinnati, The Robert Clarke Company), 'Girty, the White Indian,' 'The Traveling Church,' 'The Story of Bryan's Station,' 'The Bivouac of the Dead and its Author,' and 'Boonsborough,' an historical account published by the Filson Club. He died in 1900.

RAND, MARION HOWARD, author, was born in Philadelphia, Pa., January 5, 1824, and died in Grahamville, S.C., June 9, 1849. She lived for several years in the South. Some of the best magazines of the day, including *Godey's* and *Graham's*, published her contributions, and specimens of her verse may be found in Read's 'Female Poets of America' and in May's 'American Female Poets.' She possessed exceptional gifts, but her early death prevented the full fruition of her genius.

RANDALL, JAMES RYDER. See Biographical and Critical Sketch, Vol. X, page 4309.

RANDOLPH, ALFRED MAGILL, Protestant Episcopal bishop of Southern Virginia, was born in Winchester, Va., in 1836, the son of Robert Lee Randolph, and was educated at William and Mary College. Soon after completing his special equipment for the ministry, the war began; and for three years he was a Confederate chaplain. At the close of hostilities, he became rector of Emanuel Church, in Baltimore. Later he became bishop coadjutor of Virginia; and, finally, in 1892, bishop of Southern Virginia. He is the author of an important work entitled 'Reason, Faith, and Authority in Christianity' (New York, Thomas Whittaker). 'Sermons and Addresses' has also appeared in book form. He resides at Norfolk, Va. Bishop Randolph has received the degree of D.D. from William and Mary, the degree of LL.D. from Washington and Lee, and the degree of D.C.L. from the University of the South.

RANDOLPH, E. A. [Va.]. He wrote a 'Life of John Jasper' (1884).

RANDOLPH, EDMUND, jurist and lawyer, was born in Richmond, Va., June 9, 1820, and died in San Francisco, Cal., September 8, 1861. For several years after completing his education, he was clerk of the United States Circuit Court for Louisiana, but afterward settled in California, participated in the work of organizing the State government, and became an eminent member of the Bar. He died while advocating the claims of the United States Government in the famous Almada mine case; and for his services in this important litigation his widow received $12,000. He published 'An Address on the History of California from the Discovery of the Country to the Year 1849' (San Francisco, 1860).

RANDOLPH, EDMUND JENNINGS, statesman, was born in Williamsburg, Va., August 10, 1753, and died in Clarke County, Va., September 13, 1813. He was distinguished for scholarship and eloquence, became the first attorney-general of Virginia, served in Congress for two years, occupied the office of governor from 1786 to 1788, took an active part in the proceedings of the convention that framed the Constitution, and caused the elimination of the word "slavery" from the great document. Against the powerful opposition of Patrick Henry, he was largely instrumental in securing the ratification of the Constitution in Virginia. He subsequently entered the Cabinet of Washington, becoming first Attorney-general, and afterward Secretary of State. On relinquishing office he wrote 'The Vindication of Mr. Randolph's Resignation' and 'Political Truths; or, Animadversions on the Past and Present State of Public Affairs.' He was the victim of overwhelming misfortunes, which involved heavy loss and litigation, but he speedily resumed his place at the head of the Virginia Bar, became one of the counsel for Aaron Burr in his trial at Richmond, and wrote an important 'History of Virginia,' the manuscript of which is in the possession of the Virginia Historical Society at Richmond.

RANDOLPH, INNES, lawyer and poet, was born in Winchester, Va., October 25, 1837, and died in Baltimore, Md., April 29, 1887. He was a man of rare talents, with early predilections for both music and art, but after serving in the Confederate Army he settled in Baltimore for the practice of law and incidentally began to contribute poems and sketches to the newspapers. At length he relinquished the legal profession and became an editorial writer on the Baltimore *American,* a position which he held for the remainder of his days. Among his best known poems are "Twilight at Hollywood," "The Good Old Rebel," and an "Ode to John Marshall." After his death, a volume of his verse was edited by his son, Professor Harold Randolph.

RANDOLPH, JOHN. See Biographical and Critical Sketch, Vol. X, page 4329.

RANDOLPH, SIR JOHN, lawyer, was born on Turkey Island, Va., in 1693, and died in Williamsburg, Va., in 1737. He studied both at home and abroad, became eminent as a lawyer, and while on a visit to England to obtain a renewal of the charter of William and Mary College, his *alma mater,* he was knighted. He expected to write an historical narrative of Virginia, but on account of professional engagements he merely drafted an outline, which was subsequently expanded by William Stith, his nephew.

RANDOLPH, PEYTON, lawyer, was born in Williamsburg, Va., in 1779, and died in Richmond, Va., in 1828. For many years he was clerk of the Supreme Court of Virginia, and six volumes of 'Virginia Reports' came from his pen (Richmond, 1823-1829).

RANDOLPH, PEYTON, lawyer, was born in Williamsburg, Va., Williamsburg, Va., in 1721, and died in Philadelphia, Pa., October 22, 1775. He studied law in London and became the King's attorney for Virginia. He also served in the House of Burgesses, resisted the oppressive measures of the British Crown, carried successfully an appeal to the throne for relief against the land tax, revised the early Virginia laws, resigned his lucrative office when relations between the mother country and the colonies became tense, and was the first president of the Continental Congress. He died while attending to his legislative duties in Philadelphia; but his body was brought to Williamsburg and interred in the chapel of William and Mary College. He was several times speaker of the House of Burgesses.

RANDOLPH, SARAH NICHOLAS, author, was born in Edge Hill, near Charlottesville, Va., October 12, 1839, and was the daughter of Thomas Jefferson Randolph, Jefferson's grandson and biographer. She enjoyed excellent educational advantages and for several years conducted a school in Baltimore. She published 'The Domestic Life of Thomas Jefferson' (New York, 1871), "The Lord Will Provide," a paper on Martha Jefferson Randolph in Mrs. Wister's 'Famous Women of the Revolution' (Philadelphia, 1876), and 'Life of Stonewall Jackson,' besides frequent contributions to the periodicals. She died in 1897.

RANDOLPH, THOMAS JEFFERSON, author, was born in Monticello, Va., September 12, 1798, and died in Edge Hill, Va., October 8, 1875. His mother was the daughter of Thomas Jefferson. He acquired large means; and, after the sale of Jefferson's property, debts to the amount of forty thousand dollars were assumed by him out of regard for his grandfather's honor. As the literary executor of the great statesman he published, in four volumes, 'The Life and Correspondence of Thomas Jefferson' (Boston, 1829). He was also a financier, secured the passage of a tax bill, which put the finances of Virginia on a secure basis, and wrote 'Sixty Years' Reminiscences of the Currency of the United States,' a pamphlet of some historical interest. He was rector of the University of Virginia for seven years.

RANKIN, JOHN, clergyman, was born near Dandridge, Tenn., February 4, 1793, and died in Ironton, Ohio, March 18, 1886. He was a Presbyterian, and for several years held pastorates in Kentucky; but he afterward moved into Ohio, joined the Garrison anti-slavery crusade, and was several times mobbed for his views. He is said to have assisted Eliza, the original of one of the characters in 'Uncle Tom's Cabin,' to escape. He published 'The Covenant of Grace' (Pittsburg, 1869). His biography was written by the Rev. Alexander Richie (Cincinnati, 1876).

RANKIN, JOHN CHAMBERS. Clergyman. [N.C.]. He was born in 1816 and died in 1900. He published 'The Coming of our Lord.'

RANSOM, MATTHEW WHITAKER, soldier and statesman, was born in Warren County, N.C., October 8, 1826. He received his education at the University of North Carolina, chose the profession of law, became attorney-general of the State, opposed secession, but acquiesced in the result, attained the rank of major-general in the Confederate Army, and for several terms represented the State with great distinction in the United States Senate. He was an eloquent public speaker, cultured and brilliant. General Ransom died in 1904.

RAPER, CHARLES LEE, educator, was born in High Point, N.C., March 10, 1870. He is dean of the graduate school and professor of economics in the University of North Carolina, and author of the following works: 'The Church and Private Schools of North Carolina' (1898), 'North Carolina: a Study in English Colonial Government' (New York, The Macmillan Company, 1904), and 'The Principles of Wealth and Welfare' (New York, The Macmillan Company, 1906).

RATHBORNE, ST. GEORGE, author, was the son of Captain G. L. Rathborne, and was born in Covington, Ky., December 26, 1854. On completing his studies he became an editor, first in Chicago and afterward in New York. For several years he has spent his winters in Florida, where he owns a pineapple plantation on the Indian River. He is the author of numerous stories, chiefly for young readers, among the number being: 'Baron Sam' (New York, Street and Smith), 'Captain Tom' (*ibid.*), 'Colonel by Brevet' (*ibid.*), 'Dr. Jack' (*ibid.*), 'Dr. Jack's Wife' (*ibid.*), 'The Fair Maid of Fez' (*ibid.*), 'The Girl from Hong Kong' (*ibid.*), 'Her Rescue from the Turks' (*ibid.*), 'Major Matterson of Kentucky' (*ibid.*), 'Miss Fairfax of Virginia' (*ibid.*), 'Little Miss Millions' (*ibid.*), 'At Swords' Points' (*ibid.*), 'A Daughter of Russia' (*ibid.*), 'Sunset Ranch' (*ibid.*), 'Down in Dixie' (*ibid.*), 'Teddy's Enchantress' (*ibid.*), 'Dr. Jack's Paradise Mine' (*ibid.*), 'Young Castaways' (Akron, Ohio, The Saalfield Publishing Company), 'Boy Voyagers of the Nile' (*ibid.*), 'Down the Amazon,' and 'Adrift on a Junk' (*ibid.*).

RAVENEL, H. E. [S.C.]. He published 'The Ravenel Records' (1898).

RAVENEL, HARRIOTT HORRY. Author. She was born in Charleston, S.C., August 12, 1832, a daughter of Edward Cotesworth, of the United States Navy and Rebecca Motte Rutledge. She was educated in private schools and by tutors at home, and married, in 1851, Dr. St. Julien Ravenel, an eminent physician. Her writings, which reveal exceptional culture, include: 'Ashurst,' a novel, 'Life of Eliza Pinckney,' 'Life and Times of William Lowndes of South Carolina,' (Boston, Houghton, Mifflin and Company), and 'Charleston, the Place and the People' (The Macmillan Company). She resides in Charleston, S.C.

RAVENEL, HENRY WILLIAM, botanist, was born in St. John's Parish, Berkeley, S.C., May 19, 1814, and died in Aiken, S.C., July 17, 1887. He chose the life of a planter; and, on completing his education at South Carolina College, he settled at St. John's, pursued with great enthusiasm the study of nature, and discovered many new species of cryptograms, on which subject he became an authority of international reputation. The University of North Carolina conferred upon him the degree of LL.D. Besides contributing to the scientific journals, he published 'Fungi Caroliniani Exsiccati,' in five volumes (Charleston, 1853-1860), and, with Mordecai C. Cook, of London, 'Americani Exsiccati,' in eight volumes (1878-1882).

RAVENSCROFT, JOHN STARK, Protestant Episcopal bishop, was born near Blandford, Va., in 1772, and died in Williamsborough, N.C., March 5, 1830. He achieved distinction in the pulpit and became the first bishop of North Carolina. The degree of D.D. was conferred upon him by William and Mary College and also by Columbia. Two volumes of his sermons were published after his death, with a memoir by Bishop Wainwright (New York, 1830).

RAY, JOHN, lawyer, was born in Washington County, Mo., October 14, 1816, and died in New Orleans, La., in 1888. He achieved distinction at the Bar and became prominent in politics. In 1873 he was elected to the United States Senate by the "Kellogg" Legislature, but was not seated. He published, in two volumes, 'Ray's Digest of the Laws of Louisiana' (New Orleans, 1870).

RAYMOND, EVELYN HUNT. Author. She was born in Watertown, N.Y., November 6, 1843, a daughter of Alvin Hunt. She was educated in private schools and at Mount Holyoke Seminary. Besides numerous short stories, Mrs. Raymond has published several novels, including 'Mixed Pickles' (1892), 'Monica' (1893), 'The Mushroom Cove' (1895), and 'Among the Lindens.' She resides in Baltimore, Md.

RAYMOND, JAMES, lawyer, was born in Connecticut, in 1796, and died in Westminster, Md., in 1858. He was a lawyer of high attainments and was also versed in letters. He published a 'Digest of Maryland Chancery Decisions' (New York, 1839), and a volume in opposition to "Know-Nothingism."

RAYMOND, W. M. [Va.]. He published a work entitled 'Citronaloes.'

RAYMOND, ZILLAH. Author. [N.C.]. She wrote 'Then and Now; or, Faith's First School' (1893).

RAYNER, ISIDOR, United States Senator, was born in Baltimore, Md., April 11, 1850, and was educated at the Universities of Maryland and Virginia, and from the latter institution received also his diploma in law. He was duly admitted to the Bar, advanced rapidly to the front in his profession, and in 1886 was elected to Congress as a Democrat, after holding various offices of distinction in the State. Twice he was chosen to succeed himself in this high forum, but he declined another nomination and was elected attorney-general of Maryland, a position which he ably filled for four years. On the death of Honorable Louis E. McComas, a Republican, he was elected to succeed him in the United States Senate for the term beginning March 4, 1905. As an advocate his powers are of the very highest order; and his speeches in both Houses of Congress are masterpieces of cogent logic. Senator Rayner is one of the advisory council of 'The Library of Southern Literature.' He resides in Baltimore, Md., when official duties do not require his presence at the seat of government.

READ, OPIE. See Biographical and Critical Sketch, Vol. X, page 4357.

REAGAN, JOHN HENNINGER, statesman, was born in Sevier County, Tenn., in 1818, and spent his boyhood on a farm. After completing his education, he settled in Texas for the practice of law, was made Superior Court judge in 1852, and sent to Congress in 1857. On the organization of the Southern Confederacy, he was a delegate to the Provisional Congress at Montgomery, Ala., and was Confederate postmaster from 1862 to 1865. At the close of the war he was captured with President Davis and imprisoned at Fort Warren. It was while he was incarcerated at this place that he wrote his celebrated letter to the people of Texas, advising them to confer civil rights upon the negro and to admit the more intelligent to suffrage, lest measures still more radical should follow. For several years after the war he served in Congress; and from 1887 to 1891 he was a member of the United States Senate, resigning to become chairman of the Texas State Railroad Commission. His 'Memoirs' (New York and Washington, The Neale Publishing Company, 1900), which deal with an eventful period in the nation's life, are written in an interesting narrative vein. He died in 1905, at Palestine, Texas, the last surviving member of the Confederate Cabinet.

READE, WILLOUGHBY, educator and lecturer, was born in London, England, July 9, 1865, but came to the United States when a lad. His father was Willoughby Reade, distinguished throughout the South as a lecturer and public reader, and the son has successfully followed in the parental footsteps. For fifteen years the latter has been at the head of the department of English and elocution in the Episcopal High School of Virginia at Alexandria. He has also published several volumes, among them, 'England and the Continent' (1891), 'The Epic of King Arthur' (1900), 'When Hearts Were True,' a collection of short stories illustrative of life in Virginia (New York and Washington, The Neale Publishing Company, 1907), 'The Man at the Throttle, and Other Poems' (in press), and 'Konnarock, and Other Stories of the Virginia Mountains' (in preparation). He married, June 26, 1894, Mary W. Robertson, granddaughter of ex-Governor Wyndham Robertson of Virginia.

REAMY, THADDEUS ASBURY, physician and educator, was born in Frederick County, April 28, 1829, but early in life moved to Ohio, became an eminent medical practitioner and professor of medicine, and published a number of medical text-books.

REAVIS, LOGAN URIAH, journalist, was born in Illinois, in 1831, and died in St. Louis, in 1889. For years he conducted a campaign in the interest of securing the removal of the national capitol from Washington to St. Louis. Besides numerous pamphlets in exploitation of this idea, he published 'St. Louis, the Future Great City of the World' (1867), a 'Life of Horace Greeley, with an Introduction by Cassius M. Clay' (1882), 'Thoughts for the Young Men and Women of America' (1873), a 'Life of General William S. Harney' (1875), and other works.

REDE, WYLLYS. Clergyman. He was born in Monmouth, Ill., August 7, 1859, the son of Alvin Hart and Miriam Rede, and was educated at home and abroad. He married, in 1895, Carolyn Potter. Since entering the ministry of the Protestant Episcopal Church, most of his parishes have been in the South. He became rector of the church at Brunswick, Ga., in 1902. Besides editing *The Church in Georgia,* he has written 'Striving for the Mastery' and 'The Communion of Saints,' both published by Longmans Green and Company, New York. St. John's College gave him the degree of D.D. He resides in Brunswick, Ga.

REDFORD, A. H. Author. He wrote 'The Life and Times of Bishop Kavanaugh' (Nashville, 1884).

REDWAY, JACQUES WARDLAW, geographer, was born near Nashville, Tenn., May 5, 1849, but early in life moved to California, received his education at the University of California, and achieved distinction in the educational world of the West. He also became an extensive traveler, and published a series of geographies.

REED, JOHN CALVIN, lawyer and author, was born in Appling. Ga., February 24, 1836. On completing his collegiate course at Princeton, he studied law and became one of the foremost legal scholars at the Bar of Georgia. He published several law books, among them, 'Georgia Criminal Law' (1873), 'Practical Suggestions for the Preparation and Trial of Causes' (New York, 1875), 'American Law Studies' (Boston, 1882), and 'Conduct of Law-suits' (Boston, 1885), an enlarged edition of 'Practical Suggestions,' concerning which work Wigmore says "it is the most sensible and systematic modern book of this kind." He also published a volume entitled 'The Brothers' War' (Boston, Little, Brown and Company, 1905), a work of exceptional interest and value, which has delighted both Northern and Southern critics and contributed to the *Uncle Remus Home Magazine* a number of articles on the famous Ku Klux, of which he was one of the organizers (1908-1909). The latest production of his pen was a series of articles for 'The South in the Building of the Nation.' He also wrote numerous historical monographs. Colonel Reed died at the home of his son in Montgomery, Ala., January 12, 1910.

REED, RICHARD CLARK, Presbyterian clergyman and educator, occupies the chair of Church history in the theological seminary at Columbia, S.C. His published works include: 'The Gospel as Taught by Calvin' (Richmond, The Presbyterian Committee of Publication, 1896), and 'The History of the Presbyterian Churches of the World' (*ibid.,* 1906). He has also published a number of monographs, among them, 'Athenasius,' 'John Knox: His Field and His Work,' and 'John Calvin's Contribution to the Reformation.' The last is included in a volume of 'Calvin Memorial Addresses' (*ibid.,* 1909). He married, October 17, 1876, Mary Canty Venable. Dr. Reed has received both the D.D. and the LL.D. degrees.

REED, WALLACE PUTNAM. Editorial writer. For many years he was on the staff of the Atlanta *Constitution.* Besides contributing to 'Memoirs of Georgia' the chapter on "Literature," he published an elaborate 'History of Atlanta' (Pittsburg, D. Mason and Company), and was the author of many charming sketches and monographs. He died in 1903.

REEDER, CHARLES, manufacturer, was born in Baltimore, Md., October 31, 1817, became a constructor of marine steam-engines, and owned the *Tennessee,* the first steamship to ply between Baltimore and Europe. He published 'Caloric: a Review of the Dynamic Theory of Heat' (Baltimore, 1887).

REESE, LEVI H., clergyman, was born in Hartford County, Md., February 8, 1806, and died in Philadelphia, Pa., September 21, 1851. He was educated in the public schools of Baltimore and entered the Methodist pulpit, but afterward seceded on the organization of the Methodist Protestants. He was an ardent Prohibitionist, and at one time was chaplain to Congress. He published 'Obligations of the Sabbath' and 'Thoughts of an Itinerant.'

REESE, LIZETTE WOODWORTH. See Biographical and Critical Sketch, Vol. X, page 4379.

REESE, THOMAS. Presbyterian clergyman and educator. [S.C.]. He was born in 1742 and died in 1794. He published an able essay on 'The Influence of Religion on Civil Society' (1788), besides a number of sermons. Princeton gave him the degree of D.D.

RIVES, JUDITH PAGE WALKER, author, was born in Castle Hill, Va., March 24, 1802, and at the age of seventeen married the Honorable William Cabell Rives. She accompanied her husband on his missions to France, and embodied her recollections in two interesting volumes: 'Souvenirs of a Residence in Europe' (Philadelphia, 1842), and 'Home and the World' (New York, 1857). She also published 'The Canary-Bird' (Philadelphia, 1835), and 'Epitome of the Holy Bible' (Charlottesville, 1846). She died at Castle Hill, Va., January 23, 1882.

REEVES, MARIAN CALHOUN LEGARÉ, author, was born in Charleston, S.C., in 1854, and began her literary career some time in the 'sixties. Under the pen-name of "Fadette," she produced several interesting volumes, among them: 'Ingemisco' (New York, 1867), 'Randolph Honor,' 'Maid of Arcadie,' and 'Sea-Drift' (Philadelphia, 1869), 'Old Martin Boscawen's Jest,' with Emily Read (New York, 1878), 'Pilot Fortune' (Boston, 1883), and other works.

REICHEL, LEVIN THEODORE. Moravian bishop. For years he labored at Salem, N.C., though he was born in Bethlehem, Pa., March 4, 1812. Later he was consecrated to the Episcopacy at Herrnhut, Saxony, where he died, May 23, 1878. He published 'The Moravians in North Carolina' (1857), and a 'History of Nazareth Hall' (1855), besides leaving in manuscript a 'History of the American Branch of the Moravian Church.' William Cornelius Reichel was his nephew.

REICHEL, WILLIAM CORNELIUS, author, was born in Salem, N.C., of Moravian stock, May 9, 1824, and died in Bethlehem, Pa., October 15, 1876. For several years he was a professor in Moravian schools. He was also a writer of tireless industry and research. Among his publications are included, a "History of Nazareth Hall," written for Eagle's 'History of Pennsylvania' (Philadelphia, 1855), a 'History of Bethlehem Seminary' (1858), 'Moravianism in New York and Connecticut' (1860), 'Memorials of the Moravian Church' (1870), 'Wyalusing' (1871), 'Names Given by the Lenni Lenape, or Delaware Indians, to Rivers, etc.' (1872), 'A Red Rose from the Olden Time' (Philadelphia, 1872), 'The Crown Inn near Bethlehem' (1872), and other works. He also revised Heckwelder's 'History of the Pennsylvania Indians' (Philadelphia, 1876).

"REID, CHRISTIAN." See Tiernan, Frances Fisher.

REID, J. W. Author. [S.C.] He wrote a 'History of the Fourth Regiment of South Carolina Volunteers, 1861-1865.'

REID, SAM CHESTER, lawyer and journalist, was born in New York City, October 21, 1818, but settled in Mississippi, where he read law under John A. Quitman. He served in the Mexican War, reported the proceedings of the Louisiana Secession Convention, and during the Civil War was correspondent for several Southern papers. After the close of hostilities he resumed the legal practice. He published: 'The Scouting Expeditions of McCulloch's Texas Rangers' (Philadelphia, 1847), 'The Battle of Chickamauga' (Mobile, 1863), 'The Daring Raid of General John H. Morgan in Ohio' (Atlanta, 1864), and 'The United States Bankrupt Law of 1841,' besides several minor works. He also wrote a 'Life of Aaron Burr,' but the manuscript was destroyed by fire. He established the Mississippi Valley and Brazil Steamship Company in St. Louis, Mo.

REILEY, MARY TRIMBLE. Poet. [La.]. She published a volume of 'Poems' (Clinton, La., 1879).

REIMENSNYDER, JUNIUS BENJAMIN, clergyman, was born in Staunton, Va., February 24, 1841, received his educational equipment at Gettysburg, Pa., preached for a while in Savannah, Ga., and afterward in New York. He published 'Heavenward; or, the Race for the Crown of Life' (Philadelphia, 1874), 'Christian Unity' (Savannah, 1876), 'Doom Eternal' (Philadelphia, 1880), and 'The Six Days of Creation.' Newberry College, South Carolina, conferred upon him the degree of D.D.

RELF, SAMUEL, journalist, was born in Virginia, March 22, 1776, and died in Virginia, February 14, 1823. When a child he was taken to Philadelphia, where he owned and edited for years the *National Gazette.* He also wrote a novel entitled 'Infidelity; or, the Victims of Sentiment' (Philadelphia, 1797).

REMSEN, IRA, president of Johns Hopkins University, was born in the State of New York, February 10, 1846, and, after graduation from the College of the City of New York, took his degree in medicine from the College of Physicians and Surgeons, New York. Still later he studied at the University of Göttingen. In 1876 he was called to the chair of chemistry in Johns Hopkins University, and when Dr. Gilman resigned the presidency, in 1901, he was called to the executive helm. Dr. Remsen is an authority of world-wide note in the branch of science to which he has devoted his life-long investigations. He is also a splendid disciplinarian and a voluminous writer. His published works include: 'The Principles of Theoretical Chemistry' (1876), an 'Introduction to the Study of the Compounds of Carbon' (Boston, D. C. Heath and Company, 1885), an 'Introduction to the Study of Chemistry' (New York, Henry Holt and Company, 1887), 'The Elements of Chemistry' (*ibid.*, 1888), 'Inorganic Chemistry' (*ibid.*, 1888), a 'Laboratory Manual' (*ibid.*, 1889), and 'Chemical Experiments' (*ibid.*, 1895), besides numerous public addresses and contributions on scientific and educational subjects to periodicals and encyclopædias. He resides in Baltimore, Md.

REMY, HENRI. Author. [La.]. He wrote in French a 'Histoire de la Louisiane' (1854).

RENFROE, JOHN J. D. Baptist clergyman. [Ala.]. He published 'Representative Men of the South' (1880).

RENO, ITTI KENNEY. Author. She was born in Nashville, Tenn., May 17, 1862, and married, in 1885, Robert Ross Reno. Her writings, in addition to a number of short stories and sketches, include:

'Miss Breckinridge, a Daughter of Dixie,' and 'An Exceptional Case,' both published by J. B. Lippincott and Company, Philadelphia. She resides in Nashville, Tenn.

REQUIER, AUGUSTUS JULIAN. See Biographical and Critical Sketch, Vol. X, page 4395.

REYNOLDS, IGNATIUS ALOYSIUS, Roman Catholic bishop, was born in Nelson County, Ky., August 22, 1798, and died in Charleston, S.C., March 9, 1855. For several years he was pastor of the cathedral in Louisville, and afterward vicar-general of the diocese. In 1843 he succeeded Bishop England. He was a man of great eloquence and learning but he overtaxed his strength in the labors of his high calling and died in the meridian of his powers. He edited, in five volumes, 'The Works of Bishop John England' (Baltimore, 1849).

REYNOLDS, JAMES LAWRENCE, Baptist clergyman and educator, was born in Charleston, S.C., March 17, 1814, and died in Greenville, S.C., December 19, 1877. After graduation from the College of Charleston, he entered the theological seminary at Newton, Mass. For several years he labored with marked success in the ministry, but his scholarly attainments were such that he was called to devote much of his time to educational work. From 1855 to 1866 he was a professor in South Carolina College; from 1866 to 1873, a professor in the University of South Carolina, and the last four years of his life were given to Furman University, at Greenville. Besides contributing to current periodicals, including *DeBow's Review*, the *Southern Baptist*, and the *Confederate Baptist*, he published a series of school readers (1870). As a writer he was both vigorous and fearless. Dr. Reynolds was given the degree of D.D.

REYNOLDS, JOHN SCHREINER, lawyer, was born in Charleston, S.C., September 28, 1848, and after completing his education was admitted to the Bar. As a lawyer he takes high rank. He is a man of ripe culture and of wide information, and his work on 'Reconstruction in South Carolina' (Columbia, S.C., The State Company, 1906), makes an important contribution to the literature of an eventful period. He married, December 9, 1880, Susan Gadsden Edwards. He resides in Columbia, S.C.

REYNOLDS, THOMAS. Governor of Missouri from 1840 to 1844. Besides State papers he published an interesting commemorative address on 'The Two Hundredth Anniversary of the Discovery of the Upper Mississippi.'

RHETT, ANDREW BURNET, educator, was born in Charleston, S.C., November 22, 1877. His father was Andrew B. Rhett, and his mother, Henrietta Aiken. Besides contributing to periodicals, he wrote the sketch of William H. Trescott in 'The Library of Southern Literature.' He is principal of Mitchell School, Charleston, S.C.

RHETT, ROBERT BARNWELL, statesman, was born in Beaufort, S.C., December 24 1800, and died in St. James Parish, La., September 14, 1876. He studied law, became attorney-general of the State, served in Congress for six successive terms, and in 1851 succeeded John C. Calhoun in the United States Senate. He resigned his commission when hostilities were threatened, and afterward took his seat in the Confederate Congress. For some time Mr. Rhett owned and edited the Charleston *Mercury*, an organ of the so-called "fire-eaters." After the war he moved to Louisiana and took no further part in politics, except to attend the national Democratic Convention of 1868. He was an orator of exceptional gifts.

RHODES, ROBERT H. Poet. [Texas]. He was born in 1845 and died in 1874. He wrote a number of poems, including "Prayer," and "Under the Cactus."

RHODES, WILLIAM HENRY, lawyer, was born in North Carolina in 1822, but afterward lived in Texas, and finally removed to California, where he died about 1875. He was a man of gifts, and, besides attaining success at the Bar, he indulged his taste for literature by writing at intervals more for mental diversion than for pecuniary profit. His works include: 'Theodosia,' a play, 'The Indian Gallows, and Other Poems' (1846', and 'Caxton's Book' (San Francisco, A. L. Bancroft and Company, 1876), a work which appeared after his death, containing stories and sketches, essays and poems, edited by Daniel O'Connell.

RIBAULT, JEAN, French navigator, was born in France in 1520 and died in Florida in 1565. He made an unsuccessful effort to found a colony of Huguenots in Florida, and suffered death at the hands of the Spaniards. He published a work entitled 'The Whole and True Discovery of Florida' (1563), which is known to-day only in the English translation.

RICE, ALICE HEGAN. See Biographical and Critical Sketch, Vol. X, page 4403.

RICE, BENJAMIN HOLT, clergyman, was born in New London, Va., November 29, 1782, and died in Hampden-Sidney, Va., February 4, 1856. He was educated under the instruction of his brother, Dr. John Holt Rice, became pastor of several prominent Presbyterian churches, and taught for several years in Hampden-Sidney College. He married a sister of Dr. Archibald Alexander, and published occasional sermons, but nothing else. Interesting side-lights upon his life are furnished in a 'Discourse on the Death of Benjamin Holt Rice,' by Rev. William E. Shenck (Philadelphia, 1856). Princeton made him a D.D.

RICE, CALE YOUNG. See Biographical and Critical Sketch, Vol. X, page 4427.

RICE, DAVID, clergyman, was born in Hanover County, Va., December 29, 1733, and died in Green County, Ky., June 18, 1816. The greater part of his life was spent in Kentucky, where he became one of the pioneers of Presbyterianism. He was one of the founders of Transylvania University and a member of the convention that framed the constitution of the State. He published 'An Essay on Baptism' (Baltimore, 1789), a 'Lecture on Divine Decrees,' 'Slavery Inconsistent with Justice and Policy,' 'Two Epistles to the Citizens of Kentucky Professing Christianity,' and 'A Kentucky Protest Against Slavery' (New York, 1812).

RICE, HENRY GRANTLAND, poet and journalist, was born in Murfreesboro, Tenn., November 1, 1880. His father was B. H. Rice and his mother, Beulah Grantland. From Vanderbilt University he received the degree of B.A.; and soon after graduation he began his newspaper career. He is the author of some of the best poems that are to-day going the rounds of the press; but they have not yet been collected and published in book form. On April 11, 1906, he married Kate Hollis. His home is in Nashville, Tenn.

RICE, JOHN HOLT, clergyman, was born in New London, Va., November 28, 1777, and died at Hampden-Sidney, Va., September 3, 1831. He became an eminent Presbyterian divine, edited church papers, wrote controversial pamphlets and memoirs of friends, and published 'Historical and Philosophical Considerations on Religion.' At the time of his death he was professor of theology at Hampden-Sidney College. He declined

the presidency of Princeton, from which institution he received the degree
of D.D. William Maxwell published his 'Memoir' (Philadelphia, 1835).

RICE, MARTIN. Baptist clergyman. [Mo.]. At leisure intervals he wrote for diversion and published 'Rural Rhymes,' 'Tales of
Olden Times,' and 'The Blue River Association.'

RICE, NATHAN LEWIS, clergyman, was born in Garrard
County, Ky., December 29, 1807, and died in Chatham, Ky., June 11, 1877.
Entering the Presbyterian ministry, he became one of the foremost divines
of this denomination, edited papers, organized schools and filled eminent
pulpits. For several years he was pastor of the Fifth Avenue Presbyterian
Church of New York; after which he assumed the presidency of Westminster College, at Fulton, Mo.; and still later taught theology at Danville,
Ky., until incapacitated by ill-health. He published 'Romanism the Enemy
of Free Institutions,' 'The Signs of the Times' (St. Louis, 1855), 'Baptism,' 'Our Country and the Church,' 'Preach the Word' (New York,
1862), 'The Pulpit: Its Relations to Our National Crisis,' and 'Discourses.'

RICHARD, MARGARET ALICE. Author. [S.C.]. She was born
in 1870. Her writings include: 'Three Bells' (1894), 'Gleanings by the
Wayside' (1896), 'Prize Winning' (1897), 'Songs of Dixie,' and 'Virginia
Vaughn.'

RICHARDS, WILLIAM CAREY, Baptist clergyman and scientist, was born in England in 1818. For ten years he lived in Georgia,
where he was engaged in educational and literary work. Later he removed to Charleston, but eventually located in the North, entered the
Baptist ministry, became distinguished on the platform and in the pulpit,
and published several works, among them: 'Georgia Illustrated' (1842),
and 'Harry's Vacation,' both of which were written during his sojourn
in the South.

RICHARDSON, CHARLES. Author. [Va.]. He served in the
Army of Northern Virginia and published in the reminiscent vein two
very delightful volumes entitled 'The Chancellorsville Campaign: from
Fredericksburg to Salem Church' (New York and Washington, The Neale
Publishing Company, 1906), and 'Tales of a Warrior' (*ibid.*, 1908).

RICHARDSON, H. H., Mrs. Educator. [Va.]. She wrote an
instructive volume entitled 'Little Lessons in Plant Life for Little
Children' (1898).

RICHARDSON, JAMES DANIEL. Representative in Congress
from Tennessee for twenty years, taking his seat in 1885. He was
born in Rutherford County, Tenn., March 10, 1843, a son of John W.
and Augusta Richardson, served in the Confederate Army, first as private
and afterward as adjutant, and married, in 1865, Miss Pippen. He
is one of the foremost Masons in the United States, and is editor
and compiler of 'The Messages and Papers of the Presidents,'
also 'Messages and Papers of the Confederacy.' The sketch of Albert
Pike in the 'Library of Southern Literature' is from his pen. He resides
in Murfreesboro, Tenn.

RICHARDSON, JOHN MANLY, educator and poet, was born
in Sumter District, S.C., March 13, 1831, and died at Daingerfield, Texas,
February 4, 1898. He attained the rank of major in the Confederate
Army, became an educator of note, and besides numerous contributions
to the periodical press, among them, "The Prayer of Mary Queen of
Scots," he published two military works and translated 'Dies Iræ.' Colonel
John P. Thomas, in his 'History of the South Carolina Military Acad-

emy,' calls him "a brave soldier and a scholar crowned with bays." He was twice married.

RICHARDSON, ROBERT. Clergyman, educator, physician. [W. Va.], He was born in 1808 and died in 1876. His works include: 'Memoirs of Alexander Campbell' (1868), 'Communings in the Sanctuary' (1872), and 'A Scriptural View of the Office of the Holy Spirit' (1873).

RICHARDSON, NORVAL, diplomat and author, was born in Vicksburg, Miss. At present he is one of the Secretaries of Legation at Havana, Cuba. Besides numerous magazine stories and sketches, he has published 'The Heart of Hope' (New York, Dodd, Mead and Company, 1905).

RICHARDSON, SCUDDAY. Author. [La.]. He wrote a novel entitled 'The Youth and First Love of Philip Reynolds' (1894).

RICHARDSON, SIMON PETER. Methodist Episcopal clergyman. In the humorous style of preaching he was the forerunner of the Rev. Sam P. Jones, the noted evangelist. He was for years a power in Southern Methodism. Toward the end of his long pilgrimage he wrote an autobiographical work entitled 'Lights and Shadows of Itinerant Life' (Nashville, The M.E. Publishing House, South, 1899). He received the degree of D.D.

RICHARDSON, WARFIELD CREATH. Editor and educator. He was born in Maysville, Ky., June 23, 1823, the son of Captain Thomas Gaines Richardson. He was educated at the University of Alabama and married, in 1855, Kate Cole Jones. For more than forty years, he was a professor in the University of Alabama, occupying at different times almost every chair in the faculty of the institution. Besides numerous magazine articles, he published late in life, 'Gaspar,' a metrical romance, (Boston, Houghton, Mifflin and Company, 1873); and 'The Fall of the Alamo,' an epic. He is the oldest surviving alumnus of the University of Alabama, from which institution he received the degree of LL.D.

RIDDELL, JOHN LEONARD, physician, was born in Leyden, Mass., February 20, 1807, and died in New Orleans, La., October 7, 1867. For thirty years he occupied the chair of chemistry in the medical department of the University of Louisiana. The plant "Riddellia" was named for him, and besides numerous scientific papers he published a 'Synopsis of the Flora of the Western States' (Cincinnati, 1835).

RIDDICK, ROBERT A. Poet. [N.C.]. He wrote a volume of verse entitled 'Musings of a Bachelor' (Raleigh, 1899, paper edition, 116 pages).

RIDGAWAY, HENRY BASCOM, clergyman, was born in Talbot County, Md., September 7, 1830. For several years he served in the itinerant ranks of Methodism and occupied metropolitan pulpits, after which he became a professor in Garrett Biblical Institute at Evanston, Ill. He published 'The Life of Alfred Cookman' (New York, 1871), 'The Lord's Land: a Narrative of Travels in Sinai and Palestine' (1876), 'The Life of Bishop Edward S. Janes' (1882), 'Bishop Beverly Waugh' (1883), and 'Bishop Matthew Simpson' (1885).

RIDGELY, JAMES LOTT, author, was born in Baltimore, Md., January 27, 1807. For several years he was registrar of wills for Baltimore County, and later, under President Lincoln, became Collector of Internal Revenue. Afterward he went into business. He became an Odd Fellow in 1829 and attained high rank in the order. Besides several rituals, he wrote 'Odd Fellowship: What Is It?' 'The Odd Fellows' Pocket Companion' (Philadelphia, 1853), and other books of like character. He also edited for some time the official magazine of the order, *The Covenant.* He died in Baltimore, Md., November 16, 1881.

RIGHTOR, HENRY. Editor. He was born in New Orleans, La., January 18, 1870, the son of Nicholas Henry Rightor, and was educated at Tulane University and at Annapolis, being a cadet in the latter institution. He married, in 1886, Ella B. Earnest. He was on the *Times-Democrat,* for a number of years, and was censor for the Board of Health during the yellow fever epidemic of 1897. Later he entered the insurance field, in which he became very successful. For some time he was also chief associate editor of *The Harlequin.* His writings include: 'Harlequinade,' 'Standard History of New Orleans,' 'Moons and Marshes,' a volume of poems, and also two plays: "The Military Maid" and "The Striped Petticoat." He resides in New Orleans, La.

RILEY, BENJAMIN FRANKLIN. Clergyman and educator. He was born at Pineville, Ala., July 16, 1849. He married Emma Shaw. He was president of Howard College for several years and afterward professor of English at the University of Georgia. His most important writings are: a 'History of Alabama Baptists' and a 'History of Baptists of the Southern States East of the Mississippi.' He resides in Houston, Texas.

RILEY, FRANKLIN LAFAYETTE, educator, was born near Hebron, Miss., August 24, 1868. After graduation from Mississippi College he continued his studies at Johns Hopkins University, from which institution he received his degree of Ph.D. For one year he was president of Hillman College for Women; and in 1897 became professor of history in the University of Mississippi, a chair which he still occupies. He reorganized the Mississippi Historical Society and originated the Mississippi Department of Archives. His efforts to stimulate an interest in the collection and preservation of important data concerning the State of Mississippi have been untiring. He is a writer of vigorous and virile English, and a man of wide information. Besides editing to date some ten volumes of the Mississippi Historical Society publications, he aided in the compilation of 'The Library of Southern Literature,' being one of the assistant literary editors of this work. His writings include: 'Colonial Origins of New England Senates' (Baltimore, The Johns Hopkins Press, 1896). and a 'School History of Mississippi' (Richmond, B. F. Johnson and Company, 1900). He has also made frequent contributions to magazines and to the transactions of historical societies. The sketch of John F. H. Claiborne in 'The Library of Southern Literature' is from his pen. He married, July 15, 1891, Fannie T. Leigh.

"RIVERS, PEARL." See Nicholson, Mary Jane.

RIVERS, RICHARD HENDERSON, clergyman, was born in Montgomery County, Tenn., September 11, 1814. For several years he was president of Centenary College at Jackson, La. After the war he became an educator in Tennessee. From time to time he also filled Methodist pulpits. His writings include a 'Text-book on Mental Philosophy' (Nashville, 1860), a 'Text-book on Moral Philosophy' (1866), 'Our Young People' (1880), 'Life of Bishop Robert Paine,' and a volume of sermons. LaGrange College gave him the degree of D.D.

RIVERS, WILLIAM JAMES, educator, was born in Charleston, S.C., July 18, 1822. He was educated at the College of South Carolina, in which institution he was afterward for many years professor of the classic languages. He was a poet of local reputation, and also published a 'Catechism of the History of South Carolina' (Charleston, 1850), and a 'Sketch of the History of South Carolina,' the latter dating from 1719 to 1856.

RIVERS, WILLIAM PENN, clergyman and poet, was born in Augusta, Ga., in 1827. At leisure intervals snatched from pastoral work he wrote for the religious press. One of his poems, "A Year or Two More," is preserved in 'Songs of the South.'

RIVES, AMÉLIE. See Biographical and Critical Sketch, Vol.. X, page 4453.

RIVES, HALLIE ERMINIE. Author. She was born in Christian County, Ky., May 2, 1878, a daughter of Colonel Stephen T. Rives and descendant of Sir John Ryves, of Damory Court, Dorsetshire, England. Her mother was Mary Ragsdale Rives, who came of the line of John Tillotson, Archbishop of Canterbury. She is also a cousin of the famous author, Amélie Rives, now the Princess Troubetskoy. She married, in 1908, Post Wheeler, the poet and essayist, now filling a consular post in England. Among her writings, which are characterized by keen insight and vivid imagination, are: 'The Singing Wire,' 'A Fool in Spots,' 'Smoking Flax,' 'As the Hart Panteth,' 'A Furnace of Earth,' 'Hearts Courageous,' 'The Castaways' and others. The Bobbs-Merrill Company, of Indianapolis, Ind., are her publishers.

RIVES, WILLIAM CABELL. See Biographical and Critical Sketch, Vol. X. page 4477.

RIORDAN, JULIA THERESA, educator, was born in Atlanta. Ga., and is now teaching in the public schools, of which she is herself a finished product. No volume has yet appeared from her graceful pen; but she is the author of numerous poems and sketches of exceptional merit, some of which date from her schooldays. One of her best compositions in verse is entitled "Spring," an undergraduate production which was an easy prize-winner.

ROACH, ABBY MEGUIRE. See Biographical and Critical Sketch, Vol. X, page 4497.

ROANE, SPENCER, jurist, was born in Essex County, Va., April 4, 1762, and died in Sharon Springs, Va., September 4, 1802. He achieved distinction on the Bench; and, under the name of "Algernon Sidney," wrote numerous essays, asserting state supremacy, which were published in the Richmond *Enquirer* and widely read. He married a daughter of Patrick Henry.

ROARK, RURIC NEVELL. Educator. He was born in Greenville, Ky., May 19, 1859, the son of M. J. and Nancy Roark. He married, in 1883, Mary Creegan, and became dean of the Department of Pedagogy in the State College of Kentucky, in 1899, and president of East Kentucky State Normal School in 1907. His works, which possess much interest and value to educators, embrace: 'Psychology in Education,' (New York, D. Appleton and Company, 1895), 'Method in Education,' (*ibid.,* 1899), 'Economy in Education' (*ibid.,* 1905), and 'General Outline of Pedagogy' (1900). He was also one of the consulting editors of 'The Library of Southern Literature.' Dr. Roark died in Richmond, Ky., April 14, 1909.

ROBBINS, MARY LA FAYETTE. She wrote a volume which was published at Selma, Ala., in 1895, entitled 'Alabama Women in Literature.'

ROBERT, HENRY MARTYN, soldier, was born in Beaufort District, S.C., May 2, 1837, received his education at West Point, entered the United States Army, remained loyal to the Government, though most of his relatives were in the South, served on the staff of General McClellan, and, for many years was head of the engineering department at West Point. Later he was put in charge of river and harbor improvements at Portland, Ohio. He attained the rank of lieutenant-colonel and published 'Robert's Rules of Order' (Chicago, 1876), and 'An Index to the Reports of the Chief Engineers of the United States Army on River and Harbor Improvements' (Washington, 1881).

ROBERTS, ORAN MILO, jurist and statesman, was born in Laurens District, S.C., July 9, 1815. At first he located for the practice of law in Alabama, but afterward removed to Texas. He was several times made chief justice of the Supreme Court of the State, and from 1879 to 1883 occupied the office of governor. Later he became professor of law in the University of Texas. In 1861 he presided over the Secession Convention and in 1866 was elected to the United States Senate, but was not seated. He published an interesting descriptive volume entitled 'Governor Roberts's Texas' (St. Louis, 1881), and also wrote the volume on "Texas" for 'The Confederate Military History' (Atlanta, Ga., The Confederate Publishing Company, 1899), and the "Political, Legislative and Judicial History of Texas" (1845-1895), for 'Wooten's Comprehensive History of Texas' (Dallas, Wm. G. Scarff, 1898).

ROBERTS, WILLIAM. An Englishman who spent some time in the Southern Colonies and who wrote 'An Account of the First Discovery and Natural History of Florida.' It was published in London in 1763 and illustrated by T. Jeffreys, Geographer to His Majesty, King George III.

ROBERTSON, ARCHIBALD THOMAS. Theologian. He was born near Chatham, Va., November 6, 1863, a son of John and Ella Martin Robertson, was educated at Wake Forest College and at the Southern Baptist Theological Seminary, and married, November 27, 1894, Ella Thomas Broadus. He became professor of New Testament Interpretation in the Southern Baptist Theological Seminary in 1895. His works, which are mainly theological, include: 'Life and Letters of John A. Broadus,' (Philadelphia, American Baptist Publication Society, 1900), 'Syllabus for New Testament Study,' 'Bibliography of New Testament Greek,' 'Teaching of Jesus Concerning God the Father,' 'The Students' Chronological New Testament,' 'Keywords in the Teaching of Jesus' and 'Short Historical Grammar of New Testament Greek.' He resides in Louisville, Ky.

ROBERTSON, CHARLES FRANKLIN, Protestant Episcopal bishop, was born in New York City, March 2, 1835, and died in St. Louis, Mo., May 1, 1886. Entering the Episcopal ministry, he became the second bishop of Missouri, to which office he was elected in 1868. He received the degree of D.D. from the University of the South, the degree of LL.D. from the University of Missouri, and the degree of S.T.D. from Columbia. He published a series of important papers on "Historical Societies in Relation to Local Historical Effort" (St. Louis, 1883), "The American Revolution and the Mississippi Valley" (1884), "The Attempt to Separate the West from the American Union" (1885), and "The Purchase of the Louisiana Territory in Its Influence on the American System" (1885).

ROBERTSON, GEORGE, jurist, was born in Mercer County, Ky., November 18, 1790, and died in Lexington, Ky., May 16, 1874. Twice elected to Congress, he resigned before completing his second term, to resume the practice of law. After declining numerous political offers, he finally became judge of the Court of Appeals, and eventually chief justice. He published an 'Introductory Lecture to the Law Class' (Lexington, 1836), 'Biographical Sketch of John Boyle' (Frankfort, 1838), and a 'Scrap-book on Law, Politics, Men and Times' (1856). After his death a collection of his speeches and lectures also appeared. Judge Robertson was perhaps Kentucky's greatest jurist. He held from Centre and Augusta Colleges the degree of LL.D.

ROBERTSON, HARRISON. See Biographical and Critical Sketch, Vol. X, page 4517.

ROBERTSON, JOHN, lawyer and poet, was born near Richmond, Va., in 1787, and was educated at William and Mary College. Entering the legal profession, he achieved distinction at the Bar and in public life, becoming attorney-general of the State. It was only during the intervals of relaxation incident to the busiest life that he found opportunity for the exercise of his literary gifts; but he published three books of more than ordinary merit: 'Virginia; or, the Fatal Patent,' a metrical romance in three cantos, dealing with the separation of Virginia from the British Crown (Washington, 1825), 'Riego; or, the Spanish Martyr,' a tragedy in five acts (Richmond, 1850), and a work called 'Opuscula, Seria et Jocosa,' the product of idle moments during the eventide of an extended career. He died in Campbell County, Va., in 1873, at the age of eighty-six. Even the most casual glance at his literary productions shows that he was a man of unusual accomplishments.

ROBERTSON, SAMUEL LOWRIE, educator and poet, was born in Jackson County, Ala., November 18, 1838, and died in Birmingham, Ala., September 2, 1909. After spending two years at the University of Virginia, he took a course in law at the Richmond Hill Law School in North Carolina, and located for the practice of his profession at Charlotte, but on account of impaired health he relinquished Blackstone and returned to his former home in Alabama, where he remained until the outbreak of hostilities. During the Civil War he served in the cavalry ranks under Wheeler and Forrest. When the struggle ended he chose educational work and was for years county school superintendent of Jefferson County; organized the Teachers' Institute; and gave his energies without reserve to the uplift of the masses. At leisure intervals he exercised what was conceded to be an unusual genius for versification. One of his best-known poems is entitled "A School Room of Fifty Years Ago," which vividly portrays in verse a typical picture of the ante-bellum days. Besides several booklets he published 'Dora: or, On the Border and Other Poems' (1894) and 'Gulf Songs' (1908). Some of his best efforts were inspired by his war-time experiences and were dedicated to his old comrades-in-arms.

ROBERTSON, THOMAS BOLLING, governor of Louisiana, was born near Petersburg, Va., in 1773, and died at White Sulphur Springs, Va., November 5, 1828. For the practice of law he settled in New Orleans, La., and, attaining high rank at the Bar, he was sent to Congress, became governor of the State, attorney-general, and Judge of the United States District Court of Louisiana. He visited Paris during the last days of the Empire, and wrote a series of letters, which were afterward published in book form, entitled 'Events in Paris' (Philadelphia, 1816). He was a brother of John Robertson and of Wyndham Robertson.

ROBERTSON, WYNDHAM, governor of Virginia, was born in Chesterfield County, Va., January 26, 1803, and died in Washington County, Va., February 11, 1888. After graduation from William and Mary College he engaged in the practice of law in Richmond. On the resignation of Littleton W. Tazewell he succeeded to the governorship, having previously been chosen lieutenant-governor on the same ticket. He opposed secession, but drafted a resolution while in the Legislature declaring Virginia's intention to fight with the Southern States if attacked. Virginia, however, preferred to join her Confederate sisters. Governor Robertson wrote an interesting work entitled 'Pocahontas and Her Descendants through Her Marriage with John Rolfe' (Richmond, 1887). He also left in manuscript a vindication of Virginia's course in regard to slavery. He was a brother of John Robertson and of Thomas Bolling Robertson.

ROBINS, ELIZABETH. See Biographical and Critical Sketch, Vol. X, page 4541.

ROBINS, JOHN B. Methodist Episcopal clergyman. [Ga.]. He published 'Christ and our Country' (Nashville. M.E. Publishing House, South, 1892), and 'The Family' (Atlanta, 1896).

ROBINSON, CONWAY, lawyer, was born in Richmond, Va., September 15, 1805, and died in Philadelphia, Pa., January 30, 1884. He achieved high professional distinction, established his residence near Washington, D.C., where he practiced chiefly before the Supreme Court, and published several very important law books, including 'The Principles and Practice of Courts of Justice in England and the United States,' in two volumes (Richmond, 1855), and 'The History of the High Court of Chancery and Other Institutions of England, from the Time of Caius Julius Cæsar to the Accession of William and Mary,' which was to have been in two volumes, but he published only the first (Richmond, 1882) leaving the second in unfinished manuscript. He also took deep interest in archæological investigations and published an 'Account of the Discoveries of the West until 1519, and of Voyages to and along the Atlantic Coast of North America from 1520 to 1573' (1848). He contemplated a work on 'The Annals of Virginia,' but was diverted from this undertaking by other engagements. His legal writings are of standard value on both sides of the water.

ROBINSON, FAYETTE, author, was born in Virginia, the exact date unknown, and died in New York City, March 26, 1859. He published 'Mexico and Her Military Chieftains' (Philadelphia, 1847), 'Account of the Organization of the Army of the United States, with Biographies of Distinguished Officers' (1848), 'California and the Gold Regions' (New York, 1849), 'Grammar of the Spanish Language' (Philadelphia, 1850), 'Wizard of the Wave,' and several translations from the French.

ROBINSON, MARTHA HARRISON, Mrs. Author. [Va.]. She published a novel entitled 'Helen Erskine,' and several translations from the French.

ROBINSON, MERRITT M., lawyer, was born in Louisiana about 1810, studied law, became Supreme Court reporter, and published a 'Digest of the Penal Laws of Louisiana, Analytically Arranged' (New Orleans, 1841), and sixteen volumes of 'Louisiana Reports,' four of which were edited with marginal notes.

ROBINSON, NINA HILL, Mrs. Author. [Tenn.]. She wrote an interesting story of ante-bellum days entitled 'Aunt Dice: the Story of a Faithful Slave' (1897).

ROBINSON, SOLON, journalist and author, was born near Tolland, Conn., October 21, 1803, and died on his plantation near Jacksonville, Fla., November 3, 1880. For many years he was engaged in newspaper work in New York City; and a novel which he wrote dealing with life in the slums, entitled 'Hot Corn' (1853), sold to the number of fifty thousand copies. He also published 'Facts for Farmers' (1864), 'How to Live; or, Domestic Economy Illustrated' (1860), and 'Mewonitoc' (1867).

ROBINSON, STUART, clergyman, was born in Strabane, Ireland, November 14, 1814, and died in Louisville, Ky., October 5, 1881. He became an eminent minister of the Presbyterian Church, edited papers, filled important pastorates, and waged sharp controversies on religious questions. Dr. Robinson possessed in an eminent degree the elements of aggressive leadership. He was eloquent of speech and ready of pen; a power in the editorial sanctum, in the pulpit and in the ecclesiastical councils. He maintained the doctrine of the church's non-secular character and was expelled from the Northern Assembly in 1866 for protesting against the political deliverances of this high court of the church; but, after an earnest controversy with Dr. Robert J. Breckinridge, induced the Synod of Kentucky to unite with the Southern Assembly in 1869. He published: 'Slavery as Recognized by the Abrahamic, Mosaic, and Christian Church' (Toronto, 1865), 'The Church of God as an Essential Element of the Gospel' (Philadelphia, 1858), 'Discourses of Redemption,' a book of outlines (New York, 1866) and a volume of lectures on the Old Testament.

ROBINSON, WILLIE BLANCHE. Poet. [Texas]. Born in 1857. She published a number of patriotic poems, including one entitled "Texas to Jefferson Davis."

ROCHELLE, JAMES HENRY. Naval officer. Captain Rochelle wrote a 'Life of Rear-admiral Randolph Tucker' (New York and Washington, The Neale Publishing Company, 1906), in which he tells of the famous expedition to the River Amazon, on which he accompanied his commander, besides narrating his exploits under the Confederate flag.

ROCKWELL, ELISHA F. Author. [N.C.]. He was born in 1809 and died in 1888. He published 'Rowan County in 1774,' biographical sketches of John Thompson and James Hall, and several historical papers.

ROCKWELL, JAMES CHESTER. Poet. [N.C.]. He wrote a metrical composition entitled 'Chrystella: The Echo of a Dream' (1887, paper edition). The author, who died at a very early age, produced this work when only seventeen. He also published a number of uncollected poems.

RODGERS, J. P. Methodist Episcopal clergyman. [N.C.]. He wrote a 'Life of the Rev. James Needham' (1899), in which he gives an interesting account of a ministry of seventy years.

ROGERS, EDWARD REINHOLD. [Va.]. He published a dissertation on 'Four Southern Magazines,' which secured for him the Ph.D. degree from the University of Virginia (Richmond, The Williams Printing Company, 1902).

ROGERS, HENRY J., inventor, was born in Baltimore, Md., in 1811. The code of signals by means of flags and also the pyrotechnic system, were both his inventions, and he was also one of the practical advisers of Samuel F. B. Morse in the construction of the first electromagnetic telegraph. He published the 'Telegraph Dictionary and Seaman's Book' (Baltimore, 1845), 'American Semaphoric Signal Book' (1847), and 'American Code of Marine Signals' (1854), besides editing Rogers's 'Commercial Code of Signals for All Nations,' with Walter F. Larkin (1859).

ROGERS, JAMES WEBB, clergyman and lawyer, was born at Hillsborough, N.C., July 11, 1822, received his education at Princeton, took orders in the Episcopal Church, and became rector of St. Paul's Parish, at Franklin, Tenn. During the Civil War he fought on the Confederate side, under General Leonidas Polk. Later he became a Catholic, but was denied admission to the priesthood because of his married state; and he afterward engaged in the practice of law in Washington, D.C. His publications include several plays, among them, 'LaFitte; or, the Greek Slave' (Boston, 1870), and 'Madame Surratt: a Drama in Five Acts' (Washington, 1879). He also wrote 'Arlington, and Other Poems' and 'Parthenon' (Baltimore, 1887).

ROGERS, JOSEPH M. Author. [Ky.]. He wrote 'The True Henry Clay' (1904), an interesting study of the great Kentuckian.

ROGERS, LOULA KENDALL, Mrs. Poet and educator of Georgia. She wrote 'Toccoa, the Beautiful,' 'Twenty Years an Alien,' 'Songs,' and 'Poems.'

ROGERS, WILLIAM BARTON, educator, was born in Philadelphia, Pa., December 7, 1804, but was educated at William and Mary College, in Virginia, where his father was professor of physics. To this same chair he afterward succeeded, and still later he became professor of geology in the University of Virginia. Three brothers also attained eminence in the scientific world, James Blythe, Henry Darwin and Robert E. Besides a volume entitled 'Papers on the Geology of Virginia' (1840), he wrote 'Strength of Materials' (1838), and 'Elements of Mechanical Philosophy' (1852). He died in Boston, Mass., May 30, 1882.

ROLAND, ALICE KATE, Mrs. Author. [Ala.]. She wrote an entertaining romance entitled 'Rosalind Morton' (1898).

ROMAN, ALFRED. Jurist. He was born in St. James Parish, La., in 1824, and was the second son of Governor André Bienvenu Roman. His education was received at Jefferson College, and at the age of twenty-one he was admitted to the Bar. His success was rapid; but, the war coming on, he enlisted in the Confederate ranks and fought with distinction. Subsequent to the war he resumed law practice, and in 1880 was appointed Judge of the Criminal Court of New Orleans, receiving his commission from Governor Wiltz. This office he held for eight years. He wrote 'The Military Operations of General Beauregard' (New York, Harper and Brothers, 1883), and concerning this work Charles Gayarre said that it will be impossible to write the history of the Civil War fully without taking this important contribution into account. He died in New Orleans, September 20, 1892.

ROMANS, BERNARD, engineer and botanist, was born in Holland in 1720, received his education in England, and came to this country as a surveyor and botanist in the service of the English Government. But he became imbued with the spirit of the Revolution and gave his allegiance to the patriotic cause. Toward the end of the struggle he was made a prisoner and taken to England, where offers to exchange were refused. On his return voyage to America, in 1784, he is supposed to have been murdered. He published 'A Concise Natural History of East and West Florida,' with maps (New York, 1775), only a few copies of which are extant; 'Annals of the Troubles in the Netherlands,' in two volumes (Hartford, 1778), and 'Compleat Pilot of the Gulf Passage' (1779).

ROQUIGNY, J. DE. Author. [La.]. He published in French a work entitled 'Précis d'Histoire Ancienne.' (New Orleans, 1858).

ROSE, GEORGE B. See Biographical and Critical Sketch, Vol. X, page 4567.

ROSE, U. M. Lawyer. One of the consulting editors of 'The Library of Southern Literature.' He was born in Marion County, Ky., March 5, 1834, the son of Joseph and Nancy Rose. He married, in 1853, Margaret T. Gibbs, and settled in Little Rock, Ark., for the practice of law. While he has persistently refused to seek political preferment, and has declined numerous offices of honor and emolument, he has served on the National Democratic Committee and has presided over the deliberations of the American Bar Association. He was also a member of the Peace Conference at The Hague in 1907, with the rank of ambassador. Besides frequent contributions to law journals on American and European jurisprudence, he is the author of 'Rose's Digest of Arkansas Reports.' He resides in Little Rock, Ark.

ROSE, VICTOR M. Author. [Texas]. He wrote "Demara, the Commanche Queen,' a 'History of Victoria County,' 'The Texas Vendetta,' a 'Life of General McCulloch,' a 'Legend of Dixie,' and numerous short sketches and stories. He died in 1893.

ROSE, WILLIAM. Author of 'The Tin Owl Stories,' which appeared in 1901 (Boston, Dana Estes and Company). He resides in Independence, Mo.

ROSEBORO, VIOLA, author, was born in Pulaski, Tenn., and was educated at Fairmont College in her native state. For some time past she has resided in New York City, and besides numerous contributions to magazines, she has published two volumes of short stories entitled 'Players and Vagabonds,' 'Old Ways and New' (New York, The Century Company, 1892), and other works.

ROSELIUS, CHRISTIAN. An eminent lawyer. He was born in Germany, August 10, 1803. In order to defray the expense of his voyage to the United States, he pledged his services for a year after his arrival in port. He became attorney-general of the State of Louisiana, and is said to have declined an invitation from Daniel Webster to form a partnership with the great New England orator in Washington, D.C., for the practice of law. He was for twenty-three years professor of civil law in the University of Louisiana, and for many years was dean of the institution. His lectures on the Civil Code of Louisiana and his opinions as Attorney-general are declared to be models. He delivered an essay on "Collegiate Education" in 1865, which was afterward published in pamphlet form. His death occurred in New Orleans, September 5, 1873.

ROSENFELD, SYDNEY, dramatist, was born in Richmond, Va., October 26, 1855, and after attending for some time the public schools of his native city, he completed his education in New York. As a writer of plays he has achieved signal success. His works include: 'The Senator,' 'A Possible Case,' 'Imagination,' 'The Club Friend,' 'The Politician,' 'A Man of Ideas,' 'A House of Cards,' 'The Passing Show,' and several others, besides numerous adaptations and light-opera librettos. He resides in New York.

ROSENTHAL, LEWIS, author, was born in Baltimore, Md., September 10, 1856. On completing his education at Dartmouth, he went to Paris, where he became a journalist and a tutor. He contributed to current literature and published 'America and France; or, the Influence of the United States upon France in the Eighteenth Century' (New York, 1882).

ROSS, FREDERICK AUGUSTUS, clergyman, was born in Cobham, Va., December 25, 1796, and died in Huntsville, Ala., April 13, 1883. Entering the ministry, he became an eloquent divine of the Presbyterian faith, held numerous pulpits in the South, edited with James Gallaher and David Nelson, the *Calvinistic Magazine,* and published 'Slavery as Ordained of God' (Philadelphia, 1867).

ROSS, JAMES. Author. [Tenn.]. He was born in 1801 and died in 1878. He wrote a biography of his father entitled 'The Life and Times of the Rev. Reuben Ross' (1882).

ROSSER, LEONIDAS, clergyman, was born in Petersburg, Va., July 31, 1815. For many years he edited the *Christian Advocate* at Richmond. He filled the leading Methodist pulpits in the Virginia conference and, during the Civil War, held the important post of general missionary within the Confederate ranks. Emory and Henry College gave him the degree of D.D. He published an important work on 'Baptism' (Richmond, 1843), 'Experimental Religion,' 'Class Meetings,' 'Recognition in Heaven,' 'Open Communion', and numerous tracts and pamphlets.

ROTHWELL, WILLIAM R. Baptist clergyman and educator. He published 'Reading the Scriptures' (1889), and 'New Testament Church Order' (1890), besides several addresses.

ROUQUETTE, ADRIEN. See Biographical and Critical Sketch, Vol. X, page 4589.

ROUQUETTE, DOMINIQUE. See Biographical and Critical Sketch, Vol. X, page 4589.

ROWE, HORACE. Poet. [Texas]. He was born in 1852 and died in 1884. He wrote 'The Years of Youth, and Other Poems.'

ROWELL, A. S. ("Old Coins"). Author. [S.C.]. He wrote an interesting story of adventure for boys entitled 'The Silver Bullet; or, the Young Relic Hunters in South Carolina' (1897), besides minor works.

ROWLAND, DUNBAR, lawyer and historian, was born in Oakland, Miss., August 25, 1864. His father was Dr. William B. Rowland and his mother, Mary Bryan. He is in direct line of descent from the Rowlands and the Hairstons, who settled in Virginia in the Sixteenth Century, and one of the first of this pioneer stock to be born outside of the Old Dominion. After graduating with distinction from the University of Mississippi, he practiced law until 1902, when the Department of Archives and History was created by the State Legislature and he was elected to the chair of director. He has published 'Reports of the Mississippi Department of Archives and History,' seven volumes, 'Encyclopædia of Mississippi,' two volumes, "Mississippi from 1817 to 1861," for 'The South in the Building of the Nation,' the sketch of Sargent Smith Prentiss in 'The Library of Southern Literature,' a volume of speeches, and two volumes of the 'Official and Statistical Register,' including a "Military History of Mississippi." Dr. Rowland is one of the leaders of the crusade for historical research in foreign archives and originated the movement for the publication by the National Government of an official roster of officers and enlisted men of the Union and Confederate armies. He married Eron Opha, daughter of Major B. B. Moore. In recognition of his services to the State, the University of Mississippi, in 1906, conferred upon him the degree of LL.D.

ROWLAND, ERON OPHA, poet, was born at Okolona, Miss. Her father was Major B. B. Moore, a descendant of the Byrds of Westover. She was well educated, and in 1906 became the wife of Dr. Dunbar Rowland. Under the signature of Eron Opha Gregory, she began at an early age to write for the press. Besides numerous short stories, she wrote several hundred poems, a number of which were clipped by Editor Medill, of the Chicago *Tribune,* who paid signal tribute to the young author. One of the sweetest of her fragments of song is entitled "Some Day." Since her marriage, Mrs. Rowland has identified herself with her husband's historical work.

ROWLAND, KATE MASON, author, is a resident of Baltimore and the daughter of Major Isaac S. and Catherine Mason Rowland. For years she has been active in seeking to preserve the materials of history and has made many important contributions to the magazines, bearing upon her studious researches. Besides editing 'The Poems of Dr. Frank O. Ticknor' and 'The Real Lincoln,' by Dr. C. L. C. Minor, she has written 'The Life of George Mason,' in two volumes (New York, George Putnam's Sons), a work which includes his speeches and public papers, and 'The Life of Charles Carroll of Carrollton,' in two volumes (*ibid.*), a work of similar character.

ROYALL, ANNE, author, was born in Virginia, June 11, 1769, and died in Washington, D.C., October 1, 1854. Early in life she was stolen by the Indians, and for sixteen years she lived among the natives of the forest. She learned to read and write after her marriage to Captain Royall, a resident of Alabama. Later she removed to Washington, D.C., where she procured an old printing outfit and began to publish a sheet called *The Huntress.* Her eccentricities were numerous, and she became the terror of the Congressmen by reason not only of her vitriolic pen but of her grotesque appearance. Finally she was indicted by the Grand Jury as a scold, was tried before Judge William Cranch of the Circuit Court, and sentenced to be ducked in the Potomac River, according to the English law that was still operative in the District of Columbia; but a fine was substituted. Her books possess an odd flavor of interest and include: 'Sketches of History: or, Life and Manners in the United States by a Traveler' (New Haven, 1826), 'The Black Book; or, a Continuation of Travels in the United States' (Washington, 1828), 'A Southern Tour; or, a Second Series of the Black Book,' and 'Letters from Alabama.'

ROYALL, WILLIAM L. Lawyer and editor. [Va.]. He published an important financial work entitled 'Virginia Banks and Banking Prior to the Civil War' (New York and Washington, 1907). During the 'eighties he was sole counsel for the creditors of the State of Virginia in the prolonged contest of the famous readjuster period of State politics.

ROZIER, FIRMIN A. Author. [La.]. He published a 'History of the Early Settlement of the Mississippi Valley' (1890).

RUFFIN, EDMUND, editor and planter, was born in Prince George County, Va., January 5, 1794, and died in Amelia County, Va., June 15, 1865. By discovering the value of marl as a fertilizer he is said to have added millions of dollars to the value of land in Eastern Virginia. He edited *The Farmer's Register* for several years and made numerous experiments in agriculture. At the opening of hostilities in 1861, he went to South Carolina, where, by order of General Beauregard, his company was directed to open fire upon Fort Sumter, and being the oldest member enrolled he was permitted to fire the first gun. Within a week after the surrender at Appomattox he shot himself because he was unwilling to live under the United States Government; and the day following he died on his estate at Redmoor. Besides numerous essays on agricultural topics, he edited 'The Westover Manuscripts,' by Colonel William Byrd, of Westover (Petersburg, 1849; revised, in two volumes, 1860).

RUFFIN, MARGARET ELLEN HENRY. Author. She was born in Daphne, Ala., a daughter of Thomas and Mary Nugent Henry. and was the valedictorian of her class at St. Joseph's Academy, Emmitsburg, Md. She married in 1887, Frank G. Ruffin, of Mobile, Ala., now deceased. She is a student of languages, making a specialty of Celtic antiquities; and is also proficient in literature and music. Her verse has been very widely admired. She has written 'John Gidart' (out of print) and 'The North Star' (Boston, Little, Brown and Company), in addition to a volume of poems which appeared in 1884. Her story, 'The North Star,' drew a letter of commendation from the King and Queen of Norway. She lives in Mobile, Ala.

RUFFNER, HENRY, clergyman and educator, was born in Page County, Va., January 19, 1789, and was the son of David Ruffner, the pioneer salt manufacturer. On leaving Washington College, he entered the ministry of the Presbyterian Church; and Charleston, S.C., became for some time the field of his labors. Later he became president of Washington College. His writings include: 'The Fathers of the Desert,' in two volumes (New York, 1850), 'The Predestinarian,' 'Methodism,' 'Judith Ben-Paddi,' 'Future Punishment,' and his famous argument against slavery, which was popularly termed the "Ruffner pamphlet." He died in Malden, Va., December 17, 1861. He received the degree of LL.D. from Washington College, and the degree of D.D. from Princeton.

RUFFNER, WILLIAM HENRY. Educator and geologist. He was born in Lexington, Va., February 11, 1824, married Harriet A. Gray and later founded the State Female Normal School. Besides numerous scientific and educational reports, he is the author of an interesting 'History of Washington and Lee University.' The school law of Virginia is also the product of his pen. Washington and Lee University gave him the degree of LL.D. He resides in Lexington, Va.

RULE, LUCIEN V. Poet. [Ky.]. He wrote 'The Shrine of Love, and Other Poems' and 'When John Bull Comes A-Courtin',' a collection of political and social satires.

RUMPLE, JETHRO, clergyman, was born in Cabarrus County, N.C., March 10, 1827, studied during intervals of leisure on the farm until he was eighteen, defrayed his own expenses through college, and became an eloquent and able Presbyterian minister, laboring for more than thirty years in Salisbury, N.C. His publications include: 'The History of Rowan County, N.C.' (Salisbury, 1881), 'The History of the First Fifty Years of Davidson College' (Raleigh, 1888), and 'The History of Presbyterianism in North Carolina.' The State University gave him the degree of D.D.

RUNCIE, CONSTANCE FAUNTLEROY. Musical composer and writer. She was born in Indianapolis, Ind., January 15, 1836, a daughter of Robert Henry and Jane Dale Fauntleroy, and married, April 9, 1861, James Runcie, D.D., an Episcopal clergyman. After living for some time at Madison, Ind., she removed to St. Joseph, Mo. She organized at New Harmony, Ind., the Minerva Club, said to be the first woman's club organized in America. Her lectures on subjects of culture among women have made her widely known. She is the author of numerous productions in both prose and verse, and included among the number are: 'The Burning Question,' 'Divinely Led' (New

York, James Potts and Company), 'Poems, Dramatic and Lyric' (New York, G. P. Putnam's Sons), 'Woman's Work,' 'Felix Mendelssohn,' 'Children's Stories,' 'Fables,' and an "Essay on Woman." Two of her dramatic poems—"Anselmo, the Priest" and "Zaira, a Tale of Siberia"— are still favorites with elocutionists. Among her musical compositions is an opera, "The Prince of the Asturias," besides numerous songs, cantatas, and solos for both piano and violin. She resides at St. Joseph, Mo.

RUNNEGER, JAMES. Poet. [La.]. He published a volume of verse entitled 'Stray Leaves' (1875).

RUSSELL, IRWIN. See Biographical and Critical Sketch, Vol. X, page 4601.

RUTHERFORD, MILDRED LEWIS, educator and author, was born in Athens, Ga., July 16, 1852, a daughter of Williams Rutherford, for many years professor of mathematics in the University of Georgia, and a niece of Generals Howell and Thomas R. R. Cobb, two of Georgia's most illustrious sons. Her mother was Laura Cobb. From 1880 to 1895, Miss Rutherford was principal of the Lucy Cobb Institute at Athens; and from 1895 to 1907 she shared the responsibilities of the work with her sister, Mrs. M. A. Lipscomb, and spent alternate years in European travel. Her writings include: 'English Authors' (Atlanta, The Franklin-Turner Company, 1899), 'American Authors' (*ibid.*, 1894), 'French Authors' (*ibid.*), 'Biblical Questions on Old Testament History' (*ibid.*), 'The South in History and Literature' (*ibid.*, 1907), and 'Mannie Brown' (Buffalo, N.Y., Peter Paul Book Company, 1896). Miss Rutherford's patient and laborious researches have placed the South under grateful tribute to her pen. She resides at Athens, Ga.

RUTHERFORD, WILLIAMS. Educator. For many years he was professor of mathematics at the University of Georgia. He married Laura, a daughter of John A. Cobb of Athens, Ga., and a sister of General Howell Cobb. Professor Rutherford wrote a 'Church Members' Guide,' and 'The Family Related to Civilization.' He died in 1896 at an advanced age.

RUTLEDGE, ARCHIBALD, educator and poet, was born in McClellanville, S.C., October 23, 1883. Professor Rutledge is a teacher of English at Mercersburg, Pa., and a man of rare literary gifts. At leisure intervals he has written most charmingly in both prose and verse, and his published works include: 'Under the Pines,' a volume of poems (Winchester, Va., The Eddy Press, 1906), and 'The Banners of the Coast' (Columbia, S.C., The State Company, 1908), besides poems and short stories in *The Youth's Companion,* and other periodicals.

RUTLEDGE, EDWARD, signer of the Declaration of Independence, was born in Charleston, S.C., November 23, 1749, and died in Charleston, S.C., January 23, 1800. While pursuing his legal studies in England, he attended the law courts and the sessions of Parliament. Soon after his return to South Carolina, he was sent to the Continental Congress, took an active part in the deliberations, and became one of the signers of the Declaration of Independence. For some time during the Revolution he commanded the Charleston artillery; and, when the South Carolina metropolis fell, in 1780, he was imprisoned at St. Augustine. At the close of hostilities he resumed the practice of law, resisted with great eloquence any effort to revive the slave trade, framed the section of the State Constitution which abolishes the rights of primogeniture, declined an appointment to the Supreme Bench of the United States, and died in the executive chair of the commonwealth.

RUTLEDGE, EDWARD, clergyman, was born in Charleston, S.C., in 1797, and died in Savannah, Ga., March 13, 1832. On completing his studies at Yale, he was admitted to orders in the Episcopal Church, after which he became a professor in the University of Pennsylvania. At the time of his death he was president-elect of Transylvania University, in Kentucky. He published 'The Family Altar' (New Haven, 1822) and a 'History of the Church of England' (Middletown, 1825).

RUTLEDGE, FRANCIS HUGER, Protestant Episcopal bishop, was born in Charleston, S.C., April 11, 1799, and died in Tallahassee, Fla., November 6, 1866. He was equipped for the ministry of the Episcopal Church, pursuing his collegiate studies at Yale and his theological studies in New York. He ministered to large and important parishes, first in St. Augustine and afterward in Tallahassee, and in 1851 was consecrated bishop. The degree of D.D. was conferred upon him by Hobart College. He possessed unusual gifts of expression, but published only occasional sermons.

RUTLEDGE, JOHN, statesman and jurist, was born in Charleston, S.C., of Scotch-Irish parentage, in 1739, and died in Charleston, S.C., July 23, 1800. He was educated for the Bar in England. On his return home he acquired eminence as an advocate, opposed the Stamp Act and other oppressive measures of the British Parliament, and represented South Carolina in the first Continental Congress. Patrick Henry said of him that he was "the Assembly's greatest orator." He was made chairman of the committee to frame the constitution of South Carolina, and later president of the new state government, and commander-in-chief of the military forces. On retiring from this dual office of great responsibility at the close of the Revolution, he was returned to the national councils in Philadelphia. He declined an appointment to the Federal Bench to become chief justice of the Supreme Court of South Carolina. On July 1, 1795, he was appointed Chief Justice of the United States, and accepted, but mental infirmities made it necessary for the Senate to recall the commission. He was one of South Carolina's most illustrious sons.

RYAN, ABRAM J. (Father Ryan). See Biographical and Critical Sketch, Vol. X, page 4623.

RYLAND, CALLY. Author. She was born in Richmond, Va., a daughter of Josiah and Caroline Thomas Ryland, was educated at private schools and by tutors, and became the editor of the woman's page of the Richmond *News-Leader* in 1902. She has made some charming contributions, in both prose and verse, to the periodicals, and is the author of three very interesting volumes: 'Daphne and Her Lad' (New York, Henry Holt), written in association with M. J. Lagen, 'The Taming of Betty,' and 'Aunt Jemimy Maxim.' She resides in Richmond, Va.

SAFFORD, JAMES MERRILL. Educator. [Tenn.]. For nearly twenty-five years he was professor of natural sciences in Cumberland University, and afterward professor of chemistry in the medical department of the University of Nashville. Besides numerous minor works he published a 'Geology of Tennessee,' with a map (1869), which, with the assistance of J. B. Killebrew, was later simplified for use in the schools of the State (1899).

SAFFORD, WILLIAM HARRISON, lawyer, was born in Parkersburg, Va., in what is now West Virginia, February 19, 1821. He removed to Chillicothe, Ohio, for the practice of law and became a judge of the Circuit Court. He published 'The Life of Blennerhassett' (Chillicothe, 1850), and 'The Blennerhassett Papers' (Cincinnati, 1861).

SAGE, BERNARD JANIN. An eminent Louisiana lawyer who, in 1865, was one of the counsel selected to defend Jefferson Davis against the charge of treason. He published a work entitled 'The Republic of Republics,' in which he treats at some length of secession and coercion.

SALE, EDITH TUNIS. Author. From the pen of this writer of the old Dominion has lately come a volume entitled 'Manors of Virginia in Colonial Times' (Philadelphia, J. B. Lippincott Company).

SALE, L. M., Mrs. Author. [S.C.]. She wrote several novels, among them: 'The Saddest of All Is Loving,' 'Mabel,' and 'Beauty for Ashes,' besides a number of poems. Her maiden name was Miss Montgomery. She lived for some time in Newberry, S.C.

SALLEY, ALEXANDER SAMUEL, Jr., editor, author, compiler, was born in Orangeburg, S.C., June 16, 1871. His father was Dr. Alexander Samuel Salley, Sr., and his mother, Sally Ann McMichael. After completing his studies at the South Carolina Military Academy, he was for some time connected with the Charleston *News and Courier.* From 1889 to 1905 he was secretary and treasurer of the South Carolina Historical Society, and during his occupancy of this office he was admitted to the Bar. Mr. Salley has rendered priceless service to the historical literature of his native state by his numerous writings and compilations. They include: a 'History of Orangeburg County from the First Settlement to the Close of the Revolutionary War' (Orangeburg, 1898), 'Marriage Notices in the *South Carolina Gazette* and Its Successors, 1732-1801' (Albany, N.Y., Joel Munsey's Sons, 1902), 'Marriage Notices in the *South Carolina Gazette* and *Country Journal,* 1765-1775, and in the Charleston *Gazette,* 1778-1880' (Charleston, S.C., Walker, Evans and Cogswell Company, 1904), a 'Register of St. Philip's Parish, 1720-1758' (*ibid.,* 1904), 'The Seal of South Carolina' (Columbia, S.C., The State Company, 1905), numerous legislative journals covering early colonial and Revolutionary periods (Columbia, S.C., The Historical Commission of South Carolina, 1906-1908), a 'Tentative Roster of the Third Regiment of South Carolina Volunteers in the Confederate States' Provisional Army' (*ibid.,* 1908), and 'Documents Relating to the History of South Carolina During the Revolutionary War' (*ibid.,* 1908), besides various important individual and family histories and scores of articles contributed to periodicals. He also edited *The South Carolina Historical and Genealogical Magazine,* Vols. I to IX. He resides in Columbia, S.C.

SALYARDS, JOSEPH. See Biographical and Critical Sketch, Vol. X, page 4645.

SAMPEY, JOHN RICHARD, clergyman and educator, was born in Fort Deposit, Ala., September 27, 1863; and, on completing his educational equipment, he entered the ministry of the Baptist Church. For several years past he has been professor of Old Testament interpretation in the seminary at Louisville. He married Annis Renfroe. Since 1895 he has been a member of the International Sunday-school Lesson Committee. Besides contributing to the revision of the Old Testament Scriptures, he has published 'Thirty Years of the Southern Baptist Theological Seminary,' 'Syllabus for Old Testament Study,' and 'Lecture Notes on the Old Testament.' He received the degree of LL.D. from Howard College and the degree of D.D. from Washington and Lee.

SAMPSON, FRANCIS ASBURY. Scientist and lawyer. [Mo.]. He published 'The Natural History of Pettis County' (1882), a 'Bibliography of the Geology of Missouri' (1890), and 'The Mollusca of Arkansas' (1893).

SAMPSON, JOHN PATTERSON, negro clergyman, lawyer and author, was born in Wilmington, N.C., August 13, 1837. While in the Treasury Department in Washington, D.C., he studied law and was admitted to the Bar. At the beginning of the war he edited in Cincinnati *The Colored Citizen;* and during the days of reconstruction held political office in North Carolina. Later he entered the ministry of the A.M.E. Church and received the degree of D.D. His writings include a 'Common Sense Physiology,' 'The Disappointed Bride,' 'Temperament and Phrenology of Mixed Races,' 'Jolly People,' and 'Pastoral Theology.' He was for some time a resident of Philadelphia, Pa.

SAMS, STANHOPE, journalist, was born in Greenville, S.C., December 11, 1860. During the Spanish-American War, Mr. Sams was war correspondent for the New York *Mail;* and at different times served on other metropolitan papers. Since 1905 he has been associate and literary editor of the Columbia (S.C.) *State.* He has written numerous short stories of marked excellence, two of which were prize winners: "The Golden Age of Poincaré," in *Collier's Weekly,* and "Young Cid at Santiago," in the New York *Herald.* "Restored Identity" is the title of another short story of much interest. The sketch of J. A. B. Scherer in 'The Library of Southern Literature' is from the pen of Mr. Sams. He married, in 1888, Camilla Cantey Johnson.

SANDERS, JOHN, civil engineer, was born in Lexington, Ky., in 1810, and died at Fort Delaware, July 29, 1858. He was educated at West Point, became captain of an engineering corps, and was for many years engaged in improving the bed of the Ohio River and in making repairs in the interior defences of New York harbor. He served with credit in the Mexican War, and published 'Memoirs of the Resources of the Valley of the Ohio' (New York, 1844).

SANDS, ALEXANDER HAMILTON, lawyer and clergyman, was born in Williamsburg, Va., May 2, 1828, and died in Richmond, Va., December 22, 1887. He studied law, and, during the Civil War, was judge advocate in the Confederate Army; but shortly before his death he entered the Baptist ministry and served congregations in Virginia. Besides contributing to current periodicals, he published 'The History of a Suit in Equity' (Richmond, 1854), 'Recreations of a Southern Barrister' (Philadelphia, 1860), and 'Sermons by a Village Pastor,' in addition to a number of legal compilations.

SANDS, BENJAMIN FRANKLIN, naval officer, was born in Baltimore, Md., February 11, 1811, and died in Washington, D.C., June 30, 1883. He wrote 'From Reefer to Rear-admiral.'

SANDYS, GEORGE, poet and colonist, was born in Bishopsthorpe, England, in 1577, and died at Boxley Abbey, England, in 1644. For three years he was treasurer of the colony of Virginia and while a resident of the New World he translated ten books of Ovid's 'Metamorphoses' (London, 1626), the first literary production of any distinct value in the Western Hemisphere. He also published metrical versions of the Psalms (1636) and wrote an account of his travels in the Mediterranean lands (1615). His works were collected and published in two volumes (London, 1872).

SANFORD, SHELTON PALMER, educator and mathematician, was born in Greensboro, Ga., January 25, 1816. For over forty years he was professor of mathematics in Mercer University, from which institution he received the degree of LL.D. He published a series of algebras and arithmetics which were adopted in many states.

SASS, GEORGE HERBERT ("Barton Gray"). See Biographical and Critical Sketch, Vol. X, page 4661.

SASSNETT, WILLIAM JACOB, clergyman and educator, was born in Hancock County, Ga., April 29, 1820, and died in Montgomery, Ala., November 3, 1865. He relinquished law for theology, became a minister of the Methodist Church, South, and was for several years president of LaGrange Female College. Besides numerous magazine articles, he published 'Discussions in Literature and Religion' (Nashville, 1850), and 'Progress of the M.E. Church, South' (*ibid.*, 1855). Emory College gave him the degree of D.D.

SAUNDERS, EUGENE DAVIS. Lawyer. [La.]. He published 'Saunders on Taxation.'

SAUNDERS, MARY INGLE, Mrs., poet, was born in England in 1836, but afterward lived in Texas and published a number of commemorative odes, including "San Jacinto Day" and "Texas."

SAUNDERS, ROMULUS MITCHELL, statesman, was born in Caswell County, N.C., March 3, 1791, and died in Raleigh, N.C., April 21, 1867. He received his education from the University of North Carolina, studied law, became attorney-general of the State, served in Congress for several terms, and was appointed Minister to Spain. Later he became judge of the Superior Court and a commissioner to revise and codify the laws of the State.

SAUNDERS, WILLIAM, statesman, of North Carolina, was born in 1835 and died in 1891. He edited the 'Records of North Carolina to 1776,' in eight volumes.

"SAVOYARD." See Eugene William Newman.

SAWYER, B. F. Author. [Ga.]. He wrote several stories of Southern life, among them: 'Lucile,' 'Lady Paulina,' and 'David and Abigail' (Boston, 1894).

SAWYER, GEORGE S. Lawyer. [La.]. He published an important work entitled 'Southern Institutes: an Inquiry into Slavery' (Philadelphia, 1859). He was a member of the Bar of New Orleans.

SAWYER, LEMUEL, lawyer, was born in Camden County, N.C., in 1777, and died in Washington, D.C., January 9, 1852. He studied law, but public life was destined to claim most of his time and thought. For more than twenty years he represented North Carolina in Congress. He published a 'Life of John Randolph' (New York, 1844), an 'Autobiography' (1845), and several plays, including 'The Wreck of Honor: a Tragedy.' He was a man of eccentric habits and of singular gifts.

SCAIFE, H. LEWIS. Author. [S.C.]. He wrote 'Life at the Citadel,' 'The History of Superstition,' and 'The History and Condition of the Catawba Indians' (1896).

SCARBOROUGH, WILLIAM SAUNDERS, educator, was born in Macon, Ga., of African descent, February 16, 1852. For several years he was professor of ancient languages in Wilberforce University at Zenia, Ohio. He published 'First Lessons in Greek' (New York, 1881) and 'Theory and Functions of the Thematic Vowel in the Greek Verb.'

SCHAEFFER, CHARLES WILLIAM, clergyman, was born in Hagerstown, Md., May 5, 1813. For several years he filled Lutheran pulpits in Pennsylvania. He also edited Lutheran periodicals and taught in Lutheran schools. His publications include: 'The Early History of the Lutheran Church in America' (1857), 'Family Prayer,' and numerous translations from the German. He held the degrees of D.D. and LL.D.

SCHARF, JOHN THOMAS. An antiquarian of some note who was born in Baltimore, Md., in 1843. He served in both the military and the naval operations of the Confederate Government, was several times wounded, and once narrowly escaped death as a spy, due to his venturesome spirit and his utter disregard of danger. After the war he entered journalism in Baltimore and edited at various times the *Evening News,* the *Sunday Telegram,* and the *Morning Herald.* He devoted much time to historical investigations and made a collection of several thousand documents and pamphlets, which he gave to Johns Hopkins University. He was the author of several works of great value and importance, including: 'Chronicles of Baltimore' (1874), 'The History of Maryland,' in three volumes (1880), 'The History of Western Maryland,' in two volumes (1882), 'The History of Philadelphia,' in three volumes (1884), 'The History of the Confederate States Navy from the Time of its Organization to the Surrender of its Last Vessel' (1887), and 'The History of Delaware' (1888). He died in 1898. Dr. Scharf was given the degree of LL.D.

SCHELE DE VERE, MAXMILIAN. See Biographical and Critical Sketch, Vol. XI, page. 4687.

SCHENCK, DAVID. Lawyer. [N.C.]. Born in 1835. He published 'The Battle of Guilford Court House' (Greensboro, 1888), 'North Carolina, 1780-1781' (Raleigh, 1889), and a 'Narrative of the Battle of Cowan's Ford' (Greensboro, 1891), besides minor works. He received the degree of LL.D.

SCHERER, JAMES A. B. See Biographical and Critical Sketch, Vol. XI, page 4709.

SCHERER, MELANCTHON G. G. Clergyman. [N.C.]. He was born in 1861. He published 'The Mission of the Christian Church.'

SCHLEY, WILLIAM, governor and jurist, was born in Frederick, Md., December 15, 1786, and died in Augusta, Ga., November 20, 1858. He studied law, achieved eminence at the Georgia Bar, and became a judge of the Superior Court, a Member of Congress, and governor. He advocated the building of the first railroad in the State, and published a 'Digest of the English Statutes in Force in Georgia' (Philadelphia, 1826).

SCHLEY, WINFIELD SCOTT, naval officer, was born in Frederick, Md., October 9, 1839, a son of John Thomas and Georgiana Virginia Schley, and was educated for the navy at Annapolis. He left the academy on the eve of the Civil War and entered at once upon his eventful and dramatic career as a fighter. Promotions came rapidly; and, in the years which followed, the sphere of his operations was transferred from one part of the globe to another. In 1884 he took command of the famous Greeley Relief Expedition and rescued the explorer, with six of his men, at Cape Sabine, for which he was awarded medals and legislative honors. At the outbreak of the Spanish-American War in 1898 he held a commodore's commission; but for his dash and gallantry at the battle of Santiago Bay, in which he took active command, he was subsequently promoted to the rank of rear-admiral. On reaching the age limit in 1901 he was placed upon the retired list. Besides occasional magazine articles, his published works include: 'The Rescue of Greeley' (1886), and 'Forty-five Years Under the Flag' (1904). He married, September 10, 1863, Annie R. Franklin, of Annapolis, Md.

SCHMIDT, GUSTAVUS. Lawyer. He was born in Stockholm, Sweden, in 1793. Possessed of an adventurous nature, he crossed the ocean in early life, settled in New Orleans, and became in time one of the lights of the Louisiana Bar. An address delivered by him on "The Model Judge" is preserved in 'The Louisiana Book.' It deals with the character of Chief Justice John Marshall and abounds in scholarly touches. He died September 21, 1877, while on a visit to Virginia.

SCHMUCKER, SAMUEL MOSHEIM, clergyman, was born in Newmarket, Va., January 12, 1823, and died in Philadelphia, Pa., May 12, 1863. His father, whose sketch appears below, was one of the pioneers of American Lutheranism, and, following in the parental footsteps, the son also became an eminent clergyman and writer. In 1848 he was honorably dismissed by his synod, adopted law and literature, and published, among numerous other works, 'Errors of Modern Infidelity' (Philadelphia, 1848), 'The Spanish Wife, a Play,' including a memoir of Edwin Forrest (New York, 1854), 'Court and Reign of Catherine I' (1855), 'Life and Reign of Nicholas I,' 'Life and Times of Alexander Hamilton' (Philadelphia, 1856), 'Life and Times of Thomas Jefferson,' including 'The Yankee Slave Driver' (Philadelphia, 1857), 'Arctic Explorations and Discoveries,' 'History of Napoleon III' (Philadelphia, 1858), 'History of the Four Georges,' 'Life, Speeches and Memorials of Daniel Webster' (Philadelphia, 1859), 'Life and Times of Henry Clay,' and the first volume of a 'History of the Civil War' (1863).

SCHMUCKER, SAMUEL SIMON, clergyman, was born in Hagerstown, Md., February 28, 1799, and died at Gettysburg, Pa., July 26, 1873. He became an eminent Lutheran, prescribed the formula for the government and discipline of the church in America, taught for more than forty years in the theological seminary at Gettysburg, and published more than one hundred works, including translations. His writings include: 'Elements of Popular Theology' (1834), 'Psychology, or Elements of Mental Philosophy' (New York, 1852), 'The American Lutheran Church' (1851), 'Lutheran Manual,' and 'The Evangelical Lutheran Catechism.' Two colleges gave him the degree of D.D.

SCHOOLCRAFT, MARY HOWARD, author, was born in Beaufort, S.C., and in 1847 became the second wife of Henry Rowe Schoolcraft, the distinguished ethnologist. When her husband was confined to his chair by paralysis, she assisted him in the preparation of his later works; and she also published an entertaining volume of fiction entitled 'The Black Gauntlet, a Tale of Plantation Life in South Carolina' (Philadelphia, 1860).

SCHROEDER, JOHN FREDERICK, clergyman and educator, was born in Baltimore, Md., April 8, 1800, and died in Brooklyn, N.Y., February 26, 1865. After graduating from Princeton with the highest honors, he studied theology, became an eminent Episcopal divine, established at Flushing, L.I., a school for girls, which he afterward removed to New York; traveled abroad and lectured extensively on popular themes, and served two important Brooklyn parishes. Trinity College conferred upon him the degree of S.T.D. Besides editing several theological volumes, he published 'Maxims of Washington' (New York, 1855), 'Memoir of Mrs. Anne Boardman' (New Haven, 1849), and left unfinished 'The Life and Times of Washington,' which was completed by other hands.

SCHURZ, CARL, United States Senator and publicist, was born in Cologne, Germany, March 2, 1829, and was educated at the University of Bonn. Coming to the United States in 1852, he first located in Wisconsin. He resigned the mission to Spain to enter the Union Army and became a major-general. After the war he settled in Missouri and was sent to the United States Senate. Independent in politics, he supported Hayes in 1876 and Cleveland in 1884. For several years he edited the New York *Evening Post*. Besides contributing to various periodicals, he has published a volume of 'Speeches' (Philadelphia, J. B. Lippincott Co., 1885), a 'Life of Henry Clay' (New York, Harper and Bros., 1887), and 'Abraham Lincoln, an Essay' (*ibid.*, 1889).

SCHWEINITZ, EMIL ALEXANDER DE, chemist, was born in Salem, N.C., January 18, 1866. After graduating from the University of North Carolina, he pursued his studies at Göttingen, from which institution he received the degree of Ph.D. For many years he was professor of chemistry in Columbian University Medical School. He published a number of papers containing the fruits of his researches and won international recognition by his contributions to scientific thought, especially upon the subject of tuberculosis. He died in 1904.

SCOTT, CHARLES, lawyer, was born in Knoxville, Tenn., November 12, 1811, and died in Jackson, Miss., May 30, 1861. For several years he practiced law in Nashville, Tenn., but he afterward settled in Mississippi and became chancellor of the State. He was an active Mason and published 'The Analogy of Ancient Craft Masonry to Natural and Revealed Religion' (Philadelphia, 1849) and 'The Keystone of the Masonic Arch' (1856).

SCOTT, EDWARD, jurist, was born in Virginia in 1774, and died in Tennessee in 1852. His father was Joseph Scott, a major in the Revolution. For more than thirty years he occupied the Superior Court Bench in Tennessee and published in two volumes, 'Laws of the State of Tennessee' (Knoxville, 1821).

SCOTT, HENRY LEE, soldier, was born in New Berne, N.C., October 3, 1814, and died in New York City, January 6, 1886. He was educated at West Point, married Cornelia, the daughter of General Winfield Scott, and became an aide on the latter's staff, with the rank of colonel. He participated in the Mexican War and in the various Indian campaigns. His only work is a 'Dictionary of Military Terms' (New York, 1861).

SCOTT, JEANNE McCLAIN FORNEY, educator, was born in Tennessee in 1849, but afterward lived first in Alabama and then in Arkansas. Her stories are charmingly told, varied in plot and full of the atmosphere of Southern life. They include: 'Mars' Jeems' (1872), 'Little Miss Bettie' (1876), 'Sis and Bud' (1880), 'Render Unto Cæsar' (1886), 'Romance of the River Fields' (1891), 'At Sirat' (1892), 'Magnolias Abloom,' and 'Where the Rivers Meet' (1896).

SCOTT, JOHN. One of Mosby's men. [Va.]. He published 'Partisan Life with Mosby' (1867).

SCOTT, NANCY M. [Tenn.]. She published a biography of her grandfather entitled a 'Memoir of Hugh Lawson White, with Speeches' (1856).

SCOTT, ROBERT NICHOLSON, soldier, was born in Winchester, Tenn., January 21, 1838, and died in Washington, D.C., in 1887. His father was the Rev. William Anderson Scott, D.D. Entering the United States Army in 1857, he fought on the Union side during the Civil War. For several years he was in charge of the war records at the national capital. He was breveted a major for gallantry at Gaines's Mill, where he was wounded. He published a 'Digest of the Military Laws of the United States' (1872), an important work.

SCOTT, ROSA NAOMI, writer, was born in Knoxville, Tenn., March 29, 1871. She is engaged in journalistic work in Knoxville, but occasionally writes short stories and sketches for the magazines. Her latest bit of fiction, entitled "The Woman in the Second Row," was published in *The Woman's Home Companion*. She is also the author of the sketch of Frances Hodgson Burnett in 'The Library of Southern Literature' and the winner of a prize for the best short historical romance.

SCOTT, SUTTON SELWYN. Lawyer and planter. He was born in Huntsville, Ala., November 26, 1829, a son of James G. and Ann Scott, was educated at the University of Tennessee and married Loula Marie Hurt, of Columbus, Ga. He was Confederate Commissioner of Indian Affairs in 1863 and delegate to the Alabama Constitutional Convention in 1875. Under President Cleveland's first administration he was United States Commissioner to adjudicate claims in New Mexico and Colorado; and from 1894 to 1896 was chairman of the commission to the Indians in Utah. His writings include: 'Southbrooke: Southern Tales and Sketches,' (1880), 'The Mobilians, or Talks About the South,' (1897), and numerous articles contributed to the periodicals. He resides in Auburn, Ala.

SCOTT, WALTER, religious leader and author, was a kinsman of the famous novelist, born in Dumfriesshire, Scotland, October 31, 1796, and died in Kentucky, April 23, 1861. While not an ordained minister, he came to the support of Alexander Campbell with singular powers of eloquence, contributed to the *Christian Baptist* and published 'The Gospel Restored' (1854) and 'The Messiahship, or the Great Demonstration' (1858), besides minor works. His biography was written by William Baxter (1874).

SCOTT, WILLIAM ANDERSON, clergyman, was born in Bedford County, Tenn., in 1813; and, having been reared among the Cumberland Presbyterians, he was licensed to preach when only seventeen. But he afterward completed his theological equipment at Princeton. He was at one time pastor of the Presbyterian Church at the Hermitage, which was largely sustained by Andrew Jackson. Later he preached in New Orleans; and when the war began he was laboring in San Francisco; but on account of divided sentiment among the people on the issues of the war, he went abroad and preached for some time in Birmingham, England. He traveled extensively in foreign lands, and is said to have acquired eleven languages. His works include: 'The Christ of the Apostles' Creed' (1867), 'The Voice of the Church Against Arianism,' 'Strauss and Renan,' 'The Church in the Army, or the Four Centurians of the Gospel' (1862), 'The Wedge of Gold: or, Achan in El Dorado' (1855), 'Trade and Letters' (1856), 'The Giant Judge, or Samson the Hebrew Hercules' (1858), 'The Bible and Politics' (1859), 'Esther, the Hebrew-Persian Queen,' and 'Daniel, a Model for Young Men' (1854). He also edited the New Orleans *Presbyterian* and founded the *Pacific Expositor.* The University of Alabama gave him the degree of D.D. and the University of the City of New York the degree of LL.D.

SCOTT, WILLIAM COWPER, Presbyterian clergyman, was born in Martinsburg, Va., January 13, 1817, and died in Bethesda, Va., October 23, 1854. He published 'Genius and Faith, or Poetry and Religion in their Mutual Relation,' a work of exceptional merit evincing unusual powers of literary criticism.

SCOTT, WILLIAM J. Editor and clergyman. He was born in Clarke County, Ga., in 1826. His father was a man of distinguished classical attainments and a teacher of some note, who largely directed the education of his son. He relinquished the law for the ministry, entered the itinerant ranks of the Methodist Church and edited *Scott's Magazine,* which was published in Atlanta, Ga., just after the war. This was a periodical of exceptional merit, but on account of the impoverished condition of the section it lacked means of sustenance and collapsed. Among the published works of Dr. Scott, who frequently wrote for the religious and secular press, are: 'Lectures and Essays,' 'Historic Eras,' and 'Sketches of Ministers and Laymen of the North Georgia Conference.' The master of an elegant style, the writings of this eminent scholar possess unusual charm. He died in Atlanta, in 1899.

SCOTT, WINFIELD, an eminent American soldier, was born in Dinwiddie County, Va., June 13, 1786, and died at West Point, N.Y., May 29, 1866. He was educated at William and Mary College, practiced law for two years, entered the United States Army with the rank of captain, and rose by virtue of soldiership and courage to the supreme command. He led the American forces in the war with Mexico. In 1852 he was the candidate of the Whig party for President, and received the electoral vote of several states. Besides a pamphlet against the use of intoxicating liquors (Philadelphia, 1821), he published 'General Regulations for the Army' (1825), 'Letter to the Secretary of War' (New York, 1827), 'Letter on the Slavery Question' (New York, 1843), 'Abstract of Infantry Tactics' (Philadelphia, 1861), and his 'Memoirs,' in two volumes, giving an account of his military career. He also translated from the French a work on 'Infantry Tactics,' in three volumes (1835). Numerous biographies of General Scott have appeared, among them Edward D. Mansfield's, Joel T. Headley's, and O. J. Victor's. Besides, Lieutenant Raphael Semmes has written 'The Campaign of General Scott in the Valley of Mexico' (Cincinnati, 1852).

SCREVEN, WILLIAM, clergyman, was born in England in 1629 and died in Georgetown, S.C., in 1713. He settled first in Piscataway, N.H.; but, suffering persecutions at the hands of the Puritans, he removed to Charleston, S.C., where he organized the pioneer Baptist congregation. He wrote 'An Ornament for Church Members,' which was published after his death (Charleston, 1721).

SCRUGGS, WILLIAM LINDSAY. Lawyer, journalist, diplomat. He was born near Knoxville, Tenn., September 14, 1836, the son of Frederick and Margaret Kimbrough Scruggs, received an excellent education and was admitted to the Bar in 1861. He married Judi'h Ann Potts. He edited the Columbus *Daily Sun* and the Atl'anta *New Era* between 1862 and 1871. He was United States Minister to Colombia from 1872 to 1877, and again from 1882 to 1887, and was United States Consul in China from 1877 to 1881, United States Minister to Venezuela from 1889 to 1893, and became legal adviser and special agent of the Venezuelan Government, charged with the settlement of the Anglo-Venezuelan boundary dispute, from 1894 to 1898, bringing it successfully to arbitration. In politics he has been an Independent Republican. His writings include: 'British Aggressions in Venezuela, or the Monroe Doctrine on Trial' (Atlanta, Franklin Publishing Company, 1894), 'Official History of the Guayana Boundary Dispute' (*ibid.*, 1895), 'Lora Salisbury's Mistakes' (1896), 'Fallacies of the British Blue Book' (1896), 'The Colombian and Venezuelan Republics' (Boston, Little, Brown and Company, 1899), 'Evolution of American Citizenship' (Atlanta. Franklin Publishing Company, 1901), 'Origin and Meaning of the Monroe Doctrine' (*ibid.*, 1902), and 'The Evolution of the Fourteenth and Fifteenth Amendments' (1903), besides numerous historical, economic, and legal reviews. He resides in Atlanta, Ga.

SEABROOK, PHOEBE HAMILTON, Mrs. Author. [S.C.]. She wrote an entertaining novel of life in the South during the Civil War entitled 'A Daughter of the Confederacy' (New York and Washington, The Neale Publishing Company, 1907).

SEALS, A. B. Author. [Ga.]. For many years he was associated with his brother, Colonel John H. Seals, in the editorship of the *Sunny South,* a periodical published in Atlanta, Ga. He wrote an interesting novel entitled 'Rockford.'

SEALSFIELD, CHARLES, author, was born in Moravia, March 3, 1793, and died in Switzerland, May 26, 1864. His real name was Karl Postel, but, escaping from a convent at Prague, he came to the United States, where he was known as Charles Sealsfield. For several years he lived in Louisiana, removing afterward to Texas, and eventually to Mexico and Central America. He possessed unusual genius and wrote numerous works which were translated in English, including 'The Cabin Book; or, Life in Texas' (1844, first edition), 'North and South; or, Scenes in Mexico' (1845), 'Adventures in Central America' (1852), 'Frontier Life in the Southwest' (1853), 'The French in Louisiana' (1854), 'Adventures in Texas' (1860), 'Transatlantic Traveling Sketches,' two volumes (1833), 'Pictures of Life in Both Hemispheres,' two volumes (1834), 'Tokeah; or, the White Rose' (1828), 'Rambleton, a Romance of New York' (1836), 'The Viceroy and the Aristocracy,' a Mexican novel (1834), and several others. Two complete editions of his works have been published in German (Stuttgart, 1845-1847, fifteen volumes; 1846, eighteen volumes).

SEARING, LAURA CATHERINE, author, was born in Somerset County, Md., February 9, 1840. Her maiden name was Redden. Due to an attack of meningitis, she lost the sense of hearing when a child and later the power of speech, but she possessed an intellect of unusual vigor, acquired the languages of modern Europe during a visit abroad, made contributions to the press which attracted wide attention, and became a woman of note. She married Edward W. Searing of the New York Bar and afterward removed to California. Her verse is soulful and delicate, evincing a temperament remarkably poetic. She published 'Notable Men of the Thirty-seventh Congress' (Washington, 1862), 'Idyls of Battle,' a collection of war poems (New York, 1864), and 'Sounds from Secret Chambers' (Boston, 1874).

SEATON, WILLIAM WINSTON, editor, was born in King William County, Va., January 11, 1785, and died in Washington, D.C., June 16, 1866. After editing various journals, he located in Washington, D.C., where for more than forty years, in association with his brother-in-law, Joseph Gales, Jr., he published the *National Intelligencer,* a paper which from 1812 to 1820 exclusively reported the debates of Congress. He was for twelve consecutive years mayor of Washington. Together with Mr. Gales he published 'Annals of Congress,' forty-two volumes, from 1798 to 1824, and 'Register of Debates in Congress,' fourteen volumes, from 1824 to 1837. His 'Life' was written by his daughter (Boston, 1871).

SEAWELL, J. Playwright. [Ala.]. Author of 'Valentine, a Play in Five Acts.'

SEAWELL, MOLLY ELLIOT. See Biographical and Critical Sketch, Vol. XI, page 4729.

SEIBERT, VENITA, Miss, author, was born in Louisville, Ky., December 29, 1878. From time to time she has published numerous short stories and bits of verse which have been widely admired. She has also published a series of stories in the *American Magazine* entitled "In the Different World," and a volume of fiction entitled 'The Gossamer Thread' (Boston, Small, Maynard and Company). She reviews books for the Louisville *Courier-Journal.*

SEISS, JOSEPH AUGUSTUS, theologian, was born in Frederick County, Md., March 18, 1823. He was educated at Gettysburg, Pa., became an ordained Lutheran minister and preached for years with great power in Philadelphia, where he occupied one of the largest churches. He traveled extensively, wrote and lectured and published numerous works; among them 'Popuular Lectures on the Epistle to the Hebrews' (Baltimore, 1846), 'Lectures on the Gospels of the Church Year' in two volumes (1868), 'The Baptist System Examined' (Philadelphia, 1854), 'The Apocalypse,' in three volumes (London, 1882), and numerous others, besides liturgical works, translations and sermons.

SEJOUR, VICTOR, author and actor, was born in New Orleans, La., June 12, 1809. He spent much of his time in Paris, achieved distinction on the stage and became a writer of successful plays. Though he made his initial reputation as a man of letters in an ode to the French emperor entitled "Retour de Napoleon," it was chiefly in the line of dramatic composition that his literary activities were engaged. He published: 'Diegarias' (1844), 'La Chute de Sajan' (1849), 'Richard III' (1852), 'L'Argent du Diable' (1854), 'Les Noces Vénetiennes' (1855), 'Le Fils de la Nuit' (1857), 'André Gérard' (1857) and in association with M. Brésil, 'Le Martyr du Cœur' (1858).

SELBY, JULIAN A. [S.C.]. He wrote an interesting personal narrative entitled 'Memorabilia and Anecdotal Reminiscences of Columbia' (1905), a work which portrays some thrilling chapters in the history of the South Carolina capital. He died in Columbia, S.C., in 1907.

SELDEN, SAMUEL, physician and poet, was born at Norfolk, Va., in 1834, of good English stock. On graduating from Hampden-Sidney College, he took his degree in medicine at Charleston, S.C. For nearly twenty years he practiced his profession in his native town. The possessor of poetic gifts of no mean order, he often dipped into verse during hours of relaxation; and the year of his death witnessed the publication of his only volume entitled 'Poems' (Norfolk, 1880).

SELLERS, ALVIN V., lawyer and author, was born at Graham, Ga., September 14, 1882. He is the youngest member of the present State Senate of Georgia, 1909-1910, and published an interesting work entitled 'Classics of the Bar' (Baxley, Ga., 1909), which contains some of the masterpieces of forensic eloquence. It also reviews a number of the most celebrated trials.

SELPH, FANNIE EOLINE. Writer. She published 'Texas, or the Broken Link.'

SEMMES, ALEXANDER JENKINS, surgeon, educator, author, was born in Washington, D.C., December 17, 1828. After receiving his medical diploma, he prosecuted his studies abroad. During the Civil War he was a surgeon in Stonewall Jackson's corps. At the close of hostilities he settled in Savannah, Ga., for the practice of his profession, but he afterward took orders in the Roman Catholic Church and became president of Pio Nono College, in Macon, Ga. He was a writer of graphic resources and produced several interesting volumes, among them 'Medical Sketches of Paris' (New York, 1852), 'Gun-shot Wounds' (1864), 'Notes from a Surgical Diary' (1866), 'Surgical Notes of the Late War'

(1867), 'The Fluid Extracts' (1869), and 'Evolution the Origin of Life' (1873). He was a cousin of Admiral Semmes.

SEMMES, RAPHAEL. See Biographical and Critical Sketch, Vol. XI, page 4751.

SEMMES, THOMAS JENKINS. Lawyer and statesman. He was born in Georgetown, D.C., December 16, 1824. On settling in New Orleans for the practice of law, he advanced rapidly to the front; and during the war period he represented Louisiana in the Confederate Senate. For a time he was also professor of law in the University of Louisiana. He was called by some of his colleagues at the bar "the incarnation of logic." He wrote a 'History of the Laws of Louisiana' (New Orleans, 1873). One of his speeches entitled "The Confederate Seal" is preserved in 'The Louisiana Book' (1894).

SEMPLE, ELLEN CHURCHILL, author, was born in Louisville, Ky., in 1863, was prepared by private tutors for Vassar College, and after graduating from this celebrated institution, continued her studies abroad at Leipzig. Besides numerous contributions to scientific periodicals on both sides of the water, she published an important volume on the line of her life's work entitled 'American History and its Geographic Conditions' (1903), which is said to be the ablest treatise upon this subject in the English language, evincing not only thoroughness of research but original power of thought. It is the geography of the continent viewed in relation to the life and history of man, a masterpiece of anthropoiogical literature which has attracted wide recognition from the scientists.

SEMPLE, ROBERT BAYLOR, clergyman, was born in King and Queen County, Va., January 20, 1769, and died in Fredericksburg, Va., December 25, 1831. He became an eminent Baptist divine and published a 'History of Virginia Baptists' (1810), a 'Catechism' (1809), a 'Memoir of Elder Straughan,' and 'Letters to Alexander Campbell.' He received his degree of D.D. from Brown University.

SENOUR, WILLIAM, Mrs. Author. [Fla.]. She has published 'The Master of St. Elmo' (1904). The author resides at Faunt Le Roy, Fla.

SEVIER, CLARA DRISCOLL, author, was born in St. Mary's, Texas. Her father was Robert Driscoll and her mother Julia Fox. She married, July 31, 1906, H. H. Sevier. She is a writer of rare gifts. Her published works include 'The Girl of La Gloria' (1905), 'Mexicana' (1906), and 'In the Shadow of the Alamo' (1906). She resides in New York. The sketch of Amelia E. Barr in 'The Library of Southern Literature' is from the pen of Mrs. Sevier.

SEWALL, R. R. Presbyterian clergyman. [Fla.]. He wrote 'Sketches of St. Augustine.'

SHACKELFORD, JOSEPHUS. Baptist clergyman. [Ala.]. He wrote a 'History of the Mussel Shoals Baptist Association' (1891).

SHACKLEFORD, THOMAS MITCHELL. Jurist. He was born in Fayetteville, Tenn., November 14, 1859, a son of Daniel Park and Aletha Young Shackleford, graduated from Burritt College, Spencer, Tenn., and was married twice. He removed from Tennessee to Florida in 1882, was Associate Justice of the Supreme Court from 1902 to 1905, and then became Chief Justice. Two very interesting volumes have been the product of his leisure moments: 'Amoskohegan' and 'By Sunlit Waters,' the latter written in association with William Wilson De Hart. He resides in Tallahassee, Fla.

SHAFFNER, TALIAFERRO PRESTON, inventor and author, was born in Fauquier County, Va., in 1818, and died in Troy, N.Y., December 11, 1881. He was admitted to the Bar, but gave most of his time to inventions, of which he patented twelve. He was also at one time associated with Morse in the introduction of the telegraph and published 'The Telegraph Companion' in two volumes (New York, 1855), 'The Telegraph Manual' (1859), 'The Secession War in America' (London, 1862), 'The History of America' in two volumes (1863), and 'Odd Fellowship' (New York, 1875).

SHALER, NATHANIEL SOUTHGATE, geologist, was born in Newport, Ky., February 20, 1841, and received his education at Harvard, where he made a special study of scientific branches. For two years he served in the Union Army, after which he became a professor in the Lawrence Scientific School at Harvard, and eventually succeeded to the office of dean. Harvard conferred upon him the degree of Sc.D. His published works include: 'A First Book in Geology' (1884), 'Kentucky, a Pioneer Commonwealth' (1885), 'The United States of America,' in three volumes, with maps and illustrations (New York, D. Appleton and Company), 'Outlines of the Earth's History' (*ibid.*), and 'The Individual, a Study of Life and Death' (*ibid.*), besides numerous monographs and memoirs. He died in 1906.

SHALER, WILLIAM, author, was born in Virginia in 1778 and died in Havana, Cuba, March 29, 1833. For many years he was consul-general at Algiers, and later held the same post at Havana. He was the author of 'Sketches on Algiers,' a work which was highly praised by Jared Sparks (Boston, 1826). He also wrote a paper on 'The Language of the Berbers in Africa,' for the American Philosophical Transactions.

SHANKS, WILLIAM FRANKLIN GORE, journalist, was born in Shelbyville, Ky., April 20, 1837, became war correspondent of the New York *Herald,* and afterward served on other metropolitan newspapers. He married Mary R. Lynn, of Louisville, Ky. His publications include: 'Recollections of Distinguished Generals' (New York, 1865), 'The Noble Treason,' a tragedy, and 'The Ring Master,' a novel. He served in the Union Army, and was wounded at Chattanooga. His death occurred in 1905.

SHARKEY, T. K., Mrs. Author. [Tenn.]. She published a novel entitled 'Mate to Mate.'

SHARP, ROBERT. Educator. He was born in Lawrenceville, Va., October 24, 1857, and was educated at Randolph-Macon College and at Leipsic. In 1881 he married Blanche Herndon. For four years he was professor of English in the University of Louisiana, and since 1884 he has occupied the same chair in Tulane University. He is a writer of distinction on Anglo-Saxon topics. With Professor James A. Harrison, he has edited 'Beowolf' and 'The Fight at Finsburh,' and has edited alone Shakespeare's 'The Merchant of Venice.' He holds the degree of Ph.D.

SHAVER, LLEWELLYN ADOLPHUS. Lawyer. [Ala.]. He was born in 1847. He published a 'History of the Sixtieth Alabama Regiment, Gracie's Brigade' (1867).

SHAW, JOHN, physician and poet, was born in Annapolis, Md., and, after obtaining his medical diploma, he received a surgeon's appointment in the fleet ordered to Algiers. Later he was sent by his superior officer to London on diplomatic business, and returned by way of Lisbon. In the year following he continued his medical studies at Edinburgh, became the friend of the Earl of Selkirk, with whom he sailed for Canada to join the settlement which the nobleman was founding, but he soon returned to the United States and settled in Baltimore. He was a ready writer of verse; and soon after his death, which occurred in 1809, while on a voyage from Charleston to the Bahamas, some of his best work appeared in book form under the title 'Poems by the Late Dr. Shaw, with a Biographical Sketch.'

SHEARER, JOHN BUNYAN. Educator and divine. He was born in Appomattox County, Va., July 19, 1832. For many years he was president of Davidson College, N.C., and afterward vice-president. His writings include: a 'Bible Course Syllabus' in three volumes (Richmond, B. F. Johnson, 1895), 'Modern Mysticism,' 'The Sermon on the Mount' (Richmond, Presbyterian Committee of Publication), 'Studies in the Life of Christ' (*ibid.*), and numerous articles for the magazines and reviews.

SHEARIN, HUBERT GIBSON, educator, was born in Boyle County, Ky., near Frankfort, May 5, 1878, and received the best educational advantages, obtaining the Ph.D. degree from Yale. Besides frequent contributions to educational and popular periodicals, he has published 'The Expression of Purpose in Old English Prose' (New York, Henry Holt and Company, 1902), and has in preparation 'Outlines of English Syntax' and a 'Collection of Kentucky Mountain Ballads.' For 'The Library of Southern Literature' he wrote the sketch of Madison Cawein. Dr. Shearin is an accomplished scholar and in addition to holding the chair of English philology in Transylvania University, he is also president of Hamilton College for Women, and edits *Transylvania Studies in Philology.* He married, September 6, 1903, Ruth Marguerite Béné. He resides in Lexington, Ky.

SHECUT, JOHN LINNAEUS EDWARD WHITRIDGE, physician, was born in Beaufort, S.C., December 4, 1770, and died in Charleston, S.C., in 1836. After receiving his medical diploma he settled in Charleston, organized the first cotton factory in the State, and became the first physician to apply electricity to the treatment of yellow fever. He was fond of original research, wrote with great ease and clearness, and published several volumes, including 'Flora Caroliniensis, a Historical, Medical and Economical Display of the Vegetable Kingdom,' in two volumes (Charleston, 1806), 'An Essay on the Yellow Fever of 1817,' 'An Inquiry into the Properties of the Electric Fluid' (1818), 'Shecut's Medical and Philosophical Essays' (1819), 'Elements of Natural Philosophy' (1826), and 'A New Theory of the Earth' (1826).

SHEFFEY, MIRIAM, Miss, poet, of Virginia, published a booklet entitled 'The Spirit-Mother, and Other Poems' (New York, 1905). It is the distillation of grief, but is not depressing because of the refined sentiment which it breathes. The author's home is in Marion, Va.

SHELDON, GEORGE WILLIAM, educator and author, was born in Summerville, S.C., January 28, 1843. On completing his studies at Princeton, he became a tutor in the institution for two years and afterward a professor of Oriental languages in Union Theological Seminary, but relinquished educational work eventually for literature, and became an art critic of wide reputation. His publications include 'American Painters' (New York, 1879), 'Story of the Volunteer Fire Department of New York' (New York, Harper and Brothers), 'Hours with Art and Artists'

(New York, D. Appleton and Company), 'Artistic Homes' (*ibid.*), 'Artistic Country Seats' (*ibid.*), 'Selections in Modern Art' (*ibid.*), 'Recent Ideals in American Art' (*ibid.*), and 'Ideals of Life in France' (*ibid.*), besides contributions to numerous periodicals.

SHEPARD, SETH, jurist, was born in Washington County, Texas, April 23, 1847. His father was Chauncey B. Shepard and his mother Mary Hester Andrews. He received his education at Washington College, afterward Washington and Lee University, and served in the Confederate Army during the last years of the war in the 5th Regiment of Texas Mounted Volunteers. He was twice married. After practicing law with great success for twenty-five years, he was appointed in 1893 associate J·stice of the Court of Appeals of the District of Columbia, in add   1 to which he later became a professor in the School of Law of Georgetown University. He wrote "The Siege and Fall of the Alamo," a chapter of much interest in 'Wooten's Comprehensive History of Texas' (Dallas, W. G. Scarff, 1898), and also the Introduction.

SHEPHERD, E. H. Author. [Mo.]. He published an 'Autobiography' and 'The Early History of Missouri.'

SHEPHERD, HENRY ELLIOTT. See Biographical and Critical Sketch, Vol. XI, p. 4775.

SHEPPARD, FRANCIS H. Naval officer. [Mo.]. Born in 1846. He published 'Love Afloat,' a novel.

SHEPPARD, NATHAN, author, was born in Baltimore, Md., November 9, 1834, and died in New York City, January 24, 1888. For several years he was engaged in metropolitan journalism. During the Franco-Prussian War, while representing the Cincinnati *Gazette,* he was imprisoned in Paris, after which he wrote a diary of the siege entitled 'Shut up in Paris' (London, 1871), which was translated into French, German, and Italian. He also made numerous compilations and appeared at frequent intervals upon the lecture platform.

SHERWOOD, ADIEL, Baptist clergyman, was born at Fort Edward, N.Y., October 3, 1791, and died in St. Louis, Mo., August 18, 1879. For many years he resided in Georgia, engaged in religious and educational work, but removed to Missouri after the Civil War. He published a 'Gazetteer of Georgia' (1829; second edition, 1837), 'Christian and Jewish Churches,' and 'Notes on the New Testament.'

SHIELDS, JOSEPH DUNBAR. Author. [Miss.]. Born in 1820. Besides some interesting historical sketches of Natchez, he wrote 'The Life and Times of Sargent S. Prentiss' (Philadelphia, Lippincott and Company, 1883).

SHIELDS, M. OZELLA. Author. [Miss.]. She wrote 'Izma, or, Sunshine and Shadow' (1889), 'Sundered Hearts.' 'Vernon's Mistake,' 'A Sinless Crime,' and other novels.

SHIELDS, S. J. Author. He wrote an interesting story of life in Mississippi entitled 'A Chevalier of Dixie' (New York and Washington, The Neale Publishing Company, 1906).

SHINN, JOSIAH H. Educator and editor. [Ark.]. He was born in 1849. His writings, which bear the stamp of ripe experience and of broad scholarship, include: 'The Public School and the College' (1891), 'The South and Education' (1892), a 'History of the American People' (1893), 'Illustrated Arkansas' (1893), and other works.

SHIPP, ALBERT MICAJAH, educator, was born in Stokes County, N.C., January 15, 1819, entered the ministry of the Methodist Episcopal Church, South, became president of Wofford College, S.C., in 1859, and professor of theology in Vanderbilt University in 1874, succeeding eventually to the office of chancellor of the latter institution. He published 'The History of Methodism in South Carolina' (Nashville, Methodist Episcopal Publishing House).

SHIPP, BERNARD, author, was born near Natchez, Miss., April 30, 1813, but settled in Louisville, Ky., after completing his education, and published 'Fame and Other Poems' (Philadelphia, 1848) and 'The Progress of Freedom and Other Poems' (New York, 1852). He also compiled 'De Soto and Florida' and a volume on 'Indian Antiquities.'

SHIPP, MARGARET BUSBEE, author, was born at Raleigh, N.C., November 9, 1871. Her publications include 'Beautiful Thoughts from Browning' (New York, James Pott and Company, 1900), and 'Beautiful Thoughts from Emerson' (*ibid.* 1901). Besides, she has made frequent contributions to high-class periodicals. The quality of her work is most excellent. She married, January 17, 1894, Lieutenant William Ewen Shipp, U.S.A.

SHOBER, GOTTLIEB, Lutheran clergyman, was born in Bethlehem, Pa., of Moravian stock, November 1, 1756, and died in Salem, S.C., June 27, 1838. At an early age he settled in the South. After reaching his fiftieth year he decided to preach, but chose the Lutheran in preference to the Moravian theology because it was easier to complete the requisite course of preparation. Efforts were made by the Moravians to expel him from Salem, but he possessed large property interests and the opposition was thwarted. He translated Stelling's 'Scenes in the World of Spirits,' and published 'A Comprehensive Account of the Rise and Progress of the Christian Church, by Dr. Martin Luther.'

SHOEMAKER, MICHAEL MYERS, author, was born in Covington, Ky., June 26, 1853. After studying for two years at Cornell, he made a tour of the globe. He has been an unwearied traveler and has published numerous works descriptive of his impressions, among them 'Eastward to the Land of the Morning' (Cincinnati, The Robert Clark Company, 1893), 'The Kingdom of the White Woman' (*ibid.*, 1894), 'The Sealed Provinces of the Czar' (*ibid.*, 1895), 'Quaint Corners of Ancient Empires' (New York, G. P. Putnam's Sons, 1899), and 'Palaces and Prisons of Mary Queen of Scots' (1901). He spends much of his time in Jacksonville, Fla.

SHOEMAKER, WILLIAM LUKENS, poet, was born in Georgetown, D.C., July 19, 1822. He took his degree in medicine, but never practiced his profession. Besides making numerous translations from the German lyric writers, he published songs and ballads, some of which have been included in Piatt's 'Union of American Poetry and Art' (Cincinnati, 1881).

SHORTRIDGE, BELLE HUNT, Mrs. Author. [Texas]. She was born in 1858 and died in 1893. She wielded a versatile pen and published a volume of poems entitled 'Lone Star Lights' (1890), two novels, 'Held in Trust '(1892) and 'Circumstance' (1893), and numerous short stories and sketches.

SHOUP, FRANCIS ASBURY, soldier, educator, clergyman, was born in Franklin County, Ind., March 22, 1834. He was educated at West Point, but resigned from the Army on account of his Southern sympathies, and settled at St. Augustine, Fla., for the practice of law.

At the outbreak of the war he erected a battery at Fernandina, was commissioned a major in the Confederate Army and rose to be a brigadier-general. After the war he was for a time professor of mathematics in the University of Mississippi, and finally became an Episcopal minister. He published 'Infantry Tactics' (Little Rock, 1862), 'Artillery Division Drill' (Atlanta, 1864), 'Elements of Algebra' (New York, 1874), and 'Mechanism and Personality' (1891).

SHREVE, THOMAS H., journalist, was born in Alexandria, Va., in 1808 and died in Louisville, Ky., December 23, 1853. At first he engaged in mercantile pursuits, but he finally relinquished trade for journalism and became an editor, first in Louisville and afterward in Cincinnati. Besides a volume of fiction entitled 'Drayton, an American Tale' (New York, 1851), he published a number of excellent poems, some of which have been reprinted in William T. Coggeshall's 'Poets and Poetry of the West' (Columbus, 1860).

SHRIVER, JOHN SHULTZ, journalist, was born in Baltimore, Md., June 17, 1857, and was educated at Princeton. As correspondent of the New York *Mail and Express*, he accompanied President Harrison on his tour of the country and wrote 'Through the South and West with President Harrison.' He also published 'Almost,' a romance.

SHUCK, HENRIETTA HALL, Baptist missionary to China, was born at Kilmarnock, Va., October 28, 1817, and died in Hong Kong, China, November 27, 1844. She became the wife of the Rev. John L. Shuck, a missionary to China, shared his labors in the foreign field, and wrote a volume of exceptional interest entitled 'Scenes in China, or, Sketches of the Country, Religion and Customs of the Chinese' (Philadelphia, 1852). Jeremiah B. Jeter published her 'Life' (Boston, 1848).

SHUCK, JOHN LEWIS, Baptist missionary to China, was born in Alexandria, Va., September 4, 1812, and died in Barnwell, S.C., August 20, 1863. For years he labored at various mission stations in China and published 'Portfolio Chinensis, or, a Collection of Authentic Chinese Papers' (Macoa, China, 1840). He was one of the Gospel pioneers in the Orient.

SHUCK, L. H. Poet. [N.C.]. He wrote an historical poem entitled "Joan of Arc, the Maid of Orleans," delivered at the time of graduation from Wake Forest College, N.C. (Richmond, Va., J. W. Randolph, 1856).

SHURTER, EDWIN DUBOSE, educator and editor, was for some time instructor of oratory in Leland Stanford and Cornell universities, but is now head of the school of public speaking at the University of Texas. Besides 'Masterpieces of Modern Oratory,' he has published 'The Science and Art of Debate' (New York and Washington, The Neale Publishing Company, 1907), and 'The Oratory of the South' (*ibid.*, 1908), which contains a number of well selected extracts.

SIKES, ENOCH WALTER. Educator. He was born in Union County, N.C., in 1868, the son of John C. and Jane Austin Sikes, was educated at Wake Forest College and at Johns Hopkins University, and married, in 1897, Ruth Wingate. He is professor of history and political economy in Wake Forest College. Included among his writings are: 'From Colony to Commonwealth' (Baltimore,

Johns Hopkins University Press), 'The Confederate Congress,' and 'Joseph Hewes.' Johns Hopkins gave him the degree of Ph.D.

SIMMONS, J. F. Jurist and poet. [Miss.]. He wrote 'The Welded Link, and Other Poems' (Philadelphia, J. B. Lippincott and Company, 1881), and 'Rural Lyrics' (1884). He possessed rare gifts, but professional engagements permitted him to indulge in literary diversions only at intervals.

SIMMONS, JAMES P. Clergyman. [Ga.]. Author of 'The War in Heaven.' He lived for many years at Lawrenceville, Ga.

SIMMONS, JAMES WRIGHT, poet, was born in South Carolina and was educated at Harvard. On completing his studies, he traveled for some time in Europe; but, after returning home, he settled in the pioneer belt. Several volumes came from his pen, including 'The Maniac's Confession' (Philadelphia, 1821), 'Blue Beard; or, the Marshal of France' (*ibid.*, 1822), and 'The Greek Girl' (Boston, 1852). He published also a series of metrical tales called 'Wood-notes from the West.'

SIMMONS, WILLIAM HAYNE, physician and poet, was born in South Carolina about 1785, studied medicine in Philadelphia and settled first in Charleston and afterward in East Florida. He published an Indian poem entitled "Onea" and 'A History of the Seminoles.'

SIMMONS, WILLIAM JOHNSON, clergyman and educator, was born of African parentage in Charleston, S.C., June 29, 1849, and after studying for the Baptist ministry, was duly ordained. His writings include 'Men of Mark' (Cleveland, Ohio, 1877), and a 'History of the Colored Baptists of Kentucky.'

SIMMS, WILLIAM GILMORE. See Biographical and Critical Sketch, Vol. XI, page 4793.

SIMONTON, CHARLES H. Lawyer. [S.C.]. He published a work on 'The Federal Courts' (1899).

SIMS, ALEXANDER DROMGOOLE, lawyer, was born in Brunswick County, Va., June 11, 1803, and died in Kingstree, S.C., November 11, 1848. After receiving his diploma from the University of North Carolina, he studied law, became an eloquent advocate at the Bar, and served in Congress from 1845 till his death. He published a controversial paper on slavery and a novel entitled 'Bevil Faulcon.'

SIMS, FREDERICK WILMER, lawyer, was born in Louisa County, Va., July 23, 1862. As a member of the Bar he takes high rank. Besides occasional articles contributed to the *Virginia Law Register*, he is the author of the sketch of Patrick Henry in 'The Library of Southern Literature.' He is a member of the present State Senate of Virginia (1909).

SIMS, JAMES MARION, an eminent surgeon and author, was born in Lancaster County, S.C., January 25, 1813, and died in New York City, November 13, 1883. After receiving his medical diploma from the Jefferson Medical College, in Philadelphia, he returned home to engage in the active practice, but afterward settled in Alabama. On account of his phenomenal success in the treatment of aggravated cases of disease, and in the performance of certain delicate surgical operations, he acquired an international reputation and moved eventually to New York, where he organized the Woman's Hospital of the State of New York, and became an authority whose name commanded respect on both sides of the water. Jefferson College conferred upon him the degree of LL.D.; in France he was made a knight of the Legion of Honor, and in various other countries he was the recipient of similar honors. Besides numerous contributions to medical and scientific journals, he published a treatise on 'Ovariotomy,' and, just before his death, wrote 'The Story of My Life' (New York, 1884). Dr. Thomas A. Emmet subsequently published his 'Memoir.'

SINCLAIR, ARTHUR. Naval officer. He attained the rank of lieutenant in the Confederate States Navy and published an interesting personal narrative entitled 'Two Years of the Alabama' (Boston, Lee and Shepard, 1896).

SINCLAIR, CARRIE BELLE, poet, was born in Milledgeville, Ga., in 1839. Her father was Elijah Sinclair, a Methodist minister. She was a niece of Robert Fulton; and the story is told that while the inventor was visiting his sister, in Augusta, where the family then resided, his attention was called to the experiments of William Longstreet in steam propelling, a circumstance which may have furnished the inspiration of his famous achievement. During the war she gave much of her time to the care of wounded soldiers in the hospitals at Savannah. Miss Sinclair was the author of two very popular pieces, entitled "Georgia, My Georgia" and "The Homespun Dress," besides a number of war lyrics; and she also published a collection of her poems in a volume entitled 'Heart Whispers; or, Echoes of Song' (1872). After the war she resided in Philadelphia.

SIOUSSAT, ST. GEORGE LEAKIN. Educator. He was born in Baltimore, Md., March 13, 1878, the son of Albert W. and Annie Leaken Sioussat, graduated from Johns Hopkins University, and became professor of history and economics in the University of the South in 1904. Included among his writings, which are mainly in the line of historical research, are: 'Statistics of State Aid to Higher Education' (Baltimore, Johns Hopkins University Press), 'Highway Legislation in Maryland,' 'Economics and Politics in Maryland' (*ibid.*), and 'The English Statutes in Maryland' (*ibid.*), in addition to numerous historical papers and reviews. He resides in Sewanee, Tenn. Johns Hopkins gave him the degree of Ph.D.

SJOLANDER, J. P. See Biographical and Critical Sketch, Vol. XI, page 4833.

SKINNER, JOHN STUART, editor, was born in Maryland, February 22, 1788. At one time he was mayor of Baltimore. He edited a number of agricultural papers from time to time and translated a number of foreign works dealing with agricultural topics. He died March 21, 1851.

SKINNER, THOMAS E. Baptist clergyman. [N.C.]. He published 'Reminiscences, Sermons and Addresses' (1894).

SKINNER, THOMAS HARVEY, clergyman and educator, was born in Harvey's Neck, N.C., March 7, 1791, and died in New York City, February 1, 1871. After receiving his diploma from Princeton, he studied theology and became pastor of the Mercer Street Presbyterian Church of New York. In 1848 he became professor of sacred rhetoric and pastoral theology in Union Seminary, in New York. He was an able teacher and one of the foremost pulpit orators of the day. Besides contributing to the religious press, he published 'The Religion of the Bible' (New York, 1839), 'Aids to Preaching and Hearing' (Philadelphia, 1839), 'Hints to Christians' (1841), 'Discussions in Theology' (New York, 1868), and 'Thoughts on Evangelizing the World' (1870). He also translated 'Vinet's Pastoral Theology' and 'Vinet's Homiletics.' He received both his D.D. and his LL.D. degrees from Williams.

SLAUGHTER, PHILIP, clergyman, was born in Culpeper County, Va., October 26, 1808. He received his education at the University of Virginia, and after practicing law for five years, he entered the Episcopal priesthood, ministered to numerous parishes, and edited various periodicals. He received the degree of D.D. from William and Mary College and made large contributions to literature. His writings include: 'St. George's Parish History' (Richmond, 1847), 'Man and Woman' (1860), 'Life of Randolph Fairfax' (1862), 'Life of Colonel Joshua Fry, Sometime Professor in William and Mary Colege and Washington's Senior in Command of Virginia's Forces in 1754' (New York, 1880), "Historic Churches of Virginia," in Bishop Perry's 'Centennial History' (1882), 'Life of Hon. William Green, Jurist and Scholar' (Richmond, 1883), 'Views from Cedar Mountain, in Fifty Years of Ministry and Marriage' (New York, 1884), 'The Colonial Church of Virginia' (1885), 'Christianity the Key to the Character and Career of Washington' (1886), and 'An Address to the Minute-men of Culpeper' (1887).

SLAUGHTER, WILLIAM BANK, lawyer, was born in Culpeper County, Va., April 10, 1798, and died in Madison, Wis., July 21, 1879. He was educated at William and Mary College and practiced law for several years at Bardstown, Ky., after which he settled in the Northwest. He contributed to various periodicals and wrote 'Reminiscences of Distinguished Men I Have Met' (Milwaukee, 1878).

SLEDD, ANDREW. Educator. He was born in Lynchburg, Va., November 7, 1870, the son of Robert Newton and Frances Carey Greene Sledd, and was educated at Randolph-Macon College and Yale and Harvard universities. He married, March 14, 1899, Annie Florence, daughter of Bishop Warren A. Chandler. He was professor of Latin for four years at Emory College, and president of the University of Florida from 1904 to 1909. While he has published no books, he has frequently contributed important articles to magazines. and is one of the consulting editors of 'The Library of Southern Literature.' Dr. Sledd has received both the Ph.D. and the LL.D degrees.

SLEDD, BENJAMIN. See Biographical and Critical Sketch, Vol. XI, page 4851.

SLEDD, R. N. Clergyman. [Va.]. He published 'True Heroism, and Other Sermons' (1900).

SLENKER, ELMINA DRAKE. Author. He was born in La Grange, N.Y., December 23, 1827, a daughter of Thomas Drake, a Quaker minister who was silenced for heresy, became a free-thinker and bequeathed this independence of religious opinion to the subject of this sketch. She married, in 1856, Isaac Slenker. Under the pen-name of "Aunt Elmina," she has written a number of books. The list includes: 'Little Lessons for Liberal Sunday-schools,' 'Studying the Bible' (1870), 'The Infidel School-Teacher' (1885), 'The Handsomest Woman,' 'The Darwins,' (New York, Truth-Seeker Company), 'Little Lessons for Little Folks' (*ibid.*, 1887), and others. She resides in Snowville, Va.

SLICER, HENRY, clergyman, was born in Annapolis, Md., in 1801, and died in Baltimore, Md., April 23, 1874. He became a minister of some prominence in the Methodist pulpit, was several times elected chaplain of the United States Senate, received his degree of D.D. from Dickinson and published 'An Appeal on Christian Baptism' (New York, 1839). He also delivered and published a sermon against duelling, which aided powerfully in the passage of the act making duels illegal.

SLOAN, ANNIE L. Author. [S.C.]. She wrote an entertaining love story of colonial times in the Palmetto State, entitled 'The Carolinians' (New York and Washington, The Neale Publishing Company, 1907).

SLOAN, J. A., author, of Mississippi, wrote 'Is Slavery a Sin in Itself?—Answered According to Scriptures' (Memphis, 1857).

SMEDES, SUSAN DABNEY. See Biographical and Critical Sketch, Vol. XI, page 4863.

SMILEY, MATILDA. Poet. She published a volume entitled 'Poems by Matilda,' consisting chiefly of verse which she wrote while at school and which a friend published for her in order to raise the funds which were needed to complete her education. The promise of the work was unredeemed by any subsequent publication.

SMITH, A DAVIS. Author. [Ala.]. He published, in association with T. A. Deland, 'Northern Alabama, Historical and Biographical' (1888).

SMITH, ANNIE H., educator and author, was born in Columbia, S.C., in 1850, but soon after her marriage to Whiteford S. Smith, she removed to Atlanta, Ga., where for nearly thirty years she was actively and ably identified with the public school system, most of the time in the capacity of principal. She began her literary career by the publication of a series of lyric poems, and from time to time she also contributed short stories and sketches to periodicals. "Estranged," a novelette, appeared serially in *The Sunny South,* and attracted much attention. She also wrote 'A Christmas Story,' for children (Atlanta, J. P. Harrison and Company, 1883). But her most ambitious work was 'Rosemary Leigh: a Tale of the South,' which narrates the struggles of a brave young girl under post-bellum conditions (New York and Washington, The Neale Publishing Company, 1906). Mrs. Smith died in Atlanta, Ga., August 31, 1909.

SMITH, ASHBEL, physician and diplomat, was born in Hartford, Conn., August 13, 1805, and died in Harris County, Texas, in 1886. Locating in the Lone Star commonwealth, when it was still the Republic of Texas, he became Minister to the United States, under President Houston, and Secretary of State in the Cabinet of President Jones. During the Civil War he commanded the Second Texas Regiment of volunteers. Besides numerous medical papers, he published 'An Account of the Geography of Texas' (1851), and 'The Permanent Identity of the Human Race' (1860).

SMITH, AUGUSTINE MEADE. Lawyer. [Va.]. He published 'Commissioners in Chancery' (1887).

SMITH, BENJAMIN MOSBY, clergyman, was born in Powhatan County, Va., June 30, 1811. After receiving his diploma from Hampden-Sidney College, he studied theology, became an eminent Presbyterian divine, and filled the chair of oriental and Biblical literature in Union Seminary, New York, for fourteen years. Besides numerous sermons and addresses in pamphlet form, he published 'A Commentary on the Psalms and Proverbs' (Glasgow, 1859; Knoxville, 1883) and 'Questions on the Gospels' (Richmond, 1868). Hampden-Sidney gave him his degree of D.D.

SMITH, BUCKINGHAM, antiquarian, was born on Cumberland Island, Ga., October 31, 1810, and died in New York City, January 5, 1871. He studied law at Harvard and practiced for a while in Maine, but afterward moved to Florida. While Secretary of Legation in Mexico he made an exhaustive study of Mexican antiquities and collected many rare books and manuscripts. At Madrid, also, he made thorough researches in the Spanish archives for information respecting the colonial history of Louisiana and Florida. He became a judge of the Superior Court and a part of his library after his death was bought by the Historical Society of New York. Besides contributing to magazines, he made numerous translations of Spanish documents and manuscripts.

SMITH, BURGESS. Poet. [Ga.]. He published a volume of verse entitled 'The Vale of the Haunted Castles.'

SMITH, CHARLES ALPHONSO, educator and editor, who has lately assumed the Edgar Allan Poe professorship of English in the University of Virginia, was formerly head of the department of English and dean of the graduate department in the University of North Carolina. He was born in Greensboro, N.C., May 28, 1864, a son of the late Dr. J. Henry Smith of Greensboro, and a grandson of the late Judge Egbert R. Watson of Charlottesville, Va. After graduation from Davidson College, North Carolina, an institution of which his brother, Dr. Henry Louis Smith, is now president, he first taught in North Carolina schools, and then entered Johns Hopkins University, where he was assistant in English from 1890 to 1893. In the latter year he was elected professor of English in the Louisiana State University, a position which he resigned in 1902 to accept the chair of the English language in the University of North Carolina. He was appointed to his present position in the spring of 1909. While a member of the faculty of the Louisiana State University, Dr. Smith spent one year abroad in study at the British Museum, the University of Paris, and the University of Berlin. He is a member of the executive council of the Modern Language Association of America, and has twice been president of the Central Division. He was also at one time president of the State Literary and Historical Association of North Carolina, and vice-president of the National Educational Association. Before accepting his present position he received the appointment of Roosevelt professor of American literature in the University of Berlin, 1910-1911. He is a member of the Phi Beta Kappa Society, the American Dialect Society, and the Shakespeare Society of Germany. Besides his contributions to foreign and American journals, and his published addresses, he is the author of the following books: 'Repetition and Parallelism in English Verse' (New York, 1894), 'Anglo-Saxon Grammar and Exercise Book' (Boston, 1896; fourth edition, 1903), 'Macaulay's Essays on Milton and Addison' (Richmond, 1901), 'An English-German Conversation Book,' with Dr. Gustav Krüger of Berlin (Boston, 1902), 'Our Language: Grammar' (Richmond, 1903), 'Our Language: Second Book' (Richmond, 1906), and 'Studies in English Syntax' (Boston, 1906). Dr. Smith was one of the associate editors of 'The World's Orators,' a work of ten volumes (New York, 1901), and is also associate literary editor of 'The Library of Southern Literature.' He was married, November 8, 1905, to Susie McGee Heck, of Raleigh, N!C. He received the degree of Ph.D. from Johns Hopkins University and the degree of LL.D. from the University of Mississippi.

SMITH, C. ERNEST. Clergyman. [Md.]. He published 'Religion under the Barons of Baltimore' (1899).

SMITH, CHARLES HENRY ("Bill Arp"). See Biographical and Critical Sketch, Vol. XI, page 4885.

SMITH, CHARLES LEE. Educator. He was born in Wilton, N.C., August 29, 1865, the son of Louis Turner and Nannie G. Smith, graduated from Wake Forest College, and afterward prosecuted his studies at Johns Hopkins University. Later he went abroad. He became professor of history and political science in William Jewell College, at Liberty, Mo., in 1891. He married Sallie Lindsay Jones. Dr. Smith is the author of a 'History of Education in North Carolina' (United States Bureau of Education, 1883), and 'The Money Question' (1894). Johns Hopkins gave him the degree of Ph.D.

SMITH, DAVID THOMAS, physician and lawyer, was born in Hardin County, Ky., November 12, 1840. Besides numerous medical works, he has published 'The Philosophy of Memory, and Other Essays' (Louisville, Ky., John P. Morton and Company, 1899). He resides in Louisville, Ky.

SMITH, EGBERT WATSON, clergyman, was born in Greensboro, N.C., January 15, 1862. His father was the Rev. J. Henry Smith, D.D., and his mother, Mary Kelly Watson. After graduation from Davidson, he studied theology at Union Seminary, in Richmond. For twelve years he was pastor of the First Presbyterian Church of Greensboro, N.C. Since 1906 he has been pastor of the Second Presbyterian Church of Louisville, Ky. Besides numerous sermons, he has published a work of standard value on 'The Creed of Presbyterianism' (New York, Baker and Taylor Company, 1901). He married, April 15, 1891, Mary Wallace. Davidson College gave him the degree of D.D.

SMITH, EUGENE ALLEN. Scientist and educator. He has been professor of geology in the University of Alabama since 1871 and State Geologist since 1873. He was born in Autauga County, Ala., October 24, 1841, the son of Dr. Samuel P. and Adelaide Smith, and was educated at the University of Alabama, at Göttingen and at Berlin. He is the author of numerous important geological papers and reports. The University of Michigan gave him the degree of Sc.D.

SMITH, FRANCIS HENNEY, soldier and educator, was born in Norfolk, Va., October 18, 1812. He was educated at West Point and became an assistant professor in the academy, but resigned in 1836 to become professor of mathematics at Hampden-Sidney; and, later, on the organization of the Virginia Military Institute, he became superintendent. During the Civil War he was stationed by the Confederate authorities at Norfolk in command of the fort, and he also aided in the defence of Richmond. William and Mary College conferred upon him the degree of LL.D. Besides translating Bicot's 'Analytical Geometry' from the French, he published a series of algebras and arithmetics, and wrote 'The Best Methods of Conducting Common Schools' (1849), 'College Reform' (1850), and 'Scientific Education in Europe' (1859). He reorganized the Institute at Lexington at the close of hostilities, and died in 1890.

SMITH, FRANCIS HENRY, educator, was born in Leesburg, Va., October 14, 1829. For more than fifty years he occupied the chair of natural philosophy in the University of Virginia and is still professor emeritus in the same department. His writings, in which he has crystallized his mature studies include: 'Outlines of Physics' (Charlottesville, Anderson Brothers, 1894). 'Christ and Science' (New York, Fleming H. Revell and Company, 1907), 'Nature a Witness' (Chapel Hill, The University Press, 1908), and numerous addresses on scientific and popular subjects. He also wrote the sketch of Matthew F. Maury for 'The Library of Southern Literature.' Dr. Smith married. July 21, 1853, Mary Stuart Harrison. He holds the LL.D. and the D.C.L. degrees.

SMITH, FRANCIS HOPKINSON. See Biographical and Critical Sketch, Vol. XI, page 4909.

SMITH, GEORGE GILMAN. Clergyman and historian. He was born in Newton County, Ga., in the portion which afterward became Rockdale, on December 20, 1836. He was a chaplain in the Confederate Army, entered the ministry of the Methodist Episcopal Church, South, and was twice married. Besides numerous contributions to the secular and religious press, he is the author of the following books: 'History of Methodism in Georgia and Florida' (1877), 'Life of Bishop James O. Andrew,' 'Life of Bishop George F. Pierce' (1888), 'Life of Asbury,' 'Life of John W. Knight,' and 'The Story of Georgia and the Georgia People' (Atlanta, Franklin Publishing Company, 1900). Most of his works have been issued by the Methodist Publishing House, Nashville, Tenn. Dr. Smith resides in Macon, Ga.

SMITH, GUSTAVUS WOODSON, soldier, was born in Scott County, Ky., January 1, 1822, and was educated at West Point. He served with distinction in the Mexican War, but afterward resigned from the United States Army and was employed for some time in the construction of government buildings. At the outbreak of the Civil War he returned to Kentucky, entered the Confederate service, and attained the rank of major-general. He published a volume entitled 'The Battle of Seven Pines' (New York, 1891). General Smith died in New York City, June 23, 1896.

SMITH, HOKE, governor, Cabinet officer, lawyer, was born in Newton, N.C., of sturdy colonial stock; in 1855. His father was Dr. H. H. Smith, an educator of distinction. For the practice of law he located in Atlanta, rose to the front at the Bar, purchased the Atlanta *Journal,* with which he supported Mr. Cleveland, in 1892, and became Secretary of the Interior in the latter's second Cabinet. From 1907 to 1909 he was governor of Georgia. On the hustings he has been an advocate of great power and has campaigned for the national democracy in all parts of the United States. Mr. Smith is one of the advisory council of 'The Library of Southern Literature.' He married, in 1883, Birdie, a daughter of General Thomas R. R. Cobb.

SMITH, JAMES, pioneer, was born in Franklin County, Pa., in 1737, and died in Washington County, Ky., in 1812. When a youth of eighteen he was captured by the Indians and adopted into one of the tribes, but escaped, took part in the struggle for independence, and settled after the Revolution at Cane Bridge, near Paris, Ky., and became active in State politics. He published 'Remarkable Adventures in the Life and Travels of Colonel James Smith,' a work edited by William M. Darlington (Lexington, 1799; republished, Cincinnati, 1870), a 'Treatise on the Mode and Manner of Indian Warfare' (Paris, Ky., 1804), and two tracts on 'Shakerism.'

SMITH, JAMES TINKER. Poet. He was born in St. Mary's Parish, La., in 1816. Bereft of his parents at an early age, he was sent by his guardian to Scotland for his education, and graduated in due season from the University of Edinburgh. On returning home he took active charge of an immense estate left to him by his parents. Being an excellent French scholar, he translated into English the 'Meditations of Lamartine,' and in the volume, which he published in 1852, several of his own poems were included. He died in Franklin, La., August 10, 1854.

SMITH, JOHN. See Biographical and Critical Sketch, Vol. XI, page 4929.

SMITH, JOHN AUGUSTINE, physician, was born in Westmoreland County, Va., August 29, 1782, and died in New York, February 9,

1865. For twelve years he was president of William and Mary College, his *alma mater*, after which he practiced his profession in New York and became president of the College of Physicians and Surgeons. He published numerous lectures and essays.

SMITH, JOHN LAWRENCE, chemist, was born near Charleston, S.C., December 17, 1818, and died in Louisville, Ky., October 12, 1883. After graduating from the University of Virginia, he studied medicine, spent some time in France and Germany at the scientific schools, established the *Medical and Surgical Journal* of South Carolina on his return home, and became one of the foremost authorities of the day in the analysis of soils and minerals. At the invitation of the Sultan of Turkey, he spent some time in Asia Minor, giving instruction to the farmers in regard to the culture of cotton. For several years he filled the chair of chemistry at the University of Virginia, and afterward became identified with the University of Louisville, where he remained for the rest of his days. The highest honors were paid to him by men of science and by European sovereigns. He published numerous papers, the most important of which were collected and published under the title of 'Mineralogy and Chemistry, Original Researches' (Louisville, 1873; revised, 1884). Dr. Smith's collection of meteorites, one of the largest and richest in existence, became by purchase the property of Harvard University.

SMITH, JOSIAH, clergyman, was born in Charleston, S.C., in 1704, and died in Philadelphia, Pa., in 1781. For several years he was pastor of the Presbyterian Church in Charleston. He espoused the cause of independence, and, at the fall of Charleston, was made a prisoner of war and taken to Philadelphia, where he died in prison. He was an eloquent divine, delivered numerous public addresses, and published a volume of sermons (Charleston, 1852).

SMITH, LANGDON, journalist, was born in Kentucky, January 4, 1857, and was educated in the public schools. During his boyhood he served in the Comanche and Apache wars and was afterward war correspondent in Cuba for New York papers. Besides numerous short stories and sketches he has published 'On the Panhandle,' a work of much interest.

SMITH, MARGARET VOWELL. Author. She was born in Louisville, Ky., March 2, 1839, the daughter of Francis Lee and Sarah Smith, graduated from the Virginia Female Institute, at Staunton, Va., and afterward studied languages at one of the first schools of the day in Philadelphia. She is actively connected with many patriotic organizations. Most of her writings have been in the line of historical research. They include: 'The Governors of Virginia,' 'Virginia 1492-1892,' and 'Notes on the History of the Constitution of Virginia.' She lives in Alexandria, Va.

SMITH, MARY STUART. See Biographical and Critical Sketch, Vol. XI, page 4947.

SMITH, NATHAN RYNO, physician and surgeon, was born in Concord, N.H., May 21. 1797, and died in Baltimore, Md., July 3, 1877. For thirty years he filled the chair of surgery in the University of Maryland. Besides numerous medical works he published under the penname of "Viator," a volume entitled 'The Legends of the South.'

SMITH, NELSON FORT. Lawyer and editor. He was born in 1813 and died in 1861. He wrote 'The History of Pickens County, Ala., from the First Settlement in 1817.' It was published in Carrollton, Ala., in 1856. The work throws interesting light upon the early pioneer days.

SMITH, PETER FRANCISCO, lawyer and writer, of Georgia. For several years he has been one of the leading members of the Atlanta Bar. He is an accomplished English scholar; and, besides several legal text-books, has published a work on philology which has attracted much attention.

SMITH, S. E. D., Mrs. She published 'The Soldier's Friend; or, Experiences in Southern Hospitals' (1867).

SMITH, SARA HENDERSON. Poet. She was the wife of General Francis H. Smith, who was for many years professor of mathematics in the Virginia Military Institute at Lexington. Her literary gifts were devoted largely to religious veins of thought, and her volume entitled 'Up to the Light, with Other Religious and Devotional Poems' (New York, 1884) is a work of much interest.

SMITH, SOLOMON FRANKLIN, actor, was born in Norwich, N.Y., April 20, 1801, and died in St. Louis, Mo., April 20, 1869. For many years he followed the theatrical profession and achieved a reputation as a comedian, but he afterward became a lawyer in St. Louis and rose to some prominence at the Bar. He published 'Theatrical Apprenticeship' (Philadelphia, 1845), 'Theatrical Journey Work' (1854), and an 'Autobiography' (1868).

SMITH, THOMAS BERRY. Educator. He was born near Bowling Green, Mo., December 7, 1850, the son of William Hugh and Isabella Smith, graduated from Pritchard College, and afterward pursued special studies at Yale University. He married, in 1877, Emma Marvin Newland, and became professor of chemistry and physics in Central College in 1886. From his scientific pen have come not only many important contributions to the literature of his department of thought and research, but also many graceful poems. Included among his writings are: 'Studies in Nature and Language Lessons' (New York, D. C. Heath and Company), 'In Many Moods,' a volume of poems, and numerous articles for the educational journals. His poem entitled "Two Weddings" was published separately in 1902. He resides in Fayette, Mo.

SMITH, WILLIAM, statesman, was born in North Carolina in 1762 and died in Huntsville, Ala., June 10, 1840. For some time he practiced law in Charleston, S.C., became a circuit judge, a Member of Congress, and a Senator of the United States. In the race for reëlection to the Upper Federal Chamber he was defeated by Robert Y. Hayne, but he was afterward returned by appointment to fill an unexpired term. While serving in this distinguished body he was twice president *pro tem.;* and in the campaign of 1829 he received Georgia's electoral vote for Vice-president of the United States. He declined an appointment to the Federal Supreme Court, and retired to his plantation, near Huntsville, Ala., where he died, leaving a very large estate.

SMITH, WILLIAM ANDREW, clergyman, was born in Fredericksburg, Va., November 29, 1802, and died in Richmond, Va., March 1, 1870. For twenty years he was president of Randolph-Macon College. He wielded a strong influence in the councils of Methodism, edited *The Christian Advocate,* and published 'Lectures on the Philosophy of Slavery,' (Richmond, 1860), in which he defended the institution.

SMITH, WILLIAM BENJAMIN. See Biographical and Critical Sketch, Vol. XI, page 4965.

SMITH, WILLIAM CUNNINGHAM, educator, was born at Greensboro, N.C., in 1871. His father was Samuel C. Smith and his mother, Ella Cunningham. He is head of the English department of the State Normal College, Greensboro, N.C. Besides numerous articles in educational and literary journals, he wrote the sketch of Cornelia Spencer for 'The Library of Southern Literature.' He married, in 1897, Gertrude Allen.

SMITH, WILLIAM LOUGHTON, diplomat, was born in Charleston, S.C., in 1758, and died in Charleston, S.C., in 1812. For thirteen years he studied and traveled abroad. He was elected to the First Congress over David Ramsay, the historian, who unsuccessfully made a contest. Later he represented the Government in various diplomatic capacities. His works include: 'Speeches in the House of Representatives of the United States' (London, 1794), a 'Comparative View of the Constitution' (Philadelphia, 1796) and 'American Arguments for British Rights' (London, 1806), a series of essays which were first published over the signature of "Phocion." He also wrote a pamphlet in opposition to Mr. Jefferson's election, and published several addresses, including a "Fourth of July Oration" (1796).

SMITH, W. ROY. [S.C.]. He wrote 'South Carolina as a Royal Province' (New York, The Macmillan Company, 1908), an important work.

SMITH, WILLIAM RUSSELL. See Biographical and Critical Sketch, Vol. XI, page 4985.

SMITH, WILLIAM WAUGH. Educator. He was born in Warrentown, Va., March 12, 1845, the son of Professor Richard M. Smith. He served in the Confederate Army and was twice wounded. After the war he received his collegiate education at Randolph-Macon College. He married Marion Love Howison, and became president of Randolph-Macon College in 1897. He was active in raising large sums for the institution over which he presides. Dr. Smith is the author of several text-books, among the number being: 'Outlines of Psychology' and 'A Comparative Chart of Syntax,' and a number of poems have come from his graceful pen. He resides in Lynchburg, Va. He holds the degree of LL.D.

SMITH, ZACHARIAH FREDERICK. Author. He was born in Henry County, Ky., January 7, 1827, the son of Zachariah and Mildred Smith, received a collegiate education and was twice married. He originated the present school system of Kentucky, and organized the Cumberland and Ohio Railroad. His writings include: an excellent 'History of Kentucky,' 'Memoirs of the Mother of Henry Clay' a 'School History of Kentucky,' and 'The Battle of New Orleans.' He resides in Louisville, Ky.

SMITH, ZODA G. Poet. [Tenn.]. Author of a volume of verse entitled 'Poems' (1867).

SMITHDEAL, GEORGE MICHAEL. Educator. [N.C.]. Born in 1855. He published 'Bookkeeping: Theory and Practice.'

SMITHEY, ROYALL BASCOM. Educator. He was born in Amelia County, Va., January 20, 1851, the son of Royall B. and Mary Ann Hubbard Smithey, graduated from Randolph-Macon College, and married, July 15, 1896, Annie Shackelford. He became professor of mathematics in Randolph-Macon College in 1878. Besides numerous contributions to periodicals, his writings include: 'History of Virginia' (New

York, D. Appleton and Company) and 'Civil Government in Virginia' (*ibid.*) He resides in Ashland, Va.

SMYTH, ELLISON ADGER, educator, was born at Summerton, S.C., October 26, 1863. At present he is professor of biology in the Virginia Polytechnic Institute. Besides the sketch of John Bennett in 'The Library of Southern Literature' he has written numerous papers on insects in the *Entomological News,* notes on birds in the *Auk,* and various bulletins from the Virginia Experiment Station. He married Grace C. Allen, of Charleston. The University of Alabama gave him the degree of LL.D.

SMYTH, JOHN FERDINAND. British soldier. During the middle of the Eighteenth Century he traveled extensively in the United States, and for several years cultivated a plantation in Maryland. At the outbreak of the Revolution he remained loyal to England and taking refuge in the Dismal Swamp of Virginia, he was captured only to make another escape, and finally he obtained secret passage back home. He published in two volumes, 'A Tour of the United States of America' (London, 1784; France, 1781), a work concerning which John Randolph observed that while it was replete with calumny and falsehood, it contained the truest picture extant of the state of society in Virginia.

SMYTH, THOMAS, clergyman, author, scholar, was born in Belfast, Ireland, July 14, 1808, and died in Charleston, S.C., August 20, 1873. He received his collegiate education at the Royal College of Belfast, after which he continued his studies in London. On coming to the United States in 1830 he entered Princeton Seminary to prepare for his ministerial career, and two years later became pastor of the Second Presbyterian Church of Charleston, S.C., a charge which he served continuously for more than forty years. He was a profound thinker, a gifted theologian, and a voluminous writer; by virtue of which qualifications he became a power in the councils of Southern Presbyterians. The bibliography of this eminent divine includes the following works: 'Lecutres on the Prelatical Doctrine of Apostolic Succession' (1840), an 'Ecclesiastical Catechism of the Presbyterian Church' (1841), 'Presbytery and Not Prelacy, the Scriptural and Primitive Polity' (1843), 'The History, Character and Results of the Westminster Assembly of Divines' (1844), 'Calvin and His Enemies' (1844), 'The Romish and Prelatical Rite of Confirmation Examined' (1844), 'The Name, Nature and Functions of Ruling Elders' (1845), 'Union to Christ and His Church' (1846). 'The Nature and Claims of Young Men's Christian Associations' (1857), 'Faith, the Principle of Missions' (1857), 'Why Do I Live?' (1857), 'The Well in the Valley' (1857), and 'Obedience, the Life of Missions.' Dr. Smyth held both the D.D. and the LL.D. degrees; and left at the time of his death a library of 12,000 volumes.

SMYTHE, JAMES M. Author. [Ga.]. He wrote a novel entitled 'Ethel Somers; or, the Fate of the Union' (1857).

SNEAD, GEORGIA TILLMAN. Author. [Va.]. She published 'Beneath Virginia Skies' (1904).

SNEAD, MARTHA GEORGE TILLMAN, Mrs. Author. Her birthplace is unknown, but is credited by Miss Manly to the South. She wrote 'My Soul's Experience in the Unseen World' (1900).

SNEAD, THOMAS L. See Biographical and Critical Sketch, Vol., XI, page 5009.

SNEED, JOHN LOUIS TAYLOR, soldier and jurist, was born in Raleigh, N.C., May 12, 1820, settled in Memphis, Tenn., for the practice of law, became a brigadier-general in the Confederate Army, a judge of the Supreme Court, and published 'Reports of the Supreme Court of Tennessee, 1854-1859.'

SNIDER, DENTON J., author, was born at Mount Gilead, Ohio, but, after completing his studies at Oberlin College, he settled in St. Louis, Mo. for his life's work. His writings include: 'Commentaries on the Literary Bibles,' in nine volumes, (three on Shakespeare and two each on Goethe, Dante, and Homer), 'Walks in Hellas,' 'The Free-burgers,' a novel, 'World's Fair Studies,' 'Commentaries on Froebel's Play Songs,' 'Psychology and the Psychosis,' 'The Will,' 'The Psychology of Froebel's Play Gifts,' 'The Life of Frederick Froebel,' 'The Father of History: Herodotus,' 'Social Institutions,' 'The State,' 'Ancient European Philosophy,' 'Modern European Philosophy,' 'Architecture,' and 'A Tour in Europe.' Besides, he has also written much in verse, including "Delphic Days," "Agamemnon's Daughter," "Homer in Chios," and "Johnny Appleseed's Rhyme." On the lecture platform he is in very great demand.

SNODDY, J. S. Educator. [Mo.]. He edited a 'Little Book of Missouri Verse' (1898).

SNYDER, ANN E. HILL, Mrs. Author. [Tenn.]. She published 'My Scrap Book,' 'On the Wautauga and the Cumberland,' and 'The Civil War' (1893).

SNYDER, HENRY NELSON. Educator. He was born in Macon, Ga., January 14, 1865, a son of H. N. and Ann Hill Snyder, graduated from Vanderbilt University and spent four years in pursuing special studies both at home and abroad. He married, July 9, 1889, Lula E. Ewbank. He became professor of English literature in Wofford College in 1890 and president in 1902, and is one of the consulting editors of 'The Library of Southern Literature.' Besides numerous articles in reviews and magazines on literary and educational subjects, he is the author of 'Sidney Lanier: A Study.'. He resides in Spartanburg, S. C. Dr. Synder holds the degrees of Litt.D. and LL.D.

SOMERVILLE, WILLIAM CLARKE, author, was born in St. Mary's County, Md., March 25, 1790, and died in Auxerre, France, January 5, 1826. He was a man of means who purchased Stratford House, the home of General Henry Lee, became minister to Sweden and published 'Letters from Paris on the Causes and Consequences of the French Revolution' (Baltimore, 1822), besides political essays and poems. At the time of his death he was engaged to Cora, the daughter of Edward Livingston. In earlier life he took part in the struggles of the South American States for independence and was given large grants of lands.

SORREL, G. M. Soldier and merchant. [Ga.]. During the Civil War he was, first, Longstreet's chief of staff and afterward brigadier-general in the Army of Northern Virginia. He died at his home in Savannah, Ga., in 1901. General Sorrel wrote an exceedingly interesting personal narrative entitled 'Recollections of a Confederate Staff Officer' which was published with an introduction by Senator John W. Daniel, of Virginia (New York and Washington, The Neale Publishing Company, 1900).

SOULÉ, PIERRE. One of the foremost orators and public men of Louisiana during the ante-bellum period. He was born at Castillon, France, in 1802. Detected in a plot against the Bourbons, in 1825, he was subsequently pardoned and allowed to proceed to Paris; but his editorial expressions while on the staff of one of the papers gave renewed offence to the royal court. This time he decided to quit the country rather than endure longer the restraint upon his freedom of thought. After moving from place to place, he finally settled in New Orleans. Years later he was first appointed and afterward elected to represent Louisiana in the Senate of the United States. Subsequently he became Minister to Spain. He supported Stephen A. Douglas for President in 1860 and opposed secession. His speeches, which are preserved in the *Congressional Globe,* are full of the fire of the advocate and show him to have been the possessor of an eloquence of the highest type. (See 'The Louisiana Book,' 1894.) He died in New Orleans, March 26, 1870.

'SOUTH CAROLINA WOMEN IN THE CONFEDERACY,' a work of much interest to which contributions were made by various authors.

SOUTHWORTH, EMMA DOROTHY ELIZA NEVILLE, author, was the eldest daughter of Captain Charles L. Neville, a Virginian, and was born in Washington, D.C., December 26, 1819. Her mother was Susan Wailes, of Maryland. She was indebted to her stepfather, Joshua Henshaw, of Boston, for her education and after graduating from his select school she began to teach. Later, in 1840, she became the wife of Frederick H. Southworth, but her marriage was not an ideal one and she resumed her place in the school-room. Domestic sorrows almost overwhelmed her, but she struggled through the deep waters, began to write for the periodicals in a vein which caught the fancy of the public, and ere long earned an income which made her independent. Few writers of fiction have possessed an imagination more vivid or wielded a pen more graphic and fluent. Her stories which aggregated more than sixty in number were eagerly read by the English-speaking masses and some of them were translated into foreign languages. She has faithfully mirrored Southern life and character in many of the incidents which she portrays. Included among her best-known works, most of which first appeared serially in the New York *Ledger,* are 'Retribution,' 'Unknown,' 'The Hidden Hand,' 'An Exile's Bride,' 'The Irish Visitor,' 'Gloria,' 'The Trail of the Serpent,' 'Nearest and Dearest,' 'The Mother's Secret,' 'Children of the Isle,' 'The Curse of Clifton,' 'Mark Sutherland,' 'The Haunted Home,' 'The Deserted Wife,' 'Shannondale,' 'The Fatal Secret,' and 'Rose Elmer.' For twenty-five years her home was on the Virginia side of the Potomac overlooking the city of Washington. She afterward removed to Yonkers, N.Y.; but eventually returned to Washington where she died June 30, 1899.

SPALDING, JOHN LANCASTER, Roman Catholic bishop, was born in Lebanon, Ky., June 2, 1840. At an early age he entered Mount St. Mary's College, at Emmitsburg, Md., and, after receiving his diploma from this institution, he continued his studies abroad, first in Belgium and afterward in Rome. On his return to the United States he became secretary to the bishop of Louisville and organized for the Catholic negroes of Louisville the Church of St. Augustine, for which he also built a house of worship. Still later he became chancellor of the diocese. In 1872 he engaged in missionary work in the parish of St. Michael in New York, where his reputation as an eloquent preacher and lecturer brought him into wide recognition. When the diocese of Peoria was created in 1877, his preëminent fitness for the office of bishop was so apparent that he was duly consecrated to the care and oversight of the diocese; nor was choice ever more wisely made, if the phenomenal prosperity of the diocese is the standard by which we are to judge. For the great Catholic University he was also an ardent worker from the start, being one of the pioneers of this splendid educational enterprise. In the realm of letters Bishop Spalding has deservedly taken high rank by reason of the scholarship and vigor of his writings. Besides a biography of his uncle, Archbishop M. J. Spalding, he has published 'Essays and Reviews,' 'The Religious Mission of the Irish People,' 'Lectures and Discourses,' 'Education and the Higher Life,' 'Things of the Mind,' 'Means and Ends of Education,' 'Thoughts and Theories of Life and Education,' 'America and Other Poems,' 'The Poet's Praise,' 'Songs,' 'Agnosticism and Education,' 'Aphorisms and Reflections,' 'Socialism and Labor,' 'The Spalding Year Book,' and 'Religion and Art.' The verse of Bishop Spalding is characterized by emotional warmth and by artistic finish. He resides in Peoria, Ill.

SPALDING, MARTIN JOHN, Roman Catholic clergyman and Archbishop of Baltimore, was born near Lebanon, Ky., in 1810. His education was begun in this country but completed at Rome, Italy; and it was at this fountain-head of the Church that he was ordained to the priesthood. In 1848 he became bishop coadjutor; in 1850, bishop; and finally in 1864 Archbishop of Baltimore. His published works include: 'Early Catholic Missions in Kentucky' (1846), 'Lectures on the General Evidences of Christianity' (1847), a work which passed into several editions; 'The Life of the Right Rev. B. J. Flaget' (1852), his predecessor at Louisville, 'Miscellanea' (1855), and 'The History of the Protestant Reformation' (1860). He died in Baltimore, Md., February 7, 1872. Bishop Spalding was an able administrator, a vigorous writer and a profound theologian.

SPARKS, WILLIAM HENRY, author, was born on St. Simon's Island, Ga., January 16, 1800, and died in Marietta, Ga., January 13, 1882. For ten years he was a partner of Judah P. Benjamin in the practice of law in New Orleans. He also owned and operated at one time an extensive sugar plantation near Natchez, Miss. During the latter years of his life much of his time was given to literary composition, and he published an interesting volume of reminiscences entitled 'Memories of Fifty Years' (Philadelphia, 1870), and numerous poems. He left at his death enough written material for another volume of reminiscences, besides three stories in manuscript: 'Father Anselmo's Ward,' 'Shilecah,' and 'The Woman with the Iron-gray Hair.'

SPARROW, WILLIAM, Protestant Episcopal clergyman and educator, was born in Charlestown, Mass., March 12, 1801, and died in Alexandria, Va., January 17, 1874. For nearly twenty-five years he was professor in the seminary at Alexandria and both as a sermonizer and as a scholar he took high rank. During his lifetime he published only an occasional sermon or tract but after his death numerous selections from his manuscripts were published in a volume entitled 'The Life and Correspondence of the Rev. William Sparrow, D.D.' (Philadelphia, 1876).

SPECHT, Mrs. Author. [Mo.]. She wrote a novel entitled 'Alfrieda.'

SPEECE, CONRAD, clergyman, was born in New Lebanon, Va., November 7, 1776, and died in Staunton, Va., February 15, 1836. For twenty-two years he was pastor of the Baptist Church at Staunton, a man of eloquence and of power. He published 'The Mountaineer,' a volume of essays, besides occasional poems. Princeton gave him the degree of D.D.

SPEED, JOHN GILMER. Author and editor. He was born in Kentucky, September 24, 1853, the son of Philip and Emma Keats Speed, was an engineer by profession, but subsequently entered journalism and edited first *The American Magazine* and afterward *Leslie's Weekly*. His writings, which are terse and graphic, include: 'A Life of John Keats,' 'A Fall River Incident,' 'The Gilmers in America,' 'A Deal in Denver,' and 'The Horse in America.' Besides, he edited 'The Letters and Poems of John Keats,' and contributed numerous sketches and stories to the leading magazines. He died at Mendham, N.J., in 1909.

SPEED, THOMAS. Lawyer. He was born in Bardstown, Ky., November 26, 1841, the son of Thomas Spencer and Sarah Whitney Speed, received a collegiate education, served in the Union Army, and participated in numerous engagements. He studied law at the University of Michigan and in the office of James Speed, President Lincoln's attorney-general. He married Lucy Buckner. In 1902 he became clerk of the United States Court. His writings include: 'Records and Memorials of the Speed Family' (1892), 'The Union Regiments of Kentucky,' 'The Union Cause in Kentucky, (New York, G. P. Putnam's Sons, 1897), and 'The Wilderness Road,' published by the Filson Club, of which he was one of the organizers. He died in 1906.

SPEER, EMORY. Lawyer. United States Judge for the Southern District of Georgia and an eminent orator. He was born in Colloden, Ga., September 3, 1848, a son of the Rev. Eustace W. and Anne E. Speer, and served in the Confederate Army while still a youth. He graduated from the University of Georgia, studied law, was admitted to the Bar, and soon afterward became Solicitor-general. He represented the Ninth District in Congress for two consecutive terms, from 1879 to 1883, and was an independent Democrat until, taking issue with his party on important public questions, he became a Republican. After being United States Attorney for two years, he was appointed in 1885 United States Judge. He married, first, September 8, 1869, Sallie Dearing and, second, July 14, 1881, Eleanor Morgan. His published works include: 'The Removal of Causes' (Boston, Little, Brown and Company, 1888), 'Lectures on the Constitution' (Macon, J. W. Burke Company, 1897), 'Lincoln, Lee, Grant and Other Biographical Addresses' (Washington and New York, The Neale Publishing Company, 1910). To enumerate the addresses which this distinguished public speaker has delivered in various parts of the country is beyond the scope of this brief sketch; but they constitute too imporant a contribution to literature to be underestimated. The most notable are: "The Education of Woman," annual address, Wesleyan Female College, Macon, Ga., 1888; "Our Country," annual address, Chi Phi Convention, New York, 1892; "General James Edward Oglethorpe," an address before the Georgia Society of the Sons of the American Revolution, Savannah, Ga., 1894; "General U. S. Grant," an address before the Grant Birthday Association, at Galena, Ill., 1898; "The War with Spain," an address at the Peace Jubilee in Chicago, 1898; "A New America," the Centennial Alumni Oration at the University of Georgia, Athens, Ga., 1901; "Robert E. Lee," annual address at Emory College, Oxford, Ga., 1904; the opening address at the Cotton States and International Exposition, Atlanta, Ga., 1905; the Storr Foundation Lectures before the Law School of Yale University, New Haven, Conn., comprising "Alexander Hamilton," "John Marshall," "Joseph E. Brown," "Robert E. Lee," and "The Initiative of the President," 1906; "Thomas, Lord Erskine," an address before the American Bar Association, Seattle, Wash., 1908; "Abraham Lincoln," an address on the one-hundredth birthday of the martyred President, New York, 1909; and numerous others, in addition to speeches delivered in Congress, before juries, and on political platforms. For several years Judge Speer has been dean of the Law School of Mercer University. He resides at "The Cedars," Macon, Ga.

SPELMAN, HENRY, colonist, was born in England about 1600, and died in Virginia in 1622. Under Captain Rutcliff he was one of a party of reconnoiterers who fell into the hands of the Indians, all of whom were slain except himself. As in the case of Captain Smith, his life was saved by Pocahontas, but he was afterward rescued and, having acquired the language of the savages, he became an interpreter whose services were of great value. However, he was eventually killed by the redmen. At the time of his death he left a manuscript entitled a 'Relation of Virginia' which over two centuries later fell into the hands of James F. Hunnewell of Massachusetts, who privately printed an edition of the work (London, 1872).

SPENCE, IRVING, author, was a brother of United States Senator John Shelby Spence, lived in Maryland, and wrote 'The Early History of the Presbyterian Church' (Philadelphia, 1835).

SPENCE, W. J. D. Author. [Tenn.]. In collaboration with David L. Spence he wrote a 'History of Hickman County' (1900).

SPENCER, CORNELIA. See Biographical and Critical Sketch, Vol. XI, page 5049.

SPENCER, EDWARD. Dramatic editor. [Md.]. Born in 1834. He wrote a play entitled "Kit."

SPENCER, JOHN HENDERSON. Baptist clergyman. [Ky.]. He published a 'Life of J. T. Fisher' (1866) and a 'History of Kentucky Baptists' (1886).

SPENCER, WILLIAM LORING, Mrs., author, was born in St. Augustine, Fla. Her father was Albert A. Nunez and her uncle, for whom she was named, was General William W. Loring. She married General George E. Spencer and published several volumes of fiction, including 'Salt Lake Fruit' (Boston, 1883), 'Dennis Day, the Carpetbagger' (New York, 1884), 'Calamity Jane,' and other works. Her masculine name caused her to be dubbed "major."

SPIEKER, GEORGE FREDERICK, theologian, was born at Elk Ridge Landing, Md., November 17, 1844. He became an eminent educator and divine of the Lutheran faith, settled in Pennsylvania and published several translations from the German. Roanoke College gave him the degree of D.D.

SPIERS, MARY BUCKNER. Poet. [Va.]. She published a volume of verse entitled 'The Giant of the Blue Ridge, and other Poems,' a work of merit (New York and Washington, The Neale Publishing Company, 1903).

SPOFFORD, HENRY MARTYN, jurist, was born in Gilmanton. N.H., September 8, 1821, and died at Red Sulphur Springs, W. Va., August 20, 1880. He settled in New Orleans for the practice of law, rose to the Supreme Bench, and was elected to the United States Senate by the "Nicholls" Legislature, but was not seated. Amherst made him an LL.D. He was co-author of 'The Louisiana Magistrate and Parish Official Guide.' Ainsworth R. Spofford, for many years the librarian of Congress, was his brother.

SPOTSWOOD, ALEXANDER, royal governor of Virginia, was born in Tangier, Africa, in 1676, and died in Annapolis, Md., June 7, 1740. He was the first among the adventurous spirits of the colony to explore the Appalachian Mountains, and the story of his expedition is one of the most thrilling of the Virginia legends. He was the patron and friend of William and Mary College; and, despite an occasional disagreement with the burgesses, enjoyed great popularity during his administration of the colonial affairs. 'The Official Letters of Alexander Spottswood, Lieutenant-governor of Virginia, 1710-1722,' have been published in the collections of the Virginia Historical Society, with an introduction by Robert A. Brock (Richmond, 1882-1885). His speeches in the assembly have been preserved in William Maxwell's 'Virginia Historical Register,' Volume IV.

SPRAGINS, ANNA WARD, Mrs., poet, was born in Alabama but afterward removed to Texas. She wrote "Shiloh," "Farewell to Texas" and other poems. She died in 1876.

SPRAGUE, JOHN TITCOMB. Soldier. Though of Northern birth and an officer in the Union Army he served in the Florida War, was military governor of Florida during reconstruction and wrote a volume entitled 'The Origin, Progress and Conclusion of the Florida War' (New York, 1848).

SPRUNT, JAMES, author, was born in Scotland in 1846 but afterward came to America and located in North Carolina. He wrote a story of the Wilmington blockade entitled 'What Ship is That?' (Wilmington, 1883), 'A Colonial Plantation' (1893), 'Tales and Traditions of the Lower Cape Fear' (1896), and 'A Colonial Apparition' (1898).

SRYGLEY, FLETCHER DOUGLAS, clergyman and educator, was born in Alabama but afterward lived in Tennessee. He wrote 'Larimore and his Boys' (1879), and 'Seventy Years in Dixie' (1891).

ST. CÉRAN, TULLIUS. Poet. [La.]. He published 'Rien ou Moi' (1837), '1814 et 1815' an epic poem of the second war for independence (1838), and 'Les Louisianais' (1840).

STABLER, JENNIE L., Mrs. Author. [Va.]. Under the penname of "Jennie Woodville," she wrote numerous stories and sketches. Her best work is a novel entitled 'Left to Herself' (1871). She lived at Lynchburg, Va.

STACY, JAMES, clergyman, was born in Liberty County, Ga., June 2, 1830. For more than forty years he was pastor of the Presbyterian Church, at Newnan, Ga., where he still resides. He published an interesting 'History of Old Midway Church,' one of the most famous organizations in America, an essay on "The Observance of the Holy Sabbath," which was awarded a prize, and numerous tracts and sermons. Arkansas College conferred upon him the degree of D.D.

STANARD, MARY NEWTON. Author. [Va.]. From the pen of this talented Virginia woman have come two charming historical works entitled 'The Story of Bacon's Rebellion' (New York and Washington, The Neale Publishing Company, 1907) and 'The Dreamer' (Richmond, The Bell Book and Stationery Company, 1909), the latter being an intimate study of Edgar Allan Poe.

STANARD, WILLIAM GLOVER. Editor. He was born in Richmond, Va., October 2, 1858, a son of Captain Robert C. and Virginia M. Stanard, was educated at William and Mary College and at Richmond College, and married, April 17, 1900, Mary Mann Page Newton. He is corresponding secretary of the Virginia Historical Society and editor of the *Virginia Magazine of History and Biography*. Besides numerous historical pamphlets, he published 'The Colonial Virginia Register.' He resides in Richmond, Va.

STANLEY, M. C., Mrs. Writer. This talented Southern woman has contributed some excellent verse to *Harper's* and other popular magazines. She resides at present in Tucson, Ariz.

STANTON, FRANK LEBBY. See Biographical and Critical Sketch, Vol. XI, page 5061.

STANTON, HENRY THROOP. See Biographical and Critical Sketch, Vol. XI, page 5083.

STANTON, RICHARD HENRY, jurist, was born in Alexandria, Va., September 9, 1812, settled in Marysville, Ky., for the practice of law, became a judge of the Superior Court and a Member of Congress, edited two newspapers, and published a 'Code of Practice in Civil and Criminal Cases in Kentucky' (Cincinnati, 1855), 'Practical Treatises for Justices of the Peace' and a 'Manual for Executors.'

STEARNS, EDWARD JOSIAH, Protestant Episcopal clergyman, was born in Massachusetts in 1810 and died in Maryland in 1890. The greater part of his life was divided between Annapolis and Baltimore. He published 'Notes on Uncle Tom's Cabin' (Philadelphia, 1853), a 'Practical Guide to English Pronunciation' (Boston, 1878), and 'The Faith of Our Fathers' in reply to Cardinal Gibbons (New York, 1879), besides minor works.

STEINER, BERNARD C. Educator. [Md.]. He wrote a 'History of Education in Maryland' (1894) and a sketch of Sir Robert Eden (1898).

STEINER, LEWIS HENRY, physician and educator, was born in Frederick, Md., May 4, 1827. During the Civil War he was sanitary inspector for the Army of the Potomac. He published a 'Diary Kept During the Rebel Occupation of Frederick, Md.' (New York, 1862), and 'Cantate Domino,' a collection of sacred anthems, in which he was assisted by Henry Schwing (Boston, 1859), besides numerous translations, monographs and lectures.

STEMPEL, M. G. T. Author. [La.]. He wrote a novel entitled 'The Finished Web' (New Orleans, 1892).

STEPHENS, ALEXANDER HAMILTON. See Biographical and Critical Sketch, Vol. XI, page 5097.

STEPHENS, EDWIN LEWIS, educator, was born in Natchitoches Parish, La., November 27, 1872, and was educated at the Louisiana State University, afterward taking his Ph.D. degree from the University of New York. Since 1900 he has been president of the Southwestern Industrial Institute at Lafayette, La. For three years he edited the *Louisiana School Review*. Besides numerous contributions to periodicals, he was co-author of the Louisiana supplement to 'Tarr and McMurry's Geography' (New York, The Macmillan Company, 1907) and published a narrative of European travels. The sketch of Ruth McEnery Stuart in 'The Library of Southern Literature' is from his pen. He married, July 14, 1902, Beverly Randolph.

STEPHENS, THOMAS, author, was a son of William Stephens, president of the colony of Georgia and wrote a work entitled 'The Castle Builder, or, the History of William Stephens of the Isle of Wight' (London, 1742; second edition, 1759), in which he discusses the causes which retarded the history of Georgia.

STEPHENS, WILLIAM, president of the colony of Georgia, was born on the Isle of Wight, England, January 28, 1681, and died in Georgia, in 1753. For some time he was a Member of Parliament, but in 1730 he came to South Carolina to survey a tract of land, became an intimate friend of Oglethorpe, and, on the recommendation of the latter, was made secretary to the board of trustees of Georgia, and afterward colonial president. He wrote 'A Journal of the Proceedings in Georgia,' which was published in three volumes (London, 1742), a work of great value and importance because of the light which it throws upon the early annals of the commonwealth.

STEPHENSON, NATHANIEL. Educator and author. He was born in Cincinnati, Ohio, July 10, 1867, the son of Reuben Henry and Louisa Stephenson, taught English in the State University of Iowa and also in the Indiana University, was also for a time editorial writer on the Cincinnati *Tribune,* and afterward editor of the Cincinnati *Commercial Tribune.* He became professor of history in Charleston College in 1902. He is the author of several interesting novels including: 'They That Took the Sword (New York, John Lane), 'The Beautiful Mrs. Moulton (*ibid.*), and 'Eleanor Dayton (*ibid.*). He resides in Charleston, S.C.

STEVENS, SHEPPARD. Author. She was born in Mobile, Ala., September 18, 1862, a daughter of the Rt. Rev. Henry Niles Pierce, bishop of Arkansas, was educated in private schools and by tutors at home, and married, October 12, 1882, William C. Stevens, son of the Rt. Rev. William Bacon Stevens, bishop of Pennsylvania. She is the author of several charming stories, among them, 'I Am the King' (Boston, Little, Brown and Company, 1898), 'The Sword of Justice' (*ibid.*, 1899), 'In the Eagle's Talons' (*ibid.*, 1901), and others, besides numerous stories and sketches contributed to the periodicals.

STEVENS, WALTER B. Journalist. He was born in Meriden, Conn., July 26, 1848, a son of the Rev. A. A. Stevens, was educated at the University of Michigan, and was for many years Washington correspondent of the St. Louis *Globe-Democrat.* His writings include: 'Through Texas,' 'The Ozark Uplift,' and 'The Forest City' (St. Louis, N. D. Thompson). He resides in St. Louis.

STEVENS, WALTER LE CONTE. Educator. He was born in Gordon County, Ga., June 17, 1847, a son of Dr. Josiah P. and Ann Le Conte Stevens. On the maternal side he comes of the distinguished Georgia family which produced the noted scientists, John and Joseph Le Conte. He graduated from the University of South Carolina, and married, August 29, 1900, Virginia Lee Letcher, daughter of the war governor of Virginia. He pursued special studies in European universities, was professor of physics in Rensselaer Polytechnic Institute from 1892 to 1898; and then was called to the same chair in Washington and Lee University. Besides revising 'Steele's Physics,' he contributed to Appleton's 'Physical Geography' all parts involving the application of the principles of physics. He is also the author of numerous articles contributed to the encyclopædias and to the scientific periodicals. The University of Georgia gave him the degree of Ph.D. He resides in Lexington, Va.

STEVENS, WILLIAM BACON, Protestant Episcopal bishop, was born in Bath, Me., July 13, 1815, and died in Philadelphia, Pa., June 11, 1887. For two years he traveled abroad. On his return home, he studied medicine and settled in Savannah, Ga., where he practiced his profession for several years. During this period he became State historian for Georgia, and published a number of volumes dealing with Georgia annals. Afterward he entered the Episcopal priesthood and in 1865 became bishop of Pennsylvania. He published 'Discourses before the Historical Society of Georgia' (Savannah, 1841), 'History of Silk Culture in Georgia' (1841), 'History of Georgia,' in two volumes (Philadelphia, 1847), 'Parables of the New Testament Unfolded' (1855), 'The Bow in the Cloud,' (1855), 'Home Service' (1856), 'The Lord's Day' (1857), 'History of St. Andrew's Church, Philadelphia,' (1858), 'Sabbaths of Our Lord' (1872), 'Sermons' (New York, 1879), and numerous tracts and essays. Union College gave him the degree of LL.D., and the University of Pennsylvania the degree of D.D.

STEVENSON, ADLAI EWING, former Vice-president of the United States, was born in Christian County, Ky., October 23, 1835. After graduating from Centre College, he settled in Bloomington, Ill., for the practice of law, became prominent in politics, served four years in Congress as a Democrat, and was elected Vice-president of the United States on the ticket with Grover Cleveland in 1892. On retiring from office he was appointed a member of the commission to Europe in the interest of bi-metallism. He was the Democratic nominee for Vice-president on the ticket with William J. Bryan, in 1900, but was defeated. He is an effective public speaker, a vigorous writer, and an independent thinker.

STEVENSON, R. RANDOLPH. Physician. He wrote an interesting work entitled 'The Southern Side; or, Andersonville Prison' (Baltimore, 1876).

STEWART, AUSTIN, author, was born of African parentage in Prince William County, Va., in 1793. He escaped from bondage, became a merchant in Rochester, N.Y., took an active part in the Anti-Slavery Crusade and wrote 'Twenty-two Years a Slave and Forty Years a Freeman' (Rochester, 1859). He died in 1860.

STEWART, FREDERICK CAMPBELL. Physician. [Va.]. He published a work entitled 'Hospitals and Surgeons of Paris' (1843).

STEWART, ROBERT ARMISTEAD, educator, was born in Portsmouth, Va., March 9, 1877. At present he is engaged in educational work in Richmond, occupying a chair of modern languages. He was assistant editor of the Virginia edition of 'Poe's Complete Works' (New York, T. Y. Crowell and Company, 1903), in addition to which he has published 'Knights of the Golden Horseshoe, and Other Lays' (Richmond, The Evans Press, 1909). For 'The Library of Southern Literature' he wrote the sketch of Gordon McCabe. He is a Ph.D. and a member of the Society of the Cincinnati.

STEWART, WILLIAM H. Lecturer and writer. Colonel Stewart served with gallantry during the Civil War. On the platform he has also attained distinction and his work entitled 'The Spirit of the South,' which contains some of his best essays and orations, is a volume of much interest (New York and Washington, The Neale Publishing Company, 1908).

STIBBES, AGNES JEAN. Author. [Ga.]. She wrote 'The Earls of Sunderland,' besides numerous short stories.

STILES, JOSEPH CLAY, clergyman, was born in Savannah, Ga., December 6, 1795, and died in Savannah, Ga., March 27, 1875. He was educated at Yale and at Andover, became an eminent Presbyterian divine, gave an impetus to Presbyterianism in Georgia by an evangelistic campaign of great power and effectiveness, and held numerous important pastorates. He published 'Modern Reform Examined; or, the Union of the North and the South on the Subject of Slavery' (Philadelphia, 1858), 'The National Controversy; or, the Voice of the Fathers upon the State of the Country' (New York, 1861), and 'Future Punishment' (St. Louis, 1868). Transylvania University gave him his degree of D.D., and the University of Georgia his degree of LL.D.

STILES, ROBERT. Author. [Va.]. Major Stiles served with gallantry in the Army of Northern Virginia and wrote one of the most realistic narratives of the struggle in a work entitled 'Four Years with Marse Robert' (New York and Washington, The Neale Publishing Company, 1906).

STILES, WILLIAM HENRY, lawyer, was born in Savannah, Ga., in 1808 and died in Savannah, Ga., December 20, 1865. He studied law, became a Member of Congress, received the appointment of Chargé d'Affaires in Austria, commanded a regiment of Confederate troops, and published a 'History of Austria, 1848-1849,' in two volumes, (New York, 1852).

STILLMAN, ANNIE RAYMOND, author, was born in Charleston, S.C., in 1855. On account of defective eyesight she could read or study but little in childhood, but her bright intellect was quick to grasp. She has lived a life of beautiful consecration and published two rich volumes entitled 'How They Kept the Faith,' a story of the Huguenots (New York, A. D. F. Randolph, 1888), and 'Fool's Gold' (Chicago and New York, Fleming H. Revell Company, 1902). She resides in Tuscaloosa, Ala.

STITH, WILLIAM, an early American historian of colonial times, was born in Virginia in 1689. On completing his education in England he decided to enter the ministry and was ordained to the priesthood in the Established Church on his return to America. He became one of the most influential clergymen of the day; was chaplain of the House of Burgesses in 1738; was rector of Henrico Parish for some time; and from 1752 to 1755 he was president of William and Mary College. His claims to remembrance rest chiefly upon his work entitled 'The History of Virginia from the First Settlement to the Dissolution of the London Company.' It was first published in 1747 and afterward reëdited, with bibliographical data, in 1766. While an unfinished work, it possesses very great value because of its ancient date and, in the main, because of its accurate information. But the style is somewhat diffuse; and, to this extent, the work incurred the criticism of Jefferson. The author died at Williamsburg, Va., in 1755.

STOCKARD, HENRY JEROME. See Biographical and Critical Sketch, Vol. XI, page 5119.

STOCKARD, SALLIE. Poet. She published "The Lily of the Valley," a dramatic arrangement of the 'Songs of Solomon' (1900). The author was born in North Carolina but afterward removed to Arkansas. She is now Mrs. Magness.

STOCKTON, WILLIAM T., author, was born in Philadelphia, Pa., October 8, 1812, and died at Quincey, Fla., March 4, 1869. Educated for the Army at the United States Military Academy he served in the Florida War; but, resigning after several years, he made his home in the State which had witnessed his campaigning. He was also an officer in the Confederate service, rising from captain to lieutenant-colonel.

Under the pen-name of "Cor-de-Chasse" he wrote a number of stories and sketches for the press on hunting; which were afterward published in a volume entitled 'Dog and Gun.'

STODDARD, AMOS. Soldier. [La.]. He was born in 1762 and died in 1813. He published a volume just before his death entitled 'Sketches, Historical and Descriptive, of Louisiana' (Philadelphia, 1812).

STOKES, J. L. Methodist Episcopal clergyman. [S.C.]. He published a work entitled 'Eldon Drayton.'

STONE, ALFRED HOLT, planter and author, was born in New Orleans, La., October 16, 1870. His father was Walter Wilson Stone, and his mother, Eleanor Holt. On completing his studies at the University of Mississippi Law School, he was admitted to the Bar, and in 1896 married Mary Bailey Ireys. For some time he has been extensively engaged in cotton planting, at Dunleith, Miss., and at leisure intervals he has bestowed deep thought upon economic studies, especially in relation to the negro question. Besides numerous contributions to the magazines, he has published an exceptionally able work entitled 'Studies in the American Race Problem' (New York, Doubleday, Page and Company). He belongs to numerous scientific organizations.

STONE, ALFRED M., lawyer, was the author of an important paper read before the Mississippi Historical Society in the city of Natchez on "The Early Slave Laws of Mississippi."

STONE, BARTOW WARREN, clergyman, was born near Port Tobacco, Md., December 24, 1772, and died in Hannibal, Mo., November 9, 1844. After adhering for several years to the Presbyterian standards he renounced Calvinism, organized an independent movement, wrote what was termed "the first declaration of religious freedom in the Western Hemisphere," and published 'Letters on the Atonement' (1805), and several hymns.

STONE, CORNELIA BRANCH, president-general of the United Daughters of the Confederacy, was born at Nacogdoches, Texas, February 13, 1840, when the Lone Star State was an independent republic. She is a leader in various patriotic organizations and a woman of extraordinary gifts. Her girlhood days having been spent in the frontier belt, she was denied an academic training, but her acquisitive powers of mind have placed her far in advance of many of the finished products of the schools. She married, April 16, 1856, Henry Clay Stone. Besides numerous articles and addresses, Mrs. Stone is the author of a catechism for the instruction of the children of the Confederacy. The sketch of Mrs. Jefferson Davis in 'The Library of Southern Literature' is from her pen.

STONE, WILLIAM MURRAY, Protestant Episcopal bishop, was born in Somerset County, Md., June 1. 1779, and died in Salisbury, Md., February 26, 1838. He studied theology, became rector of several important parishes, and in 1830 was consecrated bishop. He published a number of sermons, pastoral letters, and charges. Columbia gave him the degree of D.D.

STORK, CHARLES AUGUSTUS, clergyman and educator, was born near Jefferson, Md., September 4, 1838, and died in Philadelphia, Pa., December 17, 1883. His father was Theophilus Stork. At Williams College he was a room-mate of James A. Garfield. He became a professor in the Lutheran Seminary at Gettysburg, Pa., and a pastor in Baltimore, edited Lutheran papers and wrote 'Light on the Pilgrim's

Way,' a posthumous work which was edited by his brother, **Theophilus B. Stork** (Philadelphia, 1885). He held the degree of D.D.

STORK, THEOPHILUS, clergyman, was born near Salisbury, N.C., in 1814, and died in Philadelphia, Pa., March 28, 1874. He was educated at Pennsylvania College, attained distinction in the Lutheran pulpit, edited Church papers, and became president of Newberry College, South Carolina. He published 'The Life of Martin Luther and the Reformation in Germany' (Philadelphia, 1854), and numerous theological and religious sketches and monographs. After his death a volume of his sermons was published by his sons. He received the degree of D.D.

STOVALL, A. W. Lawyer. [Tenn.]. He published 'The Life, Lectures, and Poetry of the Rev. E. H. Osborne' (1897).

STOVALL, PLEASANT ALEXANDER, editor and publisher, was born in Augusta, Ga., July 10, 1857. His father was Bolling Anthony Stovall and his mother, Martha Wilson. On completing his education at the University of Georgia he entered journalism, with which profession he has since been actively identified. For several years he has owned and edited the Savannah *Press,* one of the brightest newspapers in the State. His publications include: a 'Life of Robert Toombs' (New York, Cassell and Company, 1892), 'Free Silver Fallacies' (1895), 'Colonial Savannah' (New York, G. P. Putnam's Sons, 1901), 'The Statue of Lee' (1903), and 'Frederica' (1904). He married, January 7, 1885, Mary Ganahl of Augusta, Ga.

STRACHEY, WILLIAM. Colonial secretary of Virginia and pioneer author. Very little is known of him beyond the fact that he belonged to the English gentry and came to Virginia with Sir Thomas Gates in 1609, serving in the rôle of secretary of the colony for three years. But his writings are of very great value, because they belong to the earliest period of colonization in North America and represent the first fruits of Southern authorship. On the way over, the vessel in which he traveled, the *Sea Venture,* was wrecked on the Bermuda Islands, and, from the account that he subsequently gave of this dramatic experience, it is said that Shakespeare drew the scene of the storm in his play, "The Tempest." The style of this author is naturally quaint. He employs the archaic forms of the Seventeenth Century; but, if his sentences are sometimes involved, the interest of his narrative offers full atonement. The work that contains the story of his thrilling adventure is entitled 'A True Repertory of the Wracke and Redemption of Sir Thomas Gates Upon and From the Islands of the Bermudas' (1609). He wrote also 'A Historie of Travaile in Virginia Britiania' (1602), and edited 'Lawes, Divine, Moral, and Martial.'

STRANGE, ROBERT, author, was born in Virginia in 1769 and died in North Carolina, in 1854. He wrote 'Eoneguski: or, the Cherokee Chief' (Washington, D.C., 1839), a work which was published in two volumes. The scene of the story is laid on the banks of Homony Creek, one of the small mountain tributaries of the French Broad.

STRATTON, JOHN ROACH, clergyman and lecturer, was born of Southern parentage at Evansville, Ind., April 6, 1875. His father was the Rev. H. D. D. Stratton. On his mother's side he is related to the Carters of Virginia. Eloquent and gifted, Dr. Stratton is pastor of one of the largest Baptist congregations of Baltimore, Md., and is also one of the most popular speakers on the lecture platform. His publications include: 'Rag-time Religion' (Louisville, Ky., Charles T. Darwin, 1903).

'Outlines of Oratory' (Atlanta, Ga., Byrd Publishing Company, 1903), 'Will Education Solve the Race Problem?' (New York, Harper and Brothers, 1902), 'The Salvation of Society' (Baltimore, 1908), and "Portland, Oregon, and the Great Northwest," an essay which won the one thousand dollar prize offered by the Portland Commercial Club (1908). He married, November 2, 1903, Georgia Hillyer of Atlanta, Ga.

STRATTON, JOSEPH BUCK, clergyman, was born in 1815. He wrote "The Presbyterian Church in Mississippi" for Goodspeed's 'Memoirs,' also 'Extracts from an Elder's Diary,' and several religious and devotional works.

STRAUS, OSCAR SOLOMON, merchant, author, Cabinet officer, diplomat, was born in Otterberg, Rhenish Bavaria, December 23, 1850, a son of Lazarus Straus. When only four years old he was brought to America, together with his brothers, Isidor and Nathan, and for more than ten years the family resided at Talbotton, Ga., where the boys were partly educated. Oscar subsequently took a course at Columbia University, after which he entered the firm of Straus and Sons, importers, of New York. He arose to very high prominence in the business world, but perhaps his greatest success was achieved in diplomacy. First under President Cleveland and later under President McKinley, he ably represented the United States Government at the Court of Constantinople. During the administration of President Roosevelt he held the portfolio of Commerce and Labor, the first representative of his race in the history of the Government to occupy a place in the Cabinet; and still later, under President Taft, he was again commissioned United States Minister to Turkey, a position which he still retains. Besides numerous contributions to magazines on economic and political subjects, his published works include: 'The Origin of the Republican Form of Government in the United States' (New York, G. P. Putnam's Sons, 1886); 'Roger Williams, the Pioneer of Religious Liberty' (New York. The Century Company, 1894); 'The Development of Religious Liberty in the United States' (1896), and 'Reform in the Consular Service' (1897), besides minor works. He holds the L.H.D. and the LL.D. degrees.

STRICKLER, GIVENS BROWN, theologian and educator, was born at Strickler's Springs, Rockbridge County, Va., April 25, 1840. His father was Joseph Strickler and his mother Mary Brown. At the outbreak of the Civil War he was an undergraduate student at Washington College, Lexington, Va., and joining the Army he went to the front in the famous "Stonewall Brigade." After the struggle he completed his academic studies and still later matriculated in Union Theological Seminary, Richmond, Va., where he obtained his special preparation for his life's work. From the Tinkling Spring Presbyterian Church, an historic old landmark in the Valley of Virginia, which he served for thirteen years, he was called in 1883 to the Central Presbyterian Church in Atlanta, Ga., where he remained for an equal period, and finally in 1896 he accepted the chair of systematic theology at Union, a position of very great distinction which he still occupies. He married, November 6, 1871, Mary Frances Moore, since deceased. Dr. Strickler is one of the profoundest thinkers and one of the ripest scholars in the ranks of Southern Presbyterianism but he has been too busily engaged in pastoral and school-room work to give much thought to publication. However, his lectures which alone constitute a library of precious value to the Church will doubtless at no distant day be published in book form. Besides numerous contributions to religious periodicals, he has published an occasional volume of sermons. He holds both the D.D. and the LL.D. degrees. The latest of Dr. Strickler's publications is a volume of select sermons (Chicago and New York, The Fleming H. Revell Company, 1910).

STROBEL, PHILIP. Author. He was a native of South Carolina, but lived for some time in Georgia and published a 'History of the Salzburg Colony at Ebenezer.'

STROBEL, WILLIAM DANIEL, clergyman, was born in Charleston, S.C., May 7, 1808, and died in Rhinebeck, N.Y., December 6, 1884. He entered the Lutheran ministry, preached for some time in South Carolina and afterward served churches in Maryland and New York. He contributed to the periodicals and published numerous tracts and pamphlets. Hamilton College made him a D.D.

STRONG, GEORGE V. Poet. [N.C.]. He wrote 'Francis Herbert: a Romance of the Revolution, and Other Poems,' a work of unusual creative power and imagination (New York, Leavitt, Trow and Company, 1847).

STROTHER, DAVID HUNTER. See Biographical and Critical Sketch, Vol. XI, page 5131.

STUART, ALEXANDER HUGH HOLMES, statesman, was born in Staunton, Va., April 2, 1807. Under President Fillmore he held the office of Secretary of State, and he also served one term in Congress. He opposed secession and, after the surrender at Appomattox, he was one of the leaders in the first movement in the South to establish peaceful relations. Besides numerous speeches, he published a 'Narrative of Virginia' (1869). He was a cousin of General J. E. B. Stuart, the famous Confederate cavalryman.

STUART, RUTH McENERY. See Biographical and Critical Sketch, Vol. XI, page 5145.

STUBBS, ELIZABETH SAUNDERS. Author. She published 'Early Settlers of Alabama' (New Orleans, 1899), besides a sketch of Colonel James Edmonds.

SUARES, M. R. Baptist clergyman. [S.C.]. Born in 1812. He published a volume of verse entitled 'The Sabbath, and Other Poems' (1871).

SUMMERS, L. P. Author. [Va.]. He wrote an interesting 'History of Southwestern Virginia.'

SUMMERS, THOMAS OSMUND, clergyman and educator, was born in Dorsetshire, England, in 1812; but, coming to the United States in early life, he was admitted to the ranks of the Methodist Church and became an influential minister of the Gospel. For several years he was professor of theology at Vanderbilt. His published works include: 'Commentaries on the Gospel,' 'The Acts,' 'The Ritual of the M.E. Church, South,' and 'Talks.' He was also editor for some time of the Nashville *Christian Advocate.* His death occurred in 1882. He held the D.D. and the LL.D. degrees.

SURGHNOR, F. M., Mrs. Author. [La.]. She published a work entitled 'Uncle Tom of the Old South.'

SWAIN, DAVID LOWRY, governor and college president, was born in Asheville, N.C., January 4, 1801, and died in Chapel Hill, N.C., September 3. 1868. He was educated at the University of North Carolina, chose the legal profession. and became Supreme Court judge and governor. On retiring from the latter office he was elected president of the University of North Carolina, a position which he held for the remainder of his life. He wrote: 'The British Invasion of North Carolina,' which appeared in the *University Magazine,* and published a volume of lectures entitled 'Revolutionary History of North Carolina' (New York, 1853). Princeton and Yale conferred upon him the degree of LL.D.

SWAIN, MARGIE P. Author. [Ala.]. She published a work entitled 'Lochlin' (Selma, Ala., 1864).

SWARTZ, JOEL, clergyman and poet, was born in Shenandoah County, Va., August 18, 1827. He entered the ministry of the Lutheran Church, held important pastorates in the South, and eventually settled at Gettysburg, Pa. He edited *The Lutheran Observer* for sixteen years and published two volumes of verse: 'Dreamings of the Waking Heart' (1877) and 'Lyra Lutherana' (1883). Wittenberg College gave him the degree of D.D.

SWEET, ALEXANDER EDWIN. Journalist. [Texas]. He was born in New Brunswick, Canada, in 1841. He published 'Three Dozen Good Stories from Texas Siftings.'

SWETT, CHARLES. Author. [La.]. He published a work entitled 'A Trip to British Honduras' (New Orleans, 1815).

SWIGGETT, GLEN LEVIN, educator, was born in Cambridge City, Ind., September 15, 1867. On completing his studies at the University of Indiana he attended lectures at Johns Hopkins and later spent several years at the German universities (Ph.D.). Since 1902 he has filled the chair of modern languages in the University of the South. He founded the Tennessee Philological Society and edited for some time the *Pathfinder.* Besides frequent contributions to magazines and reviews, he has published 'Schiller—the Message in His Life' (Sewanee, 1905), Milton's 'Ode on the Nativity' (Sewanee, 1906), and Storm's 'Im Sonnenschein' (New York, The American Book Company, 1906). For 'The Library of Southern Literature' he wrote the sketch of Virginia Frazer Boyle.

SWISHER, BELLE FRENCH, Mrs., editor, was born in Georgia but afterward lived in Wisconsin and still later removed to Texas. She published a 'History of Brown County, Wis.,' a novel entitled 'Struggling Upward to the Light,' and numerous poems, including one on "The San Antonio River."

SWITZLER, WILLIAM F., historian of Missouri, published an interesting 'History of Missouri' (St. Louis, C. R. Barnes, 1879), with profuse illustrations.

TABB, JOHN B. See Biographical and Critical Sketch, Vol. XII, page 5163.

TAILFER, PATRICK. Colonist. For a while he resided in Georgia, but, growing dissatisfied with the management of affairs in the colony, he crossed the river into South Carolina, and published, in association with other parties, a 'True and Historical Narrative of the Colony of Georgia in America' (London and Charleston, 1741), in which he harshly criticizes General Oglethorpe. As a polemic, Professor Moses Coit Tyler considers it one of the best in our early literature, though the author himself may have been at the head of a party of malcontents.

TALLEY, SUSAN ARCHER, author, was born in Hanover County, Va., in 1835. During the Civil War she fell in love with Colonel Weiss, a Union soldier at Richmond, and married him; but this alliance proved to be an unhappy one and she was compelled to sue for legal separation. She was also awarded possession of her child, but she refused to accept alimony from her husband. She possessed literary gifts of high order, contributing to *Harper's Magazine* and *Scribner's Magazine;* and, in 1859, she published a volume of her poems, which received flattering notices from the press. Her best-known poem is entitled "Ennerslie," In rhythm it resembles Tennyson's "Lady of Shalott."

TANEY, MARY FLORENCE. Author. [Ky.]. She published an interesting biographical work entitled 'Kentucky's Pioneer Women' (1898).

TANEY, ROGER BROOKE, former Chief Justice of the Supreme Court of the United States, was born in Calvert County, Md., March 17, *.*777, and died in Washington, D.C., October 12, 1864. He studied law; and, after locating in Baltimore, divided with William Wirt the leadership honors of the Maryland Bar. In the Cabinet of President Jackson he became Attorney-general, but relinquished this portfolio to become Secretary of the Treasury; and, on assuming the latter office, issued an order for the removal of Government deposits from the United States Bank. Though the President favored this course, it proved to be unpopular and produced financial depression. The refusal of the Senate to confirm the appointment of Taney to the new position caused his resignation; but he afterward succeeded Chief Justice Marshall on the Supreme Bench, and for twenty-nine years presided over the deliberations of this august tribunal. In the famous Dred Scott case, which was decided in 1857, he held that the territories were open to slavery and the acceptance of this interpretation of the fundamental law became the issue in the ensuing campaign. The opinions of Chief Justice Taney are contained in the Supreme Court Reports of Benjamin R. Curtis, Benjamin C. Howard, and Jeremiah S. Black. He is credited with having written the farewell address of President Jackson. At an advanced age he began his autobiography, but made little progress. The fragment forms the introduction to the 'Memoir of Chief Justice Taney,' by Samuel Tyler (Baltimore, 1872).

TANNEHILL, WILKINS, journalist, was born in Pittsburg, Pa., March 4, 1787, and died in Nashville, Tenn., June 2, 1858. From time to time he edited various papers in Nashville, was an ardent Whig, and supported Henry Clay with great zeal and power. He published a 'Freemason's Manual,' 'Sketches of the History of Literature' (1827), and 'Sketches of the History of Roman Literature' (1846).

TAPP, SIDNEY CALHOUN. Lawyer and author. He was born in North Carolina, September 5, 1872, a son of Ruffin R. Tapp, graduated at Furman University, and afterward took a special course of instruction at the University of Chicago. He located in Atlanta, Ga., for the practice of law. He was presidential elector in 1904 on the Democratic ticket; but withdrew from the national organization to form an independent party, from which he received the nomination to the highest office in the nation's gift. His published works include: 'The Story of Anglo-Saxon Institutions, or the Development of Constitutional Government' (New York, G. P. Putnam's Sons), 'The Struggle' (*ibid.*), and 'The Story of the French Revolution.'

TARDY, MARY, Mrs., ("Ida Raymond"). Author. [Ala.]. She published a work entitled: 'Southland Writers,' in two volumes (Philadelphia, 1870). It contains biographical and critical sketches of female authors who were living at the time, and numerous extracts.

TARLETON, BANISTRE. Soldier. [England]. He was born in 1754 and died in 1833. Colonel Tarleton commanded the famous British legion which bore his name during the American Revolution, and afterward published a 'History of the Campaigns of 1780 and 1781 in the Southern Provinces of North America' (London, 1787).

TAYLOR, ALEXANDER SMITH, ethnologist, was born in Charleston, S.C., April 16, 1817, and died near Santa Barbara, Cal., July 27, 1876. For several years he traveled in the West Indies and in the Orient, and eventually settled in California, where he became a writer of note, contributing articles to the magazines and newspapers on American antiquities. Under the title of 'The First Voyage to California,' he published a translation of the diary of Cabrillo and wrote a "History of Grasshoppers and Locusts of America," in the 'Smithsonian Reports' (1853), "The Indianology of California," in *The California Farmer* (1860-1864), and "Bibliographia California," in the Sacramento *Union* (1863-1866).

TAYLOR, CHARLES ELISHA. Educator. He was born in Richmond, Va., October 28, 1842, a son of the Rev. James B. and Mary Taylor, graduated from the University of Virginia, and was professor of Latin in Wake Forest College for fourteen years. In 1884 he became president of the institution. He married, September 11, 1873, Mary Hinton Pritchard. His writings include: "Gilbert Stone," a poem (1891), 'How Far a State May Educate' (1894), and 'The Story of Yates' (1898). He resides in Wake Forest, N.C. Richmond College gave him the degree of D.D.

TAYLOR, GEORGE BOARDMAN, clergyman and educator, was born in Richmond, Va., in 1832. His father was the Rev. James Barnett Taylor, and his mother Mary Williams. On completing his educational equipment, he became the first pastor of the Franklin Square Church, in Baltimore. In 1873, under the appointment of the Southern Baptist Board of Missions, he went to Rome, Italy. Here, his wife, who was Susan Braxton, died. Since 1901, he has been teaching in the Baptist Theological School at Rome. His works include: 'Oakland,' stories for children; 'Coster Grew,' 'Roger Bernard, the Pastor's Son,' 'Walter Ennis: a Tale of the Early Virginia Baptists,' 'Baptists: Who They Are and What They Have Done,' in four volumes; 'Italy and the Italians,' and 'An Italian Text-book on Systematic Theology.' Richmond College gave him the degree of D.D.

TAYLOR, HANNIS. See Biographical and Critical Sketch, Vol. XII, page 5179.

TAYLOR, JAMES BARNETT, clergyman, was born in Barton-on-Humber, England, March 19, 1804, and died in Richmond, Va., December 22, 1871. After coming to America, he entered the Baptist ministry and accepted a call to a church in Richmond, where his power as a preacher began to attract attention. On the organization of the Southern Baptist Convention, he became corresponding secretary and continued to hold this office for more than twenty-five years. He traveled extensively over the South, edited for some time the *Religious Herald* and other papers, and published several works, among them: 'The Life of Lot Cary' (Baltimore, 1837), 'Lives of Virginia Baptist Ministers' (Richmond, 1837), and a 'Memoir of Luther Rice, One of the First Missionaries in the East' (1841). He also left in manuscript a 'History of Virginia Baptists.' 'The Life and Times of James B. Taylor,' a work of much interest, was published by his son, Dr. George Boardman Taylor.

TAYLOR, JOHN, statesman, was born in Orange County, Va., in 1750, and died in Caroline County, Va., August 20, 1824. When Richard Henry Lee resigned from the United States Senate he was appointed to succeed him, and at intervals he frequently represented Virginia in this high forum. He published 'An Inquiry into the Principles and Policies of the United States' (Fredericksburg, 1814), 'Arator: a Series of Agricultural Essays, Practical and Political,' which passed into several editions (Petersburg, 1818), 'Construction Construed and the Constitution Vindicated' (Richmond, 1820), 'Tyranny Unmasked' (Washington, 1822), and 'New Views of the Constitution of the United States' (Washington, 1823). He was a graduate of William and Mary College and by occupation a planter.

TAYLOR, JOHN LOUIS, jurist, was born in London, England, March 1, 1769, and died in Raleigh, N.C., January 29, 1829. At the age of twelve he came to America, settled in North Carolina, studied law, and became chief justice. He was a commissioner to revise the statutes of North Carolina and a compiler of numerous legal volumes, including 'Cases in the Superior Courts of Law and Equity' (New Berne, 1802), 'The North Carolina Law Repository,' in two volumes' (1814-1816), 'Term Reports' (Raleigh, 1818), and a treatise 'On the Duties of Executors and Administrators' (1825).

TAYLOR, JOSEPH JUDSON. Baptist clergyman. He was born in Henry County, Va., November 1, 1855, and received the best educational equipment. He married, in 1882, Anna Hinton. For four years he was president of Georgetown (Ky.) College. At present he is the pastor of the First Baptist Church of Knoxville, Tenn. Besides several religious tracts and pamphlets, and numerous contributions to the press, he is the author of 'Daniel G. Taylor, a Country Preacher' (Louisville, Southern Baptist Concern). He holds the D.D. and the LL.D. degrees.

TAYLOR, JOSEPH WALTERS. An Alabama lawyer of some prominence. He was born in 1820, and several occasional addresses tell of his gifts as a speaker. At Lexington, Va., soon after the war, he made an eloquent plea for making Washington and Lee University a memorial in the best sense of the word, to Robert E. Lee. He also delivered an eloquent eulogy on Henry Clay. He died several years ago.

TAYLOR, MARSHALL WILLIAM, clergyman, was born in Lexington, Ky., July 1, 1846, and died in Louisville, Ky., September 11, 1887. He was of African parentage, but was free from birth. For several years he worked on a steamboat, but he acquired an education, served in the Army of the Cumberland, entered the ministry of the Methodist Church, labored for some time in Ohio and Indiana, returned to Kentucky, and afterward settled in New Orleans, where he edited the *Southwestern Christian Advocate*. He possessed unusual gifts and published a 'Handbook for Schools' (Louisville, 1871), 'Life of the Rev. George W. Downing' (1878), 'Plantation Melodies and Revival Songs of the Negroes' which passed into several editions, 'Life and Travels of Amanda Smith' (1886), and 'The Negro in Methodism' (1887).

TAYLOR, OLIVER. Historian. [Tenn.]. He published an important work entitled 'Historic Sullivan' (Bristol, Tenn., 1909), which contains an abundance of information concerning the earliest authentic records of the State.

TAYLOR, RICHARD. See Biographical and Critical Sketch, Vol. XII, page 5199.

TAYLOR, ROBERT LOVE. Lawyer and statesman. He was born in Happy Valley, Tenn., July 21, 1850, and was educated at Pennington, N.J. He was admitted to the Bar, and was a Member of Congress from 1879 to 1881. He was elected governor of Tennessee some years later, defeating his brother Alfred; and was afterward sent to the United States Senate, of which body he is still a member. Besides jointly editing the *Trotwood Taylor Magazine,* he has delivered numerous lectures and addresses in all parts of the United States, and some of these have been published in book form. His most celebrated lecture is entitled "The Fiddle and the Bow." It acquired great popularity, not only because it revived the humor of the old-time negro, but because in the race for governor of Tennessee he employed the fiddle and the bow to captivate voters. He was twice married, and resides in Nashville, Tenn.

TAYLOR, THOMAS HOUSE, clergyman, was born in Georgetown, S.C., October 18, 1799, and died in West Park, N.Y., September 9, 1867. He studied theology, entered the Episcopal priesthood, and was rector for thirty-three years of Grace Church, in the city of New York. After his death a volume of his selected discourses was published under the title of 'Sermons Preached in Grace Church' (New York, 1869).

TAYLOR, THOMAS JONES. Lawyer and jurist. He was born in 1829 and died in 1894, having been for many years a probate judge in Alabama. He is the author of a work entitled 'The Early History of Madison County and Incidentally of Northern Alabama,' which contains some very important information.

TAYLOR, WALTER HERRON, soldier and banker, was born in Norfolk, Va., June 13, 1838. After graduation from the Virginia Military Institute, he entered commercial life, but at the outbreak of the Civil War he enlisted in the Confederate Army, and became adjutant-general on the staff of General Lee, with the rank of lieutenant-colonel. When hostilities were over he resumed the banking business in Norfolk. He published an interesting personal narrative of adventure entitled 'Four Years with General Lee' (New York, 1878).

TAYLOR, WILLIAM, missionary bishop of the Methodist Episcopal Church, South, was born in Rockbridge County, Va., in 1821, and reared on a farm. Entering the ministry of the Methodist Church, he first went to California, where he developed a number of missions. Later, he went to Canada, afterward to Australia, and finally to Africa, everywhere scattering the seed of the Kingdom. On account of his zeal in the cause of disseminating religious truth, he was elevated to the Episcopal Bench. His writings include: 'Seven Years' Street Preaching in San Francisco,' 'The Model Preacher,' 'Reconciliation; or, How to Be Saved,' 'Infancy and Manhood of Christian Life,' 'Christian Adventures in South Africa,' 'Four Years' Campaign in India,' 'Pauline Methods of Missionary Work,' 'The Flaming Torch in Darkest Africa,' and 'The Story of My Life.' He died in 1902.

TAYLOR, ZACHARY. See Biographical and Critical Sketch, Vol. XII, page 5217.

TEASDALE, SARA TREVOR, writer, was born in St. Louis, Mo., August 8, 1884. Miss Teasdale is the author of a volume of verse entitled 'Sonnets to Duse' (Boston, Poet Lore Publishing Company, 1908). Her work has appeared in high-class periodicals like *Harper's Magazine* and *Putnam's Magazine.* She resides in St. Louis.

TEASDALE, THOMAS COX. Baptist clergyman. [Miss.]. He was born in 1808 and died in 1891. He published 'Reminiscences of a Long Life' (1887).

TEDFORD, LINTON, writer and real estate dealer, was born in Maryville, Tenn., October 2, 1875. For several years he was on the staff

of the Atlanta *Constitution*, after which he removed to California. Besides
two sketches produced in Atlanta, he wrote 'The Greater Claim' (1909),
a drama which was presented with great success at the Burbank Theater,
in Los Angeles. Mr. Tedford is engaged at present upon another play
which is likely still further to increase his reputation. He married, in
1903, Evelyn Wiswall, and resides in Pasadena, Cal.

TEMPLE, OLIVER PERRY. Lawyer. He was born in Green
County, Tenn., January 27, 1820, a son of James and Mary Craig
Temple, graduated from Washington College, and married, September 9,
1851, Scotia C. Hume. He was one of the Bell-Everett electors in 1860;
but delivered the first Union speech in Tennessee after the election of
Lincoln. He was one of the chancellors of Tennessee from 1866 to 1878.
Afterward became postmaster of Knoxville. His writings include: 'The
Covenanter, the Cavalier and the Puritan' (Cincinnati, The Robert Clark
Company, 1897), 'East Tennessee and the Civil War' (*ibid.*, 1899), and
'Union Leaders of East Tennessee' (*ibid.*, 1902).

TERHUNE, MARY VIRGINIA ("Marion Harland"). Author.
Her maiden name was Mary Virginia Hawes. She was born in Amelia
County, Va., December 21, 1831, and was given the best educational advantages, with the result that at the age of fourteen her bright intellect was
so quickened that she began to contribute to the press. Nor was it long
before she stood in the front rank of Southern writers of fiction. Her
books are devoid of melodramatic or sensational elements, but are full
of wholesome interest and are pure in sentiment, elevated in thought, and
pleasing in style. Besides many novels, she has published several books
on household economics, and has been editorially connected with various
magazines and newspapers. Her principal works are: 'The Story of Mary
Washington,' 'Alone,' 'Moss Side,' 'The Hidden Path,' 'Common Sense
in the Household,' 'Common Sense in the Nursery,' 'The Cottage Kitchen,'
'The Dinner Year-book,' 'Breakfast, Luncheon, and Tea,' 'Loitering in
Pleasant Paths,' 'The Old Field School-girl,' 'Judith,' 'Handicapped,' 'Ne-
mesis,' 'At Last,' 'Helen Gardner's Wedding Day,' 'Jessamine,' 'With
the Best Intentions,' 'True as Steel,' 'Sunny Bank,' 'From My Youth Up,'
'My Little Love,' 'A Gallant Fight,' 'The Royal Road,' 'His Great Self,'
'Mr. Wyat's Wife's Sister,' 'Eve's Daughters,' 'When Grandmama Was
New,' 'Some Colonial Homesteads,' 'More Colonial Homesteads,' 'Where
Ghosts Walk,' 'Literary Hearthstones,' and 'Dr. Dale: a Story without a
Moral,' written in association with her son, Albert Terhune. Most of her
literary work has appeared under the pen-name of "Marion Harland."
She married, in 1856, Rev. Edward Payson Terhune, a Congregational
minister, and became for many years a resident of New Jersey.

TERRELL, ALEXANDER WATKINS, jurist, lawyer, diplomat,
was born in Patrick County, Va., November 7, 1827. His father was
Dr. Christopher J. Terrell. On completing his studies at the University
of Missouri he practiced law for a while at St. Joseph, after which he
located at Austin, Texas, where he became a judge of the District Court.
During the Civil War he commanded a regiment of Texas cavalry; after
the struggle he was for four years a member of the House, and for
ten years a member of the Senate of Texas; and under President Cleveland's second administration, he was United States Minister to Turkey.
By resolution of the Legislature, his portrait has been hung upon the
walls of the State Capitol beside General Sam Houston's, and under it
is this inscription: "Alexander W. Terrell, the author of more good
laws for Texas than any other man living or dead." He is now engaged
in writing his 'Memoirs,' which besides some thirty public addresses, will
contain an account of his adventures as a soldier under Marshal Bazaine
in Mexico, and as a diplomat at the Court of Constantinople at the time
of the Armenian massa-----

TERRELL, KATE SCURRY. Author. [Texas]. She contributed to 'Wooten's Comprehensive History of Texas' (Dallas, W. G. Scarff, 1898), two interesting chapters, "The Runaway Scrape," which deals with an episode of the Mexican Invasion of 1836 and "The Texas Rangers."

TERRELL, P. L. Poet. [N.C.]. The author of 'Una Grames: a Southern Girl in War Times' (Statesville, N.C., 1902).

TESTUT, CHARLES. Physician and author. [La.]. He published several works in French, among them: 'Les Échoes' (1849), 'Portraits Litteraires de la Nouvelle Orléans, (New Orleans, 1850), 'Les Vieux Solomons' (New Orleans, 1870), and 'Les Filles de Monte Cristo.'

TEUSLER, MARY JEFFERSON. Educator. [Va.]. She published 'Outlines of German Literature' (1896).

TEVIS, JULIA, Mrs., educator, was born in Virginia but afterward lived in Kentucky and published an 'Autobiography.'

THARIN, ROBERT SEYMOUR SYMMES, lawyer, was born near Charleston, S.C., January 10, 1830. For some time he practiced law in Wetumpka, Ala., a partner of William L. Yancey; but the partnership was dissolved and on account of his anti-slavery sentiments he was threatened by the mob and forced to leave the State. During the war he resided in Indiana. Afterward he resumed his law practice in Charleston. He published 'Arbitrary Arrests in the South' (New York, 1863) and 'Letters on the Political Situation' (Charleston, 1871).

THAYER, MARTIN RUSSELL, jurist, was born in Petersburg, Va., January 27, 1819. He settled in Philadelphia for the practice of law, served in Congress and became a judge of the District Court. He published 'The Duties of Citizenship' (Philadelphia, 1862), 'The Great Victory: Its Cost and Value' (1865), 'The Life and Works of Francis Lieber' (1873), and other works.

THIERRY, CAMILLE. Poet. [La.]. He published in French a volume of verse entitled 'Les Vagabondes' (1842).

THOM, WILLIAM TAYLOR. Educator. [Va.]. He was born in 1849. He published 'Shakespeare and Chaucer Examinations' (1887) and a 'Course of Shakespeare Historical Reading' (1889).

THOMAS, ALLEN CLAPP, educator and minister of the Society of Friends, was born in Baltimore, Md., December 26, 1846. Since 1878 he has been professor of history and librarian of Haverford College. He has published 'Edward Lawrence Scull: a Memoir' (1891), a 'History of the United States for Schools and Academies' (1900), an 'Elementary History of the United States' (1900), and, with Dr. Richard Henry Thomas, a 'History of the Society of Friends in America' (1894), besides contributions to periodicals. He resides in Haverford, Pa.

THOMAS, AUGUSTUS, playwright, was born in St. Louis, Mo., January 8, 1859. For six years he was a page in Congress. It was in the capacity of a writer on St. Louis and Kansas City papers that he developed his peculiar gifts. Besides the dramas, which have brought him worldwide celebrity, viz.: 'Alabama,' 'In Mizzoura,' and 'Arizona,' he has published numerous other plays, among them: 'The Man Upstairs,' 'Oliver Goldsmith,' 'On the Quiet,' 'New Blood,' 'The Hoosier Doctor,' and 'The Burglar.' He resides at New Rochelle, N.Y.

THOMAS, CYRUS, ethnologist, was born in Kingsport, Tenn., July 27, 1825. For years he was archæologist in the United States Ethnological Bureau, and published 'Reports on the Rocky Mountain Locust,' in two volumes (1878-1880), 'Synopsis of the Acridæ of North America' (1873), 'Study of the Manuscript Troano' (1882), 'Notes on Certain Maya and Mexican Manuscripts' (1884), and 'Burial Mounds of the Northern Section of the United States' (1888).

THOMAS, EBENEZER SMITH, journalist, was born in Lancaster, Mass., in 1780, and died in Cincinnati, Ohio, in 1844. At the age of sixteen he became a bookseller in Charleston, S.C., where for several years he also edited the *Gazette*. He afterward settled in Baltimore, and finally removed to Cincinnati, where he edited at different times the *Daily Advertiser* and the *Evening Post*. He published 'Reminiscences of the Last Sixty-five Years,' in two volumes (Hartford, 1840), and 'Reminiscences of South Carolina,' in two volumes (1840).

THOMAS, FREDERICK WILLIAM, author, was born in Charleston, S.C., in 1811 and died in Washington, D.C., September 30, 1866. At the age of four he became a cripple. Though he studied law, journalism became his life's work and he edited various papers. At different times he was also a clerk in Washington, D.C., a minister of the Methodist Church, a professor of rhetoric in the University of Alabama, and a lecturer on the public platform. Besides contributing to magazines, he published several volumes in a variety of veins, among them: "The Emigrant; or, Reflections When Descending the Ohio," a poem (Cincinnati, 1833), 'Clinton Bradshaw' (Philadelphia, 1835), 'East and West' (1836), 'Howard Pinckney' (1840), 'The Beechen Tree, a Tale Told in Rhyme, and Other Poems' (New York, 1844), 'Sketches of Character and Tales Founded on Fact' (Louisville, 1849), and 'John Randolph of Roanoke, and Other Sketches of Character' (Louisville, 1853). He was a son of Ebenezer S. Thomas.

THOMAS, J. A. W. Baptist clergyman. [S.C.]. He wrote a 'History of Marlborough County, S.C.,' a work which was completed by his son.

THOMAS, JOHN PEYRE. Educator and historian. [S.C.]. Colonel Thomas published an interesting 'History of the South Carolina Military Academy' (1893). He resides in Columbia, S.C.

THOMAS, JOSEPH, clergyman and poet, was born in Virginia. His 'Poetical Descant on the Primæval and Present State of Mankind,' which was published at Winchester, Va., in 1816, is not unlike 'The Course of Time' in general scope, but in execution it falls short of the masterpiece of Pollok.

THOMAS, LEWIS FULKE, editor and poet, was born in Baltimore, Md., in 1815, and died in Washington, D.C., in 1868. He was a son of Ebenezer S. Thomas. For some time he edited *The Daily Herald* of Louisville, Ky.; and later he published at St. Louis what was said to be the first book of poetry to be issued west of the Mississippi. It was entitled: 'Inda, and Other Poems.' He also wrote two plays: "Osceola" (New Orleans, 1838), and "Cortez, the Conqueror" (Washington, 1857), both tragedies.

THOMAS, MARTHA McCANNON, author, was a daughter of Ebenezer S. Thomas, and was born in Baltimore, Md., November 15, 1823. She published two interesting stories, 'Life's Lesson' (New York, 1846) and 'Captain Phil: a Story of the Civil War' (1882).

THOMAS, MARY VON ERDEN, author, was a daughter of Ebenezer S. Thomas and was born in Charleston, S.C., December 8, 1825. She became a clerk in the employ of the Government at Washington, D.C., and published a novel entitled 'Winning the Battle' (Philadelphia, 1882).

THOMAS, OLIVIA TULLY. Poet. She resided in Mississippi during the Civil War and wrote an exquisite poem entitled "The Southern Republic"; but no other fragment of song has been found from her pen.

THOMAS, RICHARD HENRY, physician and minister of the Society of Friends, was born in Baltimore, Md., January 26, 1854. For several years he was dean of the Woman's College of Baltimore. His published works include: 'Echoes and Pictures,' a volume of verse (London, 1895), 'Penelve; or, Among the Quakers,' a story (1898), and, in collaboration with Professor A. C. Thomas, a 'History of the Society of Friends in America' (1894), besides pamphlets and papers. He resides in Baltimore, Md.

THOMAS, THEODORE GAILLARD, physician, was born on Edisto Island, S.C., November 21, 1831. After receiving his medical diploma, he located in New York, became an eminent specialist, and published a 'Treatise on Diseases of Women' (Philadelphia, 1868), which was translated into several foreign languages.

THOMAS, WILLIAM HOLCOMBE, jurist and orator, was born near Oak Bowery, Ala., July 10, 1867, of vigorous Revolutionary stock. On completing his education at Emory College, Georgia, he read law under James R. Dowdell, the present chief justice of the Supreme Court of the State. In 1902 he became associate judge of the City Court of Montgomery and, in 1909, judge of the same tribunal. Judge Thomas was a member of the committee which, in 1903, secured the passage of the child labor bill by the Legislature of Alabama. In 1904 he was a member of the International Congress of Arts and Sciences, and in the same year a delegate to the Universal Congress of Judges and Lawyers in St. Louis. He is deeply interested in the educational progress of the South, and is a member of the educational conference which meets annually in the South to discuss the great problem of education. He also belongs to various organizations, scientific and political, social and patriotic. He was married, June 4, 1891, at Lowndesboro, Ala., to Lula Marion. Included among the published writings of Judge Thomas are: 'The Birth and Growth of the Constitution of Alabama' (1900), 'Tribute to Honorable W. J. Sanford, Governor of Alabama' (1901), 'Governor Sanford's Last Christmas' (1902), "Individualism vs. Law," an address before the International Congress of Arts and Sciences (1904), 'College Men and World Currents' (1906), "The New South," an address delivered before the Congregational Club of Boston, Mass.' (1908), and "The Jefferson Davis Anniversary Celebration," an address delivered before the Confederate Veterans, at Waverly, Ala. (1909), besides a number of others upon practical and vital topics.

THOMPSON, AGNES. Author. [La.]. She wrote 'Old Aunt Tilda, and Other Sketches' (New Orleans, 1892), in which she charmingly portrays life in the South.

THOMPSON, C. C. Poet. [N.C.]. The author of a poem entitled "The Christ" (New York, The Broadway Publishing Company, 1903).

THOMPSON, EDWARD PORTER. Historian. [Ky.]. Besides numerous historical monographs and essays he wrote a 'History of Kentucky,' a 'History of the Orphan Brigade,' and other novels.

THOMPSON, GEORGE WASHINGTON, lawyer, was born in St. Clairsville, Ohio, May 14, 1806, and died near Wheeling, W.Va., February 24, 1888. After studying law in Richmond, Va., he settled west of the Allegheny Mountains, in what was afterward West Virginia, served in Congress and became an occupant of the Bench. Besides contributing to the periodicals, he published a 'Dissertation on the Historical Right of Virginia to the Territory Northwest of the Ohio,' 'Life of Linn Boyd,' 'The Living Forces of the Universe' (Philadelphia, 1866), and 'Deus Semper.' At the age of fourscore years he published a poem entitled "The Song of Eighty," which he circulated among his friends.

THOMPSON, HOLLAND. [N.C.]. He wrote 'From the Cotton Field to the Cotton Mill: A Study of the Industrial Transition of North Carolina' (New York, The Macmillan Company, 1908).

THOMPSON, HUGH MILLER, clergyman and educator, was born in Londonderry, Ireland, in 1830. Coming to America in early youth, he was educated at the University of the South and received into the ministry of the Episcopal Church. For several years he taught in one of the theological schools; but in 1876 he was called to Trinity Church, New Orleans, and in 1887 he was made bishop of Mississippi. His writings include: 'Copy: Essays from an Editor's Drawer' (1872), 'Unity and Its Restoration' (1860), 'First Principles' (1863), 'Kingdom of God' (1873), 'Sin and Penalty' (1863), 'The World and the Logos' (1885), 'The World and the Man' (1890), 'The World and the Kingdom' (1888), 'The World and the Wrestlers' (1895), 'Absolution' (1864), 'Is Romanism the Best Religion for the Republic?' and others. He died in 1902. Hobart College gave him the degree of S.T.D. He also held the D.D. and the LL.D. degrees.

THOMPSON, JOHN, political writer, was born in 1777, the exact place unknown, and died in Petersburg, Va., in 1799. Under the pen-names of "Casca" and "Gracchus," he published a number of articles in the Petersburg *Gazette,* assailing the administration of John Adams, and also a number of letters over the signature of "Curtius," addressed to Chief Justice John Marshall, which were afterward published in book form (1804). George Hay wrote his memoir.

THOMPSON, JOHN REUBEN. See Biographical and Critical Sketch, Vol. XII, page 5227.

THOMPSON, MAURICE. See Biographical and Critical Sketch, Vol. XII, page 5255.

THOMPSON, RICHARD WIGGINTON, lawyer, and Cabinet officer, was born in Culpeper County, Va., June 9, 1809. He removed first to Kentucky and afterward to Indiana, studied law, became a Member of Congress, a Judge of the Court of Claims, and Secretary of the Navy in the Cabinet of President Hayes. He was a power in political conventions and a writer of party platforms. Several volumes came from his pen: 'The Papacy and the Civil Power' (New York, 1876), and a 'History of the Tariff' (Chicago, 1888), 'Personal Recollections of Sixteen Presidents,' and 'Footprints of the Jesuits.' He died in 1900.

THOMPSON, WADDY, lawyer and author, was born in Pickensville, S.C., September 8, 1798, and died in Tallahassee, Fla., November 23, 1868. He studied law, became a Member of Congress, a brigadier-general of militia, and United States Minister to Mexico. In the last-mentioned sphere of service, he negotiated two important treaties and procured the release of one hundred and fifty Texan prisoners. On returning home he published 'Recollections of Mexico' (New York, 1846), a work of much interest, which accurately portrayed conditions on the other side of the Rio Grande on the eve of hostilities. He was a cotton planter of large means.

THOMPSON, WADDY. Author. He was born in Columbia, S.C., August 13, 1867, a son of Hugh Smith and Elizabeth Anderson Thompson, graduated from the University of South Carolina, and married, October 30, 1895, Pauline Spain. He was engaged in active journalism for eight years; but relinquished newspaperdom for life insurance. He is fond of historical studies, and his leisure hours have borne fruit in two excellent volumes: 'A History of the United States' (New York, D. C. Heath and Company), and 'Life of Andrew Johnson.' He resides in Columbia, S.C.

THOMPSON, WILL H. Lawyer. He was born in Calhoun, Ga., March 10, 1848, a son of the Rev. Grigg M. Thompson, and was educated in the local schools, and at the Georgia Military Institute. Though only a lad, he served in the Confederate Army. He practiced law for several years at Crawfordsville, Ind., and afterward settled in Seattle, Wash., becoming one of the general attorneys of the Great Northern Railway system. He was first a Democrat, but became a Republican on the issues of 1896. In addition to numerous magazine articles, he is the author of several interesting publications: 'How to Train in Archery,' written in collaboration with Maurice Thompson, 'The Lion Heart,' a libretto, 'High Tide at Gettysburg,' and 'Bond of Blood.'

THOMPSON, WILLIAM T. See Biographical and Critical Sketch, Vol. XII, page 5283.

THOMSON, SAMUEL HARRISON, clergyman, was born in Nicholas County, Ky., August 26, 1813, and died in Pasadena, Cal., September 2, 1882. He became an ordained minister of the Presbyterian Church, but devoted his life mainly to teaching in colleges and published 'The Mosaic Account of Creation' (1852), 'Geology an Interpreter of Scripture' (1860), and several pamphlets.

THORNTON, JAMES BANKHEAD, lawyer, was born in Mount Zephyr, Va., August 28, 1806, and died in Memphis, Tenn., October 12, 1867. He studied law, settled in Memphis for the practice of his profession, and published a 'Digest of the Conveyancing, Testamentary, and Registry Laws of the States of the Union' (Philadelphia, 1847). He also compiled a work on 'Assignments,' but the manuscript was burned accidentally.

THORNTON, THOMAS C., clergyman, was born in Dumfries, Va., October 12, 1794, and died in Mississippi, March 23, 1860. He studied theology, joined the Baltimore conference of the Methodist Church, became president of a college in Mississippi, left the Methodist for the Episcopal Church, but eventually returned to his first allegiance and published a work entitled 'An Inquiry into the History of Slavery in the United States' and 'Theological Colloquies.'

THORNTON, WILLIAM MYNN, educator, was born in Cumberland County, Va., October 28, 1851. After graduation from Hampden-Sidney College, he continued his studies at the University of Virginia, in which latter institution he has filled the chair of mathematics for nearly thirty-five years. He is now also dean of the department of engineering. For several years he edited *The Annals of Mathematics*. The sketch of Basil L. Gildersleeve in 'The Library of Southern Literature' is from the pen of Dr. Thornton. Hampden-Sidney College gave him the degree of LL.D.

THORNWELL, JAMES H. See Biographical and Critical Sketch, Vol. XII, page 5309.

THORPE, THOMAS BANGS, author and artist, was born in Westfield, Mass., March 1, 1815. On account of ill health he left college prior to graduation and came South, locating first in Louisville, Ky., and afterward in New Orleans. As a humorist he acquired wide celebrity, and he was also something of an artist. He published 'Tom Owen, the Bee Hunter' and 'The Big Bear of Arkansas,' besides numerous magazine articles. He also edited various papers. He died in New York City, in 1878.

THRALL, HOMER S. Methodist Episcopal clergyman. **[Texas].** He wrote 'Methodism in Texas,' an interesting work.

THRASHER, JOHN S., journalist, was born in Portland, Me., in 1817, and died in Galveston, Texas. November 10, 1879. For several years he was a merchant in Havana, Cuba. Afterward he embarked in journalism on the island, but his paper was suppressed by the Spanish authorities and his life was for months imperiled. Later he returned to the United States, settled first in New Orleans and then in New York, traveled extensively in Central and South America, and finally settled in Texas, where he married a lady of wealth. He published a translation of Humboldt's 'Personal Narrative of Travels' (New York, 1856), and wrote a number of essays.

THRUSTON, GATES PHILLIPS. Lawyer. He was born in Dayton, Ohio, June 11, 1835, and was valedictorian of his class at Miami College. Afterward he studied law. He entered the Union Army, and became brigadier-general. He was twice married, and is the author of 'Antiquities of Tennessee and Adjacent States' (1890), besides numerous contributions to magazines. He resides in Nashville, Tenn.

THRUSTON, LUCY M. See Biographical and Critical Sketch, Vol. XII, page 5327.

THWAITES, REUBEN G., antiquarian, was not a Southerner but he edited an important work entitled 'Jesuit Relations and Allied Documents' (Cleveland, Ohio, 1896-1901), which recounts the travels and explorations of the Jesuit missionaries in New France, from 1610 to 1791.

TICE, J. H. [Mo.]. Author of a work entitled 'Over the Plains and on the Mountains.'

TICKNOR, FRANK O. See Biographical and Critical Sketch, Vol. XII, page 5353.

TIDBALL, THOMAS ALLEN. Protestant Episcopal clergyman. He was born in Virginia. Since 1892, he has been rector of the Church of St. Luke in Philadelphia. He has published 'Christ in the New Testament' (New York, Thomas Whittaker, 1891).

TIERNAN, CHARLES B. Lawyer. He was born in Baltimore, Md., September 4, 1840. At the Maryland Bar he has for years taken high rank. His publications include: 'The Tiernan Family in Maryland' (1898) and 'The Tiernan and Other Families' (1901).

TIERNAN, CHARLES COMFORT. Protestant Episcopal clergyman. Born in 1829. For several years he was rector of Zion Church in New York City, but in 1893 became archdeacon. His publications include: 'Expression in Church Architecture,' 'Modern Atheism,' 'The Protestant Episcopal Church' (New York, Charles Scribner's Sons, 1895), and 'The Prayer-book and the Christian Life' (*ibid.*, 1897).

TIERNAN, FRANCES FISHER ("Christian Reid"). See Biographical and Critical Sketch, Vol. XII, page 5369.

TIERNAN, MARY SPEAR NICHOLAS, Mrs. Author. [Md.]. She wrote 'Homoselle, 'Suzette,' 'Jack Horner,' and other novels.

TIFFANY, OLIVE. Poet. [Mo.]. She published a volume of verse entitled 'Floral Poems' (1893).

TIFFANY, OSMOND. Author. He was born in Baltimore, Md., July 16, 1823. While engaged in business pursuits, he also indulged his taste for literary work, and, besides contributing to periodicals, published: 'The Canton Chinese' (Boston, 1849), 'Brandon: a Tale of the American Colonies' (New York, 1851), and 'Sketch of the Life of General Otho H. Williams' (Baltimore, 1851). He also edited 'Patriarchs and Prophets of Biblical Story' (Springfield, Mass., 1860).

TIGERT, JOHN JAMES. Clergyman and editor. He was born in Louisville, Ky., in 1856. On completing his education at Vanderbilt University, he was received into the ministry of the M.E. Church, South. For several years he was professor of moral philosophy at Vanderbilt, and afterward became editor of the *Methodist Review*. He married, in 1878, Amelia McTyeire. His writings include: 'Handbook of Logic,' 'Systematic Theology,' 'Theology and Philosophy,' 'The Preacher Himself,' 'Passing Through the Gates,' 'A Voice from the South,' 'Constitutional History of American Episcopal Methodism,' 'The Journal of Thomas Coke,' 'A Manual of Christian Doctrine,' 'The Making of Methodism,' and 'Theism,' all of which are issued by the M. E. Publishing House, South. He died in 1906. Dr. Tigert held the D.D. and the LL.D. degrees.

TILFORD, TILDEN. Author. [Texas]. He published a story of cowboy life entitled 'Butternut Jones' (1903).

TILLETT, WILBUR FISK. He was born at Henderson, N.C., August 25, 1854. His father was Rev. John Tillett and his mother, Elizabeth Wyche. On completing his educational equipment, he was received into the ministry of the M.E. Church, South. He married, first, Kate Schoolfield and, afterward, Laura E. McLoud. He became professor of systematic theology in Vanderbilt University, in 1884, and two years later assumed the additional duties of vice-chancellor. His writings include: 'Our Hymns and Their Authors' (Nashville, M.E. Publishing House, South), 'Discussions in Theology' (*ibid.*), 'Personal Salvation,' (*ibid.*), 'The Doctrines of Methodism' (*ibid.*), and 'A Statement of the Faith of World-wide Methodism,' besides numerous papers and reviews. He held the D.D., the S.T.D. and the LL.D. degrees.

TILLEY, MORRIS PALMER. Educator. He was born in Norfolk, Va. His father was Thomas C. Tilley and his mother, Lois Frances Miller. He holds the assistant professorship of English in the University of Michigan. He has contributed articles of interest and value to 'Modern Language Notes' and to high-class popular periodicals like *The Nation* and *The Dial*. The sketch of James Barron Hope in 'The Library of Southern Literature' is also from his pen. He holds the degree of Ph.D.

TILLMAN, BENJAMIN RYAN. United States Senator. He was born in Edgefield County, S.C., August 11, 1847. Before completing his education he entered the Confederate Army and, due to exposure, he was stricken with severe illness which involved the loss of his left eye. He followed the pursuit of farming but took an active interest in public affairs, became twice governor of the State and, on retiring from office, in 1894, was sent to the United States Senate, a position to which he has twice been reëlected. He founded Clemson College, for boys, and Winthrop Normal and Industrial College, for girls, at John C. Calhoun's old home place, and originated the dispensary system of selling liquor under State control. He married Sallie Starke in 1868. On the floor of the United States Senate he has been a power. Unconventional and outspoken, he is also fearless and independent, a strong man of the people. On the lecture platform he has often spoken to large assemblies. He resides at Trenton, S.C., and is in politics a Democrat.

TILLMAN, JOHN NEWTON. Jurist and educator. He was born in Springfield, Mo., December 13, 1859. His father was N. J. Tillman and his mother, Mary Mullins. After graduating from the University of Arkansas, he studied law and became a judge of the District Court and a State Senator. In 1905 he was made president of the University of Arkansas, his *alma mater*. Besides a number of short stories for magazines, he is the author of several popular lectures, among them: "Nation-wide Prohibition," "College Life," "The Glory Jest and Riddle of the World," and "The Folly of Failure." He is also one of the consulting editors of 'The Library of Southern Literature.' He married, March 5, 1885, Tempy Walker. He holds the degree of LL.D.

TIMROD, HENRY. See Biographical and Critical Sketch, Vol. XII, page 5391.

TIMROD, WILLIAM H. Poet. He was born near Charleston, S.C., in 1792, and was the son of Henry Timrod, a native of Germany. At an early age he evinced unusual talent; but, due to modest circumstances, he was in the main self-educated. Besides numerous poems of rare power, he wrote a five-act drama, which he considered his masterpiece; but it was unfortunately lost. Washington Irving remarked of one of his poems, "To Time," that no finer lyric had come from the pen of Tom Moore. When he was only nineteen, he married a belle who was three years younger than himself, by the name of Miss Prince; and from this union sprang the celebrated Henry Timrod. He died in 1837.

TODD, CHARLES SCOTT. Diplomat and soldier. He was born near Danville, Ky., January 22, 1791, and died in Baton Rouge, La., May 14, 1871. After leaving William and Mary College, he studied law and located for the practice of his profession in Lexington, Ky.; but the war fever seizing him, he became an aide to General Harrison in the regular Army, won distinction for his prowess, and retired in 1815 with the rank of colonel. For a short time he was Secretary of State in the Cabinet of President Madison, and for a full term Minister to Russia under President Tyler. In conjunction with Benjamin Drake he prepared a sketch of his civil and military career, which was published in book form (Cincinnati, 1840).

TOLMAN, HERBERT CUSHING. Educator. He was born in Massachusetts, November 4, 1865, of Puritan ancestors, received the best educational advantages of both Europe and America, and won numerous prizes. He is one of the foremost linguists of the day, an authority on many languages both ancient and modern. He married, August 26, 1891, Mary Wells, and became professor of Greek in Vanderbilt University in 1894. Besides editing the 'Vanderbilt Oriental Series,' he is the author of numerous Greek and Latin textbooks of standard value and has made frequent contributions to periodicals. Yale University gave him the degree of Ph.D. He resides in Nashville, Tenn.

TOMLINSON, G. A. R. Poet. [Ga.]. He published 'The Old Brigade, and Other Poems.'

TOMPKINS, DANIEL A. Mechanical engineer and manufacturer. He was born in Edgefield County, S.C., October 12, 1852, a son of DeWitt Clinton and Hannah Virginia Tompkins, was educated at South Carolina College and Rensselaer Polytechnic Institute and has since become one of the foremost factors in the industrial development of the South since the war, being interested largely in cotton mills. He is the author of many articles bearing upon the commercial and industrial phases of the subject of cotton. He resides in Charlotte, N.C.

TONER, JOSEPH MEREDITH, physician, of Alabama, was born in 1825 and died in 1896. He was the author of an important paper read before the American Public Health Association, of New York, in 1873, on "Contributions to the Study of Yellow Fever." It was printed in pamphlet form and created such wide interest that several editions were exhausted.

TOOMBS, ROBERT. See Biographical and Critical Sketch, Vol. XII, page 5417.

TOULMIN, HENRY. Jurist. He was born in Taunton, England, in 1767, and died in Washington County, Ala., November 11, 1823. He came to America at an early age and settled first in Norfolk, Va., but he afterward removed to Kentucky, where he filled the office of Secretary of State for several years. Later he was appointed judge of the United States District Court of Mississippi; but he spent his last years in Alabama, where he assisted in framing the State constitution. He published a 'Description of Kentucky' (1792), a 'Magistrate's Assistant,' a 'Collection of the Acts of Kentucky' (Frankfort, 1802), a 'Review of the Criminal Law of Kentucky,' with James Blair (1804), and a 'Digest of the Laws of the State of Alabama' (Cahaba, 1823).

TOWNS, SAMUEL A. [Ala.]. He wrote a 'History of Marion, Ala.' (1844).

TOWNSEND, BELTON O'NEALL. Poet. [S.C.]. He published a volume of verse entitled 'Plantation Lays, and Other Poems' (1884).

TOWNSEND, JOHN WILSON. Author. He was born near Lexington, Ky., November 2, 1885, and was educated at the University of the State, afterward attending lectures at Harvard. Despite his youth, two volumes of unique interest have already come from his pen: 'Richard Hickman Menefee' (New York and Washington, The Neale Publishing Company) and 'Kentuckians in History and Literature' (*ibid.*). The sketch of Thomas H. Chivers in 'The Library of Southern Literature' is also from the pen of Mr. Townsend.

TOWNSEND, MARY A. See Biographical and Critical Sketch, Vol. XII, page 5441.

TOY, CRAWFORD HOWELL. Educator. He was born in Norfolk, Va., March 23, 1866. a son of Thomas D. and Amelia Toy, graduated from the University of Virginia and afterward studied at Berlin. He married, in 1888, Nancy Saunders. He was professor of Hebrew in the Southern Baptist Theological Seminary for ten years, and in 1880, became professor of Oriental Languages at Harvard. Among his more important works are: 'The Religion of Israel' (1882), 'Quotations in the New Testament' (New York, Charles Scribner's Sons, 1884), 'Judaism and Christianity' (Boston, Little, Brown and Company, 1890), 'Hebrew Text and English Translation of Ezekiel' (New York, Dodd, Mead and Company, 1899), and 'Commentary on Proverbs' (New York, Charles Scribner's Sons, 1899). He resides in Cambridge, Mass., and holds the degree of LL.D.

TRABUE, ISAAC HODGEN. Lawyer and planter. He was born in Russell County, Ky., March 25, 1829, a son of the Rev. Chasteen and Elizabeth T. Trabue, the paternal name being of Huguenot origin. He received an excellent education, and married, in 1865, Virginia Taylor of Savannah, Ga. He served in the Confederate Army, and, being a large slaveholder, he put his male slaves to work in the commissary department and his female slaves in the hospitals. He was prominent in Kentucky politics after the war, and one of the best chess-players of the day, defeating Zuckertort, the world's champion, in 1883. He made and codified the rules for playing four-handed chess, founded the town of Punta Gorda in Florida, and became the chief factor in opposing the removal of the State capital from Tallahassee. His published works are: 'Hobson Blowing up the Merrimac in Santiago Bay,' a drama, 'Black Wench,' a novel, and 'Rules and Directions for Playing Four-Handed Trabue, American Chess.' In politics he is a Socialist and in religion a free thinker. He resides at Punta Gorda, Fla.

TRACY, S. M. Educator. [Miss.]. He published 'Mississippi as It Is' (1895).

TRAIL, FLORENCE. Author. She was born in Frederick, Md., September 1, 1854. Though she belonged to one of the wealthiest families of Maryland, she believed in the doctrine of self-support and left home to engage in teaching, first in Kentucky and North Carolina, and afterward in New York and Connecticut. On returning from an extended tour of Europe, she published 'My Journal in Foreign Lands' (New York, 1885). This was followed by other volumes, among them: 'Studies in Criticism' (New York, 1888), 'Under the Second Renaissance' (Buffalo, 1894), and 'A History of Italian Literature.'

TRAMMELL, WILLIAM DUGAS. Author. He was born in Georgia, in 1850, and died in Texas in 1884. He wrote a novel entitled 'Ca Ira' (New York, 1874).

TRAYLOR, ROBERT LEE. Business man and collector of rare books. He was born at Midway Mills, Va., September 23, 1864, the son of Albert Washington and Mary Elizabeth Traylor. For many years he was engaged in railway development, afterward becoming interested in insurance and banking. He is the owner of perhaps the largest private library in the South, the collection including many rare and precious volumes. He married, in 1887, Annie Gavin. Among other works, he is the author of an important monograph entitled 'Some Notes on the First Recorded Visit of White Men to the Site of the Present City of Richmond.' He resides in Richmond, Va.

TRENHOLM, WILLIAM. Author. He was born in South Carolina in 1836 and died in New York in 1901. He wrote a work on finance entitled 'The People's Money' (1896).

TRENT, WILLIAM PETERFIELD. See Biographical and Critical Sketch, Vol. XII, page 5457.

TRESCOT, WILLIAM HENRY. See Biographical and Critical Sketch, Vol. XII, page 5483.

TREZEVANT, EVA WHITTHORNE. She was born in Arkansas in 1866, but afterward removed to Texas, where she published 'In Maiden Meditation' (Chicago, A. C. McClurg and Company, 1893), and 'The Reflections of a Lonely Man' (*ibid.*, 1895). Both works passed into several editions.

TROTT, NICHOLAS. Jurist. He was born in England in 1663 and died in Charleston, in 1740. For some time he was governor of the Bahama Islands. After coming to Charleston, he became speaker of the assembly, councillor, and judge. He revised 'The Laws of South Carolina before 1734,' in two volumes (Charleston, 1736), and published 'Clavis Lingæ Sanctæ' (1817), and 'Laws Relating to Church and Clergy in America.' He was a scholar of unusual attainments.

TROOST, GERARD. Mineralogist. He was born in Bois le Duc, Holland, March 15, 1776, and died in Nashville, Tenn., August 14, 1850. He organized the first alum works in the United States at Cape Sable, Md., was one of the founders of the Academy of Natural Sciences in Philadelphia, and for more than twenty years filled the chair of geology and chemistry in the University of Nashville. Besides numerous contributions to the transactions of learned societies, he translated Humboldt's 'Aspects of Nature' and published a 'Geological Survey of the Environs of Philadelphia' (Philadelphia, 1826), and nine volumes of the 'Geological Reports of Tennessee' (Nashville, 1835-1848).

TROUP, GEORGE MICHAEL. Statesman. He was born at McIntosh Bluff, on the Tombigbee River, in what is now Alabama, but what was then Georgia, September 8, 1780, and died in Laurens County, Ga., May 3, 1856. After graduating from Princeton, he studied law, located in Savannah, achieved eminence at the Bar and distinction in politics. From 1806 to 1815 he served in Congress, where he supported the war measures of 1812. On the resignation of William W. Bibb, he became United States Senator. Later, for two successive terms, he held the office of governor of Georgia. During his administration he insisted upon the removal of the Cherokee and Creek Indians by the United States Government, in compliance with an old agreement. He stood boldly for States' rights in a clash which subsequently ensued between State and Federal authorities, and won the fight. At the governor's mansion in Milledgeville he entertained Lafayette. Later, he was returned to the United States Senate. 'The Life of George M. Troup' was written by Edward J. Harden (Savannah, 1859).

TRUEDELL, SAMUEL O. [New Orleans, La.]. He published a work entitled 'A Wonderful Discovery in the Book of Job' (Philadelphia, 1890).

TRUITT, JULIA PHIFER. Poet. [La.]. She published a volume of verse entitled 'Birds of Passage' (1890).

TUCKER, BEVERLEY. See Biographical and Critical Sketch, Vol. XII, page 5501.

TUCKER, BEVERLEY DANDRIDGE. Bishop-coadjutor of the Protestant Episcopal Church. He was born in Richmond, Va., the son of Nathaniel Beverley and Jane Ellis Tucker. He was educated in England and Switzerland and at the University of Toronto. On July 22,

1873, he married Anna Maria, daughter of Colonel John Augustus Washington, of Mount Vernon. During the Civil War he served in the West Virginia artillery; and it was from this experience that he drew his inspiration for his 'Confederate Memorial Verses.' He was ordained bishop-coadjutor in 1896. Roanoke College gave him the degree of D.D.

TUCKER, GEORGE. See Biographical and Critical Sketch, Vol. XII, page 5512.

TUCKER, HENRY HOLCOMB. Clergyman and educator. He was born in Warren County, Ga., May 10, 1819. After graduating from Columbian University, he studied law and practiced for two years. He then entered the Baptist ministry, became an eminent educator and divine, and at different times was president of Mercer University and chancellor of the University of Georgia. He also owned and edited the *Christian Index*. In addition to a series of letters on 'Religious Liberty,' addressed to Alexander H. Stephens, he published 'The Gospel in Enoch; or, Truth in the Concrete' (Philadelphia, 1868), 'The Old Theology Restated' (1884), and numerous sermons, one of which, on the subject of baptism, has been translated into several different languages. He met his death by an accidental fall, in Atlanta, Ga., September 6, 1889. Columbian University gave him the degree of D.D.

TUCKER, HENRY ST. GEORGE. Lawyer. He was born in Winchester, Va., April 5, 1853, a son of John Randolph and Laura Powell Tucker, received his collegiate and legal education at Washington and Lee University and married, first, Henrietta Preston Johnston, and second, Martha Sharpe. He was a Member of Congress for eight years, and succeeded his father in the chair of constitutional and international law at Washington and Lee University in 1897, but resigned that position in 1903 to become dean of the Law School of George Washington University, Washington, D.C. Besides numerous speeches and addresses, he is the author of many important contributions to educational and law journals and the editor of 'Tucker on the Constitution' (New York, Charles Scribner's Sons, 1899). He was elected president of the American Bar Association in 1904, succeeded Fitzhugh Lee as president of the Jamestown Tercentennial Exposition of 1907, and was narrowly defeated for governor of Virginia in 1909. The University of Mississippi gave him the degree of LL.D. He resides at Staunton, Va.

TUCKER, JOHN RANDOLPH. Statesman and educator. He was a son of Henry St. George Tucker and was born in Winchester, Va., December 24, 1823. After completing his studies at the University of Virginia, he chose the profession of law and rose to distinction. For several years he was a professor in the legal department of Washington and Lee University, but relinquished his chair to enter Congress; and from 1874 to 1887 he was one of the most conspicuous figures in the arena of national legislation. As an orator he possessed few equals, his speeches in Congress being masterpieces both of eloquence and of statesmanship. He was occupying the office of president of Washington and Lee University at the time of his death. Yale gave him the degree of LL.D.

TUCKER, NATHANIEL. Poet. He was born in Bermuda, Va., in 1750, and wrote in verse 'The Bermudian' (1774).

TUCKER, NATHANIEL BEVERLEY. Lawyer. He was the son of St. George Tucker, an eminent jurist of the early national period, and stepbrother of John Randolph of Roanoke. He was born in Williamsburg, Va., in 1784, and was educated at William and Mary College. For several years he practiced law in Missouri, which he knew both as a territory and as a state; but he returned to Virginia in 1830 and soon afterward became professor of law in the famous old school from which he graduated. Besides taking an active part in the political affairs of the day, he was a man of literary inclinations and accomplishments, and wrote in numerous veins. His published works include two novels: 'The Partisan Leader, a Tale of the Future,' in which he distinctly foreshadowed the course of events down to 1861, and 'George Balcombe.' He was also the author of a 'Life of John Randolph,' a volume on 'Political Science,' a volume on 'The Principles of Pleading,' and a number of essays which appeared in the *Southern Literary Messenger.* He died in 1851.

TUCKER, ST. GEORGE. Jurist and educator. He was born in the Bermudas, in 1752, but came to Virginia early in life and married Mrs. Francis Bland Randolph, the mother of the famous John Randolph of Roanoke. He became an eminent jurist, attaining the chief-judgeship of the Virginia Court of Appeals and serving for some time also in the United States District Court of Virginia, besides holding the professorship of law at William and Mary College. He possessed literary gifts of high order and wrote with ease in both prose and verse. His writings include: 'Days of My Youth, and Other Poems,' 'Probationary Odes of Jonathan Pindar, Esq.,' a group of satires; a 'Commentary on the Constitution,' and a 'Dissertation on Slavery, or Letters on Alien and Sedition Laws,' besides annotating an edition of Blackstone's 'Commentaries.' He also left at his death some unpublished dramas. He died in 1828.

TUCKER, ST. GEORGE H. Lawyer. He was born in Winchester, Va., in 1828, a grandson of St. George Tucker, and was at one time clerk of the Virginia Legislature. He served in the Confederate Army and rose to the rank of lieutenant-colonel, but died from exposure in the Seven Days' Battle around Richmond. He was the author of an interesting historical romance entitled 'Hansford, a Tale of Bacon's Rebellion,' which vividly portrays the life of an eventful era. He died in 1862.

TUDOR, HENRY. Poet. [Mo.]. He wrote a poem on the death of President McKinley entitled: "Ite, Missa Est," which is preserved in 'Missouri Literature.'

TUNNARD, W. H. [La.]. He wrote a 'History of the Third Regiment of Louisiana Infantry' (1866).

TUNSTALL, NANNIE W. Author. [Va.]. She wrote 'Number 40' and numerous short stories.

TUOMY, MICHAEL. Geologist. He was born in Cork, Ireland, September 29, 1808, and died in Tuscaloosa, Ala., March 30, 1857. He was for some time professor of geology and chemistry in the University of Alabama and State geologist. Besides numerous geological reports, he published a 'Geology of Alabama' (1850), which was revised after his death by John W. Mallet (1858).

TUPPER, HENRY ALLEN. Clergyman. He was born in Charleston, S.C., February 29, 1828. On completing his educational equipment, he was received into the ministry of the Baptist Church. For nearly twenty years he was a pastor at Washington, Ga., but for a part of this time he was at the front, performing the duties of a chaplain in the C.S.A. He afterward became corresponding secretary of the Foreign Missionary

Board of the Southern Baptist Convention. His writings include: 'Foreign Missions of the Southern Baptist Convention' (1880), 'Two Centuries of the First Baptist Church of South Carolina' (1889), 'The Carpenter's Son' (1889), 'Truth in Romance,' and 'American Baptist Missions in Africa.' He died in 1902. Madison University conferred upon him the degree of D.D.

TUPPER, KERR BOYCE. Clergyman. He was born in Washington, Ga., February 2, 1854, a son of the Rev. H. A. Tupper, received his collegiate education at Mercer University, Macon, Ga., and married, November 21, 1875, Lucilla Sloan, of Greenville, S. C. He became pastor of the First Baptist Church of Philadelphia, and attained success on the lecture platform, his most popular subjects being: "Robert Burns," "Shelley," "William Ewart Gladstone," "Optimism Versus Pessimism," "Ideal Manliness," "The Old Book from God," and "An Evening at Home." His published works include: 'English Synonyms,' 'Popular Treatise on Christian Baptism' (1885), 'Robertson's Living Thoughts' (1890), 'Seven Great Lights' (1892), 'Gladstone, and Other Addresses' (1898), and 'Life of Diaz.' He is also an editorial contributor to *The Baptist Commonwealth*. Mercer University gave him the degree of LL.D. and Central University, Iowa, the degree of D.D. He resides in Philadelphia, Pa.

TURNBULL, ROBERT JAMES, political writer, was born in New Smyrna, Fla., in 1775, and died in Charleston, S.C., June 15, 1833. He was educated in England and, on his return home, was admitted to the Bar; but the life of a planter was more attractive to him than the profession of law. He became one of the foremost writers of the day on political topics, espoused the nullification movement, and wrote for the Charleston *Mercury*, a series of letters, afterward published in book form under the title of 'The Crisis' (1827-1832), which became the text-book of the nullifiers. He also published 'The Tribunal of Last Resort' (1830), besides numerous monographs and speeches. Most of his newspaper articles were written over the signature of "Brutus."

TURNER, EDWARD. Jurist. He was born in Fairfax County, Va., November 25, 1778, and died in Natchez, Miss., May 23, 1860. For many years he was an occupant of the Supreme Bench of Mississippi and became chief justice. He published 'Statutes of the Mississippi Territory' (Natchez, 1816).

TURNER, FRANCIS M. He wrote a 'Life of John Sevier' (New York and Washington, The Neale Publishing Company, 1909).

TURNER, HENRY M., bishop of the African Methodist Episcopal Church, was born at Newberry, S.C., February 1, 1834. For years he has been an eminent leader of his race, and has advocated with great warmth the return of his people to Africa. His published works include: a 'Hymn Book of the A.M.E. Church,' a 'Catechism' and 'Methodist Polity,' besides numerous sermons. He resides in Atlanta, Ga.

TURNER, THOMAS SLOSS. Poet. He was born in Kentucky, in 1860, but afterward removed to Texas. He wrote 'Life's Brevity,' and other poems.

TURNER. WILLIAM MASON. Physician. He was born in Virginia in 1835, but for the practice of his profession settled in Philadelphia. At leisure intervals he wrote several entertaining works of fiction, among them: 'Under Bail,' 'The Ruby Ring,' and other stories.

TURNER, WILLIAM WILBERFORCE. Author. [Ga.]. Born in 1830. He wrote 'Jack Hopeton.'

TURRENTINE, MARY E. ARRINGTON, Mrs. Writer. She was born in Arkansas, but afterward removed to Texas. She wrote "To a Mocking-Bird" and other poems, besides short stories and sketches.

TUTHILL, C. L. Residence unknown. The author of 'Virginia Dare; or, the Colony of Roanoke.'

TUTTLE, JOSEPH K. Methodist Episcopal clergyman. [Mo.]. He published a series of lectures entitled 'Ecce Christus' (1887).

TUTTLE, R. M. Poet. [Texas]. Besides 'The Mountain Idyl: or, the White Cliff Souvenir' (1889), he published 'Tuttle's Poems' (Dallas, Texas, William Warlick, 1905), a voluminous work which evinces wide range of thought.

TUTWILER, JULIA STRUDWICK. Educator and poet. She was born at Tuscaloosa, Ala., a daughter of Dr. Henry Tutwiler, who was a classmate of Edgar Allan Poe at the University of Virginia. For some time past, she has been president of the Alabama Normal College, at Livingston. It was due largely to her efforts that the University of Alabama was opened to the girls of the State; and the trustees of the institution have named the Woman's Annex in her honor. She has long been an ardent advocate of prison reform. At the Paris Exposition, in 1878, she represented *The International Journal of Education.* Besides numerous contributions to the periodicals, she is the author of some fine songs, among them: "Alabama," "The Dixie Now," "The Southern Yankee Doodle," and "Duty," all of which are used in the public schools of Alabama. The last of the four was composed for the Lee Centennial.

"TWAIN, MARK." See Clemens, Samuel Langhorne.

TYDINGS, RICHARD. Clergyman. He was born in Anne Arundel County, Md., June 16, 1783, and died in Bullitt County, Ky., October 3, 1865. He joined the Baltimore conference of the Methodist Church, but labored with success in many fields and wrote a work entitled 'Apostolic Succession' (Louisville, 1844).

TYLER, JOHN. See Biographical and Critical Sketch, Vol. XII, page 5539.

TYLER, LYON GARDNER. Educator. He was born in Charles City, Va., in 1853, a son of John Tyler, the tenth President of the United States, graduated from the University of Virginia, and married, November 14, 1878, Annie B. Tucker. He practiced law in Richmond, Va., for several years, but relinquished the legal profession in 1888 to become president of historic old William and Mary College. Among his published works are: 'The Letters and Times of the Tylers,' 'Parties and Patronage in the United States' (New York, G. P. Putnam's Sons), and 'The Cradle of the Republic' (1900). He is also the author of numerous addresses and articles, including "The Contribution of William and Mary College to the Making of the Union." He is editor and proprietor of the *William and Mary College Quarterly Magazine* and editor of 'Narratives of Early Virginia, 1606-1625' (New York, Charles Scribner's Sons). Trinity College, N.C., gave him the degree of LL.D. He resides in Williamsburg, Va.

TYLER, ODETTE (Elizabeth Lee Kirkland). Author and actress. She wrote 'Boss: a Story of Virginia Life.'

TYLER, ROBERT. Lawyer. He was born in New Kent County, Va., in 1818 and died in Montgomery, Ala., December 3, 1877. He was a son of John Tyler, president of the United States, by his first wife, Letitia Christian. After graduating from William and Mary College, he studied law, and practiced his profession for several years in Philadelphia. At the beginning of hostilities he returned to Virginia and espoused the Confederate cause. Later he edited the Montgomery *Mail and Advrtiser*. He published "Ahasuerus," a poem based on the legend of "The Wandering Jew" (New York, 1842), 'Death; or, Medora's Dream' (1843), and two open letters, "Is Virginia a Repudiating State?" and "The States' Guarantee" (Richmond, 1858).

TYLER, SAMUEL. Author. He was born in Prince George County, Md., October 22, 1809, and died in Georgetown, D.C., December 15, 1878. For several years he was professor of law in Columbian College. The cast of his mind was metaphysical, and he contributed numerous articles to magazines and reviews on reflective topics. One of his earliest productions was 'The Baconian Philosophy' (Baltimore, 1844). It attracted the attention of Sir William Hamilton, who praised it in the most cordial terms and became the author's fast friend. Other volumes followed, among them: 'Robert Burns as a Poet and as a Man' (New York, 1848), 'The Progress of Philosophy in the Past and in the Future' (Philadelphia, 1858), and a 'Memoir of Roger Brooke Taney' (Baltimore, 1872). The College of South Carolina gave him the degree of D.D.

TYNG, DUDLEY ATKINS. Clergyman. He was born in Prince George County, Md., January 12, 1825, and died near Philadelphia, Pa., April 19, 1858. After studying at Alexandria, Va., he was admitted to orders and became pastor of the Church of the Epiphany in Philadelphia. He published 'Vital Truth and Deadly Error' (Philadelphia, 1852), 'Children of the Kingdom' (1850), and 'Our Country's Troubles' (1857). He died from an accident and his memoir was written by his father, Dr. Stephen H. Tyng.

TYSON, PHILIP THOMAS. Chemist. He was born in Baltimore, Md., June 23, 1799, and died in Baltimore, Md., December 16, 1877. When the gold fever broke out, in 1849, he went to California and made numerous geological researches which he embodied in an important work entitled: 'The Geology and Industrial Resources of California' (Baltimore, 1851). Later he became State agricultural chemist of Maryland, published two volumes of reports, and became the first president of the Academy of Sciences.

ULLOA, ANTONIO DE. First Spanish governor of Louisiana. He was born in Seville, Spain, January 12, 1716, and died on the Island of Leon, July 3, 1795. He was sent to the Azores under sealed orders to take command, at Havana, of an expedition for the reconquest of Florida, but intent upon his scientific observations, he neglected to read his instructions and returned to Cadiz after cruising for two months. He was tried by a court-martial, but acquitted. He published, in five volumes, 'Relación Historica del Viaje á la América Meridianal y Observaciónes Sobre Astronomia y Fisica' (Madrid, 1748, French and English translations), besides minor works.

"UNCLE REMUS" (See Joel Chandler Harris).

UNDERWOOD, J. L. Baptist clergyman. He received his master of arts degree from Mercer University, at Macon, Ga., was both a captain and a chaplain in the Confederate Army, and wrote an excellent work entitled 'The Women of the Confederacy' (New York and Washington, The Neale Publishing Company, 1906), to which the introduction was written by the Rev. J. B. Hawthorne, D.D.

UNDERWOOD, JOSEPH ROGERS. Statesman. He was born in Goochland County, Va., October 24, 1791, and died near Bowling Green, Ky., August 23, 1876. At an early age he removed to the frontier belt, studied law, took part in the military operations along the Canadian border in the War of 1812, became a Member of Congress from Kentucky, a judge of the Court of Appeals, and a United States Senator.

UPSHAW, MARY JANE STITH. Poet. She was born in Accomac County, Va., April 7, 1828, received her education at home, and began at an early age to write for periodicals. Under the pen-name of "Fanny Fielding," she published in the *Home Monthly*, a paper issued in Nashville, Tenn., an interesting historical novel entitled "Confederate Notes." She became the wife of Josiah R. Sturgess of New York.

UPSHAW, WILLIAM DAVID. Editor and lecturer. He was born in Coweta County, Ga., October 15, 1866. On account of injuries received in early boyhood, his educational advantages were curtailed, but the discipline of affliction was the best of teachers. He began his literary career by contributing to the *Sunny South*, and eventually published 'Earnest Willie; or, Echoes from a Recluse' (Atlanta, The Franklin-Turner Company, 1898), a work which passed into several editions. He is the founder and editor of the *Golden Age*, has won success on the lecture platform, and is an eloquent advocate of prohibition. He married Margaret Beverley of Thomasville, Ga., in 1909.

UPSHUR, ABEL PARKER, statesman, was born in Northampton, Va., June 17, 1790, and died near Washington, D.C., February 28, 1844. For several years he practiced law in Richmond, after which he became a judge. In the Cabinet of President Tyler he was Secretary of the Navy until the resignation of Daniel Webster, when he became Secretary of State. He was killed by the bursting of a gun on board the United States schoolship *Princeton*, while witnessing some experiments in company with the President. Besides a number of essays and speeches, he published a 'Brief Inquiry into the True Nature and Character of Our Federal Government' (Petersburg, 1840).

VAIL, THOMAS HUBBARD. Protestant Episcopal bishop. He was born in Richmond, Va., October 21, 1812. On completing his education, he was admitted to orders and became rector of several important parishes in the North. In 1863 he went to Iowa, and one year later was consecrated the first bishop of Kansas. He published 'The Comprehensive Church' (New York, 1841), and 'Hannah,' a sacred drama (Boston, 1839). He received the degrees of D.D. and LL.D.

VALENTINE, MILTON. Theologian. He was born near Uniontown, Md., January 1, 1825. He became an eminent Lutheran educator and divine, was for twenty years president of Pennsylvania College, edited *The Lutheran Quarterly Review*, and published 'Natural Theology and Rational Theism' (Chicago, 1885): He received the degrees of D.D. and LL.D.

VANCE, JAMES ISAAC. Clergyman. He was born in Arcadia, Tenn., September 25, 1862, the son of Charles Robertson and Margaret Newland Vance, graduated at King College, Tenn., and at the Union Theological Seminary, Va., and married, December 22, 1886, Mamie Stiles Carroll. He has held important Presbyterian pastorates in Nashville and Chicago, and, in 1900, became pastor of the North Reformed Church, of Newark, N.J. He is also an eloquent platform speaker. His writings include: 'Young Man Four-square' (1894), 'Church Portals' (1895), 'The College of Apostles' (1896), 'Predestination' (a pamphlet, 1898), 'Royal Manhood' (1899), 'The Rise of a Soul,' 'Simplicity in Life,'

'A Young Man's Make-up,' and numerous contributions to magazines and reviews. King and Hampden-Sidney colleges gave him the degree of D.D. He resides in Newark, N.J.

VANCE, JOSEPH ANDERSON. Clergyman. He was born in Sullivan County, Tenn., November 17, 1864, the son of Charles Robertson and Margaret Newland Vance, and was educated at King College, Tenn., and at the Union Theological Seminary, Va. After filling pulpits in Louisville and Baltimore, he was called to the Hyde Park Presbyterian Church in Chicago. He married, January 15, 1890, Mary B. Forman. Among his published works are: 'The Westminster Assembly and Its Confession for God,' 'Home,' 'Religion and Money,' 'American Problems,' and 'The True and the False in Christian Science.' He resides in Chicago, Ill., and holds the degree of D.D.

VANCE, ROBERT B. Soldier, Congressman, poet. He was born in Buncombe County, N.C., April 28, 1828. At the outbreak of the war he was engaged in mercantile pursuits. He enlisted in the Confederate Army, attained the rank of brigadier-general and made an excellent record of soldiership. After the war he served several terms in Congress. Besides political speeches and occasional addresses, he published a volume of verse entitled 'Heart Throbs from the Mountains' (Nashville, The M.E. Publishing House, South, 1887).

VANCE, SALLY ADA REEDY, Mrs. Poet. She was born in Mississippi, but afterward removed first to Kentucky and then to Arkansas. She published numerous poems, including "The Sisters."

VANCE, ZEBULON BAIRD. See Biographical and Critical Sketch, Vol. XII, page 5555.

VAN EPPS, HOWARD. Lawyer, jurist and author of legal text-books. He was born in Eufaula, Ala., December 21, 1847, and died in Florida, December 25, 1909. On completing his studies at the University of Georgia, he settled in Atlanta for the practice of law, achieved distinction at the Bar, and became judge of the City Court. He was the author of numerous law-books, including an 'Index Digest of Georgia Reports, Vols. 1 to 100,' compiled in association with John W. Akin (1899), an 'Index Digest of Georgia Reports, Vols. 100 to 120' (1905), an 'Index Digest of Georgia Reports, Vols. 120 to 130,' 'Georgia Supreme Court and Georgia Court of Appeals, Vols. I and II' (1909), 'Van Epps's Code Supplement' (1901), 'Van Epps's Georgia Form Book' (1907), 'Van Epps's Georgia Reports, Annotated, Vols. 1 to 33, with Supplement,' and 'Georgia Decisions, Van Epps's Annotations,' Vol. I containing the "Charlton Reports" and Vol. II, the "Dudley Reports." Judge Van Epps was also an orator of rare accomplishments, and extracts from some of his literary addresses have been preserved in Knight's 'Reminiscences of Famous Georgians,' Vol. I. He married, February 12, 1873, Minnie C. Thomas.

VAN NOPPEN, LEONARD CHARLES. Editor, author, lecturer. He was born in Holland, January 8, 1868, but at the age of six was brought by his parents to the United States. After completing his education, he was admitted to the Bar of North Carolina, but his love of literature proved stronger than his allegiance to Blackstone. He spent some time abroad, specialized in the study of Dutch literature, on which subject he has delivered lecture courses at various institutions, including Columbia and Princeton universities, and translated into English verse Vondel's 'Lucifer,' besides also translating other works by the same author. Dr. Van Noppen has contributed poems and critiques to magazines, and has rendered important service to literature by his splendid lecture work. As a writer of prose he is both logical and luminous; as a poet he is governed by high literary ideals. He married, September 28, 1902, Adah Maud Stanton Becker of Jamestown, N.Y.

VARDAMAN, JAMES KIMBLE, ex-governor, editor, and lawyer, was born in Jackson County, Texas, July 26, 1861, but in early boyhood was taken by his parents to Mississippi, where he studied law, and was in due time admitted to the Bar. He also became an active factor in journalism, and, after editing various papers, founded in 1906 *The Commonwealth.* During the Spanish-American War he went to the front and served in the Cuban campaign. Both in 1892 and in 1896 he was an elector on the National Democratic ticket; and from 1904 to 1908 he filled the office of governor of Mississippi. He is an uncompromising advocate of the repeal of the constitutional amendments which confer the rights and privileges of citizenship upon the negro. On the lecture platform Governor Vardaman has become quite a favorite because of his radical views and his rare oratorical gifts.

VASCONCELLOS, ANDRES DE. Portuguese navigator. During the early part of the Sixteenth Century he accompanied Hernando de Soto to Florida and commanded the *Buena Fortuna.* As the result of his explorations along the coast lines, he published 'Relação da Viajem do Almirante Dom Hernando de Soto, Descripção da Provincia da Florida,' which was translated into Spanish (Seville, 1545), and also into French (Paris, 1685), because of the important information which it gave of "the Land of Flowers."

VASS, LACHLAN CUMMING. Presbyterian clergyman. [N.C.]. Born in 1831. He wrote an interesting 'History of the Presbyterian Church in New Bern, N.C.

VAUGHAN, GEORGE TULLY. Surgeon. He was born in Arrington, Va., June 27, 1859. For more than twenty years he has been surgeon in the United States Marine Hospital, in Washington, D.C. During the Spanish-American War he was brigade surgeon in the Seventh Corps. Besides medical papers on various subjects, he has published 'The Principles and Practice of Surgery' (New York and Washington, The Neale Publishing Company, 1901).

VEGA, GARCILASSO DE LA. Spanish historian. He published an interesting work entitled 'La Florida del Inca, Historia del Adelantado de Soto' (Lisbon, 1605).

VELASQUEZ, LORETTA JANETA, Madame. Heroine. She was born in Havana, Cuba, June 26, 1842. Her girlhood days were spent in Texas. At the outbreak of the Civil War, she donned male attire, adopted the name of Harry T. Buford, and entered the Confederate ranks. The narrative of her adventures is told in 'The Woman in Battle' (Hartford, Conn., T. Beliknap, 1876).

VELTHUSEN, JOHANN CASPER. Clergyman. [N.C.]. He published in German four interesting reports entitled 'News of the Church in North Carolina' (1786-1792).

VENABLE, CHARLES SCOTT. Mathematician. He was born in Prince Edward County, Va., April 19, 1827. After graduating from Hampden-Sidney College, he studied abroad and, on his return to America, held professorships in various institutions. During the Civil War he was an aide-de-camp on the staff of General Robert E. Lee. At the close of hostilities he became professor of mathematics at the University of Virginia and published a series of mathematical text-books. The University of Virginia made him an LL.D.

VENABLE, FRANCIS PRESTON. Educator and author. He was born in Prince Edward County, Va., November 17, 1856, the son of Charles Scott and Cantey McDowell Venable. He received the best educational advantages, supplemented by post-graduate studies at Göttingen, and married, November 3, 1884, Sallie Charlton Manning. He was professor of chemistry in the University of North Carolina, from 1880 to 1900, and became its president in 1900. He is a member of the American Association for the Advancement of Science, of the American Philosophical Society, of the American, German, and London Chemical Societies, and of various other scientific organizations. He was chosen president of the American Chemical Society in 1905. His researches and experiments have been of the greatest scientific value and his publications include: 'Qualitative Chemical Analysis' (1883), 'History of Chemistry' (New York, D. C. Heath and Company, 1893), 'Development of Periodic Law' (1896), 'Inorganic Chemistry According to Periodic Law' (1898), and 'Study of the Atom.' He resides at Chapel Hill, N.C., and is one of the consulting editors of 'The Library of Southern Literature.' His degrees are Ph.D., Sc.D. and LL.D.

VILLENEUFUE, LE BLANC DE. Dramatist. [La.]. He wrote in French a tragedy entitled 'Poncha Houma' (New Orleans, 1814).

VILLIERS DU TERRACE, BARON M. DE. Author. [La.]. He wrote in French an interesting work entitled 'Les Dernières Années de la Louisiane Française' (1903).

VERNER, SAMUEL PHILLIPS. Explorer. He was born in South Carolina in 1863. After graduating from the University of South Carolina, he taught for several years at Stillman Institute, Tuscaloosa, Ala., became interested in the subject of African exploration, made an expedition to Central Africa, which was so productive of results that others followed. His discoveries have been numerous and have brought him into wide recognition. Besides contributing to magazines and periodicals, he has published 'Pioneering in Africa,' 'The Cape to Cairo Railway,' 'The Baluba Language,' and 'The Pigmies.'

.**VEST, GEORGE GRAHAM.** See Biographical and Critical Sketch, Vol. XII, page 5575.

VIEL, ÉTIENNE BERNARD ALEXANDRE. Clergyman. He was born in New Orleans, La., October 31, 1736, and died in France, at the College of Juilly, December 16, 1821. For many years he labored at Attapakas, La., in the ranks of the Jesuits. He was gifted both as a poet and as a linguist; translated into Latin verse Fénélon's 'Télémaque,' and into French the 'Ars Poetica' of Horace, and several of the 'Odes'; and also published 'Miscellanea Latino-Gallica' (1816).

VIGNAUD, JEAN HENRI. Author. He was born in New Orleans, La., of an old Creole family, November 27, 1830. For several years he engaged successfully in journalism and established a number of papers. During the Civil War he was a captain in the Confederate Army until captured in New Orleans, and, on being released, he was appointed assistant secretary of the Confederate diplomatic commission in Paris. After the struggle he was sent upon numerous errands abroad by the United States Government. Besides contributing to various periodicals, he published 'L'Anthropologie' (1861), a 'History of the Formation of the American Union,' and a 'History of the Discovery and Occupation of the Territory of the United States.'

VIGNE, CHARLES DE LA. Soldier. He was born in Southern France about 1530, and died at Fort Caroline, Fla., September 20, 1565. While chief of the night watch in charge of the fort, he was surprised and killed by the Spaniards. He wrote an interesting account of the founding of the French colony in Florida (Paris, 1565).

VIGNOLES, CHARLES. Author. [La.]. He published a 'History of the Floridas' (1824).

VINCENT, JOHN HEYL. Bishop of the M.E. Church and chancellor of the Chautauqua system. He was born in Tuscaloosa, Ala., February 23, 1832. At eighteen he began to preach. After holding numerous pastorates he was ordained bishop in 1888. He originated the famous Chautauqua movement, edited, for many years, the Sunday-school publications of his denomination, and published 'Little Footprints in Bible Lands,' 'The Chautauqua Movements,' 'Earthly Footsteps of the Man of Galilee,' 'The Modern Sunday-school,' 'Better Not,' 'Outline History of Greece,' 'Outline History of England,' 'Our Own Church,' and several other works. He holds various degrees, including D.D., S.T.D., and LL.D.

VOORHIES, FELIX. Author. [La.]. He wrote 'Blanche Duvart: a Louisiana Romance' (1876).

WADDEL, JAMES. Clergyman. He was born in Newry, Ireland, in 1739, and died in Louisa County, Va., September 17, 1805. Before his death he ordered that his manuscripts be burned, but tradition speaks with one voice to the effect that he was the ablest Presbyterian divine and the foremost pulpit orator of his day in Virginia. "Under his preaching," says William Wirt, "audiences were irresistibly and simultaneously moved, like the wind-shaken forest." Patrick Henry classed him with Samuel Davies as one of the two greatest orators to whom he ever listened. One of his daughters married Dr. Archibald Alexander of Princeton; and his memoir was written by the Rev. James W. Alexander, D.D.

WADDELL, ALFRED MOORE, lawyer, was born in Hillsboro, N.C., September 16, 1834. After graduating from the University of North Carolina, he studied law, became clerk of the Court of Equity, and edited the Wilmington *Herald*. During the Civil War he served in the Confederate Army and attained the rank of lieutenant-colonel. From 1871 to 1879 he represented his district in Congress, published two interesting volumes entitled: 'A Colonial Officer and His Times' (Raleigh, Edwards and Broughton, 1891), 'Some Memories of My Life' (*ibid.*, 1908), and is now engaged upon a 'History of New Hanover County, N.C.' He holds the degree of LL.D. The sketch of Maurice Moore in 'The Library of Southern Literature' is also from his pen.

WADDELL, JAMES D. Lawyer. [Ga.]. During the Civil War he was a colonel in the Confederate Army. He published a 'Life of Linton Stephens' (1877).

WADDELL, JOHN NEWTON, clergyman and educator, was born in Willington, S.C., April 2, 1812. After graduating from the University of Georgia, he entered the ministry of the Presbyterian Church, and achieved eminence in the educational world. For several years he was chancellor of the University of Mississippi and afterward chancellor of the Southwestern Presbyterian University, at Clarksville, Tenn., where he died at an advanced age. He published 'Memorials of an Academic Life,' giving an interesting account of the Waddells. The University of Nashville gave him the degree of D.D. and the University of Georgia, the degree of LL.D.

WADDELL, JOSEPH ADDISON. [Va.]. He published "Annals of Augusta County, Va.," and other historical papers.

WADDELL, MOSES, clergyman and educator, was born in Rowan County, N.C., July 29, 1770, and died in Athens, Ga., July 21, 1840. He was a landmark of Presbyterianism in the South. At Willington, S.C., he taught for many years a select school, and John C. Calhoun, William H. Crawford, Hugh S. Legaré and James L. Pettigru were among his pupils. He afterward became president of the University of Georgia, and pastor of the First Presbyterian Church, of Athens. In addition to numerous sermons and addresses, he published 'Memoirs of Miss Catherine Elizabeth Smelt' (Augusta, 1819). The College of South Carolina made him a D.D.

WADDELL, WILLIAM HENRY. Editor. For years he was professor of ancient languages at the University of Georgia. He was a son of Professor James P. Waddell, and a grandson of Dr. Moses Waddell, both eminent educators. He published a 'Greek Grammar for Beginners,' and a number of poems, including one entitled "Regret," which Dr. A. A. Lipscomb pronounced a masterpiece. He died in Milford, Va., in 1878.

WADDILL, E. M. Poet. [N.C.]. He wrote "The Song of the Soldier's Home," an extended poem (Raleigh, Edwards and Broughton, 1895).

WAGSTAFF, HENRY McGILBERT, educator, was born in Roxboro, N.C., January 27, 1876. Besides a number of historical monographs, he has published 'State Rights and Political Parties in North Carolina, 1776-1860' (Baltimore, The Johns Hopkins Press, 1906). He also wrote the sketch of Francis Lester Hawks for 'The Library of Southern Literature.' He holds the chair of history in the University of North Carolina. Johns Hopkins gave him the degree of Ph.D.

WAKELEE, KATE C., author, was born in Connecticut but afterward lived in Georgia and wrote 'The Forest City Bride' and 'India Morgan,' besides other entertaining stories.

WALDO, J. CURTIS. Author. [La.]. He published 'Mardi Gras: a Tale of Ante-Bellum. Times' (1871), and a 'Roll of Honor: the Citizen Soldiery Who Saved Louisiana' (New Orleans, 1877).

WALES, PHILIP SKINNER, surgeon, was born in Annapolis, Md., February 27, 1837. After practicing medicine for several years in Baltimore and Washington, he became a surgeon in the United States Navy, and published 'Mechanical Therapeutics' (Philadelphia, 1867), and numerous papers on scientific topics.

WALKE, HENRY, naval officer, was born in Princess Anne County, Va., December 24, 1808. At an early age he removed to Ohio, but afterward entered the United States Navy and attained the rank of rear-admiral. He published 'Naval Scenes in the Late War' (New York, 1877).

WALKER, ALEXANDER. Lawyer and editor. He was born in Alexandria, Va., October 13, 1819. Early in life he removed to New Orleans and became an active force in journalism while engaged successfully at the same time in the practice of law. For a number of years he edited *The Picayune*. Later he shifted his residence to Cincinnati and edited *The Enquirer*, but returned to New Orleans and became Judge of the City Court. He was a member of the Secession Convention of Louisiana in 1861. His writings include: 'The Life of

Andrew Jackson,' 'Jackson and New Orleans' (1856), 'The History of the Battle of Shiloh,' and 'Butler at New Orleans.' For elegance of style he has few equals, his language at times being almost rhythmic. He died in New Orleans, January 24, 1893.

WALKER, CORNELIUS, clergyman, was born near Richmond, Va., June 12, 1819. On completing his education he was admitted to orders, became rector of Christ Church, Winchester, Va., for twelve years, and in 1866 accepted the chair of Church history in the Theological Seminary of Virginia, which he held until accepting the chair of divinity and homiletics. Besides contributing articles to reviews and magazines, he published a 'Biography of the Rev. William Duval' (Richmond, 1854), 'Life and Correspondence of the Rev. William Sparrow, D.D., Professor in the Theological Seminary, Va.' (Philadelphia, 1876), a 'Biography of the Rev. Charles W. Andrews, D.D.' (1877), and 'Sorrowing Not without Hope' (New York, 1887). William and Mary College gave him the degree of D.D.

WALKER, JAMES MURDOCK, lawyer, was born in Charleston, S.C., January 10, 1813, and died in Charleston, S.C., September 18, 1854. After graduating from South Carolina College, he studied law, attained high rank in the profession, and served several terms in the Legislature. He published 'The State Versus the Bank of South Carolina' (Charleston 1836), 'An Inquiry Concerning the Use and Authority of Roman Jurisprudence in the Law Concerning Real Estate' (1850), 'The Theory of Common Law' (1852), and a tract on 'Government' (1853).

WALKER, JEANIE MORT. Author. [New Orleans, La.]. The Life of Captain Joseph Fry, the Cuban Martyr' (Hartford, Conn., 1875) was her only production.

WALKER, NATHAN WILSON. Educator. He was born in Currituck County, N.C., March 7, 1875. He holds the professorship of secondary education in the University of North Carolina. Besides monographs and sketches contributed to various periodicals, he wrote 'The Biographical History of North Carolina' (Greensboro, Charles Van Noppen), a 'Hand-book for High School Teachers' (1907), and the memoir of James Johnston Pettigrew in 'The Library of Southern Literature.' He resides at Chapel Hill, N.C.

WALKER, ROBERT JOHN. Statesman. He was born in Northumberland, Pa., July 23, 1801, and died in Washington, D.C., November 11, 1869. After practicing law for some time in Pittsburg, Pa., he settled in Mississippi, was twice elected to the United States Senate, supported James K. Polk for President, became Secretary of the Treasury in the latter's Cabinet, and was also governor of Kansas. He was the author of numerous political essays and speeches; and in 1863 joined James R. Gilmore in the conduct of the *Continental Monthly,* a paper published in Washington, D.C., in the interest of emancipation. He also represented the United States Government as financial agent in Europe.

WALKER, WILLIAM, an American adventurer, was born in Nashville, Tenn., in 1824. He studied both law and medicine and took special courses of study at Edinburgh and at Heidelberg. But the spirit of adventure caused him to relinquish both professions, and he organized an expedition, which was partially successful, for the conquest of the Mexican State of Sonora, and afterward undertook an expedition of like character against Nicaragua, which was prosecuted with varying fortunes until September 22, 1860, when he was shot, under order of court martial, at Truxillo. Nothing could be done by the United States Government in the prisoner's behalf because of his violation of the neutrality laws. He was the author of a volume entitled 'The War in Nicaragua' (New York and Mobile, 1860).

WALL, HENRY. Clergyman and poet. In a vein of blended humor and satire he published a volume on 'Fashion,' which suggests the lilt of Butler's 'Hudibras' (Richmond, 1870).

WALL, HENRY CLAY. [N.C.]. He published a 'Sketch of the Peedee Guards' (1876).

WALL, MARY VIRGINIA. Author. [Va.]. She wrote an interesting story of the lost colony of Roanoke, entitled: 'The Daughter of Virginia Dare' (New York and Washington, The Neale Publishing Company, 1908).

WALLACE, DAVID DUNCAN. Educator. Dr. Wallace was born in Columbia, S.C., May 25, 1874. For several years past he has filled the chair of history and economics in Wofford College, his *alma mater.* Besides a thesis on "The Constitutional History of South Carolina, 1725-1775," which earned for him the Ph.D. degree at Vanderbilt, he has published 'A Chapter of South Carolina Constitutional History' (Nashville, 1900), and 'The Civil Government of South Carolina and the United States' (Dallas, Texas, The Southern Publishing Company, 1906). He is at present engaged upon a 'Life of Henry Laurens.'

WALLACE, JOHN H. Author. [Ala.]. He wrote an interesting work entitled 'The Senator from Alabama' (1904).

WALLACE, WILLIAM ROSS, author, was born in Lexington, Ky., in 1819; and, after receiving his education in Indiana, he moved to New York for the practice of law. But he found the muses more attractive than the courts, and gave his time almost exclusively to literary work. Besides contributing poems and sketches to the periodicals, he published: 'The Battle of Tippecanoe' (Cincinnati, 1837), 'Wordsworth' (New York, 1846), 'Alban, the Pirate' (New York, 1848), 'The Loved and the Lost,' and 'Meditations in America, and Other Poems' (New York, 1851). He died in 1881.

WALLIS, SEVERN TEACKLE. See Biographical and Critical Sketch, Vol. XII, page 5593.

WALSH, ROBERT. Journalist and author. He was born in Baltimore, Md., in 1784, and died in Paris, France, February 7, 1859. He edited the first quarterly review ever published in the United States. From time to time he was also identified with other representative periodicals. During the last six years of his life he was United States Consul in Paris. His publications include: a 'Letter on the Genius and Disposition of the French Government' (Philadelphia, 1810, republished in England), 'Correspondence Respecting Russia,' with Robert Goodloe Harper (1813), an 'Essay on the Future State of Europe' (1813), an 'Appeal from the Judgment of Great Britain Respecting the United States' (1819), 'The Museum of Foreign Literature and Science' (1822), and 'Didactics: Social, Literary and Political,' in two volumes (1836). He also edited several works and wrote numerous essays and sketches.

WALSH, THOMAS TRACY. Protestant Episcopal clergyman. [S.C.]. He published a work entitled 'Facts and Principles Pertaining to the Protestant Episcopal Church.'

WALSINGTON, MARY, author, was born in Charleston, S.C., about 1835, but was taken by her parents in infancy to New Orleans, where she was well educated and became a writer of note, contribut-

ing both stories and poems to current periodicals. "The Palmetto
Swamp," a war tale, is her best known prose production, while her
poetic work includes "The Old Tomb," "Shot," and other favorites.

WALTER, THOMAS. Botanist. He was born in Hampshire,
England, in 1745, and died near Charleston, S.C., in 1800. On his plantation in St. Stephen's Parish he cultivated most of the specimens which
he describes. He published 'Flora Caroliniana' (London, 1788).

WALTON, AUGUSTUS Q. Author, of Alabama. He wrote
'The History of the Detection and Conviction of John A. Murel, the
Great Western Land Pirate,' which appeared in 1835.

WALTON, GEORGE. Signer of the Declaration of Independence. He was born in Frederick County, Va., in 1740, and died in
Augusta, Ga., February 2, 1804. By the light of pine-knots, while serving
an apprenticeship, he acquired the rudiments of an education, removed to
Georgia, when released from his contract, studied law, and became one of
the most zealous champions of liberty in the colonies. He served in the
Continental Congress, signed the immortal instrument which severed the
ties of allegiance to England, commanded a regiment in the field, twice
occupied the chair of governor, received an election to the Senate of the
United States, became chief justice of the State, and died an occupant
of the Superior Court Bench. Mr. Walton was an eloquent brand in kin-
dling the flames of revolution in Georgia, a thinker of original and independent cast of mind, and a writer of superior gifts. At the time of
his death, he was preparing a history of Georgia. He married the daughter of an English nobleman.

WALTON, WILLIAM CLAIBORNE. Presbyterian clergyman
and evangelist. He was born in Hanover County, Va., November 4, 1793,
and died in Hartford, Conn., February 18, 1834. By his wonderful powers
as a revivalist, it is said that he brought 100,000 persons into the Church
communion. He published only one volume of sermons, besides a number
of separate discourses and a sketch of his daughter, Margaret Ann.
Joshua N. Danforth wrote his biography (New York, 1837) and Mrs.
Lydia H. Sigourney dedicated to him a poem.

WALTZ, ELIZABETH CHERRY. Author. [Ky.]. She has
published a number of charming stories of Kentucky life, among them:
'Pa Gladden, the Story of a Common Man' (New York, Charles Scribner's
Sons, 1904), and 'The Ancient Landmark.'

WALWORTH, JEANNETTE H. Author. She was born in
Mississippi in 1838, but afterward removed to Louisiana. She published
a volume of sketches entitled 'Southern Silhouettes' (1886), 'Stories of
a Southern County,' 'A Little Radical,' 'A Splendid Egotist,' 'That Girl
from Texas,' 'On the Winning Side,' and other charming works of fiction.

WAPD, GEORGE. An ante-bellum Florida poet. He was first
major ard afterward colonel, and was the author of some excellent verse,
some of which has been preserved in old scrapbooks.

WARD, LYDIA, A. C. Poet. [Va.]. She was born in 1845. At
odd moments she has written both poems and sketches, and has published
'Under the Pines, and Other Verses.'

WARD, MATT FLOURNOY. Author. He was born in Scott
County, Ky., May 19, 1806, and died in Helena, Ark., September 30, 1862.
After completing his education, he engaged in cotton planting in Arkansas,
but he also devoted some time and thought to literature and published
'Letters from Three Continents' (New York, 1850), and 'English Items;

or, Microscopic Views of England and Englishmen' (1852). He was killed before his house by a Confederate officer who mistook him for a Federal soldier.

WARDEN, ROBERT BRUCE, author, was born in Bardstown, Ky., January 18, 1824. For the practice of law, he settled in Cincinnati, Ohio, and became associate justice of the Supreme Court of the State. He wielded an industrious pen and wrote 'A Familiar Forensic View of Man and Law' (Columbus, 1859), 'A Voter's Version of the Life and Character of Stephen Arnold Douglas' (1860), 'An Account of the Private Life and Public Services of Salmon Portland Chase' (Cincinnati, 1874), and 'A View of Land and Life.' He also published several volumes of 'Ohio Reports.'

WARDER, GEORGE WOODWARD. Lawyer. He was born in Richmond, Mo., May 20, 1848, the son of Luther Fairfax and Ellen Warder, received a collegiate education and married Virginia D. McWilliams. He was admitted to the Bar and also became a large investor in Kansas City real estate, building many handsome structures, among them the Warder Grand Opera House. His leisure hours have been spent in scientific studies and in literary diversions. On the platform he has been a favorite. His principal works are: 'Poetic Fragments,' 'Eden Dell, or Love's Wanderings,' 'Utopian Dreams and Lotus Leaves,' 'After Which, All Things' (a novel), 'The New Cosmogony,' 'Invisible Light, or the 'Electric Theory of Creation,' 'The Conflict Between Man and Mammon,' 'The Cities of the Sun,' 'The Stairway to the Stars,' 'The Universe a Vast Electric Organization,' and 'Life in Celestial Sun Worlds.' He resides in Kansas City, Mo.

WARE, ELEANOR PERCY. Poet. She was born in Mississippi, becoming in after years the wife of Henry Lee, of Virginia. With her sister, Catherine Anne Ware, who afterward became Mrs. Warfield, the famous novelist, she wrote two volumes of verse which were quite successful: 'The Wife of Leon, and Other Poems,' and 'The Indian Chamber, and Other Poems.' She died, a victim of yellow fever, in 1849.

WARE, MARY, poet, was born in Madisonville, Tenn., in 1828. Her father was George Harris, an eminent lawyer, who practiced his profession first in Tennessee and afterward in Alabama. It was in the latter state that her literary gifts first found expression; and for more than half a century she was a contributor of splendid verse to current periodicals. She married in 1863, Horace Ware, a native of Massachusetts, but a pioneer in the development of the South's iron industries. At the ripe age of fourscore years Mrs. Ware still retains her intellectual faculties but little dimmed by time's encroachments and resides in Birmingham, Ala., on "The Highlands."

WARE, NATHANIEL A. Author. He was born in Massachusetts, in 1789, and died in Galveston, Texas, in 1854. For several years he taught school in South Carolina, where he also studied and practiced law. Later he removed to Natchez, Miss., became territorial secretary, acquired a fortune by the judicious purchase of land, and specialized in the study of the natural sciences. He published 'Views of the Federal Constitution,' 'Notes on Political Economy' (New York, 1844), and a work on the Pestalozzian system of education. He was the father of the famous novelist, Catharine Ann Warfield.

WARFIELD, BENJAMIN BRECKINRIDGE. Eminent theologian and divine, professor of didactic and polemic theology in the Presbyterian Seminary at Princeton, New Jersey. He was born in

Lexington, Ky., November 5, 1851, the son of William Warfield and Mary Cabell Breckinridge, was educated at Princeton University and at Leipsic, and married, August 3, 1876, Anna Pearce Kinkead, of Lexington. From 1878 to 1887 Dr. Warfield was professor of New Testament language and literature in the Western Theological Seminary at Alleghany, Pa. In the latter year he was called to the chair which he now holds. Besides editing *The Presbyterian and Reformed Review* and *The Princeton Review,* he has contributed numerous essays and articles on doctrinal themes to the encyclopædias and religious periodicals, and has also published the following works, which are of standard value among conservative Presbyterians: 'The Divine Origin of the Bible' (1881), 'Introduction to the Textual Criticism of the New Testament' (1886), 'Inspiration' (1886), 'St. Augustine's Anti-Pelagian Treatise' (1887), 'The Idea of Systematic Theology' (1888), 'On the Revision of the Confession of Faith' (1890), 'The Gospel of the Incarnation' (1893), 'Two Studies in the History of Doctrine' (1893), 'The Right of Systematic Theology' (1897), 'The Significance of the Westminster Standards' (1898), 'Acts and Pastoral Epistles' (1902), and 'The Power of God Unto Salvation,' a volume of sermons. Dr. Warfield lives in Princeton, N.J. His degrees are D.D. and LL.D.

WARFIELD, CATHARINE ANNE. See Biographical and Critical Sketch, Vol. XII, page 5617.

WARFIELD, ETHELBERT DUDLEY. Educator and divine, president of Lafayette College, at Easton, Pa., the son of William Warfield and Mary Cabell Breckinridge. He was educated at Princeton University, Columbia Law School, and Oxford University, England. He practiced law for two years in Lexington, and married, first, Sarah Lacy Brooks, and second, Eleanor F. Tilton. He was ordained to the ministry of the Presbyterian Church in 1899 and became president of Lafayette College in 1891. His published works include: 'The Kentucky Resolutions of 1798,' an historical study (1887), 'At the Evening Hour' (1898), and a 'Memoir of Joseph Cabell Breckinridge, U.S.A.' (1898). He resides at Easton, Pa. His degrees are D.D. and LL.D.

WARING, MALVINA SARAH. Author. She was born in Newberry, S.C., November 12, 1842, a daughter of John Blair and Elizabeth Ann Sheppard Black. She graduated from Limestone College and married, first, William Morena Gist, and second, Clark Waring. She is one of the foremost women of the State in all patriotic and public enterprises, and has frequently represented South Carolina on the great industrial exposition boards. In lecture work she has been deservedly popular. Some of her poems possess unusual merit, and in short stories and sketches she has done some excellent work. The volumes by which she is best known are: 'The Lion's Share' (1889), and 'That Sandhiller' (Washington, The Neale Publishing Company). She resides in Columbia, S.C.

WARNER, BEVERLEY ELLISON. Clergyman and author. He was born in Jersey City, N.J., October 14, 1855. After completing his education he was admitted to orders and became rector of Trinity Church in New Orleans, La., a charge which he has ably filled for thirty years. His writings evince an exceptional versatility of thought. They include: 'Troubled Waters,' a novel (Philadelphia, J. B. Lippincott Company, 1885), 'English History in Shakespeare's Plays' (New York, Longmans, Green and Company, 1894), 'The Facts and the Faith' (New York, Thomas Whitaker, 1897), 'The Young Man in Modern Life' (New York, Dodd, Mead and Company, 'The Young Woman in Modern Life' (*ibid.,* 1905), and 'Famous Introductions to Shakespeare's Plays' (*ibid.,* 1906). The University of the South has given him the degree of D.D., and Tulane University the degree of LL.D.

WARNER, ZEBEDEE. Clergyman. He was born in Pendleton County, Va., February 28, 1833, entered the ministry of the United Brethren in Christ, taught theology for several years, and published a number of books, among them: 'Christian Baptism' (Parkersburg, W.Va., 1864), 'Rise and Progress of the United Brethren' (1865), 'Life and Times of the Rev. Jacob Bachtel' (Dayton, Ohio, 1867), and 'The Roman Catholic not a True Church' (Parkersburg, 1868). Otterbein University gave him the degree of D.D.

WARREN, E. W. Baptist clergyman. [Ga.]. For several years he was pastor of the First Baptist Church of Atlanta, Ga. He wrote a novel entitled 'Nellie Morton.'

WARROCK, JOHN. Publisher. He was born in 1774 and died in 1858 in Richmond, Va., where he published annually for forty years 'Warrock's Almanac.'

WASHINGTON, BOOKER TALIAFERRO. The recognized leader of the negro race in the United States. He was born near Hale's Ford, Va., about 1859, of African descent, graduated from Hampton Institute, Va., and married a woman of his own race. He taught at Hampton Institute until called to take charge of the school at Tuskegee, Ala., in 1881. From an obscure beginning this school, which he planned and organized, has become the most widely known and the most handsomely endowed institution in the world for the education of the negro race. On the platform an effective speaker, and on the printed page an effective writer, he wields an immense influence and possesses the confidence and esteem of his white brethren in both sections. As principal of the Tuskegee Normal and Industrial Institute, he eschews offensive partisan politics and commands recognition on the ground of meritorious service and of high character. His published works include: 'Sowing and Reaping,' 'Up from Slavery' (New York, Doubleday, Page and Company), 'Future of the American Negro' (Boston, Small, Maynard and Company), 'Character Building' (New York, Doubleday Page and Company), 'Story of My Life and Work' (*ibid.*), 'Working With Hands' (*ibid.*), 'Life of Fred. Douglass' (Philadelphia, G. W. Jacobs), and 'Tuskegee and Its People,' besides numerous platform addresses. He resides in Tuskegee, Ala., and holds the degree of LL.D.

WASHINGTON, BUSHROD. Jurist. He was born in Westmoreland County, Va., June 5, 1762, and died in Philadelphia, Pa., November 26, 1829. He was the son of John Augustine Washington, a younger brother of General Washington. For more than thirty years he was an associate justice of the Supreme Court of the United States; and on the death of Martha Washington he inherited the mansion at Mount Vernon, with four hundred acres. He published 'Reports of Cases Argued and Determined in the Court of Appeals of Virginia' (1798-1799, two volumes), and 'Reports of Cases Determined in the Circuit Court of the United States for the Third Circuit,' edited by Richard Peters (1826-1829, four volumes). Horace Binney published 'The Life of Bushrod Washington' (Philadelphia, 1858).

WASHINGTON, GEORGE. See Biographical and Critical Sketch, Vol. XIII, page 5633.

WASHINGTON, JAMES MADISON, Mrs. Author. [La.]. She published some charming little sketches of life in Louisiana during war times, entitled: 'How Beauty Was Saved, and Other Memories of the Sixties' (New York and Washington, The Neale Publishing Company, 1907).

WASHINGTON, LAURENCE. [Va.]. He published 'A Romance.'

WASHINGTON, WILLIAM A. [Ky.]. He published a work entitled 'Rural Minstrelsy' (1860).

WATERHOUSE, S. Educator. [Mo.]. He published 'Resources of Missouri' (1867), 'The Westward Movement of Capital' (1890), and 'St. Louis, the Site for the World's Fair' (1889).

WATERS, NICHOLAS BAKER, physician, was born in Maryland in 1764 and died in Philadelphia, Pa., in 1796. He published an abridged edition of a 'System of Surgery,' by Benjamin Bell of Edinburgh (Philadelphia, 1791).

WATERS, PHILEMON BERRY. [S.C.]. He published a volume of genealogical data entitled 'The Waters and Kindred Families' (1902).

WATKINS, EDGAR, lawyer, received his law diploma from the University of Georgia in 1889 and settled in Texas, where he became one of the foremost young lawyers of the State; but he returned to Georgia in 1908, locating in Atlanta, where he has since resided. He published an authoritative work entitled: 'Shippers and Carriers of Interstate Freight' (Chicago, T. H. Flood and Company, 1909).

WATKINS, JOHN ELFRETH, civil engineer, was born in Ben Lomond, Va., May 17, 1852. For several years past he has been superintendent and curator of technological collections of the United States National Museum. He was educated at Lafayette College. Several volumes have come from his pen, among them: 'The History of the Pennsylvania Railroad, 1846-1896,' 'The Evolution of the Railway Passenger Car' (New York, Harper and Brothers), and numerous papers on engineering topics.

WATKINS, MAY L. Author. [Ala.]. She wrote 'My Lady Primrose.'

WATKINS, MILDRED CABELL. Educator. She was born in Virginia in 1860, but afterward removed to North Carolina. Besides a 'Primer of American Literature' (1894), she published numerous short stories of rare excellence.

WATKINS, SAMUEL, soldier and planter, was born in Tennessee in 1838, but afterward removed to Oklahoma. He published in a semi-humorous vein, 'Company Aytch, Maury Grays, of the First Tennessee Regiment; or, a Side-show of the Big Show' (1882).

WATKINS, TOBIAS. Physician. He was born in Maryland in 1780 and died in Washington, D.C., November 14, 1855. During the War of 1812 he was a surgeon in the United States Army, and afterward assistant surgeon-general. With his brother-in-law, Stephen Simpson, he edited in Philadelphia 'The Portico,' in four volumes (1816-1820). Besides contributing to periodicals, he translated Xavier Bichat's 'Physiological Researches upon Life and Death,' and Louis de Onis's 'Memoir upon the Negotiations between Spain and the United States, which led to the Treaty of 1819' (Baltimore, 1822).

WATSON, ANNAH ROBERTSON, Mrs., poet, was born near Louisville, Ky., but became in after years a resident of Memphis, Tenn. Her poem, "Bereft," which is preserved in 'Songs of the South,' betrays genuine poetic feeling. She also wrote essays and sketches.

WATSON, ASA R. Journalist and poet. He was born in Virginia but removed to Georgia in early manhood and became active in journalism, editing various papers. He also wrote occasional verse. One of his poems, "Kin," is preserved in 'Songs of the South.'

WATSON, HENRY CLAY, author, was born in Baltimore, Md., in 1831, and died in Sacramento, Cal., July 10, 1869. At an early age he settled in Philadelphia, entered journalism, and afterward removed to California. He published several delightful volumes of adventure, including 'Camp-fires of the Revolution' (Philadelphia, 1851), 'Nights in a Block House' (1852), 'Old Bell of Independence' (1852), 'The Yankee Teapot' (1853), 'Lives of the Presidents of the United States' (Boston, (1853), 'Heroic Women of History' (Philadelphia, 1853), 'The Ladies' Glee Book' (New York, 1854), 'The Masonic Musical Manual' (1855), and 'Camp-fires of Napoleon' (Philadelphia, 1856).

WATSON, THOMAS E. See Biographical and Critical Sketch, Vol. XIII, page 5681.

WATTERSON, HENRY. See Biographical and Critical Sketch, Vol. XIII, page 5707.

WATTS, WILLIAM COURTNEY. Author. [Ky.]. He wrote 'Chronicles of a Kentucky Settlement' (1897).

WAUCHOPE, GEORGE ARMSTRONG. Educator and editor. He was born of Scotch-Irish ancestry at Natural Bridge, Va., May 26, 1862. After graduation from Washington and Lee University, he prosecuted his studies in Berlin. For four years he was assistant professor of English in the University of Missouri, and afterward, for two years, professor of English in the University of Iowa. He then became a graduate student at Harvard. Since 1898 he has filled the chair of English at the University of South Carolina, a position to which he has brought the resources of an exceptional equipment. Among men of letters Dr. Wauchope is distinguished for his ripe scholarship and for his critical powers of analysis. His editorial labors have borne fruit in several works of standard value, including De Quincey's 'Confessions of an Opium-eater' (Boston, D. C. Heath and Company, 1898), De Quincey's 'Revolt of the Tartars' (*ibid.*, 1897), George Eliot's 'Silas Marner' (*ibid.*, 1898), Lamb's 'Selected Essays,' and 'Essays of Elia,' two volumes (1903-1908), Longfellow's 'Courtship of Miles Standish, and Other Poems' (1902), Spenser's 'Faerie Queene,' Book I (New York, The Macmillan Company), and Pope's 'Rape of the Lock, and Other Poems' (in press). He has also published "The Burning of the University of Missouri," a pamphlet (1892), "From Generation to Generation," a poem (1905), and 'The Writers of South Carolina' (in press). Dr. Wauchope is one of the assistant literary editors of 'The Library of Southern Literature.' He has visited Oxford and Cambridge Universities and made literary pilgrimages through England and Scotland; he has delivered lectures on the great English and American poets, including the tercentenary oration on Milton, at the University of Virginia, and was awarded the Poe centenary medal by the University of Virginia. He has contributed numerous short stories, poems and essays to high-class periodicals. For 'The Library of Southern Literature' he wrote the sketches of Caroline Gilman and William J. Grayson. He married, August 8, 1899, Elizabeth Bostedo. Washington and Lee University gave him the degree of Ph.D.

WAYLAND, JOHN WALTER, educator and writer, was born in Mount Jackson, Va., December 8, 1872. His father was John Wesley Wayland. He occupies the chair of history in Harrisonburg State Normal School. Besides numerous historical papers, he has published several volumes of exceptional interest, among them: 'Paul, the Herald of the Cross' (Elgin, Ill., The Brethren Publishing House), 'The Twelve Apostles' (*ibid.*), 'The German Element of the Shenandoah Valley of Virginia' (Charlottesville, The Mitchie Company), and 'The Political Opinions of Thomas Jefferson' (New York and Washington, The Neale Publishing Company, 1906). He wrote the sketches of Samuel M. Janney and Joseph Salyards for 'The Library of Southern Literature.' He has received the degree of Ph.D.

WAYNE, HENRY CONSTANTINE, soldier, was born in Savannah, Ga., September 8, 1815, and died in Savannah, Ga., March 15, 1883. After graduating from West Point, he entered the United States Army, and became a major. He resigned his commission in 1861 and received the appointment of adjutant-general of the State of Georgia. He published 'The Sword Exercise, Arranged for Military Instruction' (1856).

WEAVER, W. T. G. Poet. He was born in Missouri in 1834 and died in Texas in 1877. He published a volume of verse entitled 'Hours of Amusement.' Among his most popular airs are included: "The Song of the Texas Rangers," "Houston's Address to His Men," and "The Girl in Red." He possessed unusual gifts.

WEBB, LAURA S. ("Stannie Lee"). [Ala.]. She published a volume of verse entitled 'Heart Leaves.'

WEBB, ROBERT ALEXANDER, clergyman and educator, was born in Oxford, Miss., September 20, 1856. His father was Robert Clark Webb and his mother, Elizabeth Dortch. On completing his theological studies, he was received into the ministry of the Southern Presbyterian Church and for several years filled important pastorates. In 1892 he became professor of systematic theology in the Southwestern Presbyterian University, and in 1907 he was called to the same chair in the Theological Seminary at Louisville. His only published work, 'The Theology of Infant Baptism,' is one of the religious standards. He married, October 23, 1883, Roberta C. Beck, of Columbia, S.C. He holds the D.D. and the LL.D. degrees.

WEBBER, CHARLES WILKINS, author, was born in Russellville, Ky., May 29, 1819, and died in Nicaragua, Central America, April 11, 1856. During the war for Texan independence he served in a company of rangers and experienced numerous adventures. Later he studied for the Presbyterian ministry at Princeton, but abandoned this intention and settled in New York, where he devoted himself to literature and published a number of thrilling stories, among them: 'Old Hicks, the Guide' (New York, 1849), 'Gold Mines of the Gila' (1849), 'The Hunter Naturalist' (Philadelphia, 1851), 'A Texan Virago; or, the Tailor of Gotham' (1852), 'The Wild Girl of Nebraska' (1852), 'Tales of the Southern Border' (1853), 'Spiritual Vampirism' (1853), 'Shot in the Eye,' 'Adventures with Texas Rifle Rangers' (London, 1853), 'Wild Scenes and Song Birds' (New York, 1854), and 'History of Mystery' (Philadelphia, 1855). He fell in an ambuscade in the battle of Rivas in Central America, whither he went in the fall of 1855 to join William Walker.

WEBER, JOHN LANGDON. Author. [S.C.]. He wrote a 'History of South Carolina.'

WEBER, WILLIAM LANDER. Educator. He was born in Lenoir, N. C., April 14, 1866, a son of the Rev. S. A. Weber, D.D. was educated at Wofford College and took special work in English at the University of Chicago and at Johns Hopkins University. He married, August 27, 1891, Bettie, daughter of Bishop A. W. Wilson. and became professor of English in Emory College in 1899. His published works include: 'Word-Lists for the Study of English Etymology' and 'Selections from the Southern Poets' (New York, Macmillan Company, 1901), besides frequent contributions to the periodicals. He resides in Oxford, Ga.

WEBSTER, M. M., Mrs. Poet. She was born in Virginia, of the line of Pocahontas, the celebrated Indian princess, and was the author of a work of distinct merit entitled: 'Pocahontas: a Legend, with Historical and Traditionary Notes' (Philadelphia, 1840).

WEEDEN, HOWARD. See Biographical and Critical Sketch, Vol. XIII, page 5721.

WEEKS, RAYMOND. Poet, of Missouri. One of his fragments of verse entitled, "In Normandie," is preserved in 'Missouri Literature.'

WEEKS, STEPHEN BEAUREGARD, educator, author, editor, was born in North Carolina, February 2, 1865, the son of James Elliott and Mary Louisa Mullen Weeks, graduated from the University of North Carolina, and married, first, Mary Lee Martin, and second, Sallie Mangum Leach. Dr. Weeks is the owner of perhaps the largest book collection in existence dealing with the State of North Carolina. He was more than twenty years gathering this library, which contains more than three thousand books and pamphlets. In 1899 he became superintendent of the United States Indian Service, rising to this position from the chair of principal teacher. Besides numerous contributions to encyclopædias and reviews, his writings include: 'The Press of North Carolina in the Eighteenth Century' (1891), 'The Lost Colony of Roanoke: Its Fate and Survival,' 'Religious Development in the Province of North Carolina' (Baltimore, Johns Hopkins University Press), 'Church and State in North Carolina' (*ibid.*), 'History of Negro Suffrage in the South,' 'General Joseph Martin and the War of the Revolution in the West,' 'A Bibliography of the Historical Literature of North Carolina' (1895), 'Libraries and Literature in North Carolina in the Eighteenth Century,' 'Southern Quakers and Slavery' (*ibid.*, 1896), 'American Learned and Educational Societies,' 'Beginning of the Common School System in the South,' 'Bibliography of Confederate Text-Books,' 'Index to North Carolina Colonial and State Records,' 'Life and Times of W. P. Mangum, United States Senator from North Carolina,' and numerous minor works. He resides in Trinity, N.C. His degrees are Ph.D. and LL.D.

WEEMS, MASON L. See Biographical and Critical Sketch, Vol. XIII, page 5731.

WEIDEMEYER, JOHN WILLIAM, author, was born in Fredericksburg, Va., April 26, 1819. For several years he taught in various institutions, after which he engaged in commercial enterprises in New York. The love of nature was the passion of his earlier years, and he gathered many rare specimens and curiosities. He published a 'Catalogue of North American Butterflies (Philadelphia, 1864); two plays, 'The Vagabonds' and 'Cæsar and Cleopatra,' a volume of poems entitled 'Real and Ideal, by John W. Montclair' (Philadelphia, 1865), 'Themes and Translations' (New York, 1867), and 'American Fish and How to Catch Them' (1885).

WEIR, JAMES, Jr. Physician. He was born in Owensboro, Ky., October 17, 1856, a son of James and Susan Charlotte Weir, was valedictorian of his class at the University of Louisville. He subsequently studied medicine and received the finishing touches of his education in the best hospitals of the North and East. His writings constitute an important contribution to the literature of his profession, including: 'Religion and Lust,' 'The Dawn of Reason,' 'Intelligence in the Lower Animals,' and 'The Physical Correlation of Religious Emotion and Sexual Desire.' He resides in Owensboro, Ky.

WELBORN, DRUMMOND. Poet. [Texas]. He published 'An American Epic. and Other Poems.'

WELBY, AMELIA B. See Biographical and Critical Sketch, Vol. XIII, page 5751.

WELD, ANGELINA EMILY GRIMKÉ, reformer, was born in Charleston, S.C., February 20, 1805, and was the daughter of John F. Grimké. With her sister, Sarah, she joined the Society of Friends in Philadelphia, emancipated her slaves, became an advocate of this line of policy upon the public rostrum, wrote 'An Appeal to the Women of the South,' which was reproduced in England, and also published 'Letters to Catharine E. Beecher' (Boston, 1837). The controversy which the appearance of the Grimké sisters awoke is said to have been the beginning of the crusade for equal suffrage in the United States.

WELLS, EDWARD L. Author. [S.C.]. He published an authoritative work of much interest entitled 'Hampton and His Cavalry' (Richmond, B. F. Johnson Company, 1899), which was followed by another interesting volume entitled 'Hampton and Reconstruction.'

WELLS, J. M. Lawyer. [Miss.]. He published 'The Chisholm Massacre: or, a Picture of Home Rule in Mississippi' (1877).

WELLS, WILLIAM CHARLES. Physician and scientist. He was born in Charleston, S.C., in 1757, and died in London, England, September 18, 1817. He received his degree from the University of Edinburgh. The achievement upon which his reputation as a scientist rests is his "Essay on Dew" (London, 1814), and the conclusions which he announced are to-day accepted by men of science with only slight modifications. He received numerous medals and honors. After his death a collection of his essays, with an autobiographical memoir, appeared (Edinburgh, 1818).

WELSH, MARY. An Alabama author who wrote 'The Model Family' (1858) and 'Aunt Abbie' (1859). In the 'Transactions of the Alabama Society' will also be found a contribution from her pen entitled "Reminiscences of Old St. Giles."

WENDLING, GEORGE R. Lecturer. He resides at Charlestown, W.Va. As an orator he is unsurpassed on the lecture platform. His work is characterized by breadth of thought and by independence of treatment. The South's favorite heroes, Robert E. Lee and Stonewall Jackson, have inspired two of his most superb efforts. His other lectures include: "The Man of Galilee," "Saul of Tarsus," "Unseen Realities," and "The Hebrew Law-giver." He has published 'The Man of Galilee' in book form (Charlestown, W.Va., The Olcott Publishing Company, 1909), in deference to numerous requests for the preservation of this masterpiece, and others will doubtless follow.

WEST, ANSON, clergyman, was born in Robertson County, N.C., September 3, 1832, and was the son of Alfred West. For fifty years he was an influential minister of the gospel in the Methodist Episcopal Church, South. He was twice married. His writings include: 'The State of the Dead' (Philadelphia, J. B. Lippincott Company), 'The Old and the

New Man' (Nashville, M.E. Publishing House, South), and 'The History of Methodism in Alabama' (*ibid.*).

WEST, CHARLES NEPHEW, lawyer, was born in Savannah, Ga., August 31, 1844, served in the Confederate Army, practiced law in Savannah and wrote the chapter on "Georgia's Bench and Bar" in 'Memoirs of Georgia' (Atlanta, The Southern Historical Association, 1895).

WEST, FLORENCE DUVAL, Mrs. Author. She was born in Florida but afterward removed to Texas. Besides a collection of sketches entitled 'The Land of the Lotus Eaters,' she wrote 'The Marble Lily, and Other Poems.' She died in 1881.

WESTMORELAND, MARIA JOURDAN. Author. [Ga.]. Besides several dramas, which were produced with thrilling effect during the Civil War, she wrote two entertaining novels of Southern life, 'Clifford Troup' (New York, 1873) and 'Heart Hungry' (*ibid.*, 1874).

WESTON, JAMES A. Protestant Episcopal clergyman. Besides sermons and tracts, he published a 'Life of Peter Stuart Ney' (1893), and contributed to religious periodicals.

WETMORE, ELIZABETH BISLAND. See Biographical and Critical Sketch, Vol. XIII, page 5767.

WHALING, THORNTON. Clergyman. He was born in Bradford, Va., June 5, 1858, a son of Alexander Lewis and Agatha Whaling, and was educated at Davidson and Roanoke colleges. Choosing the ministry, he went first to New York and afterward to Columbia, S.C., for his theological education. He was for several years pastor of the Presbyterian Church at Lerington, Va., the one in which Stonewall Jackson was a Deacon. At present, he is pastor of the First Presbyterian Church of Dallas, Texas. Dr. Whaling is the author of 'The Church and Education.'

WHAREY, JAMES, clergyman, was born in Rutherford County, N C., June 15, 1789, and died in Goochland County, Va., April 29, 1842. He was a Presbyterian, served churches in various parts of Virginia and published 'Sketches of Church History,' and a work on 'Baptism.'

WHARTON, CHARLES HENRY, clergyman, was born in St. Mary's County, Md., June 5, 1748, and died in Burlington, N.J., July 22, 1833. He was educated for the Roman Catholic priesthood, but soon after the Revolution he adopted the creed of the Church of England, became rector of parishes in Delaware and New Jersey, and declined an offer of the presidency of Columbia College, in New York. His first excursion into the field of literature was a rhythmic epistle to General Washington, with a sketch of his life, which was published for the benefit of American prisoners in England (Annapolis, 1779; London, 1780), 'Letter to the Roman Catholics of Worcester' (Philadelphia, 1784), 'Reply to an Address (by Bishop Carroll) to the Roman Catholics of the United States' (Philadelphia, 1785), 'Inquiry into the Proofs of the Divinity of Christ' (1796) and 'Concise View of the Principal Points of Controversy between the Protestant and Roman Churches' (New York, 1817). He also edited religious reviews. His memoirs were published by Bishop George W. Doane, in two volumes (Philadelphia, 1834).

WHARTON, EDWARD C. Author. [La.]. Besides several comedies, he wrote a 'Life of Charles Gayarré.' 'The War of the Bachelors: a Story of the Crescent City' (New Orleans, 1882), and translated from the French 'The New World' (New Orleans, 1855).

WHARTON, HENRY M., clergyman and author, was born in Culpeper County, Va., in 1848. His father was Malcolm H. Wharton and his mother, Susan Roberts Colvin. Though only a lad, he wore the Confederate uniform during the closing days of the war, being sixteen when he surrendered. On completing his studies, he practiced law for five years, but abandoned this profession to enter the ministry of the Southern Baptist Church. He afterward became the leading exponent of his faith in Baltimore; but, under an imperative conviction of duty, he relinquished his influential charge to engage in evangelistic work. On the lecture platform and in the public press he has been a power. His writings include: 'Pulpit, Pen, and Platform,' 'Travels in Palestine,' 'Sermons,' 'The War Songs and Poems of the Confederacy,' 'D. L. Moody: His Work and Workers,' and a novel entitled: 'White Blood' (New York and Washington, The Neale Publishing Company, 1906). Among his lectures are: "On Horseback in the Holy Land," "The Ups and Downs of Life," "The Man in the Moon," "The Confederate Soldier," and "Rambles in Europe." He holds the degree of D.D.

WHARTON, JOHN. Physician and poet. At Winchester, Va., in 1814, appeared from the pen of this author a volume of poems entitled: 'The Virginia Wreath,' which is said to have contained some fair verse, the best of the collection being an "Ode to Washington." He studied medicine at Edinburgh.

WHARTON, MORTON BRYAN. Clergyman and author. He was born in Orange County, Va., April 6, 1839, a son of Malcolm H. and Susan Roberts Wharton. He was a student in the Virginia Military Institute when the war began, and left college to enter the Confederate Army in 1861. He married Mary Belle Irwin, of Lee County, Ga. He held several important Baptist pastorates, edited the *Christian Index,* spent some time in European travel and was a writer of unusual charm and interest. Among his published works are: 'European Notes,' 'Famous Women of the Old Testament' (New York, E. B. Treat), 'Famous Women of the New Testament' (*ibid.*), 'Pictures from a Pastorium,' and 'Sacred Songs to Popular Airs.' Dr. Wharton died in 1908.

WHEAT, JOHN THOMAS, clergyman, was born in Washington, D.C., November 15, 1800, and died in Salisbury, N.C., February 2, 1888. For several years he conducted a school in Washington. Afterward he was admitted to orders in the Episcopal Church and served parishes in North Carolina, Tennessee, and Arkansas. He published a work on 'Preparation for the Holy Communion' (New York, 1860), which became a standard. The University of Nashville gave him the degree of D.D.

WHEELER, JOHN HILL, author, was born in Murfreesboro, N.C., August 6, 1806, and died in Washington, D.C., December 7, 1882. After completing his studies at Columbian University, he took a course of law at the University of North Carolina, became superintendent of the mint at Charlotte, treasurer of the State of North Carolina, and United States Minister to Nicaragua. For ten years he was occupied in collecting materials for his 'History of North Carolina' (Philadelphia, 1851), a work which has deservedly taken high rank. He also published a 'Legislative Manual of North Carolina' (1874), 'Reminiscences and Memoirs of North Carolina' (Columbus, Ohio, 1884), and edited Colonel David Fanning's 'Autobiography' (Richmond, 1861). He spent his last years in Washington, D.C., in labors on statistics.

WHEELER, JOSEPH. Soldier and statesman. He was born in Augusta, Ga., September 10, 1836, graduated from the United States Military Academy at West Point in 1859, and married Daniella Jones. He became lieutenant-general in the Confederate Army and a noted cavalry commander. He was three times wounded, in addition to losing sixteen horses, which were shot from under him. He represented the Eighth Alabama District in Congress for eighteen years, resigning his seat to serve the United States Government in the war with Spain. Being made a brigadier-general in the United States Army, he served with distinction both in Cuba and in the Philippines. Besides numerous contributions to the magazines, and speeches in Congress and upon the platform, his published works include: 'An Account of the Kentucky Campaign,' 'Cavalry Tactics,' 'Military History of Alabama,' 'History of the Santiago Campaign,' 'History of Cuba,' 'History of the Effect Upon Civilization of the Wars of the Nineteenth Century.' He died in New York, while on a visit to his sister, in 1906, being at the time an officer on the retired list of the United States Army. He received the degree of LL.D.

WHEELER, JUNIUS BRUTUS. Soldier. He was born in Murfreesboro, N.C., February 21, 1830, and died in Lenoir, N.C., July 15, 1886. At the outbreak of the Mexican War, he left the University of North Carolina to enlist for the struggle, and became a lieutenant. Later he entered the academy at West Point and attained eventually the rank of major of engineers. He published a series of military text-books, which are not only authoritative in character but systematic in arrangement, including a work on 'Civil Engineering' (New York, 1877), 'Art and Science of War' (1878), 'Elements of Field Fortifications' (1882), and 'Military Engineering,' in two volumes (1884-1885).

WHELAN, JAMES. Roman Catholic bishop. He was born in Kilkenny, Ireland, December 8, 1823, and died in Zanesville, Ohio, February 18, 1878. When quite a lad he crossed the water, locating with his parents in Kentucky, where he began his theological studies. On the death of Bishop Miles, of Nashville, he succeeded to the vacant See. He wrote 'Catena Aurea; or, a Golden Chain of Evidences Demonstrating from Analytical Treatment of History That Papal Infallibility Is No Novelty' (1871), an able discussion of this subject.

WHIPPLE, LEON RUTLEDGE, educator, was born in St. Louis, Mo., September 19, 1882. He holds the instructorship of English writing at the University of Virginia and contributes short stories and sketches to current periodicals. The sketch of Kate Chopin in 'The Library of Southern Literature' is from his pen.

WHITAKER, ALEXANDER, clergyman, was born in Cambridge, England, in 1585 and died in Henrico County, Va., after 1613. He took orders in the Church of England, ministered to an English parish for several years before coming to America, baptized Pocahontas, officiated at the marriage of the Indian maiden to John Rolfe, and published 'Good News from Virginia' (London, 1613), one of the earliest books written in the English colonies.

WHITAKER, BESSIE LEWIS. Educator. Miss Whitaker is a native of Halifax County, N.C. At present she is engaged in teaching in Birmingham, Ala. Besides numerous essays and sketches, she is the author of a thesis on "The Provincial Council and the Committees of Safety in North Carolina," published in the 'James Sprunt Historical Monograph' (Chapel Hill, N.C., The University Press, 1907). She also wrote for 'The Library of Southern Literature' the sketch of Mary Bayard Clarke.

WHITAKER, DANIEL KIMBALL, editor, was born in Sharon, Conn., April 13, 1801, and died in New Orleans, La., April 10, 1881. For a while he practiced law in South Carolina, but he leaned toward literature and, abandoning the profession of law, he organized and edited in succession numerous periodicals, including the *Southern Literary Journal, Whitaker's Magazine,* the *Southern Quarterly Review,* and the New Orleans *Monthly Review.* Of these, the *Southern Quarterly Review* was the most successful, running from 1841 until 1861, when it was discontinued by the outbreak of hostilities.

WHITAKER, LILY C. Poet. She was a daughter of Daniel K. Whitaker and was born in Charleston, S.C., about 1850. She received her education in New Orleans, contributed to the *Southern Quarterly Review,* of which her father was the editor, and published "Donata" and other poems (New Orleans, 1880).

WHITAKER, MARY S., author, was born in Beaufort, S.C., February 22, 1820, and was the daughter of the Rev. Samuel Furman. She was educated in Edinburgh, contributed her first poems to the Scottish press under the auspices of Thomas Campbell, married first a Scotchman, John Miller, and afterward, on her return to America, an editor, Daniel K. Whitaker. Besides numerous magazine articles, she published a volume of 'Poems' (Philadelphia, 1850), and a novel entitled 'Albert Hastings' (1868).

WHITAKER, WALTER CLAIBORNE. Clergyman. He was born at Lenoir, N.C., January 28, 1867. His father was Lucius F. Whitaker and his mother, Rowena Oates. He is rector of St. John's Church, Knoxville, Tenn. Several volumes have come from his pen: 'The Prodigal Son' (1890), 'Dives and Lazarus' (1898), 'History of the Protestant Episcopal Church in Alabama' (1898), and 'Richard Hooker Wilmer: a Biography' (1907), besides occasional pamphlets. He also edited for several years the *Alabama Church Record* and the *Mississippi Church News.* He married, March 30, 1891, Isabel Preston Royall. The University of the South gave him the degree of D.D.

WHITE, CHARLES IGNATIUS, clergyman, was born in Baltimore, Md., in 1807, and died in Washington, D.C., April 1, 1877. He was educated at St. Mary's College, became a Roman Catholic priest, and was for twenty years pastor of St. Matthew's Church, in Washington, D.C. Besides editing numerous periodicals, he translated Balme's 'Protestantism and Catholicity, Compared in Their Effects upon the Civilization of Europe' (New York, 1850), 'Chateaubriand's Genius of Christianity' (1856), and wrote a 'Life of Mrs. Eliza A. Seton' (1853).

WHITE, EDWARD LUCAS. Educator. His father was Thomas H. White and his mother, Kate Butler Lucas. He was born in Bergen, N.J., May 18, 1866. On completing his studies at Johns Hopkins, he became a teacher of the classic languages in Baltimore. He is the author of 'Narrative Lyrics' (1908). The sketch of Marguerite E. Easter in 'The Library of Southern Literature' is also from his pen.

WHITE, GEORGE. Clergyman. He lived in Georgia and wrote two books of very great value to the student of State antiquities, viz.: 'Historical Collections of Georgia' (New York, 1854), and 'Statistics of Georgia,' each of which contains a mine of information concerning the political subdivisions of the State, its social life, its leading men and its salient outlines of progress from the earliest times.

WHITE, GREENHOW. Protestant Episcopal clergyman and educator. [Tenn.]. He published 'The Philosophy of American Litera ture' (1890), 'The Philosophy of English Literature' (1895), 'A Saint of the Southern Church,' comprising a biography of Bishop Cobbs (1897), 'An Apostle of the Western Church' (1899), and numerous contributions to periodicals.

WHITE, HENRY ALEXANDER. Theologian. He was born in Greenbrier County, Va., April 15, 1861, a son of William Orr and Mary White, graduated from Washington and Lee University, and afterward took theological work at Union Seminary, in Virginia, and at Princeton, N. J. He married, July 18, 1899, Fannie Beverley Wellford. He was professor of history in Washington and Lee University for thirteen years; and in 1902 was called to Columbia Theological Seminary. His published works include: 'The Pentateuch in the Light of the Ancient Monuments' (Richmond, B. F. Johnson), 'Robert E. Lee and the Southern Confederacy' (New York, G. P. Putnam's Sons), 'History of the United States' (New York, Silver, Burdett and Company), 'History of South Carolina,' 'Beginners History of the United States' (New York, D. Appleton and Company), and 'Life of Stonewall Jackson' (Philadelphia, G. W. Jacobs Company). The sketch of John C. Calhoun in 'The Library of Southern Literature' is also from his pen. He resides in Columbia, S.C. His degrees are D.D. and LL.D.

WHITE, HENRY CLAY. Educator. He was born in Baltimore, Md., December 30, 1850, a son of Levi S. and Louisa White, was educated at the University of Virginia and married, December 19, 1872, Ella Frances Roberts. He was made professor of Chemistry at the University of Georgia in 1872 and president of the Georgia State College of Agricultural and Mechanic Arts in 1890. He belongs to numerous learned societies on both sides of the water. His writings include: 'Elementary Geology of Tennessee,' with William Gibbs McAdoo (1873), 'Complete Chemistry of the Cotton Plant' (1874), 'Lectures and Addresses,' in two volumes (1885-1891), and minor works. He also wrote the sketch of Joseph Le Conte for 'The Library of Southern Literature.' On the platform Dr. White is an attractive speaker. He resides in Athens, Ga. His degrees are Ph.D., D.C.L. and LL.D.

WHITE, HUGH LAWSON, jurist and statesman, was born in Iredell County, N.C., October 30, 1773, and died in Knoxville, Tenn., April 10, 1840. Under General Sevier, he fought against the Cherokees when a youth of seventeen. Afterward he studied law in Philadelphia, settled in Knoxville, Tenn., for the practice of his profession, achieved distinction by reason of his rare talents, became judge of the Supreme Court and Senator of the United States, incurred the hostility of General Jackson, but was sustained by the Legislature of the State, and in the campaign of 1836 received the electoral votes of Tennessee and Georgia. His integrity of character earned for him the soubriquet of "The American Cato." One of his descendants, Nancy N. Scott, published 'A Memoir of Judge White, with Selections from His Speeches and Correspondence' (Philadelphia, 1856).

WHITE, ISRAEL CHARLES. Geologist. He was born in Monongalia County, W.Va., November 1, 1848. For fifteen years he was professor of geology in the University of West Virginia. At the present time he is State geologist. Besides compiling several volumes of geological reports, he has contributed at frequent intervals to scientific journals.

WHITE, JOHN BLAKE. Artist and author. He was born near Eutaw Springs, S.C., September 2, 1781, and died in Charleston, S.C., August 24, 1859. Besides producing a number of celebrated portraits, he published several dramas, among them: 'Foscari; or, the Venetian Exile' (1805), 'Mysteries of the Castle' (1806), 'Modern Honor' (1812), 'The Triumph of Liberty; or, Louisiana Preserved' (1819), and 'Intemperance' (1839). Both in literature and in art he was one of the pioneers of the South.

WHITE, JOHN ELLINGTON, clergyman, was born at Clayton, N.C., December 19, 1868. His father was the Rev. James M. White and his mother, Martha Ellington. For several years he has occupied the pulpit of the Second Baptist Church, of Atlanta, Ga., one of the largest congregations in the South. Several pamphlets have come from his pen, containing literary material of more than ordinary value, among them: 'Noble Anglo-Saxonism,' 'The Silent Southerners,' 'My Old Confederate,' 'The True and the False in Southern Life,' 'The Mountaineers,' 'Prohibition the Task and the Opportunity of the South,' 'The Backward People,' 'A White Man's Program,' and 'The Blind Strength of the Mountaineer's Child.' He married, October 12, 1892, Effie L. Guess. He holds the degree of D.D.

WHITE, JOSEPH M., lawyer, was born in Franklin County, Ky., May 10, 1781, and died in St. Louis, Mo., October 19, 1839. For the practice of law he settled in Pensacola, Fla., where his familiarity with French and Spanish brought him numerous clients. He was an eloquent speaker, a ready debater, a fluent writer, served six consecutive terms in Congress, and published a 'New Collection of Laws, Charters, etc., of Great Britain, France and Spain relating to Concessions of Lands, with the Laws of Mexico,' in two volumes (Philadelphia, 1839).

WHITE, OCTAVIUS AUGUSTUS, physician, was born in Charleston, S.C., February 8, 1826. After graduating from the College of South Carolina he pursued his studies at the South Carolina Medical College, became an eminent practitioner of Charleston, served as a surgeon in the Confederate Army, and at the close of the war settled in New York. He invented a number of surgical instruments, discovered new methods of treatment and made important contributions to medical literature in the way of reports and papers.

WHITE, ROBERT. Lawyer. Colonel White commanded the Twenty-third Regiment of Virginia Cavalry during the Civil War. He achieved distinction at the Bar and was honored by his comrades in the order of United Confederate Veterans with the command of the West Virginia Division. He wrote the volume on "West Virginia" for the 'Confederate Military History' (Atlanta, Ga., The Confederate Publishing Company, 1899).

WHITE, S. V. Poet. [N.C.]. Four of the author's poems were published by his daughter in a work entitled 'Selections from Portfolio' (New York, 1893).

WHITEFIELD, GEORGE, clergyman and orator, was born in Gloucester, England, December 7, 1714, and died in Newburyport, Mass., September 30, 1770. He followed the Wesleys to Georgia, organized the Bethesda Orphanage, near Savannah, and devoted his rare gifts of eloquence to raising funds for this benevolent institution. He originated the Calvinistic Methodists. As an orator he was peerless among the preachers of either hemisphere; and to reach the multitudes who flocked to hear him most of his meetings were conducted in the open air. The journals which he kept of his frequent visits to Georgia are included in his published works, which appeared soon after his death, in six volumes. The earliest of his biographers was his friend, the Rev. John Gillies, D.D., who wrote a volume of 'Memoirs' (1772). Some of his sermons were published with an introductory sketch by Samuel Drew (1833). But the most exhaustive and thorough account of his wonderful career is given by the Rev. Luke Tierman, in two volumes entitled 'The Life of George Whitefield.' One of the counties of Georgia bears the name of the great evangelist.

WHITEHEAD, PAUL. Methodist Episcopal clergyman. [Va.]. He published 'The Odd Hour; or, Recreations of a Presiding Elder.'

WHITELOCK, LOUISE CLARKSON. Author and artist. She was born in Baltimore, Md., in 1865. Her maiden name was Louise Clarkson. She writes not only charming prose but very graceful verse; and for the most of her books she has furnished the illustrations. Her published works include: 'Violet with Eyes of Blue,' 'The Gathering of the Lilies,' 'The Rag Fair,' 'Indian Summer,' 'Heartsease and Happy Days,' 'Fly Away Fairies,' and 'Little Miss Stay-at-Home,' all of which are dainty bits of artistic work, the two last-named being for children. She has published also 'The Shadow of John Wallace,' a novel, 'How Hindsight Met Provincialitis,' a collection of short stories, 'Madcap Madonna,' and others. She married George Whitelock, a lawyer of Baltimore.

WHITELOCK, WILLIAM WALLACE. Author. He was born at Mount Washington near Baltimore, Md., April 1, 1869, and was the son of William and Jane Stockton Whitelock. His education was received at Johns Hopkins and at Munich (Ph.D.). On January 10, 1901, he married, in London, England, Baroness Mary von Stockhausen. For some time he was engaged in New York journalism. During the Spanish-American War he was chief yeoman on the United States ship *Gloucester*. His writings have touched the popular chord. They include: 'When the Heart Is Young' (New York, E. P. Dutton and Company), 'The Literary Guillotine' (New York, John Lane), 'Just Love Songs,' 'Foregone Verse' (Boston, R. G. Badger and Company), and 'When Kings Go Forth to Battle' (Philadelphia, J. B. Lippincott Company). He resides in New York.

WHITESIDE, MARY BRENT, author, was born at Shelbyville, Tenn., in 1882. Her father was James Robinson Whiteside and her mother, Frances Smith, a sister of the Honorable Hoke Smith, former governor of Georgia and Secretary of the Interior under President Cleveland. She possesses unusual literary gifts, writing with ease in both prose and verse. Two little volumes which have come from her pen have won for her much praise. They are: 'Bill Possum: His Book' (Atlanta The Byrd Company), suggested by the visit of Mr. Taft to the South on the eve of his inauguration; and 'The Caprice of Capri,' a libretto. She has also made frequent contributions to the periodicals.

WHITNEY, E. L. Educator. [S.C.]. He has made some very exhaustive researches and besides a 'Bibliography of Colonial South Carolina' (1896) has published an interesting work on the 'Government of the Colony of South Carolina' (1895).

WHITSETT, WILLIAM HETH. Clergyman and educator. He was born in Nashville, Tenn., November 25, 1841, and was educated at Union University in Tennessee. He served in the Confederate Army and resumed his studies after the war, spending some time at the University of Leipsic. He held several important pastorates after entering the ministry, but relinquished pastoral for educational work. He was a professor in the Southern Baptist Theological Seminary for nearly twenty-five years, and its president from 1895 to 1899. Later he became professor of philosophy in Richmond College, Va. His writings include: 'The Origin of Infant Baptism,' 'History of Communion Among Baptists,' 'The Origin of the Disciples of Christ,' 'Life and Times of Judge Caleb Wallace' (1888), and 'A Question in Baptist History.' The sketch of John A. Broadus in 'The Library of Southern Literature' is also from his pen. He resides in Richmond, Va. His degrees are D.D. and LL.D.

WHITSETT, WILLIAM THORNTON. Educator. He was born in Guilford County, N.C., August 6, 1868, and was educated at the University of North Carolina. For more than twenty years he has been president of Whitsett Institute. He has written a number of excellent poems, including "To a Lark" and "Bob White." He resides at Whitsett, N.C.

WHITTEN, MARTHA ELIZABETH HOTCHKISS. Poet. [Texas]. She wrote some very clever verse, including 'The Old Home, and Other Poems.'

WHITTET, ROBERT. He was born in Scotland. For many years he has lived in Virginia, but the idiom of his boyhood has continued to be the favorite vehicle of his thought and much of his poetry is cast in the quaint molds of the Highlands. He is the author of two volumes entitled 'The Bright Side of Suffering, and Other Poems' (Richmond, 1882), and 'Sonnets, Mostly on Scripture Themes' (Richmond, 1900).

WHITTLE, WALTER ANDREW. Baptist clergyman. He was born in Alabama, but afterward lived in Kentucky and published 'A Baptist Abroad' (1890).

WHITTLESEY, SARAH JOHNSON COGSWELL. Author. She was born in Williamston, N.C., about 1825. After receiving her education, she removed to Alexandria, Va., where she began to write for the press. She contributed articles of merit both in prose and in verse to the current periodicals and published 'Heart Drops from Memory's Urn' (New York, 1852), 'The Stranger's Stratagem; or, the Double Deceit, and Other Stories' (1860), 'Herbert Hamilton; or, the Bas Bleu' (1867), 'Bertha, the Beauty' (Philadelphia, 1871), and, with her brother, 'Spring Buds and Summer Blossoms' (1888).

WHYTE, WILLIAM PINKNEY. United States Senator. He was born in Baltimore, Md., August 9, 1824. After completing his law studies at Harvard, he was admitted to the Bar and became one of the foremost lawyers of Maryland. When Reverdy Johnson was appointed Minister to England, Mr. Whyte succeeded him in the United States Senate. He afterward became governor of Maryland, but resigned the office to return to the United States Senate. He spoke with great effectiveness and power in the debates of the Upper Chamber. In politics he was a Democrat. The University of Maryland gave him the degree of LL.D.

WIER, A. M. Writer. For years over the signature of "Sarge Plunkett," he has contributed to the Atlanta *Constitution* weekly letters full of rustic philosophy and humor. Some of them have been published in book form under the title of 'Old Times in Georgia' (1900).

WIGGINS, BENJAMIN LAWTON. Educator. He was born at Sand Ridge, S.C., September 11, 1861. After graduating from the University of the South, he pursued post-graduate studies at Johns Hopkins. In 1882 he accepted the chair of Greek in the University of the South, a position which he continued to hold until his death. For more than fifteen years he also filled the office of vice-chancellor. Besides occasional contributions to magazines and reviews, he wrote the sketch of Sarah

Barnwell Elliott in 'The Library of Southern Literature.' He married, January 20, 1886, Clara Quintard. Three separate institutions conferred upon him the degree of LL.D. He died at Sewanee, Tenn., June 14, 1909.

WIGHTMAN, FRANCIS P. He compiled and edited 'Little Leather Breeches, and Other Southern Rhymes' (New York, J. F. Taylor and Company, 1899), and 'Jingle Jingle,' another collection of negro songs (*ibid.,* 1899).

WIGHTMAN, WILLIAM MAY, bishop of the M. E. Church, South. He was born in Charleston, S.C., January 29, 1808, and died in Charleston, S.C., February 15, 1825. For several years he edited the *Southern Christian Advocate* in Charleston, and afterward became chancellor of the Southern University. He was ordained a bishop in New Orleans. Randolph-Macon College gave him the degree of D.D., and the College of Charleston, the degree of LL.D. He edited 'The Autobiography of Bishop William Capers,' with an interesting memoir (Nashville, Tenn., 1858).

. WILCOX, CADMUS MARCELLUS. Soldier. He was born in Wayne County, N.C., May 29, 1826. He was educated at West Point and served with distinction in the Mexican War, but at the outbreak of hostilities, in 1861, he resigned his captain's commission, entered the Confederate service and became a major-general. He translated 'Evolutions of the Line' (1860), wrote 'Rifles and Rifle Practice' (New York, 1859), and a 'History of the Mexican War.' He died in 1890.

WILDE, JENNY. Poet. [La.]. She published a volume of verse entitled 'Why, and Other Poems' (1888).

WILDE, RICHARD HENRY. See Biographical and Critical Sketch, Vol. XIII, page 5789.

WILDS, SAMUEL, jurist, was born in Darlington District, S.C., March 4, 1775, and died near Cheraw, S.C., March 9, 1810. Before reaching the age of thirty he was elevated to the Bench. His unique powers of eloquence were never more signally displayed than when pronouncing sentence upon criminals. On such occasions the effect was most dramatic. Some of his addresses from the Bench are preserved in Bishop Gregg's 'History of the Old Cheraws.'

WILEY, CALVIN HENDERSON. See Biographical and Critical Sketch. Vol. XIII, page 5805.

WILEY. EDWIN. Librarian. He was born near Knoxville. Tenn., in 1872. His father was Edwin F. Wiley and his mother, Catharine McAdoo. He is employed in the Library of Congress in the department of classification. At leisure intervals he has published 'The Old and the New Renaissance' (1903), and 'The Rationale of Southern Literature' (1895). He also wrote "Presses in Tennessee and Kentucky," in the 'Proceedings of the Bibliographical Society of America,' "Libraries in the South," for 'The South in the Building of the Nation,' and the sketch of Olive T. Dargan in 'The Library of Southern Literature.' He married, in 1902, Garnet Noel, of Nashville, Tenn.

WILEY, GARNET NOEL. Writer. She was born in Nashville, Tenn., April 9, 1883. Numerous short stories and sketches have come from the pen of this talented woman, besides rhymes for children and poems of rare grace for older heads. She is the author of 'Santa Claus in Wonderland,' a cantata (London, The Curwen Press), 'The Ballad of Lady Yolande' (The Olympian, 1903), "King Ulad's Woe" (*Bob Taylor's Magazine,* 1904), 'Urla's Quest' (*ibid.,* 1905), and contributions both in prose and in verse to *St. Nicholas, Harper's Magazine, Putnam's Magazine, The Independent*, and other periodicals. She married Edwin Wiley, August 7, 1902, and resides in Washington, D.C.

WILEY, GEORGE EPHRAIM. Physician. He was born at Emory and Henry College, Virginia, October 19, 1857, the youngest child of the Rev. Ephraim Emerson Wiley, D.D., for thirty-six years president of Emory and Henry College, a kinsman of Ralph Waldo Emerson, and a preacher of great power. The son chose the medical profession, in which he has risen to high distinction. At leisure intervals he has exercised his literary gifts by writing a volume entitled 'Southern Plantation Stories and Sketches' (New York, The Broadway Publishing Company, 1907), in which he preserves some delightful bits of negro dialect and humor. Dr. Wiley is said to have been the first person to undertake the humane task of providing local homes for the worn-out ex-slaves. He resides in Bristol, Va.

WILKINSON, ANDREW. Author. [La.]. He wrote 'Sketches of Plantation Life' (1884).

WILKINSON, ELIZA, writer, was born in St. Paul's Parish, S.C., February 7, 1857, a daughter of Francis Yonge, Sr., and a granddaughter of Honorable Robert Yonge, associate-justice of the Supreme Court of South Carolina. During the occupation of Charleston by the British she wrote a series of graphic and brilliant letters, which were afterward edited by Caroline Howard Gilman (1839). They throw an interesting light upon this dramatic period. Several of Mrs. Wilkinson's unpublished letters, written subsequent to the Revolution, are also preserved in Charleston.

WILKINSON, JAMES. An officer of the Revolution, who attained the rank of brigadier-general. He was born in Baltimore, Md., in 1757. Although a gallant soldier, he was implicated in certain affairs of intrigue which seriously injured his reputation. After resigning his commission in 1781 he removed to Kentucky and acquired wide influence along the border, but he is charged with having connived with the Spaniards in Louisiana for the absorption of the Western country by Spain. It is also asserted that at the same time he was engaged with Aaron Burr in a scheme for the conquest of Mexico. He was exonerated of this charge and subsequently was advanced to the rank of major-general in the second war with England, but was finally superseded. He afterward removed to Mexico and took part in the operations that were then in progress. He died in 1828. The last years of his life were spent in an unsuccessful effort to collect from the Mexican Government a sum that was due him for munitions of war. To vindicate his good name, he published in 1808 a work entitled 'The Aaron Burr Conspiracy Exposed,' and in 1816 he gave to the public in three volumes his 'Memoirs of My Own Times.'

WILKINSON, JOHN, naval officer, was born in Norfolk, Va., November 6, 1821. The lure of the sea constrained him to enter the United States Navy, in which he attained the rank of lieutenant; but at the outbreak of the Civil War he resigned his commission, entered the Confederate service, encountered a number of thrilling adventures in command of different vessels, and published an interesting account of his exploits entitled 'The Narrative of a Blockade Runner' (New York, 1877).

WILL, ALLEN SINCLAIR. Author. [Va.]. He wrote 'The World-Crisis in China.'

WILLARD, FLORENCE J. Author. [La.]. She published a volume of 'Poems' (1879).

WILLET, JOSEPH EDGERTON. Educator. He was born in Macon, Ga., November 17, 1826. After receiving his education at Mercer, he became a professor in the institution and taught the natural sciences. During the Civil War he was employed by the Confederate Government to superintend the manufacture of ammunition. Besides a course of lectures on "Science and Religion," he published a volume on 'The Wonders of Insect Life' (1869).

WILLEY, WAITMAN THOMAS. United States Senator. He was born in Monongalia County, Va., in what is now West Virginia, October 18, 1811, and studied law. When Virginia seceded, he was elected by the Unionist Legislature at Wheeling to succeed James M. Mason in the United States Senate; and later, on the creation of West Virginia into an independent state, he was commissioned to represent the new commonwealth in the Upper Chamber; and was subsequently reëlected. He contributed to magazines and reviews and delivered a series of lectures on "Methodism." Alleghany College gave him the degree of LL.D.

WILLIAMS, BESSIE W. JOHNSON, Mrs. Writer. She was born in South Carolina but afterward lived in Georgia. She published "In Memory of Captain Herndon," a poem, and 'Ciaromski and His Daughter.'

WILLIAMS, ESPY WILLIAM HENDRICKS. Dramatist. He was born in New Orleans, La., January 30, 1852, the son of William H. and Lavinia M. Williams, was educated in the grammar schools, and married, April 15, 1879, Nannie Bowers. He engaged in business operations, devoting his leisure intervals to literary work. Some of his dramatic productions have received the favor of the highest critics and have been successfully staged on both sides of the ocean. Besides a volume of poems entitled 'A Dream of Art,' he is the author of the following plays: "Parrhasius," a tragedy produced by Robert Mantell, "The Husband," a society drama, produced by the same, "The Queen's Garter," a romantic play, produced by the same, "The Man in Black," a drama, produced by Walter Whiteside, "A Cavalier of France," a drama, produced by Louis James; "The Duke's Jester," a romantic comedy, produced by Frederick Warde; "Unorna," a romantic play, produced by Mrs. Brune, "The Emperor's Double," a romantic comedy, produced by Clarence Brune, "A Royal Joke," a comic opera, produced by the Metropolitan Opera Company, "Ollamus," a comic opera, "Eugene Aram," a tragedy, and "The Last Witch," a play. He resides in New Orleans.

WILLIAMS, EUSTACE LEROY. Journalist. He was born in Culpeper, Va., September 29, 1874, a son of L. E. and Flora Williams, was well educated, and married, in 1900, Elizabeth Smith. He is the author of 'The Mutineers' (Lothrop) and 'The Substitute Quarterback' (Dana Estes). He resides in Louisville, Ky.

WILLIAMS, FLORA McDONALD. Author. She wrote an interesting story of the Confederacy entitled: 'The Blue Cockade' (New York and Washington, The Neale Publishing Company, 1907).

WILLIAMS, JOHN G. Author. [S.C.]. He published 'The Invasion of the Moor.'

WILLIAMS, JOHN LEE. Civil engineer and lawyer. He was born in Salem, Mass., in 1775, and died in Picoloto, Fla., in 1856. After graduation from Hamilton College, N.Y., he practiced law for a while in Virginia, but later, on the exchange of flags, removed to 'Florida. He traveled over the entire territory, made extensive surveys and observations, and together with Dr. W. H. Simmons, was appointed to select the site of the State capitol. His published works include: 'A View of East Florida,' 'A View of West Florida,' and his 'Journal,' all of which are works of very great value to historical students because of the light which they throw upon the early territorial history of the peninsula. He was a man of cultured attainments, enjoyed the friendship of eminent writers and thinkers, and accompanied Audubon on more than one expedition.

WILLIAMS, JOHN SHARP, United States Senator, Congressman, lawyer, was born in Memphis, Tenn., July 30, 1854. During the Civil War, when he was still a lad, his parents moved to Mississippi, where he spent his boyhood days. He enjoyed the best educational advantages, including courses both at the University of the South and at the University of Virginia, after which he completed his studies at Heidelberg. He studied law and also became a cotton planter; achieved early distinction in politics, attended the National Democratic Conventions in 1892 and 1904, presiding over the latter in the capacity of temporary chairman; served in Congress from 1893 to 1909, becoming minority leader and was finally elected to succeed Honorable H. D. Money in the United States Senate, defeating ex-governor James K. Vardaman. As a debater, Senator Williams is without a superior. He is also an accomplished parliamentarian, a ripe scholar and a sound thinker upon political and economic questions.

WILLIAMS, JOHN WILSON MONTGOMERY, clergyman, was born in Portsmouth, Va., April 7, 1820. He was educated at Columbian College and at Newton Theological Seminary, and was for a number of years pastor of the First Baptist Church, of Baltimore, Md. He published 'Pastor and People: a Lecture' (Washington, 1867), 'Reminiscences of a Pastorate of Thirty-three Years' (1884), 'Training of our Members in the Distinctive Principles of Our Denomination a Duty and a Necessity' (Philadelphia, 1855), and a number of tracts and sermons. Columbian College gave him the degree of D.D.

WILLIAMS, JOSEPH S. Author. [Tenn.]. He has preserved many delightful incidents and traditions of pioneer life in a work entitled 'Old Times in Tennessee, by a Descendant of One of the First Settlers' (1873).

WILLIAMS, MARTHA McCULLOCH. Author. She was born in Montgomery County, Tenn., and married Thomas McCulloch Williams. She began her literary career after removing to New York in 1887. Besides numerous short stories and sketches, she is the author of several interesting serials, among them: 'Field Farings' (New York, Harper and Brothers), 'Two of a Trade,' 'Milre,' and 'Next to the Ground' (New York, McClure, Phillips and Company). One of her short stories—"In Jackson's Purchase"—won the prize in McClure's competition. She resides in New York City.

WILLIAMS, MARY BUSHNELL. Author. She was born in Baton Rouge, La., in 1826. Her father was Judge Charles Bushnell, a native of Boston. She was educated by Professor Alexander Dimitry, a distinguished scholar, and became the wife of Josiah P. Williams, a planter. She contributed to current periodicals, wrote a number of poems which were greatly admired, among them, one entitled "The Serfs of Chateney," and published a volume of 'Tales and Legends of Louisiana.'

WILLIAMS, R. GRAY. Lawyer. He was born in Leesburg, Va., July 10, 1878. During the leisure intervals of a life somewhat crowded by professional engagements he has exercised his literary gifts. Besides magazine and newspaper work, he has published occasional speeches, and a memoir of Edgar Allan Poe. He is also the founder and editor of *Things and Thoughts,* a Southern literary periodical. The sketch of Mrs. Burton Harrison in 'The Library of Southern Literature' is from the pen of Mr. Williams.

WILLIAMS, RICHARD D'ALTON. Physician and man of letters. He was born in Dublin, Ireland, October 8, 1822. Under the pen-name of "Shamrock," he began to contribute verses to the press in early youth. Later he became one of the founders and editors of the *Irish Tribune,* and on account of the extreme sentiments of the paper, he was charged with treason against the Queen. In the prosecution that followed he was represented by the celebrated Samuel Ferguson, who, in the course of his argument, declared him to be the first living poet of Ireland, next to Thomas Moore. Soon after his acquittal he emigrated to the United States. For a while he was professor of *belles-lettres* at Spring Hill College in Alabama; but he afterward settled at Thibodaux, La., dividing his time between the practice of medicine and the labor of authorship. He died July 5, 1862.

WILLIAMS, WALTER. Editor. He was born in Boonville, Mo., July 2, 1864, received a high-school education, learned the printer's trade, and established in 1895 *The Country Editor,* a monthly magazine in the interest of newspaper men. He was made vice-president of the International Press Congress at Berne, Switzerland, and was chosen delegate from the General Assembly of his church to the Pan-Presbyterian Council in Scotland. He has been an extensive traveler, organized the World's Press Parliament at St. Louis, in 1904, and married, June 30, 1892, Hulda Harned. He teaches a Bible class of more than four hundred members. His writings include: 'How the Cap'n Saved the Day,' 'Some Saints and Some Sinners in the Holy Land,' and 'The State of Missouri.' At present he is editor of the Columbia *Herald.* The sketch of J. N. Baskett in 'The Library of Southern Literature' is also from his pen. He resides in Columbia, Mo.

WILLIAMSON, HUGH. Physician. Though born in Pennsylvania in 1735, he located in North Carolina at the close of the Revolution, served in the Continental Congress from 1784 to 1786, was a member of the convention that framed the Constitution of the United States, and published, in two volumes, a 'History of North Carolina' (Philadelphia, 1812), besides numerous minor works. Late in life he removed to New York City, where he died in 1819.

WILLIAMSON, J. J. Author. He published an interesting volume entitled 'Mosby's Rangers' (1896).

WILLIAMSON, MARY LYNN. Educator and author. She was born near Charlottesville, Va., May 4, 1850, a daughter of P. R. and Mary Harrison. She received a collegiate education and married, November 2, 1874, M. W. Williamson. The greater part of her life has been devoted to educational work; and in connection with her school duties she has endeavored to simplify biography for the benefit of her youthful pupils. Among her books are: 'The Life of Robert E. Lee' (1866), 'The Life of General T. J. Jackson' (1899), and 'The Life of Washington' (1901). She lives in New Market, Va.

WILLIS, BYRD CHARLES and **RICHARD HENRY.** They were born in Virginia, but afterward removed to Arkansas, where they jointly compiled a work of genealogy entitled 'The Willis Family of Virginia' (1899).

WILLIS, HENRY PARKER. Economist and educator. He was born in Weymouth, Mass., August 4, 1874, a son of John Henry Willis, and received a collegiate education supplemented by postgraduate studies abroad. He married, and was for some time leading editorial writer on the *New Evening Post,* and later Washington correspondent for Eastern papers. In 1905 he became the professor of economics and political science in Washington and Lee University. His writings include: 'The History of the Latin Monetary Union,' 'Reciprocity' (in collaboration with Professor J. L. Laughlin), and 'The Philippines Problem.' The University of Chicago gave him the degree of Ph.D. He resides in Lexington, Va.

WILLIS, MARY JASPER BOCOCK. Educator. Mrs. Willis is a native of Virginia and a daughter of the Rev. John Holmes Bocock, an eminent Presbyterian minister. She married Richard B. Willis. For several years she has been State historian for Arkansas of the United Daughters of the Confederacy, and each year has prepared an address on the work in Arkansas to be published in the minutes. Besides magazine articles and poems of high merit, she is also the author of an exceptionally interesting volume entitled 'American History in the South' (Richmond, Va., B. F. Johnson and Company, 1900). She resides in Fayetteville, Ark.

WILLOUGHBY, WESTEL WOODBURY. Educator. He was born in Alexandria, Va., July 20, 1867. After graduation from Johns Hopkins, he practiced law for several years in Washington, D.C., and then became associate professor of political science at Johns Hopkins. His writings, which bear the impress of profound scholarship, include: 'The Supreme Court of the United States, Its History and Administrative Importance' (Baltimore, The Johns Hopkins Press, 1890), 'The Government and Administration of the United States' (*ibid.,* 1891), 'The Nature of the State: a Study in Political Philosophy' (New York, The Macmillan Company, 1896), and 'The Rights and Duties of American Citizenship' (New York, The American Book Company, 1898), besides numerous minor works, including contributions to magazines and reviews. Johns Hopkins gave him the degree of Ph.D.

WILLOUGHBY, WILLIAM FRANKLIN. Expert in the United States Department of Labor. He was born in Alexandria, Va., July 20, 1867, a twin-brother of Dr. Westel W. Willoughby, and was educated at Johns Hopkins. He has several times represented the Department of Labor at international congresses, has received the Cross of the Legion of Honor from the French Government, and has delivered lectures on economics at Johns Hopkins. He has also published a volume entitled 'The Working Man's Insurance' (New York, Thomas Y. Crowell and Company, 1898), besides other writings.

WILLSON, BYRON FORCYTHE. Editor and poet. He was born in Alleghany County, N.Y., April 10, 1837, but afterward removed with his parents to Covington, Ky., and later became an editorial writer on the Louisville *Journal.* He wrote a number of poems, including "The Old Sergeant." Just before his death he published a collection of his verse (Boston, 1866).

WILMER, RICHARD HOOKER. See Biographical and Critical Sketch, Vol. XIII. page 5823.

WILMER, WILLIAM HOLLAND, clergyman, was born in Kent County, Md., October 23, 1782, and died in Williamsburg, Va., July 24, 1827. On completing his education, he was admitted to orders, became rector of St. Paul's Church in Alexandria, Va., founded the Virginia Protestant Episcopal Seminary, in which he taught, and became president of William and Mary College. He published a number of sermons, edited the *Theological Repertory,* and published an 'Episcopal Manual' (1815). Brown University gave him the degree of D.D.

WILSON, ALPHAEUS WATERS, bishop of the Methodist Episcopal Church, South. He was born in Baltimore, Md., February 5, 1834; and, after completing his studies at Columbian College, he joined the itinerant ranks of Methodism. He became secretary of the Board of Missions in 1878 and bishop in 1882. Three separate times he has made Episcopal tours of the globe, besides visiting remote fields on separate occasions. He delivered the Cole Lectures at Vanderbilt, in 1894; and these were afterward published in a volume entitled 'Witnesses to Christ' (Nashville, Publishing House of the M.E. Church, South). On March 4, 1857, he married Susan B. Lipscomb.

WILSON, ALPHAEUS WATERS, Mrs. [Md.]. She published an interesting series of "Letters from the Orient."

WILSON, AUGUSTA EVANS. See Biographical and Critical Sketch, Vol. XIII, page 5841.

WILSON, D. L. Author. [Va.]. In association with J. C. Lester, he wrote 'The Ku Klux Klan, Its Origin, Growth, and Disbandment' (New York and Washington, The Neale Publishing Company, 1907).

WILSON, FRANKLIN, clergyman, was born in Baltimore, Md., December 8, 1822. He was educated at Brown University and studied theology, but on account of physical infirmities he held no pastorates. Besides editing *The True Union,* he published a number of essays and tracts, one of which on "The Duties of Churches to Pastors" secured a prize.

WILSON, JAMES SOUTHALL. Educator. He was born in Bacon's Castle, Va., November 12, 1880. His father was John Wilson and his mother, Mary E. Jordan. He is professor of history and associate professor of English in William and Mary College, Williamsburg, Va. Besides several magazine articles, he has published 'Alexander Wilson, Poet, Naturalist' (New York and Washington, The Neale Publishing Company, 1906), and 'Pausanius: a Dramatic Poem,' with Charles William Kennedy (*ibid.,* 1907). Princeton University gave him the degree of Ph.D. The sketch of F. A. Pollard in 'The Library of Southern Literature' is from his pen.

WILSON, JOHN LEIGHTON, missionary, was born in Sumter County, S.C., March 25, 1809, and died near Maysville, S.C., July 13, 1886. After completing his theological equipment, he went on an exploring expedition to West Africa, the result of which was the establishment of a mission station at Cape Palmas. Afterward he developed other fields in the same region. He reduced the language of the natives to writing and made grammars in order to reach them with the message of the Gospel, and the results were marvelous. But, on account of impaired health, he returned to the United States. For many years he was secretary of the Board of Foreign Missions of the Presbyterian Church, first of the united organization and afterward of the Southern branch. Besides frequent contributions to the *Southern Presbyterian Review,* he published

'Western Africa: Its History, Condition, and Prospects' (New York, 1857). Lafayette College gave him the degree of D.D.

WILSON, JOHN LYDE, lawyer, was born in Marlborough District, S.C., May 24, 1784, and died in Charleston, S.C., February 12, 1849. He studied law, achieved distinction at the Bar, and on the hustings and became governor. He fought several duels and published a 'Code of Honor,' which he designed for the purpose of regulating the resort to hostile weapons. He was a writer of exceptional vigor, caused the abolition of the Court of Appeals by an attack in the public prints, and published 'Cupid and Psyche: from the Golden Ass of Apuleius' (Charleston, 1842).

WILSON, JOHN S. Presbyterian clergyman and educator. He was one of the religious pioneers of North Georgia, organized the First Presbyterian Church in Atlanta, and published a 'Necrology' (1869) and 'Atlanta as It Is' (1871).

WILSON, LIZZIE. Poet. [Ky.]. She published a volume of verse entitled 'Poems by Lizzie' (1860).

WILSON, LOUIS ROUND. Librarian of the University of North Carolina. He was born at Lenoir, N.C., December 27, 1876. Besides the sketch of Archibald Murphey in 'The Library of Southern Literature,' he is the author of a work entitled 'Chaucer's Relative Constructions' (Chapel Hill, N.C., The University Press, 1906), and numerous library articles. He is also chairman of the North Carolina Library Commission and holds the degree of Ph.D.

WILSON, RICHARD HENRY ("Richard Fisquill"). Educator and author. He was born in Christian County, Ky., March 6, 1870. His father was Richard Henry Wilson and his mother, Margaret Field Smith. On completing his education in this country, he continued his studies abroad; and, while in Paris, he married, June 24, 1893, Marie Louise Rourceret. For several years past he has been the professor of Romance languages at the University of Virginia. Among the delightful products of his leisure hours, in addition to numerous magazine articles, are 'Mazel' (New York, Henry Holt and Company) and 'The Venus of Cadiz,' an extravaganza (*ibid.*). He resides at Charlottesville. Johns Hopkins gave him the degree of Ph.D.

WILSON, ROBERT BURNS. See Biographical and Critical Sketch, Vol. XIII, page 5865.

WILSON, SAMUEL FARMER. Lawyer and journalist. He was born in Connecticut in 1805 and died in New Orleans, La., in 1870. After practicing law, first in North Carolina and afterward in Alabama, he engaged in journalism in New Orleans and published a 'History of the American Revolution' (Baltimore, 1834), which passed into several editions.

WILSON, THOMAS. [N.C.]. "Mr. Daniel Parke Custis, of Tallahassee, Fla., credits Dr. Wilson with a volume (of verse), which as a boy he remembers but which was lost in Newbern during the Civil War."—Dr. Hight C. Moore.

WILSON, WILLIAM LYNE. Statesman and educator. He was born in Jefferson County, Va., May 3, 1843. After graduating from Columbian College, he began a course of study at the University of Virginia, but the Civil War intervened. He served in the Confederate ranks, and at the close of hostilities became a professor in Columbian College, after which he settled in Charleston, W.Va., for the practice of law. In 1882 he was made president of the University of West Virginia, but resigned to accept an election to the National House of Representatives. From 1883 to 1895 he was a Member of Congress, took the leadership of the Democratic side, and wrote the famous tariff bill which bore his name. On retiring from Congress he accepted the office of Postmaster-general in the Cabinet of President Cleveland, and at the conclusion of his term of service became president of Washington and Lee University, a chair which he filled until his death, which occurred in 1900. He was an eloquent public speaker, and on economic questions, an authority of the highest character. Columbian gave him the degree of LL.D.

WILSON, WOODROW. See Biographical and Critical Sketch, Vol. XIII, page 5881.

WINANS, WILLIAM, clergyman, was born in Pennsylvania, November 3, 1788, and died in Mississippi, August 31, 1857. He was a pioneer of Methodism in the South, and published 'Discourses on Fundamental Religious Subjects,' edited by the Rev. Thomas O. Summers, D.D.

WINCHESTER, BOYD. [Ky.]. Author of 'The Swiss Republic.'

WINCHESTER, SAMUEL GROVER. Clergyman. He was born in Rock Run, Md., February 17, 1805, and died in New York, August 31, 1841. For several years he was pastor of a Presbyterian church at Natchez, Miss. He published 'Companion for the Sick' (1833), 'Christian Counsel to the Sick' (1836), 'Family Religion' (1841), and 'The Theater' (1841).

WINEBRENNER, JOHN, clergyman, was born in Frederick County, Md., March 24, 1797, and died in Harrisburg, Pa., September 12, 1860. For several years he proclaimed the doctrines of Luther, but eventually departed from the strict standards and organized a denomination which he called "the Church of God," in which the washing of feet was made obligatory and approval given to fasts. He edited periodicals and, with Isaac D. Rupp, wrote the 'History of Religious Denominations in the United States' (Hartford, 1844). He also published a 'Pronouncing Testament and Gazetteer' (Harrisburg, 1836), 'Brief Views of the Church of God' (1840), 'Practical and Doctrinal Sermons' (1860), and 'The Church Hymn-Book.'

WINGARD, E. A. Lutheran clergyman. [S.C.]. He published a volume of verse entitled 'Echoes, and Other Poems' (1899).

WINGFIELD, EDWIN MARIA. English merchant and colonist. He was born in England about 1570, took an active part in colonizing Virginia, sailed with the first company of emigrants and was named the first president of the colony in the sealed instructions; but an unfortunate quarrel with Captain John Smith caused him to be deposed, after which he returned to England. He wrote 'A Discourse of Virginia,' which was edited with notes by Charles Deane from the original manuscript (Boston, 1860).

WINKLER, A. V., Mrs. Editor. She was born in Virginia, but afterward lived in Texas. She wrote 'The Confederate Capitol' and 'Hood's Texas Brigade.'

WINLOCK, JOSEPH. Astronomer. He was born in Shelby County, Ky., February 6, 1826, and died in Cambridge, Mass., July 11, 1875. He was educated at Shelby College. For several years he was professor of astronomy at Harvard, and completed before his death thirty-five plates of the most interesting objects in the heavens. He also published 'The Tables of Mercury,' and made contributions to scientific journals.

WINN, MARY POLK. Author. [La.]. She wrote an interesting novel of old Creole days entitled 'The Law and the Letter' (New York and Washington, The Neale Publishing Company, 1907), the scenes of which are laid in the Province of Louisiana at the time of the War of 1812.

WINSTON, ANNIE STEGER. Writer. She was born in Virginia, the daughter of Charles H. Winston, professor of physics in Richmond College. She is a frequent contributor to periodicals, including *The Century Magazine,* and is also the author of an interesting volume, 'The Memoirs of a Child.' She lives in Richmond, Va.

WINSTON, ROBERT WATSON, jurist and lawyer, was born in Windsor, N.C., September 12, 1860. His father was the Honorable Patrick Henry Winston and his mother, Martha E. Byrd. Besides numerous monographs on historical and economic subjects, magazine articles and occasional lectures, he is the author of the sketch of Edwin Wiley Fuller in 'The Library of Southern Literature.' He was for some time president of the Historical Society of North Carolina. He married, December 12, 1882, Sophronia Horner, and resides at Raleigh, N.C.

WINSTON, ROSALIE BANKHEAD, Mrs. Author. This Virginia lady in 1885 published at Petersburg a volume of mingled prose and verse entitled 'Pilate's Question: or, What is Truth?'

WINTER, LOVICK PIERCE, Methodist clergyman, was born in Oglethorpe County, Ga., December 18, 1850. The master of an entertaining style, he frequently contributes to the press. Two of his latest articles are entitled "Marry Your Neighbor's Daughter" and "Sketches of Georgia Books and Authors." He has recently been engaged by one of the publishing houses to write a 'Life of Martin Luther.' He married, September 26, 1900, Wilhelmina McAvoy, and resides at Hepzibah, Ga.

WIRT, ELIZABETH WASHINGTON, author, was born in Richmond, Va., January 30, 1784, and died in Annapolis, Md., January 24, 1857. She was the daughter of Colonel Robert Gamble, became the second wife of William Wirt, the distinguished orator and statesman, and published a volume entitled 'Flora's Dictionary' (Baltimore, 1829), which became for years the authorized interpreter of the language of flowers.

WIRT, WILLIAM. See Biographical and Critical Sketch, Vol. XIII, page 5903.

WISE, BARTON H. Lawyer. [Va.]. He published an interesting volume of biography entitled 'The Life of Governor Henry A. Wise' (1899), in which he vividly portrays the turbulent times of which this distinguished Virginian was one of the dominant figures.

WISE, GEORGE. [Va.]. He wrote a 'History of the Seventeenth Virginia Infantry' (1870).

WISE, HENRY A. See Biographical and Critical Sketch, Vol. XIII, page 5921.

WISE, JOHN S. See Biographical and Critical Sketch, Vol. XIII, page 5937.

WISSER, JOHN PHILIP, soldier, was born in St. Louis, Mo., July 19, 1852. He was educated at West Point, served on the staff of General John Gibbon during the Chinese troubles on the Pacific Coast, taught various branches of science in the academy for years, studied at the Royal School of Mines in Frieberg, attained the rank of major in

1901, and is at present military attaché at Berlin. On topics relating to the artillery branch of the service, he is an authority of recognized standing among critics of the art of war. His writings include: 'Gun Cotton' (New York, D. Van Nostrand Company), 'Practical Problems in Minor Tactics and Strategy' (New York, D. Appleton and Company), 'By Land and Sea' (Philadelphia, Hamersley and Company), various articles on military subjects in Johnson's 'New Universal Cyclopædia' (Richmond, B. F. Johnson and Company), 'Explosive Materials' (New York, D. Van Nostrand and Company), 'The Second Boer War' (Kansas City, Hudson-Kimberly Company), 'Tactics of Coast Defence' (*ibid.*), 'Practical Field Exercises' (*ibid.*), and 'A Military and Naval Dictionary' (Philadelphia, Lutheran Publishing Society), besides contributions to numerous periodicals.

WITHERS, ALEXANDER SCOTT. Lawyer. [Va.]. He was born in 1792 and died in 1865. He published a work entitled 'Border Warfare' (1831).

WITHERS, EMMA, Miss. Poet. [W. Va.]. She published a volume of verse entitled 'Wildwood Chimes' (Cincinnati, 1891).

WOLFE, C. TOLER. He was born in Virginia, in 1810, and was the author of a work entitled 'A Book of Odds and Ends' (Winchester, 1852). Somewhat of a rover, he memorialized each place he visited; and we can follow him in his wanderings by turning the pages of his work. He took authorship none too seriously, but there are glints of genius which bespeak his brilliant talents.

WOMACK, NELLIE. Poet. [Ga.]. She published a volume of verse entitled 'Waifs and Wild Meadows' (Atlanta, The Foote and Davies Company, 1898).

WOOD, ANNIE C. Author. [Va.]. She wrote two entertaining novels entitled 'Diana Fontaine' (1891) and 'Westover's Ward' (1892)

WOOD, BENJAMIN. Journalist. He was born in Kentucky in 1820, but afterward engaged in journalism in New York City, where he attained distinction and wrote a novel of the Civil War period entitled 'Fort Lafayette; or, Love and Secession.' He died in 1900.

WOOD, HENRY. He was born in New Bedford, Mass., July 8, 1849, and studied at Berlin and Leipsic (Ph.D.). He fills the chair of German at Johns Hopkins University. He is the author of various monographs on German and English literature and the editor of a critical edition of 'Faust.' He resides in Baltimore, Md.

WOOD, JEAN MONCURE, Mrs. Poet. She was born in Virginia, her father being the Rev. John Moncure. She enjoyed fair educational advantages and married General James Wood, who distinguished himself in the Revolution and was governor of Virginia from 1796 to 1799. On account of her Scotch parentage, she wrote with ease and charm in the Highland dialect. She died in 1832, leaving a volume of poems in manuscript, which was favorably reviewed by the *Southern Literary Messenger,* and afterward published by John Lewis in 'Flowers and Weeds of the Old Dominion' (Frankfort, Ky., 1857).

WOOD, JOHN, author, was born in Scotland in 1775 and died in Richmond, Va., in 1822. For several years he edited newspapers, first in Kentucky and afterward in Washington, D.C. Besides numerous minor works he published a 'Full Statement of the Trial and Acquittal of Aaron

Burr' (Alexandria, 1807), a work which has been severely criticized by James Parton. He also published a 'History of Switzerland' (Edinburgh, 1799), and a 'History of the Administration of John Adams' (New York, 1802), the latter of which was suppressed by Burr, but it was afterward edited with notes by John Henry Sherburne and republished (Philadelphia, 1846).

WOOD, THOMAS L. Editor. He compiled a work of much interest entitled: 'Arcade Echoes,' a collection of poems culled from the *University Magazine* between the years 1859 and 1890.

WOOD, WILLIAM MAXWELL, surgeon, was born in Baltimore, Md., May 27, 1809, and died at Owen's Mills, Md., March 1, 1880. He became surgeon-general of the United States Navy and published 'Wandering Sketches of People and Things' (New York, 1849), 'A Shoulder to the Wheels of Progress' (New York, 1849), 'Hints to the People on the Profession of Medicine' (Buffalo, 1852), and Fankwei; or, the San Jacinto in the Seas of India, China, and Japan' (New York, 1859).

WOODROW, JAMES. See Biographical and Critical Sketch, Vol. XIII, page 5957.

WOODS, ALVA. Educator and divine. He was born in 1794 and died in 1887. He was the first president of the University of Alabama. His only work extant is entitled 'Literary and Theological Addresses,' published in 1868.

WOODS, KATE PEARSON. See Biographical and Critical Sketch, Vol. XIII, page 5979.

WOODS, W. H. Clergyman. [Baltimore, Md.]. Several poems have come from the pen of this ripe scholar. He holds the degree of D.D.

WOODWARD, AUGUSTUS B. Jurist. He was born in Virginia, in 1775, and died in Florida, in 1827. Besides attaining distinction at the Bar, he was also a student of the sciences. His published works include: 'Considerations on the Substance of the Sun' (1801), 'Considerations on the Executive Government of the United States' (1809), and 'A System of Universal Science' (1816).

WOODWARD, CALVIN MILTON. Educator. He was born at Fitchburg, Mass., August 25, 1837. His father was Isaac Burnap Woodward and his mother, Eliza Wetherbee. On completing his studies at Harvard he engaged in educational work, but his labors were interrupted by the outbreak of the Civil War, and he enlisted in Company A of the Forty-eighth Massachusetts Volunteers. For nearly forty years he has been identified with Washington University at St. Louis, in the chair of mathematics and mechanics; and for this same length of time he has been dean of the School of Engineering. He also originated, in 1879, the St. Louis Manual Training School. For several years he was president of the Board of Regents of the University of Missouri. His writings include: 'History of the St. Louis Bridge,' 'The Manual Training School' (Boston, D. C. Heath and Company), and 'Manual Training in Education' (New York, Charles Scribner's Sons). Harvard University gave him the degree of Ph.D. and Washington University, the degree of LL.D.

WOODWARD, FRANKLIN COWLES. Educator. He was born in Virginia, May 27, 1849, and was educated at Randolph-Macon College. He entered the ministry of the Methodist Episcopal Church, South, and married, in 1879, Mary P. Leary. He was professor of English in Wofford College from 1887 to 1897; and president of that institution from 1897 to 1902. At present he is professor of English in Richmond College. He is the author of 'English in the Schools' and 'English Analysis.' He resides in Richmond, Va., and holds the degree of Litt.D.

WOODWARD, THOMAS SIMPSON. Born in 1797 and died in 1861. He was a major-general of Georgia Volunteers and wrote: 'Reminiscences of the Creek and Muscogee Indians,' a rare book (Montgomery, 1859).

WOODWARD, W. S. Methodist Episcopal clergyman. [Mo.]. He published 'The Annals of Methodism in Missouri' (1893).

WOOLWINE, THOMAS LEE. This Southern author has published a volume entitled 'In the Valley of the Shadow' (New York, Doubleday, Page and Company).

WOOTEN, DUDLEY G., lawyer and editor, published in two quarto volumes, 'A Comprehensive History of Texas' (Dallas, Wm. G. Scarff, 1898), which embodies Yoakum's pioneer work and continues the narrative down to the last century's end. It contains contributions from various writers, is an authoritative work of great value, and deals fully with the political, legislative and judicial history of the Commonwealth. The splendid chapter on "The Land Titles of Texas" is from the pen of Mr. Wooten. He also wrote "The Results of Fifty Years of Progress in Texas."

WORMELEY, MARY ELIZABETH. Author. She was born in London, England, July 26, 1822. Her father was Admiral Ralph Randolph Wormeley of the British Navy, a native of Virginia, and a kinsman of the Randolphs. For some time preceding his death he resided in the United States, and his daughter, Mary Elizabeth, married Randolph Latimer, of Baltimore. But she was already well known by this time to the reading public through her books. She wrote 'Forest Hill: a Tale of Social Life' (London, 1846, in three volumes), 'Anabel: a Family History' (New York, 1853), 'Our Cousin Veronica' (1856), and 'Familiar Talks on Some of Shakespeare's Comedies' (Boston, 1857), besides several translations and frequent contributions to periodicals. She was a woman of rare gifts. The author's mother was a niece of Commodore Edward Preble.

WORMELY, ARINA RANDOLPH. [Va.]. She published 'The Coming Woman,' a comedy (1870).

WORMLEY, CARTER W. Journalist and poet. He published a volume of lyrics entitled 'Poems' (New York, 1904). He resides in Richmond, Va.

WORTHINGTON, JANE TAYLOR LOMAX. Writer. [Va.]. Mrs. Worthington published numerous essays and poems, chiefly in the *Southern Literary Messenger*.

WREN, MARGARET BRECKINRIDGE. Poet. This Virginia lady published a volume of verse entitled 'Echoes from the Heart' (Richmond, 1887). Most of her poems are introspective in character and tinged with sadness.

WRENSHALL, LETITIA H. YONGE. Writer. She was born in Washington, D.C. For many years she lived in Augusta, Ga., but her home is at present in Baltimore, Md. She married John C. Wrenshall. The writings of this gifted Southern lady have not been numerous, but they have dealt with very important subjects. She has published 'Aboriginal Relics from the Stone Graves of Tennessee,' a lecture delivered before the Maryland Academy of Sciences; "Incantation and Popular Healing in Maryland and Pennsylvania," an essay in the *Journal of American Folk Lore;* "Odd Corners in Southern Europe," a series of letters in the Baltimore *Sun;* the sketch of Lizette Woodworth Reese in 'The Library of Southern Literature,' and numerous contributions to periodicals.

WRIGHT, CHARLES E. Editor and author. He wrote a story of modern social life entitled 'Three Beautiful Women.' Mr. Wright is engaged in journalistic work at Vicksburg, Miss.

WRIGHT, JAMES CORNELIUS. He was born in Tennessee in 1851. The only product of his pen is a biography of his father, the Rev. A. B. Wright (1895).

WRIGHT, JEAN. Poet. [Ky.]. She published a volume of verse entitled 'Poems' (1892).

WRIGHT, LOUISE SOPHIE W. Author. [Md.]. She wrote an interesting story entitled 'A Southern Girl.'

WRIGHT, M. E. Author. [Ga.]. She wrote a 'History of Missions of the Southern Baptist Convention' (Philadelphia, The American Baptist Publication Society, 1900), and afterward became Mrs. Wilbur.

WRIGHT, MARCUS JOSEPH, soldier, was born in Purdy, Tenn., June 5, 1831. For some time he practiced law in Memphis; but at the outbreak of the Civil War he entered the Confederate service and attained the rank of brigadier-general. He was afterward appointed by the War Department at Washington to collect Confederate records for publication. He wrote 'Reminiscences of the Early Settlement and Early Settlers of McNairy County, Tenn.' (Washington, 1882), and a 'Life of Governor William Blount' (1884).

WRIGHT, MARIE ROBINSON. Author. She was born in Georgia in 1866. She published 'Picturesque Mexico.' Mrs. Wright resides in New York City.

WRIGHT, ROBERT. Author. [England]. He published the most complete and thorough biography of the founder of the colony of Georgia in a work entitled 'The Memoirs of General James Edward Oglethorpe' (London, 1867).

WRIGHT, WILLIAM HENRY, engineer, was born in Wilmington, N.C., in 1814, and died in Wilmington, N.C., December 29, 1845. After graduating from William and Mary College he studied law, but relinquished the legal profession to enter West Point. He attained the rank of first lieutenant in the engineering corps, superintended the construction of Fort Warren, in Boston Harbor, and published a 'Brief, Practical Treatise on Mortars, with an Account of the Processes at the Public Works in Boston Harbor' (Boston, 1845).

WYETH, CHARLES A. Author. [Ky.]. He wrote 'The Basket of Flowers' and 'Rosa of Linden Castle; or, Filial Affection,' besides minor works.

WYETH, JOHN ALLAN. See Biographical and Critical Sketch, Vol. XIII, page 6001.

WYLIE, LOLLIE BELLE. Poet and special writer. She was born of distinguished colonial and revolutionary stock, in Bayou Coque d'Inde on the Gulf Coast of Alabama. Her maiden name was Lollie Belle Moore. She became the wife of Hart Wylie, of Atlanta. Ga.. the marriage occurring June 4, 1877. Mrs. Wylie is a woman of exceptional gifts. She has been editorially connected with numerous periodicals and has taken an active interest in the progressive movements of her sex. Besides hundreds of sketches, descriptive and biographical, she has published 'Memoirs of Judge Richard H. Clark' (Atlanta, 1898), a 'Legend of the Cherokee Rose,' a volume of verse (1887), and 'Ashes of Love,' a novelette (1890).

WYMAN, WILLIAM STOKES. Educator. He was born in Montgomery, Ala., November 23, 1830, received a collegiate education and married Melissa A. Dearing. He was for forty-six years professor of Latin in the University of Alabama. He declined the presidential office several times, but served in this capacity *pro tempore* on four different occasions, and finally, in 1902, accepted an election, but soon afterward retired. Besides numerous contributions to the magazines, he is the author of 'The Syntax of the Latin Compound Sentence' and 'The Trial of Milo.' He resides in Tuscaloosa, Ala., and holds the degree of LL.D.

WYNNE, EMMA MOFFETT, Mrs. Author. She was born in Alabama in 1844 but afterward lived in Georgia and published 'Crag Font' and 'Crown Jewels.'

WYNNE, THOMAS HICKS. Author. He was born in Virginia in 1820, but lived for some time in North Carolina. He published 'Historical Documents of the Old Dominion' (1860-1874), 'Historical Documents of the Old North State,' and a 'Narrative of Colonel David Fanning' (1861).

WYNNE, WILLIAM AMOS. Draughtsman. He was born in Texas in 1877. Besides a number of essays, he has published a volume of verse entitled 'Be Thou Thankful, and Other Poems' (1899).

WYTHE, GEORGE. Signer of the Declaration of Independence. He was born in Elizabeth City, Va., in 1726, and died in Richmond, Va., June 8, 1806. As a lawyer he stood at the head of the Virginia Bar. He espoused the patriotic cause with great ardor, signed the immortal charter of independence, and would also have signed the Constitution of the United States, but was absent from the proceedings of the convention on the last day. Later he held for twenty years the chancellorship of the High Court of Equity in Virginia. While in the full possession of his faculties at the age of eighty years, he died from poisoning. Thomas Jefferson has paid the highest tribute both to his purity of character and to his rare force of intellect. He published 'Decisions in Virginia by the High Court of Chancery, with Remarks upon Decrees by the Court of Appeals' (Richmond, 1793); the second edition with a memoir by Benjamin B. Minor (1852).

YANCEY, WILLIAM LOWNDES. See Biographical and Critical Sketch, Vol. XIII, page 6021.

YANDELL, LUNSFORD PITTS, physician, was born near Hartsfield, Tenn., July 4, 1805, and died in Louisville, Ky., February 4, 1878. For years he taught in medical colleges and edited medical journals. He published numerous essays and monographs, one of which on "Fever" was awarded a prize.

YEAMAN. GEORGE HELM, lawyer, was born in Harden County, Ky., November 1, 1829. He became a judge, a Member of Congress, and, by appointment of President Johnson, Minister to Denmark. Besides several pamphlets, he published a 'Study of Government' (Boston, 1870). After his return from Europe he practiced law in New York.

YERGER, GEORGE SHALL. Lawyer. He was born in Hagerstown, Md., August 23, 1801, and died in Bolivar County, Miss., April 20, 1860. He located in Nashville, Tenn., for the practice of law and was for many years Supreme Court reporter. Later he removed to Jackson, Miss. While engaged in a deer hunt he died of heart disease, falling upon stag which he had just shot. He published ten volumes of 'Tennessee Reports' (Nashville, 1832-1838), besides essays and sketches.

YOAKUM, HENDERSON. Lawyer and historian. He was born in Claiborne County, Tenn., in 1810, and died in Houston, Texas, November 29, 1856. After graduating from West Point, he served in the Black Hawk War with the rank of second lieutenant, but resigned from the Army, entered the legal profession, and practiced law, first in Tennessee and afterward in Texas. He fought in the Mexican War and later became colonel of militia. Besides contributing to numerous periodicals, he published an authoritative work entitled 'A History of Texas from Its First Settlement under La Salle, in 1685, to Its Annexation to the United States in 1845' (New York, 1855).

YOCUM, WILBUR FISK, clergyman and educator, was born in Salem, Ohio, July 20, 1840, being the son of Elmore and Jane Riley Yocum. On completing his educational equipment, he became an ordained minister in the Methodist Episcopal Church and organized the first public school in Walla Walla, Wash. Subsequently he taught in various colleges. For thirty years he has lived in Florida and is at present professor of education at the University of the State, which is situated at Gainesville. His work entitled 'Civil Government in Florida' is an important text-book for the student. He married, in 1871, Sarah Hanchett of Chicago.

YONGE, FRANCIS. Colonist. [S.C.]. Besides an account of a voyage to Virginia, he published 'The Proceedings of the People of South Carolina in 1719.'

YOUNG, BENNETT HENDERSON. Lawyer. He was born in Nicholasville, Ky., May 23, 1843, the son of Robert and Josephine Henderson Young. He received the best educational advantages, pursuing his studies in Kentucky, at Toronto, Canada, and at Belfast, Ireland. He married, first, Mattie R. Robinson and, second, Ella S. Sharp. He served in the Confederate Army under General John H. Morgan, and was brigadier-general on the staff of General John B. Gordon, Commander-in-Chief of the United Confederate Veterans. He is prominent at the Bar and in the lay councils of the Presbyterian Church. Included among his published works are: 'A History of Constitutions in Kentucky,' 'A History of Evangelistic Work in Kentucky,' 'A History of Jessamine County,' 'A History of Presbyterian Church Division in Kentucky,' and 'A History of the Battle of the Thames.' The sketch of John C. Breckinridge in 'The Library of Southern Literature' is also from his pen. He resides in Louisville, Ky., and holds the degree of LL.D.

YOUNG, EDWARD. Poet. He was born in Bristol, England, in 1818, but came to America in childhood and settled in South Carolina. He published a volume of verse entitled 'The Ladye Lillian, and Other Poems.'

YOUNG, LUCIEN. Naval officer. He was born in Lexington, Ky., March 31, 1852, and was educated at Annapolis. He wrote 'The Real Hawaii.'

YOUNG, MARTHA. See Biographical and Critical Sketch, Vol. XIII, page 6043.

YOUNG, MAUD J. FULLER. Author. She was born in North Carolina in direct line of descent from Pocahontas. Afterward she resided in Texas and wrote 'The Song of the Texas Rangers,' a text-book entitled 'The Botany of Texas,' and 'Cordova: a Legend of Lone Lake.'

YOUNG, R. E., Miss. Author. [Mo.]. She published 'Sally of Missouri' (1903).

YOUNG, ROBERT ANDERSON. Methodist Episcopal clergyman. [Tenn.]. He was born in 1824. His published works include: 'Personages' (1857), 'A Reply to Ariel' (1866), and 'Sketches of Foreign Travel,' besides minor writings.

YOUNG, STARKE. See Biographical and Critical Sketch, Vol. XIII, page 6065.

YOUNG, VIRGINIA DURANT. Journalist and author. She was born in Marion, S.C. Her maiden name was Durant. She wielded a pen of rare gifts, wrote newspaper editorials and sketches, and published several works, among them: 'Beholding as in a Glass' (New York, The Arena Publishing Company, 1895), 'A Tower in the Desert' (*ibid.*, 1896), and 'One of the Blue Hen's Chickens' (1901). She married, December 22, 1880, Dr. N. J. Young, and resided in Fairfax, S.C. She died November 2, 1906.

YULEE, C. WICKLIFFE. Author. He wrote an interesting novel of life at the national seat of Government entitled 'The Awakening' (New York and Washington, The Neale Publishing Company, 1906).

ZACHARIE, JAMES S. Author. [La.]. He published 'The New Orleans Guide' (New Orleans, 1889), and 'New Orleans—Its Old Streets and Places' (Louisiana Historical Society, 1900), besides essays on prison reform.

ZIMMERMAN, LEANDER M. He was born in Manchester, Md., August 29, 1866, the son of Henry and Leah Zimmerman, graduated from Pennsylvania College, at Gettysburg, and was ordained to the Lutheran ministry in 1878. He is now a pastor in Baltimore. His books are numerous. They include: 'How to Be Happy When Married,' 'The Little Grave,' 'Daily Bread for Daily Hunger,' 'Sunshine,' 'Pearls of Comfort from Tennyson's "In Memoriam,"' 'Expository Thoughts on Pilgrim's Progress,' 'Paths That Cross,' 'A Wedding Token,' 'The Family,' 'Oil of Kindness,' 'Yvonne,' 'Book of Verses,' and 'A Word to the Troubled.' He resides in Baltimore, Md., and holds the degree of D.D.

ZOGBAUM, RUFUS FAIRCHILD. Artist and author. He was born in Charleston, S.C., August 28, 1849, and studied art in New York and Paris. He is well known as a delineator of military and naval subjects. He has also written and illustrated several entertaining works, among them: 'Foot, Horse, and Dragoons; or, Sketches of Army Life,' 'All Hands,' and 'Ships and Sailors.' He resides in New York City.